# Transnational Financial Crime

**The Library of Essays on Transnational Crime**
*David Nelken*

**Titles in the Series:**

**Transnational Organized Crime**
*Margaret E. Beare*

**Transnational Terrorism**
*Steven M. Chermak and Joshua D. Freilich*

**Transnational Financial Crime**
*Nikos Passas*

**Human Trafficking**
*Marie Segrave*

**Transnational Environmental Crime**
*Rob White*

# Transnational Financial Crime

*Edited by*

## Nikos Passas

*Northeastern University, USA*

**ASHGATE**

Published by
Ashgate Publishing Limited
Wey Court East
Union Road
Farnham
Surrey GU9 7PT
England

Ashgate Publishing Company
110 Cherry Street
Suite 3-1
Burlington, VT 05401-3818
USA

www.ashgate.com

**British Library Cataloguing in Publication Data**
A catalogue record for this book is available from the British Library.

**The Library of Congress has cataloged the printed edition as follows:** 2013945933

ISBN: 9781409448884

Printed in the United Kingdom by Henry Ling Limited, at the Dorset Press, Dorchester, DT1 1HD

*To my charming and inspiring Jani (Yanni)*

# Contents

## PART III   CONTROL ISSUES

# Acknowledgements

Ashgate would like to thank the researchers and contributing authors who provided copies, along with the following for their permission to reprint copyright material.

American Society of Criminology for the essay: Tomson H. Nguyen and Henry N. Pontell (2010), 'Mortgage Origination Fraud and the Global Economic Crisis: A Criminological Analysis', *Criminology and Public Policy*, **9**, pp. 591–612. Copyright © 2010 American Society of Criminology.

Boom uitgevers Den Haag for the essay: Nikos Passas (1999), 'Globalization, Criminogenic Asymmetries and Economic Crime', *European Journal of Law Reform*, **1**, pp. 399–423. Copyright © 1999 Kluwer Law International.

Case Western Reserve University, School of Law for the essay: Nikos Passas (2012), 'Financial Controls and Counter-Proliferation of Weapons of Mass Destruction', *Case Western Reserve Journal of International Law*, **44**, pp. 747–63.

De Gruyter for the essay: John S. Zdanowicz (2009), 'Trade-Based Money Laundering and Terrorist Financing', *Review of Law and Economics*, **5**, pp. 855–78.

Elsevier for the essays: Richard B. Freeman (2010), 'Financial Crime, Near Crime, and Chicanery in the Wall Street Meltdown', *Journal of Policy of Modeling*, **32**, pp. 690–701. Copyright © 2010 Society for Policy Modeling; Rodger Jamieson, Lesley Pek Wee Land, Donald Winchester, Greg Stephens, Alex Steel, Alana Maurushat and Rick Sarre (2012), 'Addressing Identity Crime in Crime Management Information Systems: Definitions, Classification, and Empirics', *Computer Law and Security Review*, **28**, pp. 381–95. Copyright © 2012 Rodger Jamieson, Lesley Pek Wee Land, Donald Winchester, Greg Stephens, Alex Steel, Alana Maurushat and Rick Sarre.

Emerald Group Publishing Limited for the essays: Herbert Snyder and Anthony Crescenzi (2009), 'Intellectual Capital and Economic Espionage: New Crimes and New Protections', *Journal of Financial Crime*, **16**, pp. 245–54. Copyright © 2009 Emerald Group Publishing Ltd; Nicholas Dorn, Michael Levi and Simone White (2008), 'Do European Procurement Rules Generate or Prevent Crime?', *Journal of Financial Crime*, **15**, pp. 243–60. Copyright © 2008 Emerald Group Publishing Ltd.

Tom Ginsburg and Thomas S. Ulen for the essay: Tom Ginsburg and Thomas S. Ulen (2007), 'Odious Debt, Odious Credit, Economic Development, and Democratization', *Law and Contemporary Problems*, **70**, pp. 115–36. Copyright © 2007 Tom Ginsburg and Thomas S. Ulen.

## Publisher's Note

# Series Preface

This international series explores the increasingly important area of transnational crime and criminal justice. As with other well established Ashgate publications in this field, this too aims at being a major resource by bringing together the most significant journal essays in contemporary criminology, criminal justice and penology. Five key areas of transnational crime and criminal justice are analysed. The volume by Margaret Beare discusses types of organised crime, the way they are classified, the role of groups, networks, and markets and the harm that such activities cause. The collection by Nikos Passas explores the definition, types and control of transnational financial crime. That on transnational environmental crime, by Rob White, deals with the often neglected victimisation produced by such crimes, their variety and how they may best be combated. The collection on human trafficking, by Marie Segrave, analyses the framework for dealing with this increasingly debated crime; it then goes on to examine what we know about it and describes current responses (and the possible alternatives). Finally, the work on transnational terrorism, by Steven Chermak and Joshua Freilich considers the patterns, causes, impact of this behaviour and the way nation states and others seek to deal with this threat. As this collection in particular well illustrates, studying the response to transnational crime raises important questions about the legitimacy of state, and international and transnational definitions of threatening behaviour. In all cases, however, the collections make available to researchers, teachers and students a range of essays that are indispensable for obtaining an overview of the latest theories and findings in this fast-changing area. The authoritative introductions to each volume set the selected essays in context and explain their significance.

DAVID NELKEN
*Distinguished Research Professor of Law,*
*Cardiff University, UK*
*Series Editor*

# Introduction

The significance of transnational financial crime has been frequently illustrated by recent cases that made headlines and commanded public policy attention. Global powerhouses have been found and sanctioned for allowing or facilitating – sometimes quite deliberately, sometimes due to gross negligence or recklessness – misconduct associated with criminal enterprises active in drug trafficking, embargo busting, bribery or state crimes. Some are in the past century (US House Committee on Energy and Commerce, 1982; Truell and Gurwin, 1992; Mantius, 1995), others quite recent (Taibbi, 2013). Certain acts and practices have bordered or crossed the threshold of serious crime in business transactions deemed at best imprudent and too risky, with financial costs to the company, shareholders, customers and taxpayers (Barofsky, 2012; Morgenson and Rosner, 2012). The negative consequences transcend financial victimization as they include legitimacy crises, loss of confidence in private and state institutions or even security (Gori and Paparela, 2006; Edelbacher *et al.*, 2012).

In many instances, the costs are not limited to one country or region. The negative impact is not always quantifiable, yet plainly quite extraordinary. From misconduct leading to the financial crisis that brought the world economy to its knees to money laundering, corruption, banking scandals and violations of sanctions designed to prevent the proliferation of weapons of mass destruction, this type of crime affects virtually all areas of public policy: economic growth, security, the legitimacy of state institutions, law, public health, environment, human rights and everything that affects democratic governance and quality of life are simply touched by transnational financial crimes and malpractices. Nevertheless, the term is hard to define and can capture a very wide range of acts.

There is neither an international convention on this issue nor a universally accepted definition of 'financial crime', which refers to different acts in different jurisdictions and contexts. Some definitions even include violent acts leading to financial losses, while others only include non-violent offences towards financial gain. For example, the FBI refers to acts that are 'characterized by deceit, concealment, or violation of trust and are not dependent upon the application or threat of physical force or violence. Such acts are committed by individuals and organizations to obtain personal or business advantage.' The FBI's financial crime investigations focus on 'corporate fraud, securities and commodities fraud, health care fraud, financial institution fraud, mortgage fraud, insurance fraud, mass marketing fraud, and money laundering' (FBI, 2010–11).

In the United Kingdom, according to the Financial Services Authority (FSA), financial crime 'includes any offence involving money laundering, fraud or dishonesty, or market abuse', thus covering bribery and corruption, terrorism finance, sanctions violations and fraud.[1] The UK Financial Services and Markets Act (FSMA) defines financial crime as including 'any offence

---

[1]    http://www.fsa.gov.uk/about/what/financial_crime. The FSA is now split into the Financial Conduct Authority (www.fca.org.uk) and the Prudential Regulation Authority (at www.bankofengland. co.uk).

involving (a) fraud or dishonesty; (b) misconduct in, or misuse of information relating to, a financial market; or (c) handling the proceeds of crime or funds connected to terrorism'. Again, the list of acts widely considered to be financial crimes is not exhaustive.

'Transnational' is a relatively easier concept. For our purposes, we can distinguish between international crimes and transnational ones. The former includes offences defined under international law (Passas, 2003c), while the latter covers misconduct involving perpetrators or victims located or operating through more than one jurisdiction (Passas, 1999b).

Along the lines of these definitions, this volume seeks to cover transnational financial crime and illustrate the above problems as comprehensively as possible with chapters covering offences relative to state revenue collection, criminal enterprises, money laundering, the use of new technologies and methods, corruption, terrorism, proliferation of weapons of mass destruction (WMD), sanctions, financial institutions, third-world debt, procurement, tele-communications, cyberspace, the defence industry and intellectual property. The objective is to cover as many types of offences while at the same time addressing theoretical and policy issues.

As the works move from one kind of offence to another, the book is organized into three parts: (1) 'Theoretical Frameworks'; (2) Types of Transnational Financial Crime'; (3) 'Control Issues'. The first part seeks to furnish a conceptual framework within which these crimes, causes and vulnerabilities can be understood and explained. The second part contains a series of case studies into a broad range of crimes and the costs or victimization they produce. Finally, the third part continues to expand the range of misdeeds covered while focusing specifically on social control issues.

## Theoretical Frameworks

Drawing on, but also transcending classical criminological theories, several attempts have been made recently to develop conceptual frameworks for a better understanding and analysis of globalization and crime in general (Pearce and Woodiwiss, 1993; Aas, 2007; Findlay, 2008; Van Dijk, 2008) and specifically the underlying causes of transnational economic crime. In the first chapter of this part, 'Globalization, Criminogenic Asymmetries and Economic Crime' (Chapter 1), Nikos Passas explores three main questions: What factors cause transnational crime? How does the process of globalization affect such crime? How does globalization affect crime control efforts? He introduces the concept of 'criminogenic asymmetries', which he defines as structural discrepancies, mismatches and inequalities in the realms of the economy, law, politics and culture. Three ways in which asymmetries are conducive to crime are (1) by fuelling the demand for illegal goods and services; (2) by generating incentives for people and organizations to engage in illegal practices; and (3) by reducing the ability of authorities to control crime. He then argues that globalization multiplies, activates and intensifies the criminogenic potential of these asymmetries.

In the next chapter, 'Global Anomie, Dysnomie, and Economic Crime: Hidden Consequences of Neoliberalism and Globalization in Russia and Around the World' (Chapter 2), Passas focuses more on economic crime and advances the criminogenic asymmetries argument by building on the globalization literature and previous efforts in the anomie tradition that elaborated the Durkheimian and Mertonian formulations into an analytical framework most appropriate for the study of white-collar and organizational crime (Vaughan, 1983, 1995;

Passas, 1990, 1997; Messner and Rosenfeld, 1994). He argues that means–ends disjunctions are systematically generated, as neo-liberal policies in the global village foster needs and desires that are frustrated. Moreover, neo-liberalism and globalization set in motion processes that lead to global anomie,[2] dysnomie[3] and economic crimes by activating the criminogenic potential of economic, political, legal and cultural asymmetries as well as by creating new asymmetries. While he tests this argument with a case study of social change in Russia, global anomie theory has clear applications in other contexts as well, such as Iraq or Somalia (Passas, 2005a; Twyman-Ghoshal, 2012).

In the next chapter, 'Enron et al.: Paradigmatic White Collar Crime Cases for the New Century' (Chapter 3), David Friedrichs looks into the Enron case (Vallette and Wysham, 2002; Klinger and Sklar, 2005; Michalowski and Kramer, 2006) in an attempt to find some common threads with other important corporate scandals of recent years, such as Adelphia, Worldcom, Tyco and Global Crossing. Friedrichs (Chapter 3) argues that these instances require a multilevel theoretical effort that encompasses structural, organizational, dramaturgic and individualistic dimensions within the context of an 'emerging postmodern society' and 'hyperreality' (Baudrillard, 1994), a 'circumstance wherein images breed incestuously with each other without reference to reality or meaning' (p. 71). He further remarks that: 'When we increasingly experience our world in terms of simulations, and can no longer clearly differentiate between conventional reality and simulations, then we have entered the realm of hyperreality' (p. 71).

Eric Wilson's contribution, 'Criminogenic Cyber-Capitalism: Paul Virilio, Simulation, and the Global Financial Crisis' (Chapter 4), also makes use of Baudrillard and Passas' earlier chapters on asymmetries and global anomie, but mostly draws on Virilio, as he switches attention to the global financial crisis and 'criminogenic cyber-capitalism'. He makes a three-part argument: (1) the global credit crisis is a kind of 'accident', signifying the emergence of power crime,[4] or the 'criminogenic', as a systemic property of a cyber-capitalist global economy; (2) this accident in global finance, widely understood as a 'fast moving event', is governed by wider trends that are necessary attributes of what is generally described as 'globalization'; and (3) the work on the notion of simulation by Baudrillard and, more importantly, Paul Virilio's theory of speed politics provide the conceptual framework to re-formulate our understanding of the nature of the world-economy represented as a criminogenic phenomenon. As Wilson (Chapter 4) notes, 'Simulation and power crime merge on the level of the criminogenic manipulation of reality, resulting in the "accident" of the global credit crisis. Power crime is the criminogenic medium through which the periodic crises of global capitalism will now occur' (p. 79).

In the last chapter of this part, 'Counterfeiting as Corporate Externality: Intellectual Property Crime and Global Insecurity' (Chapter 5), Simon Mackenzie takes us to the issue of intellectual property (IP) crimes, which he constructs as a corporate externality in a way that parallels similar analyses of several other industries and their 'lawful, but awful' practices (Passas and Goodwin, 2004; Passas, 2005b). The trade in counterfeit products has

---

[2]   Weakened guiding power of conventional norms.

[3]   Absence of an effective global norm-making mechanism, inconsistent enforcement of existing international rules and the existence of a regulatory patchwork of diverse and conflicting legal traditions and practices.

[4]   The criminogenic 'substance' of global capitalism.

been debated vigorously also in conjunction with terrorism finance and criminal enterprises (Bach, 2003; United States. Congress. House. Committee on International Relations, 2003; United States. Congress. House. Committee on the Judiciary. Subcommittee on Courts the Internet and Intellectual Property, 2003; Naim, 2005; Phillips, 2005; United States. Congress. Senate. Committee on Homeland Security and Governmental Affairs, 2005). Mackenzie offers a different perspective and reveals the more complex role of corporations. He argues that IP crimes constitute a predictable but hidden corporate externality generated by branding and advertising activities, which create 'needs' and desires. At the same time, outsourcing production to low cost developing countries creates the opportunities to copy and sell goods in unauthorized ways. He points out that the cost of counteracting such misconduct outweighs the damage of IP crimes to the companies involved. A more important negative effect of IP crimes is the creation of profitable illegal markets that sometimes produce serious health and safety issues.

## Types of Transnational Financial Crime

The financial crisis and the growth in the external debt of several governments have rendered authorities more sensitive and occasionally aggressive relative to revenue collection. Swiss–US exchanges and the demand that secret account information be shared with tax authorities are a case in point. Media and other reports on corporations planning their taxes in ways to minimize taxation drastically have added fuel to ongoing debates on the boundaries between tax evasion or fraud and tax avoidance (McBarnet, 1992; Brooks, 2013) or the acceptability of some transfer pricing practices (Picciotto, 1992; Bhat and Deutsches Institut für Entwicklungspolitik, 2009; Reuter, 2012). In the first chapter of this part, 'A Good Century for Tax? Globalisation, Redistribution and Tax Avoidance' (Chapter 6), John Braithwaite discusses tax avoidance as a problem of globalization and refers also to profit shifting in and out of tax havens as another important method. He points out that aggressive competition among accounting and other advice professionals based in big financial centres, such as New York and London, has now driven professional conduct beyond the spirit of the law. Similarly to Passas' concept of 'criminogenic asymmetries', Braithwaite (Chapter 6) refers to 'structural discontinuities' (p. 125) among various jurisdictions, which are exploited – with New York emerging as the leading centre of advice for such practices. For example, differential tax treatments of the same activities and transactions furnish arbitrage and avoidance opportunities. In this way 'Corporations can double dip, taking one position on the meaning of a transaction for US tax purposes, another in a second country that creates tax benefits under both sets of rules' (p. 125). For a more effective control of tax planning that borders the illegal or unethical, he calls for strategic, collaborative, international and evidence-based approaches involving a responsive regulatory pyramid seeking voluntary compliance but escalating to intensive audits and enforcement steps when that does not work.

Money laundering is a par excellence transnational financial crime with extensive literature and coverage (Levi, 1991a, 1991b; Passas and Groskin, 2001; Gilmore, 2004; Masciandaro, 2004; Pieth and Aiolfi, 2004; Reuter and Truman, 2004; Levi and Reuter, 2006; Beare and Schneider, 2007; Chaikin and Sharman, 2009; Sharman, 2011). In this volume we have two chapters that deal with special issues relative to money laundering. Firstly, Michael Levi's 'E-Gaming and Money Laundering Risks: A European Overview' (Chapter 7) focuses on fraud and money laundering vulnerabilities in electronic gaming, another issue giving rise to discussions around the world (Hörnle and Zammit, 2010; United States. Congress. House. Committee on Financial Services, 2010; Williams *et al.*, 2012). Levi offers a European overview of the issues and outlines the wide range of measures that have been adopted by the regulated industry. He finds that the industry measures reduce money laundering risks, which are lower in comparison with the off-line gaming and financial services sectors.

In the next chapter, 'Trade-Based Money Laundering and Terrorist Financing' (Chapter 8), John S. Zdanowicz addresses a problem that relates to all types of financial crime: trade-facilitated crime and the comparative inattention of authorities to the lack of transparency in cross-border commercial activities (Passas and Nelken, 1993; Zdanowicz *et al.*, 1996; Passas, 2004b, 2006, 2011; DeKieffer, 2005; Wilkinson and Ellingwood, 2011). Zdanowicz suggests that international trade has been used for a long time to conceal the existence and movement of illicit funds and correctly argues that government authorities largely neglect mis-invoicing and other techniques used by financial offenders. He explains how false invoicing enables the international fund transfers to go undetected. Importantly, he shows that the analysis of existing trade databases can assist significantly in the measurement, detection and monitoring of irregular and illicit transnational flows.

Passas' chapter, 'Demystifying Hawala: A Look into Its Social Organization and Mechanics' (Chapter 9), takes us to an issue that shows the tight connection between commercial and financial flows as well as ways in which the formal and informal economies intersect. He focuses on hawala, a very old informal fund and value transfer method which originated in the Indian subcontinent but is now global. Even though the overwhelming majority of the customers send honestly earned money, just like any other financial intermediary, hawala has been abused for capital flight, tax evasion, money laundering, terrorism finance, corruption and other crimes (Passas, 1999a, 2003b, 2004a; Maimbo, 2003; International Monetary Fund. Monetary and Financial Systems Dept, 2005; Thompson, 2006, 2011). Passas describes the routine practices and mechanics of hawala and dispels several myths about it, such as the lack of money movement or the absence of paperwork and trails for investigators. He notes that expatriates and their extended families at the home country are among the most important legitimate beneficiaries of hawala. He focuses on Pakistani hawala modus operandi and money itineraries. As it becomes clear that these mechanics make both economic and cultural sense, this chapter seeks to promote more sensitive, informed, fair and consensual law enforcement practices.

The next two chapters turn attention to the origins of the global financial crisis and the contributing role of criminal acts. Richard B. Freeman in 'Financial Crime, Near Crime, and Chicanery in the Wall Street Meltdown' (Chapter 10) raises the following questions:

> How substantial was white collar crime, near crime or chicanery in the 2007–2009 financial crisis? What motivates those in top positions in banks and other institutions that deal primarily with money to engage in illegal and sleazy business practices? To what extent might more vigorous monitoring of those practices provide an early warning system of impending crises in finance that might prevent or ameliorate the malfunctioning of the financial sector? (p. 190)

Freeman reports that the crisis was indeed preceded by numerous crimes as well as 'near crime and chicanery', but the warning signs were ignored. Underlying the crimes and the crisis are issues discussed for quite some time but with no reforms or effective action: excessive compensation and bonuses for executives; perverse incentives; and undue rewards. Particularly when taxpayers shoulder the remedial cost, system-wide risks, illegal and unethical practices must be monitored, prevented and fairly sanctioned. We have seen some accountability imposed on players involved in the savings and loan disaster, Enron, the Madoff fraud and creative accounting at AIG. However, the bulk of unethical and illegal practices have gone unpunished and the risks remain despite Freeman's (Chapter 10) statement that they constitute 'a cancer on capitalism that deserves the greatest social vigilance and opprobrium that society can muster' (p. 190).

Tomson H. Nguyen and Henry N. Pontell in 'Mortgage Origination Fraud and the Global Economic Crisis: A Criminological Analysis' (Chapter 11) undertook a study into mortgage origination fraud to shed light on the way of thinking and rationalizations of those who engaged in mortgage crimes and on the effect of these crimes on the subprime crisis. They find that mortgage frauds resulted from inadequate regulation, the indiscriminate use of alternative loan products and a lack of accountability in the industry. Addressing these problems and preventing such misconduct necessitates major reform in the policies and practices especially with respect to red flags and early warning systems, stronger regulation and government oversight, loan qualification requirements and better underwriting standards.

Financial crises at the national level have been linked to another type of misconduct termed 'odious debt', 'odious lending' or 'illegitimate loans', when it comes to substantial loans to a country made against the interests and without the consent of its people (Hanlon, 2006; Nehru and Thomas, 2008; Michalowski and Bohoslavsky, 2009; Manolopoulos, 2011; Wong, 2012). When creditors knowingly lend kleptocrats and corrupt regimes huge amounts that are wasted and mismanaged, should they be free of responsibility? Should the people and succeeding governments be forced to honour such loans and pay them back in full or at all? In the next chapter, 'Odious Debt, Odious Credit, Economic Development, and Democratization' (Chapter 12), Tom Ginsburg and Thomas S. Ulen turn to this issue and add the question of whether a corrupt dictator should thus be allowed to steal not only from the past but also from the future of a country that struggles to regain its footing and proceed with a democratic government, but collapses under the weight of such debt. Ginsburg and Ulen (Chapter 12) argue that the odious debt doctrine and possible forgiveness ought to focus on three considerations. Firstly, it must be considered as part of 'an overall foreign-policy goal of democratization' (p. 244); secondly, consider the action of 'odious creditors' or national and international actors happy to support corrupt regimes; thirdly, focus also on the incentive structure of international financial institutions and actions that produce moral hazards for creditors. In their view, if the goal of advancing democracy is taken seriously by lenders, borrowing countries will benefit more and the agency problem in donor countries is alleviated. At the same time, a fund could be set up to support new lending to victim countries and lower the cost of debt repudiation. We will not end up in a perfect world but more clarity on risks and potential losses and accountability would make for a more viable and fairer approach.

Bridging issues of international finance and corruption with development, governance, arms procurement and security agendas, Susan Willett's chapter, 'Defence Expenditures, Arms Procurement and Corruption in Sub-Saharan Africa' (Chapter 13), takes a critical look into the sub-Saharan African region and assumptions behind certain initiatives of the development community. She challenges the one-sided assumption in much of the development literature that corruption is mostly a problem in emerging economies and brings in the supply side and corrupt practices in the defence industry (Klare, 1988; Hartung, 1994; Naylor, 1995, 2001; Phythian, 1996; Cilliers and Mason, 1999; Gupta *et al.*, 2001; Bondi, 2004; Passas, 2007; Spector, 2011), including British arms firms. Willett discusses the UK Department for International Development's (DFID) 'Transparency in Defence Expenditure' (TIDE) initiative, which aimed at fighting corruption in military expenditures and procurement. She points out that DFID's focus on the demand side of corruption left it open to charges of double standards and hypocrisy. Her argument is that the best approach is to tackle the global web of corruption involving Western arms companies, licensing governments, corrupt foreign officials and offshore financial institutions. However, this calls for major reforms at the level of global governance, rather than just improving sub-Sahara governance procedures.

Michael Johnston's chapter, 'Why Do So Many Anti-Corruption Efforts Fail?' (Chapter 14), focuses on corruption, takes stock of a significant body of literature on the topic (Klitgaard, 1988; Heidenheimer *et al.*, 1989; Nye, 1989; Rose-Ackerman, 1999; Quah, 2003; Johnston, 2005) and poses the question why do so many anti-corruption efforts fail. It is an enormous task, which he undertakes through two main arguments. Firstly, corruption control is to be considered both as a set of legal measures and administrative controls, and, very importantly, as 'a long-term *political* process through which people defend themselves against abuses by others – or as Madison had it, through which they "*oblige* [government] to control itself"' (p. 267, emphases and square brackets in original). Secondly, corruption manifests itself diversely in different societies. The quantitative and qualitative differences reflect diverse interests, socio-political and economic contexts, opportunities and institutional weaknesses. As a result, reforms efforts confront different challenges and starting points. Johnston focuses on two sets of problems: challenges inherent to anti-corruption efforts anywhere and those corresponding to specific sets of cases.

Passas' chapter, 'The Genesis of the BCCI Scandal' (Chapter 15), focuses on the Bank of Credit and Commerce International (BCCI) scandal, which involved not only corruption of different sorts but also numerous types of transnational financial crime, ranging from money laundering and illegal acquisition of foreign banks to accounting fraud, facilitation of coffee smuggling and illicit technology transfers, the Iran-Contra and arming of Iraq scandals and capital flight (Pizzo, 1991, 1992; Timmerman, 1991; Adams and Frantz, 1992; Bingham Report, 1992; Kerry Report, 1992; Passas, 1992, 1993, 1994, 1995, 1996, 2001; Truell and Gurwin, 1992; Mantius, 1995; Passas and Groskin, 2001). Illegal operations by, through and against BCCI took place over a long period of time and involved several powerful state and non-state actors, while the root causes and demand for BCCI's illegal services remain unattended. So why was a good part of them exposed at all or at the time they were? After outlining some basic facts about the bank and the international scandal, Passas inquires into the conditions enabling the creation of a scandal and exposure of many types of illegal activities. Contrary to conspiracy theories, he explores internal and external factors that created the context in which prosecutors and investigators could reveal misconduct and close down the bank globally. He considers structural arrangements and argues that the most important factors in the genesis and development of the scandal were geopolitical changes that deprived BCCI of its past instrumentality and usefulness to powerful interests and groups.

Levi's chapter, 'Organized Fraud and Organizing Frauds: Unpacking Research on Networks and Organization' (Chapter 16), turns to crime networks and organized fraud. He draws on his earlier work and the broader fraud and white-collar crime literature (Levi *et al.*,

1991; Weisburd *et al.*, 1991; Levi, 1993, 2008; Schlegel and Weisburd, 1992) to look into the settings, opportunities and victim-centred typology of fraud. He describes the different actors, the ways in which they collaborate with each other (Passas, 2003a), the organization and growth of the 'fraud business'. Levi (Chapter 16) finds quite diverse commitment to, mobility and size of groups engaging in fraud and concludes that:

> the globalization of crime is part of contingent relationships between settings, with their rich and varied opportunities (reflecting patterns of business, consumer and investment activities), the variable abilities of would-be perpetrators to recognize and act on those opportunities (the 'crime scripts' perspective), and their interactions with controls (including, but not restricted to, law enforcement). (p. 309)

Neal Shover, Glenn S. Coffey and Dick Hobbs explore new crime opportunities and centre on telemarketing fraud perpetrators in 'Crime on the Line: Telemarketing and the Changing Nature of Professional Crime' (Chapter 17). They interviewed 47 criminal telemarketers and report on their characteristics, attitudes and way of life. They suggest that these offenders pursue a hedonistic lifestyle and 'employ an ideology of legitimation and defence that insulates them from moral rejection' (p. 341), similar to professional thieves described in previous studies. However, they come disproportionately from middle class and entrepreneurial backgrounds, are very individualistic vis-à-vis each other and the police and their organizations appear more conventional than those of blue-collar offenders. Shover *et al.* find that the new vocational predators reflect contemporary criminal opportunities embedded in the same environment that furnishes legitimate entrepreneurial pursuits. Shover *et al.* (Chapter 17) conclude that:

> it is the bourgeois who have emerged with the education and ideological flexibility to engage with lucrative contemporary professional crime, which is located not with the proletarian outpost of traditional transgression, but within rhetorics that legitimate and enable the entire 'spectrum of legitimacy'. (p. 354)

In the next chapter, 'The Insurgent Economy: Black Market Operations of Guerilla Organizations' (Chapter 18), R.T. Naylor, a long-term student of transnational crimes that could just as easily have been part of this volume (Naylor, 1987, 1995, 1995/96, 1996; 2002; 2004, 2007, 2008), switches attention to 'the insurgent economy', black markets and the finance of guerrilla groups. He argues that insurgent groups are more than simply extensions of the criminal economy. Their outlaw economic activities are motivated by considerations of political advantage rather than of profit. While criminal organizations function in para-political ways attempting to control and regulate in order to increase income, insurgent groups work in a reversed sequence, using their income to promote their activities as underground governments. He suggests that a 'model' guerrilla movement evolves through stages and describes each one of them in detail. Naylor also points out that the expenditure obligations of guerrilla groups are derivative from not merely the scale but also the form of the guerrilla struggle.

The chapter by Rodger Jamieson, Leslie Pek Wee Land, Donald Winchester, Greg Stephens, Alex Steel, Alana Maurushat and Rick Sarre, 'Addressing Identity Crime in Crime Management Information Systems: Definitions, Classification, and Empirics' (Chapter 19), is on identity in crime management information systems (IS). Identity crime continues to defy attempts at a comprehensive and universally accepted definition (Chryssikos *et al.*, 2008). It is considered as an 'emerging' type of crime characterized by diversity and addressed in different ways around the world (UNODC, 2011). Jamieson *et al.* argue that the lack of specific identity crime laws could explain why perpetrators are not classified as identity offenders but under other law such as benefit fraud, or credit card fraud, which in turn can cause bias in crime management IS. Having collected quantitative and qualitative data, the authors add to our understanding of identity crime through hierarchical classes and definitions.

Transnational cybercrime is the subject of Rob McCusker's chapter, 'Transnational Organised Cyber Crime: Distinguishing Threat from Reality' (Chapter 20). This is yet another emerging crime topic with significant policy implications (CSIS Global Organized Crime Project and Center for Strategic and International Studies, 1998; Grabosky, 2007; Brenner, 2010, 2012; Leman-Langlois, 2012; Yar, 2013). He points out that cybercrime is now an integral part of the transnational threat landscape and conjures up images of nefarious and increasingly complex and organized cybercriminality. Yet strong evidence has not been produced so far on whether this is a new type of organized criminal activity or simply an evolution with new technological tools. In his view, the key question is whether those advances have merely facilitated the commission of physical crime or whether in fact they have led to the creation of a new wave of traditional, but virtual, organized crime.

The chapter by Herbert Snyder and Anthony Crescenzi, 'Intellectual Capital and Economic Espionage: New Crimes and New Protections' (Chapter 21), is about intellectual capital (IC) and economic espionage, including through the cyberspace. They explore the IC- and cyberspace-related crime risks and seek to assess the effectiveness of current laws and measures for the protection of IC. Their conceptual analysis suggests that traditional legal remedies are largely ineffective and that prevention is the only reasonable means for protecting IC. Thus, they recommend emphasis on legal protections geared towards the protection of sensitive data at their source, instead of reactive measures and legal actions after the offence is committed.

Having discussed multiple kinds of transnational financial crime and offenders, this part ends with a chapter that explores the ways in which legal and illegal transnational actors interface. In 'Cross-Border Crime and the Interface between Legal and Illegal Actors' (Chapter 22) Passas wishes to transcend an individualization of the problem and attempts to pave the ground for more structural analyses both for theoretical and policy purposes. He separates analytically 'enterprise crime' from 'political crime', while recognizing that the two are often combined in practice. He then proceeds to construct a typology of legal–illegal links and associations, in order to better organize the existing knowledge and data on this subject. Against some conventional wisdom that criminal entrepreneurs invariably act against the interests and actors in mainstream society, Passas emphasizes both antithetical and symbiotic relationships, while illustrating diverse types of associations within each broader category, and concludes with policy implications.

**Control Issues**

As criminological theories and empirical evidence have shown, not all control efforts succeed or bring about the intended and desired results. This will be highlighted in several of the remaining essays. Unanticipated and negative consequences of sanctions regimes and related controls are the subject of the first chapter in this part, 'Criminalizing Consequences of Sanctions: Embargo Busting and Its Legacy' (Chapter 23) by Peter Andreas. He recognizes the scholarly work on sanctions, their effects and humanitarian consequences (Hufbauer *et al.*, 1983; Cortright and Lopez, 1995, 2000; Weiss, 1997; Garfield, 1999; Simons, 1999; Chan and Drury, 2000; Barnhizer, 2001; Naylor, 2001; Rowe, 2001; Zucconi, 2001; Wallensteen and Staibano, 2005; Hufbauer, 2007; Spadoni, 2010; Carisch and Rickard-Martin, 2011), but points out the neglect of the sanctions' criminalizing consequences and legacy in post-sanctions periods.

Andreas first develops an analytical framework identifying and categorizing the potential criminalizing effects of sanctions across place (within and around the targeted country) and time (during and after the sanctions period). He applies then his framework to a detailed examination of the case of Yugoslavia. Andreas (Chapter 23) proceeds to test the applicability of the argument to the cases of Croatia and Iraq, all of which suggests that 'sanctions can unintentionally contribute to the criminalization of the state, economy, and civil society of both the targeted country and its immediate neighbors, fostering a symbiosis between political leaders, organized crime, and transnational smuggling networks' (p. 465). Importantly, these symbiotic interfaces that fit in Passas' typology in the previous chapter, survive the sanctions regimes and continue to fuel corruption and other serious crimes that undermine the rule of law. A key implication of this work is such consequences from sanctions and related control regimes ought to be an integral part of cost–benefit analysis and sanctions evaluation.

Continuing with sanctions regimes, Passas delves into financial controls against the proliferation of weapons of mass destruction in 'Financial Controls and Counter-Proliferation of Weapons of Mass Destruction' (Chapter 24). In February 2012, proliferation finance became part of the 40 Recommendations of the Financial Action Task Force (FATF; Recommendation 7) culminating earlier initiatives that linked FATF's work with that of the UN Security Council, which has issued numerous Resolutions on this new type of control, especially against the proliferation efforts of Iran and North Korea. These Resolutions were issued under Chapter VII of the UN Charter, which means they are automatically binding for all member states, who are also obligated to report to the Security Council how they have implemented them. Passas outlines the basic provisions of these Resolutions and reviews member state reports revealing a very wide range of approaches with regard to financial vigilance measures. He notes several challenges ranging from the resulting legal asymmetries at the global level and growing sophistication of proliferators to capacity problems, lack of political will, commercial interests, national inaction and diverse interpretation of key terms of the Resolutions. Adding to the difficulties faced by member states is the parallel introduction of national sanctions regimes by countries such as the USA and Canada or country blocks, like the European Union. Some of these regimes go beyond mandatory provisions of the UN Resolutions, so there are further uncertainties on the precise duties and responsibilities of private sector actors too (financial institutions, trading and export companies, etc.). Like Andreas, Passas refers to criminalization effects of sanctions for both state and non-state actors. He discusses the need for the following five key issues as required for more effective proliferation finance controls: (1) evidence-based policy making; (2) practices that transcend the current fragmentation of controls that focus on particular offences; and (3) a strategic approach that (4) includes outreach and partnership with the private sector as well as the academic community and (5) ensures that data on the global flows of information, commerce and finance are collected, rendered traceable, analysed and matched in order to identify irregular and suspicious activities, to piece together the bigger picture of serious financial misconduct and networks, illuminating the economic activity currently taking place in the shadows.

Financial controls against criminal enterprises and money laundering have also come under critical scrutiny (Naylor, 1999; Van Duyne and de Miranda, 1999), as illustrated by the next chapter by Petrus C. Van Duyne, Marc S. Groenhuijsen and A.A.P. Schudelaro, 'Balancing Financial Threats and Legal Interests in Money-Laundering Policy' (Chapter 25). They consider the justifications behind the current global anti-money laundering (AML) regime as far from self-evident. They point to the lack of empirical support regarding the significant size and destabilizing effects of criminal assets, while they find arguments about threats against the integrity of the financial systems incoherent and unconvincing. Yet, such arguments continue to have traction and overrule an evidence-based balance of legal interests and foundations, in contrast to the approach adopted relative to computer crime legislation, in which restraint was balanced with the requirement to update legal tools to an adequate level of effectiveness against the electronic criminal environment. They argue that this clarity is in stark contrast with the rhetoric underlying the AML regime, where they find neither restraint nor clarity.

The chapter by Nicholas Dorn, Michael Levi and Simone White, 'Do European Procurement Rules Generate or Prevent Crime?' (Chapter 26), deals with European public procurement rules and how effective they are against corruption and crime. They focus on Procurement Directive 2004/18 on the co-ordination of procedures for the award of contracts for public works, public supply and public services by public bodies. They find that some risks have not been adequately addressed with respect to the preparation of specifications: they relate to insider-driven specifications; low visibility of procurement processes; and ample opportunities for renegotiation of terms. Dorn *et al.* recommend risk reduction approaches through quality standards and pre-award publicity, but they also wonder whether modernization and traditional practices may outpace measures against procurement fraud.

In the next chapter, 'Criminal Profits, Terror Dollars, and Nonsense' (Chapter 27), Naylor critiques the AML and terrorism finance regime introduced in the aftermath of 9/11. He outlines five basic features of the US AML/CFT approach, which are intrusive, affect the relations of bankers, their clients and police and have not shown they can reduce the size of the criminal economy. He proposes instead the employment of ordinary fiscal measures and procedures to seize unreported income, which can be equally effective with fewer negative externalities to legitimate interests.

In the following chapter, 'Asset and Money Laundering in Bolivia, Colombia and Peru: A Legal Transplant in Vulnerable Environments?' (Chapter 28), Francisco E. Thoumi and Marcela Anzola examine the process of 'legal unification' of money laundering laws in Bolivia, Colombia and Peru, three countries that are the source of illegal cocaine and which have adopted national legislations that follow the international guidelines. They find that despite substantial institutional arrangements and legal developments, actual results in terms of prevention, detection and suppression on money laundering have been very modest. The implementation process has not been successful and the results are unsatisfactory. Thoumi and Anzola (Chapter 28) argue that the experience in these countries is not unique but can be found around the developing world and find the root cause of this problem is 'that the domestic legislation is more the result of an international initiative of legal unification in response to a global problem than the product of a domestic initiative. This constitutes a typical case of what in comparative law has been called "a legal transplant"' (p. 569) – foreign principles operating under assumptions that do not hold in these countries are transferred into a strange body that does not welcome or integrate them.

Finally, in 'Testing the Global Financial Transparency Regime' (Chapter 29) J.C. Sharman touches on a heated debate on whether the worst weaknesses in the global financial control regime are located in offshore centres in the global South or in the largest economies of the North (Levi and Gilmore, 2002; Masciandaro, 2004; Deneault, 2007; Levi, 2010; Christensen, 2012). In fact he tested the global financial transparency regime to assess the extent to which rules are actually applied in practice. His data come from his own solicitation and purchase of anonymous shell companies from 45 corporate service providers in 22 countries. He has found that the prohibition on anonymous corporations is relatively ineffective and is flouted much more in G7 countries than in tax havens. Sharman's essay (Chapter 29) 'contributes to and extends the work of realist scholars in international political economy, both in their skepticism of formal rules and focus on the effects of power' (p. 587).

## References

Aas, K.F. (2007), *Globalization and Crime*, Los Angeles, CA: London: Sage.

Adams, J. and Frantz, D. (1992), *The Full Service Bank*, New York: Pocket Books.

Bach, W. (2003), 'Drugs, Counterfeiting, and Arms Trade The North Korean Connection', Testimony before the Senate Committee on Governmental Affairs, 20 May.

Barnhizer, D. (2001), *Effective Strategies for Protecting Human Rights: Economic Sanctions, Use of National Courts and International Fora and Coercive Power*, Aldershot and Burlington, VT: Ashgate/Dartmouth.

Barofsky, N.M. (2012), *Bailout: An Inside Account of How Washington Abandoned Main Street While Rescuing Wall Street* (1st Free Press hardcover edn), New York: Free Press.

Baudrillard, J. (1994), *Simulacra and Simulation*, Ann Arbor, MI: University of Michigan Press.

Beare, M.E. and Schneider, S. (2007), *Money Laundering in Canada: Chasing Dirty and Dangerous Dollars*, Toronto: University of Toronto Press.

Bhat, G. and Deutsches Institut für Entwicklungspolitik (2009), *Transfer Pricing, Tax Havens and Global Governance*, Bonn: German Development Institute.

Bingham Report (1992), *Inquiry into the Supervision of the Bank of Credit and Commerce International*, London: HMSO.

Bondi, L. (2004), 'Externalities of the Arms Trade', in N. Passas and N. Goodwin (eds), *It's Legal But It Ain't Right: Harmful Social Consequences of Legal Industries*, Ann Arbor, MI: University of Michigan Press, pp. 43–73.

Brenner, S.W. (2010), *Cybercrime: Criminal Threats from Cyberspace*, Santa Barbara, CA: Praeger.

Brenner, S.W. (2012), *Cybercrime and the Law: Challenges, Issues, and Outcomes*, Boston, MA: Northeastern University Press.

Brooks, R. (2013), *The Great Tax Robbery: How Britain Became a Tax Haven for Fat Cats and Big Business*, London: Oneworld.

Carisch, E. and Rickard-Martin, L. (2011), *Global Threats and the Role of United Nations Sanctions*, New York: Friedrich Ebert Stiftung.

Chaikin, D.A. and Sharman, J.C. (2009), *Corruption and Money Laundering: A Symbiotic Relationship* (1st edn), New York: Palgrave Macmillan.

Chan, S. and Drury, A.C. (2000), *Sanctions as Economic Statecraft: Theory and Practice*, Houndmills: Palgrave Macmillan.

Christensen, J. (2012), 'The Hidden Trillions: Secrecy, Corruption, and the Offshore Interface', *Crime, Law and Social Change*, **57**, pp. 325–43.

Chryssikos, D., Passas, N. and Ram, C. (eds) (2008), *The Evolving Challenge of Identity-Related Crime: Addressing Fraud and the Criminal Misuse and Falsification of Identity*, Milan: ISPAC.

Cilliers, J. and Mason, P. (eds) (1999), *Peace, Profit or Plunder? The Privatisation of Security in War-Torn African Societies*, Halfway House, South Africa: Institute for Security Studies.

Cortright, D. and Lopez, G.A. (1995), *Economic Sanctions: Panacea or Peacebuilding in a Post-Cold War World?*, Boulder, CO: Westview Press.

Cortright, D. and Lopez, G.A. (2000), *The Sanctions Decade: Assessing UN Strategies in the 1990s*, Boulder, CO: Lynne Rienner Publishers.

CSIS Global Organized Crime Project and Center for Strategic and International Studies (1998), *Cybercrime – Cyberterrorism – Cyberwarfare: Averting an Electronic Waterloo*, Washington, DC: CSIS Press.

DeKieffer, D. (2005), 'Trade Diversion as a Fund Raising and Money Laundering Technique of Terrorist Organizations', unpublished paper, 6 November.

Deneault, A. (2007), 'Tax Havens and Criminology', *Global Crime*, **8**, pp. 260–70.

Edelbacher, M., Kratcoski, P.C. and Theil, M. (2012), *Financial Crimes: A Threat to Global Security*, Boca Raton, FL: CRC Press.

FBI (2010–11), 'Financial Crimes Report to the Public: Fiscal Years 2010–11', at: http://www.fbi.gov/stats-services/publications/financial-crimes-report-2010–2011.

Findlay, M. (2008), *Governing through Globalised Crime: Futures for International Criminal Justice*, Devon: Willan.

Garfield, R. (1999), *The Impact of Economic Sanctions on Health and Well-Being*, London: Overseas Development Institute.

Gilmore, W.C. (2004), *Dirty Money: The Evolution of Money Laundering Counter-Measures* (3rd edn), Strasbourg: Council of Europe Press.

Gori, U. and Paparela, I. (2006), *Invisible Threats: Financial and Information Technology Crimes and National Security*, Amsterdam: Ios Press.

Grabosky, P.N. (2007), *Electronic Crime*, Upper Saddle River, NJ: Pearson Prentice Hall.

Gupta, S., Mello, L.D. and Sharan, R. (2001), 'Corruption and Military Spending', *European Journal of Political Economy*, **17**, pp. 749–77.

Hanlon, J. (2006), 'Lenders, Not Borrowers, Are Responsible for "Illegitimate" Loans', *Third World Quarterly*, **27**, pp. 211–26.

Hartung, W.D. (1994), *And Weapons for All*, New York: HarperCollins.

Heidenheimer, A.J., Johnston, M. and LeVine, V.T. (eds) (1989), *Political Corruption: A Handbook*, New Brunswick, NJ: Transaction.

Hörnle, J. and Zammit, B. (2010), *Cross-Border Online Gambling Law and Policy*, Cheltenham, UK: Edward Elgar.

Hufbauer, G.C. (2007), *Economic Sanctions Reconsidered* (3rd edn), Washington, DC: Peterson Institute for International Economics.

Hufbauer, G.C., Schott, J.J. and Elliott, K.A. (1983), *Economic Sanctions in Support of Foreign Policy Goals*, Washington, DC and Cambridge: Institute for International Economics; Distributed by MIT Press.

International Monetary Fund. Monetary and Financial Systems Dept (2005), *Regulatory Frameworks for Hawala and Other Remittance Systems*, Washington, DC: Monetary and Financial Systems Dept, International Monetary Fund.

Johnston, M. (2005), *Syndromes of Corruption: Wealth, Power, and Democracy*, Cambridge: Cambridge University Press.

Kerry Report (1992), *The BCCI Affair*, Washington, DC: GPO.

Klare, M.T. (1988), 'Secret Operatives, Clandestine Trade: The Thriving Black Market for Weapons', *Bulletin of Atomic Scientists*, **44**, pp. 16–24.

Klinger, S. and Sklar, H. (2005), 'Titans of the Enron Economy: The Ten Habits of Highly Defective Corporations', in N. Passas and N. Goodwin (eds), *It's Legal But It Ain't Right: Harmful Social Consequences of Legal Industries*, Ann Arbor, MI: University of Michigan Press, pp. 230–52.

Klitgaard, R. (1988), *Controlling Corruption*, Berkeley, CA: University of California Press.

Leman-Langlois, S. (2012), *Technocrime, Policing, and Surveillance* (1st edn), New York: Routledge.

Levi, M. (1991a), 'Pecunia non Olet: Cleansing the Money-Launderers from the Temple', *Crime, Law and Social Change*, **16**, pp. 217–302.

Levi, M. (1991b), 'Regulating Money Laundering', *British Journal of Criminology*, **31**, pp. 109–25.

Levi, M. (1993), *The Investigation, Prosecution, and Trial of Serious Fraud*, London: HMSO.

Levi, M. (2008), *The Phantom Capitalists: The Organization and Control of Long-Firm Fraud* (rev. edn), Aldershot: Ashgate.

Levi, M. (2010), 'Serious Tax Fraud and Noncompliance', *Criminology & Public Policy*, **9**, pp. 493–513.

Levi, M. and Gilmore, B. (2002), 'Terrorist Finance, Money Laundering and the Rise and Rise of Mutual Evaluation: A New Paradigm for Crime Control?', *European Journal of Law Reform*, **4**, pp. 337–64.

Levi, M. and Reuter, P. (2006), 'Money Laundering', *Crime and Justice*, **34**, pp. 289–375.

Maimbo, S.M. (2003), *The Money Exchange Dealers of Kabul: A Study of the Hawala System in Afghanistan*, Washington, DC: World Bank.

Levi, M., Bisset, P. and Richardson, T. (1991), *The Prevention of Cheque and Credit Card Fraud*, London: Home Office Crime Prevention Unit.

Manolopoulos, J. (2011), *Greece's 'Odious' Debt: The Looting of the Hellenic Republic by the Euro, the Political Elite and the Investment Community*, London: Anthem Press.

Mantius, P. (1995), *Shell Game*, New York: St Martin's Press.

Masciandaro, D. (2004), *Combating Black Money: Money Laundering and Terrorism Finance, International Cooperation and the G8 Role*, *Universita di Lecce Economics Working Paper No. 56/26*.

McBarnet, D. (1992), 'Legitimate Rackets: Tax Evasion, Tax Avoidance and the Boundaries of Legality', *Journal of Human Justice*, **3**, pp. 56–74.

Messner, S.F. and Rosenfeld, R. (1994), *Crime and the American Dream*, Belmont, CA: Wadsworth.

Michalowski, R.J. and Kramer, R.C. (2006), *State–Corporate Crime: Wrongdoing at the Intersection of Business and Government*, New Brunswick, NJ: Rutgers University Press.

Michalowski, S. and Bohoslavsky, J. (2009), 'Ius Cogens, Transitional Justice and Other Trends of the Debate on Odious Debts: A Response to the World Bank Discussion Paper on Odious Debts', *Columbia Journal of Transnational Law*, **48**, pp. 59–113.

Morgenson, G. and Rosner, J. (2012), *Reckless Endangerment: How Outsized Ambition, Greed, and Corruption Created the Worst Financial Crisis of Our Time*, New York: St Martin's Press.

Naim, M. (2005), *Illicit: How Smugglers, Traffickers and Copycats Are Hijacking the Global Economy*, New York: Doubleday.

Naylor, R.T. (1987), *Hot Money and the Politics of Debt*, New York: Simon and Schuster.

Naylor, R.T. (1995), 'Loose Canons: Covert Commerce and Underground Finance in the Modern Arms Black Market', *Crime, Law and Social Change*, **22**, pp. 1–57.

Naylor, R.T. (1995/96), 'From Underworld to Underground', *Crime, Law and Social Change*, **24**, pp. 79–150.

Naylor, R.T. (1996), 'The Underworld of Gold', *Crime, Law and Social Change*, **25**, pp. 191–241.

Naylor, R.T. (1999), 'Wash-Out: A Critique of Follow-the-Money Methods in Crime Control Policy', *Crime, Law and Social Change*, **32**, pp. 1–57.

Naylor, R.T. (2001), *Economic Warfare: Sanctions, Embargo Busting and Their Human Cost*, Boston, MA: Northeastern University Press.

Naylor, R.T. (2002), *Wages of Crime: Black Markets, Illegal Finance, and the Underworld Economy*, Ithaca, NY: Cornell University Press.

Naylor, R.T. (2004), 'The Underworld of Ivory', *Crime, Law and Social Change*, **42**, pp. 261–95.

Naylor, R.T. (2007), 'The Alchemy of Fraud: Investment Scams in the Precious Metal-Mining Business', *Crime, Law and Social Change*, **47**, pp. 89–120.

Naylor, R.T. (2008), 'The Underworld of Art', *Crime, Law and Social Change*, **50**, pp. 263–91.

Nehru, V. and Thomas, M. (2008), *The Concept of Odious Debt: Some Considerations*, Washington, DC: World Bank.

Nye, J.S. (1989), 'Corruption and Political Development: A Cost–Benefit Analysis', in A.J. Heidenheimer, M. Johnston and V.T. LeVine (eds), *Political Corruption: A Handbook*, New Brunswick, NJ: Transaction, pp. 963–83.

Passas, N. (1990), 'Anomie and Corporate Deviance', *Contemporary Crises*, **14**, pp. 157–78.

Passas, N. (1992), *Regulatory Anaesthesia or the Limits of Criminal Law: The Prosecution of BCCI for Money Laundering in Tampa, FL*, Washington, DC: Drug Policy Foundation.

Passas, N. (1993), 'Structural Sources of International Crime: Policy Lessons from the BCCI Affair', *Crime, Law and Social Change*, **20**, pp. 293–305.

Passas, N. (1994), 'I Cheat, Therefore I Exist? The BCCI Scandal in Context', in W.M. Hoffman, J. Kamm, R.E. Frederick and E. Petry (eds), *Emerging Global Business Ethics*, Newport, CO: Quorum Books, pp. 69–78.

Passas, N. (1995), 'The Mirror of Global Evils: A Review Essay on the BCCI Affair', *Justice Quarterly*, **12**, pp. 377–419.

Passas, N. (1996), 'Accounting for Fraud: Auditors' Ethical and Legal Dilemmas in the BCCI Affair', in W.M. Hoffman, J. Kamm, R.E. Frederick and E. Petry (eds), *The Ethics of Accounting and Finance*, Newport, CO: Quorum Books, pp. 85–99.

Passas, N. (1997), 'Anomie, Reference Groups, and Relative Deprivation', in N. Passas and R. Agnew (eds), *The Future of the Anomie Tradition*, Boston, MA: Northeastern University Press, pp. 62–94.

Passas, N. (1999a), *Informal Value Transfer Systems and Criminal Organizations: A Study into So-Called Underground Banking Networks*, The Hague: Ministry of Justice.

Passas, N. (1999b), *Transnational Crime*, Aldershot: Ashgate.

Passas, N. (2001), 'False Accounts: Why Do Company Statements Often Offer a True and Fair View of Virtual Reality?', *European Journal on Criminal Policy and Research*, **9**, pp. 117–35.

Passas, N. (2003a), 'Cross-Border Crime and the Interface between Legal and Illegal Actors', *Security Journal*, **16**, pp. 19–37.

Passas, N. (2003b), 'Hawala and Other Informal Value Transfer Systems: How to Regulate Them?', *Journal of Risk Management*, **5**, pp. 39–49.

Passas, N. (2003c), *International Crimes*, Aldershot and Burlington, VT: Ashgate/Dartmouth.

Passas, N. (2004a), 'Indicators of Hawala Operations and Criminal Abuse', *Journal of Money Laundering Control*, **8**, pp. 168–72.

Passas, N. (2004b), *The Trade in Diamonds: Vulnerabilities for Financial Crime and Terrorist Finance*, Vienna, VA: FinCEN, US Treasury Department.

Passas, N. (2005a), 'Global Anomie Theory and Crime', in S. Henry and M. Lanier (eds), *The Essential Criminology Reader*, Boulder, CO: Westview Press, pp. 174–82.

Passas, N. (2005b), 'Lawful But Awful: "Legal Corporate Crimes"', *Journal of Socio-Economics*, **34**, pp. 771–86.

Passas, N. (2006), 'Setting Global CFT Standards: A Critique and Suggestions', *Journal of Money Laundering Control*, **9**, pp. 281–92.

Passas, N. (2007), *Procurement Fraud and Corruption: Report to the Institute for Fraud Prevention*, Boston, MA: Northeastern University.

Passas, N. (2011), 'Terrorist Finance, Informal Markets, Trade and Regulation: Challenges of Evidence in International Efforts', in C. Lum and L.W. Kennedy (eds), *Evidence-Based Counterterrorism Policy*, New York: Springer, pp. 255–80.

Passas, N. and Goodwin, N. (eds) (2004), *It's Legal, But It Ain't Right: Harmful Social Consequences of Legal Industries*, Ann Arbor, MI: University of Michigan Press.

Passas, N. and Groskin, R.B. (2001), 'Overseeing and Overlooking: The US Federal Authorities' Response to Money Laundering and Other Misconduct at BCCI', *Crime, Law and Social Change*, **35**, pp. 141–75.

Passas, N. and Nelken, D. (1993), 'The Thin Line between Legitimate and Criminal Enterprises: Subsidy Frauds in the European Community', *Crime, Law and Social Change*, **19**, pp. 223–43.

Pearce, F. and Woodiwiss, M. (eds) (1993), *Global Crime Connections: Dynamics and Control*, Toronto: Universisty of Toronto Press.

Phillips, T. (2005), *Knockoff: The Deadly Trade in Counterfeit Goods: The True Story of the World's Fastest Growing Crime Wave*, London: Kogan Page.

Phythian, M. (1996), *Arming Iraq: How the U.S. and Britain Secretly Built Saddam's War Machine*, Boston, MA: Northeastern University Press.

Picciotto, S. (1992), *International Business Taxation*, New York: Quorum Books.

Pieth, M. and Aiolfi, G. (2004), *A Comparative Guide to Anti-Money Laundering: A Critical Analysis of Systems in Singapore, Switzerland, the UK and the USA*, Cheltenham: E. Elgar Publishing.

Pizzo, S. (1991), 'The West Bankers: Behind the Big BCCI Scandal Lies a Strange Alliance – Arab Sheikhs and Pro-Israel S&Ls', *Mother Jones*, Nov./Dec., pp. 28–29.

Pizzo, S. (1992), 'Family Values', *Mother Jones*, Sept., pp. 28–33, 66–68.

Quah, J.S.T. (2003), *Curbing Corruption in Asia: A Comparative Study of Six Countries*, Singapore: Eastern Universities Press.

Reno, W. (2009), 'Illicit Markets, Violence, Warlords, and Governance: West African Cases', *Crime, Law and Social Change*, **52**, pp. 313–22.

Reuter, P. (2012), *Draining Development? Controlling Flows of Illicit Funds from Developing Countries*, Washington, DC: World Bank.

Reuter, P. and Truman, E.M. (2004), *Chasing Dirty Money: The Fight against Money Laundering*, Washington, DC: Institute for International Economics.

Rose-Ackerman, S. (1999), *Corruption and Government: Causes, Consequences, and Reform*, Cambridge: Cambridge University Press.

Rowe, D.M. (2001), *Manipulating the Market: Understanding Economic Sanctions, Institutional Change, and the Political Unity of White Rhodesia*, Ann Arbor, MI: University of Michigan Press.

Schlegel, K. and Weisburd, D. (eds) (1992), *White-Collar Crime Reconsidered*, Boston, MA: Northeastern University Press.

Sharman, J.C. (2011), *The Money Laundry: Regulating Criminal Finance in the Global Economy*, Ithaca, NY: Cornell University Press.

Simons, G.L. (1999), *Imposing Economic Sanctions: Legal Remedy or Genocidal Tool?*, London: Pluto Press.

Spadoni, P. (2010), *Failed Sanctions: Why the U.S. Embargo against Cuba Could Never Work*, Gainesville, FL: University Press of Florida.

Spector, B.I. (2011), *Negotiating Peace and Confronting Corruption: Challenges for Postconflict Societies*, Washington, DC: United States Institute of Peace.

Taibbi, M. (2013), 'Gangster Bankers: Too Big to Jail', *Rolling Stone*, 28 February, at: http://www.rollingstone.com/politics/news/gangster-bankers-too-big-to-jail-20130214.

Thompson, E.A. (2006), 'The Nexus of Drug Trafficking and Hawala in Afghanistan', in D. Buddenberg and W.A. Byrd (eds), *Afghanistan's Drug Industry: Structure, Functioning, Dynamics, and Implications for Counter-Narcotics Policy*, Washington, DC: The World Bank, pp. 155–88.

Thompson, E.A. (2011), *Trust Is the Coin of the Realm: Lessons from the Money Men in Afghanistan*, Karachi: Oxford University Press.

Timmerman, K.R. (1991), *The Death Lobby: How the West Armed Iraq*, Boston, MA: Houghton Mifflin.

Truell, P. and Gurwin, L. (1992), *False Profits*, Boston, MA: Houghton Mifflin.

Twyman-Ghoshal, A. (2012), *Understanding Contemporary Maritime Piracy*, Boston, MA: Northeastern University.

UNODC (2011), *Handbook on Identity-Related Crime*, Vienna: UN Office of Drugs and Crime.

US House Committee on Energy and Commerce (1982), *SEC and Citicorp*, Washington, DC: US Government Printing Office.

United States. Congress. House. Committee on Financial Services (2010), *Internet Gambling Regulation, Consumer Protection and Enforcement Act Report Together with Dissenting Views (to Accompany H.R. 2267) (Including Cost Estimate of the Congressional Budget Office)*, Washington, DC: US GPO.

United States. Congress. House. Committee on International Relations (2003), *Intellectual Property Crimes: Are Proceeds from Counterfeited Goods Funding Terrorism? Hearing before the Committee on International Relations, House of Representatives, One Hundred Eighth Congress, First Session, July 16, 2003*, Washington, DC: US GPO.

United States. Congress. House. Committee on the Judiciary. Subcommittee on Courts the Internet and Intellectual Property (2003), *International Copyright Piracy: A Growing Problem with Links to Organized Crime and Terrorism: Hearing before the Subcommittee on Courts, the Internet, and Intellectual Property, One Hundred Eighth Congress, First Session, March 13, 2003*, Washington, DC: US GPO.

United States. Congress. Senate. Committee on Homeland Security and Governmental Affairs (2005), *Counterfeit Goods: Easy Cash for Criminals and Terrorists: Hearing Before the Committee on Homeland Security and Governmental Affairs, United States Senate, One Hundred Ninth Congress, First Session, May 25, 2005*, Washington, DC: US GPO.

Vallette, J. and Wysham, D. (2002), *Enron's Pawns*, Washington, DC: Sustainable Energy and Economy Network/Institute for Policy Studies.

Van Dijk, J. (2008), *The World of Crime: Breaking the Silence on Problems of Security, Justice, and Development across the World*, Los Angeles, CA: Sage Publications.

Van Duyne, P. and de Miranda, H. (1999), 'The Emperor's Clothes of Disclosure: Hot Money and Suspect Disclosures', *Crime, Law and Social Change*, **27**, pp. 245–71.

Vaughan, D. (1983), *Controlling Unlawful Organizational Behavior*, Chicago, IL: Chicago University Press.

Vaughan, D. (1995), 'Anomie Theory and Organizations: Culture and the Normalization of Deviance at NASA', in N. Passas and R. Agnew (eds), *The Future of Anomie Theory*, Boston, MA: Northeastern University Press, pp. 95–123.

Wallensteen, P. and Staibano, C. (2005), *International Sanctions: Between Words and Wars in the Global System*, London: Routledge.

Weisburd, D., Wheeler, S., Waring, E. and Bode, N. (1991), *Crimes of the Middle Classes*, New Haven, CT: Yale University Press.

Weiss, T.G. (1997), *Political Gain and Civilian Pain: Humanitarian Impacts of Economic Sanctions*, Lanham, MD: Rowman & Littlefield.

Wilkinson, T. and Ellingwood, K. (2011), 'Cartels Use Legitimate Trade to Launder Money, U.S., Mexico Say', *LA Times*, 19 December, at: http://articles.latimes.com/print/2011/dec/2019/world/la-fg-mexico-money-laundering-trade-20111219.

Williams, R.J., Wood, R.T. and Parke, J. (2012), *Routledge International Handbook of Internet Gambling*, London: Routledge.

Wong, Y. (2012), *Sovereign Finance and the Poverty of Nations: Odious Debt in International Law*, Cheltenham: Edward Elgar.

Yar, M. (2013), *Cybercrime and Society* (2nd edn), Thousand Oaks, CA: Sage Publications.

Zdanowicz, J.S., Welch, W.W. and Pak, S.J. (1996), 'Capital Flight from India to the United States through Abnormal Pricing in International Trade', *Finance India*, **10**, pp. 881–99.

Zucconi, M. (2001), *The Effects of Economic Sanctions: The Case of Serbia*, Milan: Franco Angeli.

# Part I
# Theoretical Frameworks

# [1]

# Globalization, Criminogenic Asymmetries and Economic Crime

Nikos Passas*

## A. Introduction

We are inundated by press reports and official statements on the danger of transnational crimes, ranging from drug trafficking, terrorism and political corruption to car theft, the smuggling of aliens, nuclear materials and money laundering. The issue is high on the agenda whenever Heads of States meet. Topical as it has become, the problem is hardly new. Sophisticated criminals have always been able to transcend national borders. Governments, corporations, white-collar professionals, as well as illegal enterprises and professional crooks have been committing transnational offences for ages. There is a plethora of documented cross-border crimes, such as piracy, arms trafficking, genocide, environmental pollution and the ruthless exploitation of Third World countries by multinational corporations.[1]

What is new in the 1990s, however, is the intense official concern about transnational crime. Just about every international and regional agency has been proposing and implementing policy initiatives and concrete measures. Some of these proposals are quite controversial and risky, as they involve the merging of law

---

\* Nikos Passas, Philadelphia. The author of this article would like to acknowledge the financial support of Temple University, which allowed him to concentrate exclusively on his research activities during a sabbatical leave.

[1] G.J. Andreopoulos, *Genocide: Conceptual and Historical Dimensions* (Philadelphia, University of Pennsylvania Press, 1994); A.A. Block, *Masters of Paradise: Organized Crime and the Internal Revenue Service in the Bahamas* (New Brunswick NJ, Transaction 1991); J. Braithwaite, *Corporate Crime in the Pharmaceutical Industry* (London, Routledge and Kegan Paul 1984); W.J. Chambliss, *On the Take: From Petty Crooks to Presidents* (Bloomington, Indiana University Press 1988, 2nd ed.); M.B. Clinard, *Corporate Corruption: The Abuse of Power* (New York, Praeger 1990); R. Falk, 'Nuremberg: Past, Present, and Future' in (1971) 80 *Yale Law Journal*, at pp. 1501–1528; A. Labrousse, *La Drogue, L'Argent et les Armes* (Paris, Fayard 1991); R.J. Michalowski and R.C. Kramer, 'The Space Between Laws: The Problem of Corporate Crime in a Transnational Context' in (1987) 34 *Social Problems* 1, at pp. 34–53 reprinted in N. Passas, (ed.), *Transnational Crime* (Aldershot, Dartmouth 1998).

enforcement and intelligence services, a certain militarization of policing, privacy piercing methods and the use of undercover operations.[2] This begs the question: is the threat of transnational crime growing so fast that draconian measures are indispensable or are we overreacting? Is it possible that the proposed cures are as harmful as the problem they seek to solve? Some of these policies are quite drastic and carry risks to democratic principles and transition processes in many countries.

Unfortunately, discussions about the nature and extent of transnational crime are often based on speculation, exaggerations, soft data or false information. We do not have even a universally accepted definition of 'transnational crime'. In the absence of reliable evidence, the task of policymakers and social scientists is to analyse current conditions and carefully outline what we might expect at least theoretically. This is the first and most essential step before taking policy measures we might later regret. In this paper, the author poses three interrelated questions:

(1)  What factors cause transnational crime?
(2)  How does the process of globalization affect such crime?
(3)  How does globalization affect crime control efforts?

It will be argued that cross-border crime is the product of 'criminogenic asymmetries': conflicts, mismatches and inequalities in the spheres of politics, culture, the economy and the law. Globalization multiplies and intensifies such asymmetries. At the same time, there is no widely accepted and effective transnational law making and law enforcement body or mechanism. While the international community becomes a global village, controllers are generally constrained by their divergent domestic rules and limited within their jurisdiction. Precisely when we need better controls, the world is characterized by *dysnomie*.

Yet, there is no need to panic. The problem appears to be neither new nor out of control. Despite a gradual loss of autonomy, states are still able to do something about transnational crime. The author concludes with policy implications and argues that the best strategy is to make full use of new formal and informal control opportunities, which are also produced by the process of globalization.


# B. A Definition of Transnational Crime

While the public debate is ongoing, the definition of transnational crime remains relatively unclear. Some equate transnational crime to stereotyped 'organized crime',

---

[2]  P. Andreas, 'The Rise of the American Crimefare State' in (1997) 14 *World Policy Journal* 3, at pp. 37–45; R.T. Naylor, 'From Cold War to Crime War: The Search for a New 'National Security' Threat' in (1995a) 1 *Transnational Organized Crime* 4, at pp. 37–56; N. Passas and J. Blum 'Intelligence Services and Undercover Operations: The Case of Euromac' in *Invading the Private? Accountability and the New Policing in Europe* (Stewart Field and C. Pelser (eds.)) (Aldershot, Dartmouth in press).

which crosses national borders. The problems with employing the term 'organized crime' or limiting it to Mafia type ethnic associations are well known from the study of domestic forms of criminal enterprises.[3] Others distinguish between international crime and transnational crime. International crimes are those proscribed by international law and custom.[4] Transnational crimes, on the other hand, are sometimes defined as acts prohibited by the penal laws of more than one country.[5]

In the past, only state actors were subject to international law or could refer to it for the resolution of their disputes. Recent developments, however, have completely changed the situation. Individuals can now bring action against state actors and can be prosecuted for breaches of international criminal laws. In this new context, the distinction between the above-mentioned two types of crime is not particularly helpful. More importantly, the reliance on national laws for the definition of transnational crime leads to an impasse. Powerful domestic or international actors can and do influence the laws of nation states. This means that what is a crime and what is not can be decided by corrupt legislators, dictators, ruthless corporations, resourceful lobbies, etc. Should such forces influence the scope of a social scientist's object of study or a public policymaker's actions? In addition, even if all legislative processes were well-intentioned and lawful, there is a substantial diversity of laws and standards in the global community. So, we need substantive criteria for the definition of the concept of transnational crime.

In the search for a definition, which avoids the use of one or a few nation states' standards, one might be tempted to adopt completely non-legal criteria. Yet, this approach can easily lead to a subjective or relativist definition. So, the point is to define transnational crime in an inclusive manner, but without distancing ourselves too much from the law. As a first approximation, the following definition is proposed: transnational crime is cross-border misconduct, which entails avoidable and unnecessary harm to society, which is serious enough to warrant state intervention and similar to other kinds of acts criminalized in the countries concerned or by international law. Crime will be viewed as cross-border when the offenders or victims are located in or operate through more than one country.

---

[3] N. Passas, (ed.), *Organized Crime* (Aldershot, Dartmouth 1995).

[4] E.g., aggression, piracy, war crimes, genocide, etc.: C. Bassiouni, (1983) 'The Penal Characteristics of Conventional International Criminal Law' in (1983) 15 *Case Western Reserve Journal of International Law*, at pp. 27–37; T.L.H. McCormack and G.J. Simpson, 'The International Law Commission's Draft Code of Crimes Against the Peace and Security of Mankind: An Appraisal of the Substantive Provisions' in (1994) 5 *Criminal Law Forum* 1, at pp. 1–55.

[5] A. Bossard, *Transnational Crime and Criminal Law* (Chicago, Office of International Criminal Justice 1990).

# C. Criminogenic Asymmetries and Economic Crime

This article focuses on economic crime, which includes state crime, corporate and individual white-collar crime, as well as illegal enterprises (popularly called 'organized crime'). Most analyses of contemporary transnational economic crime concentrate on control issues, which reflect a certain anxiety on the part of (primarily Western) governments who realize that their ability to address even domestic forms of crime is diminishing. However, a complete explanation of any sort of crime requires adequate accounts with respect to illicit opportunities, motives to take advantage of such opportunities and wanting controls.

Students of global crimes have noted the influence and importance of wars, embargoes, protectionist policies, economic crises, political instability or oppression, supply shortages, differences in values and priorities among states, etc.[6] These and many other forces contributing to economic crime can be examined under the umbrella concept of 'criminogenic asymmetries', which refers to structural discrepancies, mismatches and inequalities in the realms of the economy, law, politics, and culture. Asymmetries can cause crime:

(1) by fuelling the demand for illegal goods and services;
(2) by generating incentives for people and organizations to engage in illegal practices; and
(3) by reducing the ability of authorities to control crime.

The cases illustrating the criminogenic effects of asymmetries are legion.

For example, regulatory discrepancies along with substantial economic and political asymmetries have given rise to an enormous illegal market for toxic waste. Many Third World countries either do not regulate toxic waste or do so much less

---

[6] W.J. Chambliss, 'State-Organized Crime' in (1989) 27 *Criminology* 2, at pp. 183–208; J.P. Eaton, 'The Nigerian Tragedy, Environmental Regulation of Transnational Corporations and the Human Right to a Healthy Environment' in (1987) 15 *Boston University International Journal*, at p. 261 et seq.; P.L. Margules, 'International Art Theft and the Illegal Import and Export of Cultural Property: A Study of Relevant Values, Legislation, and Solutions' in (1992) 15 *Suffolk Transnational Law Journal*, at pp. 609–647, reprinted in N. Passas (ed.) *Transnational Crime* (Aldershot, Dartmouth 1998); R.T. Naylor, 'The Insurgent Economy: Black Market Operations of Guerilla Organizations' in (1993) 20 *Crime, Law and Social Change*, at pp. 13–51; R.T. Naylor, 'Loose Canons: Covert Commerce and Underground Finance in the Modern Arms Black Market' in (1995b) 22 *Crime, Law and Social Change*, at pp. 1–57, reprinted in N. Passas (ed.) *Transnational Crime* (Aldershot, Dartmouth 1998); Observatoire Géopolitique des Drogues, *The Geopolitics of Drugs* (Boston, Northeastern University Press 1996); N. Passas, 'Structural Sources of International Crime: Policy Lessons from the BCCI Affair' in (1993) 20 *Crime, Law and Social Change* 4, at pp. 293–305; W.R. Swinyard, H. Rinne and A.K. Kau, 'The Morality of Software Piracy: A Cross-Cultural Analysis' in (1990) 9 *Journal of Business Ethics*, at pp. 655–664.

rigorously than industrial states. This provides the opportunity for companies to get rid of their dangerous waste in areas where rules are lax or non-existent. Rich and 'filthy' countries ship their waste to other countries, less able to adequately deal with the ultimate disposal of such imported 'goods'.[7]

The huge financial and competitive advantages that can be gained by regulatory and cost asymmetries are a strong incentive to profit from illicit opportunities. Additional companies join in because their competitors do it and their survival is at stake. Power and economic asymmetries lead recipient countries to allow all this to go on because of their dependence on foreign investment, the need for cash in order to service external debt and the desire to create jobs. Economic and knowledge asymmetries shape the motivation of local participants in this questionable trade, too. The decision to go along reflects their lack of understanding of the full extent or nature of the hazard, their desperate need for additional income, or corruption.

Asymmetries contribute in complex ways to the absence of adequate controls. In some cases there are simply no controls at all. Technological and knowledge asymmetries are again at play, as local expertise or resources necessary to recognize the risks and deal with the waste are in short supply. Political and power asymmetries play their role when people notice the negative effects, but oppressive regimes disallow protests and ensure that poisoning practices continue unimpeded.[8] Bribes may be paid to ensure that officials' eyes remain blind to the injustice and exploitation that takes place in their jurisdiction. Even when governments of affected countries seek redress and international instruments to remedy the situation, powerful Western governments undermine corrective actions.[9]

Many criminal practices are both the result and a cause of asymmetries in a vicious circle. Corruption, for example, is a conservative force that maintains or increases asymmetries. In the Third World, it has seriously hampered social, economic and political progress. Through the transfer of illicit payments to the West, corruption undermines economic development. This, in turn, leads to political instability as well as poor infrastructure and social services, lower education standards, and the non-completion of projects. Funds are allocated unfairly and inefficiently, which frustrates skilled and honest citizens, and increases the general population's level of distrust. As a consequence, a lot of foreign aid disappears, productive capacity is weakened, administrative efficiency is reduced and the

---

[7] U. Beck, *The Risk Society* (London, Sage 1992) at p. 40; Center for Investigative Reporting and B. Moyers, *Global Dumping Ground: The International Traffic in Hazardous Waste* (Washington DC, Seven Locks Press 1990).

[8] M.B. Clinard, *Corporate Corruption: The Abuse of Power* (New York, Praeger 1990).

[9] E.g. see the disagreements over the language in the Basel Convention: M. Critharis, 'Third World Nations are Down in the Dumps: The Exportation of Hazardous Waste' in (1990) 6 *Brooklyn Journal of International Law* 2, at pp. 311–339, reprinted in N. Passas (ed.) *Transnational Crime* (Aldershot, Dartmouth 1998).

legitimacy of political order is undermined.[10] Political violence and other conflicts are likely to spring up in such contexts, which then give rise to illegal weapons markets and possible connections with drug trafficking as a source to finance arms purchases.[11]

Corruption is also a consequence of asymmetries. Companies operating in countries with slow and inefficient administrations are tempted to pay 'speed money', in order to 'get the job done'. In other cases, a company may lose contracts, if it is squeamish about matching the bribes offered by other companies. The more non-meritocratic and unequal societies are, the higher is the preparedness of individuals to pay bribes in order to secure a job or other favours.

In that process, controls are weakened; widespread rationalizations of bribery as a necessary evil ease the minds of corporate managers. Diverse interpretations of the public interest may turn a corrupt practice into a patriotic act.[12] Economic asymmetries foster attitudes justifying corruption as functional to local economies and as a way of redistributing wealth.[13] The more generalized a clientelist system is, the less participants feel that they are doing something objectionable. Moreover, legal asymmetries provide a shield against the discovery or sanctioning of corruption. The funds may end up in a secrecy jurisdiction with anonymous accounts. Additional protection is offered by the differential treatment of bribes to foreign officials. In some countries they are a serious offence, while in others they constitute tax deductible business expenses.

# D. Globalization and Asymmetries

These problems increase significantly as a result of the dynamics of globalization, whereby asymmetries are multiplied, intensified and their criminogenic potential is

---

[10] M. Johnston, 'Corruption, Inequality and Change' in *Corruption, Development and Inequality* (P.M. Ward (ed.)) (London and New York, Routledge 1989) pp. 13–37; R. Klitgaard, *Controlling Corruption* (Berkeley, University of California Press 1988); N. Passas, 'Promotion and Maintenance of the Rule of Law and Good Governance: Action Against Corruption' in (1997a) 3 *International Journal of Technical Co-operation* 2, at pp. 237–253.

[11] R.T. Naylor, 'The Insurgent Economy: Black Market Operations of Guerilla Organizations' in (1993) 20 *Crime, Law and Social Change*, at pp. 13–51; R.T. Naylor, 'Loose Canons: Covert Commerce and Underground Finance in the Modern Arms Black Market' in (1995b) 22 *Crime, Law and Social Change*, at pp. 1–57, reprinted in N.Passas (ed.) *Transnational Crime* (Aldershot, Dartmouth 1998); Observatoire Géopolitique des Drogues *supra* note 6.

[12] J. Kwitny, *The Crimes of Patriots: The True Tale of Dope, Dirty Money, and the CIA* (New York, W.W. Norton & Co 1987).

[13] E.g., in some underdeveloped regions of the EU, the fight against fraud in cases involving money coming from Brussels has not been a high priority in the past; N. Passas, 'European Integration, Protectionism and Criminogenesis: A Study on Farm Subsidy Frauds' in (1994) 5 *Mediterranean Quarterly* 4, at pp. 66–84.

activated. In a nutshell, globalization refers to a set of contradictory processes and dynamics resulting into the transformation of the world order through the multiplication and intensification of linkages and interconnectedness. Capital, goods, services, people and ideas cross borders with increasing speed, frequency and ease. Actions in one country have consequences and significance in distant places. Local events and destinies can hardly be interpreted and understood without looking beyond national boundaries. The world is being reconstituted as 'one place' with global communications and media, transnational corporations, supranational institutions, integrated markets and a financial system that trades 24 hours a day.[14]

As the world is shrinking, both space and time are 'compressed'.[15] The time space compression is most visible in the economic domain, especially in finance and manufacturing. It has enhanced the global mobility of capital and led to a new international division of labour. Further, globalization extends and intensifies the linkages of the local with the global, thereby leading to a conflation of 'presence' with 'absence'. Social relations no longer require simultaneous presence in a single location.[16] Giddens[17] has pointed to the intensified process of 'disembedding' social relations, which are taken out of local contexts and reconstituted across space and time. In the sphere of business, the internationalization of capital can be conceptualized as 'territorial non-coincidence of capital'.[18] The fall of trade barriers and technological advances enable the expansion of transnational corporations and financial networks which seek to take advantage of regions with low production costs and new markets.

Cultural identities also become disembedded as a result of easy travelling and global consumerism. The more global media networks spread and promote foreign styles and images, the more identities become detached from specific time and space.[19] This process is illustrated by the TV series 'Hercules' and 'Star Trek'. Typically American ways of thinking, manners of speech, Manicheism, virtues, flaws and weaknesses are projected well into the past and the future. 'Hercules' reconfigures age old mythological personalities, while 'Star Trek' suggests that the future of earth will look very much like the core of 'good' US values. Both series thereby effectively universalize things American as they are shown to a world audience.

---

[14] T. McGrew, 'A Global Society?' in *Modernity and its Futures* (S. Hall, D. Held and T. McGrew (eds.)) (Cambridge, Open University Press 1992) pp. 62–102; L. Sklair, *Sociology of the Global System* (New York and London, Prentice Hall and Harvester Wheatsheaf 1995).

[15] D. Harvey, *The Condition of Postmodernity* (Oxford, Basil Blackwell 1989).

[16] A. Giddens, *Modernity and Self-Identity* (Cambridge, Polity 1991); D. Harvey, *The Condition of Postmodernity* (Oxford, Basil Blackwell 1989).

[17] A. Giddens, *The Consequences of Modernity* (Cambridge, Polity 1990).

[18] R. Murray, 'The Internationalization of Capital and the Nation-State' in (1971) 67 *New Left Review*, at pp. 84–109.

[19] S. Hall, 'The Question of Cultural Identity' in *Modernity and its Futures* (S. Hall, D. Held, and T. McGrew (eds.)) (Cambridge, Open University Press 1992) pp. 273–316.

In the processes of globalization, the nation state is being increasingly transcended and considered inadequate as the basis for social analysis.[20] Society and the nation state are becoming conceptually distinguishable. Moreover, the independence, sovereignty and autonomy of nation states are systematically undermined by external actors and supranational bodies. Monetary and fiscal policies in one country deeply affect those in other countries. Decisions which constituted and symbolized sovereign powers now have to be shared and co-ordinated. Regional and international organizations are emerging as major players who foster further expansion of global capital and a degree of homogenization in world markets. The World Bank, the IMF, the OECD, and the European Union (the 'EU') exemplify agents of harmonization. The EU more clearly illustrates the process of 'pooling of sovereignty' among interdependent nation states, as powers and functions are transferred to supranational institutions.[21]

All these developments have inherent criminogenic consequences, as they multiply and intensify existing asymmetries. Just as globalization serves well the needs of legal capital, so does it facilitate criminal enterprises. Just as ordinary international business transactions can be concluded at the speed of light, so can unethical and illegal ones. Just as local destinies often cannot be explained without taking into account global factors, local crime victimization may not be fully understood without reference to global forces. Just as social relations do not require a simultaneous 'presence' in a given place, no longer are all elements of serious crimes in one country or region. The social organization of crime is increasingly international and sophisticated rendering national control mechanisms obsolete. As the autonomy of nation states is reduced, even domestic crimes can increasingly neither be prevented nor sanctioned without cross national collaboration.

In the past we have seen how organizations became a weapon for crime.[22] We have also seen how they served to distantiate the criminal hand from the criminal mind.[23] In the global age, this distance is stretched even further as the organizations are more compartmentalized and spread throughout the world. In addition, both criminal hands and criminal minds may be absent, far away from the locus of the crime. In many instances, crimes are so well camouflaged that only specialists can detect them and realize the risks involved.

Globalization reinforces inequalities of power and wealth both within nation states and among them. It maintains and intensifies global hierarchies of privilege,

---

[20] Z. Bauman, *Intimations of Postmodernity* (London, Routledge 1992).
[21] R.O. Keohane and S. Hoffman, (1990) 'Institutional Change in Europe in the 1980s' in *The New European Community: Decisionmaking and Institutional Change* (R.O. Keohane and S. Hoffman (eds.)) (Boulder, Westview 1990) pp. 1–39.
[22] S. Wheeler and M.L. Rothman, 'The Organization as Weapon in White-Collar Crime' in (1982) 80 *Michigan Law Review*, at pp. 1403–1427.
[23] J. Braithwaite, 'Criminological Theory and Organizational Crime' in (1989) 6 *Justice Quarterly* 3, at pp. 333–358.

wealth and control.[24] Power asymmetries can be discerned in most spheres of social and economic interactions in different forms. For instance, knowledge asymmetries and risk distribution asymmetries end up systematically attracting and linking the powerful with the powerless.[25] This is clearly demonstrated in the case of toxic waste (non-) regulation discussed above. Technological asymmetries are also increased in global markets, leading to underground markets for nuclear and other material that is embargoed or in short supply.[26] By reproducing and intensifying divisive social relations,[27] globalization inevitably generates poles of resistance and opposition.

The tendency towards universalization is countered by a resurgence of nationalism and emphasis on ethnic identities.[28] This contradictory dynamic combines with asymmetric power relations and politics in various parts of the world to give rise to fundamentalisms. These, in turn, nurture all sorts of illegal markets as conflicts may translate into armed confrontations, which necessitate weapons, information, and skills that are in short supply because of prohibitions and embargoes. Treaties aiming at the non-proliferation of particular weapons or dual use technology may be proposed and promoted by nation states which already possess them. This adds fuel to the fire of geopolitical, religious or ethnic conflicts. More to the point for the purposes here, this series of power, ideological and demand supply asymmetries create illegal markets for technology, arms and other controlled goods and services. In addition, such illegal markets will be interconnected with drug trafficking, terrorism, corruption, money laundering, capital flight, etc. Plenty of arguments and justifications will enable numerous individuals, groups or organizations to participate in those markets. Some will be motivated by profit, others by religious or ideological convictions, and still others by the pursuit of the perceived national interest. In that context, blind eyes will be easy to secure and border controls will become porous.

The time space compression activates the criminogenic potential of existing power and economic asymmetries too. Power asymmetries are again at work when transnational corporations employ global media to market their goods and services in places where substantial numbers of people cannot afford them. Disjunctions between goals and means may be very few in rigidly stratified societies that do not encourage high social mobility. In such societies, people may not feel that they are lacking something, even if they are 'objectively' deprived. As Durkheim and Merton have shown, societies in turmoil or characterized by structural and cultural

---

[24] R. Walker, *One World, Many Worlds* (New York, Lynne Riener 1988).

[25] U. Beck *supra* note 7.

[26] M.T. Klare, 'Secret Operatives, Clandestine Trade: The Thriving Black Market for Weapons' in (1988) 44 *Bulletin of Atomic Scientists* 3, at pp. 16–24; M.T. Klare, *Rogue States and Nuclear Outlaws: America's Search for a New Foreign Policy* (New York, Hill and Wang 1995).

[27] G. Modelski, *The Principles of World Politics* (New York, Free Press 1972).

[28] D. Harvey, *The Condition of Postmodernity* (Oxford, Basil Blackwell 1989); I. Wallerstein, *Historical Capitalism* (London, Verso 1983).

contradictions can expect high rates of deviance. Whenever a culture promotes ambitions that the society cannot help fulfil, there are frustrations and strains towards crime. Globalization breaks societal barriers and encourages new needs, desires, fashions. In this way, it promotes the adoption of non-membership reference groups for comparisons that can be unfavourable and upsetting. Globalization systematically causes in other words, relative deprivation, which may lead to deviance and crime.[29] It creates or dramatically broadens awareness of pre-existing economic asymmetries, which only now are criminogenic.

The criminogenic potential is activated through the cultivation of awareness of economic asymmetries and the widespread interpretation of them as unnecessary and changeable. Newly constructed needs, new ideals that are culturally promoted, legitimated and widely regarded as attainable, old and intensified economic asymmetries combine to increase discontent. Shortages of desired goods give rise to smuggling operations and black market networks, as illustrated by the illegal car trade between Eastern and Western Europe and the illegal trade in various commodities between China and Hong Kong.[30] People from deprived areas are strongly motivated to emigrate to the places where the 'goodies' are available.[31] Many become vulnerable to serious crime as they are prepared to naively trust fraudsters who guarantee them decent jobs in promised lands, only to end up in forced prostitution.[32] When quotas are imposed on new immigrants, highly corrupt and exploitative smuggling operations develop for those who wish to emigrate.[33]

Many criminogenic effects of political asymmetries, economic asymmetries and relative deprivation can be seen in the aftermath of the collapse of the USSR and disillusionment with Western democratic policies and capitalism.[34] Relative deprivation has a revolutionary potential too.[35] Cross-border communications convey the evitability of injustice and inequality, inspire change and foster rebellion. In the past, the ideals of the French Revolution generated violent upheavals in the Balkan peninsula against the autocratic Ottoman rule.[36] In the process of

---

[29]  N. Passas, (1997b) 'Anomie, Reference Groups, and Relative Deprivation' in *The Future of the Anomie Theory* (N. Passas and R. Agnew (eds.)) (Boston, Northeastern University Press 1997b) pp. 62–94.

[30]  J. Vagg, 'The Borders of Crime' in (1992) 32 *British Journal of Criminology* 3, at pp. 310–328.

[31]  S. Hall *supra* note 19.

[32]  L. Shelley, 'Post-Soviet Organized Crime' in (1994) 2 *Demokratizatsiya* 3, at pp. 341–358.

[33]  W.H. Myers, 'The Emerging Threat of Transnational Organized Crime from the East' in (1995–1996) 24 *Crime, Law and Social Change* 3, at pp. 181–222.

[34]  S. Handelman, 'The Russian "Mafiya"' in (1994) 73 *Foreign Affairs* 2, at pp. 83–96; L. Shelley *supra* note 32.

[35]  U. Eco, *Travels in Hyperreality* (London, Picador 1987).

[36]  R.G. Hovannisian, 'Etiology and Sequelae of the Armenian Genocide' in *Genocide: Conceptual and Historical Dimensions* (G.J. Andreopoulos (ed.)) (Philadelphia, University of Pennsylvania Press 1994) pp. 111–140.

globalization now events in one corner of the planet can affect feelings and encourage people located in another corner, to rebel against aggression by a neighbouring state. East Timor is a case in point. The independence of the Baltic States and the UN response to Iraq's annexation of Kuwait 'have given rise to unequivocal statements about the unacceptability of aggression by a big power against its small neighbor and the sacrosanct nature of that right to self determination of which the Timorese were so cynically deprived'.[37]

Globalization renders cultural asymmetries criminogenic and brings about another sort of more questionable and criminal type of disembeddedness. The increased contact between countries with art-rich pasts and countries with art collecting presents results in illicit transfers of national treasures from their original sites to artificial contexts. There is a huge global market of art items which are removed or stolen from primarily economically underdeveloped countries and channelled to Western private collections, museums or galleries. In the process of rooting paintings or frescoes out of their original context, many pieces of art are destroyed or damaged.[38]

A combination of legal and cultural asymmetries leads to the cleansing of stolen art through countries with laws that conveniently legitimate the ultimate possessors, in a way reminiscent of money laundering.[39] In addition, there is a market in counterfeit art, as supply is insufficient to satisfy the thirst of international art collectors. Again, the profits in these markets are substantial and the risks of punishment low. Economic problems in some Third World countries motivate counterfeiters to sell fake art to rich foreigners. This activity 'is looked on favourably as a source of income that can improve the standard of living in the villages where the counterfeiters work'.[40]

Other institutions facilitate the globalization of trade by promoting exports of domestic products. They often do this, however, through protectionist policies which produce a number of asymmetries. Protectionism generates incentives for the diversion of trade, adds inequalities, creates strains among traders from various countries, and introduces disincentives for effective controls. The EU's Common Agricultural Policy (the CAP) and similar programmes, for example, create demand and supply asymmetries, maintain artificial price asymmetries for the same goods, perpetuate unequal economic exchanges (something-for-nothing transactions), and

---

[37] J. Dunn, 'East Timor: A Case of Cultural Genocide?' in *Genocide: Conceptual and Historical Dimensions* (G.J. Andreopoulos (ed.)) (Philadelphia, University of Pennsylvania Press 1994) at p. 186.

[38] P.L. Margules *supra* note 6.

[39] J.E. Conklin, *Art Crime* (Westport CT, Praeger 1994).

[40] J. Brooke, 'Faced with a Shrinking Supply of Authentic Art, African Dealers Peddle the Illusion', *New York Times*, 17 April 1988 at H51.

enhance global inequalities.[41] Differential pricing depending on the country of origin or final destination encourages smuggling activities, false declarations and 'phantom trade'. Subsidies and price supports foster surplus production of goods that not infrequently have to be destroyed. Ironically, as people in many parts of the world die of starvation, people in other parts destroy food supplies in order to keep the prices high.

Third World countries are then even more dependent on Western/Northern countries for their development. The aid they receive, however, is often 'imposed' or of debatable quality.[42] In addition, aid programmes themselves are criminogenic. They facilitate fraud against recipient countries, which are anxious to receive as much as possible and therefore unlikely to complain if a part of the aid is rotten or sub-standard. Not surprisingly, we have seen cases of powdered milk sent to drought areas or machines delivered without training staff and manuals. Moreover, much of what is officially recorded as aid comes in the form of military equipment and weapons, which fuels conflict and the associated illegal markets (Rwanda and the 'aid' from European countries preceding the genocidal events is a case in point).

# E. Globalization, Dysnomie and 'Crimes Without Lawbreaking'

As the world becomes increasingly interconnected and asymmetries are multiplied, crime rates should be expected to rise unless effective control systems are in place. Yet, official controls are weakened by processes leading to *dysnomie*; that is, to conditions undermining the ability of authorities to control individual and organizational behaviour. In this respect, *dysnomie* has some affinity to *anomie*, which connotes the relative absence of norms or people's weak allegiance to prevailing norms. In contrast to *anomie*, however, *dysnomie* is constituted by:

(1) the absence of a widely accepted transnational normative framework to regulate cross-border activities; and
(2) the existence of many different, inconsistent and often conflicting legal frameworks.

So, *dysnomie* refers to an ineffective regulatory patchwork and fragmented controls, which make possible the commission of 'crimes without lawbreaking'.

---

[41] N. Passas *supra* note 13; M.J. Roarty, 'The Impact of the Common Agricultural Policy on Agricultural Trade and Development' in (February 1987) *National Westminster Bank Quarterly Review,* at pp. 18–28.
[42] EU Court of Auditors (1987). Special Report No. 1/87 on The Quality of Food Aid. Brussels, OJ No. C 219/1.

More than ever before, international law is a *conditio sine qua non* for the maintenance of world order and security. This, however, requires additional shifts of competence and power from nation states to transnational institutions. The more powerful a government is, the more it has to lose by contributing to such pooling of sovereignty. Hence the resistance by countries in the North to the establishment of international norms and procedures. US President Bush's rhetoric about a 'new world order' and enthusiastic commitment to some international laws lost its momentum after the end of the Persian Gulf War. The promise of a more active UN proved to be illusory and the re-election of its 'daring' Secretary General was vetoed by the US. The UN has limited independence and cannot be expected to act against the countries that finance it or have veto power.

Indeed, the US and other prominent members of the coalition against Iraq have blocked the development of an international criminal code and permanent court. The same applies to specific initiatives regarding *inter alia* aggression, genocide, the protection of the environment or the prevention of theft of natural and cultural property from countries in the South.[43] International law used to legitimate policies and practices of powerful nation states (e.g., slavery). Now, its role is more ambiguous, as it can be used against powerful states (see *Nicaragua v. USA* before the World Court, although the ruling was never enforced). Further, as the US–USSR bi-polarity disappeared, the geopolitical context that supported international law for decades disappeared, leaving little to replace it.[44]

Transnational institutions have failed to provide a comprehensive normative framework and enforcement mechanisms to ensure predictability in economic activity and the control of illegal transactions. It is true that the UN, the World Trade Organization, the OECD, the EU, the Council of Europe, and other organizations have assumed a growing number of responsibilities in directly regulating international transactions or in influencing national regulation and promoting processes of harmonization.[45] These organizations' guidelines and suggestions, however, are only occasionally and inconsistently followed by national governments. Experience shows that even when some regimes, principles, laws or 'gentlemen's agreements' (e.g., the Basle Concordat on banking practices) are in place, their implementation or enforcement is most of the time purely symbolic and

---

[43] M. Critharis *supra* note 9; R. Falk *supra* note 1; R. Falk, 'Rethinking the Agenda of International Law' in *Beyond National Sovereignty: International Communication in the 1990s* (K. Nordenstreng and H.I. Schiller (eds.)) (Norwood NJ, Ablex 1993) pp. 418–431; B.B. Ferencz, 'An International Criminal Code and Court: Where They Stand and Where They're Going' in (1992) 30 *Columbia Journal of Transnational Law*, pp. 375–399; P.L. Margules *supra* note 6.

[44] R. Falk *supra* note 43.

[45] R. Cox, *Power, Production and World Order* (New York, St. Martin's Press 1987); N. Passas *supra* note 13; N. Passas *supra* note 10.

selective (compare the long list of unenforced UN resolutions with the determination to punish Iraq's invasion of Kuwait).

In effect, both regulatory and criminal law enforcement functions are stubbornly in the hands of national bodies which pursue objectives and employ methods that are inconsistent with each other. Regionalism, nationalism, and the insistence on exclusive competence to enact and enforce laws within national territories bring about further asymmetries. This is because gaps generated by the resistance to global control mechanisms are filled by national measures. At the same time, despite efforts to harmonize standards and approaches in some areas (e.g., copyright, drugs), legal traditions remain extremely diverse and often incompatible. The internationalization of business, the frequent travel and the familiarization of executives with conflicting rules further facilitate misconduct. In such cases of confusing polynomie, globalization leads to a relativization of norms and to law violations without pangs of conscience.[46]

Thus, the globalization of markets and enterprises entails increasingly fragmented regulation. The more a company grows into new markets, the less amenable it becomes to control, accountability and consolidated supervision. These processes foster the *par excellence* global crime, the 'crime without lawbreaking'. Misconduct falling under our substantive definition of crime may be committed in such ways that the criminal laws of no country are violated. Criminals can slip through the cracks of the parochial regulatory patchwork.[47] We have seen how this is possible in the description of the trade in toxic waste and of corrupt practices. Lawyers, accountants, former government or military officials who act as consultants or private businessmen can offer advice on how to engage in harmful practices without breaking the laws of the countries where different operations take place. Transactions criminalized in various parts of the world can be concluded in countries that allow or welcome them. Transactions can be structured so that no country's laws are broken although the final outcome is clearly unethical or 'criminal'. Compartmentalized corporate structures effectively raise firewalls protecting both the company and its executives from knowledge of wrongdoing and liability. Financial transactions that are disallowed or must be reported can be booked to offshore subsidiaries and branches. Research, experiments, manufacturing and distribution of commodities or services that are outlawed or controlled in some countries can take place in countries with friendlier regulations.

The pharmaceutical industry illustrates how such opportunities are maintained and exploited by transnational corporations. The initial testing of drugs can be conducted in the Third World where safeguards are lower, civil lawsuits are unlikely, and other forms of protest have slim chances of success. Countries with lax standards are used for first approval and manufacture, so that Third World markets

---

[46] This is consistent with the more general 'compliance crisis' noted by J. Rosenau, *Turbulence in World Politics* (Brighton, Harvester Wheatsheaf 1990).

[47] R.J. Michalowski and R.C. Kramer *supra* note 1.

can be entered, before final approval is made by more demanding First World agencies. Components of dangerous and banned drugs can be made in places allowing their manufacture and then marketed in countries that have not banned them.[48] The Third World is not only used as a laboratory with guinea pigs, but also as a dumping ground for dangerous products. Drugs with serious side effects are exported to several countries with the list of side effects getting shorter the farther to the South the drugs are going. Defective and harmful products, such as the Dalkon Shield IUD, can be exported and sold around the world despite their ban in the home country.[49]

Other examples of crimes without lawbreaking include the use of child labour in poor countries that condone it by companies that then export the manufactured goods to countries that criminalize the practice. Taxes may be evaded legally through the practice of price transfer, which allows the profits to be booked in countries with no income tax.[50] Dirty money can be laundered in countries requiring no reporting of even substantial amounts of cash deposits and then transferred to Western banks that may not know its criminal origin (and do not care to find out).[51] Globalization has enabled financial institutions to do overseas what they are disallowed to do at home. As the BCCI has shown, it has become possible for a financial institution to not have a home at all.[52]

Secrecy and anonymity hinder investigators by covering the tracks of the 'global offender'. Illegal financial transactions and losses that must be reported can be conducted and hidden through offshore entities of global enterprises, practically pulling the wool over the eyes of controllers. Secrecy jurisdictions serve as a 'black box' through which all manner of illegal activities can be shielded against prosecution and punishment.[53] In a sense, this sort of black box makes serious crimes disappear. Few, if any, outsiders know that they have been committed. Victims realize their losses only when it is too late (all these systemic problems are highlighted by the recent financial scandals of BCCI, Barings, Daiwa and Sumitomo).

---

[48] J. Braithwaite *supra* note 1.
[49] P. Cashman, 'The Dalkon Shield' in *Stains on a White Collar* (P. Grabosky and A. Sutton (eds.)) (Sydney, The Federation Press 1989) pp. 92–117.
[50] S. Picciotto, *International Business Taxation* (New York, Quorum Books 1992).
[51] M. Levi, 'Pecunia non Olet: Cleansing the Money-Launderers from the Temple' in (1991) 16 *Crime, Law and Social Change*, at pp. 217–302. Interestingly, the very criticism of the role and responsibility of Swiss banks relative to 'Nazi gold' during the Second World War could be made of the role and responsibility of big Western banks today. Just as the neutral Swiss could tell that the gold coming from Germany was forcibly taken from Jews, banks can at least suspect that the hundreds of billions of dollars coming from the Third World are proceeds from drug and arms trafficking, dictators' plunder, flight capital, corrupt payments, evaded taxes, etc.
[52] N. Passas, 'The Mirror of Global Evils: A Review Essay on the BCCI Affair' in (1995b) 12 *Justice Quarterly* 2, at pp. 801–829.
[53] J. Blum, and A. Block, 'Le Blanchiment de l' Argent dans les Antilles: Bahamas, Saint Maartin et Iles Caïmans' in *La Planète des Drogues* (A. Labrousse and A. Wallon (eds.)) (Paris, Seuil (1993) pp. 73–102.

In short, to the extent that transactions take place within one jurisdiction or within jurisdictions with similar legal traditions, the task environment is relatively easy to handle. Businesses are clear about the rules of the game, while supervisors can regulate more readily. To the extent that transactions cross jurisdictions with differing legal traditions and cultures, both compliance and control become highly problematic. In addition to these problems, legal cacophonies are accompanied by jurisdictional conflicts, nightmares in collaboration, cultural conflicts and power differentials among both actors and regulators.

European integration and the regulation of EU programmes, such as the CAP, highlight the clash between centralizing forces of globalization and attempts at decentralization. Powers and competence to make decisions and policies affecting its 15 members are shifted to EU organs. Despite the pooling of sovereignty, national authorities remain in charge of enforcing EU regulations and policing the borders.[54] There is no EU power to enact or enforce criminal law. As a result, the EU funds, to which Member States contribute unequally, are protected by national and local authorities, whose priorities lie elsewhere and may be reluctant to prosecute contributors to the regional economy. Despite good efforts at harmonization,[55] the national penal laws applicable to EU frauds vary substantially. EU regulations and fraud are hard to explain to juries, boring and unintelligible to national judges and law enforcers.[56] Efforts to resolve jurisdictional issues for multinational cases started in the 1970s and are still ongoing.

EU regulations are not only imperfect but also too numerous for national controllers to keep up with. The changing national moods and ruling parties in Member States, shifting priorities and commitment to European integration, the enlargement of the EU and the need to remedy problems created by loopholes in previous regulations, make for constant amendments and rule proliferation. The combined effect of the uneven process of European integration, piecemeal controls, regulatory inflation with intended ambiguities is to render some EU programmes inherently dysnomic. The whole process leads to an over legalization of certain areas, which requires increased reliance on legal and accounting experts. This in turn leads to reduced visibility, accountability and detectability of misconduct.[57]

If the problems are serious within the relatively developed and integrated EU, they are barely manageable in the global markets. By operating in countries with conflicting standards corporations not only have higher compliance costs, but they can also find it hard to abide by the laws of all countries where they operate. Occasions arise when they may have to break the laws of one country, if they observe

---

[54] With the exception of the very contested powers of the EU Commission with respect to competition and anti-trust rules.

[55] M. Delmas-Marty (ed.), *Corpus Juris* (Paris, Economica 1997).

[56] N. Passas and D. Nelken, 'The Fight Against Fraud in the European Community: Cacophony Rather Than Harmony' in (1991) 6 *Corruption and Reform,* at pp. 237–266.

[57] N. Passas *supra* note 13.

those of another. In such cases, globalization produces yet another type of crime: 'crime due to respect of domestic law'. Cases from the banking sector exemplify this dilemma. Many financial institutions operate both in the US and in 'black box' jurisdictions in the Caribbean, the Pacific, and Europe. As criminal clients use the offshore banking facilities for their transactions, US law enforcers ask the US branches of these institutions to produce the records, which are indispensable for prosecution. Since the records are physically within secrecy jurisdictions, the banks cannot comply with US court orders. The governments in such secrecy jurisdictions regard these demands as a violation of their sovereignty and take further measures to ensure that US attempts to obtain confidential records are frustrated. Caught in the middle are the banks, the non-party witnesses, who are required to either ignore a US court order and face contempt of court charges or to produce the records and violate banking and criminal laws of the country in which the records are located.[58]

At stake is not only the question of sovereignty, but also strong financial interests. Tax havens and secrecy jurisdictions derive substantial revenues from the banking industry. It is tax advantages and confidentiality that draws legitimate and illegitimate businesses to offshore locations. Given the lack of universal tax and regulatory standards, globalization has unleashed a competitive struggle among nation states to attract as many investments and businesses as possible. Given the gigantic market for secrecy and tax advantages,[59] countries have succumbed to the temptation to regulate more laxly than others. In other words, at precisely the time when better regulation was needed, globalization has fostered 'competitive deregulation'.[60]

In the end, attempts to regulate nationally and curb globalization are doomed to fail. In fact, they become a Sisyphean task given that 'much of the globalization today is the result of regulatory barriers, which drove borrowers and investors to find ways around national regulation'.[61] We finally come full circle. We started with processes whereby globalization undermines state autonomy and increases or activates asymmetries, including discrepancies in legal traditions and regulatory practices. We now see that it is also independent actions of states and asymmetric national regulations that make for globalization.

---

[58] H. Harfield and R.E. Deming, 'Extraterritorial Imperatives' in (1988) 20 *Case Western Reserve Journal of International Law*, at pp. 393–403; S.B. Piñera-Vàzquez, 'Extraterritorial Jurisdiction and International Banking: A Conflict of Interests' in (1988) 43 *University of Miami Law Review*, at pp. 449–491.

[59] I. Walter, *Secret Money: The World of International Financial Secrecy* (London, George Unwin & Allen 1985).

[60] R. Dale, *The Regulation of International Banking* (Cambridge, Woodhead-Faulkner 1984).

[61] L.L. Bryan, *Bankrupt: Restoring The Health and Profitability of Our Banking System* (New York, Harper Business 1991) at p. 183.

# F. Conclusion and Policy Implications

If globalization is inevitable, what can be done about the economic crime problems that accompany it? Globalization has brought into closer contact, interaction and interdependence countries with unequal power and diverse cultures, legal traditions, economic and political outlooks. The roots of the growing problem of economic crime have been located in the criminogenic asymmetries that offer illegal opportunities, create motives to use such opportunities, and make it possible for offenders to get away scot free. Asymmetries will continue to exist, some of them will even grow. In fact many asymmetries ought to remain, especially in the sphere of culture. Crime fighting cannot and should not seek the standardization of everything on a global level. The task is to diminish or eradicate undesirable asymmetries and to reduce the criminogenic effect of those we wish to preserve or cannot do much about.

There are also some reasons why the problem is not as grave as one may fear. First of all, criminal entrepreneurs have no desire to destroy the state. Only politically motivated offenders seek the overthrow of government and a change in political regime. Economic offenders, however, benefit from the relative certainty, predictability and other services provided by the government. They often have a symbiotic relationship with legitimate business and other organizations,[62] as they use the same infrastructure or offer goods and services in demand by conventional society. Similarly to domestic illegal entrepreneurs, they only wish to neutralize the state and use it to their advantage.[63] So, self-preservation of criminal entrepreneurs dictates minimal confrontation with state actors and no attacks on the economic system, as such.

In addition, serious offenders have always crossed borders with little difficulty. The problem is not as new as some media and sensationalist reports make it appear. The difference now is that cross-border crime is becoming more of an equal opportunity employer than before. Globalization and new technologies make it possible for small time criminals and small non-state related groups to also commit transnational offences. This is the most worrying aspect in some respects, because the degree of predictability is lower. However, just as transnational crime is in a sense 'democratized', so is the control of such misconduct. Communication technologies and the wider use of the Internet enable coalition building, sharing of ideas and information, and thereby can support informal control mechanisms (the internet can also assist criminal justice efforts). Non-governmental organizations and

---

[62] N. Passas, (1998) 'Transnational Crime: The Interface Between Legal and Illegal Actors' presented at the *National Research Council Workshop on Transnational Organized Crime* (Washington DC 1998).

[63] D.C. Smith, 'Some Things That May Be More Important to Understand About Organized Crime Than Cosa Nostra' in (1971) 24 *University of Florida Law Review* 1, at pp. 1–30.

pressure groups can be quite effective even when they take on powerful opponents. As has been pointed out, there is also a process of 'globalization from below'.[64] In other words, small communities and countries are empowered in some respects.[65] The cases of *Shell* and *Nestlé* illustrate the point. More recently, Colombian indigenous people waged a successful battle against Occidental Petroleum.[66] The effect of informal controls can be bolstered through boycotts, the shaming of powerful actors into socially responsible practices, and the use of civil law suits.

At the same time, policymakers need to work towards a reduction of legal asymmetries through harmonization of provisions and sanctions. Fewer regulatory asymmetries will lower both criminogenesis and compliance costs. Corporations are more likely to comply with rules they accept than with rules they perceive as arbitrary and unwarranted.[67] It may be possible, thus, to collaborate with companies for better all round results without resort to criminal law.[68] In the banking sector, there are serious efforts underway by think tanks, academics and financial institutions to develop international standards that the industry can live with and the regulators can enforce. The same process may be encouraged in other industries.

National authorities must resist the temptation to use asymmetric powers and enforce their laws extraterritorially without genuine consent by concerned governments. Unilateral actions and selective enforcement must be shunned, because they are counterproductive. They may produce short-term results (i.e., the capture and punishment of certain offenders). Yet, in the long term, they undermine the legitimacy of international norms. National bodies ought to collaborate constantly and consistently. Furthermore, they need to promote and encourage the development of an international criminal code and the establishment of a permanent international criminal court.

Powerful states and corporations will not always participate whole heartedly in processes that ultimately involve power sharing. Co-operation, harmonization of rules and the emergence of international regimes require a degree of consensual knowledge, a shared understanding of common risks and problems to be solved.[69] A vital element of a strategy to fight global economic crime, therefore, is to contribute to consensual knowledge about its causes and consequences. Policymakers and the

---

[64] R. Falk, 'Rethinking the Agenda of International Law' in *Beyond National Sovereignty: International Communication in the 1990s* (K. Nordenstreng and H.I. Schiller (eds.)) (Norwood NJ, Ablex 1993) pp. 418–431.

[65] J. Braithwaite *supra* note 1; J. Rosenau *supra* note 46.

[66] *The Economist*, 7 June 1998.

[67] M.D. Ermann, and J.R. Lundman, 'Deviant Acts by Complex Organizations: Deviance and Social Control at the Organizational Level of Analysis' in (1978) 19 *Sociological Quarterly*, at pp. 55–67.

[68] B. Fisse and J. Braithwaite, *Corporations, Crime and Accountability* (Cambridge, Cambridge University Press 1993).

[69] E.B. Kapstein, 'Resolving the Regulator's Dilemma: International Co-ordination of Banking Regulations' in (1989) 43 *International Organization* 2, at pp. 323–347.

public must be made aware of the boomerang effects of their country's domestic and foreign policies and the practices of transnational corporations.

Most importantly, the crime problem must be addressed at its root. It must be emphasized that, despite the gradual loss of nation states' power to act and influence their own environment without external constraints, it is the exercise of state power that ultimately contributes to global crime opportunities and crime facilitation. Reduced national autonomy does not make states less responsible for crime causation. It is national policies, the exercise of asymmetric state powers, an obsession with sovereignty and nationalist resistance against international regulation that account for many criminogenic asymmetries.

Almost all asymmetries discussed above are the making of national authorities. Their economic policies bear responsibility for relative and objective deprivation. It is their protectionism and subsidization of domestic industries, while they preach 'free markets' and 'liberalization of trade' to others, that impair the efforts of less developed countries to narrow the gaps. It is their monetary policies and control of international organizations that preserve asymmetric development and growth. It is authoritarian regimes that cause ethnic and political violence. It is their hegemonic policies and support for dictatorial regimes overseas that provoke international terrorism and fundamentalisms. It is their selective control and promotion of domestic military industries that fuel armed conflicts (note that industries from the permanent members of the UN Security Council produce the overwhelming majority of weapons). It is their unwillingness to share knowledge, information and technology that breeds unease and inequalities. It is their prohibitions of commodities and services in demand that create illegal opportunities. It is their inability or unwillingness to reduce the demand for prohibited goods and services that perpetuates the illegal markets. It is their imposition of quotas for new immigrants that gives rise to the inhumane smuggling of illegal aliens. It is their resort to criminal justice methods to deal with the consequences of their policies that provide incentives for more sophisticated organization of crime and raise the price of corruption. In many instances, conflicts between foreign policies and covert activities of secret services generate illegal markets and facilitate crime.

In some cases, state actors are direct participants in transnational crimes.[70] In other cases, the creation of illegal opportunities is an unintended consequence of

---

[70] E.g., in piracy: W.J. Chambliss, 'State-Organized Crime' in (1989) 27 *Criminology* 2, at pp. 183–208; the misuse of nuclear capability: D. Kauzlarich and R. Kramer, *Crimes of the American Nuclear State* (Boston, Northeastern University Press 1998); the Iran–Contra affair: L.E. Walsh, *Final Report of the Independent Counsel for Iran/Contra Matters* (Washington DC, US Court of Appeals for the District of Columbia Circuit 1993); the illegal arming of Iraq: M. Phythian, *Arming Iraq: How the US and Britain Secretly Built Saddam's War Machine* (Boston, Northeastern University Press 1996).

governmental policies, as seen in the war on drugs,[71] or subsidy programmes. In yet other cases, governments simply do not wish to act. Secrecy jurisdictions, for example, are routinely demonized for the crimes they facilitate. The same governments, which complain about these jurisdictions can take effective action against them. However, there are many important users of these jurisdictions with influence over government policies. In addition to criminals, secrecy jurisdictions are also used by government agencies, business people and corporations,[72] who are bound to resist aggressive action through lobbying and political campaign contributions. The problem, thus, is one of government unwillingness rather than powerlessness. Transnational crime is the hidden cost of certain government policies. The main point for our purposes, however, is that to the extent that there is a government responsibility to transnational crime causation, there is also a government capacity to do something about it.

As we have seen, globalization causes crime as well as possibilities for its control. Nation states lose autonomy, but they are still able to influence crime patterns (at least some of them). Due to the lack of sound empirical data, we cannot be sure exactly how much transnational crime is being committed and whether it is rising. There is an urgent need for systematic research into different forms of transnational crimes. The author's final point is that, until we develop a solid empirical database on this problem and we implement policies resulting from careful theoretical analyses, we should avoid the adoption of controversial measures, which risk undermining the very freedoms we wish to preserve and promote.

# G. References

P. Andreas, 'The Rise of the American Crimefare State' in (1997) 14 *World Policy Journal* 3, at pp. 37–45.

G.J. Andreopoulos, 'Genocide: Conceptual and Historical Dimensions' (Philadelphia, University of Pennsylvania Press, 1994).

C. Bassiouni, (1983) 'The Penal Characteristics of Conventional International Criminal Law' in (1983) 15 *Case Western Reserve Journal of International Law*, at pp. 27–37.

Z. Bauman, *Intimations of Postmodernity* (London, Routledge 1992).

U. Beck, *The Risk Society* (London, Sage 1992).

A.A. Block, *Masters of Paradise: Organized Crime and the Internal Revenue Service in the Bahamas* (New Brunswick NJ, Transaction 1991).

---

[71] A.A. Block, and A.W. McCoy, (eds.), *War on Drugs: Studies in the Failure of US Narcotics Policy* (Boulder, CO: Westview Press 1992); E.A. Nadelmann, 'Commonsense Drug Policy' in (1998) 77 *Foreign Affairs* 1, at pp. 111–126; Observatoire Géopolitique des Drogues *supra* note 6.

[72] Walter *supra* note 59.

A.A. Block, and A.W. McCoy, (eds.) *War on Drugs: Studies in the Failure of US Narcotics Policy* (Boulder CO, Westview Press, 1992).

J. Blum, and A. Block, 'Le Blanchiment de l' Argent dans les Antilles: Bahamas, Saint Maartin et Iles Caïmans' in *La Planète des Drogues* (A. Labrousse and A. Wallon (eds.)) (Paris: Seuil (1993) pp. 73–102.

A. Bossard, *Transnational Crime and Criminal Law* (Chicago, Office of International Criminal Justice 1990).

J. Braithwaite, *Corporate Crime in the Pharmaceutical Industry* (London, Routledge and Kegan Paul 1984).

J. Braithwaite, 'Criminological Theory and Organizational Crime' in (1989) 6 *Justice Quarterly* 3, at pp. 333–358.

J. Brooke, 'Faced with a Shrinking Supply of Authentic Art, African Dealers Peddle the Illusion', *New York Times,* 17 April 1988 at H51.

D.A. Bryan, 'Consumer Safety Abroad: Dumping of Dangerous American Products Overseas' in (1981) 12 *Texas Tech Law Review*, at pp. 435–458.

P. Cashman, 'The Dalkon Shield' in *Stains on a White Collar* (P. Grabosky and A. Sutton (eds.)) (Sydney, The Federation Press 1989) pp. 92–117.

Center for Investigative Reporting and B. Moyers, *Global Dumping Ground: The International Traffic in Hazardous Waste* (Washington DC, Seven Locks Press 1990).

W.J. Chambliss, *On the Take: From Petty Crooks to Presidents* (Bloomington, Indiana University Press 1988, 2nd ed.).

W.J. Chambliss, 'State-Organized Crime' in (1989) 27 *Criminology* 2, at pp. 183–208.

M.B. Clinard, *Corporate Corruption: The Abuse of Power* (New York, Praeger 1990).

J.E. Conklin, *Art Crime* (Westport CT, Praeger 1994).

R. Cox, *Power, Production and World Order* (New York, St. Martin's Press 1987).

M. Critharis, 'Third World Nations are Down in the Dumps: The Exportation of Hazardous Waste' in (1990) 6 *Brooklyn Journal of International Law* 2, at pp. 311–339, reprinted in N. Passas (ed.) *Transnational Crime* (Aldershot, Dartmouth 1998).

R. Dale, *The Regulation of International Banking* (Cambridge, Woodhead-Faulkner 1984).

M. Delmas-Marty, (ed.) *Corpus Juris* (Paris, Economica 1997).

J. Dunn, 'East Timor: A Case of Cultural Genocide?' in *Genocide: Conceptual and Historical Dimensions* (G.J. Andreopoulos (ed.)) (Philadelphia, University of Pennsylvania Press 1994) pp. 171–190.

J.P. Eaton, 'The Nigerian Tragedy, Environmental Regulation of Transnational Corporations, and the Human Right to a Healthy Environment' in (1997) 15 *Boston University International Law Journal,* at p. 261.

U. Eco, *Travels in Hyperreality* (London, Picador 1987).

M.D. Ermann, and J.R. Lundman, 'Deviant Acts by Complex Organizations: Deviance and Social Control at the Organizational Level of Analysis' in (1978) 19 *Sociological Quarterly,* at pp. 55–67.

R. Falk, 'Nuremberg: Past, Present, and Future' in (1971) 80 *Yale Law Journal*, at pp. 1501–1528.

R. Falk, 'Rethinking the Agenda of International Law' in *Beyond National Sovereignty: International Communication in the 1990s* (K. Nordenstreng and H.I. Schiller (eds.)) (Norwood NJ, Ablex 1993) pp. 418–431.

B.B. Ferencz, 'An International Criminal Code and Court: Where They Stand and Where They're Going' in (1992) 30 *Columbia Journal of Transnational Law*, at pp. 375–399.

B. Fisse and J. Braithwaite, *Corporations, Crime and Accountability* (Cambridge, Cambridge University Press 1993).

A. Giddens, *The Consequences of Modernity* (Cambridge, Polity 1990).

A. Giddens, *Modernity and Self-Identity* (Cambridge, Polity 1991).

S. Hall, 'The Question of Cultural Identity' in *Modernity and its Futures* (S. Hall, D. Held, and T. McGrew (eds.)) (Cambridge, Open University Press 1992) pp. 273–316.

S. Handelman, 'The Russian "Mafiya" ' in (1994) 73 *Foreign Affairs* 2, at pp. 83–96.

H. Harfield and R.E. Deming, 'Extraterritorial Imperatives' in (1988) 20 *Case Western Reserve Journal of International Law*, at pp. 393–403.

D. Harvey, *The Condition of Postmodernity* (Oxford, Basil Blackwell 1989).

R.G. Hovannisian, 'Etiology and Sequelae of the Armenian Genocide' in *Genocide: Conceptual and Historical Dimensions* (G.J. Andreopoulos (ed.)) (Philadelphia, University of Pennsylvania Press 1994) pp. 111–140.

M. Johnston, 'Corruption, Inequality and Change' in *Corruption, Development and Inequality* (P.M. Ward (ed.)) (London and New York, Routledge 1989) pp. 13–37.

E.B. Kapstein, 'Resolving the Regulator's Dilemma: International Co-ordination of Banking Regulations' in (1989) 43 *International Organization* 2, at pp. 323–347.

D. Kauzlarich and R. Kramer, *Crimes of the American Nuclear State* (Boston, Northeastern University Press 1998).

R.O. Keohane and S. Hoffman, (1990) 'Institutional Change in Europe in the 1980s' in *The New European Community: Decisionmaking and Institutional Change* (R.O. Keohane and S. Hoffman (eds.)) (Boulder, Westview 1990) pp. 1–39.

M.T. Klare, 'Secret Operatives, Clandestine Trade: The Thriving Black Market for Weapons' in (1988) 44 *Bulletin of Atomic Scientists* 3, at pp. 16–24.

M.T. Klare, *Rogue States and Nuclear Outlaws: America's Search for a New Foreign Policy* (New York, Hill and Wang 1995).

R. Klitgaard, *Controlling Corruption* (Berkeley, University of California Press 1988).

J. Kwitny, *The Crimes of Patriots: The True Tale of Dope, Dirty Money, and the CIA* (New York, W.W. Norton & Co 1987).

A. Labrousse, *La Drogue, L'Argent et les Armes* (Paris, Fayard 1991).

M. Levi, 'Pecunia non Olet: Cleansing the Money-Launderers from the Temple' in (1991) 16 *Crime, Law and Social Change*, at pp. 217–302.

P.L. Margules, 'International Art Theft and the Illegal Import and Export of Cultural Property: A Study of Relevant Values, Legislation, and Solutions' in (1992) 15 *Suffolk Transnational Law Journal*, at pp. 609–647, reprinted in N. Passas (ed.) *Transnational Crime* (Aldershot, Dartmouth 1998).

T.L.H. McCormack and G.J. Simpson, 'The International Law Commission's Draft

Code of Crimes Against the Peace and Security of Mankind: An Appraisal of the Substantive Provisions' in (1994) 5 *Criminal Law Forum* 1, at pp. 1–55.

T. McGrew, 'A Global Society?' in *Modernity and its Futures* (S. Hall, D. Held and T. McGrew (eds.)),(Cambridge, Open University Press 1992) pp. 62–102.

R.J. Michalowski and R.C. Kramer, 'The Space Between Laws: The Problem of Corporate Crime in a Transnational Context' in (1987) 34 *Social Problems* 1, at pp. 34–53 reprinted in N. Passas (ed.) *Transnational Crime* (Aldershot, Dartmouth 1998).

G. Modelski, *The Principles of World Politics* (New York, Free Press 1972).

R. Murray, 'The Internationalization of Capital and the Nation-State' in (1971) 67 *New Left Review*, at pp. 84–109.

W.H. Myers, 'The Emerging Threat of Transnational Organized Crime from the East' in (1995–1996) 24 *Crime, Law and Social Change* 3, at pp. 181–222.

E.A. Nadelmann, ' Commonsense Drug Policy' in (1998) 77 *Foreign Affairs* 1, at pp. 111–126.

R.T. Naylor, 'The Insurgent Economy: Black Market Operations of Guerilla Organizations' in (1993) 20 *Crime, Law and Social Change*, at pp. 13–51.

R.T. Naylor, 'From Cold War to Crime War: The Search for a New 'National Security' Threat' in (1995a) 1 *Transnational Organized Crime* 4, at pp. 37–56.

R.T. Naylor, 'Loose Canons: Covert Commerce and Underground Finance in the Modern Arms Black Market' in (1995b) 22 *Crime, Law and Social Change*, at pp. 1–57, reprinted in N. Passas (ed.) *Transnational Crime* (Aldershot, Dartmouth 1998).

Observatoire Géopolitique des Drogues. *The Geopolitics of Drugs* (Boston, Northeastern University Press 1996).

N. Passas, 'Structural Sources of International Crime: Policy Lessons from the BCCI Affair' in (1993) 20 *Crime, Law and Social Change* 4, at pp. 293–305.

N. Passas, 'European Integration, Protectionism and Criminogenesis: A Study on Farm Subsidy Frauds' in (1994) 5 *Mediterranean Quarterly* 4, at pp. 66–84.

N. Passas, (ed.) *Organized Crime* (Aldershot, Dartmouth 1995).

N. Passas, 'The Mirror of Global Evils: A Review Essay on the BCCI Affair' in (1995b) 12 *Justice Quarterly* 2, at pp. 801–829.

N. Passas, 'Promotion and Maintenance of the Rule of Law and Good Governance: Action Against Corruption' in (1997a) 3 *International Journal of Technical Co-operation* 2, at pp. 237–253.

N. Passas, 'Anomie, Reference Groups, and Relative Deprivation' in (1997b) *The Future of the Anomie Theory* (N. Passas and R. Agnew (eds.)) (Boston, Northeastern University Press) pp. 62–94.

N. Passas, (1998) 'Transnational Crime: The Interface Between Legal and Illegal Actors' presented at the *National Research Council Workshop on Transnational Organized Crime* (Washington, DC 1998).

N. Passas and J. Blum 'Intelligence Services and Undercover Operations: The Case of Euromac' in *Invading the Private? Accountability and the New Policing in Europe* (Stewart Field and C. Pelser (eds.)) (Aldershot, Dartmouth in press).

N. Passas and D. Nelken, 'The Fight Against Fraud in the European Community: Cacophony Rather Than Harmony' in (1991) 6 *Corruption and Reform*, at pp. 237–266.

S. Picciotto, *International Business Taxation* (New York, Quorum Books 1992).

S.B. Piñera-Vàzquez, 'Extraterritorial Jurisdiction and International Banking: A Conflict of Interests' in (1988) 43 *University of Miami Law Review*, at pp. 449–491.

M. Phythian, *Arming Iraq: How the US and Britain Secretly Built Saddam's War Machine* (Boston, Northeastern University Press 1996).

M.J. Roarty, 'The Impact of the Common Agricultural Policy on Agricultural Trade and Development' in (1987) *National Westminster Bank Quarterly Review*, *February*, at pp. 18–28.

J. Rosenau, *Turbulence in World Politics* (Brighton, Harvester Wheatsheaf 1990).

L. Shelley, 'Post-Soviet Organized Crime' in (1994) 2 *Demokratizatsiya* 3, at pp. 341–358.

L. Sklair, *Sociology of the Global System* (New York and London, Prentice Hall and Harvester Wheatsheaf 1995).

D.C. Smith, 'Some Things That May Be More Important to Understand About Organized Crime Than Cosa Nostra' in (1971) 24 *University of Florida Law Review* 1, at pp. 1–30.

W.R. Swinyard, H. Rinne and A.K. Kau, 'The Morality of Software Piracy: A Cross-Cultural Analysis' in (1990) 9 *Journal of Business Ethics*, at pp. 655–664.

J. Vagg, 'The Borders of Crime' in (1992) 32 *British Journal of Criminology* 3, at pp. 310–328.

L.E. Walsh, *Final Report of the Independent Counsel for Iran/Contra Matters* (Washington, DC, US Court of Appeals for the District of Columbia Circuit 1993).

R. Walker, *One World, Many Worlds* (New York, Lynne Riener 1988).

I. Wallerstein, *Historical Capitalism* (London, Verso 1983).

I. Walter, *Secret Money: The World of International Financial Secrecy* (London, George Unwin & Allen 1985).

S. Wheeler and M.L. Rothman, 'The Organization as Weapon in White-Collar Crime' in (1982) 80 *Michigan Law Review*, at pp. 1403–1427.

# [2]

# Global Anomie, Dysnomie, and Economic Crime: Hidden Consequences of Neoliberalism and Globalization in Russia and Around the World

## Nikos Passas

## Introduction

TRANSNATIONAL CRIME HAS RECENTLY ACQUIRED A PROMINENT PLACE IN PUBLIC debates. It is commonly presented as the most significant crime problem at the turn of the millennium (Myers, 1995–1996; Shelley, 1995). Many have even suggested that it represents a serious domestic and international security threat (Paine and Cillufo, 1994; Williams, 1994). The argument is also made that a wave of transnational crime undermines neoliberal policies and the functioning of an increasing number of market economies around the globe (Handelman, 1995; Shelley, 1994). As a consequence, the proposed remedies are often quite drastic and involve undercover operations, privacy-piercing approaches, and the participation of intelligence services in the fight against global crime (Andreas, 1997; Naylor, 1999; Passas and Blum, 1998; Passas and Groskin, 1995).

Yet, little attention and virtually no systematic research has been devoted to understanding the causes, structure, extent, and effects of serious cross-border misconduct (Passas, 1998). The risks it poses may be grossly exaggerated (Naylor, 1995; Lee, 1999). The draconian measures being contemplated and implemented in different countries, therefore, are essentially an exercise in shooting in the dark. Chances are good that the target will be missed and substantial "collateral damage" may be caused by ill-conceived policies in this "war" on crime. This risk is

NIKOS PASSAS is Associate Professor in the Department of Criminal Justice at Temple University (529 Gladfelter Hall, Philadelphia, PA 19122; e-mail: npassas@nimbus.temple.edu). The author specializes in the study of white-collar crime, corruption, organized crime, and international crime. He is the author of *Informal Value Transfer Systems and Criminal Organizations: A Study into So-called Underground Banking Networks* (1999) and the editor of *The Future of Anomie Theory* (1997), *Transnational Crime* (1999), and *Organized Crime* (1995). Dr. Passas has authored numerous papers and research reports. He serves as Northeastern University Press series editor on transnational crime. He has acted as a consultant to various bodies, including the United Nations Centre for International Crime Prevention, the Commission of the European Union, the German Parliament, and a number of governments. The author wishes to thank warmly Bob Weiss for his constructive feedback and patience.

particularly high in countries in transition toward a market democracy. It would be much wiser, thus, to carefully study the problem before taking ineffective and possibly damaging actions.

This article seeks to make a contribution by concentrating on the causes of transnational economic crime. The main argument is that, contrary to conventional wisdom, neoliberalism and globalization contribute to processes leading to global anomie, dysnomie, and, ultimately, economic misconduct. They do so by activating the criminogenic potential of economic, political, legal, and cultural asymmetries, as well as by creating new such asymmetries (Passas, 1999). These asymmetries cause crime by furnishing opportunities for misconduct, by generating motives for actors to take advantage of such opportunities, and by weakening social controls. More specifically, means-ends disjunctions are systematically created, as neoliberal policies foster new needs and desires that are all too often left unfulfilled. Promises of more freedom, prosperity, and happiness for a larger number of people have turned out to be chimerical. Economic and power inequalities have widened within and across countries in the last two decades. The number of poor has reached unprecedented levels, while welfare programs and safety nets are reduced or abolished. Enormous populations have become more vulnerable to exploitation, criminal victimization, and recruitment in illicit enterprises or rebel and fundamentalist groups. Normative standards and control mechanisms are weak or completely absent exactly when they are needed the most.

This article begins with some basic conceptual clarifications and outlines the theoretical framework so far applied to the analysis of U.S. organizational and individual deviance. Then, the main features of globalization and neoliberalism are presented, followed by a contrast of promises made by proponents of neoliberal policies and their actual consequences. Attention then shifts to specific criminogenic effects of these outcomes and the case of Russia, which illustrates the different stages in the processes leading up to serious misconduct and anomie. The chief policy implication of this analysis is that the recently unleashed forces of neoliberalism need to be reined in and held in check, while government policies ought to better shield the least privileged from the adverse effects of globalization.

## Some Conceptual Clarifications

Although there is no universally accepted definition of transnational crime, many commentators seem to think of it as a globalized form of the stereotypical "organized crime." This, however, leaves out corporate and governmental crimes, whose effects can be far more harmful than those of "professional" criminals and ethnic groups involved in the business of illegal goods and services. We therefore need a definition that is inclusive enough without becoming too relativistic and subjective. For our purposes, transnational crime refers to cross-border misconduct that entails avoidable and unnecessary harm to society, is serious enough to warrant state intervention, and is similar to other kinds of acts criminalized in the countries concerned or by international law. Crime will be viewed as transnational when the offenders or victims are located in or operate through more than one country (Passas, 1999).

Globalization is another term that is often used without clear definition. In the simplest sense, it refers to a growing interconnectedness and multilateral linkages across national borders. According to Keohane and Nye (2000: 104),

> globalism is a state of the world involving networks of interdependence at multicontinental distances. The linkages occur through flows and influences of capital and goods, information and ideas, and people and forces, as well as environmentally and biologically relevant substances (such as acid rain or pathogens).

Globalism has several dimensions, such as economic, cultural, environmental, or military, not all of which take place at the same time. So, whenever globalism increases and becomes thicker or more intense, we can speak of globalization. When globalism decreases, we can speak of de-globalization.

Finally, the term "criminogenic asymmetries" refers to structural discrepancies and inequalities in the realms of the economy, law, politics, and culture. Such asymmetries are produced in the course of interactions between unequal actors (individual or organizational) or systems with distinctive features. All asymmetries contain some criminogenic potential. Durkheim argued that crime cannot be eliminated, because we are and always will be different from each other. Even in a society of saints, minor deviations would be considered serious offenses. In modern societies, crimes are those behavioral differences (asymmetries) that have been outlawed by legislative bodies. There is always the opportunity for powerful actors to victimize less privileged ones (economic, political, and power asymmetries). This potential is not always materialized. Criminal opportunities are not necessarily taken advantage of. Mostly this is because actors do not always seek or wish to make use of illegal opportunities. They may not regard such action as appropriate (due to socialization, internalization of norms) or fear adverse consequences. The criminogenic potential is most likely to be activated when opportunities, motives, and weak controls are all present.

For example, a combination of legal/regulatory asymmetries with economic and political asymmetries has given rise to a huge illicit market for toxic waste disposal. Many Third World countries either did not regulate toxic waste or did so much less rigorously than did industrialized states. This provided an opportunity for maximum-profit-seeking companies to get rid of their hazardous waste in areas where rules were lax or nonexistent (Center for Investigative Reporting and Moyers, 1990; Critharis, 1990). Power and economic asymmetries between rich and poor countries have led waste recipients to allow this to go on because of their dependence on foreign investment, the need for cash to service external debt, or the desire to create jobs (Korten, 1995). Economic and knowledge asymmetries also shaped the motivation of local participants in this questionable trade. The decision to go along reflects an incomplete understanding of the extent or nature of the hazard, their desperate need for additional income, an effort to be competitive and attractive to foreign companies (race to the bottom), or corruption.

## Anomie and Deviance

Both Durkheim (1983) and Merton (1968) have stressed how high rates of deviance should be expected when social expectations are out of balance with realistic opportunities to reach the desired goals. According to Durkheim, this means-ends discrepancy is caused by society's inability to regulate people's naturally limitless desires. This problem was particularly acute in the commercial and business sector, in which anomie was chronic during the industrial revolution, opening up new horizons and undermining society's ability to contain aspirations. A similar situation can be observed in contemporary societies, where electronic, information, and biological technologies constantly redefine what is possible and break new ground.

According to Merton, unrealistic hopes and expectations are not simply natural, but socially constructed and promoted. Structural problems are at the heart of the means-ends disjunction. The U.S. culture and the ideology of the American Dream encourage lofty expectations, while society fails to provide equal access to legal opportunities. Meanwhile, there is a cultural overemphasis on success goals at the expense of normative behavior (as further elaborated by Messner and Rosenfeld, 1994). Both of these factors make for deviance and anomie.

Without ignoring the differences between the two sociologists, it has been possible to use an elaborated version of their anomie theories to explain corporate crime in the context of capitalist economies (Passas, 1990). Regardless of whether people strive for "more" due to natural drives or because of cultural encouragement, the point is that market economies cannot perform without lofty aspirations, consumerism, emphasis on material/monetary goals, and competition. All this leads to the pursuit of constantly moving targets and systematic sources of frustration. A synthesis of anomie theory with reference group analysis made clear how means-ends discrepancies are socially generated and experienced by people in all social strata. It also showed how this theoretical framework is applicable to the analysis of crime without strain or problems (i.e., anomie theory is not a strain theory) and to "organized crime" even after discrimination or blockage of legitimate opportunities no longer affects minority groups (Passas, 1997).

In brief, the dynamic social process leading to structurally induced strain, anomie, and deviance without strain is as follows. Means-ends discrepancies are caused by a strong cultural emphasis on monetary or material success goals for all members of society, while a good number of them do not have a realistic chance to attain them. Socially distant comparative referents are constantly introduced and sustained through the school, family, politics, workplace, media, advertising, and even religion (Passas, 1994). Regardless of their social background and the social capital available to them, people are urged to desire more than they have. Success stories of going from rags to riches make the American Dream even more believable. As this cultural theme is internalized, competitive forces and consumerism foster normative referents on what is "normal" and appropriate. The widely internalized egalitarian discourse clashes in practice with widespread inequality (power and economic asymmetries). Consequently, those members who fail to meet such comparative and normative standards are likely to experience relative deprivation and frustration. This strain, combined with the culturally induced overemphasis on goals and the concomitant underemphasis on the proper methods, makes for deviance of various types (see Merton's typology). A good part of the deviance is an individual search for a solution to these structural problems. If the deviant solution is successful (i.e., perpetrators are not caught or adequately punished), this adaptation may become normative for others in a similar social context. To the extent that this solution is available to them (demand for illicit goods or services, access to illegitimate opportunity structures), they may adopt this role model — and may be expected by their significant others to follow this path — even though the original source of strain has by now been eclipsed. Unless effective control measures are taken, this process continues in a vicious circle toward higher rates of deviance and widespread anomie (for a schematic representation of this process, see Figure 1 at the end of the article).

In the literature, anomie is often conceptually confused with its causes or effects. To keep its explanatory potential, this mistake should be avoided. Anomie is a withdrawal of allegiance from conventional norms and a weakening of these norms' guiding power on behavior. This is caused by structural contradictions and affects deviance in two ways. One is associated with strain, the other is not. The former is caused by relative deprivation, frustrations, and the almost obsessive focus on goals. This makes deviance thinkable, as conventional norms are regarded as nonbinding, at least temporarily. Rationalizations enable departures from otherwise accepted/internalized social rules, as actors convince themselves that in their particular circumstances an exception is acceptable (Aubert, 1968; Sykes and Matza, 1957). Through interactive processes, techniques of neutralization and rationalizations contribute to a context in which newly socialized actors may adopt normative referents and deviant behavior as a matter of course. If "this is the way business is done around here," people may engage in price fixing or misleading advertising without experiencing any prior frustration or problem.

## Globalization and Neoliberalism

These structural problems have been most prominent in the USA. However, a very similar process is now being reproduced throughout the world through globalism and neoliberalism. Promises are made that are not fulfilled. People's expectations are exalted at a time when economic and power asymmetries increase and become less justifiable and intolerable in the eyes of the people affected. The logic of the market permeates popular thinking and introduces rationalizations, making the adoption of a criminal or unethical solution more acceptable. The horizontal lines in Figure 1, rather than representing controlling influences, at the global level point to the criminogenic impact of globalization and neoliberal policies.

Nowadays, globalism and neoliberalism seem to be indistinguishable empirically or even conceptually (Cox, 1993; Stewart and Berry, 1999). Nevertheless, I think it is useful to try to separate them analytically. As noted earlier, globalism refers to the degree of interconnectedness and the increase or decrease of linkages. By contrast, neoliberalism refers to an economic and political school of thought on the relations between the state on the one hand, and citizens and the world of trade and commerce on the other. Because it espouses minimal or no state interference in the market and promotes the lifting of barriers to trade and business transactions across regional and national borders, it certainly becomes a motor of globalization.

Globalization in the last two decades shows clear signs of deeper and thicker interconnections that affect many more people than ever before. The effects are now much faster, as shown by the financial crisis in Thailand in 1997. The world has shrunk and become "one place," with global communications and media, transnational corporations, supranational institutions, and integrated markets and financial systems that trade around the clock (McGrew, 1992; Sklair, 1995). The cultural landscape has changed under the influence of mass media. Through their ads, TV programs, movies, and music, they contribute to cultural globalism, target young children, and foster consumerism (e.g., "Image Is Everything," "Just Do It," or "Coke Is It"). Information technology is making for "distant encounters and instant connections" (Yergin and Stanislaw, 1998). Fresh normative and comparative ideals are thus promoted, legitimated, and presented as attainable. Scholars attribute the momentum of this process to the forces of capitalism (Wallerstein, 1983), technology (Rosenau, 1990), the presence of a hegemon (Gilpin, 1987), or a combination of them all (Giddens, 1990).

Neoliberalism, in particular, has made a major contribution to the dynamic and contradictory processes of globalization since the elections of Ronald Reagan, Margaret Thatcher, and Helmut Kohl. During the 1950s and 1960s, the dominant concerns revolved around distributive justice, neocolonialism, and dependency theory. These were displaced in the 1980s and into the 1990s by discourses of "free markets," individualism, and self-help (Woods, 1999). Policies of deregulation, privatization of state assets, and removal of tariffs implemented the doctrine that the state should get out of the way of free enterprise. Unemployment, inequality, and poverty were no longer explained by structural contradictions or constraints. The problems became individualized and blamed on corrupt administrations or on the poor themselves. The proposed medicine was more liberalization of the economy, free competition, privatization of inefficiently managed government agencies, abolition of capital controls, and permitting foreign capital to enter all markets.

The ideological underpinning of globalization, thus, has been the primacy of economic growth, which is thought to be benefiting the whole planet. Consistent with that prime directive, country after country has been persuaded (or forced) to promote "free trade" and consumerism, to reduce government regulation of business, and to adopt the same economic model regardless of local specificities and differences between industrialized and developing countries (Bello, 1999; Mander, 1996).

More specifically, shifts in the North, the East, and the South have been quite remarkable. In the North, the welfare state that used to care for citizens "from cradle to grave" has been replaced by a "pay as you go" social service system. Even public utilities have been privatized and have begun to charge "economic prices," as former subsidization systems were abolished. Further, "industrial intervention-ism and labour protection have given way to laissez-faire; and...tax systems whose major purpose was to correct inequalities have been transformed into systems mainly intended to promote incentives and economic efficiency" (Stewart and Berry, 1999: 151).

In developing countries, similar shifts took place as a result of hegemonic influences from the North. Western-educated Third World "technocrats" returned to their home countries eager to introduce neoliberal policies (Burbach et al., 1997: 86; *Newsweek*, June 15, 1992). As the bandwagon of liberalization took off, few countries wished to be left out. As a World Bank official warned, "lagging countries risk being left farther behind.... For economies that remain inward-looking, the risk of being marginalized is greater than ever" (cited in Klak, 1998: 21).

Yet, the shifts have not always been voluntary. A host of measures and conditions consistent with the neoliberal agenda were imposed on countries through international institutions, such as the International Monetary Fund (IMF), the World Bank, the OECD, the European Union, the G7, etc. Countries drowning in external debt sought additional loans to pay off their older ones — chiefly to banks from the industrialized world. Billions of dollars were made available to them, but only if they introduced Structural Adjustment Programs (SAPs). Despite important differences among the various economies, SAPs shared the same basic elements: long-term "structural" reforms to deregulate the economy, liberaliza-tion of trade, removal of restrictions on foreign investment, promotion of an export orientation of the economy, wage reductions and controls, privatization of state enterprises, and short-term stabilization measures such as cutbacks in government spending, high interest rates, and currency devaluation (Bello, 1996; 1999).

Changes along these lines also took place in the East, where the switch from state-managed economies toward "free market" and parliamentary democracy has been quite drastic and swift (Glinkina, 1994; Woods, 1999). The problem is that the introduction of global neoliberalism has brought about enormous economic and political asymmetries, as its promises and theoretical expectations remain unfulfilled.

## The Promises of Global Neoliberalism

The supporters of global neoliberalism make a series of claims. For instance, the world is shrinking following greater connectivity (IBM claims to offer "solutions for a smaller planet"). The distinction between core and periphery states is presumed to be getting fuzzier and irrelevant, as there are only winners from now on. Investment, trade, and development opportunities are more widely distributed around the world. There is a marked convergence into one world economy, in which everyone can find a market niche. Media and cultural influences are more widespread and multilateral, as foods, music, and art are imported to the North and integrated into local cultures. Finally, people are more integrated thanks to telecommunication technologies and immigration (Klak, 1998).

To economists, all these trends are positive, even if short-term hardship is deemed necessary for some parts of the population. Global welfare is expected to be enhanced, as the forces of free competition within and between countries will encourage more efficient resource allocation and bring about higher productivity (Oman, 1999). A more open, trade-creating world should, therefore, benefit everyone, if unevenly. Trickle-down effects of wealth creation would ensure that virtually everyone will participate in this welcome trend (Korten, 1996).

The objective of SAPs was to render developing economies more efficient, drive up growth rates, and provide foreign exchange that could be used to repay debt. Higher growth rates are empirically associated with comparatively more equal income distribution (Alesina and Rodrik, 1994). Hence, neoliberal policies would bring about not only more economic growth, productivity, a better division of labor (multistate production and wider participation), lower unemployment, more wealth and prosperity, but also more democracy, less poverty, and fewer inequalities. Unfortunately, in most countries, these virtuous circles did not occur.

### The Consequences of Global Neoliberalism

Throughout the world, the expectations raised by neoliberal theorists have not materialized despite the extensive application of their policy recommendations. Instead, most economies "fell into a hole" of low investment, decreased social spending and consumption, low output, decline and stagnation. Both the World Bank and the IMF retreated from SAPs and acknowledged their failure (Bello, 1999; Katona, 1999; *Multinational Monitor*, June 2000; Watkins, 1997).

In the North, GDP growth was lower in the 1980 to 1990 period than in the 1950s and 1960s. We also witness a higher volatility in growth (e.g., booms and busts). Lost in all the talk about huge technological advances ushering in the computer and Internet era is the fact that productivity growth now is half that of levels in the 1950s and 1960s. Unemployment in OECD (Organization for Economic Cooperation and Development) countries has risen from eight million in 1970 to 35 million in 1994. In the midst of U.S. prosperity and economic expansion, inequalities increased. The number of people living under the officially defined poverty level grew from 11.4% of the population in 1978 to 13.5% in 1990. Almost one in four new babies in the U.S. are born into poverty, while the top one percent of Americans saw their real income shoot up by 50% (Levy, 1998; Wilterdink, 1995). Also noteworthy is that U.S. and Western European international trade relative to GDP was greater a century ago than in recent years (Hirst and Thompson, 1996).

Neoliberal dreams proved to be even more chimerical in the South. Role models, like South Korea, Malaysia, and Indonesia plunged into crises in the 1990s. Mexico and Brazil, which faced their own scary periods, experienced growth of three percent in the last two decades, whereas that rate was six percent during the *dirigiste* period of 1950 to 1980. Wage gaps widened. Even in Costa Rica and Chile, models of success in Latin America, the results have been an unmitigated disaster for the lower social classes. The number of Costa Ricans below the poverty line rose from 18.6% in 1987 to 24.4% in 1991, while 42% of all Chileans are also living in poverty (Burbach et al., 1997: 86). Half of the investment flows to developing countries went to just three countries (China, Mexico, and Argentina). In addition, some investments had negative local effects. For instance, as diverse agriculture was converted into monocultures or to export-oriented flower plantations, self-sufficiency was undermined (Clinard, 1990; Klak, 1998).

Moreover, the core-periphery distinction is as relevant as ever. Its real meaning relates to power, authority, and the accumulation of wealth, where the gaps (asymmetries) are increasing. Although production (of certain items) is more dispersed, the concentration of power, control, and benefits has become more pronounced. In 1991, 81% of the world stock of direct foreign investment was in the core triad of the USA, the European Union, and Japan — up from 69% in 1967. The appearance of integrated markets also obscures the fact that 80% of all world trade is within the core triad, in which resides less than 20% of the planet's population (Hirst and Thompson, 1996; Klak, 1998).

In Latin America, debt jumped from $230 billion in 1980 to $600 billion in 1997. Capital had been fleeing those countries up to the early 1990s, when net inflows were the result of casino capital — seeking short-term gains and likely to abandon those countries at the first hint of trouble. Consequently, new debts were created with a new round of borrowing (Robinson, 1998–1999). An important reason why developing countries cannot pay off their debt is that trade protectionism in the North has kept them from penetrating those markets. Trade liberalization has been inconsistent in that rich countries demand more open markets abroad, while continuing to subsidize their own economic sectors, such as agriculture (Andreas, 1999; UNDP, 2000; Watkins, 1997). Compounding these problems, aid to poor countries has been cut back. Whatever assistance is offered comes with strings attached, including the reduction of state intervention, which could have softened the effects for the most vulnerable (Watkins, 1997; Woods, 1999). These policies further undercut food security, cause poverty, and increase economic and power asymmetries. For instance, the cost of living in the Caribbean and the U.S. is quite comparable. In 1997, however, per capita income in Trinidad and Tobago, the richest Caribbean state, was less than half that of Mississippi, the poorest U.S. state. The gap between skilled and unskilled workers widened even more: Haitian workers made clothing with Disney logos for less than 60 cents per hour, while Disney's CEO made $9,700 per hour (Klak, 1998).

The claim of multilateral and even cultural influences also masks tremendous asymmetries. Even though we listen to reggae in the North, 95% of TV programs in St. Lucia come from the U.S. The most widely read newspaper in the Caribbean is the *Miami Herald*. Consequently,

> U.S. affluence and opportunity, often romanticized, is especially well-known, deeply ingrained, and alluring to the Caribbean...[where] people are prone to set their living standard goals in accordance with what the U.S. media ascribe to the United States. And the imbalance in media flows is increasing with the Caribbean's economic crisis and neoliberalism, as local media have been slashed (Klak, 1998: 11).

As dreams of consumption are disseminated, 86% of total private consumption expenditures is accounted for by 20% of the world's people in industrialized countries (UNDP, 1998). For the people who live outside the consumption geographical area, big banks offer credit to only 10% of the people in developing countries, whereas ads for credit cards and consumer items are omnipresent (Barnet and Cavanagh, 1994). Well over one billion people are deprived of basic consumption needs. For hundreds of millions, basic sanitation, clean water, adequate housing, and health services are unattainable luxuries. Two billion people live on less than two dollars a day and 1.3 billion on less than one dollar a day (ICFTU, 2000). Struggling to survive, some decide to sell their body parts to make ends meet, which is the ultimate symbol of commodification (Scheper-Hughes, 2000).

A negative effect of the Internet is that it alters the relationship between our place of residence and our cultural preferences, experiences, and identities. A spreading global virtual reality disconnects locality from culture, weakens the bonds to particular communities, and estranges people from each other (Minda, 2000). Ladakh, a Himalayan province that prospered for a millennium despite harsh weather conditions, illustrates how (especially cultural) globalization devastated local communities (Norberg-Hodge, 1996). In 1962, isolated Ladakh was linked to the rest of India by an army-built road. The modernization that began in 1975 took about a decade to change the pride Ladakhis felt until then into a collective inferiority complex. Tourism and the media conveyed a picture of wealth, technology, power, and work that was alien and irresistible to them. Village life by comparison began to appear "primitive, silly, and inefficient" (*Ibid.*: 35). Ladakhis felt ashamed of their culture and strove for consumer items that symbolize modern life, such as sunglasses and Walkmans. As Western educational standards penetrated Ladakh, the intergenerational learning experience that helped them provide for themselves in their rough terrain gave way to schools that used texts imitating Indian and British models that were completely irrelevant to their lives (e.g., figuring out the angle of the Tower of Pisa and learning how to keep a London-like bedroom tidy). There used to be no such thing as a "paying job"; there was no money economy. Gradually, however, unemployment — previously nonexistent — became a serious problem, because naturally available resources were abandoned, cheap imports made local farming redundant, and people flocked to the cities to compete for scarce jobs. Radios and TVs chased away the traditions of singing together and group story telling. The points of reference ceased to be real people living nearby, but geographically and socially remote ideals. Consumerism bred new "needs," which could hardly be materialized. Family and other bonds disintegrated and divisions emerged between old and young, Buddhists and Muslims. The result was unprecedented violence, community breakdown, and anomie.

### Criminogenic Effects: Systemic Strains and Global Anomie

What makes the ideology of the American Dream unique is a focus on money and material goods, a strong emphasis on "winning" (often, by all means), and success for everyone in a society where many opportunities for material advancement are available and plenty of "rags to riches" stories lend legitimacy and credibility to the egalitarian discourse. Legal opportunities, however, for achieving the lofty goals are inaccessible to most Americans. In such a consumption-driven culture, which highly values competition and individualism, the means-ends disjunction has entailed a significant criminogenic risk, much greater than in the rest of the world. Crime has been the flip side of economic growth, innovation, and better living standards for certain segments of the population. What sheltered other countries from this negative potential were things absent or minimized in the USA, such as rigid social stratification, low rates of social mobility, less materialism and time spent before TV boxes, safety nets for the underprivileged, more emphasis on other priorities (e.g., solidarity), etc.

This made it possible to explain the higher crime rates in the U.S. compared to other developed or developing countries. These protective factors, however, are now being gradually lost. Disjunctions between socially induced goals and legal means are few in societies that do not encourage high social mobility. In such societies, people may not feel that they are lacking anything, even when they are "objectively" deprived. Economic or other asymmetries are unknown or not experienced and perceived as intolerable. Global neoliberalism breaks down societal barriers and encourages new needs, desires, and fashions. It promotes the adoption of nonmembership reference groups for comparisons that can be unfavorable and upsetting. New normative reference groups define what is "cool" to do. People's ideals in the South and the East may not be about getting from "a log cabin to the White House." However, they are being systematically driven to abandon old ways and values in order to consume. They do not necessarily think that they can be "like Mike," but they do fancy those pricey athletic shoes. So, fresh normative and comparative models create new "needs," together with the expectation that the fulfillment of such needs is vital and achievable.

Yet, as needs and normative models are "harmonized," people become conscious of economic and power asymmetries, and directly experience their impact. Globalization and neoliberalism heightened this awareness, further widened the asymmetries, and fostered the interpretation of them as unnecessary and changeable. In the end, most people realize that the attainment of their lofty goals and lifestyles is beyond reach, if they are to use legitimate means. The success in spreading neoliberalism has brought about a series of failures: more poverty, bigger economic asymmetries, ecosystem deterioration, slower and unsustainable growth patterns. At the time that societies most needed the shield of the state to cushion these effects, welfare programs, safety nets, and other assistance to the poor (individuals, companies, and states alike) forcibly declined or disappeared. Thus, global neoliberalism systematically causes relative deprivation as well as absolute immiseration of masses of people. In effect, it has generated new sources of criminogenesis and removed existing antidotes to it.

All this provides multiple motivations for criminality, as many would turn left and right for solutions and illicit opportunity structures become more international and accessible. At the same time, many weak states lose their autonomy, come to depend more on international organizations and transnational capital, and are unable to cope with emerging crime threats from criminal enterprises and powerful corporations. So, globalism and neoliberalism replace the "egalitarian discourse" of the American Dream in the scheme represented in Figure 1 in a process occurring in the industrialized world, developing countries, and those in transition from Communism to market democracies. Nowhere are these results more clearly visible than in the former USSR.

## The Case of Russia

No one argues that there was no appetite for consumer goods in the years of the USSR or that such goods were widely available. Crime, corruption, illegal markets, and even underground factories could be found behind the official facade of the command system before *glasnost* and *perestroika*, although black marketers were not numerous and lived modestly. The government turned a blind eye to these activities, because they served as a safety valve in an inefficient system (Gleason, 1990; Handelman, 1995; Naylor, 1999b). Discontent, enormous structural problems, and an inability to deal with them characterized the pre-transition years. This is particularly true for the 1960s, when Khrushchev pledged that the USSR would overtake the U.S. in the production of industrial goods by the 1980s. Yet, as inefficiencies precluded such progress, demands for more consumer items "from an increasingly educated, by now self-assured, population, started to put pressure on government...as a loyal expression of the citizens' request for the gradual delivery of promised well-being" (Castells, 2000: 25).

In the 1990s, however, the rates of fraud, prostitution, drug trafficking and abuse, alcoholism, smuggling, white-collar crime, violence, and corruption skyrocketed (Castells, 2000; Handelman, 1995; Holmes, 1997; Lee, 1994; Shelley, 1994). To be sure, Russia is unique in the degree of chaos and disintegration that accompanied the transition to a market economy and the implementation of neoliberal reforms. Few countries have experienced the speed and intensity of privatization, deregulation, and the lack of political leadership and administrative skills we witness in Russia. Indeed, it is the closest we can come to a social state of anomie, without a total collapse and anarchy. This does not mean that Russia is atypical. Very similar, albeit less intense, processes have occurred throughout the world (Lee, 1999; Mander and Goldsmith, 1996; van Duyne et al., 2000). Nevertheless, precisely because it is such an extreme case, it illustrates the theoretical points made here and the process toward anomie and economic crime.

*Enter Neoliberalism*

In the 1985 to 1989 period, reforms took place while the Communist Party was still in control. The Law on Cooperatives (1986) and the Law on Individual Labor Activity (1987) paved the way for further reforms, such as legalization of small businesses in 1989. Between 1990 and 1991, the USSR Supreme Soviet, with Yeltsin as chairman, introduced laws that made state and private enterprises equal, allowed state companies relative independence from government managers, abolished most restrictions on property bought by citizens, promoted privatization, and allowed foreign companies to operate in Russia. Such reforms did not take place at the same pace throughout the USSR. This set Russia apart from the Union and Yeltsin from Gorbachev. Legal asymmetries made the task of law enforcers impossible, as they did not know which laws to prioritize and apply (Afanasyef, 1994). Up to the 1991 coup and the collapse of the USSR, reforms were cautious and gradual, and had not challenged the core of the command economy system. Following the failed coup and under Yeltsin, however, this changed dramatically. Demagogy and erroneous judgments on the feasibility of a swift transition to a market democracy compounded the problem. The Russian government was warned of the dire consequences of a speedy transition to a market economy without previous establishment of the necessary institutions and legal infrastructure. The chairman of an international advisory committee, which repeatedly issued warnings in 1992, was told that "forces in the Kremlin" favored a less "regulatory approach that would provide greater freedom of manoeuvre. Gaidar, supported by the IMF, believed firmly in the intrinsic capacity of market forces to remove obstacles by themselves, and people could use their vouchers to acquire shares" (Castells, 2000: 188). Prices were liberalized, imports and exports became free, domestic trade restrictions were abolished, government intervention was minimized, and public property was massively privatized. By June 1994, officials were self-congratulatory over the fact that 70% of state assets had passed into private hands (Kuznetsova, 1994).

### New Normative and Comparative Referents

The reforms initiated by Andropov and Gorbachev (*perestroika* and *glasnost*) allowed some freedom of speech and openness that let globalization and media influences into the USSR. The post-1991 changes, however, offered new hope out of the severe problems people were facing. Russian leaders fostered heightened aspirations by declaring that the country would soon be modernized and join the "civilized world." Authorities in the former Soviet republics made the same promise, arguing that "'since we got rid of the Russians,' all obstacles to prosperity have been removed and Western standards are within reach" (Burbach et al., 1997: 118). There were forceful and impressive presentations of consumerist lifestyles as "desirable," "modern," and feasible. Distant comparative and normative referents were thus promoted by the media and advertising. Indeed, the yearning for Western lifestyles and consumption items made the initial acceptance of neoliberalism by the population much easier (*Ibid.*). Neoliberalism strengthened that desire and made consumerist dreams appear realistic. Even young Russians now would like to be like Mike and wear the same type of shoes or eat the same breakfast. As Glinkina (1994: 385) put it, an important factor contributing to the criminalization of the economy has been "a drastic stratification of the population's standard of living with a simultaneous loss, in a considerable part (especially among the youth), of socially important goals — replacing them with consumption ideals...."

It must be noted that the normative shift was far more radical in the former USSR and Eastern Europe than it was in Third World countries. The transition from socialism to capitalism by overzealous authorities espousing the new dogma of neoliberalism has had its own direct anomic effects, as will be seen below.

### The Consequence: Means-Ends Discrepancies

The worldwide consequences of neoliberal policies were replicated in Russia. However, the effects have been far more disastrous than elsewhere: lower productivity, high unemployment, much steeper inequalities, increased levels of absolute poverty, disappearance of familiar safety nets, and administrations paralyzed by ineptness and corruption. The ensuing means-ends discrepancies are far more than a theoretical construct. They are painfully experienced by large numbers of people who realize that they simply cannot attain their goals. Within one year, inflation wiped out most people's life savings, while the buying power of most wages dropped to the level of the 1950s. In the winter of 1993, funds were often insufficient to heat residential buildings (Burbach et al., 1997; Handelman, 1993).

As a new bourgeoisie emerged from the ashes of the Communist regime, one-third of the population became impoverished. The gap between the rich and the poor opened up suddenly and grew out of proportion. Official data indicate that in 1994 the difference between them was elevenfold. Researchers argue that the difference between the top 10% and the bottom 10% is 28-fold (Kuznetsova, 1994). Even the chair of the Privatization Commission admitted that the process created "pauper-proprietors" who "cannot survive without state protection" (cited in Burbach et al., 1997: 120).

*Relative and Absolute Deprivation*

The rising expectations of the 1960s led to disenchantment with Communism and paved the way for radical social change. The abandonment of the Soviet conservative model and very rapid implementation of neoliberal policies fueled hopes that a much better future was within reach. Russians rejected rigid stratification and strove for a socially mobile ideal. As has been noted,

> [the middle classes] believed that capitalism could offer even more. Thus, the modernization that had been promised by the neoliberals was perceived by the majority of the population as the modernization of consumption.... The Western model of consumption has finally triumphed, at least in the main cities. But for the majority of the people, the price is that even the former Soviet way of life has become an unattainable dream (Burbach et al., 1997: 124).

The aspiring yuppies have ended up as "dumpies," while a growing polarization makes them see a few of their compatriots enjoy luxuries attained by looting the remnants of the former USSR.

Thus, the post-Soviet Russian dream turned out to be a nasty nightmare (Handelman, 1995). As happened in many other countries, austerity, belt tightening, and lower (in some cases, no) salaries were imposed as consumerism took hold. The impact of these experiences on personal feelings is much more widespread, intense, and unpleasant due to the higher expectations. Even people who are not objectively deprived now feel relatively deprived. Comparisons between their present and past situations are unfavorable: "Formerly privileged sections of the Russian population, such as teachers, doctors, miners, and workers in the oil and gas industry, went on strike, for they could no longer survive on 50 to 70 dollars per month salaries" (Burbach et al., 1997: 125–126).

East-West political and administrative asymmetries, economic asymmetries, and relative deprivation in the aftermath of the collapse of the USSR and disillusionment with Western policies and capitalism have been clearly crimino-genic (Handelman, 1994; Shelley, 1994). Motives for various types of crime became abundant, illegal opportunity structures multiplied, and control systems have been seriously damaged and undermined. The Mertonian category of "conformity" has almost become a rarity, as crime rates increased sharply. Even worse is the problem of economic crime. Recorded economic crimes rose almost 23% during the first seven months of 2000, compared with the same period in 1999 (Radio Free Europe/Radio Liberty, August 17, 2000). Strains and discontent have translated into a range of predatory misconduct, corruption, political violence, a variety of illegal markets, and expressive misconduct.

## Search for Solutions and Anomie

In this context, many can be expected to "innovate," to employ illegal methods for survival or the satisfaction of their basic and newly acquired needs. Methods range from petty property crimes and prostitution to criminal enter-prises and white-collar crime, depending on the social position of the offender. An electronics engineer, for example, could not live on his three dollars per month and moonlighted as a taxi driver. When his taxi broke down, he turned to selling poppy straw (OGD, 1996). Unpaid and depressed professionals with access to more valuable commodities, such as nuclear material, pose an even more serious threat (Lee, 1999). Consumerist teasing increased demand for goods made unavailable (e.g., cars or electronics) by the economic collapse, fueling smug-gling operations, black market networks, and associated illegal enterprises. Shortages of other desired goods are artificially created by quickly adapting entrepreneurs.

Similar conditions outside Russia explain the illegal car trade between Eastern and Western Europe (van Duyne et al., 2000) and the illegal trade in various commodities between China and Hong Kong before unification (Vagg, 1992). In Russia, many took advantage of such supply-demand asymmetries, including the *vory v zakonye* (commonly described as "thieves in law"), who had been the dominant type of professional offenders in the USSR. Structural changes and globalization, however, brought about more competition from ethnic groups (Armenians, Azeris, Chechens, Georgians, etc.) in drugs and arms trafficking, as well as from loose and ad hoc associations of criminals in certain locations or industries. Unsettling reports assert a symbiotic relationship between criminal groups and active or retired intelligence officials. Deteriorating economic condi-tions have facilitated recruitment for employees in growing illegal markets.

Criminal enterprises, for instance, have "…invested heavily in the opium business, financing much of the new cultivation by hiring peasants and even entire villages to plant and protect the poppy crops" (Lee, 1994: 401).

Another source of criminal opportunities sprang from the disintegration of institutions and the disarray in law enforcement. Legitimate businesses are exposed to blackmail and other criminal victimization, but the authorities are unable to assist them. Consequently, many domestic and foreign companies deal with criminal groups and seek their protection, rather than rely on the government (Lee, 1994). Not surprisingly, the majority of Russian experts consider the strengthening of criminal groups to be a "very significant" social consequence of the market reforms introduced in 1992 (Afanasyef, 1994).

Other illicit opportunities were furnished by the privatization process, such as selling state assets at extremely low prices or driving down the prices of privatized companies so as to cheaply purchase vouchers owned by individuals desperate to make ends meet. Privatization in countries with an existing bourgeoisie and experienced managers and entrepreneurs facilitated certain corporate crimes and abuses of power by respected professionals. In Russia, the mix of offenders was different: former company directors, the *nomenklatura*, professional criminals, and new entrepreneurs with a black market background (Glinkina, 1994; Kuznetsova, 1994; Shelley, 1994). The attempt of former Communist officials to dominate this field did not prove lasting. Many were not competent to run private businesses and had to sell them or lose control. The main beneficiaries seem to be former black marketers and outsiders to the old order (Naylor, 1999b). The abuse of privatization has had an anomic effect as the impunity of offenders became widely known, to the point that Russians began to refer to privatization (*privatizatsiya*) as *prikhvatizatsiya*, which means "grabbing" (Handelman, 1995: 104).

Crime and corruption in the midst of privatization fervor are not unique to Russia. (On other previously Communist states, see Popescu-Birlan, 1994; on Latin America, see Saba and Manzetti, 1996–1997.) As a former World Bank official put it, "everything we did from 1983 onward was based upon our new sense of mission to have the south privatized or die; towards this end we ignominiously created economic bedlam in Latin America and Africa" (cited in Katona, 1999). Another similarity with other parts of the world is the degree of authoritarianism that accompanied neoliberal policies. While stimulating rapid accumulation of private capital, the role of the state is reduced to implementing financial austerity. When people started to oppose such measures, "Yeltsin resorted, with Western support, to establishing a semi-authoritarian regime. Making Russian 'reformers' invincible to political and legal challenges inside the country contributed to further criminalization of the Russian State, which acquired an oligarchic character" (Beare, 2000: 6). As similar processes occurred around the world, from Pinochet's Chile to Suharto's Indonesia, one wonders if such reforms would have been possible in a democracy.

Legal organizations also "innovate" by cutting corners and breaking the law due to the environment created by unsystematic legal reforms. Unable to navigate a sea of legal gaps and inconsistencies, "...most managers of private as well as state-owned enterprises cannot run their businesses without committing crimes" (Afanasyef, 1994: 437). Many companies cannot handle the competitive challenges generated by globalism and require state protection. The subsidization of privatized companies, however, introduces further regulatory and price asymmetries that foster the smuggling of goods across newly created borders within the former USSR (see below on nonferrous materials). Enterprises that do not enjoy state intervention are at a disadvantage and may be forced into bankruptcy or crime as a last resort. This is analogous to the situation in all countries that abolish trade barriers, let transnational corporations in, and eliminate preferential treatment for domestic industries.

High-level corruption and banking crimes have become quite common, as the networks of mobsters, financiers, businessmen, and high-level officials extend beyond Eurasia (Beare, 2000). The ongoing investigations into billions of dollars (possibly IMF-provided funds) laundered through the Bank of New York have expanded to include British, Swiss, and Italian entities and actors.

Moreover, pyramid schemes and other frauds have devastated gullible investors, as is the case with other post-Communist countries. Independent Oil, Lenin Trade and Financial Corporation, Aldzher (a security corporation), and other companies defrauded more than a million depositors and investors. Just as the Lincoln Savings and Loan frauds were committed in midst of obsessive deregulation in the U.S. against "the weak, the meek, and the old," Russian pensioners have been the main fraud victims (Glinkina, 1994).

Economic asymmetries among countries produce another set of criminal opportunities, as many become strongly motivated to flee the problem and search for a better future in the West, where the "goodies" are available. However, neoliberalism has promoted the free movement of everything but labor. Quotas and restrictions in promised lands generate demand for illegal services such as the smuggling of humans (Chin, 1999). This leads to opportunities for criminal exploitation, corruption, child/cheap labor, slavery, and forced prostitution.

Women, who are increasingly breadwinners but make up two-thirds of the newly unemployed in Russia, are even more vulnerable in this respect. Economic desperation drives many of them to prostitution or high risk taking. Lack of opportunity makes Russians and East Europeans softer targets for human traffickers. They are more likely to be lured to the West with promises of well-paying, respectable jobs only to end up blackmailed, beaten up, and forced into prostitution (Bruinsma, 1999; Shelley, 1994). The same problems faced by Thai, Mexican, and other women in the U.S. have led to a public hearing before the House Subcommittee on International Operations and Human Rights (September 14, 1999).

Relative deprivation and experience of injustice have a revolutionary potential too. International communications convey the message that injustice and inequality are avoidable. Events in one corner of the earth affect feelings and encourage people elsewhere to rebel against aggression. This may inspire change and foster rebellion. Just as the ideals of the French Revolution led to rebellions in the Balkans against the Ottoman rule (Hovannisian, 1994), the independence of the Baltic states and the U.N. response to Iraq's invasion of Kuwait inspired the East Timorese to fight against the Indonesian autocratic rule (Dunn, 1994). The uprising of Zapatistas in Mexico was deliberately started on January 1, 1994, the day NAFTA went into effect, "as a highly symbolic way to protest neoliberalism and globalisation in Mexico and Latin America" (Robinson, 1998-1999: 123–124).

Repressed nationalism, globalism, and bad times have jointly contributed to several armed conflicts and rebellions in the former USSR (the Caucasus, Moldova, Crimea, Tajikistan, and Chechnya). Rebellion and illegal markets become interconnected, as armed conflicts necessitate training, weapons, intelligence, and financing. The cases of Chechnya, Tajikistan, Afghanistan, and Colombia show how political revolts are associated with corruption, money laundering, the traffic in arms, drugs, and even nuclear material and other crimes that go unpunished (Kuznetsova, 1994: 445; Lee, 1999; Naylor, 1999b; OGD, 1996). Chechnya, which survives thanks to donations from criminal organizations based in other parts of Russia, has become such a paradise for these activities that some depict the war there as "a crusade against a 'mafia republic,'" while others think of it as "a conflict between opposing criminal elites for the control of oil and the financial resources held by the government in Grozny" (Politi, 1998: 44).

Finally, "retreatism" is the only option left to those lacking access to illegal opportunities or who are unwilling to assume the associated risks of violence and arrest. Hence, expressive crimes could be expected. More important, the rates of alcohol and drug abuse (further facilitated by the decriminalization of drug use in Russia in 1991) increased geometrically, especially in the cities, and fueled the demand for things provided in illegal markets (Lee, 1994; OGD, 1996).

*Anomie*

The transition from a command to a market economy practically legalized large parts of the black market and made legal business dependent on criminals' protection. The dismantling of borders and increased contact among previously isolated ethnic groups contributed to the formation of new, wider networks of illegality (Politi, 1998). The result was that one could hardly tell criminals from businessmen, particularly when some outlaw groups act on instructions from government officials or the police (Handelman, 1993). Given official efforts to ensure that the transition to a market economy would occur before substantial opposition could build and that the changes would be irreversible, too many shady actors were allowed to take advantage of this official shield (Glinkina, 1994; Naylor, 1999b). In this light, common views on government-criminal interfaces and symbiosis are plausible, although difficult to prove. Surveys in 1994 showed that the concern of Russians over organized crime was second only to their fears of triple-digit inflation (Afanasyef, 1994). At the perceptual level, therefore, this interface is real and has real consequences: demoralization and anomie.

The corrupted process of privatization has generated widespread rationalizations, such as, "it is OK to steal from the state" or "everyone is doing the same thing." Taking an example pointing to international security risks, Lee (1999: 21) has noted that, "perhaps the most serious problem is the growth of a privatization mentality within the nuclear complex. Economic reform has meant a license to steal. This has resulted in broad systemic corruption and a variety of insider threats and conspiracies."

An additional sign of anomie is what has been described as a "culture of urgency" among young killers:

> For them there is no hope in society, and everything, particularly politics and politicians, is rotten. Life itself has no meaning, and their life has no future.... So, only the moment counts, immediate consumption, good clothing, good life, on the run, together with the satisfaction of inducing fear, of feeling powerful with their guns (Castells, 2000: 210).

Only effective social controls can halt the process toward further deviance and a higher degree of anomie (deviance without strain). Unfortunately, in Russia and elsewhere, a decreased level of autonomy for certain states, the increased power of international organizations and transnational corporations, and dysnomie add to the fuel.

*Dependence, Deregulation, and the Race to the Bottom*

> "Just between you and me, shouldn't the World Bank be encouraging more migration of the dirty industries to the LDCs (lesser developed countries)?" "I think the economic logic behind dumping a load of toxic waste in the lowest wage country is impeccable and we should face up to that.... I've always thought that underpopulated countries in Africa are vastly under-polluted; their air quality is vastly inefficiently low compared to Los Angeles or Mexico City" (1991 memo attributed to World Bank official Lawrence Summers, who later became U.S. Secretary of Treasury; it is widely believed that he did not write it, even though he has accepted responsibility for it. At any rate, this illustrates the neoliberal mindset).

The loss of autonomy and reduced sovereignty of the state relative to capital referred to earlier (Korten, 1996; Watkins, 1997) is particularly acute in the former

Communist countries. Speculative capital will quickly flee each country at the first sign trouble or wavering over neoliberal reforms. External debt grew in all former Communist countries, but especially in Russia, which bears the marks of Africa-like dependent capitalism and "colonial subjugation. The country exports fewer and fewer industrial products and more and more raw materials. Meanwhile, it imports low-quality mass consumption goods, obsolete and hence cheap technology, luxury items and radioactive waste" (Burbach et al., 1997: 120–121). An instance of the direct and blatant interference of foreign governments and transnational corporations in domestic matters was when Chase Manhattan urged the Mexican government to crush the Zapatista rebellion to calm down U.S. investors (Silverstein and Cockburn, 1995; see also Clinard, 1990).

Ironically, the higher degree of dependency in the South and East has lowered the accountability of politicians and corporations. They can now blame globalization for the loss of jobs and lower wages, and prescribe more "efficiency," deregulation, short-term austerity, and declining levels of public spending so as to keep capital in place or attract more. Thus, economic and political leaders appear to be protectors of the public interest and a stabilizing force, while they dismantle existing safety nets (economic neoliberalism has also undermined political liberalism; Klak, 1998).

The Russian government's aversion to regulation (Glinkina, 1994) is observable in other countries, where deregulation turned into competitive deregulation and a race to the bottom. Even in the U.S., the savings and loan disaster and the asymmetric regulation of hazardous wastes demonstrate how criminogenic this process has been. This made it possible to dump legally in Pennsylvania what was prohibited in New Jersey, in what has been termed "crimes without law violations" (Passas, 1999). Such crimes are most likely in the global context given the overwhelming influence of TNCs over national laws and macroeconomic policies. This has prompted some to speak of "rationalized corporate colonialism" (Mander, 1996). Such asymmetries of power make for legal norms that allow overseas that which is, for good reason, criminalized in the base country (e.g., toxic waste dumping, testing drugs on humans, bribery, tax evasion, as well as the patenting of life forms by biotechnology companies and other outrageous practices) (see King and Stabinsky, 1998–1999; Shiva, 1997). The legal asymmetries and uneven power of transnational corporations that create or perpetuate these and other asymmetries give rise to crimes without law violations. Thus, entire countries become vulnerable to victimization by TNCs, a significant problem that is often neglected in conventional discussions of transnational crime. The volatile combination of low wages, bad working conditions, tax breaks only for the rich/corporations, lower environmental standards, deregulation, and less corporate and political accountability with the government relegated to the protection of the international free trade system has predictably made for crises (e.g., Korea, Malaysia, Indonesia, Mexico, and Brazil). It also makes for dysnomie.

### Dysnomie and Further (Global) Anomie

Dysnomie literally means "difficulty to govern" and obtains when the following three conditions are present: a lack of a global norm-making mechanism, inconsistent enforcement of existing international rules, and the existence of a regulatory patchwork of diverse and conflicting legal traditions and practices. Russia is in this respect a microcosm that reflects what is happening in the entire world.

Since reforms took place at an uneven pace in each Soviet Republic, an asymmetry grew wider following the collapse of the USSR. In addition, this collapse suddenly created thousands of miles of new borders that had to be policed, just as state resources were diminished. This made for porous borders that offered no resistance to smugglers. This is how Estonia became the largest exporter of nonferrous materials, even though it does not produce any (Glinkina, 1994). Extensive legal changes accelerated the transition to a market economy, but they were marked by inconsistencies and lacked the necessary legal and institutional infrastructure (Handelman, 1995). For example, the law against private entrepreneurship and commercial mediations was repealed only on December 5, 1991. The law against black market transactions, which defined them as "the buying up and reselling of goods or other items for profit-making," was first amended in February 1990 to increase penalties for certain offenses, was then officially reinterpreted to refer only to trade in commodities sold at state-fixed prices (October 1990), and was finally repealed in February 1991 (Afanasyef, 1994: 429). Lack of resources made the problem worse, as underpaid, ill-equipped, and outgunned police could not be expected to do an effective job.

Weak controls allow criminals to get away and to regard themselves as successful. Deviant "solutions" came to be seen as keys to "success." Successful deviance then becomes a normative referent, contributing to a wider normative breakdown and overemphasis on goals at the expense of normative means. In the context of massive cultural shifts — from the criminalizing of private profit and the hiring of labor outside the household to making them central values for a new social order — the sense of right and wrong became fuzzy. As the deputy minister of Internal Affairs admitted at a 1992 press conference, "even our specialists find it difficult to determine the legal from the illegal — to determine, for instance, what is profiteering and what is honest trade" (cited in Handelman, 1993). Corruption grew so much that up to 30% of illegal gains are reportedly paid to government officials (Glinkina, 1994; Lee, 1999). In the end, distinctions between white-collar crime, organized crime, corruption, and legitimate business are almost impossible to make. Lawbreaking behavior and success are fused. As a businessman told Handelman (1995: 139), "the truth is, everything you see around you, all our success, is not thanks to our wonderful economic laws. It's thanks to the fact that we do not obey them."

Dysnomic conditions also bring about anomie at the global level. As argued elsewhere (Passas, 1999), international law is more essential now than ever for the maintenance of world order and security. Yet, big powers are reluctant to contribute to the required pooling of sovereignty and have been blocking the development of an international criminal code and specific legislation to restrain their corporations. Dependent on rich countries for its operations, the U.N. has not been overly aggressive in pursuing these aims or in establishing a permanent international criminal tribunal. Globalism has thus run ahead of the creation of a desperately needed normative and enforcement infrastructure.

Existing international laws are applied selectively and never against one of the permanent members of the U.N. Security Counsel. This ad hoc approach and the extraterritorial application of national laws undermine the legitimacy of current laws and procedures. We are left with a legal patchwork of inconsistent and conflicting rules. An example of the effect of such asymmetries is the secrecy and anonymity available in certain jurisdictions that hinder investigative work by covering the tracks and proceeds of global offenders, de facto shielding them against prosecution and punishment. By exploiting the cracks between diverse state rules, companies continually commit crimes without law violation. Globalism also leads to a relativization of norms and facilitates law violations with a clear conscience (rationalizations and techniques of neutralization).

Finally, the border-policing problem in the former USSR is not unique, even if the underlying causes were specific to it and other European countries (Yugoslavia, Czechoslovakia). More generally, borders become porous, as technology and mobility enabled people, money, goods, and ideas to travel quickly and cheaply. Criminals can take advantage of this shrinking world, but law enforcement agencies are constrained by parochial laws and procedures. Though the reasons for the porousness may differ, the process and results are the same.

## Conclusion

Tremendous structural strains have overwhelmed even the usually patient and submissive Russians. The economic situation deteriorated further, hopes were dashed, opportunities for criminal gain and for looting the USSR's assets multiplied, and the anomic societal context offered no assistance to anyone seeking to restore some law and order. In Russia and around the world, the neoliberal operation was successful, but the patients are being systematically frustrated, are starving, and subject to exploitation by corporations, criminal enterprises, and corrupt politicians. In short, globalization and neoliberalism spread analytically similar criminogenic processes that were once unique to the U.S. culture of the American Dream in a context of structural inequalities. Just as the world supposedly became freer, wealthier, more democratic, more enjoyable, and more equal, people find themselves poorer, more exploited, and facing increased hardships. Just as the need for strong normative guidance grows, norms break down or lose their legitimacy. Just as effective controls become necessary to slow down or stop the vicious cycle leading to higher rates of crime, a dysnomic regulatory patchwork remains in place largely because of nationalist insistence on sovereignty and states' unwillingness to allow the introduction of common principles and law enforcement mechanisms.

Two main points need to be reiterated here. First, it appears that global neoliberalism and serious crime go hand in hand. However, it would be erroneous to argue that stereotypical organized criminals are giving capitalism a bad name and undermining neoliberal policies. The implication is that, were we to rid ourselves of some very bad apples, everything would be fine. Rather, it appears that serious organizational misconduct is a consequence of such policies. Second, when we discuss transnational crime, we should bear in mind that it is not just the stereotyped ethnics who cause most problems. It may be that the biggest threat emanates from legitimate corporations and other organizations.

Detailed discussion of policy implications is beyond the scope of this article. The horizontal arrows in Figure 1 hint at the points of possible policy intervention. Myriad concrete ideas can be found in the literature, ranging from legal changes to informal controls, grass-roots movements, integration of economic growth with environmental and social protection, relocalization of production and consumption, etc. The most important ray of hope, however, is implicit in the foregoing analysis. Neoliberal policies and globalization are largely the fruit of (some) governments. They affect and are affected by governance. Therefore, governments have the ability to reverse some of these processes and to mitigate their adverse consequences. Otherwise, the current processes of globalization and neoliberalism will prove to be unsustainable and at a huge cost.

### Figure 1:
### Social Processes Leading to Anomie and Deviance

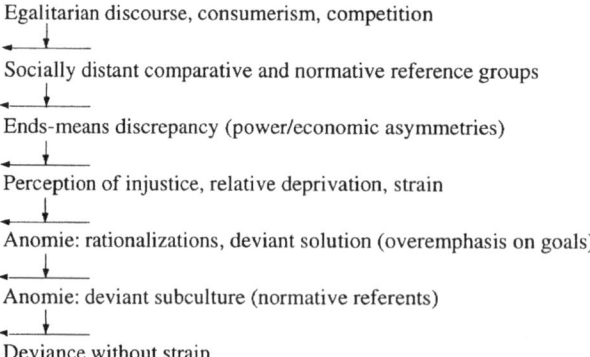

Egalitarian discourse, consumerism, competition

Socially distant comparative and normative reference groups

Ends-means discrepancy (power/economic asymmetries)

Perception of injustice, relative deprivation, strain

Anomie: rationalizations, deviant solution (overemphasis on goals)

Anomie: deviant subculture (normative referents)

Deviance without strain

The horizontal lines point to policy implications. This is where interventions can be attempted in order to block this process and prevent misbehavior. In the context of neoliberal globalism, they represent criminogenic influences.

# REFERENCES

Afanasyef, V.
1994            "Organized Crime and Society." *Demokratizatsiya* 2,3: 426–441.
Alesina, A. and D. Rodrik
1994            "Distributive Politics and Economic Growth." *Quarterly Journal of Economics* 109,2: 465–490.
Andreas, P.
1999            "Smuggling Wars: Law Enforcement and Law Evasion in a Changing World." T. Farer (ed.), *Transnational Crime in the Americas*. London: Routledge: 85–98.
1997            "The Rise of the American Crimefare State." *World Policy Journal* 14,3: 37–45.
Aubert, V.
1968            "White-Collar Crime and Social Structure." G. Geis (ed.), *White-Collar Criminal: The Offender in Business and the Professions*. New York: Atherton Press: 173–184.
Barnet, R.J. and J. Cavanagh
1994            *Global Dreams: Imperial Corporations and the New World Order*. New York: Simon and Schuster.
Beare, M.
2000            "Russian (East European) Organized Crime Around the Globe." Paper presented at the "Transnational Crime Conference," organized by the Australian Institute of Criminology, Australian Customs Service, and Australian Federal Police, Canberra.
Bello, W.
1999            "Is the 'Structural Adjustment' Approach Really and Truly Dead?" *BusinessWorld, Internet Edition* (November 8), downloaded from Internet site http://www.bworld.com.ph/current/today.html.
1996            "Structural Adjustment Programs: 'Success' for Whom?" J. Mander and E. Goldsmith (eds.), *The Case Against the Global Economy*. San Francisco: Sierra Club Books: 285–293.
Bruinsma, G.J.N. and G. Meershoek
1999            "Organized Crime and Trafficking in Women from Eastern Europe in the Netherlands." *Transnational Organized Crime* 4: 105–118.
Burbach, R., O. Núñez, and B. Kagarlitsky
1997            *Globalization and Its Discontents*. London: Pluto Press.
Castells, M.
2000            *End of Millennium* (2nd ed.). Oxford: Blackwell.
Center for Investigative Reporting and B. Moyers
1990            *Global Dumping Ground: The International Traffic in Hazardous Waste*. Washington, D.C.: Seven Locks Press.
Chin, K.L.
1999            *Smuggled Chinese: Clandestine Immigration to the United States*. Philadelphia: Temple University Press.
Clinard, M.B.
1990            *Corporate Corruption: The Abuse of Power*. New York: Praeger.
Cox, R.W.
1993            "Structural Issues of Global Governance: Implications for Europe." S. Gill (ed.), *Gramsci, Historical Materialism, and International Relations*. Cambridge: Cambridge University Press.
Critharis, M.
1990            "Third World Nations Are Down in the Dumps: The Exportation of Hazardous Waste." *Brooklyn Journal of International Law* 6,2: 311–339.

Dunn, J.
  1994                "East Timor: A Case of Cultural Genocide?" G.J. Andreopoulos (ed.),
                      *Genocide: Conceptual and Historical Dimensions*. Philadelphia: University of
                      Pennsylvania Press: 171–190.
Durkheim, E.
  1983                *Le Suicide*. Paris: Presses Universitaires de France. (Originally published
                      1930.)
Gambetta, D.
  1993                *The Sicilian Mafia*. Cambridge: Harvard University Press.
Giddens, A.
  1990                *The Consequences of Modernity*. Cambridge: Polity.
Gilpin, R.
  1987                *The Political Economy of International Relations*. Princeton: Princeton
                      University Press.
Gleason, G.
  1990                "Nationalism or Organized Crime? The Case of the 'Cotton Scandal' in the
                      USSR." *Corruption and Reform* 5: 87–108.
Glinkina, S.P.
  1994                "*Privatizatsiya* and *Kriminalizatsiya*: How Organized Crime Is Hijacking
                      Privatization." *Demokratizatsiya* 2,3: 385–391.
Handelman, S.
  1995                *Comrade Criminal*. New Haven: Yale University Press.
  1994                "The Russian 'Mafiya.'" *Foreign Affairs* 73,2: 83-96.
  1993                "Why Capitalism and the Mafia May Mean Business." *The New York Times*
                      (January 24).
Hirst, P. and G. Thompson
  1996                *Globalisation in Question: The International Economy and the Possibilities of
                      Governance*. Cambridge: Polity.
Holmes, L.
  1997                "Corruption and the Crisis in the Post-Communist State." *Crime, Law, and
                      Social Change* 27: 275–297.
Hovannisian, R.G.
  1994                "Etiology and Sequelae of the Armenian Genocide." G.J. Andreopoulos (ed.),
                      *Genocide: Conceptual and Historical Dimensions*. Philadelphia: University of
                      Pennsylvania Press: 111–140.
ICFTU (International Confederation of Free Trade Unions)
  2000                *Globalising Social Justice: Trade Unionism in the 21st Century*. Durban:
                      ICFTU.
Katona, D.
  1999                "Challenging the Global Structure Through Self-Determination: An African
                      Perspective." *American University International Law Review* 14: 1439–1472.
Keohane, R.O. and J.S. Nye
  2000                "Globalization: What's New? What's Not? (And So What?)." *Foreign Policy*
                      118: 104–119.
King, J. and D. Stabinsky
  1998-99             "Biotechnology Under Globalisation: The Corporate Expropriation of Plant,
                      Animal, and Microbial Species." *Race and Class* 40,2–3: 73-89.
Klak, T.
  1998                "Thirteen Theses on Globalization and Neoliberalism." T. Klak (ed.),
                      *Globalization and Neoliberalism*. Lanham, MD: Rowman and Littlefield: 3–
                      23.
Klak, T. and G. Myers
  1998                "How States Sell Their Countries and Their People." T. Klak (ed.), *Globaliza-
                      tion and Neoliberalism*. Lanham, MD: Rowman and Littlefield: 87–109.

Korten, D.C.
  1996         "The Failures of Bretton Woods." J. Mander and E. Goldsmith (eds.), *The Case Against the Global Economy*. San Francisco: Sierra Club Books: 20–30.
  1995         *When Corporations Rule the World*. West Hartford, CT: Kumarian Press.
Krasner, S.D.
  1985         *Structural Conflict: The Third World Against Global Liberalism*. Berkeley: California University Press.
Kuznetsova, R.W.L.F.
  1994         "Crime in Russia: Causes and Prevention." *Demokratizatsiya* 2,3: 442–452.
Lee, R.W.
  1999         "Transnational Organized Crime: An Overview." T. Farer (ed.), *Transnational Crime in the Americas*. London: Routledge: 1–38.
  1994         "The Organized Crime Morass in the Former Soviet Union." *Demokratizatsiya* 2,3: 392–411.
Levy, F.
  1998         *The New Dollars and Dreams: American Incomes and Economic Change*. New York: Russell Sage Foundation.
Mander, J.
  1996         "Facing the Rising Tide." J. Mander and E. Goldsmith (eds.), *The Case Against the Global Economy*. San Francisco: Sierra Club Books: 3–19.
Mander, J. and E. Goldsmith (eds.)
  1996         *The Case Against the Global Economy*. San Francisco: Sierra Club Books.
McGrew, T.
  1992         "A Global Society?" S. Hall, D. Held, and T. McGrew (eds.), *Modernity and Its Futures*. Cambridge: Open University Press: 62–102.
Merton, R.K.
  1968         *Social Theory and Social Structure*. New York: The Free Press.
Messner, S.F. and R. Rosenfeld
  1994         *Crime and the American Dream*. Belmont, CA: Wadsworth.
Minda, G.
  2000         "Book Review: The Globalization of Culture." *Colorado Law Review* 71: 589–643.
Myers, W.H.
  1995–1996    "The Emerging Threat of Transnational Organized Crime from the East." *Crime, Law, and Social Change* 24,3: 181–222.
Naylor, R.T.
  1999a        "Wash-out: A Critique of Follow-the-Money Methods in Crime Control Policy." *Crime, Law, and Social Change* 32,1: 1–57.
  1999b        *Patriots and Profiteers: On Economic Warfare, Embargo Busting, and State-Sponsored Crime*. Toronto: McClelland and Stewart.
  1995         "From Cold War to Crime War: The Search for a New 'National Security' Threat." *Transnational Organized Crime* 1,4: 37–56.
Norberg-Hodge, H.
  1996         "The Pressure to Modernize and Globalize." J. Mander and E. Goldsmith (eds.), *The Case Against the Global Economy*. San Francisco: Sierra Club Books: 33–46.
OGD, Observatoire Géopolitique des Drogues
  1996         *The Geopolitics of Drugs*. Boston: Northeastern University Press.
Oman, C.
  1999         "Globalization, Regionalization, and Inequality." Ngaire Woods and A. Hurrell (eds.), *Inequality, Globalization, and World Politics*. Oxford: Oxford University Press: 36–65.
Paine, L.P. and F.J. Cilluffo (eds.)
  1994         *Global Organized Crime: The New Empire of Evil*. Washington, D.C.: CSIS.

Passas, N.
   1999          "Globalization, Criminogenic Asymmetries, and Economic Crime." *European
                 Journal of Law Reform* 1,4: 399–423.
   1998          "Transnational Crime: The Interface Between Legal and Illegal Actors."
                 Presented at the National Research Council Workshop on "Transnational
                 Organized Crime." Washington, D.C.
   1997          "Anomie, Reference Groups, and Relative Deprivation." N. Passas and R.
                 Agnew (eds.), *The Future of the Anomie Tradition*. Boston: Northeastern
                 University Press: 62–94.
   1994          "The Market for Gods and Services: Religion, Commerce, and Deviance."
                 *Religion and Social Order* 4: 217–241.
   1990          "Anomie and Corporate Deviance." *Contemporary Crises* 14,3: 157–178.
Passas, N. and J. Blum
   1998          "Intelligence Services and Undercover Operations: The Case of Euromac." S.
                 Field and C. Pelser (eds.), *Invading the Private? Accountability and the New
                 Policing in Europe*. Aldershot: Dartmouth.
Passas, N. and R.B. Groskin
   1995          "International Undercover Operations." G. Marx and C. Fijnaut (eds.),
                 *Undercover: Police Surveillance in Comparative Perspective*. Amsterdam:
                 Kluwer: 291–312.
Politi, A.
   1998          "Russian Organised Crime and European Security." E.U. Directorate-General
                 for External Relations (ed.), *Illicit Trade and Organised Crime: New Threats
                 to Economic Security?* Luxembourg: European Communities: 31–57.
Popescu-Birlan, L.
   1994          "Privatization and Corruption in Romania." *Crime, Law, and Social Change*
                 21,4: 375–379.
Robinson, W.I.
   1998–1999     "Latin America and Global Capitalism." *Race and Class* 40,2–3: 111–131.
Rosenau, J.
   1990          *Turbulence in World Politics*. Brighton: Harvester Wheatsheaf.
Saba, R.P. and L. Manzetti
   1996–1997     "Privatization in Argentina: The Implications for Corruption." *Crime, Law,
                 and Social Change* 25,4: 353–369.
Scheper-Hughes, N.
   2000          "The Global Traffic in Human Organs." *Current Anthropology* 41,2: available
                 on the Internet at http://www.journals.uchicago.edu/CA/journal/issues/v41n2/
                 002001/002001.html.
Shelley, L.
   1995          "Transnational Crime: An Imminent Threat to the Nation-State?" *Journal of
                 International Affairs* 48,2: 463–489.
   1994          "Post-Soviet Organized Crime." *Demokratizatsiya* 2,3: 341–358.
Shiva, V.
   1997          *Biopiracy: The Plunder of Nature and Knowledge*. Boston: South End Press.
Silverstein, K. and A. Cockburn
   1995          "Major U.S. Bank Urges Zapatista Wipe-Out: 'A Litmus Test for Mexico's
                 Stability.'" *Counterpunch* 2,3.
Sklair, L.
   1995          *Sociology of the Global System* (2nd ed.). New York and London: Prentice
                 Hall and Harvester Wheatsheaf.
Stewart, F. and A. Berry
   1999          "Globalization, Liberalization, and Inequality: Expectations and Experience."
                 Ngaire Woods and A. Hurrell (eds.), *Inequality, Globalization, and World
                 Politics*. Oxford: Oxford University Press: 150–186.

Sykes, G.M. and D. Matza
    1957       "Techniques of Neutralization: A Theory of Delinquency." *American Sociological Review* 22,6: 664–670.
UNDP (United Nations Development Programme)
    2000       *Poverty Report*. New York: Oxford University Press.
    1998       *Human Development Report: Consumption for Human Development*. New York: United Nations.
Vagg, J.
    1992       "The Borders of Crime." *British Journal of Criminology* 32,3: 310–328.
van Duyne, P.C., V. Ruggiero, M. Scheinost, and W. Valkenburg (eds.).
    2000       *Cross-Border Crime in a Changing Europe*. Tilburg and Prague: Tilburg University and Prague Institute of Criminology and Social Prevention.
Wallerstein, I.
    1983       *Historical Capitalism*. London: Verso.
Watkins, K.
    1997       *Globalisation and Liberalisation: Implications for Poverty, Distribution, and Inequality*. Occasional Paper 32: U.N. Development Program.
Williams, P.
    1994       "Transnational Criminal Organisations and International Security." *Survival* 36,1: 96–113.
Wilterdink, N.
    1995       "Increasing Income Inequality and Wealth Concentration in the Prosperous Societies of the West." *Studies in Comparative International Development* 30,3: 3–23.
Woods, N.
    1999       "Order, Globalization, and Inequality in World Politics." Ngaire Woods and A. Hurrell (eds.), *Inequality, Globalization, and World Politics*. Oxford: Oxford University Press: 8–35.
Yergin, D. and J. Stanislaw
    1998       *The Commanding Heights: The Battle Between Government and the Marketplace That Is Remaking the Modern World*. New York: Simon and Schuster.

# [3]

# ENRON ET AL.: PARADIGMATIC WHITE COLLAR CRIME CASES FOR THE NEW CENTURY

DAVID FRIEDRICHS
*University of Scranton*

**Abstract**. The Enron et al. cases (i.e., the series of "corporate scandal" cases emerging in 2001–2002, beginning with Enron, and including such cases as WorldCom, Global Crossing, Adelphia, and Tyco) are the first major American white collar crime cases of the new century. This article identifies some of the key attributes of these cases. The Enron et al. cases can only be understood by applying criminological theory on several different levels; structural, organizational, dramaturgic and individualistic dimensions are applied to the Enron case in particular. The Enron et al. cases must also be understood in the context of an emerging postmodern society. The specific role of criminologists in explaining and responding to these paradigmatic new white collar crime cases is addressed. The article ends with some conjectures on the potential outcomes of the Enron et al. cases.

## Enron as Metaphor

The Enron et al. cases of 2001–2004 are the largest scale white collar crime cases since the S & L and insider trading cases of the 1980s. The Microsoft antitrust case of the late 1990s could also be classified as a major white collar crime case, although it was pursued by federal and state antitrust lawsuits that did not attempt to convict Microsoft executives of criminal charges (Auletta 2001; Heilemann 2001). In terms of overall impact on the economy, the political and legal environment, and public perceptions of business-related crime and ethical lapses, it was evident from quite early in 2002 on that the Enron case, in conjunction with related cases, was overshadowing many earlier cases of white collar crime, and at least potentially could have transformative effects. These cases involved an exceptionally broad range of leading corporate and financial executives and institutions.

The term "Enron et al." is invoked here to refer to the specific cases involving the Enron corporation and some of its top personnel, but also to the linked case of the Andersen accounting firm, and a series of cases that surfaced in the wake of the Enron case. Enron, then, becomes a metaphor for a series of other cases, part of a domino effect: these cases, in alphabetical order, include Adelphia Communications, Computer Associates, Dynergy, Global Crossing, Qwest, Rite Aid, Tyco International, WorldCom, and Xerox (Berenson 2002b). In the case of each of these corporations, either the corporation itself and/or top executives were under criminal and/or civil investigation for some form of gross misrepresentation on financial statements or outright accounting fraud, typically involving inflation of sales, numbers of customers and profits, sham off-the-books partnerships, transactions and trades, concealment of expenses, bonus payments or loans to top executives, or some combination of these activities. A common thread in at least most of these cases was the extraordinary levels of compensation for top executives, and large paper losses for investors following revelations of the misrepresentations or misstatements (Oppel and Atlas 2001; Barboza 2002a; Greider 2002). Questions were subsequently raised about the financial statements of other major corporations (e.g., see Berenson 2003; Morgenson 2003). The legitimate fear that there might be many corporations that issued misleading financial statements contributed to a precipitous erosion of investor confidence and dramatic declines in stock market indices, despite claims of some analysts that many market fundamentals were relatively positive (Berenson 2002a; Morgenson 2002a). The common thread of inflating apparent profits or concealing losses and costs, in the interest of pushing the stock price up or avoiding a decline in the stock price, is more striking than the various devices or techniques to achieve this end (McLean 2001; Barboza 2002b). The immense rewards in various forms enjoyed by the top insiders in these corporations, significantly based upon basic misrepresentation of the corporation's financial balance sheet, are another common thread (Leonhardt 2002a, b). The cooperative involvement of a broad network of other parties – including independent boards of directors, accounting firms, law firms, investment banking firms, and stock analysts – is still another common theme (Eichenwald and Barboza 2002; Madrick 2002).

## Enron et al. as Crime

In addition to massive civil lawsuits, the Enron et al. cases have inspired numerous criminal investigations, leading to some guilty pleas, indictments and pending trials (Eisenberg 2002b; Thomas 2002; Eichenwald 2004; Feder and Eichenwald 2004). Claims of criminal conduct have been vigorously contested in most cases, although some concessions of such conduct have been forthcoming as a part of plea negotiations. In the narrow, technical sense, willful violation of criminal laws will have to be demonstrated to make the case that crimes occurred. Alternative constructs on the misrepresentations of corporate financial balance sheets are likely to include the following: the various accounting strategies were technically legal and generally accepted practices, or were so certified by professionals (accountants and lawyers) overseeing the process; judgment calls, as opposed to willful intent to defraud, was involved; unanticipated circumstances and bad luck, rather than criminal conduct, can be blamed for the financial meltdowns (Eichenwald 2002b; Toobin 2003). The inherent ambiguity of some of the relevant laws, the complexity of the schemes themselves, and the resources of first-class legal talent to challenge government characterizations of these activities, all contribute to the difficulties inherent in successfully applying a legal designation of crime to the Enron et al. activities.

The crime question can also be considered more broadly. Sutherland (1949), in his original study of corporate crime, adopted the broader conception of corporate crime to encompass violations of civil law and regulatory law, as well as criminal law, on the premise that the corporations disproportionately influence the adoption of criminal laws in ways that favor their interests. This claim certainly still has merit. More broadly still, progressive criminologists would characterize the activities of Enron et al. as criminal simply on the basis that policies were adopted that can be shown to have had demonstrably exploitative and harmful consequences (for workers; for consumers; for investors; for citizens; and so on) (Henry and Lanier 2001; Tifft and Sullivan 2001). Indeed, the actual and potential scope of demonstrable harm attributable to Enron et al. is extraordinary, and includes: for tens of thousands of people, lost jobs; lost pensions; lost opportunities for higher education; higher prices; higher rates of interest; less money for investment in legitimate businesses; less money for charities; and so on (Fusaro and Miller 2002). To the extent that government resources have to be directed toward addressing these activities, government resources for other concerns (including socially beneficial programs) can be affected. Somewhat more abstract but very real costs are possible, and include: enhanced physical and mental distress for those most directly affected; erosion of trust in major institutions; and intensification of inter-group resentment and conflicts. Of course, those who adopt some version of a Marxist perspective would regard the activities of Enron et al. as simply the more manifestly obvious forms of crime that are inherent to capitalist enterprise (Lynchy, et al. 2000; Russell 2002). In sum: While there are many indications of criminal conduct in the narrowest legal sense, crime may also be said to be involved in the Enron et al. cases in terms of broader conceptions of the term crime.

### Applying Criminological Theory to Enron et al.

Greed is a term commonly used as an explanation for Enron et al. and surely greed played a role. But such a simplistic, one-dimensional explanation does not take us very far. At the other end of the spectrum, Enron et al. can be explained as an outcome of a complex interaction of many different factors and variables, operating on various levels. Accordingly, an integrated theoretical approach is called for in these cases (Barak 1998; Vold et al. 2002). If we aspire to understand Enron et al. on a truly sophisticated level, it is useful to identify as many potentially applicable variables and factors as possible, with at least some such factors either eliminated or relegated to a minor role in the development of a comprehensive explanatory scheme.

### *Structural Level*

Enron et al. occurs within the context of a capitalist political economy that establishes the fundamental conditions for the operation of private corporations, and is linked with certain cultural values promoting free market competition, the pursuit of profit, and the expansion of markets, or growth, among other things. Russell's (2002) brief on behalf of the on-going relevance of a Marxist framework applies here. In the wake of the collapse of the Soviet Union, capitalism was widely celebrated as triumphant, and a political and cultural environment of intensified celebration of capitalist values prevailed throughout the 1990s and into the new century. Mitchell (2001) has critiqued the current form of orientation of American corporate capitalism as favoring stock price maximization over values. The focus on short-term enhancement of stock price has many harmful consequences, but top corporate executives who make the often ruthless decisions (e.g., laying off thousands of workers) are relatively insulated from confronting the painful human costs of these decisions.

The late 1990s bull market created expectations of substantial stock price growth, and put CEOs under immense pressure to produce numbers that would promote such price growth, or at a minimum would not lead to a decline in stock price. If reported quarterly numbers were below expectations, the corporate stock price would fall dramatically, generating substantial losses and making it more difficult to raise further capital. During the same period of time, the expansion of stock option plans, bonuses and other forms of rewarding top executive personnel were much more fully developed. An escalating stock price was arguably the surest way to riches for corporate managers, and provided strong additional incentives for encouraging aggressive or blatantly fraudulent accounting in connection with the production of corporate financial statements.

The political and legal context of the present era must also be taken into account. Although many political leaders and legislators expressed outrage over Enron et al., they also played a key role in creating the legal environment that facilitated the illegal and unethical activities of these corporations (Labaton 2002a). For example, legislation in 1995 was passed shielding companies and accountants from investor lawsuits, and in 2000 regulators were forced to dilute proposed restrictions on accountants. Altogether, during this period of time, legislation relating to investor lawsuits imposed tougher burdens of proof on plaintiffs; shortened the statute of limitations for filing such suits; put limits on pretrial discovery, and on accountant liability; and imposed the obligation on plaintiffs who lost such suits to pay the legal costs. The sum effect of such legislation was to provide corporations and their auditors with a sense of relative immunity for any financial manipulations they might undertake causing losses to investors.

Deregulatory legislative initiatives cannot be understood independently of the political environment. In an era of costly political campaigns, political office-holders have become increasingly dependent upon the donations of major corporations and wealthy corporate executives, who in return expect favorable responses to their lobbying on behalf of laws favorable to their economic well-being. Indeed, the entire Enron et al. phenomenon could be said to lend support to Mills' (1959) thesis about the power elite: that the top corporate, political, and military people make the important decisions for the rest of us, are closely linked with each other and engage in "higher immorality" in the pursuit of their own interests. Although these propositions apply to both political parties, and all recent administrations, the extent of these interlocks and mutual interests are especially pronounced in the administration of President George W. Bush, as has been widely documented (Duffy and Dickerson 2002; Fusaro and Miller 2002). The earlier career and actions of the President, the Vice President, and other high-level officials in this administration raised questions in many

118                          DAVID FRIEDRICHS

quarters about the depths of their commitment to address emerging corporate scandals.

One can also argue that an emerging postmodern cultural environment fostered an increasing disconnect between traditional criteria for reality toward hyperreal orientations privileging simulations and abstract projections as real (Schwartz and Friedrichs 1994). This postmodern dimension of the Enron et al. cases is explored more fully in the section that follows; however, it can be observed here that high-level executives in Enron et al. may have become increasingly insulated from a conventional form of a real world, creating a self-delusional and mutually reinforcing world of ever-expanding opportunities for profit and growth (Wolff 2002). Financial deals and the use of financial instruments such as derivatives became so complex the executives involved may no longer have fully comprehended what was involved (Altman 2002b), The distribution of very large political donations and the cultivation of political connections could have also contributed to an illusion of immunity from political or justice system interference in their schemes (Greider 2001; Van Natta 2002). If high-level executives did not on some level buy into these various illusions, they were consciously engaged in profoundly self-destructive activities.

*Networks and Interlocks*

Contemporary capitalist corporations such as Enron are best understood as operating as part of a network of organizations and entities with which they establish ties of mutual interdependence. In the public realm – as noted above – corporations develop ties with political leaders and parties upon whom they are dependent for favorable policy decisions, and who are dependent on them, in turn, for political campaign donations. The interconnections between public and private interests, then, incorporate fundamental conflicts of interest, with the practical benefits of accommodating corporate donors often trumping other considerations by political decision-makers. In the private sector, entities include accounting firms, investment banking houses, stock brokerages, stock analysts, and law firms. These networks are increasingly structured to have inherent conflicts of interest that lead to enabling fraudulent activity as opposed to acting as checks and balances on such activities (Gullotta 2001; Atlas 2002; Berenson 2002b; Levin 2002; Morgenson 2002b).

Two of the more blatant conflicts of interest highlighted in the wake of the exposure of Enron et al. are as follows: Auditing firms derive a substantial proportion of their income from consulting contracts with the corporations they are auditing; a fear of losing these lucrative consulting contracts inhibits the accounting firms from pressing the corporation on financial statement discrepancies, or leads to willing participation in the production of misrepresented financial statements. As another example, stock analysts are affiliated with investment banking operations that derive their principal income from underwriting and consulting deals with corporate clients, as opposed to truly independent and honest evaluation of the corporation's stock. As the top people in the corporation have much to lose if the stock price declines, stock analysts serve their own firm best by evaluating the stock of corporate clients (or prospective clients) in positive terms.

The notion of independent boards overseeing corporate financial arrangements was also severely compromised by the various benefits derived by board members from not challenging or seriously questioning corporate practices (Stellin 2002). Even investors and employees were not strongly inclined to challenge the actions of the corporate leadership as long as they seemed to be reaping high rates of return on their investments. Altogether, effective preventive checks and balances on unwarranted or outright fraudulent activities were largely absent. External entities did not adequately compensate for the conflicts of interest and lack of internal oversight: e.g., credit rating agencies failed to identify misrepresentations in corporate financial statements; the SEC was neither adequately staffed nor appropriately organized to proactively investigate these corporate financial statements; and the media – disproportionately owned and controlled by large corporations – also largely failed to reveal the financial misrepresentations of these corporations, until they became self-evident as the corporate finances began unraveling (Lewis 2002; McNamee et al. 2002; White 2002). Criminologists have to attend to the various ways in which these networks, interlocks, inherent conflicts of interest, and inadequate forms of oversight promote a criminogenic environment.

*Organizational Factors*

On an organizational level, an environment of intense competitiveness, intimidation toward compliance with the organizational agenda established by company leadership, and the promotion of a strong ethos of corporate pride, loyalty, and superiority was also significant. At Enron, for example, a "rank and yank" system of evaluating employee's performance was put into place: employees who fell below a certain ranking at the periodic evaluation points would lose their jobs (Fusaro and Miller 2002: 51). Employees who failed to comply with corporate directives were also in jeopardy. On the positive side, employee loyalty was promoted by much celebratory activity and rhetoric within the corporation, all geared to promoting the perception that the corporation was superior to most others, had an excellent business plan and outstanding prospects for the future, and so forth.

The pay incentive structures adopted at Enron et al. are another organizational feature of these cases. At Enron, specifically, huge bonuses were paid in 2000 to executives who made stock-price targets; these bonuses exceeded $300 million (Eichenwald 2002a). The period of these bonus awards coincides with the period when Enron was engaged in various accounting maneuvers to inflate the appearance of profits from its operations. Accordingly, one has evidence of a financial motivation for these maneuvers, and to the extent that they turn out to be illegal, criminal intent. Furthermore, generous loans in the millions were made to many top executives at these companies, enabling the executives to increase their pay while satisfying demands to increase their holding in the corporation's stock (Leonhardt 2002a). These loans gave executives incentives to pursue risky strategies to keep the stock price up, since this would make it easier to repay the loans with higher value stocks, profiting greatly from the difference in the original price of the stock. By paying back loans with stocks, executives avoided having to report that they were selling shares in their own corporation; and generous stock option plans provided such executives with parallel incentives to do whatever was necessary to drive up stock price.

Some of these corporate organizations – and again, Enron in particular – proudly proclaimed themselves to be models of a new, more creative, more visionary form of management than was true of "old economy" corporations, and they were praised in some quarters for pioneering new approaches to business in a rapidly evolving information age (Barboza 2001). In the case of Ford Motor Company, it is clear what business they are in: they produce automobiles. In the case of Enron (and some of the other companies) the nature of their business was far less clear, and the stress was on trades and deals, not products and assets. In hindsight, this form of corporate organization is especially likely to foster management obfuscation and illegal financial manipulations.

Modern corporate organizations have become increasingly complex in terms of how they are organized. Transnational conglomerates are going to be far more complex than traditional, domestic corporations with a single, core product or service. In addition, highly complex financial instruments have been adopted by these corporations. "Derivatives" exemplify such instruments. According to Altman (2002b) "derivatives are contracts that promise payments from one investor, and 'counter-party,' to another, depending on future events. These events can be as ephemeral as changes in the prices of securities or commodities from which the contracts are derived – hence the name – or as concrete as weather changes.... ." Derivatives were developed as a useful hedge on certain types of business-related risks, and can serve a legitimate purpose, but they also tend to be highly complex, are not transparent, and incorporate risks that may not be well understood. Enron specifically used derivative trades as a means of hiding loans. Accordingly, the complexity of many of the new corporate organizations – especially those in emerging businesses such as telecommunications and energy trading – created expanded opportunities for illegal and unethical financial manipulations.

*Dramaturgic Level*

On a dramaturgic level, the Enron corporation was for some time very successful in conveying an image of ultra-respectability that largely insulated it from external challenge, and also reinforced an internal legitimation of its business practices. This projection of ultra-respectability was fostered by: the cultivation of and friendship with top political leaders (including both Presidents Bush) by Chairman Kenneth Lay; the construction of an emblematic headquarters in Houston; the naming of Houston's stadium as Enron Field; the conspicuous local philanthropy; and so on. Lay, the son of a Baptist minister, as the "face" of Enron, projected an image of decency, generosity, charm, and – or so it seemed – integrity (Thomas and Murr 2002). Enron was able to capitalize on an especially high level of trust that was in turn, in important ways, a function of its image of ultra-respectability.

*Individualistic Level*

Sutherland (1949) dismissed the notion that personality or individual attributes could significantly explain white collar crime, and this has generally been the line adopted ever since. But character and personality should not be wholly irrelevant. The top personnel at Enron et al. – or those most directly implicated in wrongful conduct – are quite uniformly described as lacking in basic integrity, and greedy. It seems excessively cynical to declare that integrity is irrelevant, and that any executive operating in the environment in which the Enron et al. executives operated would make exactly the same decisions. But to the extent that these individuals had any ethical bearings or concerns, they seem to have been clearly trumped by other considerations, and priorities. The media has also reported on the greed, in the traditional sense, of at least some of the key executives in these cases: multi-million dollar mansions, extravagant vacation homes, yachts, private jets or helicopters, fancy art collections, and so on (Eichenwald 2002a; Leonhardt 2002a, b). Many of these executives (who in some cases came from very humble circumstances) were also greedy for acceptance by political and social elites, and surely some of their campaign contributions and philanthropic endeavors were inspired by the desire for acceptance. Finally, in an oft-cited proposition, money becomes a way of "keeping score": that is, at least some of these executives seemed to have a bottomless need to run up the numbers of their compensation simply as a way of proving to themselves (and others) their superior place in the society's "scoreboard" of winners and losers.

Of course many highly successful corporate leaders who do not get in trouble with the law have some mixture of such attributes. These attributes by themselves may not necessarily lead to engaging in unlawful and unethical practices, but in conjunction with some of the conditions described earlier may well facilitate law-breaking. These high-level executives may be more fearful of failing, of losing their position and losing face, than of what may be quite unthinkable or unimaginable to them: that they might be indicted for crimes and go to prison (Schwartz 2002). Accordingly, they engage in risky strategies. The process of getting into trouble with high-risk decisions is often incremental, and gradual. In a vein somewhat parallel to the thinking of embezzlers, who first embezzle small sums fully expecting to replace the embezzled money, and then due to unanticipated losses get in deeper and deeper, so it is with at least some of these executives (Cressey 1953). Their past success has imbued them with an unwarranted optimism, and an assumption that they will be able to overcome any crisis, with a combination of various factors working in their favor. Things get out of control, however. Ever since the Watergate case, it has been a commonly advanced axiom that the cover-up is worse (and more damaging) than the original crime (Eichenwald 2002d; Schwartz 2002). Some efforts at cover-up continue to be the norm in Enron et al. cases, however, and may reflect a fundamental unwillingness to face up to losing one's privileged position and all that goes with it, and the inherently arrogant sense that one is too smart to get caught.

One of the striking – and arguably especially disheartening – aspects of the Enron et al. cases was the absence of individuals who took a stand against illegal or unethical practices, refused to cooperate, or reported such matters to the proper authorities (McLean and Elkind 2003). In the case of Enron, one high-level official had apparently expressed some concerns about the irregular financial arrangements, resigned, and then appears to have committed suicide when the public scandal surfaced (although some suspicion remains that it wasn't a suicide) (Fusaro and Miller 2002; Yardley 2002). In his suicide note this individual expressed his unbearable pain over the turn of events; but such a response seems to have been highly atypical.

### Enron et al.: Modern or Postmodern White Collar Crime?

The question now turns to whether the Enron/Andersen case – or Enron et al. cases – is best understood as a modern or a postmodern phenomenon; whether it is something new in white collar crime, or simply an exemplification of long-standing, familiar forms of white collar crime. This question, 1 believe, does not have a single, straightforward answer, but it is surely worth addressing.

It is not uncommon to differentiate between traditional, modern, and emerging future (or postmodern) societies (Friedrichs and Friedrichs, 2004). Traditional societies are characterized by agriculture as the central form of productive activity, hand-tool technology, farming villages as the typical community, the family structure as the dominant form of organization for farms and shops, interpersonal communication, and social and geographical stability as the normative expectation. In modern societies, industrial activity is the central form of productive activity, the machine displaces hand tools in the technological realm, urbanization and city life dominate, bureaucracies displace families as the dominant form of organization, mass communication becomes increasingly important, and both social and geographical mobility are normative expectations. In an emerging postmodern society, information services (broadly defined) increasingly become central to productive activity, the computer displaces the machine at the center of modern technology, the megalopolis and virtual communities become increasingly important, adhocracies (or more flexible, adaptable forms of bureaucracy) emerge, interactive communication (exemplified by video, cable, the internet, and television/computer link-ups) spreads, and social and geographical fluidity – i.e., moving in and out, back and forth – is increasingly internalized as an expectation.

Needless to say, the foregoing is a broad, generalized, and selective characterization of social change. Furthermore, it makes sense to acknowledge that traditional, modern, and postmodern patterns of social existence co-exist, that tensions and conflicts between these patterns are central elements of our social existence, and that the schematic comparison of traditional, modern, and postmodern societies reflects mainly a matter of degree in the existence of different elements at a particular point in time. Any attempt to demarcate a specific time frame for the transformation from a traditional to a modern, or from a modern to a postmodern, society is necessarily arbitrary. Nevertheless, if one accepts such qualifications and caveats, the comparative endeavor is a necessary and useful exercise.

Instances of white collar crime, broadly defined, can be found in the earliest historical records, and various forms of fraud have been a persistent feature of human history. But white collar crime as it has been conventionally conceived of – since Sutherland – is principally a modern phenomenon, because the conditions of modernity promote the amplification of such crime. Many forms of corporate crime, in particular, reflect in some form the conditions generated by a modern, industrial society. The literature on corporate crime has especially attended to corporate violence in the forms of crimes against citizens (e.g., pollution), crimes against workers (e.g., unsafe working conditions, such as exposing workers to asbestos), and crimes against consumers (e.g., unsafe products, such as the Pinto and the Dalkon Shield). Corporate crime also takes the form of abuses of power, fraud, and economic exploitation, including crimes against taxpayers (e.g., defense contract fraud), crimes against consumers (e.g., price fixing), crimes against employees (e.g., economic exploitation), crimes against competitors (e.g., theft of trade secrets), and crimes against owners and creditors (e.g., managerial self- dealing and strategic bankruptcy).

In certain respects, the Enron et al. crimes are manifestations of frauds with a long lineage. The South Sea Bubble case of the 18th century is one example of such fraud (Robb 1992; Balen 2003). The South Sea Company was chartered in London in 1711 to engage in slave trade and commerce in South America, Over a period of about 10 years, investors lost large fortunes because the whole enterprise was quite fraudulent, driven by bribery, false financial statements, and stock manipulation. In some interpretations, the Enron et al. cases simply exemplify – on a grand scale – the classic, enduring "pump and dump" schemes where insiders drive up stock prices on the basis of some form of misrepresentation, and then bail out of their own positions at the top, with other investors incurring huge losses when the scheme inevitably collapses. On the other hand, it is also possible to identify some dimensions of the Enron et al. cases that are at least relatively novel, and may be taken to reflect emerging postmodern attributes of social existence.

First, the corporate crime literature to date has principally focused on corporations that manufacture some type of product. The Enron et al. cases disproportionately involve corporations engaged in the provision of some form of service (e.g., relating to energy, telecommunications, entertainment, and the like). In the case of corporations like Exxon, Ford, Johns-Manville, or A.H. Robbins, everyone understands the core nature of their business; in the cases of Enron, Global Crossings, WorldCom and Tyco International, however, the real nature of what they do or what kind of business they are in is far less clear. Second, those involved in the Enron et al. cases can in many cases be characterized as "paper entrepreneurs." Unlike Henry Ford they did not make their fortune by developing (or inventing) and producing a product for which there was a large and expanding public demand so much as that they found ways of acquiring and manipulating financial assets. Third, the companies involved are increasingly likely to be transnational in their operations, and organized to take advantage in every way (e.g., on corporate tax liability) of this transnational character.

The concept of hyperreality introduced by Baudrillard (1994) can usefully be applied to the Enron et al. cases. Hyperreality has been characterized as a circumstance wherein images breed incestuously with each other without reference to reality or meaning. When we increasingly experience our world in terms of simulations, and can no longer clearly differentiate between conventional reality and simulations, then we have entered the realm of hyperreality. The related term "hypermodernism" has been applied to the hyper-intensification of modernism, and a circumstance where technology and economics merge (Appignanesi and Garratt 1995: 126). Hyperreal finance is a world of 24 hour hook-ups between worldwide financial markets, where transactions in cyberspace become dominant.

In the various accounts of the Enron et al. cases, one is struck by a fundamental disconnect between the presumed modernist assumptions of most ordinary investors – that they are investing in something real, in

126                          DAVID FRIEDRICHS

an appropriately assessed product or service with a good potential for
growth – and the apparent postmodernist or "hyperreal" orientation of
some of the central figures in these cases, whose primary concern seemed
to be the manipulation of assets and numbers in ways that maximized
their own short-term gain, with almost complete indifference to the
demonstrable value of the product or service at the center of their
business. The question of whether the key figures in these cases were
deliberately and consciously engaging in transactions they knew to be
fraud, or that on some level they were no longer able to clearly dis-
criminate between simulated transactions and transactions of substance,
is not entirely resolved. In more colloquial terms, did these key figures
on some level confuse the "smoke and mirrors" they were generating
with something of substance? Did they operate in an environment
promoting a "dematerialization of the real," and a disconnect with the
conventional reality of capitalist economy?

   The concept of intertextuality as it has emerged from postmodernist
discourse may also have some relevance here. This term refers to the
idea that there is a complex and infinite set of interwoven relationships,
"an endless conversation between the texts with no prospect of ever
arriving at or being halted at an agreed point" (Bauman 1990; 42).
Absolute intertextuality assumes that everything is related to everything
else. In the Enron et al. cases, as they have been emerging, one is struck
first by the complexity of the many suspect deals, financial arrangements
and instruments (e.g., derivatives), to the point that it seems possible
that at a certain juncture, none of the key players can any longer fully
grasp the scope and character of the financial edifice they have constructed. Second, and relatedly, one is struck by the direct and indirect
intertwined involvement of so many different parties in these transactions: i.e., corporate executives, corporate boards, auditors, investment
bankers, stock analysts, lawyers, credit rating agencies, and the like. On
the one hand, none of these different entities may have a complete
handle on all aspects of the complex financial transactions involved; on
the other hand, these different entities may mutually reinforce on at
least some level the basic disconnect with conventional reality.

   None of the propositions stated in the previous paragraph should be
interpreted as excusing the culpability of the different parties from their
fiduciary responsibilities; denying the significant forms of conscious
wrong-doing, unethical or illegal activity involved; or overlooking the
role of greed and personal enrichment as motivating factors in individual and collective involvement in fraudulent transactions. But at the
same time, a deeper understanding of the Enron et al. crimes calls for

attention to the potential role of an emerging postmodern environment in the corporate world.

## Challenges for Criminology

What specific contribution can criminologists make to the under-standing of these cases? First, if the term crime is to be applied here, it is criminologists who should be best qualified to clarify different ways in which this term is most appropriately applied to these cases (Henry and Lanier 2001). More specifically, criminologists can clarify what forms of white collar crime are involved in these cases. In another vein, Snider's (2000) work on the decriminalization of corporate crime, in the recent era, provides an important point of departure for critical criminologists addressing the definitional issues.

Second, criminologists can engage in what Barak (1998: 294) calls "newsmaking criminology." The media coverage of Enron et al. – variously characterized as corporate scandals, corporate transgressions, or a corporate crime wave – has arguably been the most substantial, pervasive, and sustained coverage of white collar crime (in some form) in American history. Criminologists can engage in the systematic study of this media coverage and its influence on public policy. On the applied level, criminologists can contribute more directly to the popular media coverage of Enron et al. crimes, challenging some of the common misrepresentations of such crime in the media. Criminologists are especially well-qualified to address the question of the real costs of these crimes in relation to more conventional forms of crime.

Third, criminologists can initiate the systematic criminological study of Enron et al. cases, through the exploration of primary data, and ethnographic or participant observer studies. The present articles relies largely on journalistic sources, in part because as a practical matter – with many legal cases pending – primary data and interviews with participants are not yet a feasible option. Over time, this should change, and articles such as this can hopefully provide a useful point of departure for such directly engaged research. In this connection, as well, criminologists will face challenges of obtaining funding for this type of research.

Fourth, there is the question of theory and explanation: Which theories – most typically, developed to explain conventional forms of crime and delinquency – are usefully applied to the understanding of the Enron et al. cases? This article has attempted to make a preliminary contribution to this endeavor. But much further work is called for, especially in terms of the application of sophisticated forms of critical theories of the political economy to an understanding of this type of crime. The relevance of some significant work being done within the framework of mainstream approaches, such as an emerging network science, has to be considered. Altogether, refinements of existing initiatives toward the development of integrated criminological theories will be necessary if we are to obtain a profound understanding of Enron et al. crime.

Finally, criminologists are especially qualified to identify some of the challenges of policing and prosecuting the Enron et al. cases. They can identify what has been learned about the prevention and control of other forms of crime that is applicable to crimes of this nature. Furthermore, they can build upon pioneering work of Benson and Cullen (1998) on the prosecution of corporate crime, studying the complex decision-making process involved in the pursuit of the Enron et al. cases.

In sum, a specifically criminological analysis of the Enron et al. cases should complement and enrich analyses generated by commentary and interpretation coming from many other sources.

## Conclusion

Enron et al. might well be described as a paradigmatic form of white collar crime, because they incorporated in almost pure form some of the key – and sometimes contradictory – attributes that Sutherland had in mind when he promoted the concept of white collar crime: The crimes were committed by privileged, respectable members of society, violating a fundamental trust, through major corporations, for purposes of financial gain (and to avoid financial loss), with devastating economic consequences for many ordinary members of society. Sutherland's interest in white collar crime was significantly inspired by his revulsion with the manipulations of financial elites during the 1920s, culminating in the stock market crash of 1929 and contributing to the depression of the 1930s. At the same time, the Enron et al. cases also incorporate some elements distinctive to an emerging postmodern information age.

One can envision a number of different outcomes for the Enron et al. cases. First, it is possible they will largely recede from public consciousness; prosecutors will encounter insurmountable barriers to successfully pursuing most of these cases, or convictions will be reversed on appeal; various lobbying entities will successfully defeat any serious efforts for new laws and regulatory initiatives; and the cases will simply become part of an evolving list of white collar crime cases, devoid of a special status. The likelihood of such a scenario is importantly linked with other developments in the larger world, including the course of international terrorism and the response to it. More specifically, if major new terrorist attacks along the lines of 9/11 occur, or the occupation of Iraq becomes increasingly costly and chaotic, governmental and public attention (and resources) are proportionally less likely to focus on corporate crime cases.

In a second scenario, Enron et al. will continue to be a focus of some on-going public interest. They will lead to some successful prosecutions, focused principally on individual executives identified as having initiated illegal actions, and convictions will generally be upheld. But in this scenario, the stress will be on the enforcement of existing laws and regulations, with some possible fine-tuning, but no fundamental reforms. This might be described as the scenario generally favored by the administration of President George W. Bush and the Republican congressional leadership.

In a third scenario, Enron et al. will reemerge as matters of significant on-going public interest. They will produce major prosecutions of not only individual executives but errant corporations as well, and convictions will be quite uniformly upheld. These cases will lead to the adoption of laws and regulations tougher in fundamental ways in response to the types of activities involved in these cases. This is a scenario most likely to be embraced by liberal democrats.

Finally, there is this: Enron et al. might hypothetically evolve into criminal cases so large in scope that they will lead to a fundamental transformation of the public perception of white collar crime, and a structural transformation of the political and economic system fostering these forms of white collar crime. Such a transformation could lead to broad support for preventive measures and basic deterrence of Enron et al. types of crime. Those of a progressive orientation have long awaited the white collar crime "tsunami", a white collar crime wave so devastating and broad in scope that it will produce just such a transformation.

If past history is any guide, perhaps the expectation of a minor or moderate impact of the Enron et al. cases is the most probable scenario. However, the fostering of a broader consciousness in the direction of a major or transformative impact of the Enron et al. cases is a worthwhile objective toward which white collar crime criminologists – and

130 DAVID FRIEDRICHS

especially those with a critical criminological orientation – should orient themselves.

## References

Altman, D. (2002a). Finding gems of genius among Enron's crumbs. *The New York Times* (February 3), Wk3.

Altman, D. (2002b). Contracts so complex they imperil the system. *The New York Times* (February 24), 3/1.

Appignanesi, R. and Garratt C. (1995). *Introducing Postmodernism*. New York: Totem Books.

Atlas, R. (2002). Market place. *The New York Times* (June 13), C3.

Auletta, K. (2001). *World War 3.0: Microsoft and Its Enemies*. New York: Random House.

Balen, M. (2003). *The Secret History of the South Sea Bubble: The World's First Great Financial Scandal*. New York: HarperCollins.

Barak, G. (1998). *Integrating Criminologies*. Boston: Allyn & Bacon.

Barak, G. (2001). Crime and crime control in an age of globalization: A theoretical discussion. *Crticial Criminology* 10, 57–72.

Barboza, D. (2001 ). Victims and champions of a Darwinian Enron. *The New York Times* (December 12), C4.

Barboza, D. (2002a). Officials got a windfall before Enron's collapse. *The New York Times* (June 18), C1.

Barboza, D. (2002b). Former officials say Enron had gains during crisis in California. *The New York Times* (June 23), A1.

Barboza, D. and Schwartz, J.(2002), The financial wizard ties to Enron's fall. *The New York Times* (February 6), A1.

Baudrillard, J. (1994). *Simulacra and Simulation*. Ann Arbor: University of Michigan Press.

Bauman, Z. (1990). Philosophical affinities of postmodern sociology. *Sociological Review* 38, 411–444.

Benson, M. and Cullen, F.T. (1998). *Combating Corporate Crime: Local Prosecutors at Work*. Boston: Northeastern University Press.

Berenson, A. (2002a). The biggest casualty of Enron's collapse: Confidence. *The New York Times* (February 10), 4/1.

Berenson, A. (2002b). Three-decade-old echoes, awakened by Enron. *The New York Times* (February 24), Cl.

Berenson, A. (2003). Report says Freddie Mac misled investigators. *New York Times* (July 24), Cl.

Bradley, W. (2002). Enron's end. *The American Prospect* (January 1–14), 30–31.

Callahan, D. (2002). Private sector, public doubts. *The New York Times* (January 15), A21.

Cressey, D.R. (1953) *Other People's Money*. Glencoe, IL: Free Press.

Duffy, M. and. Dickerson, J.F. (2002). Enron spoils the party. *Time* (February 4), 19–25.

ENRON ET AL.: PARADIGMATIC WHITE COLLAR CRIME CASES    131

Eichenwald, K. (2002a). Enron paid huge bonuses in '01: Experts see a motive in cheating. *The New York Times* (March 1), Al.

Eichenwald, K. (2002b). White-collar defense stance: The criminal-less crime. *The New York Times* (March 3), Wk/3.

Eichenwald, K. (2002c). How the trial at Andersen could hurt a fraud case. *The New York Times* (May 24), Cl .

Eichenwald, K. (2002d). Andersen guilty of shredding files in Enron scandal. *The New York Times* (June 16), Al.

Eichenwald, K. (2002e). Ex-Enron official admits payments to finance chief. *The New York Times* (August 22), AI.

Eichenwald, K. and Barboza, D. (2002). Enron criminal investigation is said to expand to bankers. *The New York Times* (June 13), Al.

Eisenberg, D. (2002a). Dennis the Menace, *Time* (June 17), 48–49.

Eisenberg, D. (2002b). Jail to the chiefs? *Time* (August 12), 24–25.

Friedrichs, D. (2004), *Trusted Criminals: White Collar Crime in Contemporary Society,* 2nd edition. Belmont, CA: Wadsworth.

Friedrichs, D. and Friedrichs, J. (2004). Postmodernist theory. In A. Thio and T. Calhoun (eds.), *Readings in Deviant Behavior*, 3rd edition. Boston: Pearson, pp. 70–76.

Fusaro, P.C, and Miller, R.M. (2002). *What Went Wrong at Enron.* New York: John Wiley.

Greider, W. (2001). Enron's rise and fall. *The Nation* (December 24), 5–6.

Greider, W. (2002). Crime in the suites. *The Nation* (February 4), 11–14.

Gullotta, M. (2001). The SEC's auditor independence rule Missing the boat on independence. *Santa Clara Law Review* 24; 221–146.

Heilemann, J. (2001). *Pride Before the Fall: The Trials of Bill Gates and the End of the Microsoft Era.* New York: HarperCollins.

Henry, S. and Lanier, M. (eds.) (2001). *What is Crime? Controversies over the Nature of Crime and What to do About It,* Lanham, MD: Rowman & Littleheld.

Labaton, S. (2002a). Now who, exactly, got us into this? *The New York Times* (February 3), 3/1.

Labaton, S. (2002b). Downturn and shift in population feed boom in white-collar crime. *The New York Times* (June 2), Al .

Leonhardt, D. (2002a). A prime example of anything goes executive pay. *The New York Times* ( June 4), Cl.

Leonhardt, D. (2002b). Slivers of support for shackling corporate pay. *The New York Times* (July 13), C1.

Levitt, A. (2002). Who audits the auditors? *The New York Times* (January 17), A29.

Lewis, R. (2002). Media, mostly big businesses, fail to report on big business. *The Scranton Times* (February 4), Editorial page.

Lynch, M.J., Michalowski, R. and Groves, W.B.(2000). *The New Primer in Radical Criminology: Critical Perspectives on Crime, Power, and Identity.* Monsey, NY: Criminal Justice Press.

Madrick, J. (2002). Enron: Seduction and betrayal. *The New York Review of Books* (March 14), 21–24

McLean, B. (2001). Why Enron went bust. *Fortune* (December 24), 59–68.

McNamee, M., Borrus, A. and Henry, D. (2002). The reluctant reformer. *Business Week* (March 25), 72–82.

Mills, C.W. (1959). *The Power Elite.* New York: Oxford University Press.

132                          DAVID FRIEDRICHS

Mitchell, L. (2001). *Corporate Irresponsibility: America's Newest Export*. New Haven: Yale University Press.

Morgenson, G. (2002a). Worries of more Enrons to come give stock prices a pounding. *The New York Times* (January 30), C11.

Morgenson, G. (2002b). Requiem for an honorable profession. *The New York Times* (May 5), 3/1.

Morgenson, G. (2003). Financial disclosure the Barry Diller way. *New York Times* (July 24), C1.

New Republic (2002). The real Enron scandal. *The New Republic* (January 28),7.

Oppel, R.A. Jr. and Atlas, R. (2001). Enron struggles to find financing to remain in business. *The New York Times* (December 1 ), C1.

Rich, F. (2002). All the president's Enrons. *The New York Times* (April 6), A13.

Robb, G. (1992). *White-Collar Crime in Modern England: Financial Fraud and Business Morality-1845–1929*. Cambridge, UK: Cambridge University Press.

Russell, S. (2002). The continuing relevance of Marxism to critical criminology. *Critical Criminology* 11, 113–135.

Sargent, M.A. (2002). The real scandal, *Commonwealth* (March 8), 10–12.

Schwartz, J. (2002). Choosing whether to cover-up or come clean. *The New York Times* (July 1), C1.

Schwartz, M. and Friedrichs, D. (1994). Postmodern thought and criminological discontent: New metaphors for understanding violence. *Criminology* 32, 221–246.

Scott, J. (2002). Once bitten, twice shy: A world of eroding trust. *The New York Times* (April 21), Wk5.

Snider, L. (1999). Relocating law: Making corporate crime disappear. In. E. Comack (ed.), *Locating Law*, Halifax, NS: Fernwood Publishing Co, 183–207.

Snider, L. (2000). The sociology of corporate crime: An obituary. *Theoretical Criminology* 4, 169–206

Stellin, S. (2002). Directors ponder new, tougher rules. *The New York Times* (June 30), 3/16.

Sutherland, E.H. (1940). White collar criminality. *American Sociological Review* 5, 1–12.

Sutherland, E.H.( 1949). *White Collar Crime*. New York: Holt, Rinehart & Winston.

Thomas, C.B. (2002). Called to account. *Time* (June 24), 52.

Thomas, E. and Murr, A. (2002). The gambler who blew it all. *Newsweek* (February 4), 19–24.

Tifft, L. and Sullivan, D.(2001). A needs-based, social harms definition of crime. In S. Henry and M. Lanier (eds.), *What is Crime? Controversies over the Nature of Crime and What to do About it*. Lanham, MD: Rowman & Littleheld, 179–206.

Van Natta, D. Jr. (2002). Enron spread contributions on both sides of the aisle. *The New York Times* (January 21), A13.

Vold, G.B., Bernard, T.J. and Snipes, J.B. (2002). *Theoretical Criminology*. 5th-edition. New York: Oxford University Press.

White, L. (2002). Credit and credibility. *The New York Times* (February 24), Wk13.

Wilentz, S. (2002). A scandal for our time. *The American Prospect* (February 25), 20–22.

Wolff, M. (2002). Spread thin. *New York* (March 4) 1, 20–21.

Yardley, J. (2002). Critic who quit top Enron post is found dead. *The New York Times* (January 26), A1.

Zweig, P. (2002). Learning old lessons from a new scandal. *The New York Times* (February 2), A11.

# [4]

# Criminogenic Cyber-Capitalism: Paul Virilio, Simulation, and the Global Financial Crisis

Eric Wilson

**Abstract**  This essay is a manifesto expounding the relevance of the critical theory of Paul Virilio to critical criminology. I interpret the global credit crisis as a criminogenic 'event', explicable in terms of Virilio's theory of speed-politics. The trans-national space(s) of globalization are inherently criminogenic. 'Power crime' is the criminogenic 'substance' of global capitalism. Globalization—intensity, extensity, velocity, and impact—equates with cyber-capitalism, which ensures the operational primacy of simulation. Simulation, the fast moving manipulation of post-reality, causes the 'disappearance of the real', which underlines the epistemological crisis that attenuates global economic catastrophe. Simulation equates with the 'logistics of perception', which manifests itself through both pure war and speed-politics. Simulation and power crime merge on the level of the criminogenic manipulation of reality, resulting in the 'accident' of the global credit crisis. Power crime is the criminogenic medium through which the periodic crises of global capitalism will now occur.

*The day when virtual reality becomes more powerful than reality will be the day of the big accident.—Paul Virilio.*

*Accident is statistically inescapable.—Yi-Fu Tuan.*

## Introduction

My paper advances three propositions: (1) That the global credit crisis constitutes a form of 'accident', signifying the emergence of power crime, or the 'criminogenic', as a systemic property of the cyber-capitalist world-economy; (2) That this accident in global finance, widely understood as a 'fast moving event', is governed by wider trends that are necessary attributes of what is generally described as 'globalization'; (3) That the work on the notion of simulation by the critical theorists Jean Baudrillard and, more crucially, Paul Virilio provide us with the conceptual tools and philosophical imaginary that we need in order to

E. Wilson (✉)
Faculty of Law, Monash University, Melbourne, Australia
e-mail: Wilson@law.monash.edu.au

re-formulate our understanding of the nature of the world-economy which now stands revealed as a criminogenic phenomenon.


## Globalisation and Simulation

'I don't claim to define the situation, I try to reveal tendencies.'—Paul Virilio

In this paper I adopt the (provisional) definition of globalization offered by David Held.

> [A] process (or set of processes) which embodies a transformation in the spatial organization of social relations and transactions—assessed in terms of their extensity, intensity, velocity and impact—generating transcontinental or interregional flows and networks of activity, interaction, and the exercise of power. (Held et al. 1999 at 15)

Historical materialists such as Robert Brenner have argued powerfully that the current global credit crisis is merely the most recent event within the long term systemic crisis of over-accumulation and the declining rate of profitability.[1] However, what orthodox Marxist analysis ordinarily elides is the extent to which the speed of the crisis can itself serve as the primary indicator of the nature of the globalized economy within which the event is embedded. Non-Marxist scholars, such as William Greider, evidence a clear awareness of a qualitative transformation of the nature of late capitalism.

> The essence of this industrial revolution, like others before it, is that commerce and finance have leapt inventively beyond the existing order and existing consciousness of peoples and societies. The global system of trade and production is fast constructing a new functional reality for most everyone's life, a new order built upon its own dynamics and not confined by the traditional social understandings. (Greider 1997 at 15)

Within this imaginary, global economic catastrophe is discursively equated with an even more foundational ontological crisis; 'The most important breakthrough, by far, was in an obscure realm of high finance that is utterly unfamiliar to most citizens and, for that matter, do most politicians: the decontrol of capital movement itself' (Greider 1997 at 33).[2]

There is considerable evidence that within the mainstream media, the most important shaper of public conceptions, a fundamental but indiscernible shift in the nature of late capitalist relations has taken place, one that serves to unite a metaphysics of chaos with an epistemology of radical uncertainty, underlying a wider but equally ineffable cultural crisis. The popular writings of the international financial speculator George Soros is an outstanding example of this fledging attempt at collective re-conceptualization. Soros formally eschews the orthodox view that 'uncertainties' are currently 'impeding the normal functioning of the financial market.' For him, 'Misinterpretations of reality and other kinds of misconceptions play a much bigger role in determining the course of events than generally recognized' (Soros 2008 at 11). Misrepresentation is not an anomaly but 'a causal force in history': the 'current financial crisis can be directly attributed to a false

---

[1] See below.

[2] An 'economistic' ontology, with, of course, a concomitant political catastrophe; 'The wondrous machine of global revolution [i.e., 'globalization'] is oscillating out of control, widening the arcs of social and economic instabilities in its wake. The destructive pressures building up within the global system are leading toward an unbearable chaos that, even without a dramatic collapse will likely provoke the harsh, reactionary politics that can shut down the system' Greider (1997, 316).

interpretation of how financial markets function' (Soros 2008 at 50).[3] Indeed, there 'has to be some form of credit or leverage and some kind of misconception or misrepresentation involved for a boom-bust process to develop' (Soros 2008 at 78). Yet, somewhat curiously, Soros goes on to insist with equal moral and intellectual certainty that 'Markets will not be fully re-assured until all hidden liabilities are fully disclosed' (Soros 2008 at 128).[4] In the end, then, Soros ironically re-affirms the very epistemological realism ('truth') that has already been put into doubt by the global dimension of a crisis that seems to have resulted from the system-wide commodification of 'debt' as 'asset', a global loss in the ability to distinguish between positive and negative value.[5] I suggest that the site where popular economic discourse would most greatly benefit from a direct engagement with critical theory lies along this precise juncture: that the nature, structure, and operation of the current global political economy renders impossible, both in ontological and epistemological terms, the recovery, or 're-discovery', of the Real.

**Simulation: Speed**

> The question of modernity and postmodernity is superseded by that of reality and post-reality.—Paul Virilio

The complex manipulation of suspect financial instruments that appears to have caused the crisis strongly bring to mind the critical, almost poetic, reveries of the French theorist Jean Baudrillard on what he de-notes as 'simulation', the onto-epistemological transformation of the 'real' into the 'virtual'. Like a good simulationist, Baudrillard defines his key notion in binary opposition to simulation's Other, dissimulation.

> To dissimulate is to feign not to have what one has. To simulate is to feign to have what one hasn't. One implies a presence, the other an absence. But the matter is more complicated, since to simulate is not simply to feign...Thus, feigning or dissimulating leaves the reality principle: the difference is always clear, it is only masked; whereas simulation threatens the difference between 'true' and 'false', between 'real' and 'imaginary' (Baudrillard 1983 at 5).[6]

---

[3] A point labored at great length by Greider. 'The power of global finance includes an extraordinary ability to create its own version of reality and persuade others to believe in it. When investment analysts determine the financial outlook for a company or nation, their portraiture [sic] is based on statistical indicators, market trends and political intelligence—an analysis clearly abstracted from the messy facts of daily life. The financial data seems so concrete and logical, so consistent with orthodox principles of economics, that others are regularly seduced by the markets self-confident assumptions. Governments, press and politicians typically embrace these financial projections and amplify them into a general metaphor of economic progress' Greider (1997, 259).

[4] Soros' account touches directly on the vital question over the role that *trust* plays in economic transactions. The classic discussion is Akerlof (1970).

[5] 'Freed by deregulation, the banks found new business converting consumer debt into tradeable securities and then selling those securities to the [pension and mutual] funds (or other banks).' Blackburn (2008, at 67; also 74). See the summary provided by Wark (1994, 200). Published in 1994, Wark's 'Site #4: Wall Street, New York City, Planet of Noise' is an utterly prescient anticipation of the global financial catastrophe of September 2008. Idem, 165–247. In particular, chapter eight, 'Crash!', is an early Virilian analysis of the then newly emergent cyber-capitalism. Idem, 205–247.

[6] For the role played by simulation in contemporary critical theory, see Cubitt (2001).

For Baudrillard, the era of simulation is a 'post-theological' one, in which we have collectively repudiated the traditional hierarchy of evaluation of the 'true' and 'false' a relic of the lingering superstitious belief in God.

> The transitions from signs which dissimulate something to signs which dissimulate that there is nothing, marks the decisive turning point. The first implies a theology of truth and secrecy (to which the notion of ideology still belongs). The second inaugurates an age of simulacra and simulation, in which there is no longer any God to recognize his own, nor any last judgement to separate the true from false, the real from its artificial resurrection, since everything is already dead and risen in advance. (Baudrillard 1983 at 12)

The 'highest' value (in the Nietzschean sense) of the Baudrillarian Text lies is that it enables the parodic inversion of classical Marxism. Like Nietzsche, Baudrillard is not concerned with 'truths', but with values. Both undertake a critical, and highly subversive, form of axiology: 'As Nietzsche said: "Down with all hypotheses that have allowed belief in a real world"' (Baudrillard 1993 at 61). From this perspective, both the Liberal and Marxist belief in the objective 'truth' of the law of exchange(s) stand revealed as a 'superstition' (metaphysics) or, even worse, a 'prejudice' (morality). Baudrillard's project is not to construct a metaphysical counter-reality but to undertake an ironic analysis of a pataphysical (i.e., 'post-Real') phenomenon, the 'liquidation of meaning'. Baudrillard is not a metaphysician but a radical anthropologist; all of his later writings are supremely ironic, and intensely poetic, commentaries upon the contemporary 'violence perpetuated against meaning', interrogating the current legitimacy of the Reality Principle as the master-sign of social and cultural value by means of deliberately ironical quasi-metaphysical postulates.

Contrary to popular perceptions, therefore, the Baudrillarian text is a critical excavation not of 'reality' but of 'meaning'; the uncovering of the infinitely self-referential nature of the 'structural law of value' lies at the very heart of his work. (Gane 1993 at x) Baudrillard has even worked out a (primitive) historical chronology of the successive domains of simulation, each era governed by its own form of simulacra, a regime of value controlled by a temporally specific circulation/exchange system of signs. These historically successive 'orders of the sign' are, respectively

1. First-order simulacra = the 'Baroque" (16th–18th centuries; Baudrillard 1993 at 55–57)
2. Second-order simulacra = the 'Industrial' (19th–20th centuries; the use-value vs. exchange-value of classical Marxism, or the law of equivalent value/commodity form-exchange; Baudrillard 1993 at 55–57)
3. Third-order simulacra = The 'Code' (late twentieth Century; the subsumption of the illusory binary opposition between use- and exchange-value; Baudrillard 1993 at 57–61)

For Baudrillard, our current age of the sign-system/simulacra of the code is signified by 'a neo-capitalist cybernetic order'. (Baudrillard 1993 at 57–61) This seminal notion of a cybernetic form of capitalism, or, more pithily, cyber-capitalism, is equally central to the work of Baudrillard's contemporary Paul Virilio, whose treatment of simulation, I would like to suggest, is actually more germane to my efforts to develop a criminological model of the global credit crisis.[7]

---

[7] In this paper I will be focusing on Virilio's earlier writings where he develops the seminal notions of speed-politics and pure war. In my opinion, these are the Virilian concepts of the most direct relevance to critical criminology. Virilio's later work on phenomenology, while of great interest to me, are not of the

For Virilio, and unlike Baudrillard with whom he is frequently and somewhat misleadingly linked, the central feature of cyber-capitalism is not the mimetic replacement of reality with the virtual but, in a sort of ontological practical joke, the 'mis-taking' of the model for the reality.[8] Like Baudrillard, Virilio advances a radically circulationist notion of power; however, for him, while simulation equals 'exchange' it does not equal 'substitution'. 'We face a duplication of reality. The virtual and the "real" reality double the relationship to the real, something that, to the best of my knowledge, results in clear pathological consequences' (Virilio 1995a). In Virilio's own words, as against

the opinion of Baudrillard, I have to say that reality never vanishes. It constantly changes. Reality is the outcome of a pre-determined epoch, science or technique. Reality must be re-invented, always. To me, it is not the simulation of reality that makes the difference, it is the replacement of a pre-determined reality by another pre-determined reality. I proceed from the antagonism between real and virtual reality, and I notice that both will shortly constitute one single reality...(Virilio 1995a)

Reality is not eliminated; however, neither is it merely being mis-perceived. Rather, the phenomenological conduits of reality/perception have themselves been fundamentally altered through both new social relations and new technologies.[9] This point has been forcefully made by Mike Gane in his authoritative studies of Baudrillard.

What separates Baudrillard and Virilio...[is] essentially a dispute about the theory of the real as a referant for simulation, and particularly the social as referant ...Virilio's 'simulations' are representations of the real world, representations which are substituted for one another as technology develops. Baudrillard's conception of these relations is more complex: the real is not a brute given, but a historically and socially evolved form of appropriation of the world (and replaces other forms through their constant and systematic destruction). For Baudrillard then, representation 'stems from the principle of the equivalence of the sign and the real' whereas simulation, 'on the contrary, stems...from the radical negation of the sign as value, from the sign as inversion...of every reference.' In this new situation, 'there is no longer a Last Judgement to separate the false from the true' (Gane 2000 at 95).

---

Footnote 7 continued
greatest importance here. However, I hope to visit the applicability of neo-phenomenology to critical criminology at a later time.

[8] 'We lose, in simulation, the grounds of our metaphysical certainty concerning the difference between the real and the abstraction, the real and the representation, the real and knowledge about it. The difference is the crucial thing that we have lost, since without that difference that separates the two poles of any of these systems of truth, picturing or science, we cannot distinguish one from the other. This is the profound implication of the indifference of simulation, its assimilation of all separations into an indefinite cloud of self-generating models' Cubitt (2001, 50).

[9] See Wark on this point: 'The "economic real" is in some quite fundamental ways, elusive, ineffable, unknowable. To assume that there is a "true" price or set of prices at which buyers and sellers will match up perfectly and the market will clear, assumes away everything dynamic and changing in the market. It assumes away time itself. To assume that there is a knowable correspondence between prices and the value of the goods and services they represent assumes that one has access to a knowledge of the movements of the economy which is independent of the institutions and discourses that make it manifest by representing it...The vector [of finance capitalism] feeds information into the market, but the "efficiency" of the market's response depends on being able to *interpret* that information in an appropriate way' Wark (1994 176 and 185; see also, 181–182).

In this sense, Virilio's notion of simulation-as-representation is more appropriate to the global credit crisis which is based upon the inability to maintain the dichotomy between the false and the true. Strictly speaking, in Baudrillard's view the global credit crisis should never have happened, as it signifies the retention of an almost 'superstitious' belief in the existence of true value; the collapse of global markets as the occurrence of the apocalyptic Last Judgement that Baudrillard precludes as an historical possibility. Employing the terminology of theoretical physics as a source of metaphor, Virilio, contra Baudrillard, holds that 'In the past, reality was a matter of mass; then it became mass + force. Today, reality is the outcome of mass + force + information. Matter has now become three dimensional. This is a clear break' (Virilio 1995a).

Virilio's penchant (often criticized) for the scientific imaginary leads him to formulate his central critical notion, one that effectively folds simulation/simulacra into a much wider framework of critical re-presentation: that of speed. I would argue that Virilio's notion of speed—or, more precisely, of *speed-politics*—is a crucial innovation for two reasons. The first reason is that the concept permits us to advance beyond the neo-Marxist impasse that refuses to allow for any re-conceptualization of capitalism in a non-dialectical manner. On the one hand, speed would appear to serve as an updating of Marx's classic account of space/time compression that figures so largely in innovative contemporary Marxist scholarship, such as David Harvey's seminal *The Limits to Capital*. For Harvey

> Marx depicts the consequent impulse to revolutionize transport relations in very general terms. Capital, he writes, must 'strive to tear down every spatial barrier to ...exchange, and conquer the whole earth for its market,' it must 'annihilate this space with time' in order to reduce the turnover time of capital to 'the twinkling of an eye'. (Harvey 1999 at 377)

While Marx's 'annihilation of space with time' is materialist, Virilio's notion of speed as effecting a 'disappearance' of reality/truth is phenomenological, annihilation corresponding to a condition that is as much existential as it is historical.[10] I understand Virilian speed as a non-dialectical expression of space/time compression in which the measurable rate, or velocity, of transaction/exchange is itself the primary mode of production and not a merely derivative aspect of production; as Mckenzie Wark perceptively points out, Marx's entire account of 'the annihilation of space by time' wholly fails to take into account 'the *separation* of communication from transport, or the development of two distinct *velocities* of movement' (Wark 1994 at 221). Conceived in phenomenological terms, speed directly correlates with globalization theory's notion of the critical variable of 'real time communication', defined by Held as 'the manner in which globalization appears to shrink geographical time and distance; in a world of instantaneous communication, distance and time no longer seem to be a major constraint on patterns of social organization or interaction' (Held et al. 1999 at 15 fn. 2).[11]

---

[10] A notion that Greider intuitively grasps in a non-theoretical manner. 'The world, one could say, was now divided by three different planes of consciousness in terms of how people thought about time. The global financial market and its electronic participants traded continuously around the clock and no longer paused to recognize day or night. Most people in modern society measured time in segments of hours and days, weeks or months. But the primitive [sic] among us, still existing in many places, continued to think and function according to the ancient cycles of seasons' Greider (1997, 349).

[11] In Wark's own account, the 'vector' of high speed Finance Capitalism 'responded enthusiastically to immaterial [information] technology, making one suspect a close affinity between the abstract social force that is money and the principles of the new technologies...Now, the vector and capital are complicit in this, but the vector and capital are not identical. Capital drives the vector further and harder, forcing its

The second reason should, by now, be obvious: Virilio's notion of speed allows us to ground theory in a far more direct manner in the material contours of contemporary capitalism. In my working definition of globalization, taken from Held, speed equates with velocity, which is one of the four cardinal features of globalized political economy. Velocity as the 'growing extensity and intensity of global interconnectedness may also imply a *speeding up* of global interactions and processes as the development of worldwide systems of transport and communication increase the potential velocity of the global diffusion of ideas, goods, information, capital and people' (Held et al. 1999 at 15). As I will now show, Virilian speed-politics is essential to the most fundamental operations of cyber-capitalism.[12]

## Pure War and the Logistics of Perception

> I don't believe in explanations. I believe in suggestions, in the obvious quality of the implicit.—Paul Virilio

Progressive scholars have regularly pointed to the long term stagnation of the world economy from 1973 onwards. (Brenner 2002 7–47, 268 and 285–286)[13] Contemporary capitalism, or what I de-note as cyber-capitalism, is inherently unstable; the systemic crisis of profitability can be categorized in two ways, each one corresponding to the operation of cyber-capitalism in a different zone of territorial space. Within inter-national space, the crisis is one of capital over-accumulation, as described by Giovanni Arrighi.

> Over-accumulation crises occur because there is such an over-abundance of capital seeking investment in established channels of trade and production that competition among its possessors enables real wages to rise in step with, or even faster than, increases in labour productivity. Over-production crises, in contrast, occur because the possessors of capital are so successful in shifting competitive pressures onto labour that real wages fail to keep up with increases in labour productivity, thereby preventing aggregate demand from expanding in step with aggregate supply. (Arrighi 2007, 81–82)

---

Footnote 11 continued

technologies to innovate, but at the same time it tries to commodify the fruits of this development. The vector may have other properties, values that escape the restriction of its abstract potential to the commodity form...the vector and capital are not the same thing...and the vector is not always a functional tool for capital' Wark (1994, 168, 171 and 222). For a similar themed account, see Sassen (2006, chapter seven), 'Digital Networks, State Authority, and Politics', 323–376. Once established, 'expanded decentralization and simultaneous integration enabled by global digital networks produce threshold effects. Today's global electronic capital market can be distinguished from earlier forms of international financial markets due to some of the technical properties of the new [information and communication technologies], notably the orders of magnitude that can be achieved through decentralized simultaneous access and interconnectivity and through the softwaring of increasingly complex instruments.' Idem, 376. Contrast Wark and Sassen with Brenner's tepid account of information technology which reduces the whole of digitalization to yet one more opportunity for over-investment and financial speculation. Brenner (2002, 223–229). As is typical for a neo-Marxist, Brenner is unable to conceive of technology apart from the commodity form.

[12] For much of what follows, see Wilson (2009b).

[13] For the flattening of the profitability of the world-economy, see Brenner (2006, xxi, xxii, 1–9, 101). For the absolute decline in real wages, see idem, xxviii, 2–3, 193, 201, 208–211.

Within intra-national space, the crisis is experienced as one of systemic over-production; the standard recent account is provided by Robert Brenner; 'A lasting decline in the rate of profit in the international *manufacturing* sector, caused by the persistence of over-capacity and over-production, has been, and continues to be, fundamentally responsible for reduced profitability and slow growth on a system-wide scale over the long term' (Brenner 2002 at 285). In fact, both aspects of the crisis of capitalism are obverse phenomena, over-accumulation on a global scale exercising downward pressure(s) on domestic earnings and consumption.[14] On a deeper structural level, the interminable crisis of profit has led to two concomitant events of fundamental importance: (1) the net shift within developed economies away from industry and towards financial services, most importantly international banking[15]; and (2) the radical de-regulation of these same financial sectors. The moves towards finance capitalism and de-regulation were paralleled, in turn, by the increase in the centrality of speed and simulation to the operations of the world economy, one that is increasingly dominated by both the technology and the order of signs/simulacra of the cybernetic. I will discuss the centrality of speed and simulation to the 'deep structure' of the global credit crisis later in this paper.[16] For the present, I want to examine the ways in which the fast-moving world economy directly corresponds to Virilio's notion of speed-politics and its particular manifestation of what he de-notes as *pure war*.

For Virilio, both politics and economics are understood as manifestations of a single geo-strategic phenomenon that is governed by variables of speed, not only in terms of conventional tactical considerations of military force but also in the practice of the domestic politics of the technologically developed state. Speed reduces the being of the state to the panoptical effect of an unlimited transparency that is ultimately self-consuming, what Virilio calls 'the aesthetics of disappearance'; 'The state's only original existence is as a visual hallucination akin to dreaming' (Virilio 1989, 33). Politics *disappears into aesthetics* precisely through its inability to successfully uphold the 'reality principle', which is premised upon conventional representational demarcations between the 'real', the 'visual', and the 'virtual'. (Virilio 1991a) Virilio identifies this ontological and political 'loss of reality' with the *kinematic*, which assumes two forms. 'Kinematic optics', or 'cinematic motion', effectively 'dissolves' substance through the acceleration of perception; time supplants space which 'deletes' Being.[17] 'Kinematic acceleration' is realized through the 'dismemberment' of space/time into isolated 'frames', or editorial 'cuts'. In both instances of the kinematic the virtual re-presentation of reality is now governed by alterations in the rate, or speed, of perception: 'It is reality [that] we have to

---

[14] This forms the essence of Arrighi's critique of Brenner's orthodox neo-Marxist account of the credit crisis: 'Despite Brenner's characterization of the late twentieth-century long downturn as a situation of over-production, what he actually describes is a variant of the kind of over-accumulation of capital that, in Smith's theory of economic development, drives down the rate of profit and brings economic expansion to an end' Arrighi (2007, 165–166).

[15] This transition must not be simplistically mistaken as a movement away from the 'true' and towards the 'false'. As Baudrillard has argued, industrial value, which broadly corresponds to a form of use-value, is itself a form of simulacra; 'Up to this point, we have considered production and labour as potential, as force and historical process, as a generic activity: an energetic-economic myth proper to modernity. We must ask ourselves whether production is not rather an intervention, a *particular* phase, *in the order of signs*— whether it is basically only one episode in the line of simulacra, that episode of producing an infinite series of potentially identical beings (object-signs) by means of technics' Baudrillard (1993, 55).

[16] See below.

[17] To '*save phenomena is to save their speed of apperception*' Virilio (1999, 45). Cubitt rightly places the cinematic—which connotes simulation—at the center of Virilio's oeuvre; idem, 54–64, passim. First and foremost, Virilio is a 'simulationist'; speed is the medium of simulation.

measure in a cinematic way'.[18] The final outcome is a total 'virtualizing' of reality arising from 'the unprecedented limits imposed on subjective perception by the instrumental splitting of modes of perception and representation' (Virilio 1994 at 49).

This optical/ontological collapse of politics into speed underlines the key Virilian notion of pure war (Virilio and Lotringer 1997) a military metaphor that signifies the centrality of the panoptical to the contemporary mode of combat. 'The primacy of speed is simultaneously the primacy of the military' (Virilio and Lotringer 1997 at 51); pure war is the master-sign of a (post-) modern world-system that is governed by absolute speed, signifying the total reversibility between the political, the military, and the economic. Politics disappears into a tripartite 'logistics of perception': military, tele-cinematic, and techno-scientific (Virilio 1999).

> In geo-strategic terms, pure war is derived from the historical shift in military thought from defence to offence: 'The very long period of the supremacy of *defence* over *offence* that marked the history of fortification…is superseded today by the era of the supremacy of the *absolute speed* of weapons of interdiction on the field of battle over the movement of the *relative speeds* of mechanized forces' (Virilio 2005b at 2).

Accordingly, pure war is 'an optical, or electrico-optical confrontation; its likely slogan, "winning is keeping the target in constant sight"' (Virilio 1989 at 2)[19].

> At first, the battlefield was local, then it became worldwide and finally became global, which means satellized with the invention of video and of the spy satellites of observation of the battlefield. From now on, the battlefield is a global one. It is not worldwide any more in the sense of the First or Second World War. It is global in the sense of the planet, the geo-sphere. (Der Derian 2001 at 64)[20]

Virilian pure war has been doctrinally expressed by the Pentagon as 'Rapid Dominance' (Ullman and Wade 1998) or, in the vernacular, 'shock and awe': in 'crude terms [the invader] should seize control of the environment and paralyse or so overload an adversary's perceptions and understanding of events so that the enemy would be incapable of resistance' (Klein 2007 at 147 and 333). As is readily apparent, 'shock and awe' directly correlates with the onto-political kinematics of pure war.

> It is a war of images and sounds, rather than objects and things, in which winning is simply a matter of not losing sight of the opposition. The will to see all, know all, at every moment, everywhere, the will to universalised illumination: a scientific permutation on the eye of God which would forever rule out the surprise, the accident, the irruption of the unforeseen (Virilio 1994 at 70).

---

[18] For these technologies of 'de-realization', see Virilio (1989, 79–89). 'Ours are cinematic societies. They are not only societies of movement, but of the acceleration of the very movement. And hence, of the shortening of distances in terms of time, but, I would also add, of the relation to reality' Armitage (2000, 27).

[19] See also Virili (2005b at 78). 'Many inexperienced military observers focus their attention on the destructiveness of new weapons. While awesome power can be delivered, sharpening the point of the spear is really secondary to locating the enemy. For decades *war games* have proven that it is more important to improve the military's sensor systems and command and control processes than it is to increase firepower. Once an adversary is located, we know how to destroy him. This philosophy has driven the research and development budget' Alexander (2003, 41).

[20] See Alexander (2003 41–47).

This simultaneous projection of speed into both external and internal political space yields two extremely dangerous developments. The first one is that it establishes manifold linkages between the pure war and the practical operations of hegemony within international politics. The second one is that the logistics of perception creates the preconditions for the extra-legal manipulation of representation by entrenched political and military elites. Both of these developments culminate in the criminogenic transformation of the world system.

## Pure War and Hegemony: Exo- and Endo-Colonization

'The separate states had to compete for mobile capital, which dictated to them the conditions under which it would assist them to power.'—Max Weber

The central construct of the Virilian paradigm is that the historical meta-narrative of Modernity is the transition from total war to pure war, signified by the atomic 'disappearances' of Hiroshima and Nagaski. The new political order that results following 1945 is denoted as the 'suicidal state', marking the subordination of the world-system to both pure war and speed-politics. The contemporary State is 'suicidal' not only because it exists within the frame of atomic annihilation, but because traditional forms of political action and speech have been superseded by the requirements of pure war; in terms of political economy, this means the replacement of orthodox economies with a 'military Keynesianism', which supplements the pre-war welfare state. (Block 1977 at 105–108, 114–122 and 168) Following the Second World War, the New Deal doubled as the basis of both a new national and international order, serving as the ideological framework of the Bretton Woods Agreement that legitimated U.S. hegemony.[21] The 'outbreak' of the Cold War in 1947 and Truman's move away from Roosevelt's universalism towards a polarizing containment 'was not so much a negation of the original notion of creating a global welfare state, as its transformation into a project of creating a "warfare-welfare state" on a world scale, in competition with and opposition to the Soviet system of communist states' (Arrighi 2007 at 152).[22] For Virilio, as for other critical scholars, the Cold War was not a truly international conflict, but rather the globalization of a domestic struggle: the shift away from democratic accountability and political transparency towards the covert, or

---

[21] On the complex 'triangulation' between the New Deal, Bretton Woods, and U.S. hegemony, Helleiner (1994).The centrality of 'economic statecraft' to international relations is ordinarily overlooked by mainstream economists and international relations scholars. For an extensive consideration of international economic policy as a continuation of 'national geo-economic strategy' by other means, see Hudson (2003). 'One lesson of U.S. [hegemonic] experience is that the national diplomacy, embodied in what now is called the Washington Consensus, is not simply an extension of business drives. It has been shaped by overriding concerns for world power (euphemized as national security) and economic advantage as perceived by American strategists quite apart from the profit motives of private investors.' Idem, 1. For Bretton Woods as the mechanism facilitating the transition from U.K to U.S. hegemony, see Eichengreen (1996 91–92).

[22] See also, Hudson (2003, 12–14). It is important to note that the US was far from the only nation to do so; the shift towards 'suicide' is a phenomenon that encompasses the whole of the developed world. In his magisterial study on the post-war Japanese economic 'miracle', Chalmers Johnson places military Keynesianism at the centre of Japans success. Between 1911 and 1961, 'the Japanese Economy remained on a war footing. The goal changed from military to economic victory, but the Japanese people could not have worked harder, saved more, or innovated more ruthlessly if they had actually been engaged in a war for national survival, as in fact they were. And just as a nation mobilised for war needs a military general staff, so a nation mobilised for economic development needs an economic general staff' Johnson (1982, 241). See also idem, chapter six, 198–241, passim.

parapolitical, operations of the national security state.[23] The result was a new form of exo-colonization, the systematic subordination of global society to pure war, the US utilizing its national security state apparatus to enforce the global governance prescriptions of the newly globalized New Deal/warfare-welfare state. According to Brenner

> US multinational corporations and international banks, aimed at expanding overseas, needed profitable outlets for their foreign direct investment. Domestically based manufacturers, needing to increase exports, required fast-growing overseas demand for their goods. An imperial US state, bent on 'containing communism' and keeping the world safe for free enterprise [i.e., the cyber-capitalist-world-economy], sought economic success for its allies and competitors as the foundation for the political consolidation of the post-war capitalist order, in the face of the anaemia of domestic ruling classes supplied by war, collaboration, and defeat. All these forces thus depended upon the economic dynamism of Europe and Japan for the realisation of their own goals. (Brenner 2002 at 14–15)

The rise of US hegemony prompted a parallel shift towards international financial capitalism as a means of effectively subsidizing the global suicidal state.

> US policy-makers saw the free mobility of both short and long-term investment as a top priority, for, in their eyes, it could provide a critical prop for the macroeconomic programme that they intended to implement…The US sought increased mobility of capital not only to facilitate its plans for the domestic economy, but also to strengthen domestic financial interests. (Brenner 2002 at 127–128 and Eichengreen 1996 at 98–99)

The revitalization of the capitalist world-economy, financed by the Marshall Plan and administered by the U.S. dominated specialized agencies of the United Nations, most importantly the World Bank (the IBRD) and the International Monetary Fund (the IMF), culminated in the re-production of the earlier global economic crisis that caused the Great Depression: systemic over-accumulation of capital. Within the new Bretton Woods Agreement, however, this led to the phenomenon of what both Arrighi and Brenner describes as 'uneven development'; 'Confronted with heightened international competition (especially in trade-intensive sectors like manufacturing), higher-cost incumbent firms responded to falling returns by diverting a growing proportion of their incoming cash flows from investment in fixed capital and commodities to liquidity and accumulation through financial channels' (Arrighi 2007 at 141 and 142).[24] According to Arrighi, 'Uneven development, under US hegemony, was a process consciously and actively encouraged "from above" by a globalizing US warfare-welfare state' (Arrighi 2007 at 154). Hence, the 'particular form that uneven development assumed after the Second World War…was thoroughly embedded in, and shaped by, the forces of US world hegemony in the Cold War' (Arrighi 2007 at 151). From 1945 to 1965 the world-system was stabilized by 'a symbiosis, if a highly conflictual one, of leader and followers, of early and later developers, and of hegemon and hegemonized' (Brenner 2002 at 15). After the Second World War, uneven development

---

[23] For a full discussion of the nature and implications of parapolitics, see the Wilson (2009a).

[24] On the shift in the US economy from manufacturing to finance, see Brenner (2006, 47–50, 155, 227, 267–280, 290). For developmental strategy as a forum for inter-state rivalry, see Chang (2003).

was embedded from the beginning to end in Cold War anomalies, and was therefore thoroughly shaped by the successes and failures of the strategies and structures deployed by the hegemonic US warfare-welfare state. The intensification of inter-capitalist competition and the associated crisis of profitability were important as a sign that the long post-war boom [1945–1973] had reached its limits (Arrighi 2007 at 156).

Once this stage had been reached, there was no longer a meaningful boundary between the politics of national and international space, each having 'disappeared' into the other. 'From the very beginning…uneven economic development did entail the *relative* decline of the U.S. domestic economy. But it was also a precondition for the continued vitality of the dominant forces [that is, finance capitalism] within the US political economy' (Brenner 2002 at 14).[25] Crucially, this response to domestic decline consisted

> of a system-wide tendency, centered on the leading capitalist economy of the epoch, towards the 'financialization' of processes of capital accumulation. Integral to the transformation of inter-capitalist competition from a positive- into a negative-sum game, this tendency has also acted as a key mechanism of the restoration of prof-itability, at least temporarily, in the declining but still hegemonic centers of world capitalism (Arrighi 2007 at 118). [26]

The deeper structural problem, here, should be obvious; the alleged solution could only be medium term, as the hegemon had to perform the unsustainable dual role of global military protector and what Brenner refers to as the 'consumer of last resort'. (Brenner 2006 at 51, 161 and 189)[27] As Arrighi has pointed out, a 'situation of this kind can hardly be reproduced for any length of time without transforming into an outright tribute or "protection payment", the more than $2 billion (and counting) that the United States needs *daily* to balance its current accounts with the rest of the world' (Arrighi 2007 at 164). The true moment of crisis came in the early 1970s, with the chronic balance-of-payments dilemma engendered by the US led war in Indochina; the most important determinant of the ultimate collapse of Bretton Woods 'was neither inter-capitalist competition nor labour-capital relations but the direct and, especially, the indirect effects of the escalation of the Vietnam War on the US balance-of-payments' (Arrighi 2007 at 134). The crisis of 1971–1973, the terminus of the ascending phase of US hegemony, 'was simultaneously a crisis of profitability and a crisis of legitimacy' (Silver and Arrighi 2003 at 341); the intractable difficulties created by the war in Vietnam reached their climax in the same year as the crisis of profitability [a severe inflationary cycle], when the escalation of the war in Vietnam failed to break

---

[25] Peter Gowan has labored to demonstrate that the financialization of the world-economy constituted a strategic shift in U.S. hegemony away from 'direct power' and towards 'structural power' Gowan (1999, 23–38). 'The Nixon strategy in "liberating" international financial markets was based on the idea that doing so would *liberate the American state from succumbing to its economic weaknesses and would strengthen the political power of the American state.*' Idem, 23. Emphasis in the original.

[26] Uneven development occurs not only between economic sectors but between geographical zones. See Agnew (2005, 204–214), for an account of uneven development within the US, between the high-speed 'global cities' (New York, Boston, Miami, Chicago, Los Angeles, San Francisco) and the low-speed globally disconnected local and regional economies. 'What is clear is that U.S. cities are at the heart of the emerging U.S. economy. The leading industries in terms of contribution to U.S. GDP growth in the 1990 s have been those in information technology, processing, and telecommunications, on the one hand, and users [of] the products of these industries in finance, insurance, and real estate…on the other.' Idem, 208.

[27] See also Hudson (2003, 24, 377 and 386).

the back of Vietnamese resistance and provoked instead widespread opposition to the war in the United States itself. The collapse of the Bretton Woods regime of fixed exchange rates and the massive devaluation of the US dollar that ensued were as much the result of the escalating costs of that war—including the costs of programs aimed at stemming the tide of domestic opposition to the war—as they were the result of US responses to the crisis of profitability...Indeed, if anything, they worsened the decline by provoking a worldwide inflationary spiral that threatened to destroy the whole US credit structure and worldwide networks of capital accumulation on which US wealth and power had become more dependent than ever before. (Silver and Arrighi 2003 at 344)[28]

The termination of the (neo-) New Deal regime of Bretton Woods by the Nixon administration in 1973 signified the decisive de-stabilisation of the capitalist world-economy and the rise of what Harvey has referred to as the mutually assured destructiveness of 'the export of devaluation'; 'In the end [capitalism] has only one place to go. It has to cannibalize itself...The deepening and widening of [the global economic crises of capital over-accumulation]...transforms the cannibalistic tendencies of capitalism into so many modes of assured destruction, to be periodically unleashed as the absolute form of devaluation...' (Harvey 1999 at 438).

Thanks to the globalization of pure war and the suicidal state, devaluation may be exported not to one domain, but two: the foreign and the domestic. The export of devaluation into foreign space is well known and marks an almost atavistic return to neo-colonialism; 'At times of savage devaluation, interregional rivalries typically degenerate into struggles over who is to bear the devaluation...each [rivalry] entails the aggressive manipulation of some aspect of economic, financial or state power' (Harvey 1999 at 438). Naomi Klein's recent indispensable text offers the standard contemporary account of this process; the domestic implementation of neo-liberal 'reform' is known as 'shock doctrine' (Klein 2007), the expression in economic form of the military doctrine of 'shock and awe': either the accidental or deliberate infliction of trauma upon the state as a means of neutralizing political opposition to 'decentralized state agendas' (Ullman and Wade 1998 at 13). This introduction of a military technique into the space of political economy is, in turn, an outstanding example of Virilian pure war/speed-politics at work.

> By 'shock', we mean the ability to intimidate perhaps absolutely; to impose overwhelming fear, terror, vulnerability and the inevitability of destruction or defeat; and to create in the mind of the adversary impotence, panic, hopelessness, paralysis and the psychological incentives for capitulation. Generally, this would be achieved with great suddenness, rapidity and unexpectedness. (Ullman and Wade 1998 at 13)

---

[28] It was essential for the U.S. to repudiate the gold standard. 'The key to understanding today's dollar standard is to see that it has become a debt standard based on U.S. Treasury IOUs, not one of assets in the form of gold bullion' Hudson (2003, 35). The 'disappearance' of the 'real' world-economy of the gold standard into the 'simulated' economy of floating currencies was the unintended consequence, or 'accident', of U.S. hegemony. 'The Nixon administration was determined to break out of a set of institutionalized arrangements which limited U.S. dominance in international monetary policies in order to establish a new regime which would give it monocratic power over international monetary affairs. U.S. capital was indeed being challenged by its capitalist rivals in product markets at the time. The break-up of the Bretton Woods system was part of a strategy for restoring the dominance of U.S. capitals through turning the international monetary system into a dollar-standard regime' Gowan (1999, 19).

As Virilio would lead us to expect, the trauma of the impact of the neo-liberal agenda is strictly equivalent to the speed of its implementation.[29] Beginning in the late 1970s, the IMF oversaw the transference of the political control of the national economic policies of its member states from the federal ministries of finance to those of the central banks.[30] This raised traditional international economic competition to a new threshold, as globalized neo-liberalism and free trade worked to re-subordinate the developing economic peripheries to the developed core zone (Stiglitz 2002 at 13–16, 84, 92, 99 and 101).[31] The implementation of exo-colonization via economic liberalization reached its apogee in the East Asian financial crisis of the late 1990s, as Brenner makes clear.

> The IMF was primarily concerned, as it had been during the Latin American debt crisis, to see that US, European and Japanese banks would be repaid in full. Acting as an instrument of US foreign economic policy, it also sought to exploit this opening to compel the region's economies to liberalise their functioning and open themselves up to foreign penetrations. As a condition for the advance of bridge finance to these economies, it therefore called, in Hoover-like fashion, for the tightening of credit and the imposition of fiscal austerity, thereby radically exacerbating the domestic economic and debt crisis, and inviting depression. As part of the same package, which can only be called imperialist, it extracted the agreement from local authorities, most dramatically in Korea, to adopt wide-raging plans for the reorganisation of their economies along Anglo-Saxon lines with the goal of easing the entry of foreign capital (Brenner 2002 at 164).

What is not so clear, however, is the manner in which the export of cannibalistic devaluation has penetrated the domestic sphere. In perfect Virilian fashion, the operations of exo-colonization within international space and time are perfectly mirrored by the operations of endo-colonization within what was traditionally understood to constitute 'internal' political space and time. What links both exo- and endo-colonization is the strategic centrality of concentrated financial capitalism; that is, a network of economic

---

[29] As Klein ably shows, Chile under Pinochet is a classic example of this phenomenon: 'For the [neo-liberal] experiment to work, Pinochet had to strip [neo-Keynesian] distortions away—more cuts, more privatization, more speed' Klein (2007, 80).

[30] Throughout his text, Stiglitz naively laments the 'politicization' of IMF decision making. With greater acumen, Scheurerman expressly links the global rise of the central banks to the operation of speed-politics; 'How better to allow for financial regulation of our high-speed capitalism than by minimizing the direct interventionist instruments of slow moving legislatures while outfitting a group of financial experts with significant discretionary power to respond to fast-moving market shifts' Scheuerman (2004, 245 fn. 92). Scheuerman outlines the various recent innovations in international economic law underpinning the legal indeterminacy governing global economic regulation in idem, chapter five, 144–186. 'Although it remains true that every functioning capitalist economy requires some minimum of legal protections (private property, contracts, a system of binding dispute resolution) even that minimum is more pliable than generally acknowledged. By no means can we endorse the orthodox view that capitalism and a robust rule of law—based on a system of clear, general, stable, prospective, public norms—are likely to go hand in hand. On the contrary, economic globalization flourishes precisely where such legal forms are lacking. The overlap between economic globalization and social acceleration helps explain why. The temporal mismatch between economic activity and traditional forms of adjudication is particularly acute within global law because of the striking employment there of new possibilities for high-speed social action.' Idem, 181.

[31] Even the 'un-theoretical' Soros has acknowledged this point. For him, globalization 'has an asymmetric structure. It favors the United States and other developed countries at the center of the financial system and penalizes the less developed economies at the periphery. The disparity between the center and the periphery is not widely recognized, but it has played an important role in the development of the super-bubble' Soros (2008, 93). On the manifold linkages between global neo-liberalism and speed-politics, see idem, 96–102.

institutions and processes governed by both speed and simulation. As Brenner has argued, neo-liberalism was specifically designed

> to relieve the surfeit of capacity of production in manufacturing by provoking a purge of that great ledge of high-cost, low-profit, manufacturing firms that had been sustained by the Keynesian expansion of credit, while clearing a channel to the profitable expansion of the low-productivity service sector by further reducing employee compensation. It was aimed, finally, at bringing about a revitalisation of, and thereby shift into, domestic and international financial sectors—which had been hard hit during the 1970s by accelerating price increases and a plethora of loanable funds—by means of suppressing inflation as well as rapid moves toward deregulation, especially the elimination of capital controls (Brenner 2002 at 35).[32]

Intriguingly, Brenner has utilized Virilian terminology when de-noting the domestic importation of devaluation: 'speed up'. This term refers to the panoply of domestic neo-liberal 'reforms'—de-regulation, anti-unionism, cost reduction, the globalization of uneven development—that constitutes the direct extension of pure war into internal space; 'In fact, all of these interrelated measures of cost reduction, neo-liberalism, and globalisation[33]— unleashed with ever-increasing intensity from the shift of the 1970s by the advanced capitalist economies—constituted little more or less than the problem of reduced profitability' (Brenner 2006 at xxii). For Brenner, speed up signifies 'not so much increased efficiency—meaning more output from the same labour input—as more output from more labour input per hour' (Brenner 2006 at 334). With wages flat or actually falling from the 1970s onward, 'employers had every incentive to substitute labour for capital' (Brenner 2002 at 79). Whatever increase in profitability that

> has been achieved since the inflation of unsustainable cyclical upturns after 1973 has been made possible, probably to the greatest extent in US history, simply by means of an increase in exploitation—that is, the intensification of labour plus a shift in the distribution of income from labour to capital. Because inflated profits were extracted with relatively little recourse to increases in either labour or capital stocks, they were translated more or less directly into increases in the profit *rate* (Brenner 2006 at 335).

The global economic instability of the late twentieth century ultimately proves inextricable from 'a revival of more decentralized forms of business which rely far more on the social division of labour among production units than on the technical division of labour within units' (Arrighi 2007 at 169).

It is tempting to read these Virilian developments, expressed in more materialist terms by Arrighi and Brenner, as a useful supplement to Harvey's recent work on neo-liberalism and contemporary forms of class conflict (Harvey 2003, 2005). For Harvey, the shift from the 'slow' (or 'low velocity') sectors of manufacturing to the 'fast' (or 'high velocity') realms of international finance forms a continuation of class struggle by other means, an insight repeated in Virilio's more poetic account of a 'planet of slums' (Davis 2006); '*The*

---

[32] See also Brenner (2002, 40–43, 54, 57–58, 67, 81–89, 130, 132). For de-regulation as a form of inter-state competition, see Helleiner (1994, 167): 'The mobility of capital was behind the dynamic. When one state began to deregulate and liberalize its financial markets, other states were forced to follow its lead if they hoped to remain competitive in attracting footloose funds and financial business. The United States and Great Britain were the leaders of the competitive deregulation movement'.

[33] As with neo-liberalism frequently identified with 'Americanization'. 'Globalization is the outcome of the geographical projection of American marketplace society allied to technical advances in communication and transportation' Agnew (2005, 72).

*desert is spreading*, they say. Yet it is not the desert that is spreading over the planet, but the *urban wasteland*—that place where, without ever mixing, the multitude of ethnic microcosms survive—in the shanty towns, the half-way hostels, the sink estates...' (Virilio 2000 at 61)[34] The proliferation of this urban desert is the direct result of the globalization of the suicidal state which itself serves as the grounds for the further intensification of pure war directed towards the interior. The accelerated social decomposition resulting from the 'trauma' of pure war ultimately fractures the political consensus of the liberal state; the de-localized state is now 'founded on threat, the economic rival [and] the social adversary' (Virilio 1991b at 124).[35] In order to police the post-liberal political order, the virtual State increasingly directs its optical apparatus inwards, transposing the spatio-temporal domain of 'the enemy' from the exterior to the interior. (Virilio 2005c at 176)[36] Paradoxically, the political paranoia surrounding the domestic threat—well evidenced by the current 'War on Terror'—is a direct result of the panoptical transparency of trans-national space achieved through the global telecommunications network.[37]

In more narrowly economic—or materialist—terms, an even more intractable crisis stands revealed: speed up, which undercuts wages but inflates production, renders unsustainable any long-term re-stabilization of capitalism through the re-enforcement of declining consumption, which is itself the primary sign of the social anomie of labour. Brenner has made this point emphatically.

> Rather than setting the US and the world economy on a new course, the forces driving the New Economy actually exacerbated the fundamental problem making for long-term slowed growth–namely, persistent chronic over-capacity in manufacturing and related sectors making for secularly reduced profit rates for the economy as a whole. As a consequence, that ensured the still further extension of the long [post-1973] downturn, rendering unavoidable the equity price crash and sharp cyclical fall-off that brought a dramatic climax to the long expansion of the 1990s and opened the way to a new period of turbulence opening in the early years of the new millennium. (Brenner 2006 at 268)

Only one possible solution, or perhaps I should say 'strategy', remained: The structural transformation of the world economy, by means of simulation and speed, into a systemically criminal, or criminogenic, phenomenon.

---

[34] Mike Davis writes in a similar fashion; 'With a literal "great wall" of high-tech border enforcement blocking large-scale migration to the rich countries, only the slum remains as a fully franchised solution to the problem of warehousing this century's surplus humanity...The urban edge is a zone of exile, a new Babylon' Davis (2006, 200–201).

[35] See also 'The Consumption of Security', 119–129, in Virilio (1986). On the deleterious effects of speed-politics on the conventional operation of liberal democracy and the rule of law, see Scheuerman (2004).

[36] Davis is salient on this point. 'The demonizing rhetorics of the various international "wars" on terrorism, drugs, and crime are so much semantic apartheid: they construct epistemological walls around *gecekondus*, *favelas*, and *chawls* that disable any honest debate about the daily violence of economic exclusion. And, as in Victorian times, the categorical criminalization of the urban poor is a self-fulfilling prophecy, guaranteed to shape a future of endless war in the streets' Davis (2006, **202**).

[37] Compare Davis with Virilio on this point. 'In summary, the Pentagon's best minds have dared to venture where most United Nations, World Bank or Department of State types fear to go: down the road that logically follows from the abdication of urban reform...Indeed, in the absence of other paradigms, the Pentagon has evolved its own distinctive perspective on global urban poverty...Pentagon doctrine is being re-shaped to support a low-intensity world war of unlimited duration against criminalized segments of the urban poor. This is the true "clash of civilizations"' Davis (2006, 205 and 202–203).

## Cyber-Capitalism and Power Crime

> Markets don't reflect facts very well, partly because they create facts themselves.—
> George Soros
> Credit bubbles are hard to detect.—Ben Bernanke

It is a widely recognized fact that today's capital markets 'operate in cyberspace, using space-age technology and an unending proliferation of complex speculative instruments' (Longworth 1998 at 254). Also known as 'synthetic securities', these speculative instruments include all of the 'usual suspects' regularly identified with the structural sources of the global credit crisis: VARs (value-at-risk calculations), CDOs (collateralised debt obligation) CDS (credit default swaps), and SIVs (structured investment vehicles). What is less well understood is the degree to which these de-stabilizing innovations constitute an essential component of the dual movement(s) of exo- and endo-colonization. This is evident in one of the most disturbing aspects of cyber-capitalism: the legitimatizing of high speed financial speculation and the central role currently played by credit bubbles in wealth creation. Bubbles quite simply 'arise when banks treat the value of the real estate as if it were independent of the bank's willingness to lend against it' (Soros 2008 at 64–65). However, bubbles also double as an effective short term solution to the dilemma of capital over-accumulation and stagnating personal income. (Turner 2008 at 48)

> The downward pressure on prices of consumer goods that results from globalisation allowed central banks to keep interest rates low, driving debt levels up. The housing bubble in turn provided alternative jobs in the service sector…But they have in many cases been contingent on the credit bubble that the authorities had to create, to fill the void generated by the loss of manufacturing jobs (Turner 2008 at 69–70)[38].

Debt, in both its public (government) and private (corporate; household) forms, has been strategically deployed as a stimulus to artificially maintaining a rate of growth that is both unsustainable and, critically, 'un-realistic'.[39] 'Had it not been for the unprecedented expansion of both public and private debt in response to these recessions [1974–1975, 1979–1982, the early 1990s], the world economy could not easily have avoided a depression'. Thus, it was 'the unprecedented growth of debt of all types—government, corporate and consumer—which kept up employment and capacity utilisation and ultimately secured stability throughout most of the length of the [post-1973] downturn' (Brenner 2006 at 158).[40]

I would argue that these structural developments within cyber-capitalism can be usefully understood from a criminological perspective. By this, I mean that the contemporary world economy bears all of the necessary attributes of a criminogenic phenomenon, one in which criminal activities—or, at the very least, processes that are of marginal legality—are effectively 'folded' into accepted institutional praxis, effecting a virtual disappearance of

---

[38] For the 'housing bubble' as the continuation of the generic 'credit bubble', see Brenner (2006, 317, 318, 319, 332). 'Crudely put, rising equity prices were now enabling US economic growth to depend for its expression to an ever-greater extent on the growth of US private indebtedness' Brenner (2002, 176).

[39] Brenner (2002, 44–45, 152–153, 175–176, 199, 216, 266, 268–269, 288–289, 302, 304). 'Financialization encourages households to behave like businesses, businesses to behave like banks, and banks to behave like hedge funds' Blackburn (2008, 100).

[40] 'The Bush administration's vision of the "ownership society" somehow latched onto the codicils of Johnson's "Great Society" to encourage the poor to take on housing debt at the pinnacle of the property bubble. The quality of the arrangements…avoided the real problem, which is the true extent of property in the United States and the folly of imagining that it can be banished by waving the magic wand of debt creation Blackburn (2008, 73).

the 'criminal' into the 'lawful'. Here, I am expanding upon the notion of 'criminogenic asymmetries' as pioneered by Nikos Passas (Passas 2000). For Passas, criminogenic phenomena constitute

> structural disparities, mismatches and inequalities in the spheres of politics, culture, the economy and the law. Asymmetries are criminogenic in that (1) they generate or strengthen the demand for illegal goods and services; (2) they generate incentives for particular actors to participate in illegal transactions; (3) they reduce the ability of authorities to control illegal activities (Passas 2000 at 23).

There are two critical features to note in this definition. The first is the determining supply-and-demand logic at work that serves to underpin a mimetic relationship between licit and illicit market forces.

> Asymmetries generate the demand for goods that are illegal, unethical or embarrassing.[41] Illegal markets follow the rules of supply and demand, sometimes even more strictly than legitimate markets—because the latter often enjoy protective measures introduced by nation states or groups of states. Whenever there is a gap between local demand and supply, cross-border trade[42] is likely to develop. If the goods or services happen to be outlawed, then illegal enterprises will emerge to meet the demand. *In this respect, there is no difference between conventional and criminal enterprises* (Passas 2000 at 24).[43]

The final sentence is the crucial one. Criminogenic asymmetries subvert orthodox conceptions of legitimacy that demarcate the conventional boundaries between the 'legal' and the 'illegal'. The mimetic effect produced by the criminogenic is that legal and illegal actors begin to imitate, and even appropriate, the reasoning and behavior of the other (Passas and Nelken 1993). This leads to the second critical feature: the criminogenic does not merely denote the criminal but the far more subversive category of the supra- or extra-legal as well. The collapse of orthodox modes of juridical demarcation yields an epistemic crisis within political authority in which parallel market structures become effectively de-criminalized through the tactical alterations of public discourse; as Wark reminds us, the market 'doesn't bypass the state in the deregulated financial environment. On the contrary, it is all the more central to it. State institutions…have a powerful ability to administer the referents' (Wark 1994 at 185). Employing the same imaginary as both Wark and Held, Passas argues that 'when the business is illegal all that changes are some adjustments in *modus operandi*, technology, and the social networks that will be involved. In some cases, we have a mere re-description of practices to make them appear outside legal prohibitive provisions' (Passas 2000 at 24).[44] The realm of the criminogenic itself constitutes site of a

---

[41] Unfortunately, Passas does not elaborate on what falls into the last category.

[42] Although Passas means this to refer to trans-national geographical space, 'cross-border' may just as usefully employed to describe criminogenic migrations across domestic juridical or political spaces.

[43] Emphasis added.

[44] On this point, see also Vincenzo Ruggiero; 'today, economic enterprise is struggling to establish a new moral justification for its activity. For this reason, every economic act, even if it is illegitimate, may become normative, in that it can establish new regulations and values, and may promote new ethical codes and legitimacies' Ruggiero (2009, 122). For an outstanding example of the corporate legitimation of otherwise illicit economic practices—in this case, 'control fraud'—see Tillman (2009). See also Black (2005, 734–755). 'Frauds are a classic case of market failure due to asymmetric information…Accounting fraud is an optimal [criminogenic] strategy because it simultaneously produces record (albeit fictional) profits and prevents the recognition of real losses.' Idem, 739 and 736.

particular form of disappearance: the eradication of the border between Law and Crime.[45] This becomes even more apparent when we recall how the global credit crisis has revealed the effective disappearance of traditional demarcations between public and private spaces. 'Recent housing bubbles have not been the fault of central banks *per se*, but of governments allowing corporate power to exploit wage differentials in the pursuit of higher profit margins' (Turner 2008 at 6); as a result, 'the easy lending fostered by Western governments has fuelled mergers, takeovers and acquisitions by private equity funds that concentrates corporate power, underpinning the fundamental forces that create asset bubbles' (Turner 2008 at 12). Crucially, government created speculation operates in international as well as national space.

> The systematic tearing down of trade barriers in the absence of appropriate protection and rights for ordinary workers accelerated a two decade trend towards higher profit ratios in the West. That was unsustainable. Profit ratios can only continue to rise at the expense of a further decline in the share of national income taken as labour income, or wages. And such a divergence will increase the tendency and political pressure for consumer borrowing and house price inflation to fill the gap, between over-investment and inadequate demand. And this dichotomy will ultimately trigger a financial crisis that will lead to a sudden reversal in profit margins (Turner 2008 at 7–8).

Cyber-capitalism, along with all of its attendant risks of catastrophe, is not merely an economic system, but a method of political and social control grounded upon pure war.

> The accumulation of trade surpluses in emerging markets and huge foreign exchange reserves mirrored the explosion of consumer debt in the West. Governments in industrialised economies have appeased the process, because it fits neatly with their avowed strategy of promoting free trade, irrespective of the costs. And the asset bubbles that fill in the gap in demand allow them to deceive their citizens into believing that globalisation in its current form works (Turner 2008 at 11).[46]

---

[45] For an extended discussion of the radical iterability governing the discursive construction of both Law and Crime, see Wilson (2009a). It is important to keep in mind that the criminogenic is not identical with the 'criminal'. While crime may be defined as the violation of clearly established laws and norms—as reflected in the formal legalism preferred by orthodox criminology—the criminogenic can be usefully understood as encompassing practices that would ordinarily be denoted as criminal if not but for the operation of political or judicial processes that effectively de-criminalize the illicit behaviors. Criminognic phenomena, therefore, pose a direct challenge to the validity of mainstream criminology, which tends to reduce crime to conventional sociological categories of deviance and anti-social behavior. 'The tendency of orthodox criminology to focus on private crimes of greed, lust and rage—perhaps we should think of this as criminology's version of the "nuts, sluts and perverts" fetish that has impoverished the sociology of deviance—has rendered institutional crimes of power, that is, corporate, political and state crimes—relatively minor areas of study within criminology' Michalowski (2009, 312).

[46] Like Turner, Greider is adamant in framing the structural dynamics of globalization as the primary cause of the global credit crisis. 'Instability, in other words, flowed from the fracturing of power and responsibility that globalization has produced. The immediate force behind the more dramatic swings and currency exchange values was, after all, the monetary policy of the three major central banks [US, Japan Germany] setting interest rates and controlling virtual money supplies. But the currency traders played off those actions, kibitzing and speculating like theatre critics, occasionally vetoing the government's policy decisions by ganging up and attacking them. And each central bank was itself trapped between its own conflicting obligations—the domestic economy versus the global monetary system' Greider (1997, 251–252). Michel Albert is even more unsparing in his language; 'Divided and disunited the nation states and their puny borders can offer no real resistance to the globalized capitalist economy' Cited in Longworth (1998, 168). As Held expresses it with considerable understatement, 'In this case, the boundaries between domestic markets and global affairs may be blurred' Held et al. (1999, 15). What all three are describing could be expressed in Virilian terms as the loss, or disappearance, of the state as the referent, or the 'real', of international politics.

The ultimate Virilian irony at work here is that the suicidal state has quite literally 'disappeared' into its own logistics of perception. This is clear to even mainstream commentators like Soros; 'What is worse, the newly invented methods, and instruments were so sophisticated that the regulatory authorities lost the ability to calculate the risks involved. They came to depend on the risk control methods developed by the institutions themselves' (Soros 2008 at 116–117).[47] Most important here is the realization that credit bubbles are inseparable from speed.

> On the basis of increased borrowing and stock issuance…these same corporations…were enabled to accelerate investment *in advance of profits*, making for faster productivity growth [speed up] and even greater potential for returns. Higher 'expected profits' made for still more elevated equity prices, which enabled further stepped-up borrowing and stock issues, allowing still more rapid capital accumulation, making for further leaps forward in technology, enabling productivity growth to rise even higher, making possible even higher expected profits…issuing in what Fed chairman Alan Greenspan celebrated as a 'virtuous cycle' of economic expansion (Brenner 2006 at 268).

What both Soros and Brenner are describing, even without knowing it, is an epistemological crisis that is manifesting itself through material(ist) phenomena.

> The newly invented financial instruments and the newly introduced trading and financial techniques suffered from a fatal flaw. They were based on the assumption that financial markets tend towards equilibrium…This assumption left out of account the impact of the new instruments and new techniques which changed the functioning of financial markets out of all recognition (Soros 2008 at 115).

On an empirical level, we can trace the criminogenic transformation of cyber-capitalism through the proliferation of those illegal forms of economic institutions that emerged as key signs of the world financial economy in the 1980s (Dick 2009): off-shore tax havens, the rise of 'hot money' and money-laundering,[48] and the creation of the world-wide 'shadow banking' system (Blackburn 2008 at 68–84) that served as a vital but covert nexus between governments, national security agencies, and trans-national criminal cartels.[49]

---

[47] In Soros' opinion, the US housing bubble 'was supported by a preliminary misconception that the value of the collateral was not affected by the willingness to lend. That is the most common misconception that has fuelled bubbles in the past, particularly in the real estate area.' Idem, 83.

[48] Guilhem Fabre has implicitly identified international money-laundering as a phenomenon of speed-politics; 'political will and political means should take into account these realities and overtake this opaque system, where the methods of supervision and the rules of the game are at least a decade behind the rapidity of financial flows and the existing capacities for circumvention' Fabre (2009, 95). For a useful snap-shot of the trans-national money-laundering system during the heyday of the 'roaring nineties', see Woods (1998). Beginning in the early 1990s, it was apparent that the critical variable to transnational money-laundering was the rise of 'cyber-currency' or 'virtual money'; idem, 4, 13–14, 37, 177 and 181. See also Lilley (2003, chapter six, 115–132), passim.

[49] A critical milestone of the criminogenic evolution of the world economy was reached in 1972 with the establishment of the Bank of Credit and Commerce International, or BCCI. See Passas (1993, 1994, 1995, 1996). For an introductory treatment of the other two great criminogenic banks of the 1980s—Nugen Hand and Ambrosiano—see Lernoux (1984, chapters 4, 9 and 10). According to Passas, more attention 'has been paid to the use of BCCI for criminal purposes than to the demand for its illegal services, which reflects global structural problems' Passas (1995, 397). As we should expect, these 'global structural problems' are inseparable from speed; 'BCCI was promoting itself as the friendly "can-do" bank. It was extremely fast at providing letters of credit or loan, it was more personal than other major banks, and had "no questions asked" policies' Passas (1994, 72). The myriad linkages between the covert agencies of the State and cross-

On a more theoretically sophisticated level, criminogenic cyber-capitalism is wholly consistent with the operational requirements of what critical criminologists have de-noted as 'power crime', which I understand as the conjunction of criminogenic asymmetries with simulation.

For 'power crime', I use the definition provided by Passas (Passas 2007a): fraud and corruption by elites that possess substantial governmental power or economic power. Passas identifies two 'levels of dynamism' integral to power crime that are of particular interest to me. The first is spatial, 'that elites are able to *choose* to operate wherever the legal, political, economic and cultural environment is most criminogenic and the payoffs to abuse the greatest'. The second is causal, 'that elites are able to *change* the environment [and]... make it far more criminogenic' (Passas 2007a). If we read these definitions through Virilian 'lenses', we come to realize that the criminogenic variable that connects space with causality is speed-politics: the relationship between power and speed, therefore, is of considerable criminological importance. While Passas' account does not explicitly refer to speed, his understanding of power crime is highly conducive to a Virilian analysis, precisely because the essence of power crime is the control over definitions, perceptions, and appearances.[50] Although certainly not reducible to the visual, any critical under-standing of power crime would benefit tremendously from careful consideration of the optical dimensions of the phenomenon. 'Normal' crime, because it is a 'low-velocity' phenomenon, is highly susceptible to detection and enforcement: 'Normally, thieves face a fairly symmetrical environment: to steal more they have to take greater risks of detection, prosecution and sanction' (Passas 2007b). By contrast, power crime, precisely because it is a 'high-velocity' phenomenon operating on the level of perception, is able to effectively 'disappear' into a total criminogenic environment of its own making. Accordingly, 'elite criminals' are the very ones able to create an 'environment in which engaging in massive fraud and corruption *increases* one's political power and status and greatly reduces the risks of detection and prosecution. Elite criminals optimise by creating fraud networks that help them maximize this asymmetry of risk and reward' (Passas 2007b at 2).[51] Speed itself

---

Footnote 49 continued

border criminal organizations that first began to surface in public awareness following the Vietnam War evidences a parallel evolution of global political economy that is de-noted as *parapolitics*, 'a system or practice of politics in which accountability is consciously diminished' Scott (1972, 171). For a recent explication of the meaning of the parapolitical, see Cribb (2009).

[50] The account is provided by Ruggiero and Michael Welch is more illustrative of this. 'Perpetrators of *power crime* are offenders who possess an exorbitantly exceeding amount of material and symbolic resources when compared to those possessed by their victims...We can argue, with respect to *power crimes*, that criminal designations are controversial and highly problematic, due to the higher degree of freedom enjoyed by perpetrators. The capacity to control the effects of their actions allows those who have more freedom to conceal (or "negotiate") the criminal nature of their actions. If we translate the notion of freedom into that of resources, we can argue that those possessing a larger quantity and variety of them also have greater possibilities of attributing criminal definitions to others and repelling those that others attribute to them. They also have greater ability to control the effects of their criminal activity, and usually do not allow this to appear and be designated as such' Ruggiero and Welch (2009, 298). The author's account of the manipulation of 'symbolic resources' as a means of effecting the perceptual 'disappearance' of criminal substance is highly suggestive of a simulated event.

[51] The related phenomenon of 'control fraud' is also a direct product of the formation of systemic 'crim-inogenic institutional frameworks' throughout the 1990s. Neo-liberal policy changes 'were influenced by the argument that [high speed] New Economy industries operated under a different set of economic rules than [low speed] Old Economy industries and were largely self-regulating. Concurrent with these changes was a broader trend (particularly among New Economy industries) towards financialization—"a pattern of accumulation in which profits accrue primarily through financial channels rather than through trade and commodity production."' Tillman (2009, 370).

facilitates the transformation of the 'real' of a wholly 'virtual' form of reality that effectively supersedes the notions of legality and political accountability, an insight that has been expressed in somewhat theoretically naïve terms by Greider; 'The overall logic of [neo-liberalism] began to make more sense if one put aside the usual rationales for its policies and assumed, instead, that it was serving a deeper historical purpose: compelling people to accept capitalism's revolutionary transformation' (Greider 1997 at 314).[52] Power crime, a criminogenic phenomenon governed by both speed and simulation, constitutes an example of what Virilio would classify as an 'accident' of pure war and the logistics of perception. The 'accident' of power crime is the sign that cyber-capitalism has disappeared into a fast moving criminogenic 'post-reality'.

## The Criminogenic 'Accident'

[W]hen disillusion falls upon an over-optimistic and over-bought market, it should fall with sudden and even catastrophic force.—John Maynard Keynes
A surprising number of weaknesses were revealed in a remarkably short period of time.—George Soros
The rapidity of a phenomenon liquidates you.—Paul Virilio

The accident, a signature Virilian concept, is a '*diagnostic of technology*' (Der Derian and Virilio 1998 at 20). Constituting the 'revelation of the identity of the object' (Virilio and Lotringer 1997 at 39), the accident serves as an 'indirect kind of *oeuvre*, a consequence of substance...*An accident is in fact an assault on the propriety of substance*, an unveiling of its nakedness, of the poverty of *whatever*, *whoever* is confronted by *what happens* unexpectedly—to people as much as to their creations' (Virilio 2005a at 28). It is only through the failure of a new technology or system of social relations that the nature of the substance of the thing in question stands fully revealed. Virilio deploys the 'accident' as a Derridean pun, a textual displacement caused by a sudden realisation of the utterly fortuitous nature of all linguistic construction that blurs the operational 'distinction between [the] surface features of the discourse and its underlying logic' (Culler 1983 at 146). The subversive work of the 'pun' in this instance is accomplished through the deliberate conjunction of the double meaning of 'accident': as a derived, or contingent, ontological property and as the material result of industrial and technological praxis.

Virilio extends his techno-centric critique of pure war through drawing our attention to both the causal centrality and the constructive agency of speed: 'If to invent the substance is, indirectly, to invent the accident, then the more powerful and efficient the invention, the more dramatic the accident' (Virilio 2005c at 85). If pure war, then, is the true substance, the contingent, or accidental, properties of pure war will manifest themselves through the effects of trauma and decomposition induced by speed. The accident of speed is power

---

[52] Helleiner makes the fascinating point that the neutralization of political opposition to neo-liberalism very much depends upon the 'low visibility' of the criminogenic alterations of global finance; see idem (1994, 19–20 and 203–205). '"It is obvious that the pursuit of liberalisation of capital movements generates les conflict and less ardour than the maintenance of free trade. The reason is that trade restrictions have *quick and visible effects* on jobs and profits, whereas the impact of restrictions on capital flows is *invisible to the public* and quite often a matter of *great uncertainty* for the specialists."' Raymond Bertrand, cited in idem, 204–205. Emphasis added. There is nothing more ontologically lethal than a subversive metaphor.

crime; the contingent property that is hidden but that, when 'seen', or made transparent, reveals the essence of the substance. The accident, however, because it is catastrophic, signifies substance as *negativity*; here, the optical effect of power crime, an 'accidental' property of speed-politics. We should not be surprised, then, that the Virilian accident corresponds remarkably well with Held's definition of globalization that I used to begin this paper; 'The growing *extensity* [trans-border; interregional], *intensity* [volume] and *velocity* [speed] of global interactions may also be associated with a developing enmeshment of the local and global such that the *impact* of distant events is magnified while even the most local developments may come to have enormous global consequences' (Held et al. 1999 at 15). Not surprised, that is, because all of Virilio's seminal notions— pure war, speed-politics, the logistics of perception, disappearance, the accident—form part of a general account of globalization that Virilio describes utilizing the highly met- aphorical language and imaginary of catastrophism.

> After the globalization of telecommunications, one should expect a generalized kind of accident, a never-seen-before accident. It would be just as astonishing as global time is, this never-seen-before kind of time. A generalized accident would be something like what Epicurus called 'the accident of accidents'. The stock-market collapse is merely a slight prefiguration of it. Nobody has seen this generalized accident yet. But then watch out as you hear talk about the 'financial bubble' in the economy: a very significant metaphor is used here, and it conjures up visions of some kind of cloud, reminding us of other clouds just as frightening as those of Cherny- bol...When one raises the question about the risks of accidents on the information (super) highways, the point is not about the information in itself, the point is about the absolute velocity of electronic data. The problem here is interactivity. Computer science is not the problem, but computer communication, or rather the (not yet full known) potential of computer communication (Virilio 1995b).

The 'global credit crisis' is a criminogenic 'event'; power crime is 'the accident' of the substance of cyber-capitalism. The 'credit crunch' is nothing other than the 'irruption' of the lingering but denied presence of capital-as-the-social-as-referent: the 'crisis' is that the optical/epistemic machinery of cyber-capitalism is no longer able to objectively differentiate between the 'true' and the 'false'. What we face is the 'return of the repressed/Real' in the form of a systemic recessionary crisis

## Conclusion

> What is amazing is that the lesson has still not been learned.—George Soros
> Speed is violence.—Paul Virilio

We no longer value the truth for there is no profit in it.

The true world-historical failure of capitalism lies not within its inability to transcend its internal contradictions but in its inability to achieve a self-grounding in stable and unlimited growth. The cyber-capitalist world economy is inevitably, and necessarily, suicidal: it invariably strives to create the pre-conditions for its ultimate 'disappearance'; the orthodox cycle of boom/bust has been replaced by the traumatic repetition of bubble/ burst. We have abandoned the realm of Keynesian referents and are now governed by the fatal sovereignty of Bataille's archaic 'accursed share': the surplus product/value that must be periodically—and ritualistically—destroyed in order to preserve homeostasis (Bataille

1991).[53] Simulated cyber-capitalism was devised as the solution to the intractable problem of over-accumulation/declining profitability; yet, simulation creates the catastrophic preconditions for the 'accidental' disappearance of the world-economy. To the degree that cyber-capitalism is co-determinate with simulation, the world-economy has become 'suicidal'; that is, it has ontologically 'disappeared' through its inability to recognise itself, to maintain the dichotomy between true and false, public and private, Law and Crime—a criminogenic hyper-reality. The 'collapse' of the cyber-capitalist world economy into criminogenic hyper-reality is itself the signification of the permanent loss of the 'truth' of Crime.

## References

Agnew, J. (2005). *Hegemony: The new shape of global power*. Philadelphia: Temple University Press.

Akerlof, G. A. (1970). The market for 'lemons': Quality uncertainty and the market mechanism. *Quarterly Journal of Economics, 84*(3), 488–500.

Akerlof, G. A., et al. (1993). Looting: The economic underworld of bankruptcy for profit. *Brookings Papers on Economic Activity, 1993*(2), 1–73.

Alexander, J. B. (2003). *Winning the war: Advanced weapons, strategies and concepts for the post-9/11 world*. New York: St. Martin's Press.

Armitage, J. (Ed.). (2000). *Paul Virilio: From modernism to hypermodernism and beyond*. London: SAGE Publications.

Arrighi, G. (2007). *Adam smith in Beijing: Lineages of the twenty-first century*. London: Verso.

Bataille, G. (1991). *The accursed share: An essay on general economy* (Vol. 1). New York: Zone Books.

Baudrillard, J. (1983). *Simulations* (P. Foss, P. Patton, & P. Beitchman, Trans.). New York: Semiotext(e).

Baudrillard, J. (1993). *Symbolic exchange and death* (I. Hamilton Grant, Trans.). SAGE Publications: London.

Black, W. K. (2005). 'Control Frauds' as financial super-predators. *Journal of Socio-Economics, 34*, 734–755.

---

[53] I take with extreme seriousness Harvey's preliminary speculations in his *The New Imperialism* and *A Brief History of Neo-Liberalism*, that the orthodox and highly teleological Marxist account of the historical evolution of capitalism is fundamentally mistaken. The problem is the 'true' role played by the primitive stage of accumulation—a violent predatory capitalism that seeks out sustainable rates of profit through the direct expropriation of wealth through violence and extortion. In the seminal eighth chapter of volume one of *Capital*, Marx clearly situates primitive accumulation at the very origins of the capitalist world-economy in the 16th and 17th centuries, but then rapidly passes over this embryonic stage in favour of later and more sophisticated forms of surplus extraction. Along with Harvey and other 'open' neo-Marxists, I have come to doubt the viability of this highly teleological narrative. My own work on parapolitics has led me to conclude that primitive modes of accumulation have not been supplanted by 'modern' forms, but have co-evolved, penetrating allegedly non-extortionist forms. A more accurate model than the one offered by Marx in *Capital* is that supplied by Nietzsche in *The Genealogy of Morals*, which interprets the 'modern' not as the dialectical suspension of the primitive but as the anti-dialectical sublimation of the archaic, in which 'primitive' and 'modern' structures and practices irrationally co-exist. I would go beyond Harvey and argue that primitive accumulation not only co-exists with modern forms of production, it remains the primary means of wealth creation; it is through 'primitive' acts of violent appropriation that the fatal catastrophe of capital over-accumulation can be indefinitely postponed—but not, of course, dialectically suspended. On the centrality of systemic theft, or 'collective embezzlement' to the corporate culture of cyber-capitalism, see Akerlof et al. (1993). 'Much as violations of worker safety standards or environmental protection laws are to the industrial production process, collective embezzlement may be the signature crime of finance capitalism…Unrestrained by investments in infrastructure and with little of their own capital at stake, those who handle other people's money in the casino economy truly operate in a "criminogenic environment"' Calavita et al. (1997, 171–2). This accords well with Black's likening of control fraud to a form of 'looting' that is highly analogous to a primitive form of accumulation; Black (2005, 738). If I am right, then it becomes imperative to re-conceptualize the whole of global political economy in terms of the criminogenic, the primary analytical tool with which to express the 'dangerous supplement' of primitive accumulation.

Blackburn, R. (2008). The subprime crisis. *New Left Review, 50*, 63–106.

Block, F. L. (1977). *The origins of international economic disorder: A study of United States International Monetary Policy from World War II to the Present*. Berkeley: University of California Press.

Brenner, R. (2002). *The Boom and the Bubble: The US in the World Economy*. London: Verso.

Brenner, R. (2006). *The economics of global turbulence: The advanced capitalist economies from Long Boom to Long Downturn, 1945–2005*. London: Verso.

Calavita, K., Pontell, H. N., & Tillman, R. H. (1997). *Big money crime: Fraud and politics in the savings and loan crisis*. Berkeley: University of California Press.

Chang, H.-J. (2003). *Kicking away the ladder: Development strategy in historical perspective*. London: Anthem Press.

Cribb, R. (2009). Introduction: Parapolitics, shadow government and criminal sovereignty. In E. Wilson (Ed.), *Government of the shadows: Parapolitics and criminal sovereignty* (pp. 1–9). London: Pluto Press.

Cubitt, S. (2001). *Simulation and social theory*. London: SAGE Publications.

Culler, J. (1983). *On deconstruction: The theory and criticism of structuralism*. London: Routledge and Kegan Paul.

Davis, M. (2006). *Planet of slums*. London: Verso.

Der Derian, J. (2001). *Virtuous war: Mapping the military-industrial-media-entertainment network*. Boulder: Westview Press.

Der Derian, J., & Virilio, P. (1998). 'Is the author dead? An interview with Paul Virilio. In J. Der Derian (Ed.), *The Virilio reader* (pp. 16–21). Oxford: Blackwell.

Dick, H. (2009). The shadow economy: Markets, crime and the state. In E. Wilson (Ed.), *Government of the shadows: Parapolitics and criminal sovereignty* (pp. 97–110). London: Pluto Press.

Eichengreen, B. (1996). *Globalizing capital: A history of the international monetary system*. Princeton: Princeton University Press.

Fabre, G. (2009). Prospering from crime: Money laundering and financial crises. In E. Wilson (Ed.), *Government of the shadows: Parapolitics and criminal sovereignty* (pp. 90–96). London: Pluto Press.

Gane, M. (1993). Introduction. In Baudrillard 1993, (pp. vii–x).

Gane, M. (2000). Paul Virilio's bunker theorizing. In J. Armitage (Ed.), *Paul Virilio: From modernism to hypermodernism and beyond* (pp. 85–102). London: SAGE Publications.

Gowan, P. (1999). *The global gamble: Washington's Faustian bid for world dominance*. London: Verso.

Greider, W. (1997). *One world, ready or not: The manic logic of global capitalism*. New York: Simon and Schuster Paperbacks.

Harvey, D. (1999). *The limits to capital* (2nd ed.). London: Verso.

Harvey, D. (2003). *The new imperialism*. Oxford: Oxford University Press.

Harvey, D. (2005). *A brief history of neoliberalism*. Oxford: Oxford University Press.

Held, D., et al. (1999). *Global transformations: Politics, economics and culture*. Cambridge: Polity Press.

Helleiner, E. (1994). *States and the reemergence of global finance*. Ithaca: Cornell University Press.

Hudson, M. (2003). *Super imperialism: The origin and fundamentals of U.S. world dominance* (2nd ed.). London: Pluto Press.

Johnson, C. (1982). *MITI and the Japanese miracle: The growth of industrial policy, 1925–1975*. Stanford: Stanford University Press.

Klein, N. (2007). *The shock doctrine: The rise of disaster capitalism*. London: Penguin Books.

Lernoux, P. (1984). *In banks we trust*. Garden City: Anchor Press/Doubleday.

Lilley, P. (2003). *Dirty dealing: The untold truth about global money laundering, international crime and terrorism* (2nd ed.). London: Kogan Page.

Longworth, R. C. (1998). *Global squeeze: The coming crisis for first-world nations*. Chicago: Contemporary Books.

Michalowski, R. (2009). Power, crime and criminology in the new imperial age. *Crime, Law and Social Change, 51*(2009), 303–325.

Passas, N. (1993). Structural sources of international crime: Policy lessons from the BCCI Scandal. *Crime, Law and Social Change, 20*, 293–309.

Passas, N. (1994). I cheat, therefore i exist? The BCCI scandal IN CONTEXT. In W. Michael Hoffman, et al. (Eds.), *Emerging global business ethics* (pp. 69–78). Westport: Quorum.

Passas, N. (1995). The mirror of global evils: A review essay on the BCCI affair. *Justice Quarterly, 12*(2), 377–405.

Passas, N. (1996). The genesis of the BCCI scandal. *Journal of Law and Society, 23*(1), 57–77.

Passas, N. (2000). Globalization and international crime: Effects of criminogenic asymmetries. In P. Williams & D. Vlassis (Eds.), *Combating transnational crime: Concepts, activities and responses* (pp. 22–56). New York: Routledge.

Passas, N. (2007a). *Corruption in the procurement process and outsourcing government functions: Issues, cases, case studies, implications.* Report Prepared for the Institute of Fraud Prevention, Report to Institute for Northeastern University, Boston February 2007.

Passas, N. (2007b). *Corruption in the procurement process/outsourcing government functions.* Report to the Institute for Fraud Prevention. Shortened version prepared by W. Black. Northeastern University, Boston February 2007.

Passas, N., & Nelken, D. (1993). The thin line between legitimate and criminal enterprises: Subsidiary fraud in the European Community. *Crime, Law and Social Change, 19,* 223–243.

Ruggiero, V. (2009). Transnational crime in global illicit economies. In E. Wilson (Ed.), *Government of the shadows: Parapolitics and criminal sovereignty* (pp. 117–129). London: Pluto Press.

Ruggiero, V., & Welch, M. (2009). Power crime. *Crime, Law and Social Change, 51,* 297–301.

Sassen, S. (2006). *Territory, authority, rights: From medieval to global assemblages.* Princeton: Princeton University Press.

Scheuerman, W. E. (2004). *Liberal democracy and the social acceleration of time.* Baltimore: The Johns Hopkins University Press.

Scott, P. D. (1972). *The war conspiracy: The secret road to the second Indochina* War. Indianapolis: Bobbs-Merrill.

Silver, B. J., & Arrighi, G. (2003). Polyani's 'Double Movement': The *Belle Epoques* of British and U.S. Hegemony compared. *Politics and Society, 3*(12), 325–355.

Soros, G. (2008). *The new paradigm for financial markets: The credit crisis of 2008 and what it means.* New York: Public Affairs.

Stiglitz, J. E. (2002). *Globalization and its discontents.* New York: W.W. Norton and Company.

Tillman, R. (2009). Reputations and corporate malfeasance: Collusive networks in financial statement fraud. *Crime, Law and Social Change, 51,* 365–382.

Turner, G. (2008). *The credit crunch: Housing bubbles, globalisation and worldwide economic crisis.* London: Pluto Press.

Ullman, H. K., & Wade, J. P., Jr. (1998). *Rapid dominance—A force for all seasons. Technologies and systems for achieving shock and awe: A real revolution in military affairs.* London: Royal United Services Institute for Defense Studies.

Virilio, P. (1986). *Speed and politics* (M. Polizotti, Trans.). New York: Semiotext(e).

Virilio, P. (1989). *War and cinema: The Logistics of Perception.* Trans. Patrick Camiller. London: Verso.

Virilio, P. (1991a). *The aesthetics of disappearance* (P. Beitchman, Trans.). New York: Semiotext(e).

Virilio, P. (1991b). *Lost dimension* (D. Moshenberg, Trans.). New York: Semiotext(e).

Virilio, P. (1994). *The vision machine* (J. Rose, Trans.). Indianapolis: Indiana University Press.

Virilio, P. (1995a). The silence of the lambs: Paul Virilio in conversation: interview with Carlos Oliveria. *CTHEORY.*

Virilio, P. (1995b). Speed and information: Cyberspace alarm! *CTHEORY.*

Virilio, P. (1999). *Polar inertia.* London: SAGE Publications.

Virilio, P. (2000). *Strategy of deception Tran. Chris Turner.* London: Verso.

Virilio, P. (2005a). *City of panic* (J. Rose, Trans.). Oxford: Berg.

Virilio, P. (2005b). *Desert screen: War at the speed of light* (M. Degener, Trans.). New York: Continuum.

Virilio, P. (2005c). *Negative horizon: An essay in dromoscopy* (M. Degener, Trans.). New York: Continuum.

Virilio, P., & Lotringer, S. (1997). *Pure war* (M. Polizotti, Trans.). New York: Semiotext(e).

Wark, M. (1994). *Virtual geography: Living with global media events.* Bloomington: Indiana University Press.

Wilson, E. (2009a). Deconstructing the shadows. In E. Wilson (Ed.), *Government of the shadows: Parapolitics and criminal sovereignty* (pp. 1–55). London: Pluto Press.

Wilson, E. (2009b). Speed/pure war/power crime: Paul Virilio on the criminogenic accident and the virtual disappearance of the suicidal state. *Crime, Law and Social Change, 51*(3–4), 413–434.

Woods, B. F. (1998). *The art and science of money laundering: Inside the commerce of the international narcotics traffickers.* Boulder: Paladin Press.

# [5]

# Counterfeiting as corporate externality: intellectual property crime and global insecurity

Simon Mackenzie

**Abstract** Corporate negative externalities occur when corporations place some of the costs of their profit-seeking activity onto society. This paper suggests that the current global problem of intellectual property crime is such an externality, and that it has not been recognised as such because corporations present product counterfeiting and piracy as crimes which reduce their revenue, rather than as predictable side effects of corporate production and merchandising, including branding activity, which have considerable socially deleterious consequences. It is argued that corporate actors are responsible for the socially harmful effects of the global counterfeiting problem in the following respects. Branding, advertising, and other corporate activities drive the market for goods which have a fashion value over and above their use value. While corporations 'create' this desire, they cannot prevent it being applied to the desire for fake or replica goods. Outsourcing of corporate production activities to developing countries to take advantage of cheap manufacturing and labour costs presents considerable opportunities to producers in those countries to copy and distribute the goods in an unauthorised way. Serious measures are not taken against product counterfeiters by rights-holding corporations, since market expediency dictates that the costs of counterfeiting are not so adverse to corporations to incentivise them to change their business methods. Counterfeit and pirated goods cause a range of social harms above and beyond the spuriously-costed financial damage corporate rights-holders suggest they suffer - these include the health and safety issues created by some fake goods, and the creation and maintenance of highly profitable organised crime activity in international markets for fake goods.

## Introduction

Critical perspectives in criminology, sociology and law have in recent years borrowed the concept of corporate 'negative externalities' from the discipline of

This paper arose out of research undertaken for an overview of global trends in faking published as the chapter 'Fakes', in Brookman, Maguire, Pierpoint and Bennett (eds), *Handbook on Crime* (Willan, 2010). There is some overlap between the two texts. The core argument of this paper – of IPC as externality - appears here for the first time.

S. Mackenzie (✉)
Scottish Centre for Crime and Justice Research, University of Glasgow, Glasgow, Scotland, UK
e-mail: simon.mackenzie@glasgow.ac.uk

economics, and brought it into popular discourse as a key way to think about questions such as responsibility, accountability, culpability and ethics in relation to some of the adverse consequences of corporate activity. Mass-market texts by authors such as Noam Chomsky, Joel Bakan, Naomi Klein, and many others, have used the idea [1–4]. Negative externalities occur when corporations place some of the costs of their profit-seeking activity onto society. The standard example of this type of corporate externality involves pollution which degrades the environment, adversely affecting public health and perhaps requiring clean-up at taxpayer expense.

The concept of a corporate externality has been relatively narrowly conceived, however, and it has clearly been in the interests of corporations to try to mask the adverse social effects of certain corporate capitalist activity. Perhaps the most effective veil for negative externalities occurs when the corporation itself is a victim—in other words when the circumstances the corporation has put in train return to adversely affect the corporate interest as well as the public interest. In this paper I suggest that the current global problem of 'Intellectual Property Crime' is such an externality, and that it has not been recognised as such because corporations present product counterfeiting and piracy as crimes which reduce their revenue, rather than as predictable side effects of corporate production and merchandising, including branding activity, which have considerable socially deleterious consequences.

I suggest that corporate actors are responsible for the socially harmful effects of the global counterfeiting problem in the following respects:

- Branding, advertising, and other corporate activities drive the market for goods which have a fashion value over and above their use value;
- While corporations 'create' this desire, they cannot prevent it being applied to the desire for fake or replica fashion goods;
- Outsourcing of corporate production activities to developing countries to take advantage of cheap manufacturing and labour costs presents considerable opportunities to producers in those countries to copy and distribute the goods in an unauthorised way;
- Serious measures are not taken against product counterfeiters by rights-holding corporations, since market expediency dictates that the costs of counterfeiting are often not so adverse to corporations to incentivise them to change their business methods;
- Counterfeit and pirated goods cause a range of social harms above and beyond the spuriously-costed financial damage corporate rights-holders suggest they suffer—these include the health and safety issues created by some fake goods, and the creation and maintenance of highly profitable organised crime activity in international markets for fake goods.

There are some immediately obvious responses to such a line. First, one might suggest that it is 'blaming the victim'—something which criminology has tended to argue vehemently against in respect of other less powerful victims. Second, one might suggest that corporate actors should not be criticised for a crime problem which is most properly seen as the enterprise of criminals over whom they have no control. The answer to both of these questions lies, I suggest, in the idea of predictable consequences. In the current criminological movement away from state definitions of 'crime' and towards efforts to achieve a broader analytical purchase on 'social harm' [5, 6], the question looms large of moral liability for the predictable consequences of action. So, for example, Green and Ward have produced a compendium of 'State Crimes' which includes allegations such as against the Turkish government who are thought liable for predictable earthqudake deaths consequent upon their failure to enforce suitably stringent building regulations in an earthquake-prone area [7]. We can see, then, that powerful 'victims' can quite often be implicated in the causes of their own misfortune, and more relevant here, in the misfortune of others. As with these other analyses of the power-harm nexus, it can reasonably be argued that the current explosion of rhetoric and activity around global markets in counterfeit and pirated goods would be better oriented if it began from a platform of less ideologically-circumscribed 'crime prevention', and began to seriously acknowledge the role of corporate global business activity in creating and driving the crime problem in question.

In what follows, I will attempt to examine the theme of corporate responsibility in creating and sustaining the context of motive and opportunity which drives the counterfeit problem, and of the continuing corporate reluctance to try, in as thorough as way as possible, to mitigate the effects of that context. I will structure the argument according to the components of the argument laid out above: that corporate branding activity is instrumental in creating a market for counterfeit and pirated goods; that outsourcing of production to countries with weak legal systems and low levels of situational control on the production of fakes promotes the faking problem; that corporations do not put as much effort into anti-counterfeiting measures as they might, because it is not worth it to them, since fakes do not present a serious cost to their business models and they are therefore more concerned with mounting performative responses to suggest that they are taking the problem seriously; that the market supports the definition of the faking problem as a 'crime issue' rather than a 'business issue' as this diverts the cost of dealing with the problem onto the state and its policing functions rather than leaving the matter to be addressed at the cost of businesses themselves; and that predominantly the costs of the faking problem are borne by other actors besides the brand-holders, in particular the social costs which are imposed on the public by harmful fake products, especially in the developing world, and the organised crime activities that the attractive supply and demand dynamics of the fake trade support.

## White-collar crime and corporate externalities

In the introduction to their edited book *It's Legal but it Ain't Right*, Passas and Goodwin observe that 'many industries generate crime externalities without necessarily committing crimes themselves' [8]. Among the activities, and associated adverse crime events, which they include by way of example are 'a variety of companies exploiting child labour and turning a blind eye to violations of human rights', and 'the illegal dumping of toxic wastes generated by chemical firms'. In respect of the latter, Szasz produced a case study which allows us to see in action the process of the social externalising of the unhappy consequences of the private drive for profit [9]. Szasz built on the distinction made by Needleman and Needleman between market sectors that are 'crime-facilitative' and those that are 'crime-coercive' [10]. In crime-facilitative industries, 'the criminal activity is not forced' rather it is 'unavoidable because the conditions that make it possible are necessary to the overall functioning of that industry and could not be altered without fundamentally affecting how business is conducted in that industry'. In Szasz's study, the regulation of the disposal of hazardous waste was seen to create quite foreseeable opportunities for organised crime groups to infiltrate the process as licensed but unsupervised contractors, disposing of the waste in unhealthy ways while the businesses that generated the waste and commissioned its disposal turned a blind eye.

The 'hyper-realisation' of the concept of intellectual property by way of multi-national corporatisation, branding and merchandising [3], and the globalisation of production and supply, can also be studied as a crime-facilitative business practice. As we shall see, the range of crimes and harms it facilitates is diverse. In addition to being noted by criminological writers in the critical vein, such crime-facilitative business practices have also led in the more applied crime prevention literature to an analysis of 'crime as pollution' [11, 12], in which crime is seen as an externality of a very wide range of market-based activity:

> Many agents in society (such as manufacturers and businesses) have little or no economic incentive to act in ways that reduce crime risks for others. They may, rather, save on production costs or business costs in ways that, whether inadvertently or not, serve to effectively increase the risk of crime to others [12: 152].

Among the types of 'polluters' that Farrell and Roman identify are manufacturers of goods at particular risk of theft, such as cars and mobile phones, who save on costs by excluding anti-theft devices; and retailers who fail to follow safe practices on alcohol sales, benefiting from increased sales while experiencing little of the overall cost of crime, disorder and ill-health these practices allow to develop. In this way, manufacturers, premises managers and persons 'produce targets and situations that provide criminal opportunities' but 'do not bear the crime costs to society that they produce' [11: 53]. Other examples of crime considered as a negative externality of conventional social organisation are available across a wide range of academic literature spanning disciplines, such as where increased tourism causes crime or attracts criminals [13], or the legalisation of gambling in casinos leads to thefts, burglaries, robberies, drug use, drunk driving, domestic violence, and white-collar crimes among addicted gamblers who steal from their employers, families and friends [14, 15].

## Branding and IPC

The development of the idea of Intellectual Property Crime (IPC) has cemented the use of the language of counterfeiting beyond its more traditional use in law, where it referred to the unlawful copying of banknotes. IPC is a generic term used to describe various individual infringements contained in IP-related legislation. In the language of IPC, 'counterfeiting' is the unauthorised reproduction of branded goods, involving trademark infringement, while 'piracy' is the unauthorised copying of other copyright-protected works such as music and video. We will use the term 'counterfeiting' here as a shorthand reference to all types of IPC, as the technical differences between various modes of IP infringement are not key to the argument presented.

Although faking has many victims, and effects many varieties of harm, in some cases the most obvious supposed 'victims'—the buyers—do not see themselves as victims at all. Many counterfeit goods are bought quite willingly, by buyers who know they are fake. Sugden's ethnographic study of the underground economy surrounding Manchester United's brand provides good examples of this. While fake replica shirts sold to fans cause economic loss to the club, the counterfeit salesmen are viewed as 'Robin Hoods' by 'the impoverished mothers of fanatical kids from Manchester's run-down estates' who see the club that sells exorbitantly-priced originals as 'robbing bastards' [16: 251].

In such scenarios we can see crime as a form of problem solving in the Mertonian anomie vein—and the problem to be solved is, as ever, the strain created, maintained and manipulated by vested capitalist interests. IPC is an entirely predictable consequence of the market routines of branded fashion producers, with high mark-ups, mass advertising targeted to promote brand allegiance, and global production which as we shall see attenuates control and oversight from the centre. These practices create both motive and opportunity for IPC, the co-presence of which is to some analysts the determinant of criminal activity [17]. The argument has been forcefully made, and for some time now, that advertising not only increases consumer desire for certain goods but does so by creating desires in the consumer which are often only loosely relevant to the article advertised, but which increase desire for the object by tying its social meaning to other images such as 'power, wealth, status, sex, and so on' [18]. Galbraith observed the insatiable nature of such manufactured desires [19, 20], and the contemporary concept of 'consumerism' includes an understanding of the tension between the desire for new possessions and their inevitable failure to satisfy on more than a short-term basis given their increasingly rapid replacement with new upgraded models, and the cycles of fashion. Perhaps the most famous contemporary journalist writing about corporations and consumerism has built on these observations to mount a critique of the power of brands themselves to take on a desirable quality, for the most part independent of the goods to which they are attached [3]. Linking brands to particular desirable lifestyle and other images has been a very deliberate strategy of our contemporary multi-national corporations, precisely calculated to offer customers an opportunity to feel that their consumptive purchases have an effect on, or reflect, their idealised sense of identity. In creating brands with such power and attempting to capitalise on them by way of charging premium prices for associated products, however, IP rights-holding corporations have laid a furtile turf for a parallel market in counterfeits.

The pursuit of profit makes the faking of some items more attractive than others. Product counterfeiting is therefore structured such that the most prolific instances of faking are to be found either in markets for items which can be easily replicated in bulk at very low costs (for example CDs and DVDs burned on easily-available electronic systems) or where items are more costly or difficult to fake, in markets where these items sell for high prices (for example, aviation parts).

Where an item is known to be fake, a consumer will pay less for it than they would for the original. Thus there arises a lure for fakers to insert their product into licit markets, to be sold as apparent originals and therefore at the highest price possible. This again invites a cost-benefit and opportunity analysis. Clearly there subsist markets in fakes where no effort is made to dupe the consumer—fake Rolexes sold in street markets in the developing world would be an example—but there is also evidence that many designer clothing and luxury item fakes are being made to increasingly high standards to aid their passing off as genuine and maximise sale price.

As well as price-maximisation, some markets display other structural pressures towards passing fakes off as genuine. In the pharmaceuticals market, end consumers are hard to reach other than through the licit market, production is tightly regulated, and production can be automated to the point that once the initial costs of setting up a factory have been met, counterfeit drugs can be produced in bulk. Fakers, as well as legitimate businesses, are attracted by the economies of scale. Thus we have seen the development of highly expertly faked packaging, security labels, holograms and other brand paraphernalia which allow fake drugs to be inserted into licit chains of supply. There have in the last few years been an increasing number of instances of such fakes being discovered having been prescribed over the counter in Western countries, and these brand-infringing and sometimes highly dangerous products confirm that fakes in this market, as in others, are often all but indistinguishable from the real thing. The profit motive here has a particularly pernicious effect: those medicines which cost the most tend to be those designed to treat very serious illness. In attracting counterfeiters with the promise of high profit margin these drugs when faked and supplied without active ingredients, or with positively harmful ingredients, can be lethal.

Counterfeiters are able to 'compete' with legitimate business in heavily regulated markets since they are not constrained with the costs of having to meet the high safety standards imposed on legitimate businesses producing items for these markets. The costs involved in meeting these safety standards are passed on to consumers by way of highly priced end products, making attractive opportunities for counterfeiters who can produce at low cost and sell at high. In some markets, like that in replacement motor vehicle parts, legitimate businesses have something of a monopoly over the production of genuine spares for their vehicles, and in addition to binding the costs of meeting safety standards into these parts, choose to exploit their monopoly by keeping prices high. These choices increase the attraction of the market for counterfeiters and enable them to easily undercut the legitimate market while still turning a good profit. Counterfeiters in spare parts markets tend to focus on the high-volume sale parts; i.e. those that are most often required by consumers [21: 10].

## Outsourcing

As industrialised nations have increasingly become consumers rather than producers of goods, the locations of the production of goods destined for Western markets has shifted to 'developing' economies such as China and India, which offer labour and infrastructure at a low cost. Luxury goods, which were once produced by boutique, often family-owned, small businesses, are now mostly produced by multi-national corporations which bought out the small designer workshops, 'rationalised' their business methods, and shifted production to the Far East to expand production and take advantage of the lower cost of labour [22]. In respect of many businesses the process of outsourcing has been part of a corporate globalisation strategy that has fundamentally transformed the old model of firms which originated and produced their goods in the West. As well as becoming more 'global' and ethereal, these corporations are increasingly transforming themselves into middle-men rather than producers of commodities, selling on to consumers at home goods produced abroad at low cost, sometimes at very high mark-up. In some cases the big corporations own the factories where production occurs in the poor countries, while in others they buy from an independent supplier. These independent suppliers will in many cases produce goods only for one major corporate customer, blurring the line between corporate ownership and corporate supply.

This process of outsourcing of legitimate production, and the associated flow of objects from developing countries to Western consumer markets, has been mirrored by a similar flow of brand imitations and other fake goods which are produced in poor countries in order to feed demand in rich ones [23]. This approximates the 'industrialisation of faking', and in this process of illicit production we see China playing a major role. In 2006, 79% of the IP infringing goods which were seized at EU borders originated in China [24]. As well as China, we can identify other key locations for the production of particular types of fakes: for example India is significantly implicated in the production of fake pharmaceuticals. The industrialisation of faking can be explained with reference to the legitimate market forces and production routines it mirrors. Low-paid factory owners and workers in countries which attracted outsourcing were entrusted with product designs by the large corporations who wanted their goods made cheaply, and these designs have been used as the basis for the establishment of a massive industry in fakes. This industry ranges from very poor quality imitations, which can easily be told apart from the originals, to 'fakes' which are made on the same production line as the originals, during hours of unofficial 'overtime'. These latter are therefore only 'fake' in the sense of 'unauthorised', being on all other measures identical to the originals. Somewhat ironically, the lower quality of materials now used in 'luxury' goods make them considerably easier to fake. Increasingly, aside from the brand infringement, the actual difference between some real designer goods and imitations is becoming difficult to discern, even in the case of fakes not made on the original production line.

This pattern of eastern/southern production linking with western/northern consumption is complemented by a significant uptake of the purchase of fakes in their countries of production and other developing countries. China consumes a lot of the fakes that it makes; indeed its population is mostly too poor to buy the original items. In 2001, for example, China recorded 192,000 deaths due to counterfeit medicines, and closed down 1,300 factories producing these fakes [25: 71]. While fake lifestyle drugs such as Viagra and steroids are pumped into western consumer markets where these drugs are bought in large enough quantities to make the sale of counterfeits worthwhile (HMRC reported seizures of 735,000 pharmaceuticals in

2006), developing nations have been flooded with replicated drugs for the treatment of more serious conditions such as malaria and HIV. As mentioned above, there have been instances of fake medicinal drugs for illness being inserted into European and US markets, but to nowhere near the extent to which they have appeared in developing countries. Developing countries are characterised by high demand for these medicines combined with difficulty in paying the high prices often demanded by the pharmaceutical companies, creating opportunities to be exploited by producers of counterfeit drugs who can undercut the conventional market.

We can therefore see that there are many structural properties of contemporary market forces which create and shape the problem of the harms caused by faking on a national and international level, and that among them the outsourcing of production to economies that offer cheap production costs combined with low regulatory or practical oversight figures as one driver of the issue, with harmful effects that track the global demand for IP-protected goods.

### Anti-counterfeiting and the externalisation of the costs of control

The corporate response to IPC has been somewhat underwhelming, and this can be explained with reference to the opportunity and motivation structure of the market for the production and sale of IP-protected goods. With respect to the outline presented above of outsourcing and the 'industrialisation' of faking, although the profits of IP rights-holding corporations are clearly diluted by these practices, and their brand reputations may suffer injury,[1] they are so heavily dependent on legitimate foreign-outsourced production in supporting the profitability of their businesses that they, and indeed the host of international regulatory bodies charged with dealing with the faking problem, have been reluctant to make accusations or take decisive action that might embarrass the governments of supply countries. The stream of illicit goods has been seen as an unfortunate but acceptable by-product of profitable outsourced production. While it may be 'acceptable' in terms of the profit margins of corporations, it is clearly quite unacceptable when the fakes increase risks to the health and safety of consumers.

The overall record of detecting, regulating and preventing fakes has also been unimpressive. There are many reasons for this. As we have noted, there exists a tension in the social construction of the issue of IPC, whereby law enforcement agencies have tended to see industry as responsible for addressing its own IPC problems so far as possible, seeing IPC as a 'business issue' rather than a 'crime issue', while corporations keen to externalise the costs of policing have increasingly subscribed to the contrary view. Business has responded in a variety of ways to the perception of IPC as only a matter of trade-related concern. Most major corporations have taken some self-help measures, including employing anti-counterfeiting investigators and dedicated legal teams, and attempting to crime-proof their products through a range of target hardening measures. There are too many such measures to

---

[1] Note 'may': many commentators suggest that fakes do not generally harm the image of the brand but, so long as they are not dangerous, serve to promulgate the brand image and create more desire for the original product through making it more conspicuous.

list here: they include such things as identification codes, holographic labels, and encryption technologies [26]. As with much situational crime prevention in practice, these measures approximate a 'sticking-plaster' approach to the counterfeiting problem—the core global economic drivers of transnational markets in fakes tend to receive little attention. The common theme of these measures is that they aim to make faking harder. Target hardening measures such as those mentioned increase the effort for fakers, since they must either break the codes in the original items before piracy can ensue, or if they are counterfeiters the intricate labels and marks must be copied as well as the product itself. The continuing rise in the problem of global IPC demonstrates that these measures cannot solve the problem of this type of crime; at least while other components of situational crime prevention theory [27] remain effectively ignored, for the risks to IPC offenders remain low compared to other criminal opportunities, and the rewards are high. Some fakers have taken up the challenge of duplicating the safety features of various consumer products, increasing the sophistication of their fakes in response to upgraded security features in the originals. Studies of offender motivation in student samples of software pirates have also revealed that some people positively relish the challenge of breaking the codes that encrypt protected material [28].

At the same time as attempting to push the major costs of policing IPC onto state law enforcement agencies, corporate brand-owners have done little to mitigate those aspects of their business routines which cause severe problems for the effective policing of the issue. There is a variety of obstacles which stand in the way of the effective regulation of counterfeit and pirated goods. Rights-holders are sometimes unable to identify fakes, resulting in abandoned prosecutions. There are several reasons for this [29]. First, as noted, some 'fakes' are actually unauthorised factory over-runs: in other words they are identical to the 'authentic' goods other than that they were not made with the consent of the rights-holder. Other than where goods are stamped with serial numbers or other systems of identification, these unauthorised products will be very hard to tell apart from the originals given that they are made from the same materials, in the same way, in the same factories. Second, supply chains have become attenuated through processes of outsourcing and subcontracting to the point that a rights-holder may not have direct knowledge of the factories involved in producing their goods. The range of sub-contractors in an outsourced production chain means there will be variations in the end products depending on where they were made, and this again makes it difficult for a rights-holder to say that a given product is fake as opposed to an authorised product suffering incidental variation from the core design. Third, parallel trading results sometimes in goods with different specifications being designed for markets in different countries. This means that where, for example, a UK subsidiary of a multinational company is approached by Trading Standards to pass judgement on whether a seized product is counterfeit, they may not have the information to decide whether it is a fake or a legitimate design from a different market. Counterfeiters can abuse this uncertainty by claiming their fakes to be parallel imports, setting off time-consuming and costly investigations to determine whether this is the case. As Vagg and Harris note [29], where seized goods do turn out to be legitimate parallel imports, Trading Standards can be sued for wrongful seizure, and consequent loss of earnings. Where Trading Standards bear the risk of these legal recriminations rather than the rights-holder who mistakenly claimed the goods to be fake, they are best advised to err on the side of caution when there is doubt over the legitimacy of goods. This makes zero-tolerance approaches to IPC difficult to enforce in practice.

Public education strategies are also in play as forms of intervention in the market in counterfeits, in keeping with the underlying philosophy of the Market Reduction Approach [30]. This is the idea that by reducing the uptake of illicit purchase opportunities, a reduction in economic incentives will occur for those trafficking counterfeits which will ultimately make its way back up the chain of supply to discourage the manufacturers of counterfeits at source. Public education continues to be thought to play a leading role in discouraging consumers from purchasing illicit 'bargains'. It is telling that these approaches are so prevalent—the problem is (re) framed as one where consumers are to blame for their consumptive choices; the problem would be solved if only they could be persuaded to buy *the right things* from *the right people*. The predictable and rational consequence of the branding and advertising activities undertaken by corporate labels tend not to feature in business or law enforcement thinking about anti-counterfeiting strategies—that where similar goods are offered at a fraction of the price they will be attractive to consumers who have been exposed to the forces that create in them the desire for the brand, and for many of whom a replica is good enough.

Various strategies of intervention in the educative vein have been attempted, including alerting consumers to the idea that their seemingly relatively innocuous purchases of copied DVDs may be funding serious organised crime, and shaming purchasers by associating their actions with 'real' crime or otherwise trying to attach social stigma to such purchases. An example of the 'it's a crime' approach is the latest addition to front-end DVD material: 'you wouldn't steal a car... etc; so don't buy a counterfeit DVD'. An example of the social stigma approach is the 'don't be a Knock-off Nigel' campaign which has recently been rolled out nationally in the UK on television and in cinemas. The problem with the 'it's a crime' approach is that surveys reveal that around 80% of the public now know counterfeiting and piracy are criminal. Unfortunately the hitherto-assumed next step—that this knowledge would lead them not to purchase counterfeit goods—has not in fact materialised to a satisfactory degree. Thus we see the new strategy emerging, moving from appeals to the legal and moral status of the act of theft itself, to appeals to social stigma and attempted control through embarrassment. Legal/moral strategies have been rendered less than fully effective by the fact that consumers are often quite able to neutralise feelings of wrongfulness with reference to the nature of the perceived victim (corporate media making large profits) and the impression that the property rights gifted by IP laws may be more artificial and more obviously 'constructed' than more conventional property rights. The hope now is that the possibility of the taint of social stigma is less easily neutralised than moral/legal knowledge concerned with the act of theft, and that people will want to avoid taking on the identity of a 'Knock-off Nigel'. The success of this strategy remains to be seen.

Other recent developments include marginally less patronising plans to attempt to influence purchasing routines by educating the public as to the nature of the harms counterfeits cause; but again these are somewhat hamstrung by the need to frame counterfeits as defective products (which is not always true), to highlight physical injury to consumers (which is only a risk in relation to certain categories of fake) and to suggest links to organised crime (a term never used in its more empirically nuanced sense of networked entrepreneurs and grey markets in this discourse), while strategically ignoring the driving force behind the development of the concept of IPC (businesses' lost profits) which remains a harm to which the public appear consistently unsympathetic. These appeals are, in my analysis, to the key externalities of corporate activity in creating markets in branded goods. It is interesting that these predictable outcomes of IP protection in brand markets— parallel or intermixed flows of defective or dangerous goods, and organised criminal activity—are now being highlighted by policing and trade organisations as reasons not to buy fakes, when their production is so closely tied to the social and economic structures and forces created by legitimate markets that they are, in effect, an inevitable output of those legitimate markets.

**Externalisation of harm**

Let us look more closely at the issue of dangerous or defective counterfeits, since this is where we find much of the externalised cost of the corporate merchandising of IP-protected goods. Medicines, industrial machine parts, auto and aviation parts, food and beverage products (including alcohol) and the like which misleadingly purport to be made by a certain manufacturer are sometimes of significantly lower quality than the originals, and can pose serious health risks to users. So contrary to the view that IP infringement is primarily a matter of economic loss for the brand-holder, the practice can involve considerable risk to the health and safety of the public [31]. For example, diethylene glycol (anti-freeze) in counterfeit medicines has killed hundreds of people in a series of tragedies in Haiti, Nigeria and Bangladesh [32]. In 2002 the International Federation of Pharmaceutical Manufacturers Associations estimated that 40% of antimalarial drugs in Southeast Asia did not contain an active ingredient [25: 71]. As well as causing physical or psychological harm by underperforming or containing harmful substances, counterfeit drugs containing under-dosages can foster resistance to the active ingredients, compounding the problems experienced by developing countries suffering epidemics [33].

Estimating the harm caused by the counterfeiting problem is difficult. There is a general dearth of reliable statistical evidence on most aspects of counterfeiting. Fakes in all markets are notoriously under-reported. Many fakes will never be discovered, even when they cause accidents: the sorts of forensic investigations which might link an aircraft crash to a fake part, or a death to a fake medicine, are not usually undertaken for more common accidents and injuries, such as motor vehicle crashes, let alone where the fake in the end does its job well enough and does not cause an accident. Where one receives an electrical shock from a faulty appliance it will be more likely thrown away than examined to see if it is fake. It might, if reported, be kept as data by a trading standards body, but the various processes of attrition in the likelihood of such reporting gives an indication of just how partial a view of the market will be held in such datasets. Many fakes are bought by willing buyers and will therefore not lead to reporting, and even some buyers who are duped into buying a fake will not draw attention to the fact for fear of seeming stupid or, in the case of specialist markets like the art market, having their expertise called into question. In a 1999 report on the counterfeiting of medicines, the WHO made a point of calling attention to the reluctance of pharmaceutical companies to report the known presence of counterfeits in the market [34]. While the companies claim this is to avoid consumer alarm, it has been alleged that it is more likely fuelled by a desire to protect their brand image. Recent statements have been made by trade bodies such as the Royal Pharmaceutical Society to the effect that companies are now encouraged to make their knowledge public [35].

There are various estimates available of the size of the counterfeit segments of a range of markets. Given the risk to health, and sometimes life, some of these illicit markets represent, many of these estimates are very worrying. They tend to be made in the form of unsupported statements, however, with reports referencing other reports without making clear the precise source of the estimates or the methodology and data used to arrive at them. UNICRI produces several such estimates in its latest report on counterfeiting, asserting for example that counterfeits may make up as much as 10% of the legal market for aircraft parts in the USA, a similar percentage of the motor vehicle parts market in the UK, and in relation to pharmaceuticals, around 1% in developed countries, 10 to 30% in Africa, Asia and parts of Latin America, more than 20% in ex-Soviet republics, and more than half of all drugs sold on the internet [25: 55, 58, 68–69].

There is also the problem that many estimates of the global trade in fakes are produced by interest groups representing the legitimate trade. These groups can be suspected of not producing especially reliable figures: they are usually not expert in research methodologies, they sometimes have an interest in inflating the figures (to suggest the problem is worse than it is and exert pressure for governmental action) and sometimes in deflating them (to suggest their market is resilient in the face of fakes, and that consumers can be assured that almost all products in a given market are genuine).

Some figures and other data have been produced which are more than just rough estimates, however. These tend to be from case studies and can give us accurate local pictures of the scale and effects of some harmful faking. For example, a multinational survey in 2004 found 53% of antimalarials in Southeast Asia to be fakes containing incorrect levels of the active ingredient [36]. Seizure statistics are also available, and can give us a partial indication of the scale of the problem. We can briefly review these here in terms of global, European and UK trends.

Global trends

The OECD in June 2007 published a preliminary executive summary (the full report on which it is based remains unpublished at the time of writing) which used data from customs seizures in OECD countries to estimate that the global trade in counterfeit and pirated products 'could have been up to USD 200 billion in 2005' [37] which would represent about 2% of world trade. We need yet more caveats here: extrapolated seizure statistics will not include domestically produced and consumed counterfeit goods (i.e. those not trafficked transnationally), or digital products distributed on the internet. In 1988/89 the International Chamber of Commerce had estimated the IPC economy at 2–4% of world trade, and by 2002 its new Counterfeiting Intelligence Bureau estimated the illicit trade had risen to 5–7% of world trade [38]. Given other available information it seems unlikely that the global IPC trade has fallen between 2002 and now; it is more likely that, as we have said, the significant exclusions from the OECD's recent 2% estimate would raise that figure to an unknown degree.

European trends

In the EU, Regulation 1383/2003 (Customs Actions Against Goods Suspected of Infringing Intellectual Property Rights) sets the relevant regulatory framework for the enforcement of border measures and Regulation 1891/2004 contains provisions for implementation. Different approaches are taken to the implementation of enforcement measures at borders by different Member States, however, as they seek to apply these Regulations in terms of their own legal processes. These differences in law and application have been thoroughly documented [39]. Customs seizure statistics are published annually in an EU report; the latest version at the time of writing is for 2007 [24]. It is important to remember that these trends cannot inform us of the level of counterfeit manufacturing, transit or purchase, but only reveal the aggregated activities of customs in EU Member States.

The number of cases (i.e. the number of seizures, rather than the number of goods themselves) has increased year on year from 5,056 in 2001 to 43,671 in 2007. The number of articles tends to fluctuate quite wildly: for example in the last 3 years the figures have been 76 million (2005), 128 million (2006), and 79 million (2007). These variations are likely to some extent to be an artefact of customs activity: in 2007 for example, more seizures than previously were made in air and postal freight, producing the pattern of higher cases in that year but less articles seized, due to the small size of these types of shipments. The drop in articles seized in 2007 was due to significant falls in intercepted counterfeit cigarettes and CDs/DVDs, and the overall drop in that year thus disguises a rise in the number of articles seized in every other type of counterfeit, including a near 100% increase in toys and a 50% increase in medicines. Although around a third of cases of seizure are made in relation to passenger traffic, due to the far greater amount of goods per commercial shipment, 95% of all items seized were from interceptions of commercial traffic in 2007. Most seizures were of trademark infringing goods (92%), with 5% being patent infringements (mostly electronic equipment such as MP3 and DVD players), 2% copyright infringements (mostly CDs and DVDs, as well as items containing protected images such as well-known comic figures), and 1% design right infringements (mainly clothing, toys and cellphone accessories).

UK trends

The number of people sentenced for IPC has fluctuated over the last decade, with a notable rise since 2002. There has been a corresponding rise in the use of imprisonment for these offenders. In 2002, 441 people were sentenced in the UK for IPC, with 25 imprisoned. By 2005, the number of people sentenced had more than doubled to 995, with 195 imprisoned [40: 73]. The increasing use of imprisonment for IP criminals suggests an increase in the seriousness with which IPC is viewed by the criminal justice system, and it therefore seems likely that a proportion of the dramatic rise in IPC sentences since 2002 is due to increased law enforcement concern with the matter rather than a rise in the incidence of the crimes themselves.

The IP Crime Group also surveyed all Trading Standards services in the UK (although not all responded, rendering the data only a partial picture), in relation to their activities in 2006. By far the highest numbers of counterfeit goods seized by responding Trading Standards services (by unit) in 2006 were DVDs and software (217,274 items), followed by clothing (116,594). The next largest categories to these two were cigarettes (13,200 items) and CDs (12,719 items). The street value of the clothing seized was estimated at around £2.5 million, as against £1.1 million for the DVDs and software.

What does the future hold for IPC trends? Fraud has been predicted to rise to be 'the crime of the 21$^{st}$ century' due to the interplay of a range of factors, chief among them the new opportunities for this type of crime presented by social and technological developments, and the low likelihood of apprehension [41]. Not all IPC is fraudulent, but we might equally say that social (especially the growing importance of branding to consumers) and technological (especially the growth in copying technology) factors, as well as the global economic trends mentioned, have increased the opportunities for criminal gain in this field, and the likelihood of apprehension is low. Unless these factors change significantly we might reasonably expect the growth in IPC to continue.

As the above statistics imply, as well as physical harms counterfeit goods cause financial loss to the companies that hold the IP rights to the goods in question, and this cost of 'victimisation' would presumably be the main corporate argument against the position outlined here that most of the costs of counterfeiting are externalised by brand holders. That argument seems to find stronger support in relation to some commodity markets than others. For example, the British Phonographic Industry estimated physical music piracy cost the industry £165 million in lost retail sales in 2006 and it is well known that the music industry has lately been feeling quite severely the effects of internet file-sharing.

Yet even in relation to an industry which is famous for suffering the effects of IPC, there are good reasons to question the corporate estimate of the scale of loss. Generally, we can observe that businesses and anti-counterfeiting associations representing trade interests routinely inflate the amount of financial loss represented by brand copies. In their argument, a consumer who purchases a counterfeit product has deprived the brand-holder of a legitimate sale. Yet it is not correct to say that a consumer who chose to buy a counterfeit would otherwise have bought the original version. This is particularly the case where, as is usual, the original is priced at a point significantly higher than the fake. It may be that a fake DVD bought at £2 represents a lost legitimate sale at £10, but it may very well not, and the logic becomes even more stretched if the sale is of a fake Louis Vuitton bag at £10 where the original costs £2,000. In the latter sort of sale it is more likely that the counterfeit represents no direct financial loss to the company whatsoever, under the 'replacement' argument at least, as almost all buyers at £10 would not have bought at £2000, and almost all buyers at £2000 would not want a £10 fake. Further, even if the 'replacement' argument were thought a correct analysis, the true financial loss to the brandholder would have to be calculated using only the profit element represented by sales, rather than the full market value of the items sold. And of course internet music piracy generally involves no or negligible cost to the downloader, who would never otherwise have bought many of the albums in their new collection.

In relation to other similarly-costed estimates of the harm caused by counterfeits, the Business Software Agency conduct an annual Global Software Piracy Study which in its latest sweep (2007) estimated 38% of software used worldwide to be pirated, representing losses to industry, they say, of USD 48 billion. The median piracy rate was 61% meaning half of the 108 countries in the survey had a software piracy rate of 61% or higher [42]. In terms of 'internalised' costs, poor quality brand counterfeits may deplete consumer faith in markets generally, and the ease with which counterfeiters can copy new designs may discourage businesses from research and development [43]. Against this argument that faking has an adverse effect on innovation through discouraging R & D, there is a more critical argument that the enforcement of IP rights stifles invention [44, 45] such as by restricting the capacity of some product designers to build on and improve the ideas of others. While, therefore, the World Intellectual Property Organization (WIPO) considers IP protection an essential cornerstone of 'all social, economic and cultural development' [46: 41], this is a somewhat dubious, if widely accepted, position.

There are clearly therefore both substantial internalised and externalised costs associated with the problem of IPC, but while the internalised costs are felt by rights-holders as financial losses, the negative externalities of the legal trade in IP-protected goods are experienced by wider society as a range of harmful social outcomes. We can also of course identify 'positive' externalities in which IPC is not experienced by consumers as a social harm—the very high level of software piracy in the global survey mentioned, for instance, will include many happy users of pirated software who are pleased to have a product that is on all measures identical to the original other than being unauthorised. Still, the internalised corporate costs and positive externalities of IPC should not divert analysis from the negative externalities we have identified, which remain a distinctive corporate contribution to 'crime as pollution' and to contemporary global insecurity.

## Conclusion

The above review of research, statistics, and interventions in relation to product counterfeiting and piracy shows that the issue is important in terms of the social harm it represents, that it is a growing problem, and that it is not effectively regulated. In large part the problem of poor regulation results from IPC's 'hot potato' status—the police see business as best placed to deal with it, and businesses do not want to divert their profits into setting up larger internal anti-counterfeiting units than are absolutely necessary to suggest to outsiders that they are taking the issue seriously. The problem falls into a liminal zone of regulation where the most relevant body (in the UK) is the local trading standards office, staffed by non-police personnel and exercising limited powers with relatively little resource. The economic downturn has led to global corporations shedding jobs, and units such as anti-counterfeiting teams (or often persons) which are not at the front-line of profit generation are under threat (a personal communication to the author from a police source confirms this—a major commercial player in the UK has in the summer of 2009 made its head of anti-counterfeiting redundant, with no plans to replace him). If the fight against organised crime is really going to involve business co-operation in combating international markets in counterfeit goods, the consumptive attitude of corporations towards policing and their reluctance to take costly steps to mitigate the negative externalities of their business methods, will need to be overcome.

What are the implications of the above analysis for criminological theory? The social harm perspective has found such wide acceptance that it can now be found not only in the critical left, but also in the 'mainstream' of criminology—e.g. the 'crime as pollution' analysis mentioned above—as well as in practitioner approaches to criminal justice—e.g. the current move in the UK towards a social harm perspective in the risk assessment of organised crime, and the performance management of the specialist police who engage with it [47]. Once one begins to 'take harm seriously' [5], previously narrowly-conceived matters of criminal culpability are seen as only a rather artificially delimited part of a much larger tapestry of harmful 'effects', and also as is argued here, 'side-effects'. One productive route for criminology might be to explore the further integration of critical and applied perspectives which has informed the present analysis. The 'crime as pollution' argument, based as it is in an economic perspective and with an understanding of the externalities of legal or borderline-legal activities, has been offered by Farrell and Roman as a tool of analysis to extend the (mainly situational) crime prevention approach [12] by way of using 'market-based incentives' to encourage business to accept the cost of crime-proofing their products, such as by arranging for them to suffer financial penalty if they do not. Yet such a perspective also seems quite amenable to application as a framework for understanding the drivers of some of the pressing contemporary global security issues where these are the widely-felt externalities of international economic organisation and routines. Here, product crime-proofing might not be sufficient to unwind the criminogenic situation created by IP-related global corporate business practice. Neither would taxes on business equivalent to an estimation of the externalised costs seem appropriate, as they would be passed on to consumers by way of rises in the cost of the branded goods, and it is this high cost which is implicated in the creation of the problem of IPC in the first place. Still, the integration of the practical thinking of crime prevention specialists with the political economies of globalised capitalist production devised in the analyses of critical scholars lead us to observe that if crime is an externalised form of 'pollution', market forces pollute on a scale generally unrecognised.

## References

1. Bakan, J. (2004). *The Corporation: the Pathological Pursuit of Profit and Power*. New York: Free Press.
2. Chomsky, N. (1999). *Profit Over People: Neoliberalism and Global Order*. New York: Seven Stories Press.
3. Klein, N. (2000). *No Logo: Taking Aim at the Brand Bullies*. Toronto: Knopf Canada.
4. Klein, N. (2007). *The Shock Doctrine: the Rise of Disaster Capitalism*. Toronto: Knopf Canada.

5. Hillyard, P., Pantazis, C., Tombs, S., & Gordon, D. (Eds.). (2004). *Beyond Criminology: Taking Harm Seriously.* London: Pluto Press.

6. Friedrichs, D.O. and Schwartz, M. (Eds.) (2007). *Special Issue of Crime, Law & Social Change.* Vol. 48: Iss. 1/2.

7. Green, P. J., & Ward, T. (2004). *State Crime: Governments, Violence and Corruption.* London: Pluto Press.

8. Passas, N., & Goodwin, N. R. (Eds.). (2004). *It's Legal but it Ain't Right: Harmful Social Consequences of Legal Industries.* Ann Arbor: University of Michigan Press.

9. Szasz, A. (1986). Corporations, Organized Crime, and the Disposal of Hazardous Waste: an Examination of the Making of a Criminogenic Regulatory Structure. *Criminology, 24*(1), 1–28.

10. Needleman, M. L., & Needleman, C. (1979). Organizational Crime: Two Models of Criminogenesis. *Sociological Quarterly, 20*, 517–528.

11. Roman, J., & Farrell, G. (2002). Cost-benefit Analysis for Crime Prevention: Opportunity Costs, Routine Savings and Crime Externalities. In N. Tilley (Ed.), *Evaluation for Crime Prevention (Criminal Justice Studies Vol. 14)* (pp. 53–92). Monsey: Criminal Justice Press.

12. Farrell, G., & Roman, J. (2006). Crime as Pollution: Proposal for Market-based Incentives to Reduce Crime Externalities. In K. Moss & M. Stephens (Eds.), *Crime Reduction and the Law.* Routledge: Abingdon.

13. McPheters, L., & Stronge, W. B. (1974). Crime as an Environmental Externality of Tourism: Miami, Florida. *Land Economics, 50*(3), 288–292.

14. Kindt, J. W. (2004). The Costs of Legalized Gambling: An Economic Approach. In N. Passas & N. Goodwin (Eds.), *It's Legal but it Ain't Right* (pp. 115–137). Ann Arbor: Michigan University Press.

15. Das, S. (Ed.) (1994). *Casinos in Florida: an Analysis of the Economic and Social Impacts.* Tallahassee: Office of Planning and Budgeting, Florida Office of the Governor.

16. Sugden, J. (2007). Inside the Grafters' Game: an Ethnographic Examination of Football's Underground Economy. *Journal of Sport and Social Issues, 31*(3), 242–258.

17. Pawson, R., & Tilley, N. (1997). *Realistic Evaluation.* London: Sage Publications.

18. Crisp, R. (1987). Persuasive Advertising, Autonomy and the Creation of Desire. *Journal of Business Ethics, 6*(5), 413–418.

19. Galbraith, J. K. (1958). *The Affluent Society.* Boston: Houghton Mifflin.

20. Galbraith, J. K. (1967). *The New Industrial State.* Boston: Houghton Mifflin.

21. Brut, J.-P. (1999). Car Parts Counterfeiting. In R. E. Kendall (Ed.), *International Criminal Police Review: Special Issue on Counterfeiting.* Lyon: ICPO/Interpol.

22. Thomas, D. (2007). *Deluxe: How Luxury Lost its Lustre.* New York: Penguin.

23. Grossman, G. M., & Shapiro, C. (1989). Foreign Counterfeit of Status Goods. *Quarterly Journal of Economics, 103*, 79–100.

24. EU Taxation and Customs Union (2007). Report on Community Customs Activities on Counterfeit and Piracy: Results at the European Border—2007. *European Commission website* at http://ec.europa.eu/taxation_customs/resources/documents/customs/customs_controls/counterfeit_piracy/statistics2007.pdf (version current at 23 July 2009).

25. UNICRI (2007). Counterfeiting: a Global Spread, a Global Threat. *United Nations Inter-regional Crime and Justice Research Institute.*

26. Piquero, N. L. (2005). Causes and Prevention of Intellectual Property Crime. *Trends in Organized Crime, 8*(4), 40–61.

27. Clarke, R. V. (1992). *Situational Crime Prevention.* New York: Harrow and Heston.

28. Sims, R. R., Cheng, H. K., & Teegen, H. (1996). Toward a Profile of Student Software Pirates. *Journal of Business Ethics, 15*, 839–849.

29. Vagg, J., & Harris, J. (2000). False Profits: Why Product Counterfeiting is Increasing. *European Journal on Criminal Policy and Research, 8*, 107–115.

30. Sutton, M. (1998). Handling Stolen Goods & Theft: a Market Reduction Approach. *Home Office Research Study 178.* London: Home Office.

31. Yar, M. (2005). A Deadly Faith in Fakes: Trademark Theft and the Global Trade in Counterfeit Automotive Components. *Internet Journal of Criminology,* www.internetjournalofcriminology.com.

32. Hanif, M., Mobarak, M., Ronan, A., Rahaman, D., & Donovan, J. (1995). Fatal Renal Failure Caused by Diethylene Glycol in Paracetamol Elixir: the Bangladesh Epidemic. *British Medical Journal, 311*, 88–91.

33. Morris, J., & Stevens, P. (2006). *Counterfeit Medicines in Less Developed Countries: Problems and Solutions.* London: International Policy Network.

34. World Health Organization. (1999). *Guidelines for the Development of Measures to Combat Counterfeit Drugs*. Geneva: WHO.
35. Cockburn, R., Newton, P.N., Agyarko, E.K., Akunyili, D., and White, N.J. (2005). The Global Threat of Counterfeit Drugs: Why Industry and Governments Must Communicate the Dangers. *PLoS Medicine*, 2(4)
36. Dondorp, A., Newton, P., Mayxay, M., Van Damme, W., Smithuis, F., Yeung, S., et al. (2004). Fake Antimalarials in Southeast Asia are a Major Impediment to Malaria Control: Multinational Cross-sectional Survey on the Prevalence of Fake Antimalarials. *Tropical Medicine & International Health*, 9(12), 1241.
37. OECD (2007). The Economic Impact of Counterfeiting and Piracy: Executive Summary. *Organisation for Economic Co-operation and Development website* at http://www.oecd.org/dataoecd/13/12/38707619.pdf (version current at 23 July 2009).
38. Hetzer, W. (2002). Godfathers and Pirates: Counterfeiting and Organized Crime. *European Journal of Crime, Criminal Law and Criminal Justice*, 10(4), 303–320.
39. Vrins, O., & Schneider, M. (Eds.). (2006). *Enforcement of Intellectual Property Rights Through Border Measures: Law and Practice in the EU*. Oxford: Oxford University Press.
40. IP Crime Group. (2007). *Intellectual Property Crime Report 2007*. Newport, South Wales: UK-IPO.
41. Albanese, J. S. (2005). Fraud: the Characteristic Crime of the 21st Century. *Trends in Organized Crime*, 8(4), 6–14.
42. BSA (2008). Fifth Annual BSA and IDC Global Software Piracy Study. *Business Software Alliance website* at http://global.bsa.org/idcglobalstudy2007/studies/2007_global_piracy_study.pdf (version current at 23 July 2009).
43. International Chamber of Commerce (2005). Intellectual Property: Source of Innovation, Creativity, Growth and Progress. *ICC website* at http://www.iccwbo.org/uploadedFiles/ICC/policy/intellectual_property/Statements/BASCAP_IP_pub.pdf (version current at 23 July 2009).
44. Lessig, L. (2001). *The Future of Ideas: the Fate of the Commons in a Connected World*. New York: Random House.
45. Moohr, G. S. (2003). The Crime of Copyright Infringement: an Inquiry Based on Morality, Harm, and Criminal Theory. *Boston University Law Review, 83*, 731–783.
46. WIPO (2001). WIPO Intellectual Property Handbook: Policy, Law and Use. *World Intellectual Property Organisation Publication No. 489(E)*. Geneva: WIPO.
47. Hamilton-Smith, N. and Mackenzie, S. (forthcoming, 2010). The Geometry of Shadows: a Critical Review of Organised Crime Risk Assessments. *Policing and Society.*

# Part II
# Types of Transnational
# Financial Crime

# [6]

# A good century for tax?
## Globalisation, redistribution and tax avoidance

John Braithwaite
Australian National University

---

*It does not surprise anyone when I tell them that the most important tax haven in the world is an island. They are surprised, however, when I tell them that the name of the island is Manhattan. Moreover, the second most important tax haven in the world is located on an island. It is a city called London in the United Kingdom.*
**Marshall J. Langer**

## Tax havens and international arbitrage

Tax avoidance is now a problem of globalisation. The problem is driven by increasingly aggressive competition among advice professionals – tax lawyers, accountants, investment bankers, financial planners – in the world's financial capitals, pre-eminently New York. Once upon a time, national ethical settlements prevented these professions from competing with one another, and confined professional conduct within norms that respected a certain spirit of the law. Competition policy and globalisation are changing that. English tax lawyers discovered in the '90s that they had to compete for the first time with New York accounting firms for international tax advice to British companies. Contingency fees may have been anathema to a British tax lawyer, but now they might confront an American accounting firm proposing to clients a series of shelters that allow a wipe-out of the company's liability in return for a fee of thirty per cent of the tax saved (see Novack and Saunders, 1998). A great deal of European tax advice is now provided in New York.

Structural discontinuities, like those created by different tax treatments for the same transaction in different nations, open up opportunities for international arbitrage. Corporations can double dip, taking one position on the meaning of a transaction for US tax purposes, another in a second country that creates tax benefits under both sets of rules. Cross-border derivatives that may be characterised in different ways in different jurisdictions were cited during my recent research in the US and Australia as the emerging growth area of tax avoidance by arbitrage (Braithwaite, 2005). New York is the centre of innovation in such arbitrage, with London also having its share of 'rocket scientists' of financial engineering. This is part of what Langer refers to in the quote opening this essay. In more marginal places, like Australia, we can look across to New York and London and see the future of tax avoidance by large corporations and very wealthy individuals.

Profit shifting in and out of tax havens is another important avoidance modus operandi. The extent to which income can avoid tax will depend on the extent to which income can be shifted to havens, where income and company tax are mostly not levied. Gregory Rawlings (2004) has shown the connection between British colonial policy and tax haven constitution. Almost all of the tax havens that have been identified by the OECD as major in the present or recent past are either current colonies or crown dependencies (the British Virgin Islands, Anguilla, Turks and Caicos Islands, Montserrat, Gibraltar, Jersey, Alderney, Guernsey, Sark and the Isle of Man) or former British colonies (the Bahamas, Belize, Barbados, St Lucia, Grenada, St Christopher and Nevis, Barbuda, Antigua, Dominica, St Vincent and the Grenadines, Tonga, Vanuatu, Nauru, Seychelles and Bahrain). Other countries or territories not explicitly identified by the OECD, but which are also major tax havens or global finance centres, are also current British colonies (the Cayman Islands and Bermuda) or former colonies (Hong Kong, Singapore, Malta and Cyprus).

There are two reasons for this. One is that Britain found it convenient to nudge resource-poor island colonies toward becoming off-shore financial centres as an alternative to propping them up with foreign aid. Second, this created financial services business in the city of London that gave it a competitive advantage over New York. Paris, in contrast, was no competitor for New York, and France never nudged its colonies into being tax havens (Rawlings, 2004: 334). Rawlings (2004) has sensitively explored this difference in decolonisation policy through the intriguing case study of the Vanuatu (formerly New Hebrides) tax haven: Britain and France jointly colonised Vanuatu under a unique condominium arrangement. Britain promoted Vanuatu becoming a tax haven in a way the French did not and the regional financial power, Australia, vigorously resisted.

### 'A great century for tax'

In 2000, Christopher Hood said that the twentieth century had been 'a great century for tax collection by Western governments'. In previous centuries both the US and Australia had seen bloody tax revolts. In the US this led

to revolution. In Australia, to the Eureka Stockade in 1852, the closest thing it ever had to a revolution, with gold miners taking up arms to resist the collection of taxes which fell as heavily on those who found little gold as it did on those who made a million. The twentieth century has seen no similar revolts in these and most other Western democracies.

At the beginning of that century, few Western economies were organised well enough to be able to collect income or company tax: it was more practical to focus on the customs barrier. Meanwhile, land taxes – paid on transfer of land and on estates at the time of death – progressively became more important. When income tax was introduced in Australia in 1915, workers with annual incomes up to the considerable level of £156 paid no tax. In most of the West, it was only highly paid workers who paid income tax during the first half of the century. Between the two world wars there was growth in collections from new sales taxes and other indirect taxes.

Surprisingly, Steinmo's (1993) data show that for much of the twentieth century, the US tax system was more redistributive than the Swedish and British systems and possibly even the Australian system. This was particularly so during Franklin Rossevelt's long presidency and in the mid-30s, income tax still only affected the very wealthy with under five per cent of the US population paying anything (Steinmo 1993:24). During the '30s top marginal income tax rates in the US reached eighty one per cent and were generally higher than in Sweden, the UK and Australia. During the second world war, they rose to ninety four per cent and were still at ninety per cent under the Eisenhower administration. Later, in the '50s, a top Australian rate of eighty five per cent finally exceeded that in the US.

Income tax, company tax and sales tax steadily increased the government share of gross domestic product during the twentieth century and this was the general trend throughout the West. This is what Hood meant by the century being a good one for tax. Collectability was assisted by the corporatisation of the West (see Braithwaite and Drahos, 2000: Chapter 9). The final stage of this was financial institutions becoming more concentrated and computerised, making withholding on interest and dividends feasible. As retail organisations became larger companies, as opposed to family-owned corner stores, the collection of indirect tax became more cost-effective. When most of the Australian – and to a lesser extent, American – working class was a rural working class, itinerantly shearing sheep for graziers, cutting cane or picking cotton, collecting taxes was difficult and costly. As the working class became progressively more urban – in the employ of large city-based corporations – income tax collections from workers became a goldmine, especially after the innovation of pay-as-you-earn (withholding of tax from pay packets by employers) in the mid-century.

Taxation became less redistributive as a result with workers paying a higher proportion of their income in sales taxes and other indirect taxes than the wealthy. Just as the income tax was progressive, sales taxes were regressive. So as indirect taxes grew, the tax system became less redistributive and income tax also became less progressive. As workers became wealthier and less itinerant, eventually almost all of them were caught in the income tax net. The paradox of 'bracket creep' in a progressive tax system saw inflation bring more and more of the workforce under higher tax brackets originally targeted at the wealthy.

Most income tax in the US is still paid by the rich. In 2001, forty one per cent of income tax was paid by the wealthiest five per cent of the

US population (McIntyre, 2002: 2). They earned thirty three per cent of the nation's income. But with the proportion of income tax being paid by the very wealthy falling, as the proportion of the national income they earn rises fast, there is now only limited progression left in the income tax to counter the extreme regression of other taxes such as those on sales, excise and payrolls (Johnston, 2003: 11).

## Corporate tax competition

Microsoft, the company that builds the wealth of the wealthiest man in the world, paid $3 billion in US tax between 1996 and 2000. It also received $12 billion in tax breaks. Enron paid no income taxes at all in four of the last five years of its existence. IBM had an effective rate of 3.4 per cent for the last five years of the '90s when the tax shelter boom peaked. General Electric, the most profitable corporation in the US over this period, had an effective tax rate of only 11.5 per cent. This was in part thanks to creative lease-backs in the electric power plant market that it dominates globally (build it, sell it, then lease it back to create deductions in high tax jurisdictions and record profits where taxes are low). CSX Corporation paid no federal income tax at all in three of the four years before its CEO, John W. Snow, became Bush's Treasury Secretary.

International corporate tax competition started when the Thatcher government in the UK cut the corporate rate from fifty two per cent to thirty five per cent in 1984. The US followed in 1986 with a cut from forty six per cent to thirty four per cent. Another round of corporate tax competition raged between 1996 and 2003 when the average rate of the thirty richest countries fell from 37.5 per cent to 30.8 per cent (*Financial Times*, 2 May 2003, p.1). Capital gains is the tax that is used to capture some of the corporate wealth that is passed on

88   public policy research – June–August 2005

to build individual wealth. US capital gains tax rates were almost halved between 1987 and 2003 (Johnston, 2003: 40). In May 2003 PricewaterhouseCoopers tax partner John Whitney warned 'I believe that corporate tax is in near terminal decline. Over the next ten years governments may have to deal with a lot less corporate revenue…'

A final stage in the erosion of a redistributive tax system in the US has been a shift away from the historically much higher odds of tax audits for the wealthy compared to the poor. In 2001, for the first time, low income taxpayers (earning less than US$25,000) were targeted with a higher audit risk than high income taxpayers (earning more than US$100,000). Audits of people earning over $100,000 dropped from 74,566 in 1992 to 29,086 in 2001 even though there was a huge increase in the number earning this amount. This shift is defended by organisations like the Heritage Foundation as an accomplishment for the Bush administration, on the grounds that there are high rates of fraud on the part of the poor (Johnston, 2003: 135).

Global tax planning by large corporations was the biggest reason why most OECD countries in the latter part of the twentieth century saw the proportion of total revenue collected from company tax fall sharply (Steinmo, 1993: 20). Australia was actually an exception to this trend from the '90s to the present. But the US was part of the international trend to lower company tax collections fuelled by international tax competition, though the US fall in the percentage of tax collected from corporations has not been as steep as for some other countries such as Sweden (Steinmo, 1993 : 175). Nations competed to retain the capital of their corporations and wealthiest individuals by bidding down both top marginal income tax rates and company tax rates very sharply in the

'80s (Steinmo, 1993: 30). By 1995 Germany was collecting only 2.8 per cent of its total tax collections from corporate income tax. Even after it recovered to 4.4 per cent for the rest of the decade (Genser, 2001: 5) by 2001 corporate income tax had fallen again to 1.7 per cent of tax collected. This is so low as to raise the question whether the substantial transaction costs in collecting corporate taxes justify such miserly returns. In 2005, Germany still had the highest corporate tax rate in Europe, but is about to join a renewed round of competition with low taxing new Eastern members of the EU on its borders by cutting its rate dramatically.

The late twentieth century has also seen 'loophole madness' growing with more and more private interests being granted tax breaks. The value of tax expenditures or tax breaks in the US increased particularly sharply during the Reagan years. This phenomenon in Australia and the US created the loophole-ridden tax laws that were a major part of what enabled their late-century explosions of aggressive tax planning. Thankfully, the UK is not as deeply afflicted with this problem. Opinion polls in both the US and Australia consistently show that at the end of the twentieth century ordinary citizens felt large corporations and wealthy individuals should pay more tax and that middle- and low-income families should pay less. The imperatives of the global competition for capital and for political campaign contributions – where the corporate tax system has become a way to raise campaign funds by offering concessions – outweighed the democratic imperative to respond to the wishes of the people.

### Twenty-first century regression

A century that started with workers having itinerant wealth that was hard to track down ended with the wealthy having the mobile wealth. Wealthy corporations started to reincorporate their US operations as 'runaway headquarters' in tax havens like Bermuda to avoid paying US tax, just as they moved intellectual property such as patents, copyright and the title to the company's logo to such havens. Yes, the twentieth century was a good century for tax: a growing proportion of GDP was collected (OECD, 2001: 35-39: 86-87). It is simply not true that the Reagan and Thatcher revolutions ushered in an era of smaller government: the current Bush administration in the US is the biggest spender that nation has experienced. But it was a century where taxation was inverted from being a pre-eminent tool for the redistribution of wealth from rich to poor, to hitting – at the turn of a new century – a turning point and becoming a tool for redistribution from the poor and the middle class to the very rich.

In the large middle of the US tax system, a great amount of redistribution still goes on from the upper middle class and moderately wealthy people, down to those less well off. It is the very richest individuals and wealthy corporations that pay the lowest effective tax rates. Effective income tax rates on individuals still continue to rise slowly in the US until adjusted gross income hits $2 million, beyond which it falls (Sullivan, 2003). This situation has got worse and will deteriorate further as Bush tax changes impact. The situation is much more regressive than the official figures indicate. We know that very wealthy people receive a lot of income in the form of gifts and inheritance that are grossly undervalued for gift and inheritance tax purposes (Johnston, 2003: 86-90, 165-66), a lot of income covertly offshore and vast income in deferred, often non-taxable benefits.

Former General Electric CEO Jack Welch's recent divorce litigation revealed the multitude of untaxed or minimally taxed deferred

benefits he was receiving from GE. Just one example was a company jet arguably worth $3.5 million a year. If Welch flies in it to Paris, the cost to GE would be more than $100,000 each way if GE had to charter it, but Welch would be out of pocket just $486 each way in federal tax liabilities given the way Congress has required the IRS to value the personal use of company planes (Johnston, 2003:62). Johnston (2003:57) reports that in 2003 two hedge fund managers had more than $2 billion each in an untaxed deferral account offshore, another two more than $1 billion each. One of these was thirty five years old and looking forward to decades of untaxed compound interest on these funds until he retires or spends it. 'Deferral, the tax lawyers say, is ninety per cent of tax planning. Delay a tax for thirty years and its cost in today's money is almost nothing. Inflation and investing the unpaid tax should cover the whole bill.' (Johnston, 2003:117).

**From fiscal termites to moral termites?**

Former IMF tax policy chief Vito Tanzi (2000) has argued that the twenty-first century may not be a good century for tax. He identified eight *fiscal termites:* electronic commerce and transactions (using cyberspace to buy where there is no tax); electronic money (cutting out the financial reporting of intermediaries that allowed the efficient twentieth century growth of VAT and sales tax); intra company trade (multinationals avoiding tax by internal sales at high prices into high tax countries, low prices into low tax countries); off-shore financial centres and tax havens (with deposits which Tanzi estimates to exceed US$5 trillion); derivatives and hedge funds (about a trillion dollars flow through hedge funds each year); inability to tax financial capital (the increasing impossibility of imposing high taxes on mobile

90   public policy research – June–August 2005

financial capital that moves in response to tax rates); growing foreign activities that lead for example to tax-free non-resident accounts and, finally, foreign shopping (a spin-off from increased travel by wealthy individuals).

Subsidiaries in the top eleven tax havens accounted for twenty three per cent of foreign profits of US companies in 1988, thirty eight per cent in 1999 and forty six per cent in 2001 (Sullivan, 2004). For Australia, in contrast, funds flowing in from OECD identified tax havens fell between the peak of the aggressive tax planning boom in 1997-8 to half that level in 1999-00, and stayed around that reduced level for the next three years. Funds flowing out from Australia to tax havens fell by more than a quarter between 1997–8 and 2002–3 (Australian Taxation Office, 2004: 4). As I have examined elsewhere (Braithwaite, 2005), Australia in this period put in place some quite effective measures against corporate profit shifting, which included shifting profits into tax havens.

Fiscal termites in turn introduce *moral termites* into the tax system (Braithwaite, 2005). There is growing evidence that when ordinary people perceive the rich to be getting away with paying no tax, their commitment to voluntary compliance with tax laws erodes (Wenzel, 2002). In addition, because every one of Tanzi's eight fiscal termites are much more exploitable by the rich than the poor, they will continue the transformation of the tax system from an institution that redistributed wealth from rich to poor into the reverse. Avi-Yonah (2000a:1) sums up well how developed nations responded to capital becoming more mobile and subject to greater tax competition: 'first..shifting the tax burden from (mobile) capital to (less mobile) labor [structurally increasing inequality of wealth], and second, when further increased taxation of labor became politically and economically difficult,

by cutting the social safety net [increasing inequality again]'. Avi-Yonah (2000b: 1577) points to evidence showing that as economies become more open, taxes on capital go down while taxes on labour go up.

Facing these realities of globalisation, each nation might be seen as having to choose between attracting capital and securing growth on a small-government, low-taxation-of-capital, weak-safety-net trajectory, versus a bigger-government, lower-growth trajectory where the gulf between rich and poor is not allowed to widen. The choice is not this simple: when we allow the gulf between the rich and the poor to widen, this also substantially reduces subsequent growth, especially in the long run (Agion *et al*, 1999; Alesina and Rodick, 1992; Persson and Tabellini, 1994; Repetti, 2001: 832–840).

Increasingly the economic evidence suggests that the reason inequality dampens subsequent growth is that it causes an underinvestment in education by the poor. When a large fraction of the population under invests in education compared to the investment being made by the economies with which one competes, productivity growth falters (Agion *et al*, 1999; Perotti, 1993; Galor and Zeira, 1993). This is the most plausible account of why 'the relatively egalitarian states of East Asia have grown three times faster than the highly unequal economies of Latin America' (Mack, 2002). The poorest people of East Asia see more point in investing in the educational development of their children than Latin America's poor. Andrew Mack also points to World Bank research that high income inequality increases risks of criminal violence and armed violence between warlords. Of course civil war and unsafe streets disastrously reduce economic growth.

Finally, he points out that 'increasing inequality and social exclusion increase the risks of a backlash against the very market reforms that represent the best long-term hope of escaping the scourge of poverty' (Mack 2002: C2). Empirically, it is politically easier to do the constant economic restructuring needed to succeed in the contemporary world in nations where safety nets mean the poor do not fall into a deep hole when they lose their jobs (Leibfried and Rieger, 1995). Hence, joining a 'race to the bottom' to low tax rates is no guarantee of attracting capital and prodding growth. There is no inevitability about globalisation causing a race to the bottom.

## The state can fight back

There are alternative policy paths to making a crude choice for or against opting into low taxation of wealth and a weak safety net for the poor. This includes a variety of ways that all national tax authorities can learn together how to combat the aggressive tax planning that exploits the derivatives and tax havens that have been opening the tax gap ever wider.

For example, the Australian Tax Office enforcement programs against international profit shifting have raised about a billion extra dollars in tax for each million dollars spent on the programs. This strategy involves a responsive regulatory pyramid of more intensive audits and other enforcement tools. The idea is to drive voluntary compliance down to a culture of learning and innovation into new compliance strategies that work at the base of the pyramid. If that does not happen, enforcement against profit shifting escalates to progressively more intensive levels. Strategic, evidence-based tax administration can be advanced internationally in a way that sustains the

capability to fund a credible safety net for the poor and that shifts some of the tax burden from the backs of labour to the taxation of capital and high wealth individuals. The US and Australian tax administration have some valuable lessons for the rest of the world on how we might begin to do this.

Strategic enforcement can advance both economic growth and economic equality for the nations that are in the vanguard of introducing such administrative measures. Moreover, all nations can share in greater growth, greater equality and therefore better prospects of peace when international cooperation works to secure them globally. Very wealthy individuals and corporations of course have formidable political capabilities for resisting enforcement. However, the contrast between US tax policy that has allowed the proportion of tax collected from them to decline, and the Australian tax administration which has seen the tax share of very wealthy individuals and corporations increase sharply over the past decade, shows that there are better and worse paths for the state in managing this resistance.

Aghion P *et al* (1999) 'Inequality and Economic Growth: The Perspective of the New Growth Theories' *Journal of Economic Literature* 37: 1615

Alesina A and Rodrik D (1992) 'Distribution, Political Conflict and Economic Growth: A Simple Theory and Some Empirical Evidence.' In Cukierman A *et al* (eds.) , *Political Economy, Growth and Business Cycles*

Australian Taxation Office (2004) *Tax Havens and Tax Administration* Canberra: Australian Taxation Office.

Avi-Yonah R (2000a) 'World-Class Tax Evasion' *The American Prospect* 11 (May 22): 1-4

Avi-Yonah R (2000b) 'Globalization, Tax competition, and the Fiscal Crisis of the Welfare State' *Harvard Law Review* 113: 1573-1677

Braithwaite, J and Drahos P (2000) *Global Business Regulation* Melbourne: Cambridge University Press.

Braithwaite, J (2005) *Markets in Vice, Markets in Virtue* New York: Oxford University Press.

92   public policy research – June–August 2005

Galor O and Zeira J (1993) 'Income Distribution and Macroeconomics' *Review of Economic Studies* 60: 35-52

Genser, B (2001) *Corporate Income Taxation in the European Union: Current State and Perspectives* Canberra: Centre for Tax System Integrity Working Paper No. 17

Johnston D C 2003. *Perfectly Legal: The Covert Campaign to Rig Our Tax System to Benefit the Super Rich – And Cheat Everyone Else* New York: Portfolio

Leibfried S and Rieger E (1995) *Conflicts over Germany's Competitiveness ('Standort Deutschland'): Exiting from the Global Economy?* Occasional Paper, Centre for German and European Studies, University of California at Berkeley

McIntyre B (2002) 'White House Reveals Nation's Biggest Problems: The Very Rich Don't Have Enough Money and Workers Don't Pay Enough in Taxes.' Washington, DC: Citizens for Tax Justice.

Mack, A (2002) 'Policy is the Key to Income Inequality.' *Canberra Times*, 6 July, C2

Novak J and Saunders L (1998, December 14). 'The hustling of X rated shelters' *Forbes*: 2-8

Organization for Economic Cooperation and Development (2001) *Revenue Statistics* Paris: OECD (available online www.SourceOECD.org)

Perotti R (1993) 'Political Equilibrium, Income Distribution and Growth.' *Review of Economic Studies* 60: 755-766.

Persson T and Tabellini G (1994) 'Is Inequality Harmful for Growth?' *American Economic Review* 84: 600-621

Rawlings G (2004) 'Laws, liquidity and Eurobonds.' *Journal of Pacific History* 39: 325-341

Repetti J R (2001) 'Democracy, Taxes and Wealth.' *New York University Law Review* 76: 825-873

Steinmo, S (1993) *Taxation and Democracy: Swedish, British and American Approaches to Financing the Modern State* New Haven: Yale University Press

Sullivan M A (2004) 'Economic Analysis: US Multinationals Move More Profits to Tax Havens' *Tax Notes International* 33: 589

Tanzi V (2000) *Globalization, Technological Developments, and the Work of Fiscal Termites* Washington DC: International Monetary Fund WP/00/181

Wenzel M(2002) 'The impact of outcome orientation and justice concerns on tax compliance: The role of taxpayers' identity. *Journal of Applied Psychology*

# [7]

# E-gaming and money laundering risks: a European overview

Michael Levi

**Abstract** The article examines the fraud and money laundering risks that arise in the regulated e-gaming sector and describes the kinds of measures taken by the sector itself against such risks. It establishes that the e-gaming sector uses a broad set of techniques to reduce the risks of fraud and money laundering and that, compared to methods of customer identification and monitoring in the off-line gaming and financial services sector, the scope for substantial abuse of e-gaming for laundering purposes is modest, both for those crimes that generate cash and for those that do not.

**Keywords** E-gaming · Money laundering · Online gambling · Fraud

## 1 Introduction

This is a review of e-gaming and the money laundering risks that can and are known to arise from it, from the perspective of the EU. It may be helpful first to outline what money laundering is, and it will be argued here that there are two significantly different ways in which people use the term 'money laundering', which are often confused

Professor of Criminology, Ph.D., D.Sc. (Econ.).

This is the written version of the presentation given by the author at the conference on "Gambling in the Internal Market—Balancing state and stakeholders' interests", organised by ERA in cooperation with the Czech Presidency of the Council of the European Union on 15–16 June 2009 in Prague. Michael Levi is currently funded by a UK Economic and Social Research Council Professorial Fellowship (RES-051-27-0208). He is grateful to the ESRC and to the European Gaming and Betting Association for their support for this project.

M. Levi (✉)
Cardiff School of Social Sciences, Cardiff University, Glamorgan Build., King Edward VII Avenue, Cardiff CF10 3WT, Wales, UK
e-mail: levi@cardiff.ac.uk

or implicit. The first is to mean the hiding of the illicit origins of funds in order to make tainted wealth look legitimate. This, we suspect, is what most people who encounter the term would expect money-laundering to mean. The second—acquiring, possessing or using proceeds of crime—comprises all acts that fall within the laws and regulations against money laundering, which are intentionally framed broadly in order to stimulate business, finance and the professions to make it harder for criminals to legitimate their wealth in the first sense above. It also penalises broadly defined self-laundering by those who commit the primary money-generating crimes (often referred to as 'predicate crimes'), to the extent that almost anything they do with proceeds constitutes laundering. The preventative role in avoiding damage to the integrity of the Single European market is the reason why the European Community first (in 2001) regulated laundering under the First Pillar of the EU rather than the Justice and Home Affairs Third Pillar.

## 1.1 What is money-laundering?

Article 1 of the Third Money Laundering Directive of the European Union (2005/60/EC) requires the prohibition (in law) of money-laundering and terrorist financing in the following terms:

> "2. For the purposes of this Directive, the following conduct, when committed intentionally, shall be regarded as money laundering:
>    (a) the conversion or transfer of property, knowing that such property is derived from criminal activity or from an act of participation in such activity, for the purpose of concealing or disguising the illicit origin of the property or of assisting any person who is involved in the commission of such activity to evade the legal consequences of his action;
>    (b) the concealment or disguise of the true nature, source, location, disposition, movement, rights with respect to, or ownership of property, knowing that such property is derived from criminal activity or from an act of participation in such activity;
>    (c) the acquisition, possession or use of property, knowing, at the time of receipt, that such property was derived from criminal activity or from an act of participation in such activity;
>    (d) participation in, association to commit, attempts to commit and aiding, abetting, facilitating and counseling the commission of any of the actions mentioned in the foregoing points.
> 3. Money laundering shall be regarded as such even where the activities which generated the property to be laundered were carried out in the territory of another Member State or in that of a third country.
> 4. For the purposes of this Directive, "terrorist financing" means the provision or collection of funds, by any means, directly or indirectly, with the intention that they should be used or in the knowledge that they are to be used, in full or in part, in order to carry out any of the offences within the meaning of Articles 1 to 4 of Council Framework Decision 2002/475/JHA of 13 June 2002 on combating terrorism [10].

5. Knowledge, intent or purpose required as an element of the activities mentioned in paragraphs 2 and 4 may be inferred from objective factual circumstances."

This is a very broad prohibition of any acts that are knowingly performed with the proceeds of crime (and, in the case of terrorist financing, acts committed with legitimate-source funds that further terrorism). It also appears to encompass leisure expenditures that derive from the proceeds of crime, as well as laundering in the sense of concealing proceeds in order to reinvest with the appearance of legitimacy.

In the light of these differing constructions of money-laundering, a key policy question is how plausible it is that a significant amount of this total laundering—in the billions of Euros—would occur via e-gaming. E-gaming (as contrasted with land-based forms of gambling) does not directly feature significantly, or indeed at all, in the recent published threat assessments of Europol and other European policing organisations, or in their policing priorities. To date, generalised and understandable expressions of concerns by Europol and by the Financial Action Task Force about money laundering risks posed by the Internet have *not* been accompanied by evidence of significant laundering via *e*-gaming. Whilst it is true that the absence of evidence is not the same as the evidence of absence, it is also true that the *absence* of evidence is *not* the same as the *presence* of evidence. The review will conclude that under current EU regulatory practices, it seems unlikely that there is widespread laundering of the proceeds of other crimes via e-gaming.

### 1.2 E-gaming in Europe: the economic context

Let us look at the money laundering risks within the perspective of the size of the on-line betting and gaming industry. On-line gambling accounts for some 5% of global Gross Gaming Revenues (stakes minus winnings). European players constitute around half the global market for on-line gaming (excluding lotteries). In 2009, H2 Gambling Capital estimated Gross Gaming Revenues in the European gaming market at €85 billion for 2008, of which €6.5 billion (7.65% of the total) was in on-line gaming. Three quarters of this (€4.8 billion) went to private operators, the rest going to state monopolies. On-line gambling volumes are projected to rise significantly by 2012, but the public/private sector ratios are not expected to change. Global Betting and Gaming Consultants have produced past and projected estimates of gross gaming revenues for the European market, in US$ billion, set out below. It is within this economic context of very substantial expenditures that money-laundering risks should be viewed.

**Fig. 1** Gross Gaming Revenues (US $billion) for the European market [6]

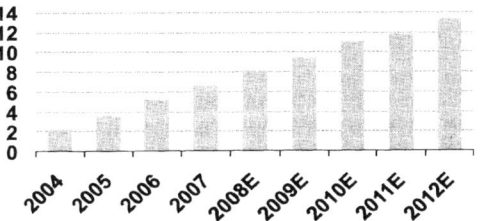

| **Table 1** Volumes and values of UK plastic card expenditure on gaming | | Volume (000s) | Value (m) | Average transaction value |
|---|---|---|---|---|
| | 2004 | 65,234 | £1,975 | £30.29 |
| | 2005 | 86,945 | £2,641 | £30.38 |
| | 2006 | 113,193 | £3,312 | £29.26 |
| | 2007 | 128,117 | £3,511 | £27.40 |
| | 2008 | 130,155 | £3,562 | £27.36 |

*Gross Gaming Revenues (billion dollars) for the European market*

Gambling (a wider category than just e-gaming) accounts for 2.2% (by volume) and 1.2% by value of total plastic card spending at UK acquired merchants. According to UK Payments (personal communication), the trends for plastic spending on gaming in the UK are in Table 1.

### 1.3 Areas of risk

E-gaming (as contrasted with other land-based forms of gambling) does not directly feature significantly, or indeed at all, in the recent published threat assessments of Europol[1] and other European policing organisations, or in the policing priorities that accompany or develop out of them.[2] The expression of concerns about possible risks of the Internet does not count as evidence of laundering via e-gaming, since the relationship between fear of crime and actual crime risks is very indirect in many spheres of crime.[3]

1. Online gaming firms can credit winnings or unused funds back to an account other than the one on which the original bet was made: an issue which gaming firms share with other business areas.

---

[1] An older Europol (2005) report, compiled under the now outdated model rather than the post-2006 Organised Crime Threat Assessment (OCTA), stated (p. 17): "In some Member States legal gambling schemes are quite a widespread modus operandi to launder money. It is estimated that the above-mentioned trend will continue and increase in the future. OC groups also make their way directly into the gambling world by buying companies in this field." The owners and directors of regulated gaming firms are required to pass 'fit and proper person' tests, so depending on the quality of regulation, we may assume that the older Europol comments are irrelevant to contemporary analysis and that the allegation is of a highly general nature. Some later threat assessments and situation reports mention risks from gambling, but not from e-gaming.

[2] Or which *should* do so: one might raise broader questions about the extent to which the Europol OCTA does in fact drive policing priorities in the Member States, but these are not germane to this article.

[3] See, more generally, *Levi* [8]. Among the sources that express broad concerns but provide *no* evidence to suggest that e-gaming is a significant source of money laundering risk are:

– *United States General Accounting Office* [11], p. 34 et seq.;
– The 2007 report of the German Financial Intelligence Unit at the *Bundeskriminalamt* [3], the relevant section of which repeats the wording from the Europol report of 2005;
– The report for the French Parliament by *Blessig/Myard* [2], pp. 89–90;
– The French *CERT-LEXSI report* [4];
– *Bauer* [1].

2. The use of 'front people' through whom to run gaming transactions.
3. Peer to peer games, where value transfers can occur between both electronic and human players as a result of deliberate losses, at a relatively low cost to the players.
4. Payment in (and out) via other financial intermediaries which are regulated for AML purposes but where Know Your Customer is of modest or variable quality.

The corrupt 'fixing' of sports results or individual events on which betting takes place, generating fraud and proceeds of crime, is sometimes considered to be money laundering. However it would be far more sensible to regard this as the making of a dishonest profit rather than hiding and transforming the proceeds of crimes that have been committed in the community. Likewise, identity fraudsters can use financial instruments they have dishonestly acquired to gamble for pleasure and to transfer modest sums to other financial media—which themselves may be traceable: but this is more fraud than it is money laundering. It is not argued here that the latter frauds are not social harms: but they are not the same as using e-gaming to conceal the proceeds from drugs and people trafficking, burglary, fraud, theft, robbery, etcetera.

## 2 Counter-measures against fraud and money-laundering in the regulated e-gaming sector

Implicit in the earlier discussion is the existence of counter-measures. It is not possible to estimate what the level of fraud and laundering via e-gaming would be in an unregulated 'state of nature': however regulation is important in reducing the collateral damage caused by e-gaming and other forms of commerce, including the prevention of gambling by under-age persons. Below are the sorts of measures taken by the regulated sector against fraud and money laundering. As noted earlier, neither this article nor industry representatives interviewed deny that there can be 'leakage' through which launderers may move some proceeds of some crimes. It would be absurd to claim a total shut-out of laundering from the e-gaming sector; nor is it a realistic policy goal for governments in a free society to eliminate money laundering risks. In respect of money laundering, the aim should be to reduce the risk that e-gaming may assist other crimes. This is done in two ways: controls over ownership and controls over the operation of e-gaming itself. One reason to prefer regulation over prohibition is to ensure that operators have to undergo a 'fit and proper person' test before receiving a licence, preventing people with links to organised crime and terrorist groups from owning what could be vehicles for laundering if there were no controls or if controls were over-ridden. The second reason is to encourage e-gaming companies to develop a set of procedures approved by regulators to reduce integrity risks. The latter are discussed in greater detail below.

### 2.1 Money laundering controls in the online gaming industry

Online gaming companies licensed in the EU have chosen to comply with the EU Directives for the prevention of money-laundering, the third of which—strictly speaking—applies only to casinos within the gaming sector. In addition, the regulated sector has developed an agreed set of standards (see footnote 1 and 2). Some of these measures (see EGBA standards, principle 3) in relation to anti money laundering include:

– Identifying their customers (including their age) and checking their information in detail;
– Preventative and detective controls or technology shall be in place to ensure that the prospect of cheating through collusion (external exchange of information between different players) is prevented.

For protection against identity theft, the Code notes:

– Confidential customer information submitted at any point in time shall be protected from unauthorised or unnecessary disclosure.
– Customer credit card numbers stored on the system shall be secured from unauthorised use.
– Making use of the watch lists containing known or suspected members of terrorist organisations, to try to ensure that they do not hold accounts.
– Using established lists of Politically Exposed Persons to implement Enhanced Due Diligence, as required.[4]
– Monitoring the gaming and in-payment/pay-out behaviour of customers.
– Limiting deposits (to a variable extent, since some firms do not have limits but rather monitor carefully those few gamblers who make large on-line deposits, e.g. over €2,000).
– Prohibiting direct payments between customers.
– Prohibiting cash payments directly (other than via regulated cash-card/voucher firms).
– Automatic blocking of payments from countries that are not the same as the registered home country of the customer.
– After identifying an attempt to launder money, reporting the information to the Financial Intelligence Unit and—depending on the jurisdiction and 'tipping off' rules—blocking the account/ending the commercial relationship.

Furthermore, they include (to a variable extent):

1. Device Fingerprinting—Taking a 'fingerprint' of a device like a laptop enables them to check whether it has already been used by an identified fraudster and/or launderer.
2. Location mismatches—Running rules looking at a customer's physical location (and from where they are logging in) and their telephone number to look for any anomalies.
3. Hotlists—Referencing information (devices, IP addresses, credit cards, debit cards, etc.) to both internal and external 'Hot' databases of stolen cards or compromised data (though the latter depends on the depth of coverage of those databases); and checking against EU and other Politically Exposed Person and terrorist lists.

---

[4]Though given that combating Grand Corruption in millions of Euros is the main driver here, it would be strange if PEPs were using e-gaming to launder funds rather than simply to enjoy gambling. If corrupt public officials and their families can defeat banking controls in the EEA and Switzerland, e-gaming firms face a big challenge!

4. Know Your Customer Checks (KYC)—Proving that the information provided in an application or transaction is correct, namely that a person actually exists and resides where they say they do.
5. Variances—Looking for changes between current and previous devices, I.P. locations and login sessions. If a customer usually logs in on their laptop from London, the e-gaming firm may question why they start logging in from an Internet café in Belgrade or Vietnam (though this may be because they are on a business trip or holiday).
6. Transaction Limits—Use of limits to minimise the attractiveness of a business to fraudsters, thus reducing the value they can derive from one unique set of compromised information.
7. Velocity Thresholds—Setting combinations of total spend over different time periods. This essentially creates 'Honey Traps' to pick up unusual patterns, which vary within the sector.
8. Unusual Data—Looking for unusual changes of personal information on accounts, particularly in the early days of a new account. For an extreme example, it is unusual to open an account on the day one moves house, so why change the registered address as soon as the account is open?
9. Associations—Looking for links between cards, bank accounts, I.P.s, devices and personal data. Fraudsters are unlikely to give up on the first attempt—if a card has been used once already for a fraud, they may well try to use it again, though mostly in a short period before they consider that it may have been hotlisted. Peer-to-peer losses in poker and other games of skill are a particular source of risk and high customer cashouts are accompanied by alerts to double-check the hands that have been played, in addition to the routine expert monitoring of peer-to-peer games.
10. Verification—Using systems such as Interactive Voice Response (IVR) to verify account applications or transaction history means that people can protect their business and the genuine consumer from identity theft or account takeover.

## 2.2 Know Your Customer (KYC)

### 2.2.1 Initial acceptance

Controls over identity frauds are primarily the task of the financial services sector and retailers who hold sometimes unnecessarily large databases of card data and other personal information on customers, which, if compromised, can then be misused to facilitate identity frauds and money-laundering. There are particular problems of information-sharing between the financial and e-gaming sectors, and the e-gaming industry ignorance of the Bank Identification Number (BIN) ranges of pre-paid cards (which banks state they cannot provide) makes it hard to develop electronic checks to know whether or not a card is pre-paid and whether higher suspicion should attach to it and to transactions on it.

Detailed requirements and controls vary (as is reasonable under a risk-based approach to money laundering controls), but before a player can play for real money, customers may be required to provide the following information: Username, Password, E-mail address, First and Last names; Date of birth—the system does not accept a date of birth that would make the player less than 18 years of age; Sex; Address information; Country; Phone number; Account currency; Preferred contact language; and Secret question and answer.

The amount of information available for verification varies in different European jurisdictions, depending on databases collected by governments and the private sector, and also the costs of verification.[5] Where possible, all real money players are verified electronically by external and internal systems to carry out age, ID and telephone verification (e.g. to check that the phone number they have given is not a professional services firm or is genuine). The telephone service telephones the number registered by the player and the player must enter the code displayed on his screen to confirm that the user is a real person with a real number. They verify that the name and address registered matches the name (last name and initial of the first name) and address of the person paying the telephone bill. The results of these verifications are put through a combined risk matrix, through which all players go on initial deposit. The category assigned determines whether or not the account requires further verification: if it does, those cases are outsourced to agents for review.

Some firms check to ensure that payment cards have not previously been registered with another player account, for multiple players sharing the same IP address, and for suspicious patterns of transactions. There is also a negative check against lists of suspected terrorists provided by the US Treasury Office of Foreign Assets Control (OFAC) and EU[6] as an (understandably) limited way of avoiding the financing of terrorism. It is accepted in official circles that terrorist finance typologies are not sufficiently well developed or widely communicated to serve as clear guidance beyond such lists.

### 2.2.2 Ongoing monitoring

A variety of approaches take place for ongoing monitoring of accounts, once accepted. One firm has stated that up to 50 different automated checks are efficiently carried out to identify any suspicious behaviour during deposits and withdrawals, and analysed by a team of experts. If suspicions are substantiated, the transactions relevant are cancelled and the accounts involved closed. No data are available as to how often this actually happens across the industry as a whole. Some firms employ staff from different countries speaking various languages, to enable them to test more rigorously whether or not conduct is suspicious and whether identity is properly established: this can be vital since models of suspicion developed for high-plastic societies

---

[5]For example banks charge the industry for checks whether a particular card number is registered to a particular person, which drives up the costs of e-gaming and which e-gaming and other e-tailers are reluctant to pay unless they already have suspicions about customers, which happens with only a tiny proportion of total customers.

[6]The issue of the constitutionality of lists is itself a serious issue that has preoccupied the European Court of Justice and led to some political reassessment. See Council Common Position 2009/468/CFSP, http://eur-lex.europa.eu/LexUriServ/LexUriServ.do?uri=OJ:L:2009:151:0045:0050:EN:PDF.

(such as the UK) may not work in high-cash societies (such as much of Central and Eastern Europe).

To ensure efficient prevention of fraud, firms define a variety of characteristics of suspicious behaviour based on previous experience. They are automatically monitored each time a user makes a deposit before being analysed by the company's internal security team (some of which have been kept confidential for the purposes of this public article):

- initial deposits of substantial sums;
- deposits not immediately used as stakes in betting;
- deposits and withdrawals made without placing any bets.

If two or more characteristics of suspicious behaviour are detected and the company's representatives conclude that there are grounds for suspicion, the user's account is closed and deposits are returned.

Some firms monitor carefully all transactions over a moderate level (a balance between keeping the sum low enough to assist but not so small as to generate too many referrals and false positives), and other indicators of *prima facie* suspicious behaviour include people who in a short time make large winnings on sports betting after a small initial deposit. (Though the latter can turn out to be just good luck.)

The following transaction details can also be verified automatically:

- Does the country of origin of the credit card match the customer's country of registration?
- Does the country of origin of the normal IP address (PC identification) coincide with the customer's country of registration? (Though allowance has to be made for mobile gaming.)
- Do any details of the transaction (credit card number, IP address, etc.) appear in any 'hot' list?
- Is the same payment card being used by more than one customer?
- Is one customer using several credit cards or payment accounts?

A payment transaction can be denied if the response to two or more of the above questions is affirmative. In addition, checks for the following parameters automatically can be made to monitor the customer's behaviour since the deposit was made:

- small or no stake placed since deposit;
- use of other payment options since last withdrawal;
- use of other withdrawal options since last withdrawal.

All of these can build up a pattern of information against which to assess the risks posed by particular customers. As in many areas of account opening and conduct, electronic profiling enables less costly judgments to be made about 'out of context' behaviour, though human intervention is always required to make threshold judgments about what course of action to pursue, and such human interventions constitute costs that are not in the narrow economic self-interest of e-gaming businesses, therefore being an effect of money laundering regulation and of corporate commitment to it.

## 2.3  Comparison with other sectors

The UK and broader European payment card industry has a number of initiatives in place to counter e-commerce frauds:

- Visa and MasterCard have introduced secure payment systems (Verified by Visa and MasterCard SecureCode) for safer online transactions. Cardholders are prompted to register with Verified by Visa and MasterCard SecureCode whenever they shop online at a participating retailer's website.
- To pass this obstacle, cardholders need to register a private password with their card company for use when shopping online at participating retailers (and to remember it!). The systems also allow financial institutions to verify for the retailer that a cardholder is genuine. More than 37 million cards—26% of all UK cards—had already been registered for these systems by December 2008 (see www.becardsmart.org.uk).
- An automated cardholder address verification (AVS) and card security code (CSC) system is available for businesses that accept phone, internet or mail order transactions in the UK. The system allows them to verify the billing address of a cardholder and cross-check the security code on the signature strip of the card. These data checks provide additional information to help e-gaming and other businesses assess fraud risks and decide whether to proceed with the transaction.

## 3  The compliance of the e-gaming sector with AML efforts

In any area of compliance, a threshold judgment has to be made about how much compliance is 'good enough', and reasonable people can disagree about whether a particular set of facts or perceived facts constitutes adequate compliance. This sort of judgment is made at the country level by FATF and the FATF-style regional bodies—MoneyVal in the case of Europe—and at the sectoral level by national regulators and collective industry bodies. Compliance levels are properly seen in terms of a range rather than a binary category, but—as in the now terminated Non Cooperating Countries and Territories 'blacklisting' process at the beginning of the 2000s—countries, firms and individuals may have to be designated non-compliant and sanctions have to be taken against them. This study[7] has not had the resources to carry out a *detailed* audit of compliance and of inter-firm consistency. Since we are focussing here upon the European regulated sector, compliance assessment is the task of the national regulators in jurisdictions where operators are licensed. However is plain that though procedures and control practices vary (as they do in all other regulated sectors such as financial services and the professions), genuine efforts are made by regulated e-gaming firms to identify customers and their suspicious behaviour, and there is some reporting to Financial Intelligence Units of transactions and account behaviour that are deemed to be suspicious.

---

[7]This applies also to a study of UK firms carried out for the Remote Gambling Association: see *MHA Consulting* [9].

Laundering controls may be demarcated into 'front end' controls such as customer identification and 'back end' controls that may be deduced from patterns of trading and other aspects of the conduct of accounts. Arguably, in analyses of money-laundering issues and in evaluations, there has been too much focus historically upon the front end of customer identification rather than the more challenging back end customer monitoring compliance issues. On the former, given that they are utilising cards that have already been subject to KYC, further customer identification by regulated firms takes place on payouts above €2,000[8]—though major firms do so on *all* payouts—often subcontracted to European electronic verification firms; on the 'back end' compliance monitoring issues, many areas of e-gaming have an advantage because the modest scale of financial transactions and their predictability makes them easier to develop risk models for. E-gaming firms vary in the extent to which they impose spending limits, and in general business sectors and financial services, this would be regarded as a purely business decision, unless their solvency was threatened, which in this case would be very unlikely. Greater diligence is (and should be) exercised where gaming limits are higher, since this generates greater laundering opportunities. Land-based betting and gaming, though on the whole well regulated, have higher average and maximum spends, and our interviews suggest that high rollers prefer the ambience of off-line gambling, even where they also game online. Unlike cash-generating trading firms, however, the underlying transactions that form the basis of online gaming firms' accounts are transparent, verifiable in principle, and therefore e-gaming firms are difficult to use as front companies or as wilfully blind conduits for laundering, with or without senior management involvement.

### 3.1 Reporting of suspicious transactions

One indicator of conformity with AML efforts might be thought to be the number of suspicious activity reports made to Financial Intelligence Units. Unfortunately this would be a serious error, since in itself, the number of reports is neither a success nor a failure indicator. First, the more effective front-line KYC and the less inherently exploitable an industry is to large post account-opening expansion of trading, the less likely a sector is to be used as a major money laundering conduit: subject to their skills and contacts, offenders will search for easier places to launder. Thus if money laundering controls are tight and are perceived by offenders to be tight (or are not contemplated at all by them as a laundering route), one might expect few SARs to be made. On the other hand, in the absence of positive evidence of preventative effectiveness, the making of no or very few reports may reasonably be taken as an indicator that a sector is not making enough efforts to develop awareness and to pass on suspicions, including the rationale behind account termination, to Financial Intelligence Units.[9] Some SARs (though tiny in percentage terms) lead to the identification of previously unsuspected offenders, while a much larger number (though again a modest percentage) enhance the intelligence picture on criminal networks and proceeds

---

[8]The threshold figure varies by jurisdiction, up to €3,000 in Alderney, depending on the interpretation given to the EC Third Directive.

[9]The reporting to FIUs of suspicions which have led to the refusal to open an account is a contentious area of AML obligation generally.

of crime: but given constraints on financial investigation resources, sometimes fewer reports generate a better yield. In the UK in 2007–2008, out of a total of 210,052 SARs, the gaming sector made 403 SARs (up from 299 in 2006–2007), of which 24 involved requests for consent to permit dealing with a person whose transactions they suspected of being proceeds of crime: however there is no breakdown for e-gaming compared with land-based gaming. By way of comparison, there were 33 reports direct from credit card companies,[10] and 280 reports from spread betting firms; 7,299 reports from money transmission firms, and 3,553 from bureaux de change.[11] One SAR from the gaming sector was considered sufficiently indicative to be transmitted to the National Terrorist Finance Unit for further investigation.

No data are available for sub-sectors EU-wide, though numbers of reports are inherently much lower in those countries where accounts are automatically frozen when a SAR is made. The numbers of SARs are not an index of vulnerability, but rather of activism by MLROs (which can include 'defensive reporting' to avoid criticism), so not much should be read into figures. To reiterate, a low number of SARs can mean either (a) low risk (perhaps because good preventative action eliminates many attempts at source) or (b) an industry 'in denial' about the risks that are generated by their activities; conversely a high number of SARs can mean that the industry is taking active steps to deal with problems, or that some or all firms are reporting suspicions without much analysis. The latter can be either to disarm potential criticisms from regulators and the media for not reporting enough, or because they have insufficient compliance resources to carry out their internal review role properly.

## 4 Conclusions

The e-gaming industry uses a broad set of techniques to reduce the risks of fraud and of money-laundering, some of which make extremely sophisticated use of the data available in this technology-intensive area of leisure activity.[12] These include (to a variable extent):

– *Manual*
  Agents flag cases they consider to be "suspicious" based on risk alerts, customer tip-offs and unusual betting and or wagering play by customers;
– *Third Party Data*
  Age Verification lists sourced from firms in the market,
  Hotlists, including the sorts of data sources used by banks to identify terrorists and foreign public officials who require 'Enhanced Due Diligence',

---

[10]Credit card issuers in the UK obtained exemption from the requirement to submit SARs after every fraud, because to do so would place an unreasonable administrative burden for no obvious enforcement/intelligence benefit since, in most cases, there is no suspect.

[11]See the *Serious and Organised Crime Agency* [10], p. 41.

[12]To avoid revealing information that may be useful to criminals, only broad outlines of measures have been detailed here. E-gaming using those Stored Value Cards (and, in the future, media such as payment-enabled mobile phones) that have *not* been through adequate KYC controls requires special attention, though not particularly by the e-gaming industry. For a more general discussion, see *Choo* [5].

Telematching,

The European Sports Security Association watch list;

- *Rules Based*

Pre-defined rules based on business knowledge and past experiences. For example limitation on the number of credit cards that can be used; device reputation models;

- *Statistical Profiling*

Outliers of transactional behaviour determined through regression analysis,

Risk scoring models;

- *Advanced Analytics—Artificial Intelligence*

Creating predictive modelling techniques,

Implementation of neural networks to assist the human thought process in detecting fraudulent trends.

As with all business areas, there is scope for debate between directors, Money-Laundering Reporting Officers and regulators about levels of resources and best practice in keeping fraud and money-laundering risks down to 'acceptable' levels. (Though philosophically, it is arguable that those levels of fraud that are fully compensated by the gaming firms and do not risk insolvency are a matter for independent business decisions rather than for governments.[13]) It may be desirable to vary controls in order to keep criminals (with or without inside collusion) uncertain about what risks they face.

In short, compared to methods of customer identification and monitoring in the off-line gaming and financial services sector, the scope for substantial abuse of e-gaming for laundering purposes is modest, both for those crimes that generate cash and for those that do not. This is partly a result of the greater recording of transactions in this industry than in most others, and partly the consequence of legitimate firms being subject to regulation. There is doubtless scope for improvement in controls over fraud and laundering, and regulators need to be vigilant (i) about the levels of private sector resourcing of anti-fraud/AML efforts, without which the risks of money laundering would rise; and (ii) inter-jurisdictionally consistent in their requirements, following deliberation between regulators, preferably (in my view) after consultation with the industry.[14] However there is also much mythology about e-gaming laundering risks, which arises from inadequate information and a tendency to project a dislike of gaming and/or private sector involvement in it into alarm about e-crime. Crime and our responses to it are dynamic activities that require regular attention to trends if we are not to find ourselves stuck in a rut of fighting previous wars on crime. From a social benefit-cost perspective, the more desirable and realistic objective is to manage

---

[13]On this principle, governments and regulators should intervene only where there is market failure or a serious risk of it. Even where compensation is paid to cardholders and/or gamblers for direct fraud losses, some externalities—economic and/or emotional costs—may fall upon those defrauded (*Levi/Burrows* [7]).

[14]Consultation is not the same as bowing to pressure: it offers the scope for rational discussion and evidence-gathering, though there must always be scepticism about evidence from all sides and sometimes, a need for further evidence-collection. In the aftermath of such efforts, even if the ruling was the same, one might hope to improve upon the quality of the evidence assessment by the ECJ in Case C-42/07 *Liga Portuguesa de Futebol Profissional and Bwin International*, Judgment of 8 September 2009, http://eur-lex.europa.eu/LexUriServ/LexUriServ.do?uri=CELEX:62007J0042:EN:HTML.

down the collateral harms generated by e-gaming opportunities, while preserving the liberty of those who wish to gamble and can afford to do so.

### References

1. Bauer, A.: Jeux En Ligne et Menaces Criminelles, Rapport au Ministre du Budget, des Comptes publics et de la Fonction publique. Institut de Criminologie de Paris, Université de Paris II, Paris (2008)
2. Blessig, E., Myard, J.: Rapport d'information sur le monopole des jeux au regard des règles communautaires (2008). http://www.assemblee-nationale.fr/13/pdf/europe/rap-info/i0693.pdf
3. Bundeskriminalamt: Annual Report 2007—Financial Intelligence Unit (2007). http://www.bka.de/profil/zentralstellen/geldwaesche/pdf/fiu_germany_annual_report_2007.pdf
4. CERT-LEXSI: Cybercriminalité des Jeux en Ligne (2006). www.lexsi.com/telecharger/gambling_cybercrime_2006.pdf
5. Choo, R.: Money laundering risks of prepaid stored value cards. In: Trends and Issues in Crime and Criminal Justice No 363. Australian Institute of Criminology, Canberra (2008)
6. Global Betting and Gaming Consultants: Global Gambling Report. http://www.gbgc.com/publications/global-gambling-report (2008)
7. Levi, M., Burrows, J.: Measuring the impact of fraud: a conceptual and empirical journey. Br. J. Criminol. **48**(3), 293–318 (2008)
8. Levi, M.: Fear of fraud and fear of crime: a review. In: Simpson, S., Weisburd, D. (eds.) The Criminology of White-Collar Crime. Springer, New York (2009)
9. MHA Consulting: The threat of money laundering and terrorist financing through the online gambling industry. Remote Gambling Association, London (2009)
10. Serious and Organised Crime Agency: The Suspicious Activity Reports Regime Annual Report 2008. SOCA, London (2008)
11. United States General Accounting Office: Internet gambling—an overview of the issues (2002). http://www.gao.gov/new.items/d0389.pdf

# [8]

# Trade-Based Money Laundering and Terrorist Financing

JOHN S. ZDANOWICZ[*]
*Florida International University*

*Money laundering can be defined, generally, as the process of concealing the existence, illegal source, or application of income derived from a criminal activity, and the subsequent disguising of the source of that income to make it appear legitimate. Deception is the heart of money laundering. The use of international trade to move money, undetected, from one country to another is one of the oldest techniques used to circumvent government scrutiny. International trade as a means of laundering money is also a technique generally ignored by most government law enforcement agencies. This article details how false international trade invoicing is used to move money across borders, undetected. This research details how the statistical analysis of the U.S. trade database can assist in measuring illegal money flows. It also details some statistical techniques that may be used to detect and monitor these abnormal transactions.*

## 1. INTRODUCTION

This research paper contributes to the literature on trade-based money laundering and terrorist financing by providing an analysis of previously unused statistical techniques and methodologies as a means of monitoring, detecting and prosecuting criminal money laundering activities. The paper describes how new statistical profiling methodologies that evaluate transactions contained in a country's international trade database can mitigate the risks associated with trade-based money laundering. This paper discusses the application of four new trade-based money laundering profiling techniques which focus on country, customs district, product, and transaction price risk characteristics.

For years, individuals who study international trade pricing patterns have reported on the evidence that abnormal pricing in trade was being used to move money across borders, undetected by governments and law enforcement agencies. It was

---

[*] John Zdanowicz: Florida International Bankers Association Professor of Finance, Florida International University, Miami, Florida 33199, john.zdanowicz@fiu.edu.

argued that abnormal trade pricing may be motivated by attempts to evade income taxes or import duties, or it may be related to moving "dirty" money earned from criminal activities. More recently, the concern has been that false trade invoicing is being used as a source of money used to support terrorist activities. Empirical evidence of trade-based money laundering has been published in both academic and professional publications (Bhagwati, 1964; Cuddington, 1987; DeBoyrie et al., 2005b; De Wulf, 1981; Gulati, 1987; Pak et al., 2003; Zdanowicz et al., 1999; Zdanowicz, 2004b).

Much of this information has generally been ignored by many individuals, law enforcement, and government agencies that have the responsibility to monitor money laundering methodologies. However, recently, three major events have revealed that there is a new focus on trade-based money laundering and terrorist financing.

*Trade Transparency Units:* The U.S. State Department and the U.S. Treasury Department supported the Immigration and Customs Enforcement Bureau (ICE) of Homeland Security with the funding necessary to establish Trade Transparency Units (TTU's) with Brazil, Argentina and Paraguay. This funding resulted in a US/Brazilian transnational investigation called "Operation Deluge." This investigation revealed $200 million in Brazilian import duty fraud due to Brazilian imports at undervalued prices. These transactions also resulted in income tax evasion in the United States. The stings conducted by ICE agents in Miami led to the arrest of two individuals and the seizure of $500,000 of merchandise awaiting export to Brazil. In Brazil, 128 arrest warrants were executed and 79 individuals were arrested. Brazilian government officials consider the trade-based money laundering scheme they detected through Operation Deluge to be the largest in Brazil's history (Coleman, 2006). The U.S. government is increasing its funding to ICE and supporting the establishment of additional TTU's with other countries. Operation Deluge has shown that an investment in analyzing and detecting trade-based money laundering has a significant positive return on investment.

*FATF: Trade-Based Money Laundering Report:* In June 2006, the Financial Action Task Force (FATF), a Paris-Based multinational agency, released the first comprehensive report on Trade-Based Money Laundering, which stated that "The international trade system is clearly subject to a wide range of risks and vulnerabilities that can be exploited by criminal organizations and terrorist financiers" (Financial Action Task Force, 2006).

The report explains that money laundering through the over- and under-invoicing of goods and services, is one of the oldest methods of transferring value across borders, and it remains a common practice today. It is accomplished by misrepresenting the price of a good or service in order to transfer money between colluding importers and exporters.

One of the key findings of the FATF report was that trade data analysis is a useful tool for identifying trade anomalies, which may lead to the investigation and prosecution of trade-based money laundering cases.

The study concludes, "trade-based money laundering represents an important channel of criminal activity and, given the growth of world trade, an increasingly important money laundering and terrorist financing vulnerability. Moreover, as the standards applied to other money laundering techniques become increasingly effective, the use of trade-based money laundering can be expected to become increasingly attractive."

*FFIEC Bank Secrecy Act Anti-Money Laundering Examination Manual:* The Federal Financial Institutions Examination Council (FFIEC) released its first Bank Secrecy Act Anti-Money Laundering Examination Manual in 2005 and revised the manual in 2006 and 2007 (Federal Financial Institutions Examination Council, 2007). Some key points in the FFIEC BSA/AML Examination Manual include:

> Objective: Bank examinations will "assess the adequacy of the bank's systems to manage the risks associated with trade financing activities, and management's ability to implement effective due diligence, monitoring, and reporting systems."

> Risk Factors: "While banks should be alert to transactions involving higher risk goods, they need to be aware that goods may be over- or under- valued in an effort to evade AML or customs regulations."

> Policies, Procedures, and Processes: "should require a thorough review of *all* applicable trade documentation to enable the bank to monitor and report unusual and suspicious activity. In addition to OFAC filtering, the monitoring process should give greater scrutiny to obvious over- or under pricing of goods and services." This requirement that banks need to detect obvious over- or under-invoiced goods has been an area of significant debate, disagreement, and questioning. One technique that can assist financial institutions in determining normal price ranges is through the statistical analysis of the U.S. trade data base.

# 2. TRADE-BASED MONEY LAUNDERING

Money may be moved out of the United States to a foreign country by under-valuing U.S. exports or over-valuing U.S. imports. Money may be moved into the United States from a foreign country by over-valuing U.S. exports or under-valuing U.S. imports.

## 2.1. EXAMPLE – OVERVALUED U.S. IMPORTS

Assume a terrorist or criminal wants to launder $1 million dollars to a foreign country. He would need to have a foreign exporter to collude on the transaction. The set of transactions used to launder the money would include:

1) Foreign exporter purchases 10,000 razor blades for $.10 per blade. ($1,000)
2) Foreign exporter exports 10,000 razor blades to a domestic importer for $100 per razor blade. (Total Invoice $1,000,000)
3) Domestic importer receives 10,000 razor blades worth $1,000 but pays the foreign exporter $1,000,000.
4) Outcome: The domestic importer has moved $1million to the foreign country less the $1,000 transactions cost of the razor blades.

## 2.2. EXAMPLE - UNDERVALUED U.S. EXPORTS

Assume a terrorist or criminal wants to launder $1 million to a foreign country. He would need to have a foreign importer to collude on the transaction. The set of transactions used to launder the money would include:

1) Domestic criminal or terrorist uses his $1 million to purchases 200 gold watches for $5,000 per watch. ($1,000,000) The watches would be purchased for cash.
2) Domestic exporter sells the 200 gold watches to a foreign importer for $5.00 per watch ($1,000).
3) Foreign importer receives the 200 gold watches and is presented with an invoice for $1,000, which he pays to the domestic exporter.
4) Foreign importer sells the gold watches at the market price of $5,000 per watch and converts the 200 gold watches into $1,000,000.
5) Outcome: The domestic exporter has moved $1million to the foreign country less the $1,000 transaction cost of the invoice payment.

## 2.3. MOTIVATIONS AND IMPACT

The motivations and impact of trade price manipulation include:

*Under-Invoiced Exports*

Money Laundering from Illegal Activities
Terrorist Financing
Income Tax Avoidance/Evasion
Capital Flight
Avoid Export Surcharges
Conceal Illegal Commissions

*Over-Invoiced Exports*

   Increase Export Subsidies

   Increase Value Added Tax Rebates

*Over-Invoiced Imports*

   Money Laundering from Illegal Activities

   Terrorist Financing

   Income Tax Avoidance/Evasion

   Capital Flight

   Justify High Domestic Prices under Price Controls

   Conceal Illegal Commissions

*Under-Invoiced Imports*

   Evade/ Reduce Import Duties

   Dumping at Below Market Prices

# 3. U.S. MERCHANDISE TRADE DATA BASE

This research on determining abnormal international trade pricing is based on the analysis of the monthly data contained in the United States Merchandise Trade Data Base. This database is produced by the U.S. Department of Commerce, Census Bureau and is used to determine the U.S. balance of trade. The database contains information at the transaction level and is reported to the U.S. Census Bureau from Shipper's Export Declarations and U.S. Customs Service Entry Summary forms, the legal documents required by U.S. Customs to be filed for any export or import. All transactions with a value of more than $2,500 for exports and $1,250 for imports are recorded, with exclusions for shipments involving the U.S. Armed Forces and diplomatic missions and for in-transit shipments through the United States. On average more than 10 million records per year are analyzed, with each record identifying the item, quantity and dollar value along with the mode of transportation, the U.S. customs district through which the goods passed and the foreign country involved in the trade. Products are classified using the international standard Harmonized Commodity Code System which contains over 17,000 categories of imports and over 9,000 categories of exports. All of the Census Bureau price data are converted to U.S. Dollar terms. If the original documents were stated in foreign currency terms, then the exchange rate at the beginning of the quarter in which the transaction occurred is used to convert to dollars, except if the exchange rate had changed by more than 5% over the quarter. In the latter case, the rate used is the end of the quarter rate. For each year analyzed, all

860 / REVIEW OF LAW AND ECONOMICS

individual transaction records on the 12 monthly United States import databases and the 12 monthly United States export databases are combined. The total data set is segmented and entered into a country/product table containing the price data for all combinations of countries and products. In this country/product table, over 232 columns represent every country and the world, while every import harmonized code and every export harmonized code are represented by over 26,000 rows. The resulting table contains over 6 million cells. Each cell in the table contains the data on the population of transactions related to the United States import or United States export of a particular commodity from or to a specific country, as well as from or to the world. Some cells are empty if no transactions existed between the United States and a country for a particular commodity.

# 4. RESEARCH METHODOLOGIES

During the past sixteen years, various methodologies have been employed to analyze abnormal international trade pricing:

## 4.1. COUNTRY AVERAGE PRICE VS. WORLD AVERAGE PRICE

In January 1992, *Money Laundering Alert* published the first article with results of an empirical analysis of trade-based money laundering. In that pioneering work, the average country price was compared to the average world price for every product (Money Laundering Alert, 1992). Abnormal international trade prices were determined based on this methodology. Some examples of abnormal export and import average prices derived from this research methodology include:

### U.S. EXPORTS AT LOW AVERAGE PRICES

| Product | Country | Country Average Price | World Average Price |
|---------|---------|----------------------|---------------------|
| Cooking Stoves | Colombia | $ 76.62/each | $ 425.65/unit |
| Erythromycin | Iran | $ 0.10/gram | $ 1.20/gram |
| Nickel Alloy Wire | Venezuela | $ 2.21/kg | $ 12.26/kg |
| Herring –Bone Tire | France | $ 7.69/each | $ 192.25/unit |
| Machine Guns | France | $ 364.08/each | $ 2,022.67/unit |
| Enriched 235 Uranium | Spain | $ 15.50/kg | $ 172.22/kg |
| Military Rifles | UK | $ 106.87/each | $ 387.55/unit |

Trade-Based Money Laundering / 861

## U.S. IMPORTS AT HIGH AVERAGE PRICES

| Product | Country | Country Average Price | World Average Price |
|---|---|---|---|
| Razors | Colombia | $ 34.81/each | $ 0.09/unit |
| Cut Emeralds | Panama | $ 974.58/carat | $ 43.63/carat |
| Industrial Miners Diamonds | Venezuela | $ 795.62/carat | $ 6.45/carat |
| Untrimmed Pillowcases | France | $ 909.29/each | $ 0.62/unit |
| Cordless Telephones | France | $ 4,232.50/each | $ 47.65/unit |
| Unrecorded Magnetic Discs | Spain | $ 698.16/each | $ 0.43/unit |
| Slip Joint Pliers | UK | $ 489.75/each | $ 0.88/unit |

One of the criticisms of comparing country average prices with world average prices was that the analysis did not account for country/product heterogeneity. It was pointed out the imported dresses from Haiti were different from imported dresses from France. This led to modifying the data analysis methodology to take into account country/product differences.

## 4.2. PRICES 50% ABOVE OR BELOW AVERAGE COUNTRY PRICE

The initial objective of this research methodology was to estimate the impact of over-invoiced imports and under-invoiced exports on the amount of money moved out of the United States during 1993. All records on the 12 monthly U.S. import databases and 12 monthly U.S. export databases for the period from January 1, 1993 through December 31, 1993, by commodity and by country were combined into an annual trade database. The commodities were defined by 10 digit harmonized commodity codes. This methodology recognized that the characteristics of import and export transactions might vary among countries. Therefore, this methodology analyzed import and export transactions relative to historical U.S./country trade. The analysis of total U.S./country imports and total U.S./country exports determined the average U.S./country import price and the average U.S./country export price for every commodity (Pak and Zdanowicz, 1994).

For every country, an analysis of every reported import and export transaction for every commodity during 1993 was determined for all U.S./country import transactions, and all U.S./country export transactions. For every country, the analysis determined all U.S. import transactions for every commodity that were 50% above the average U.S./ country import price. For every country, the analysis determined all U.S./country export transactions, for every commodity that were 50% below the average U.S./country export price.

The analysis determined the dollar amount of over-invoiced imports for every import transaction, for every commodity, for every country and determined the

862 / REVIEW OF LAW AND ECONOMICS

total dollar amount of over-invoiced imports for every country. The analysis also determined the dollar amount under-invoiced exports for every export transaction, for every commodity, for every country and determined the total dollar amount of under-invoiced exports for every country. This analysis determined the total amount of money moved out of the United States in 1993 due to transactions at import prices greater than 50% of the average U.S./country commodity price and export prices less than 50% of the average U.S./country export commodity price. This analysis was extended employing the same methodology for 1994, and 1995. The following are the estimates of money moved out of the United States:

**MONEY MOVED OUT OF THE UNITED STATES DUE TO:**
**Import Prices >150% of Average Country Import Price**
**Export Prices < 50% of Average Country Export Price**

| Year | Money Moved Out of U.S. |
|------|--------------------------|
| 1993 | $ 97.35 Billion |
| 1994 | $116.18 Billion |
| 1995 | $136.76 Billion |

The following are some examples of abnormally priced imports and exports detected by this methodology.

**ABNORMALLY HIGH U.S. IMPORT PRICES**

| Product | Country | Price |
|---------|---------|-------|
| Telephone Answering Machines | Mexico | $ 255.00/unit |
| Erythromycin | Japan | $ 1,693.83/gram |
| Dot Matrix Printers | Sweden | $ 5,493.26/unit |
| Toothbrushes | France | $ 18.00/unit |
| Safety Pins | Canada | $ 29.65/unit |
| Cassette Tape Players | Denmark | $17,314.25/unit |
| Telephones (No Features) | Japan | $ 270.43/unit |

**ABNORMALLY LOW U.S. EXPORT PRICES**

| Product | Country | Price |
|---------|---------|-------|
| Telephone Answering Machines | Mexico | $ 27.09/unit |
| Erythromycin | Japan | $ 0.08/gram |
| Men's Bathrobes | Saudi Arabia | $ 4.81/dozen |
| Generators (Int. Combustion) | France | $ 9.56/unit |
| Electric Cooking Stoves | Mexico | $ 30.55/unit |
| Refrigerators (Household) | Japan | $ 40.43/unit |
| TV Receivers (Color) | Canada | $ 31.40/unit |

## 4.3. INTER-QUARTILE RANGE PRICE ANALYSIS

One of the main criticisms of the 50% deviation analysis was that the use of a 50% filter was arbitrary. This criticism was valid. In some cases the 50% filter may have been too low and in other cases it might have been too high.

In 1994, the U.S. Internal Revenue Service issued its 482 transfer pricing regulations and stipulated that the inter-quartile price range should be used to determine the validity of transfer prices in international trade. The IRS defines suspicious prices as those import prices that exceed the upper quartile import prices and those export prices that are less than the lower quartile export price. Based on the IRS defining the definition of arms-length pricing norms, the research methodology shifted to using the product/country inter-quartile price ranges as statistical filters. The median price, lower quartile export price and the upper quartile import price for every commodity exported and imported to and from every country were determined. Every import record was evaluated and compared to the country specific import upper quartile price to determine if it was over-valued. The dollar amount of over-valuation for every import transaction was determined. Similarly, every export record was evaluated and compared to the country specific export lower quartile price to determine if it was under-valued. The dollar amount of under-valuation for every export transaction was determined. The dollar amounts of all under-valued export transactions and all over-valued import transactions for every commodity, for every country were aggregated. The following table contains the total estimated money moved out of the U.S. for 2004, 2005, and 2006 due to abnormal pricing based on the inter-quartile range analysis (International Trade Alert, 2005).

**MONEY MOVED OUT OF THE UNITED STATES DUE TO:**
**Import Prices > Upper Quartile Country Import Prices**
**Export Prices < Lower Quartile Country Export Prices**

| Year | Money Moved Out of U.S. |
|------|-------------------------|
| 2004 | $167.76 Billion |
| 2005 | $191.95 Billion |
| 2006 | $189.05 Billion |

The following are some examples of abnormally priced imports and exports detected by this methodology:

864 / REVIEW OF LAW AND ECONOMICS

### ABNORMALLY HIGH U.S. IMPORT PRICES

| Product | Country | Price |
|---|---|---|
| Toilet/Facial Tissue | China | $ 4,121.81/kg |
| Threaded Nuts | Belgium | $ 2,426.70/kg |
| Tweezers – Base Metal | Japan | $ 4,896.00/unit |
| Lawnmower Blades | Australia | $ 2,326.75/unit |
| Razors | UK | $ 113.20/unit |
| Used Clothing | Haiti | $ 260.00/kg |
| Women's Cotton Briefs | Venezuela | $ 50.00/unit |

### ABNORMALLY LOW U.S. EXPORT PRICES

| Product | Country | Price |
|---|---|---|
| Diamonds – Not Industrial | India | $ 13.45/carat |
| Forklift Trucks – Self-Propelled | Jamaica | $ 384.14/unit |
| Bulldozers – Self-Propelled | Colombia | $ 1,741.92/unit |
| Video Projectors – Color | Brazil | $ 33.95/unit |
| Missile and Rocket Launchers | Israel | $ 52.03/unit |
| Forklift Trucks – Self-Propelled | Haiti | $ 555.73/unit |
| New Automobile Tires | Russia | $ 3.97/unit |

# 5. APPLICATIONS OF INTER-QUARTILE RANGE STATISTICAL ANALYSIS

The 1994 Internal Revenue Service's specification that the inter-quartile price range is the relevant arms-length definition of normal pricing gave researchers a statistical benchmark for the analysis of international trade pricing. Thus, many additional international trade pricing studies were conducted based on the U.S. government's Merchandise Trade Data Base and the U.S. Government's definition of abnormal international trade pricing. The following are summaries of some of these studies.

## 5.1. MONEY MOVED OUT OF AND INTO THE UNITED STATES

In addition to estimating the amount of money being moved out of the United States using the inter-quartile range analysis, the estimate of the amount of money moved into the U.S. was also determined. Money can be moved into the U.S. through over-valued exports and undervalued imports. The analysis indicates that during 2004, $55.5 billion was the net capital flow into the U.S.

Trade-Based Money Laundering / 865

## TOTAL MONEY MOVED OUT OF U.S. BY COUNTRY DOLLAR VALUE
### (THROUGH UNDER-VALUED EXPORTS AND OVER-VALUED IMPORTS)
### Year: 2004

| UNDER-VALUED EXPORTS | OVER-VALUED IMPORTS | TOTAL MOVED OUT OF THE US | SHARE OF TRADE |
|---|---|---|---|
| $111,593,487,257 | $56,167,170,400 | $167,760,657,657 | 7.34% |

## TOTAL MONEY MOVED INTO U.S. BY COUNTRY DOLLAR VALUE
### (THROUGH OVER-VALUED EXPORTS AND UNDER-VALUED IMPORTS)
### Year: 2004

| OVER-VALUED EXPORTS | UNDER-VALUED IMPORTS | TOTAL MOVED INTO THE US | SHARE OF TRADE |
|---|---|---|---|
| $48,066,362,572 | $175,219,246,010 | $223,285,608,582 | 9.77% |

## 5.2. IMPACT OF NEW BANKING REGULATIONS ON MONEY MOVED OUT OF SWITZERLAND

When central banking authorities enact legislation that only focuses on financial institutions, criminals and terrorists will find alternative techniques and channels to launder their money. The conclusion of a study based on the inter-quartile range analysis supports the argument that money launderers and terrorists will shift their money laundering activities to false invoicing in international trade. In 1998, the Swiss Federal Government broadened the reach of its money laundering regulations to include not only banks, but its entire financial services sector. The law, known as the Federal Act on the Prevention of Money Laundering in the Financial Sector - Money Laundering Act (MLA), requires all financial institutions to report suspicious transactions to Switzerland's Federal Reporting Office for Money Laundering. The Act went into effect on April 1, 1998 (De Boyrie et al., 2005a).

The study measured the dollar amount of money moved from Switzerland to the United States through false invoicing, both before (1995 to 1997) and after (1998 to 2000), the date the money laundering law was enacted. In order to evaluate the possible impact of other economic factors that might increase Swiss capital outflows, a detailed statistical analysis was conducted. Other economic variables considered in the analysis included differences in U.S./Swiss interest rates, exchange rates, consumer price indices and producer price indices. The results of the statistical analysis indicated that the new law was the only factor that could explain the increase in capital outflows from Switzerland to the United States. The results of the research study determined that the dollar amount of money moved from Switzerland to the United States

866 / REVIEW OF LAW AND ECONOMICS

increased significantly after the law was enacted. The average amount of money moved increased from $253 million per month before the law to $628 million per month after the law. There was also a significant increase in money moved as a percentage of Swiss/U.S. trade. The average monthly amount of money moved as a percentage of Swiss/U.S. trade increased from 29% to 58%. Subsequent to the passage of the law, the monthly average dollar amount of money moved increased by 149% and the money moved as a percentage of Swiss/U.S. trade increased by 100%.

**MONTHLY CAPITAL OUTFLOWS FROM SWITZERLAND TO U.S.**

| Year | $ Amount/Month | % of Trade Volume |
|------|----------------|-------------------|
| 1995 | $ 222,270,140 | 29.06% |
| 1996 | $ 315,550,450 | 35.41% |
| 1997 | $ 220,770,123 | 22.31% |
| 1998 | $ 413,664,512 | 45.28% |
| 1999 | $ 900,088,394 | 83.49% |
| 2000 | $ 571,560,220 | 44.52% |

**AVERAGE MONTHLY OUTFLOWS - BEFORE VS. AFTER NEW LAW**

| Time Period | $ Amount | % of Trade Volume |
|-------------|----------|-------------------|
| Before the Law | $ 252,863,571 | 28.93% |
| After the Law | $ 628,437,709 | 57.76% |
| Percent Increase | 149% | 100% |

## 5.3. MONEY MOVED TO AL QAEDA WATCH LIST COUNTRIES

After September 11, 2001, when terrorists attacked the United States and murdered over 3,000 individuals, the Department of State issued a watch list of Al Qaeda countries that had a high probability of harboring terrorist extremists. A study employing the inter-quartile range determined that over $8.4 billion may have been moved from the United States to Al Qaeda watch list countries during 2004. A sample of some suspicious transactions is listed below. The following table contains the estimated amount of money moved by country (Freer, 2001; Zdanowicz, 2004b, 2005).

## ABNORMALLY HIGH IMPORT PRICES
## FROM AL QAEDA WATCH LIST COUNTRIES

| Product | Country | Price |
|---|---|---|
| Cotton Dishtowels | Pakistan | $ 153.72/unit |
| Glass Mirrors (less than 929 sq cm) | Indonesia | $ 164.54/sq.cm |
| Razors | Egypt | $ 22.89/unit |
| Air Pumps (hand/foot operated) | Malaysia | $ 5,000.00/unit |
| Camshafts and Crankshafts | Saudi Arabia | $ 15,200.00/unit |
| Footballs | Malaysia | $ 142.50/unit |

## ABNORMALLY LOW EXPORT PRICES
## TO AL QAEDA WATCH LIST COUNTRIES

| Product | Country | Price |
|---|---|---|
| Color Video Monitors | Indonesia | $ 22.43/unit |
| Color Video Monitors | Pakistan | $ 21.90/unit |
| Sports Footwear (Athletic Shoes) | Jordan | $ 0.40/pair |
| Radioactive Elements, Isotopes | Egypt | $ 0.01/mbq |
| Bulldozers | Saudi Arabia | $ 5,909.09/unit |
| Television Antennas | Malaysia | $ 0.30/unit |

## AL QAEDA WATCH LIST COUNTRIES
### (THROUGH UNDER-VALUED EXPORTS AND OVER-VALUED IMPORTS)
### For Countries on the Al Qaeda Watch List

| Obs | COUNTRY | UNDER-VALUED EXPORTS | OVER-VALUED IMPORTS | TOTAL MOVED OUT OF THE US | SHARE OF TRADE |
|---|---|---|---|---|---|
| | TOTAL | $5,811,961,635 | $2,537,901,565 | $8,349,863,196 | 6.75% |
| 1 | MALAYSA | $2,317,172,101 | $1,201,554,685 | $3,518,726,786 | 9.00% |
| 2 | S ARAB | $690,811,190 | $316,492,990 | $1,007,304,181 | 3.85% |
| 3 | IRAQ | $706,095,531 | $210,325,795 | $916,421,327 | 9.78% |
| 4 | INDNSIA | $397,962,961 | $330,162,743 | $728,125,704 | 5.40% |
| 5 | ARAB EM | $639,817,694 | $22,463,911 | $662,281,605 | 12.72% |
| 6 | ALGERIA | $78,935,289 | $181,162,213 | $260,097,502 | 3.10% |
| 7 | PAKISTN | $126,213,808 | $102,956,529 | $229,170,337 | 4.89% |
| 8 | EGYPT | $200,826,873 | $27,078,209 | $227,905,082 | 5.14% |
| 9 | KUWAIT | $159,018,609 | $56,749,463 | $215,768,072 | 4.54% |
| 10 | IRAN | $152,952,617 | $12,628,410 | $165,581,027 | 70.03% |
| 11 | JORDAN | $64,374,230 | $24,273,637 | $88,647,866 | 5.39% |
| 12 | OMAN | $62,421,004 | $9,353,236 | $71,774,240 | 9.60% |
| 13 | QATAR | $51,792,019 | $1,416,201 | $53,208,219 | 6.32% |
| 14 | BAHRAIN | $39,923,000 | $6,629,735 | $46,552,735 | 6.59% |
| 15 | AFGHAN | $38,156,092 | $96,595 | $38,252,686 | 20.95% |
| 16 | MOROC | $26,974,330 | $9,784,635 | $36,758,964 | 3.54% |

868 / REVIEW OF LAW AND ECONOMICS

| 17 | LEBANON | $29,554,177 | $2,411,754 | $31,965,930 | 5.95% |
|----|---------|-------------|------------|-------------|-------|
| 18 | TUNISIA | $12,256,463 | $5,566,000 | $17,822,463 | 3.81% |
| 19 | BRUNEI | $3,088,678 | $13,780,559 | $16,869,237 | 3.70% |
| 20 | SYRIA | $5,902,256 | $2,737,644 | $8,639,900 | 1.80% |
| 21 | SUDAN | $4,340,695 | . | $4,340,695 | 6.04% |
| 22 | YEMEN | $1,906,847 | $38,840 | $1,945,687 | 0.66% |
| 23 | ERITREA | $749,224 | . | $749,224 | 1.38% |
| 24 | SOMALIA | $333,418 | $1,182 | $334,600 | 3.41% |
| 25 | DJIBUTI | $330,563 | . | $330,563 | 0.75% |
| 26 | LIBYA | $51,966 | $236,599 | $288,564 | 0.08% |

## 5.4. ABNORMAL WEIGHT

The terrorist attack of September 11, 2001 transformed the world's perspective on the terrorist movement. It was an event that changed the focus of all countries regarding the monitoring of their ports of entry in an attempt to protect themselves against the importation of weapons of mass destruction (WMD) and other contraband related to terrorist activities. In the United States, the enactment of the Patriots Act and the creation of the Department of Homeland Security were attempts to minimize terrorist related money laundering and smuggling (Zdanowicz, 2003).

Based on the inter-quartile analysis of the weight characteristics of U.S. import data thousands of import transactions with abnormal weights were observed.

### ABNORMAL U.S. IMPORT WEIGHTS

| Country | Product | Weight |
|---------|---------|--------|
| Egypt | Razors | 15 kg/unit |
| Indonesia | Coffee | 1.26 kg/kg |
| France | Footwear | 46 kg/pair |
| Germany | Sweaters | 57 kg/dozen |
| Malaysia | Briefcases | 98 kg/unit |
| Pakistan | Fabric | 62 kg/sq meter |
| Indonesia | Pillows | 55 kg/unit |
| Pakistan | Towels | 2 kg/unit |

Although these examples reflect the importation of abnormally weighted cargo into the United States, they are only a sample of transactions. The implications regarding port security are crucial for the development of the policies necessary to protect the citizenry from international terrorism.

# 6. TRADE FINANCING

The U.S. government created the Federal Financial Institutions Examination Council, which adopted a common examination manual in an attempt to eliminate inconsistent bank examinations. The examination, first published in June 2005, resulted from the collaboration of the Federal Reserve Board, Office of the Comptroller of the Currency, Federal Deposit Insurance Corporation, National Credit Union Administration and the Office of Thrift and Supervision. The examination manual was revised in 2006 and 2007 based on input from the industry. A significant addition to the manual was the inclusion of trade financing as an area for bank risk monitoring and examination.

## 6.1. FFIEC MANUAL

The 2007 FFIEC Examination Manual states that financial institutions engaged in trade financing activities should give greater scrutiny to:

1) Items shipped that are inconsistent with the nature of the customer's business (e.g., a steel company starts dealing in paper products, or an information technology company starts dealing in bulk pharmaceuticals).
2) Customers conducting business in high-risk jurisdictions.
3) Customers shipping items through high-risk jurisdictions, including transit through non-cooperative countries.
4) Customers involved in potentially high-risk activities, including activities that may be subject to export/import restrictions (e.g., equipment for military or police organizations of foreign governments, weapons, ammunition, chemical mixtures, classified defense articles, sensitive technical data, nuclear materials, precious gems, or certain natural resources such as metals, ore, or crude oil).
5) Obvious over- or under-pricing of goods and services.
6) Obvious misrepresentation of quantity or type of goods imported or exported.
7) Transaction structure appears unnecessarily complex and designed to obscure the true nature of the transaction.
8) Customer directs payment of proceeds to an unrelated third party.
9) Shipment locations or description of goods not consistent with letter of credit.
10) Documentation showing a higher or lower value or cost of merchandise than that which was declared to customs or paid by the importer.
11) Significantly amended letters of credit without reasonable justification or changes to the beneficiary or location of payment. Any changes in the names of parties also should prompt additional OFAC review.

870 / REVIEW OF LAW AND ECONOMICS

Before conducting the complex price analysis of the letter of credit transaction, financial institutions should conduct character-based analysis to determine if further and more extensive analysis is warranted. According to the FFIEC, "Unless customer behavior or transaction documentation appears unusual, the bank should not be expected to spend undue time or effort reviewing all information." The analysis of trade data will provide filters to determine suspicious transactions that should be evaluated in more detail (Zdanowicz, 2007; Money Laundering Alert, 2008).

Character-based analysis requires a financial institution to evaluate the non-price characteristics about the financing transaction such as: the risk of the country of import or export, the risk of the product, the client's appearance on PEP lists, or the results of OFAC filtering. Many of the existing "Know Your Customer" policies can be applied to international trade financing activities. The FFIEC provides guidance to assess the appropriateness and comprehensiveness of a bank's customer due diligence (CDD) policies, procedures, and processes.

## 6.2. CHARACTER-BASED ANALYSIS - COUNTRY, PRODUCT AND CUSTOMS DISTRICT RISK PROFILES

The analysis of the U.S. trade database will assist financial institutions with identifying trade financing transactions that should be investigated in more detail. The analysis of the U.S. trade database may assist in evaluating six of the eleven red flags listed in the FFIEC Examination Manual (items 2, 3, 4, 5, 6 and 10 in the list above). Various risk profiles can be determined by evaluating recent U.S. international trade transactions such as:

> Country Risk Index: A risk profile of every country in the world, based on the most recent 12-month abnormal pricing history in the country's international trade.

> Product Risk Index: A risk profile of every product classification, based on the most recent 12-month abnormal pricing history of that product.

> U.S. Customs District Risk Index: A risk profile of every U.S. Customs District based on the most recent 12-month abnormal pricing history of transactions in the customs district.

Each risk index is based on the analysis of every U.S. import and export transaction, for all products, countries, and U.S. customs districts. The analysis is based on the Internal Revenue Service's 482 Transfer Pricing Regulations, which define the inter-quartile range as the arms-length pricing range in international trade. The risk indices can be updated every month as new U.S.

trade data is released to the public. The three character-based profiling risk indices discussed in this section are new statistical methodologies and will assist law enforcement and financial institutions with mitigating risk.

All three risk indices are determined by calculating the dollar amount of money moved out of the U.S. as a percentage of the total trade for a country, product or customs district. This may result in shares of trade that exceed 100%. For example, assume that the median export price for a product is $100 and that the lower price filter (lower quartile price) is $50. A reported export transaction for $10 would result in an estimated undervalued export transaction of $40. Thus, the percentage undervaluation for this transaction would be 400% ($40/$10 = 400%).

## 6.3. COUNTRY RISK INDEX

An analysis of the total dollar value of abnormal international trade pricing by country is detailed in the following table. This table contains a sample of the dollar amount of money moved out of the U.S. in 2004 through undervalued exports and overvalued imports for the top 25 countries (out of 218 countries) that trade with the U.S.. This analysis shows that the largest amount of money being moved out of the U.S. corresponds to the largest U.S. trading partners. This analysis may not be useful in identifying high-risk countries.

**TOTAL MONEY MOVED OUT OF U.S. BY COUNTRY DOLLAR VALUE**
**(THROUGH UNDER-VALUED EXPORTS AND OVER-VALUED IMPORTS)**
**Year: 2004**

| Obs | COUNTRY | UNDER-VALUED EXPORTS | OVER-VALUED IMPORTS | TOTAL MOVED OUT OF THE US | SHARE OF TRADE |
|---|---|---|---|---|---|
| 1 | CANADA | $11,039,683,286 | $7,256,738,049 | $18,296,421,335 | 4.12% |
| 2 | JAPAN | $8,151,814,635 | $5,974,212,167 | $14,126,026,802 | 7.68% |
| 3 | CHINA | $6,007,716,795 | $7,800,914,990 | $13,808,631,785 | 5.97% |
| 4 | MEXICO | $8,785,360,653 | $4,192,936,064 | $12,978,296,718 | 4.87% |
| 5 | FR GERM | $6,407,989,714 | $5,433,984,370 | $11,841,974,084 | 10.90% |
| 6 | U KING | $7,594,995,153 | $2,484,349,794 | $10,079,344,947 | 12.24% |
| 7 | KOR REP | $5,816,253,001 | $1,425,414,117 | $7,241,667,118 | 9.99% |
| 8 | FRANCE | $3,897,833,867 | $1,625,064,324 | $5,522,898,191 | 10.41% |
| 9 | TAIWAN | $3,094,430,949 | $1,698,479,949 | $4,792,910,898 | 8.51% |
| 10 | SINGAPR | $3,636,170,934 | $713,527,417 | $4,349,698,351 | 12.46% |
| 11 | PHIL R | $3,398,036,934 | $512,074,712 | $3,910,111,646 | 24.11% |
| 12 | MALAYSA | $2,317,172,101 | $1,201,554,685 | $3,518,726,786 | 9.00% |
| 13 | BELGIUM | $3,126,261,045 | $345,127,901 | $3,471,388,946 | 11.84% |
| 14 | IRELAND | $1,129,283,725 | $2,266,965,110 | $3,396,248,835 | 9.54% |
| 15 | HG KONG | $2,937,782,192 | $347,808,479 | $3,285,590,672 | 13.08% |

872 / REVIEW OF LAW AND ECONOMICS

| 16 | NETHLDS | $2,550,432,078 | $526,550,514 | $3,076,982,591 | 8.34% |
| 17 | ITALY | $1,536,748,889 | $1,489,132,352 | $3,025,881,241 | 7.80% |
| 18 | SWITZLD | $2,277,817,712 | $735,336,191 | $3,013,153,903 | 14.41% |
| 19 | BRAZIL | $2,376,524,681 | $555,731,959 | $2,932,256,640 | 8.37% |
| 20 | INDIA | $1,791,009,935 | $505,472,160 | $2,296,482,094 | 10.60% |
| 21 | AUSTRAL | $1,821,607,280 | $257,314,622 | $2,078,921,902 | 9.53% |
| 22 | THAILND | $1,181,887,099 | $729,875,756 | $1,911,762,854 | 7.99% |
| 23 | DENMARK | $1,451,172,673 | $432,241,119 | $1,883,413,791 | 31.26% |
| 24 | ISRAEL | $1,004,123,800 | $456,182,415 | $1,460,306,216 | 6.16% |
| 25 | SWEDEN | $775,593,211 | $469,080,673 | $1,244,673,884 | 7.80% |

However, the following table contains a sample (top 25 out of 218 countries) of the Country Risk Index for 2004 which measures the money moved from the U.S to all countries in the world as a percentage of their trade with the U.S. This type of character-based analysis will provide the bank with an indication that a more detailed analysis is warranted. An analysis of the Product Risk Index and the Customs District Risk Index will provide additional evidence regarding the risk of financing the transaction.

## COUNTRY RISK INDEX – 2004
### TOTAL MONEY MOVED OUT OF U.S. BY COUNTRY
### (THROUGH UNDER-VALUED EXPORTS AND OVER-VALUED IMPORTS)
### RANK ORDERED BY PERCENT OF TRADE

| Obs | COUNTRY | UNDER-VALUED EXPORTS | OVER-VALUED IMPORTS | TOTAL MOVED OUT OF THE US | SHARE OF TRADE |
|---|---|---|---|---|---|
| 1 | AZERBJN | $528,389,802 | $157,416 | $528,547,218 | 268.54% |
| 2 | YUGOSLV | $169,598,049 | $741,061 | $170,339,110 | 72.49% |
| 3 | IRAN | $152,952,617 | $12,628,410 | $165,581,027 | 70.03% |
| 4 | CUBA | $247,970,745 | . | $247,970,745 | 61.91% |
| 5 | KAZAKHS | $291,952,547 | $7,378,273 | $299,330,820 | 34.90% |
| 6 | BULGAR | $214,509,017 | $14,467,039 | $228,976,056 | 33.72% |
| 7 | ESTONIA | $156,854,211 | $9,510,139 | $166,364,350 | 31.52% |
| 8 | DENMARK | $1,451,172,673 | $432,241,119 | $1,883,413,791 | 31.26% |
| 9 | BARBADO | $99,437,204 | $820,250 | $100,257,454 | 26.08% |
| 10 | PHIL R | $3,398,036,934 | $512,074,712 | $3,910,111,646 | 24.11% |
| 11 | ANTIGUA | $31,027,519 | $1,270 | $31,028,789 | 23.94% |
| 12 | LIBERIA | $813,897 | $33,439,992 | $34,253,890 | 23.64% |
| 13 | B VIRGN | $24,263,203 | $13,856 | $24,277,059 | 21.11% |
| 14 | AFGHAN | $38,156,092 | $96,595 | $38,252,686 | 20.95% |
| 15 | ANDORRA | $2,416,758 | $21,034 | $2,437,792 | 19.44% |
| 16 | KENYA | $129,810,252 | $7,197,135 | $137,007,387 | 18.36% |
| 17 | POLAND | $429,068,286 | $52,566,628 | $481,634,914 | 17.47% |
| 18 | SLVENIA | $102,026,329 | $18,606,648 | $120,632,978 | 17.13% |

Trade-Based Money Laundering / 873

| 19 | CZECH | $350,028,716 | $62,282,789 | $412,311,505 | 15.96% |
| 20 | SWITZLD | $2,277,817,712 | $735,336,191 | $3,013,153,903 | 14.41% |
| 21 | HG KONG | $2,937,782,192 | $347,808,479 | $3,285,590,672 | 13.08% |
| 22 | ARAB EM | $639,817,694 | $22,463,911 | $662,281,605 | 12.72% |
| 23 | TURKEY | $889,053,935 | $163,868,214 | $1,052,922,150 | 12.69% |
| 24 | PORTUGL | $343,236,195 | $72,192,340 | $415,428,535 | 12.63% |
| 25 | BURKINA | $2,834,423 | $75 | $2,834,498 | 12.56% |

## 6.4. PRODUCT RISK INDEX

A similar analysis was conducted to determine a product risk index. First, the amount of money moved out of the U.S. by under-invoicing exports and over-invoicing imports for products defined by the six-digit harmonized codes were calculated. The Product Risk Index was calculated by finding and ranking the products that had the highest percentage of trade related to money moved out of the U.S. The following table is a sample of the Product Risk Index that ranks the products based on this metric. There are 4,758 six-digit product codes.

### PRODUCT RISK INDEX – 2006
### MONEY MOVED OUT OF THE UNITED STATES BY PRODUCT
### RANK ORDERED BY PERCENT OF TRADE

| Rank | Product | Money Moved Out of US $ | Percent of Trade |
|---|---|---|---|
| 1 | Cartridges for Riveting | 416,426,777 | 2,756.98% |
| 2 | Iodides and Iodides Oxides | 529,245,774 | 1,500.75% |
| 3 | Photo Plates and Film | 165,778,813 | 747.94% |
| 4 | Mechanisms for Music Boxes | 6,653,673 | 694.50% |
| 5 | Optical Fibers | 1,956,532,697 | 627.56% |
| 6 | Rare Earth Metals | 79,794,777 | 605.30% |
| 7 | Cadmium and Articles Thereof | 13,184,553 | 459.90% |
| 8 | Radioactive Elements & Isotopes | 1,617,767,386 | 416.36% |
| 9 | Recorded Media Sound or Image | 1,567,385,322 | 388.22% |
| 10 | Unrecorded Cards with Magnetic Stripe | 213,685,706 | 384.93% |
| 11 | Formic Acid | 59,890,154 | 377.94% |
| 12 | Dielectric Fixed Capacitors | 523,967,404 | 277.96% |
| 13 | Unsaturated Chlorine Derivatives | 62,813,577 | 257.24% |
| 14 | Fixed Resistors | 1,241,694,299 | 250.67% |
| 15 | Salt of Inorganic Acid | 86,570,802 | 226.22% |
| 16 | Pen Nibs and Nib Points | 73,429,037 | 197.32% |
| 17 | Phosphinates | 33,808,292 | 180.02% |
| 18 | Hydrids/Nitrids/Azids/Silicids | 312,245,013 | 174.33% |
| 19 | Electrical Insulators of Glass | 57,288,622 | 154.24% |
| 20 | Tubes, Pipes & Hoses with Fittings | 178,460,024 | 148.50% |

874 / REVIEW OF LAW AND ECONOMICS

## 6.5. CUSTOMS DISTRICT RISK INDEX

A similar analysis was conducted to determine the Customs District Risk Index. First, the amount of money moved out of the U.S. by under-invoicing exports and over-invoicing imports for each of the forty-five U.S. Customs Districts were calculated. The Customs District Risk Index was calculated by finding and ranking the customs districts that had the highest percentage of trade related to money moved out of the United States. The following table is a sample of the Customs District Risk Index that ranks the customs districts based on this metric.

### TOTAL MONEY MOVED OUT OF U.S. - CUSTOMS DISTRICT PERCENT OF TRADE (2006)
### (THROUGH UNDER-VALUED EXPORTS AND OVER-VALUED IMPORTS)

| Obs | CUSTOMS DIST | UNDER-VALUED EXPORTS | OVER-VALUED IMPORTS | TOTAL MOVED OUT OF THE US | SHARE OF TRADE |
|---|---|---|---|---|---|
| 1 | VESSELS | $10,440,522 | $62,203 | $10,502,725 | 12.65% |
| 2 | NORFOLK | $4,366,882,223 | $1,186,220,163 | $5,553,102,386 | 12.49% |
| 3 | WASH DC | $1,135,910,310 | $237,210,543 | $1,373,120,853 | 10.98% |
| 4 | CLEVLND | $3,723,789,413 | $3,774,890,944 | $7,498,680,356 | 9.67% |
| 5 | ALASKA | $1,981,926,506 | $500,164,352 | $2,482,090,858 | 9.35% |
| 6 | WILM NC | $489,857,335 | $1,224,482,864 | $1,714,340,199 | 9.20% |
| 7 | MIAMI | $5,457,244,652 | $1,172,529,595 | $6,629,774,247 | 9.20% |
| 8 | P RICO | $1,912,460,747 | $1,045,689,699 | $2,958,150,446 | 9.09% |
| 9 | SAVANNH | $4,555,773,333 | $2,808,081,132 | $7,363,854,466 | 8.93% |
| 10 | MINNPLS | $352,484,563 | $937,729,699 | $1,290,214,261 | 8.88% |
| 11 | DALLAS | $3,013,005,092 | $2,053,358,044 | $5,066,363,136 | 8.69% |
| 12 | CHICAGO | $4,694,399,341 | $5,557,520,573 | $10,251,919,914 | 8.50% |
| 13 | SAN FRN | $6,262,545,997 | $3,092,980,638 | $9,355,526,635 | 8.42% |
| 14 | BOSTON | $1,381,013,743 | $1,297,384,689 | $2,678,398,433 | 8.05% |
| 15 | LOS ANG | $18,087,424,830 | $5,272,017,132 | $23,359,441,961 | 7.09% |
| 16 | CHRLSTN | $1,914,536,435 | $1,557,621,260 | $3,472,157,695 | 7.05% |
| 17 | SAN DGO | $2,304,323,215 | $1,252,101,304 | $3,556,424,519 | 7.00% |
| 18 | NY CITY | $14,807,060,703 | $5,821,751,035 | $20,628,811,738 | 6.99% |
| 19 | NOGALES | $821,952,582 | $848,289,515 | $1,670,242,097 | 6.79% |
| 20 | ST LOUI | $89,475,979 | $715,287,030 | $804,763,008 | 6.72% |

## 6.6. INTERNATIONAL PRICE PROFILING SYSTEM – IPPS

The FFIEC BSA/AML Examination Manual stipulates that financial institutions engaged in trade financing conduct both character-based and transaction-based analysis. Transaction-based analysis is the evaluation of import or export prices to determine "obvious over- or under-pricing of goods and services." The analysis of the U.S. Merchandise Trade Data Base can produce statistical price filters to assist financial institutions with detecting abnormally priced products. This analysis is defined as the International Price Profiling System.

The "International Price Profiling System" (IPPS) is a new risk-based analysis system that evaluates the risk characteristics of prices related to international trade transactions. The details about this methodology have not been published in the academic literature. The IPPS may be employed to evaluate transactions that have a risk of being related to money laundering, terrorist financing, income tax evasion, and import duty fraud. This new International Price Profiling System is currently being used by some financial institutions as a means of mitigating trade financing risk. It has also been reported that some European countries are evaluating their international trade transactions with similar methodologies.

Money is moved across borders through false invoicing of import or export transactions. Money is moved out of a country by under-invoicing exports or over-invoicing imports. Money is moved into a country by over-invoicing exports or under-invoicing imports.

The IPPS evaluates an international trade price based on four (4) different filters.

| | |
|---|---|
| World | 5th and 95th Percentile |
| Country | 5th and 95th Percentile |
| World | Mean (-) and (+) 2 Standard Deviations |
| Country | Mean (-) and (+) 2 Standard Deviations |

The statistical filters are calculated from twelve months of international trade transaction data as reported by the U.S. Department of Commerce.

The IPPS analysis evaluates an international trade price and produces a "Risk Index" that may range between "-4" and "+4". A negative "Risk Index" reflects the potential of money being moved out of the United States to a foreign country. A positive "Risk Index" reflects the potential of money being moved into the United States from a foreign country. The magnitude of the "Risk Index" reflects the probability or likelihood that a price is over-valued or under-valued, and is determined in the following manner.

| Risk Index | Analysis | Interpretation of Price Abnormality |
|---|---|---|
| -4 | Violates 4 Filter Prices | $ Moved Out - Very Extreme Indication |
| -3 | Violates 3 Filter Prices | $ Moved Out - Extreme Indication |
| -2 | Violates 2 Filter Prices | $ Moved Out - Moderate Indication |
| -1 | Violates 1 Filter Price | $ Moved Out - Slight Indication |
| 0 | Violates 0 Filter Prices | No Risk of $ Moved Out or In |
| +1 | Violates 1 Filter Price | $ Moved In - Slight Indication |
| +2 | Violates 2 Filter Prices | $ Moved In - Moderate Indication |
| +3 | Violates 3 Filter Prices | $ Moved In - Extreme Indication |
| +4 | Violates 4 Filter Prices | $ Moved In - Very Extreme Indication |

The International Price Profiling System is based on statistical analysis and indicates suspicious prices in international trade. It does not prove that the suspicious transactions are related to money laundering, terrorist financing, or other illegal activities. There is some probability that the IPPS will generate false positives. It is the responsibility of the governmental agencies or financial institutions to conduct further investigations as to the nature of the suspicious transactions. The investigations can only lead to three mutually exclusive outcomes: (1) the suspicious price is "right" – i.e., there may be some unique characteristic that is reflected in the price; (2) the suspicious price is "wrong" – for example, it may be due to a clerical error; or (3) the suspicious price is "abnormal" and indicates a criminal activity. The IPPS is meant to be a dynamic analytical tool. Institutions should modify the price filters based on the outcomes of using the system. Some products may require wider or narrower price filters. This can only be determined by evaluating the results of the price profiling.

The following presentation demonstrates the application of the IPPS.

### 6.6.1. EXPORT OF TOMATO KETCHUP TO KUWAIT

The following is an example of the International Price Profiling System for the export of tomato ketchup to Kuwait at a price of $.14 per kilogram. This price is below the lower bounds as calculated by all four of the risk measures. Therefore it indicates a risk index of -4.

| **WORLD** | | | **KUWAIT** | |
|---|---|---|---|---|
| Transactions: | 2,378 | | Transactions: | 26 |
| | | | | |
| 95th Percentile: | $ 1.28 | | 95th Percentile: | $ 2.53 |
| MEDIAN: | $ 0.81 | | MEDIAN: | $ 0.58 |
| 5th Percentile: | $ 0.55 | | 5th Percentile: | $ 0.51 |
| | | | | |
| Mean + 2SD: | $ 2.20 | | Mean + 2SD: | $ 3.55 |
| MEAN: | $ 0.81 | | MEAN: | $ 0.76 |
| Mean – 2SD: | $ 0.30 | | Mean – 2SD: | $ 0.16 |
| | | Risk Index = - 4 | | |

### 6.6.2. IMPORT OF SOCCER BALLS FROM PAKISTAN

The following is an example of the International Price Profiling System for the import of soccer balls from Pakistan at a price of $30.00 per unit. This price is above the upper bounds as calculated by all four of the risk measures. Therefore it indicates a risk index of -4.

Trade-Based Money Laundering / 877

| WORLD | | | PAKISTAN | |
|---|---|---|---|---|
| Transactions: | 3,014 | | Transactions: | 966 |
| | | | | |
| 95th Percentile: | $ 7.14 | | 95th Percentile: | $ 7.02 |
| MEDIAN: | $ 2.79 | | MEDIAN: | $ 3.54 |
| 5th Percentile: | $ 1.35 | | 5th Percentile: | $ 2.19 |
| | | | | |
| Mean + 2SD: | $ 27.40 | | Mean + 2SD: | $ 20.61 |
| MEAN: | $ 2.96 | | MEAN: | $ 3.73 |
| Mean – 2SD: | $ 0.32 | | Mean – 2SD: | $ 0.67 |
| | | Risk Index = - 4 | | |

# 7. CONCLUSION

This paper provides new information that will contribute to the attempt to minimize trade-based money laundering and terrorist financing. It provides an analysis of previously unused statistical techniques and methodologies as a means of monitoring, detecting and prosecuting criminal money laundering and terrorist financing activities through international trade. The paper describes how new statistical profiling methodologies that evaluate transactions contained in a country's international trade database can mitigate the risks associated with trade-based money laundering. This paper discusses the application of four new money laundering profiling techniques which focus on country risk profiles, customs district risk profiles, product risk profiles, and transaction price risk characteristics. The practice of profiling as a means of detecting suspicious individuals and activities is controversial and frowned on by many. However, the statistical analysis of information and statistical profiling is crucial in the fight against money laundering and the financing of terrorist activities.

The analysis of the U.S. Merchandise Trade Data Base (and other country's trade databases) provides a vast amount of information to assist financial institutions, law enforcement and governmental agencies to detect and minimize trade-based money laundering. The inclusion of other countries databases would make the analysis even more robust. The events of September 11, 2001 have made the analysis of trade-based terrorist financing even more compelling

# References

Bhagwati, J.N. 1964. "On the Underinvoicing of Imports," 26 *Bulletin of the Oxford University Institute of Economics and Statistics* 389-97.

Coleman, Rachael. 2006. "U.S. and Brazilian Stings Nab Trade-Based Laundering Ring," *Money Laundering Alert*, August 2006.

Cuddington, J.T. 1987. "Capital Flight," 31 *European Economic Review* 382-388.

878 / REVIEW OF LAW AND ECONOMICS

De Boyrie, Maria, Simon Pak, and John Zdanowicz. 2005a. "The Impact of Switzerland's Money Laundering Law on Capital Flows through Abnormal Pricing in International Trade," 15 *Applied Financial Economics* 217-230.

_____, _____, and _____. 2005b. "Estimating the Magnitude of Capital Flight due to Abnormal Pricing in International Trade: The Russia-USA Case," 29 *Accounting Forum* 1-22.

De Wulf, L. 1981. "Statistical Analysis of Under-and Overinvoicing of Imports," 8 *Journal of Development Economics* 1981.

Federal Financial Institutions Examination Council. 2007. "Bank Secrecy Act Anti-Money Laundering Examination Manual," August 24, 2007.

Financial Action Task Force. 2006. "Trade Based Money Laundering," June 23, 2006, available at www.fatf-gafi.org .

Freer, J. 2001. "Honey Trade Launders Al Qaeda Cash," *South Florida Business Journal*, October 26, 2001.

Gulati, S.K. 1987. "A Note On Trade Misinvoicing," Institute of International Economics, October, 1987.

International Trade Alert. 2005. "International Trade Pricing Analysis – 2004: Money Moved Out of U.S. and Into the U.S.," International Trade Alert Working Paper available at www.internationaltradealert.com, June 2005.

Money Laundering Alert. 1992. "Exports, Imports Cover Flight of U.S. Drug Proceeds," January, 1992.

_____. 2008. "Mitigating Trade-Based Money Laundering Risk," March 2008.

Pak, Simon, and John Zdanowicz. 1994. "U.S. Trade with the World: An Estimate of 1993 Lost U.S. Federal Income Tax Revenues Due to Over-Invoiced Imports and Under-Invoiced Exports," Trade Research Institute Working Paper #9404-01, available at john.zdanowicz@fiu.edu , April 1, 1994.

Pak, Simon, Stelios Zanakis, and John Zdanowicz. 2003. "Detecting Abnormal Pricing in International Trade: The Greece-USA Case," 33(2) *Interfaces* 54-64.

Zdanowicz, John. 2003. "Movie Inspires New Research Into Suspicious Import Weights," *Money Laundering Alert*, May 2003.

_____. 2004a. "Who's Watching Our Back Door?," 1(1) *Business Accents Magazine*, Florida International University, Fall 2004.

_____. 2004b. "Detecting Money Laundering and Terrorist Financing via Data Mining," 47(5) *Communications of the Association of Computing Machinery* 53-55.

_____. 2005. "Trade-Based Terrorist Financing Analysis: Suspicious Trade with Al Qaeda Countries," International Trade Alert Working Paper, available at www.internationaltradealert.com, June 16, 2005.

_____. 2007. "Mitigate Trade Financing Risks with Proper Documentation, Analysis," *Money Laundering Alert*, April 2007.

_____. 2008. "Trade Finance: Mitigating Trade-Based Money Laundering Risks," *Money Laundering Alert*, March 2008.

_____, Simon Pak, and Michael Sullivan. 1999. "Brazil-United States Trade: Capital Flight Through Abnormal Pricing," 13(4) *International Trade Journal* 423-443.

# [9]

# Demystifying Hawala: A Look into its Social Organization and Mechanics[1]

NIKOS PASSAS

Northeastern University, Boston, USA

## Abstract

This paper sheds light on the routine practices and mechanics of hawala, an informal funds transfer system, which emerged in the Indian subcontinent and spread globally in recent decades. Hawala has come under suspicion of being a tool in the hands of al Qaeda and other terrorists, so a series of measures and policies have been taken internationally for its regulation and control. The paper dispels several myths about hawala, such as the lack of money movement or the absence of paperwork and trails for investigators. By focusing on the Pakistan hawala modus operandi, it also explains the routes money follows before it reaches the final destination mostly in the hands of expatriates' extended families. By showing how these mechanics make economic sense, the paper makes a contribution to more sensitive, informed, fair and consensual law enforcement.

KEY WORDS: Crime control, Economic development Hawala, Migrant remittances, Regulation, Terrorism

## Introduction

Since the late 1980s and especially during the 1990s, official concern grew about so-called 'underground banking' and its abuse by serious offenders. Media, internet postings and government reports made reference to threats posed by unregulated and informal networks that allow value transfers without leaving tracks for investigators. Some academic works echoed this concern and contributed to a conventional wisdom about what these 'underground banks' are, how they operate and what risks they represent at the domestic and international levels (Savona 1997;

Williams 1997). The first systematic study of existing, but scattered, evidence concluded that conventional wisdom about this phenomenon was shaped largely by errors and baseless or misleading statements reprinted over and over again ('facts by repetition'). The study pointed out that the terms used to describe this phenomenon were wrong, many legitimate interests were served, criminal abuse had been exaggerated and further research was necessary before any measures were taken (Passas 1999; 2000).

Western policies adopted an attitude of benign neglect about informal fund and value transfers, consistent with the freedom of movement for capital and goods. Policies in many developing countries, however, sought to control such movements and limit capital flight, tax evasion, customs frauds and violations of currency controls.

[1] Research on which this paper is based was sponsored by a National Institute of Justice (NIJ) grant for a study of 'Terrorist Finance and the Nexus with Transnational Organized Crime' (grant no. 2003-DT-CX-0001), a grant by the NIJ to look into informal value transfer systems (IVTS) (grant number 2002-IJ-CX-0001), as well as studies sponsored by the World Bank and the Dutch Ministry of Justice's Research and Documentation Centre (WODC).

Desires to control informal value transfers converged after the 9/11 attacks in the US, for fear that al Qaeda and similar groups may be channelling their funds around the globe through hawala networks. This led to a series of hurried reactions from the Financial Action Task Force (FATF), which added a special recommendation on what it calls 'alternative remittance systems', to the US Patriot Act, which assumes that Western regulatory paradigms and frameworks can apply just as well to informal ethnic networks. Even though it has become more widely accepted that the overwhelming majority of beneficiaries from these informal networks are remitting honestly earned money, much of what is accepted as true and taken for granted is still inaccurate or false (Passas (In press)).

As financial controls of terrorism became a high-priority policy issue, it became clear that a wide range of formal and informal fundraising and transfer channels can be used; yet, some of them are still neglected and unappreciated (Passas 2003a). Further, there are still substantial difficulties in flagging transactions, relationships and associations without serious disruption to normal trade and life. Some persons subject to law enforcement action in the aftermath of 9/11 have been released or removed from terrorism lists for lack of evidence. This is particularly problematic not only because of human rights and due process issues, but also because the 'collateral damage' produced by such actions includes the draining of political capital (necessary for international cooperation) and the rise of anti-US and anti-West sentiment in communities and regions needed in a coalition against terrorism.

To the extent that the targeting of financial activities or funds is inaccurate, such collateral damage is unnecessary, costly and counter-productive (Passas 2003a; 2003b; 2005; 2006; (In press); Passas and Jones 2006). Analyses from other bodies, such as the IMF and the World Bank, have come to the same conclusions and point out that ill-conceived policies are likely to cause economic costs and other collateral damage to developing countries and their citizens (el Qorchi et al. 2003; Genesis 2004; Maimbo et al. 2005; Maimbo and Passas 2004). At the same time, we do know that certain offences are also facilitated or conducted through the same networks (Carroll 1995; Financial Action Task Force 1999; Kapoor 1998; Passas 2003a; 2004a; 2004b; 2004c). Policymakers cannot ignore this aspect either.

It is vital, therefore, that we establish facts and separate them from myths and exaggerations, which make for measures and policies with negative effects. This paper seeks to contribute in this direction by outlining the main mechanics and social organization of South Asian hawala networks, often described as 'paperless' operations that leave no trails and facilitate serious financial crime and militant support.

**Method and Sources**

The research for this paper relied 1) on site visits and extensive interviews with scholars, lawyers, hawala clients and operators, officials in international organizations, regulators and law enforcers in 25 countries from all continents; 2) a critical review of legal and scholarly literature, media and government reports, and 3) dozens of cases from around the world, but mainly from the USA, UK, the Netherlands, the Middle East, Africa and South Asia. This diversity of sources and the range of primary and secondary data proved to be instrumental to gaining distance from any single perspective and views.

### Defining the Terms

The terms 'underground banking' and 'alternative remittance services' are unfortunately still used in many policy- and law-making settings. The first term is a baseless description. Banking (deposit-taking, lending, etc.) is rarely, if ever, involved in these transactions, which have been taking place quite openly in several countries. The term 'alternative' is also ill-chosen, as it obscures the fact that hawala and similar informal networks are the conventional or sole option available for legitimate transfers in many parts of the global South, where informal remitters and financiers (with a variety of names but quite similar mechanics) have been operating for a long time, before contemporary bank services, which remain inaccessible to millions of people in many countries. In Afghanistan or Somalia, for instance, hawala is the best functioning 'institution' which has been used even by aid organizations active there (Maimbo 2003; Passas 2003a). In addition, very often it is value rather than money that is transferred from place to place.

In order to avoid misleading and ethnocentric descriptions, the term informal value transfer systems (IVTS) was introduced (Passas 1999) and later refined to refer to 'mechanisms or networks of people facilitating the transfer of funds or value without leaving a trail of entire transactions or taking place outside the traditionally regulated financial channels' (Passas 2003a). A distinction between two types of IVTS has also been drawn. At one end there are informal funds transfer systems (IFTS) (see Maimbo 2003; el Qorchi et al. 2003), and at the other extreme are pure transfers of value. In between, there is a continuum of combinations that may be referred to as informal value transfer methods (IVTM) (see details in Passas 2003a).

IFTS have the following characteristics: they constitute traditional ethnic fund and value transfer operations and businesses; they have originated on the Indian subcontinent and in China, but have spread following waves of immigration and economic globalization; they are currently subject to regulations designed for so-called 'money services businesses'; and their clients and services are for the most part well established, known to their respective local community. Examples of IFTS are hawala (India), hundi (Bangladesh), fei chien (China), phoe kuan (Thailand), padala (Philippines) and other similar services (including couriers). The underlying feature is that the transfer is originated, transferred and delivered as a financial asset.

IVTM, in contrast, involve small groups or networks, which employ methods of transferring both money and value informally but mostly illegally; they share the following main features:

- They do not require the existence of wide-spread networks of people; most of them can be accomplished by a

48

couple of individuals on either an ad hoc or regular basis (hence the use of the term 'method' as opposed to 'system' or 'network').

- They involve the use of the formal financial system, but they leave no trail for anyone wishing to monitor or reconstruct the route of a transaction intended to remain secret.
- They are very often part of legitimate or legitimate-looking trade transactions, which effectively obfuscate substantial value transfers.
- They are always criminal and usually combine with other offences (e.g. tax evasion, subsidy fraud, embargo busting, capital flight, funding of militant groups, smuggling).
- They have the capacity to transfer very substantial amounts of money (much higher amounts than IFTS). So, not only terrorist financiers but, even more crucially, weapons proliferators (requiring significant amounts transferred) could potentially make use of IVTMs.

Examples of IVTM include the following: in-kind payments/transfers; use of on-line gifts services; invoice manipulation; trade diversion; stored value; illicit use of credit/debit cards, correspondent accounts, brokerage accounts, options/futures trading or electronic payments.

The distinction between IFTS and IVTM is analytical but also serves as an indicator of legitimate as opposed to suspicious activities. It highlights the large variety of channels that can be used for the transfer of value without leaving clear traces. Serious misconduct may be perpetrated or facilitated by these channels, many of which involve regulated sectors or institutions. The combination of a number of these transfer methods and the fact that illicit value transfers may be hidden behind apparently legitimate and ordinary transactions should raise regulatory concerns. This distinction also draws attention to possible unintended effects of ill-considered attempts to regulate IFTS (e.g. a displacement from IFTS to much less traceable and understood IVTM).

This paper focuses on one type of IFTS, hawala, with particular emphasis on Pakistani networks.

### The Mechanics of Hawala

Hawala originated in South Asia possibly many centuries ago and means 'reference' in Hindu (i.e. you provide a reference and receive funds or credit in exchange). The Arabic root h-w-l means transfer. Hawaladar is a hawala dealer or operator. Hawala and similar informal value transfer systems operate in many ethnic communities, such as South Asian, South-east Asian, Chinese, African, South American and Middle Eastern. Even though the particular name changes from region to region (hawala, hundi, BMPE, padala, door-to-door, etc.), the main modus operandi and operational characteristics remain essentially the same. At a minimum, there is a remitter, a recipient and two hawala operators, one in each country. As we will see, things can get a great deal more complex with agents and multiple intermediaries in the settlement process.

Hawala started within extended families or villages as a way of settling accounts among friends or relatives (i.e.

'I owe you 100 rupees; you owe my father 100 rupees; I will settle my debt to you by paying my father 100 rupees'). It resembled a bartering method, whereby payments could be made in kind. As people sought a secure system through which traders could transfer money and travellers could protect themselves from thieves and highwaymen, hawala gradually went national. The immigration waves of the 20th and 21st centuries contributed to the infrastructure of the contemporary global, reliable and efficient value transfer system.

Two main aspects can be distinguished in the hawala business: 1) the sending and receiving of money (i.e. relationships between a hawala operator (hawaladar) and his or her clients), and 2) the settlement process (i.e. relationships among intermediaries). The first aspect is relatively simple and straight forward, while the settlement process can get very complex. This paper will address them in turn and will focus on the ways in which Pakistani networks functioned in the period of the late 1990s to 2002.

The individual remitter may know from word of mouth or through advertisements in the ethnic press about hawala operators and contacts them to find out what exchange rate they offer for specific countries or regions. The rate is typically much better than what banks offer and includes the cost of delivery overseas (see concrete examples in Passas (In press)).

The hawaladar would receive the cash and make a note in a book or ledger. Hawaladars usually keep information on their clients' names, as well

as the amount to be transferred, the name, address and telephone numbers of the beneficiary overseas. These records are maintained (in hard copy, on computers, or both) at least until accounts are settled, but often are kept for several years (at least in labour-importing countries).

At the end of each business day, the hawaladar organizes the information on outgoing money transfer requests by location and sends a fax (sometimes an email or telephone call) with the payment instructions to a counterpart for delivery. Payment instructions usually include the list of recipient names, addresses, telephone numbers, amounts and a reference number for each payee (see Fig 1).

The delivery of remittances takes place commonly within 24 hours, even though it is possible for payments to be made within minutes. In remote areas, it may take up to two days.

The delivery of funds may be made to the doorstep of beneficiaries or at the South Asian hawaladar's premises (see Fig 2).

In the case of Pakistan, for example, payment instructions may be sent to counterparts in various locations (e.g. Islamabad, Peshawar, Lahore, Mirpur, etc.) or in Karachi, from where arrangements are made for delivery throughout the country. Karachi is the centre of Pakistan hawala for settlement purposes (see below), but currency exchange companies there may also undertake to arrange for delivery of funds—the big Karachi companies have their own networks of agents and sub-agents through whom deliveries can be arranged. This delivery service may incur a charge of

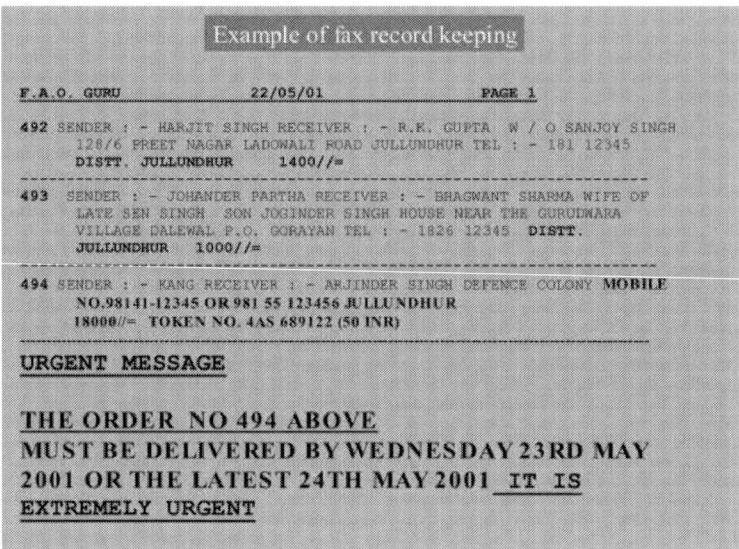

**Figure 1.** *Example of fax record-keeping. Source: A case of South Asian hawala—names and numbers have been altered.*

about 2 rupees per 1,000, while the smaller local companies often charge less (only 1 rupee per 1,000).

Because a hawaladar will wish to send funds to multiple locations, he may send more than one set of payment

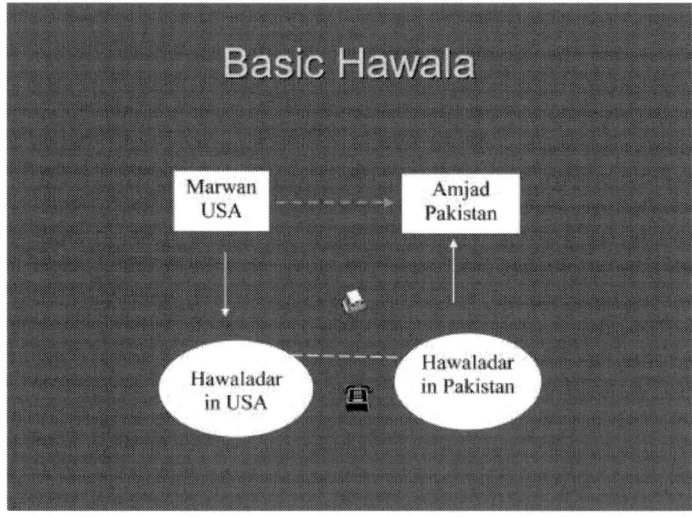

**Figure 2.**

instructions to several Pakistani (and other) counterparts.

If the remitters' (clients') funds are sent to the hawaladar by wire or check, the transfer would be executed (payment instructions would be sent) when the account is credited (this may also depend on special arrangements, amount to be sent, knowledge of customer, etc.).

Hawaladars are rarely engaged in hawala exclusively. A hawaladar may be a small business owner without the facility to arrange for overseas delivery of funds. In such cases, this person would simply act as an agent of a larger hawaladar in the same country (e.g. USA or UK) to whom he sends the funds he collects on behalf of his retail customers and the payment instructions. Large hawaladars collect funds from multiple agents and locations, pool them together and arrange for delivery.

Hawala agents and sub-agents would make a profit by offering a lower exchange rate to their clients than what is offered to themselves by the larger hawaladar. For example, if a larger hawaladar offers to deliver 62 Pakistani rupees per dollar, the agent may decide to offer his own clients 61 rupees per dollar.

Telephone or email communications between the US hawaladars would reflect the bargaining and deals made on a regular basis. As funds are pooled together by large hawaladars, payments are made fast, cheaply and conveniently in places where banking services are unavailable, expensive or unreliable. Most of the time, recipients receive cash in Pakistan, but occasionally they may receive a check or credit in their bank

account, if so desired. Trust, a defining element of hawala, makes the system extremely efficient. There are very few instances in which retail clients lost their money.

Typically, no fee is charged to retail customers or agents for the money transfer. The large hawaladars' profit (or loss) depends on what deal they have made with their overseas counterparts to whom they sell the dollars. This can be better appreciated through a brief examination of the settlement process.

Each time a hawaladar sends payment instructions to a counterpart, he creates a debt. The closer are relationships among hawaladars, the easier becomes the settlement process. Kinship and family ties made hawala work smoothly at first. In the contemporary global economy, and given the substantial amounts that are moving about, hawaladars also rely on people beyond kinship or ethnic ties.

For hawala to operate optimally, there must be pools of cash or funds on both ends of transactions. This is how each hawaladar will make payments for the other's clients and will minimize the need to move money. So, there is one cash pool in labour-importing countries like the USA on one side (pool A) and another cash pool in remittance-receiving countries, such as Pakistan on the other (pool B) (see Fig 3).

If cash pools A and B were equal, settling up would be done simply through reciprocal payments (e.g. 'you pay on behalf of my customers and I pay on behalf of yours—you keep your rupees and I keep my dollars'). This

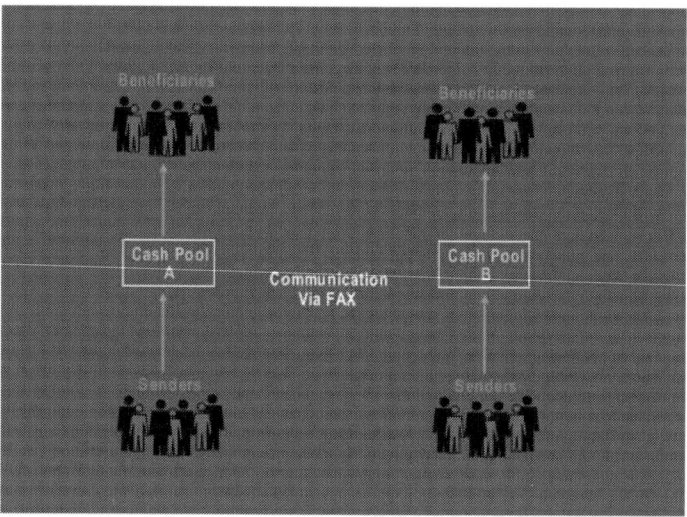

**Figure 3.**

happens to some extent, as immigrants in the USA would send remittances to their families, while traders in Pakistan would need to pay in dollars for goods they import.

Yet, these pools and money flows are always asymmetrical. Very often, each hawaladar sends payment instructions and money to several places around the world at once.

Geo-political and other events can affect these cash flows and pools too. Whenever there is an economic or political crisis in Pakistan or India, for instance, cash pool B will grow a great deal, as many people would want to get their savings out of the country. At the same time, cash pool A is likely to shrink (fewer people would wish to send funds as long as the crisis lasts). Other events can have a significant impact on these pools.

The scandal around the Bank of Credit and Commerce International

(BCCI) in 1991, for example, has had a major impact on thousands of South Asian families, especially Pakistanis (see Kerry Report 1992; Passas 1995; 1996; Truell and Gurwin 1992). In the aftermath of BCCI's closure, they were left without the vital services BCCI used to provide. As a consequence, the hawala pool in the UK grew substantially.

The nuclear test in 1998 was another watershed event that caused a liquidity crisis in Pakistan and drove higher the demand of US dollars by the government.

In certain instances, some inflows may increase, as local currencies depreciate significantly and expatriates see an opportunity to receive a higher amount of that currency against the US dollar and may also wish to help their families at a time of need. In such cases, legitimate remittance flows towards areas in crisis may grow.

Customers in the remittance-receiving countries most often demand US dollars or other strong currencies, as they seek to pay for international trade transactions. The central banks in South Asia are also keen on receiving US dollars, as this is the currency in which external debt is denominated and they wish to routinely replenish their US dollar reserves. As a result, the US dollar has been the dominant currency in which hawala operators balance their accounts.

For these reasons, the settlement process usually goes through accounts held by hawaladars or money exchange companies in key money centres, such as New York or Dubai (see Fig 4). Settlement may also take place through payments to third parties around the world. In such instances, a personal or company account in Hong Kong, Singapore or other places receiving funds from the US would be settling

the debt of a trader in Pakistan to a partner.

Settlement in some instances may involve even more complex transactions (e.g. correspondent bank accounts, in-kind payments, etc.).

The volume of immigrant remittances to Pakistan is in the billions of dollars per annum (it was at least 4 billion US dollars in 2003; see Maimbo et al. 2005), so a substantial inflow of funds is to be expected. This means that Pakistani hawaladars would need rupees to replenish their cash pool and to be able to make quick deliveries when payment instructions are faxed. The direct way of doing this would be for West-based hawaladars to wire their dollars to Pakistan. This does not happen, however, due to the specificities of the Pakistani foreign exchange market. Instead, rupees are made available to local hawaladars through big exchange companies operating with the State Bank

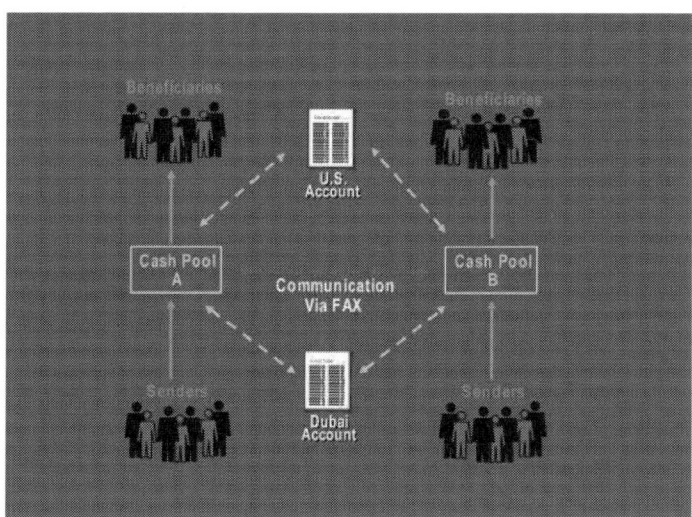

**Figure 4.**

of Pakistan and in collaboration with United Arab Emirates (UAE) intermediaries.

Historically, the Pakistani foreign exchange business has been shaped by controls and restrictions. It has not been possible to buy rupees outside Pakistan, while it is not allowed to convert rupees into foreign currency inside Pakistan, apart from authorized currency dealers. Local exchange companies can sell rupees to tourists and visiting expatriates, but they have to convert these currencies into rupees. In order to do this, they take these currencies out of the country, convert them into dollars and sell the dollars to the central bank.

The United Arab Emirates is the key place to do this due to its liberal financial regime, proximity and liquidity.

The whole currency exchange and hawala market routing changed in the aftermath of the nuclear bomb test in 1998 and the ensuing dollar shortage and liquidity crisis. Through special procedures and a formal application, the State Bank of Pakistan (SBP), the central bank of the country, allowed all currencies except dollars to be exported to the UAE, in order to be returned to the SBP as dollars.

The currencies would leave Karachi in sealed packages delivered to UAE exchange companies, such as World Link Exchange (which ceased business in 2002), Federal Exchange and Wall Street Exchange.

Pakistani currency dealers could either export their cash on their own or use the service of big Karachi companies. The Pakistani currency exporter was then obliged to repatriate at least 80% of the

value in dollars to the SBP within three days. The SBP set up a special dollar account with the National Bank of Pakistan in Bahrein. So, the UAE exchange companies would convert currencies into dollars for Pakistani companies and transfer the dollars to this designated account in Bahrein. The SBP would then make rupees available to the currency exporter, whose profit would depend on the rates at which he sold rupees for various currencies, bought dollars and then re-bought rupees.

In short, big Karachi companies would gather all foreign currency from their agents and other companies around the country, transport it to the UAE, convert it into dollars and transfer the dollars to the SBP for rupees to be distributed throughout the country. Karachi dealers would thus have accounts with the UAE companies, which in turn did most (if not all) of their settlement through their dollar correspondent accounts in New York.

One common misconception, which was echoed also in my own earliest IVTS study, was that a distinguishing feature of hawala is the transfer of funds without movement (Passas 1999; Jost and Sandhu 2000). In fact, this is a feature similar to formal fund transfers—Western banks or remittance companies do not physically transfer funds either. As with formal institutions, there are accounting entries and debts that need to be balanced. At the same time, however, there is a significant volume of wire and other transfers that do cross borders and most typically pass through the USA.

Although retail customers and many observers see the money transfer part of hawala, the core of the business is currency trading. Money transfer and currency deals are fused completely in the settlement process. That is, hawaladars essentially buy and sell different currencies. US-based operators sell dollars to Pakistani counterparts for rupees. Each operator tries to make a profit by buying a currency at a lower rate than what he sells it for. The cost of distribution to Pakistani residents/beneficiaries is either incorporated in the exchange rate agreed between US and Pakistan counterparts or a fee of about 1–2 rupees per 1,000 (see above).

As we have seen, some of the hawala business is redistribution in the same country. A US hawaladar, for example, may also receive payment instructions from Pakistan or other countries on behalf of traders who wish to pay for goods in the USA. In such cases, the US hawaladar may receive or pick up funds from his own customers and make a deposit or delivery in the US on behalf of the customers of his overseas partners. Such deliveries can be in cash, by check or deposit in a designated bank account.

The same would happen in Pakistan, as the importer's rupees will be used by the Pakistani hawaladar to deliver cash to the families of immigrant remitters.

Because of the larger dollar flows to Pakistan, however, more funds would accumulate in cash pool A; so the US hawaladar has excess dollars to sell and shops around South Asian buyers for the best rate. He may have certain favourite partners, but he may occasionally check with others, so telephone or email records would reflect this practice.

Dollars would thus typically get transferred to New York accounts held by UAE money exchange companies for further credit to the Karachi or other counterparts in Pakistan.

After that, the Pakistan-based buyers of dollars would make rupees available to a designated partner of the Western hawaladar, in order for the cash to be delivered to agents and individual beneficiaries throughout Pakistan.

In addition to the currency deals, there is also the wire transfer service to designated accounts, which could be around 0.4%–0.6% depending on bank charges at a given time period.

It is clear, thus, that Pakistani hawala networks are characterized by several levels or layers at both the sending and receiving end. At the lowest level, we find persons who act as couriers executing pick-up and delivery functions. They take no initiatives, act as they are told, and have no say in the exchange rate of the currencies involved.

At the next level, we commonly find small businesses willing to help community members by collecting their money and arranging for the delivery of funds to their beneficiaries in Pakistan.

Bigger hawaladars pool funds and coordinate delivery, while exchange companies play a key role in the settlement process that takes place in dollars sold to SBP or sent to other destinations at the request of Pakistani customers.

It is very important to emphasize that at each step of these exchanges and processes, meticulous records are kept by the various parties. Given the very large volumes that are traded through these networks, it is essential that everyone checks and confirms transactions in order to eliminate errors and resolve any disputes or questions that might arise.

Each service provider essentially profits to the extent he can buy currencies at a lower rate than he sells them. In order to determine the profit or loss of a West-based hawaladar, one has to compare the rate he has offered to his agents and retail clients with the rate he has arranged with the Pakistani counterpart/partner.

The hawala profit comes from the difference between official and unofficial currency exchange rates, or the difference between bid and ask prices for a given currency. When such differences are large, the margin widens for hawaladars who can make a good profit while offering to their customers far better rates than the bank.

In general, hawaladars try to make a profit through:

- Exchange rate differences
- Selling or 'renting' (lending) cash
- Commissions/fees
- Financing of legal or criminal trade
- Gaining of clientele for other goods and services (hawala is a loss leader)

Apart from a few instances in which expatriates offer free services to their compatriots (see Australian-African case in Passas 1999), the main aim of engaging in hawala is to make profit. This could be done indirectly. That is, by offering money transfer services for free in order to attract clients to the main business, such as a travel agency or retail store. The most common and direct way of making profit, however, is by arbitrage: exploiting the difference between the exchange rate agreed with the customer and the rate obtained in the black or other markets around the world. Table I shows the discrepancies over a 20-year period in several countries.

As can be seen, the incentive for hawala can be extraordinarily high. In those cases, the services to retail customers may be offered for free, given the substantial profits to be made in the exchange arbitrage.

Profit is typically generated in this fashion. In some cases, a commission is charged ranging from 0.25%–1.5% of the amount involved or this is roughly the margin hawaladars seek in order to protect themselves against currency price shifts between the time they agree on a rate with counterparts and the time of delivery. Hawaladars may also use their clients' cash in order to finance legal or criminal enterprises of their own or those of third parties. This would be another way of making profit. Whatever fee or commission is charged would depend largely on various factors, such as the destination, amount and urgency of the transfer. When the bid/ask price differential for currencies is wide, there is more room for a hawaladar to offer comparatively good rates to customers, who may prefer this method to a bank or official remitter for that reason alone.

The retail clientele consists primarily of ordinary people and expatriates, who wish to send remittances back home. In addition, traders, business people, companies, tourists, non-governmental organizations, or even government agencies occasionally make use of hawala. They all find it a convenient system. Sometimes, they may have no other alternative. Others prefer it due to its informality, occasional lack of records, anonymity and the difficulty authorities

Table I. *Black market exchange rate premiums, 1981–2000 (in percent of previous period official rate).*

| | 1981 | 1982 | 1983 | 1984 | 1985 | 1986 | 1987 | 1988 | 1989 | 1990 | 1991 | 1992 | 1993 | 1994 | 1995 | 1996 | 1997 | 1998 | 1999 |
|---|---|---|---|---|---|---|---|---|---|---|---|---|---|---|---|---|---|---|---|
| Algeria | 247 | 266 | 330 | 369 | 389 | 246 | 419 | 416 | 358 | 264 | 83 | 300 | 358 | 250 | 175 | 133 | 125 | 150 | 100 |
| Bangladesh | 41 | 41 | 42 | 45 | 130 | 218 | 211 | 272 | 210 | 199 | 136 | 67 | 40 | 30 | 19 | 19 | 11 | 0 | 0 |
| Ecuador | 29 | 96 | 64 | 91 | 85 | 0 | 31 | 38 | 16 | 23 | 19 | 10 | 6 | 5 | 4 | 2 | 5 | 11 | 0 |
| El Salvador | 84 | 34 | 98 | 100 | 204 | 82 | 100 | 195 | 85 | 36 | 12 | 12 | 18 | 15 | 15 | 10 | 10 | 11 | 0 |
| Guatemala | 22 | 25 | 70 | 24 | 45 | 15 | 33 | 28 | 9 | 22 | 14 | 4 | 5 | 4 | 4 | 2 | 2 | 0 | 0 |
| India | 9 | 13 | 28 | 16 | 17 | 8 | 13 | 14 | 12 | 15 | 18 | 4 | 5 | 5 | 6 | 6 | 3 | 2 | 2 |
| Indonesia | 4 | 1 | 0 | 2 | 0 | 11 | 16 | 16 | 3 | 1 | 4 | 26 | 9 | 7 | 5 | 0 | 6 | 11 | 5 |
| Iran | 403 | 379 | 320 | 562 | 557 | 977 | 1,576 | 1,030 | 1,965 | 1,965 | 3,252 | 3,360 | 88 | 100 | 150 | 193 | 186 | 150 | 400 |
| Pakistan | 41 | 25 | 30 | 11 | 0 | 1 | 19 | 10 | 0 | 6 | 9 | 8 | 8 | 8 | 6 | 6 | 11 | 25 | 20 |
| Philippines | 6 | 7 | 50 | 1 | 1 | 2 | 8 | 3 | 4 | 6 | 6 | 1 | 2 | 4 | 7 | 9 | 0 | 0 | 0 |
| Sri Lanka | 6 | 10 | 38 | 32 | 15 | 3 | 2 | 36 | 25 | 16 | 9 | 10 | 6 | 4 | 1 | 1 | 0 | 0 | 0 |
| Sudan | 3 | 57 | 54 | 102 | 43 | 122 | 85 | 270 | 344 | 915 | 52 | 95 | 78 | 50 | 25 | 10 | 0 | 11 | 5 |
| Tanzania | 193 | 205 | 301 | 287 | 281 | 248 | 139 | 100 | 35 | 50 | 59 | 36 | 9 | 8 | 6 | 10 | 7 | 11 | 5 |
| Turkey | 20 | 15 | 11 | 1 | 0 | 7 | 8 | 9 | 2 | 1 | 6 | 6 | 4 | 4 | 4 | 4 | 4 | 0 | 4 |
| Zimbabwe | 53 | 51 | 192 | 80 | 53 | 70 | 50 | 47 | 76 | 37 | 50 | 33 | 19 | 15 | 10 | 7 | 16 | 900 | 400 |

Source: el Qorchi et al. 2003
Certain missing values interpolated by the authors.

may have to trace the whole transaction. So, hawala does lend itself to criminal abuse. Criminals involved in drug trafficking, terrorism, tax evasion, capital flight, money laundering, human and commodities smuggling, illicit organ trade, and fraud have often found in hawala an attractive vehicle.

Understanding the layers of intermediaries in specific hawala networks is crucial for investigators searching for money trails and evidence that can stand up in court. Different types of records are kept by various participants in the network. Because the payment instructions go in one direction (where the final destination of the money is), whereas the funds follow a different path, putting the two together is indispensable to determine the commission of particular offences. As remitters hand their money to hawaladars in labour-importing countries, the records investigators are most likely to see are those noting the amount to be sent in local currency, the equivalent in US dollars (if not in the US), the rate for the currency to be delivered, the name of remitter (not always) and recipient, delivery location and date.

Separating the legitimate transactions from suspicious ones is essential and a set of guidelines has been produced for the benefit of both financial institutions' compliance officers and regulators or law enforcement officials (see Passas 2004c).

**Conclusion**

A growing body of work is now finding that terrorist financing, like other criminal activities, involves a mix of formal and informal methods and networks. Given the use of IVTS by legitimate and criminal actors, fully understanding its

workings will require better comprehension of transnational crimes and legal financial systems. Also, studying IVTS more in depth can contribute to a better understanding of transnational crimes. Updated indicators of IVTS abuse and some predictive model on terrorists' objectives and modus operandi would go a long way to support crime control efforts. In order to do this, a better understanding of the networks of terrorist finance, including the wider nexus with other criminal groups and legitimate organizations, is indispensable.

Extremely helpful would also be the establishment of a method enabling the connection or association of financial and trade transactions. It is possible and common in both cash-intensive and other societies to withdraw funds in cash and use them for the purchase of goods to be transferred or other transactions. Goods may then be shipped elsewhere and the proceeds of the sale transferred to another location. By shifting from financial to commercial transactions, the trail of the whole set of transactions is lost to investigators. At this point, no country makes this connection despite the availability of means to do so (Passas 2006). This is a point of vulnerability to which controllers should pay closer attention

At the same time, it is worth noting that all recent regulatory and law enforcement attention to hawala in particular has been based on the assumption that this is a favourite channel that al Qaeda extremists use to transfer their funds. This may be true in some countries, such as Afghanistan, where *everyone* uses hawala anyway. When it comes to Europe and North America, however, this is not the case. There is no evidence of hawala use by the 9/11 hijacking team. Despite very aggressive US law enforcement actions, there has been no case of terrorist finance through hawala at all—contrary to conventional wisdom to which officials and press releases have contributed, the Somali hawala (Barakat) investigation yielded no charges of terrorism (Passas (In press)). In Europe only one case of funds going to the northern part of Iraq to support the insurgency involved hawala transfers.

While it is true that the comparatively low amounts necessary for terrorist operations could potentially travel through hawala, it is doubtful that that controllers would be able to detect such flows, if hawala operators wish to protect the identity of senders and recipients. This suggests that more important is the ability to collaborate with hawaladars and the ethnic communities they serve. Cooperation is much more likely to occur when consensus or community policing earns the trust and confidence of immigrants and ethnic minorities in host countries. Over-reactions and unfair targeting of particular ethnic groups and their means of remitting needed funds to their families in the homeland cause unnecessary tensions and suffering, while they alienate the very groups who can assist most in counter-terrorism.

Thus, a balanced and evidence-based approach to hawala is not only consistent with fundamental human rights and due process, but also instrumental to more effective crime control and to the enhancement of national and international security.

The fear of the unknown in this field can be quite damaging. Too often practices and routines not well understood are treated with suspicion. In the post-9/11 context, we have seen how suspicions can be easily converted into injustice—for example, the Arar Commission Report 2006 makes very chilling and disturbing reading about government responsibilities and the treatment of an innocent Canadian citizen subject to rendition from the USA to Syria, where he spent 10 months before release without charges (see http://www.ararcommission.ca/eng/26.htm).

Many aspects of hawala and its settlement process, especially the reasons for which funds are wired to the USA or other jurisdictions rather than directly to countries of destination, have been a mystery to controllers and policymakers. It is small wonder that many responses do not serve justice, harmony, economic development or security. By outlining the basic mechanics of hawala, dismissing the myth of traceless or paperless transactions and explaining the rationale for seemingly odd fund itineraries, the hope is that this paper assists in reducing collateral damage and contributes to more sensitive, well informed, more consensual and effective law enforcement.

## References

Carroll S (1995). Anti-Money Laundering Laws and the Quasi-Banker: A Report on Alternative Banking in Australia. Sydney: AUSTRAC.

El Qorchi M, Maimbo SM, Wilson JF; International Monetary Fund (2003). Informal funds transfer systems: an analysis of the informal Hawala system. Washington, DC: International Monetary Fund.

Financial Action Task Force (**FATF**) (1999). 1998–1999 Report on Money Laundering Typologies. Paris: Financial Action Task Force, OECD.

Genesis (2004). Access to Financial Services in South Africa: A Brief Case Study of the Effect of the Implementation of the Financial Action Task Force Recommendations. Cape Town: Prepared for FinMark Trust and DFID.

Jost PM, Sandhu HS (2000). The hawala alternative remittance system and its role in money laundering. Lyon: Interpol General Secretariat.

Kapoor S (1998). Bad Money. Bad Politics: The Untold Hawala Story. South Asia Books.

Kerry Report (1992). The BCCI Affair. Washington, DC: GPO.

Maimbo SM (2003). The Money Exchange Dealers of Kabul. Washington, DC: The World Bank.

Maimbo S, Adams R, Aggarwal R, Passas N (2005). Migrant Labor Remittances in South Asia. Washington, DC: The World Bank.

Maimbo S, Passas N (2004). The Regulation and Supervision of Informal Remittance Systems. Small Enterprise Development 15(1):53–62.

Passas N (1995). The Mirror of Global Evils: A Review Essay on the BCCI Affair. Justice Quarterly 12(2):377–419.

Passas N (1996). The Genesis of the BCCI Scandal. Journal of Law and Society 23(1):52–72.

Passas N (1999). Informal Value Transfer Systems and Criminal Organizations: A Study into So-Called Underground Banking Networks. The Hague: Ministry of Justice, The Netherlands.

Passas N (2000). Facts and Myths About 'Underground Banking'. In: van Duyne PC,

Ruggiero V, Scheinost M, Valkenburg W (eds). Cross-Border Crime in a Changing Europe. 192–208. Tilburg/Prague: Tilburg University/Prague Institute of Criminology and Social Prevention.

Passas N (2003a). Informal Value Transfer Systems, Money Laundering and Terrorism. Washington, DC: Report to the National Institute of Justice (NIJ) and Financial Crimes Enforcement Network (FINCEN).

Passas N (2003b). Hawala and Other Informal Value Transfer Systems: How to Regulate Them? Journal of Risk Management 5(2):39–49.

Passas N (2004a). Informal Value Transfer Systems and Criminal Activities. The Hague: WODC. Ministry of Justice, The Netherlands.

Passas N (2004b). Law Enforcement Challenges in Hawala-related Investigations. Journal of Financial Crime 12(2):112–19.

Passas N (2004c). Indicators of Hawala Operations and Criminal Abuse. Journal of Money Laundering Control 8(2):168–72.

Passas N (2005). Ziele, Grenzen und Risiken der Finanzkontrolle von Terrororganisationen. [Goals, Limits and Risks of Financial Controls of Terrorism] In: Bundeskriminalamt. Netzwerke des Terrors—Netzwerke gegen den Terror. Wiesbaden: BKA (German Federal Police).

Passas N (2006). Setting Global CFT Standards: A Critique and Suggestions. Journal of Money Laundering Control 9(3):281–92.

Passas N (In press). Fighting Terror with Error: The Counter-productive Regulation of Informal Value Transfers. Crime, Law and Social Change.

Passas N, Jones K (2006). The Trade in Commodities and Terrorist Financing: Focus on Diamonds. European Journal of Criminal Policy and Research. Available at http://dx.doi.org/10.1007/s10610-006-9006-3.

Savona E (ed) (1997). Responding to Money Laundering—International Perspectives. Netherlands: Harwood Academic Publishers.

Truell P, Gurwin L (1992). False Profits. Boston and New York: Houghton Mifflin.

Williams P (1997). Money Laundering. The IASOC Magazine 10:1–16.

PROFESSOR DR NIKOS PASSAS
Northeastern University
Boston
USA
Email: n.passas@neu.edu

# [10]

# Financial crime, near crime, and chicanery in the wall street meltdown

Richard B. Freeman *

*Harvard University, Department of Economics, and National Bureau of Economic Research, 1050 Massachusetts Avenue, Cambridge, MA 02138, USA*

*Keywords:* Financial crime; Financial near crime; Financial chicanery; Wall street meltdown

## 1. Introduction

Following are important recent news items on the economics of financial crime:

*Fraud 'Directly Related' to Financial Crisis Probed: FBI Agents Could be Reassigned from National Security Due to Booming Caseload Feb 11, 2009 ABC NEWS* – "I don't think we've paid enough attention to the mortgage and financial fraud that have so dramatically contributed to the economic downturn ... unscrupulous mortgage brokers ... Wall Street financiers" Senate Judiciary Chairman Patrick Leahy. (http://abcnews.go.com/TheLaw/Economy/story?id=6855179&page=1)

*Obama Doesn't 'Begrudge' Bonuses for Blankfein, Dimon Feb. 10, 2010 (Bloomberg)* – President Barack Obama said he does not "begrudge" the $17 million bonus awarded to JPMorgan Chase & Co. Chief Executive Officer Jamie Dimon or the $9 million issued to Goldman Sachs Group Inc. CEO Lloyd Blankfein ... I, like most of the American people, do not begrudge people success or wealth. That is part of the free-market system." (http://www.businessweek.com/news/2010-02-10/obama-doesn-t-begrudge-bonuses-for-savvy-blankfein-dimon.html)

*SEC Charges Goldman Sachs With Fraud in Structuring and Marketing of CDO Tied to Subprime Mortgages* Washington, DC, April 16, 2010 – The Securities and Exchange Commission today charged Goldman, Sachs & Co. and one of its vice presidents for defrauding investors by

* Tel.: +1 617 588 0303; fax: +1 617 867 2742.
*E-mail address:* freeman@nber.org.

*R.B. Freeman / Journal of Policy Modeling 32 (2010) 690–701* 691

misstating and omitting key facts about a financial product tied to subprime mortgages as the U.S. housing market was beginning to falter. (http://www.sec.gov/news/press/2010/2010-59.htm)

*Prosecutors Ask if 8 Banks Duped Rating Agencies May 12, 2010 (New York Times)*. The New York attorney general has started an investigation of eight banks to determine whether they provided misleading information to rating agencies in order to inflate the grades of certain mortgage securities. Those targets are Goldman Sachs, Morgan Stanley, UBS, Citigroup, Credit Suisse, Deutsche Bank, Crédit Agricole and Merrill Lynch, which is now owned by Bank of America. (http://www.nytimes.com/2010/05/13/business/13street.html)

Financial crises often uncover widespread white collar crime through which bankers, brokers and top managers in other financial institutions made huge earnings by fraud, insider trading, options backdating, securities scams, financial misreporting and the like or by related practices on the border of illegality. The Great Depression highlighted the insider dealings and fraudulent behavior of Wall Street's leading financiers. The 1980s Savings and Loan crisis was characterized by massive criminal looting, which imprisoned as many as 3500 bankers.[1] The most famous conviction was that of Charles Keating whose efforts to limit federal regulation of Lincoln Savings and Loan Association had been supported by then-private citizen Alan Greenspan and by the "Keating five" Senators.[2]

How substantial was white collar crime, near crime or chicanery in the 2007–2009 financial crisis? What motivates those in top positions in banks and other institutions that deal primarily with money to engage in illegal and sleazy business practices? To what extent might more vigorous monitoring of those practices provide an early warning system of impending crises in finance that might prevent or ameliorate the malfunctioning of the financial sector?

This paper presents evidence on these questions. Section 1 shows that the US experienced a wave of financial crime, near crime and chicanery *before* the 2007–2009 implosion of Wall Street. In fact, the FBI gave a Paul Revere alert that "financial disaster is coming" but it was ignored. Section 2 summarizes evidence that the huge bonuses, option-related incentives, and tournament-style rewards evidence is consistent with Senator Leahy's view that we haven't paid enough attention to the economic costs of fraudulent financial behavior. The American people should "begrudge" the amoral or illegal behavior of those at the top, particularly after taxpayer bailouts saved their firms from collapse. Whether the leaders of finance and business who cut corners to make millions are convicted like Enron's management, Bernard Madoff, and the bankers who looted the savings and loan industry in the 1980s,or forced to pay huge civil fines like the AIG management who misreported profits in the early to mid 2000s, or manage to escape punishment by having kept their dishonest practices within the bounds of the law, their behavior is a cancer on capitalism that deserves the greatest social vigilance and opprobrium that society can muster.

---

[1] For the Depression see John Kenneth Galbraith, *The great crash of 1929*. (Houghton Mifflin, 1997). For the 1980s S&L crisis, see William Black. *The best way to rob a bank is to own one*. University of Texas Press (2005) and G.G.A. Akerlof & P.M. Romer. (1993). "Looting: the economic underworld of bankruptcy for profit," *Brookings papers on economic activity*. Economic Studies Program, The Brookings Institution, vol. 24 (1993-2), 1–74. The Financial Times reports that 1072 bankers were jailed for S&L crimes and another 2558 bankers were jailed for other offenses, which were often S&L-linked. Gillian Tett. "Insight: a matter of retribution". *Financial Times*. September 3, 2009. Available at http://us.ft.com/ftgateway/superpage.ft?news_id=fto090320091244573891.

[2] On Greenspan's involvement see Nathaniel Nash, *"Showdown time for Danny Wall"*. *New York Times*, July 9, 1989 http://www.nytimes.com/1989/07/09/business/showdown-time-for-danny-wall.html?pagewanted=2. On the Keating five see http://en.wikipedia.org/wiki/Keating_Five accessed May 11, 2009. Senators Cranston, DeConcini & Riegel did not to run for re-election after the Senate found they had substantially and improperly interfered with the regulatory investigation; Senator Glenn McCain was re-elected after being judged guilty of poor judgment.

692                    *R.B. Freeman / Journal of Policy Modeling 32 (2010) 690–701*

While the epidemic of criminal and near criminal behavior and chicanery were not the main cause of the 2007–2008 financial implosion and ensuing "great recession" they contributed more to the disaster than economists appreciate.

## 2. The Fuzzy boundaries among crime, near crime and chicanery

Consider the following situations:

(a) You create special purpose entities that keep losses off company balance sheets, make false statements to bankers and auditors, count failed projects as assets, and use complex derivatives to mask your firm's problems. Your financial misreporting makes the firm look profitable and allows you and fellow executives to enrich yourselves at the expense of shareholders. When the firm is about to crash, you advise employees to invest 401k pension money into shares while you cash out yours.
(b) You run a Ponzi scheme, reporting high returns on fictitious transactions. You use your connections as a respected leader of finance and member of your religious community to attract new investors to the scheme. Those who trusted you and did not cash out their investments early lose virtually all of their money.
(c) At the behest of a hedge fund manager you create an investment vehicle where the hedge fund helps pick shares likely to tank so that it can make money betting against the fund. You advise clients to invest in the fund while also betting that it fails. You sell similar financial products to non-profit institutions dependent on endowment earnings and bet that those products fail.[3]
(d) You misreport your firms' revenue by $2.1 billion and net income by $1.4 billion by allocating the revenue stream on equipment leases in ways inconsistent with general accounting practices. By doing this you gain $20 million in options as you are about to retire – 3 times the value of options in the prior 5 years.
(e) Your deceptive accounting practices mislead investors in your insurance company to believe the company met or exceeded earnings and growth targets between 2000 and 2005 when it did not. Your fraudulent reports keep share prices high and rising, which enriches you and your fellow executives.
(f) When the stock market fell after 9/11 you convinced your compensation committee to issue large options to you and other executives at the peak of the crisis. You cash in on the options when the market recovers from initial panic.
(g) The share price of your firm rose unexpectedly so you get your compensation committee to backdate options to you and other executives to the time when the share price was low.
(h) Your small bio-tech start-up is talking merger with Glaxo-Smith-Kline. You terminate the employee stock bonus plan and give participants the option to sell their shares to the company without informing them about the possible merger. After the merger Glaxo pays four times as much for shares as the price of the shares that you offered to employees.

Decision (a) produced criminal convictions against Enron's executives. Decision (b) put Bernard Madoff to prison and will presumably imprison many others who used Ponzi schemes to make money in the 2000 s. Decision (c) led the SEC to charge Goldman Sachs with fraud. Decision

---

[3] "E-mail suggests Goldman knew Harvard would lose." Beth Healy. *Boston Globe*, April 28, 2010 http://www. boston.com/business/markets/articles/2010/04/28/e_mail_suggests_goldman_knew_harvard_would_lose/.

*R.B. Freeman / Journal of Policy Modeling 32 (2010) 690–701*                          693

(d) enraged Xerox shareholders but former CEO Paul Allaire escaped being sued in civil court for financial misreporting because his contract made Xerox liable for civil offenses committed as CEO. Decision (e) led AIG to oust CEO Hank Greenberg and to pay more than $1.6 billion to settle charges of improper accounting and for Greenberg to pay $15 million to settle fraud charges. Decision (f) is presumptively legal. The legality of decision (g) depends on the particular rules governing the compensation committee. Decision (h) produced a court suit and ERISA complaint by employees against Stiefel Laboratories that has not yet been resolved at this writing.[4]

From the perspectives of the "you" who made decisions (a)–(h) and the criminal justice system it is critically important whether the decisions are ultimately judged as illegal, subject to criminal or civil proceedings and worthy of prosecution or suing in court, or as amoral and sleazy but legal. The differences send some to jail, force others to pay large fines, and let others get away with their loot. But regardless of the legal status of these decisions, all are morally reprehensible and harm the economy. Each diverts resources from productive activity to "rent-seeking". Each redistributes money from shareholders, workers or consumers whose activity contributes to national output to rent-seeking parasites whose only product is misery for their victims. Each reduces trust in business and forces the government to enact greater regulatory protections and for citizens to invest in protecting themselves from fraud, both of which increase the cost of transactions.

The term *financial crime* is a broad one. The FBI financial crime unit refers to "matters relating to fraud, theft, or embezzlement ... characterized by deceit, concealment or violation of trust, and ... not dependent upon the application or threat of physical force or violence. Such acts are committed by individuals and organizations to obtain personal or business advantage."[5] As priority areas for the FBI financial crimes unit the Agency lists corporate fraud, health care fraud, mortgage fraud, identity theft, insurance fraud and money laundering, and also includes securities and commodities fraud, telemarketing fraud, Ponzi schemes, advance fees schemes, and pyramid schemes, among others. It treats most acts as falling under criminal law. The Securities and Exchange Commission (SEC) focuses on insider trading, violations of licensing, registration or anti-fraud provisions of Securities Law. Although SEC allegations of financial misreporting often imply criminality most SEC suits fall under civil law, which allows firms and managers to sidestep admission or denial of guilt and settle charges by paying fines or restitution. The burden of proof for conviction in criminal law is "beyond all reasonable doubt" whereas the burden of proof in civil law is the "preponderance of evidence".

The term *near financial crime* is a broad one of my making. I use it to refer to situations in which there was sufficient indication of illegal activity but insufficient proof against the alleged perpetrator to win conviction or in which prosecutors or victims chose to forgo going to court because the probability of winning monetary recompense or conviction did not justify the costs of pursuing the case.[6] Without an inside whistle-blower or paper/electronic trail of discussions, it is often difficult to prove that an alleged white collar perpetrator willfully broke the law, which is often required in criminal cases. Management may have plausible deniability that allows them to

---

[4] http://www.joffelaw.com/caselaw/2010/01/04/bacon-v-stiefel-laboratories-inc-case-no-09-21871-cv-king-january-4-2010/.

[5] http://www.fbi.gov/publications/financial/fcs_report052005/fcs_report052005.htm.

[6] Smart lawyers may be able to convince a judge/jury that the evidence against the person was not beyond all reasonable doubt in a criminal offense or may muddy some key element of the claim in the case of civil charges. ("I didn't tell the accountants to cook the books, I said I wanted them to make the company look very profitable and suggested some possible ways. But I never understood accounting or those complex financial instruments. I'm just not very smart. Stupidity is not a crime").

escape judgment under the rubric that "mistakes were made but not by me." They may have left a seemingly exculpatory paper or electronic trail and followed correct procedures, as recommended by their lawyers.[7] I also include as "near crime" acts that were not illegal when committed but which led the legislature to make them illegal shortly thereafter. In a world of rapidly changing criminal innovations, the law will often be a step or two behind the discovery of a loophole in existing legislation or some new technology that opens the door for new white collar crimes not covered adequately in the criminal or civil code.

*Chicanery* refers to trickery or deception to gain an advantage that most people would view as unethical but not as criminal.

The boundaries among crime, near crime and chicanery are fuzzy. They are fuzzy in the sense of fuzzy set theory, which recognizes that given actions need not fit into 0/1 exclusive sets but can belong to several sets with "membership values" that reflects their closeness to the archetype of that set.[8] The credit card company that charges customers in obscure ways to make money so that the customer does not realize what he/she is paying, for example, would be on the border of chicanery and near crime. Its actions might have 30% membership in the near crime set and 80% membership in the chicanery set. The lender that applies borrower payments to debts with the lowest interest charges rather than to those with the highest interest charges unless the payee tells them otherwise might have 80% membership in the chicanery set and 5% membership in the near crime set. The firm that gives high paying jobs to former government officials whose public decisions favored it might have 50% membership in the chicanery set but 0% in the crime set. It is sending a signal to current government officials about how decisions might affect their future but bribes no one. The hedge fund that pays large sums to someone who may in future hold a key public job is also acting legally. Its payments might have only modest membership in the chicanery set. The line between chicanery and smart business or social practices is also a fuzzy one.

## 3. The financial crime wave

The most comprehensive indicator of potential financial crimes is the "suspicious activity reports" (SARs) that the U.S. Department of the Treasury's Financial Crimes Enforcement Network (FinCEN) gathers from banks and other money service businesses. Respondents at the business fill out FinCen form109 (http://www.irs.gov/pub/irs-pdf/ffc109.pdf) that asks about money laundering, structuring[9] and terrorist financing and provides space to report other forms of suspicious transactions. Exhibit 1 shows that between 1997 and 2006–2007, before the Wall Street implosion, the number of SARs reported to FinCen grew at near exponential rates. FinCen focus on money laundering notwithstanding, the most rapid increase in fraud related to mortgages. As Exhibit 2 shows, the number of mortgage frauds began to zoom upwards in 2003 and increased nearly ten fold through 2009. The early increase was sufficiently disturbing to the FBI that in 2004 the agency warned that "Mortgage fraud (was) becoming an 'epidemic'" that risked recre-

---

[7] Mike France & Dan Carney. "Why corporate crooks are tough to nail". *Business Week*. Online July 1, 2002 http://www.businessweek.com/magazine/content/02_26/b3789013.htm.

[8] See http://en.wikipedia.org/wiki/Fuzzy_set for a discussion of fuzzy sets and references.

[9] By which it means structuring the transaction to evade record keeping or reporting requirements of the Bank Secrecy Act.

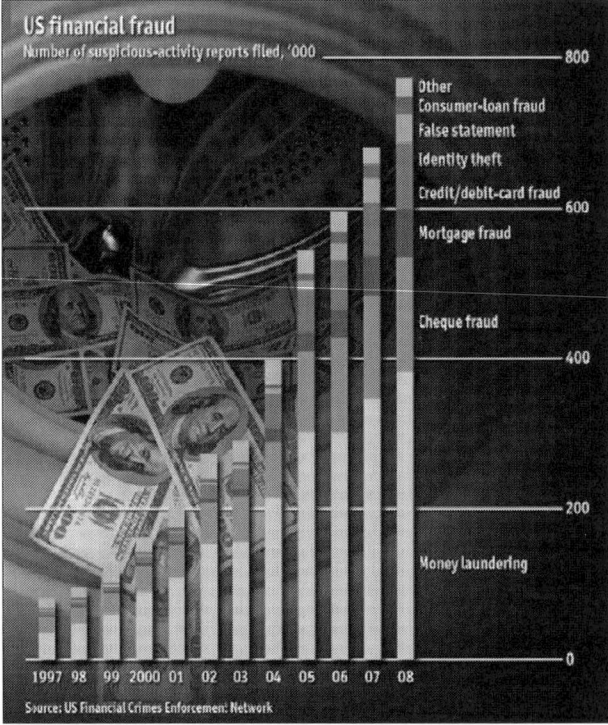

Exhibit 1. Suspicious activity reports: a leading indicator of financial crime wave. SOURCE: *The Economist*, "The rise of financial crime in America". July 21, 2009. http://www.economist.com/daily/chartgallery/displaystory. cfm?story_id=14067467.

ating the Saving & Loan crisis of the 1980s.[10] That the FBI found enough evidence of financial crime in the SARs to go public with warnings while then Federal Reserve Chair Alan Greenspan saw nothing to worry about in the housing market reflects the difference between the criminal justice mindset, which invariably seeks out suspicious events to investigate, and the ideological laissez-faire mindset, which invariably seeks to justify events as reflecting the perfect operation of perfect markets. Had the Bush Administration or Federal Reserve reacted to the FBI warning and deployed FBI or other investigators to deal with the incipient wave of financial crime, they could have dampened the housing bubble and possibly curtailed the spread of toxic assets that set off the collapse of Wall Street in fall 2008.

The second financial crime that exploded in the late 2000s were Ponzi schemes, the most famous of which Madoff's $65 billion scam.[11] The boundary scheme between Ponzi schemes and other forms of financial fraud are fuzzy. Nora Manella, then prosecuting attorney in the Central District of California, noted in discussion of one Ponzi scheme, that "in this case the victims invested in what was originally a legitimate scheme. They (the investors) were defrauded only when he

---

[10] http://www.usatoday.com/money/perfi/housing/2004-09-17-mortgage-fraud_x.htm and http://www.facebook.com/topic.php?uid=2255675352&topic=7398.
[11] See http://en.wikipedia.org/wiki/Madoff_investment_scandal.

696                    R.B. Freeman / Journal of Policy Modeling 32 (2010) 690–701

| Mortgage Fraud SARs | |
| --- | --- |
| **Fiscal Year** | **SAR Submissions** |
| 2009 | 67,190 |
| 2008 | 63,713 |
| 2007 | 46,717 |
| 2006 | 35,617 |
| 2005 | 21,994 |
| 2004 | 17,127 |
| 2003 | 6,936 |
| 2002 | 5,609 |
| 2001 | 4,210 |
| 2000 | 3,245 |

Mortgage Asset Research Institute
TWELFTH PERIODIC MORTGAGE FRAUD CASE REPORT

April 2010

Exhibit 2. Mortgage Fraud SARS, 2000–2009.

(the businessman) decided that being a con man was preferable to being a failed businessman."[12] Speculation at the height of any boom has the flavor of a Ponzi scheme. Investors buy assets at prices far above their fundamental value in the hope of selling the assets to some other investor, who buys them with the same hope.[13] A financial bubble could be defined as a market-created Ponzi scheme. Just as the FBI warned the Bush Administration and Federal Reserve about the emerging mortgage fraud pandemic, the financial fraud investigator Harry Markopolos warned the Securities and Exchange Commission about the Madoff Ponzi scheme, to no avail.[14]

In 2009 the media reported that prosecutors were bringing so many such schemes to court that ABC news declared it to be "the year of the Ponzi". The AP counted 150 or so Ponzi schemes compared to 40 schemes in 2008. At this writing the number of schemes uncovered continues to grow. On April 29, 2010 the Wall Street Journal reported that the Colorado Securities Commissioner was bringing civil charges against the perpetrator of a scheme that defrauded investors of at least 60 million dollars under the headline "Alleged Ponzi in Colorado Has Shades of Madoff Affair."[15]

The 2000s epidemic in financial crime contrasts with the falling rate of personal and property crime over the past two decades in the FBI's Uniform Crime Reports of offenses reported to the

---

[12] http://www.crimes-of-persuasion.com/Crimes/InPerson/MajorPerson/examples.htm.
[13] Wei Xiong & Jialin Yu. "The Chinese warrants bubble" NBER Working Paper No. 15481. November 2009.
[14] Harry Markopolos. *No one would listen: a true financial thriller*. Hoboken, NJ: Wiley & Sons (2010). Also see http://en.wikipedia.org/wiki/Harry_Markopolos.
[15] http://online.wsj.com/article/SB10001424052748703648304575212602804526536.html?mod=rss_whats_news_us.

*R.B. Freeman / Journal of Policy Modeling 32 (2010) 690–701*      697

police and the Bureau of Justice Statistic's National Crime Victimization Survey of households. Neither of these measures of crime provide much information on white collar crime. The National White Collar Crime Center surveyed white collar crimes in 1999 and 2005 but does not have the breadth of data available to the Department of Justice (http://www.nw3c.org/).[16]

## 4. Why a financial crime wave: the incentive of really big bucks

Observers and researchers have offered several possible explanations for the crime wave that engulfed finance and the top of major US businesses in the 2000s.

Many cite the decline of moral standards in society—the advent of Gordon Gecko morality that extolled greed and profits above all else.[17] In December 2009, Jeff Imhelt of General Electric attacked the executive class, of which he is a leading member: "We are at the end of a difficult generation of business leadership . . . tough-mindedness, a good trait, was replaced by meanness and greed, both terrible traits. Rewards became perverted. The richest people made the most mistakes with the least accountability."[18] Since, as noted, crime was falling outside of finance, it is difficult to blame the behavior on any broad trend toward amoral or illegal actions. No roaring twenties Prohibition culture was sweeping the country. It was not only the meanness and greed that was concentrated at the top, as Imholt notes, but crime as well, with relatively more white collar crimes concentrated in finance than in other sectors.

Another possible explanation for the white collar crime wave is that finance and business attracted persons with less moral reservations about acceptable money-making behavior than in the past.[19] Selectivity is important in labor supply behavior, with workers who are less risk averse than others take riskier jobs, and those with stronger physiques take on greater physical

[16] Firms that sell services to businesses to protect the firm from financial crimes provide additional data on these and other such crimes, though with limited coverage across the economy and over time. Price Waterhouse Coopers has its Global Fraud Survey, based on executive reports for 50 or so countries including the US (http://www.pwc.com/us/en/forensic-services/publications/assets/2009-global-economic-survey-us-supplement.pdf); the Association of Certified Fraud Examiners have an annual report on occupational fraud, as reported by Certified Fraud Examiners in the United States and U.S. Territories (http://www.acfe.com/resources/publications.asp?copy=rttn); Kroll has a Global Fraud Report. The annual 2009–2010 report stressed "sectors closer to the economic crisis – financial services and professional services in particular – have seen an increase in their incidence and level of fraud" (http://www.kroll.com/about/library/fraud/oct2009/).

[17] John McCain spoke of "greed, corruption and excess" as "Wall Street treated the American economy like a casino," Rick Klein. "McCain blames greed for Wall St. mess; Obama blames GOP". *ABC News*. September 16, 2008, http://abcnews.go.com/Politics/5050/story?id=5812268&page=1. Charles Colson, the Watergate criminal who found new life as an evangelical prison ministry leader, declared that the problem was "greed unchecked by any moral restraint." Charles Colson. "Tipsy on Wall Street: A President's candid comment", (July 29, 2008), http://www.crosswalk.com/news/commentary/11579703/. Greenspan referred to "an infectious greed [that] seemed to grip much of our business community" as if greed was not the putative motivating force for market capitalism. Harry Binswanger. Greenspan on "Greenspan on 'Infectious Greed'", *Capitalism Magazine*, (August 30, 2002) http://www.capmag.com/article.asp?ID=1825. Playing the Clinton mantra, one religious leader explained "it's the morality, sinner." Ed Stoddard. "Evangelicals see moral decline in Wall St. woes", *Reuters*. October 1, 2008, http://www.reuters.com/article/idUSTRE4905RF20081001.

[18] See Francesco Guerrera. "GE chief attacks executive 'Greed'", *Fin. Times*, December 9, 2009, available at http://www.ft.com/cms/s/0/fe1e3f7c-e507-11de-9a25-00144feab49a.html?nclick_check=1.

[19] Laboratory studies of public goods games found that business students made fewer socially desirable investments than students in other fields. Lorenz Goette, David Huffman & Stephan Meier. "The impact of group membership on cooperation and norm enforcement: Evidence using random assignment to Real Social Groups". *American Economic Review*, 96 (2) (2006), 212–216. Stephan Meier & Bruno Frey reported that selectivity was the main factor explaining the less socially responsible behavior of Swiss business students than others. B.S. Frey & S. Meier. "Social comparisons and pro-social behavior: testing "conditional cooperation" in a field experiment". *American Economic Review* 94 (5) (2004),

labor, and so on. But recalling the behavior of S&L bankers in the 1980s and of tobacco firm executives from the 1960s through the 1990s I am dubious of the proposition that business leaders were intrinsically less moral in the run-up to the 2007–2008 financial implosion than in earlier periods. Other analysts offer a biological explanation.[20] Research that finds men with higher testosterone levels take greater risks in a financial investment game led one news columnist to claim that "the greedy architects of the new recession—can not help themselves."[21] Excessive testosterone or insufficient dopamine receptors may contribute to individual differences in risk-taking and willingness to undertake financial crimes but my guess is that this is of second order importance in the 2000s epidemic of financial crime. The hypothesis that seems most relevant to me is the orthodox economic one that is best captured by the "every man has his price"[22] theorem of micro-economics. This theorem or law stresses the power of incentives to induce people to undertake actions they might not otherwise do. If I can fleece you of $10 I am an honest man. If I can fleece you of $1 million I think twice. If I can fleece you of "real money"—tens of millions—and if my lawyer and accountant say it is legal, I change from Mr. Honest to Mr. Gordon Gecko. Toodaloo suckahs. Caveat emptor. You want more toxic assets? Here they are. Fiduciary responsibility—what is that?

The implication of this analysis for inequality is the opposite of the usual supply-side claim that huge inequalities are needed to motivate those at the top to make the best decisions. Instead it suggests that smaller rewards at the top are needed to reduce the amount of unscrupulous risk-taking and criminality that accompanied the Wall Street boom and implosion.

There is a variety of evidence that decisions to engage in financial crime, near crime, and chicanery respond to economic incentives. Since stock options are more valuable when share prices are more variable, one way to increase the value of options is to make riskier decisions than may be in the interest of the firm. Sanders and Hambrick (2007) found that firms whose CEO compensation was loaded with options had greater variation in performance than other firms. If the gains to the winners exceed the losses to the losers, this would raise total output and possibly

---

183–192. By contrast, Elizabeth Maynes & Charles Bram Cadsby reported that nurses made socially desirable decisions. Charles Bram Cadsby & Elizabeth Maynes. "Choosing between a socially efficient and free-riding equilibrium: Nurses versus economics and business students. *Journal Of Economic Behavior & Organization*, 37 (2) (1998), 183–192. Dan Ariely reports that NY bankers cheat twice as much as others.

[20] J. M. Coates & J. Herbert. "Endogenous steroids and financial risk taking on a london trading floor" *PNAS* 105(16) (2008), 6167–6172. C.L. Apicella, A. Dreber, B. Campbell, P.B. Gray, M. Hoffman & A.C. Little. "Testosterone and financial risk preferences". *Evolution and Human Behavior*, 29(6) (November 2008), 384–390.

[21] Shannon Rupp. "Could we blame the financial crisis on too much testosterone? Harvard researchers say yes", *AlterNet*. October 20, 2008. Available at http://www.alternet.org/economy/103502/could_we_blame_the_financial_crisis_on_too_much_testosterone_harvard_researchers_say_yes/. Zald found that persons with fewer mid-brain dopamine receptors are more likely to take risks. D.H. Zald., et al. "Midbrain dopamine receptor availability is inversely associated with novelty-seeking traits in humans". *Journal of Neuroscience* 28(53) (2008), 14372–14378. Camelia Kuhnen & Brian Knutson related brain regions innervated by serotonergic and dopaminergic neural pathways to individuals' financial risk-taking behavior C.M. Kuhnen & B. Knutson. "The neural basis of financial risk taking". *Neuron* 47(5) (2005), 763–770. Knutson, et al. showed that the parts of the brain that light up with erotic pictures also light up with financial gambles and that young men make greater gambles after seeing sexually arousing pictures. B. Knutson, G.E. Wimmer, C. Kuhnen & P. Winkielman. "Nucleus accumbens activation mediates the influence of reward cues on financial risk-taking." *Neuroreport* 5(19) (2008), 509–513. C.M. Kuhnen & J.Y. Chiao. "Genetic determinants of financial risk taking". *PLoS ONE*, 4 (2) (February 2009), e4362. Find that the genes that regulate dopamine and serotonin are also significant in risk-taking in investment decisions carries the biology story a step further.

[22] See e.g., Sir Robert Walpole. 1st earl of Oxford, in *10 Notes and queries: a medium of intercommunication for Literary Men*. General Readers, Etc. 368 (1907).

*R.B. Freeman / Journal of Policy Modeling 32 (2010) 690–701*                              699

be in the interest of the broader economy. But they also found that riskier behavior produced more big losses than big gains.[23]

A growing literature in economics, management and accounting finds that financial misreporting is more likely when executives can benefit, usually through stock options and equity, from the misreporting. These studies rely on two relatively small data sources: a 2002 Government Accountability Office report on financial statement restatements and the quarterly SEC reports of Accounting and Auditing Enforcement Releases (AAER). Armstrong, Jagolinzer and Larcker (2010) report that eight of ten recent studies using these data find that improper reporting is associated with "the strength of inducements."[24] But their propensity score analysis of the AAER data finds little evidence of a positive relationship between CEO equity incentives and the incidence of accounting-related restatements, which leaves what seemed to be a general conclusion in some disarray. The extent to which the strength of inducements affects financial misreporting in general does not, however, gainsay its role in motivating the executives in the Enron, AIG and Xerox cases cited earlier. And one does not need regression analysis to interpret firms backdating stock options or writing. In a simple maze-solving laboratory experiment with modest stakes for persons solving more mazes, Alexander Gelber and I found that greater incentives for coming higher in a tournament induced participants to misreport the number of mazes they had solved.[25] The massive sums available in finance provide far greater incentive for misrepresenting performance.

As Harvard's Rakesh Kurana and Andy Zelleke have stated, during the 1990s–2000s management seemed to operate corporations "for the purpose of creating vast wealth for senior executives."[26] Just as Bernard Madoff knew he was running a Ponzi scheme, the big Wall Street firms knew what they were doing when they packaged subprime mortgages and earned their fees by selling them quickly to others; as one portfolio manager put it, "a lot of people knew this was bogus, but the money was too good."[27] In 2008, the then-chairman of the SEC testified before Congress that "if honest lending practices had been followed, much of this crisis quite simply would not have occurred."[28] The large banks that funded Enron's off-the-books deals *knew* that Enron's book-keeping was a shell game designed to make the firm appear profitable when it was not, but the banks kept making loans to it because it earned the banks and their managers huge profits.[29]

In sum, the compensation system that allows top management to earn massive amounts for meeting or *seeming to meet* performance criteria that management sets for itself seems the most likely cause of the financial crime wave of the 2000s that contributed to the Wall Street implosion

---

[23] W. G. Sanders & D.C. Hambrick. "Swinging for the fences: The effects of CEO stock options on company risk taking and performance". *Academy Of Management Journal* 50(5) (2007), 1055–1078.

[24] C. Armstrong, A.D. Jagolinzer & D. Larcker. "Chief executive officer equity incentives and accounting Irregularities". *Journal of Accounting Research*, 48(2) (May 2010), 225.

[25] R.B. Freeman & A.M. Gelber. "Prize structure and information in tournaments: Experimental evidence". *American Economic Journal: Applied Economics* 2(1) (January 2010), 149–64.

[26] Rakesh Khurana & Andy Zelleke. "You can cap the pay, but the greed will go on", *Wash. Post*, Febuary 8, 2009. Available at http://www.washingtonpost.com/wp-dyn/content/article/2009/02/06/AR2009020602794.html.

[27] Jill Drew. "Frenzy" *Wash. Post*, Dec. 16, 2008. Available at http://www.washingtonpost.com/wp-dyn/content/article/2008/12/15/AR2008121503561.html.

[28] Christopher Cox, Chairman, U.S. Sec. & Exch. Comm'n, Testimony before the Committee on Oversight and Government Reform of the U.S. House of Representatives: Testimony concerning the Role of Federal Regulators: Lessons from the Credit Crisis for the Future of Regulation (October 23, 2008). Available at http://www.sec.gov/news/testimony/2008/ts102308cc.htm (agreeing with the earlier testimony of the SEC's former chief accountant).

[29] Bethany McLean & Peter Elkind. *The smartest guys in the room. Penguin books* (2003).

and ensuing recession. In 2000 or so, American executives were making roughly 300 times the earnings of normal workers with the bulk of their earnings coming in the form of stock options and bonuses.[30] The top managers in finance were among the highest paid of all.

U.S. capitalism has not always been marked by such earnings differentials. The exceptional pay of management reflects three to four decades of rising income inequality that brought Gini coefficients and other measures of inequality to levels comparable to those before the Great Depression.[31] Much of the 1980s–2000s income gain in the U.S. went to the upper 10%, while much of the gain among the upper 10% went to the upper 1%, and much of the gain in the upper 1% went to the upper 0.1% and so on.[32] Finance benefited more than other sectors from the concentration of economic gains at the top of the income distribution. Compensation per full-time equivalent employee for security and commodity brokers in the finance sector rose from 146% above the national average of compensation per full-time equivalent employee in 1990 to 290% above average in 2007.[33] In 1990, total compensation for security and commodity brokers was 31% of the compensation for federal civilian employees.[34] In 2007, it was 93% that of federal civilian employees.[35] Much of the increased incomes went to those in the highest positions. In 2006, Wall Street paid out $62 billion in bonuses.[36] Some heads of hedge funds made around $1 billion or more a year.[37]

Finally, and more speculatively, it is possible that these incentives interacted in various ways with the Gordon Gecko style culture that developed on Wall Street to create a greater wave of criminality, near criminal behavior and chicanery than incentives by themselves might have done in a different cultural setting. If social psychologists can induce people to seemingly torture others without incentive pay, per Stanley Milgram's famous social psychology experiment,[38] imagine how easy it must be to get people to engage in shady transactions that

---

[30] G. William Domhoff. "Who rules America: Wealth, income and power" September 2005. http://sociology. ucsc.edu/whorulesamerica/power/wealth.html. Hall & Murphy (2003) & Jensen (2005) report that the ratio of average CEO total compensation to average production worker compensation increased from 150 in 1994 to 570 in 2000, due almost entirely to a rapid increase in the value of option grants as stocks rose in the 1990s bull market.

[31] See Thomas Piketty and Emmanuel Saez. "Income inequality in the United States, 1913-1998," *Quarterly Journal of Economics*, 118(1) (2003), 1–39. (Longer updated version published in A.B. Atkinson and T. Piketty eds., Oxford University Press, 2007.), supra note 75.

[32] See id.; Robert J. Gordon & Ian Dew-Becker. Controversies about the rise of American Inequality: A Survey. Nat'l Bureau of Econ. Research, Working Paper No. 13982, 2008. Available at http://www.nber.org/papers/w13982.

[33] See Bureau of Economic Analysis, Table 6.2C. Compensation of Employees by Industry, http://www.bea.gov/national/nipaweb/SelectTable.asp?Selected=N (choose table 6.2c, then choose 1990 for the "First Year" and "Last Year," then click "Update") (accessed 27.02.2010); Bureau of Economic Analysis, Table 6.2D. Compensation of Employees by Industry, http://www.bea.gov/national/nipaweb/SelectTable.asp?Selected=N (choose table 6.2d, then choose 2007 for the "First Year" and "Last Year," then click "Update") (last visited 27.02.2010).

[34] See Bureau of Economic Analysis, Table 6.2C. Compensation of Employees by Industry, http://www.bea.gov/national/nipaweb/SelectTable.asp?Selected=N (choose table 6.2c, then choose 1990 for the "First Year" and "Last Year," then click "Update") (last visited 27.02.2010).

[35] See Bureau of Economic Analysis, Table 6.2C. Compensation of Employees by Industry, http://www.bea.gov/national/nipaweb/SelectTable.asp?Selected=N (choose table 6.2c, then choose 1997 for the "First Year" and "Last Year," then click "Update") (last visited 27.02.2010).

[36] M.B. Zuckerman. "We deserve a better bailout", *U.S. News & World Rep.* March 10, 2010. Available at http://www.usnews.com/opinion/mzuckerman/articles/2008/10/03/we-deserve-a-better-bailout.html.

[37] Jenny Anderson, & Julie Creswell *New York Times*, April 24, 2007. "Top hedge fund managers earn over $240 million". J. Simons, K.C. Griffin & E.S. Lampert were listed as making over $1 billion, with George Soros falling a bit below a billion dollars http://www.nytimes.com/2007/04/24/business/24hedge.html?fta=y&pagewanted=all.

[38] Stanley Milgram. *Obedience to authority: An experimental view* (1974). In the most recent evidence on the Milgram result, Dominick Packer reports that about two-thirds of the participants in the Milgram experiment went beyond 150 volts

*R.B. Freeman / Journal of Policy Modeling 32 (2010) 690–701*                                701

rip off clients/shareholders/workers in a culture where money-making is all that matters and your behavior gets you a small fortune.

## 5. Conclusion

The 2000s experienced a financial crime wave that ranges from legally actionable criminal offenses to near crime to chicanery. The US had early warnings from the FBI that the financial crimes in mortgages risked a 1980s Savings and Loan style collapse of banking but ignored those warnings. Many of the decisions behind the financial crime wave are closely associated with the huge incentives that were available to those at the top of finance and many corporations. Those incentives are themselves linked to the rise of inequality in the period. As is usual in social science, we need more evidence on the causes and consequences of what was probably the greatest financial crime wave in our history. We need additional evidence on the elasticity of responsiveness of financial crime to the potential monetary gain and the probability of detection and penalties for such crimes; on the destruction that financial crime brings to the economy (do small deviations from honest behavior have large aggregate effects on the economy, per the Akerlof–Yellen analysis of small deviations from rationality[39] or per the studies by Shleifer, Vishny and Murphy on corruption and rent-seeking)[40]; on the impact of corporate culture on the "price" at which different people engage in financial crime and so on. But even absent such evidence, it would seem sensible to increase the number of anti-fraud investigators and investigations, to expand prosecutions and penalties for financial crime, and to listen more to the FBI and Lieutenant Colombos of the world and less to the Alan Greenspans and Bob Rubins in setting policy toward the financial world.

Book'em, Danno.

---

where the person being shocked yelled "Stop, let me out" while about half kept administering the punishment to the 450 volts at which the experiment ended. Dominic J. Packer. "Identifying systematic disobedience in Milgram's obedience experiments: A meta-analytic review". *Perspectives on Psychological Science* 3(4) (2008), 301–304. Burger replicated the finding that two-thirds went beyond the 150 volts. See Jerry Burger. "Replicating Milgram: Would people still obey today?". *American Psychologist*, 64 (1), (2009) 1–11. None of these studies have examined how such behavior responded to monetary incentives, whether more people go to the 450 volts if paid to do so than if not paid.

[39] G.A. Akerlof & J.L. Yellen. (1985). "Can small deviations from rationality make significant differences to economic equilibria?" *American Economic Review,* 75(4) (September 1985), 708–20.

[40] K. M. Murphy, A. Shleifer & R. W. Vishny. "Why is rent-seeking so costly to growth?" *American Economic Review, Paper and Proceedings,* 83 (2) (May 1993), 409–14. Also K. M. Murphy, A. Shleifer & R. W. Vishny. "The allocation of talent: Implications for growth". *Quarterly Journal of Economics,* 106 (2) (May 1991), 503–30.

# [11]

# Mortgage origination fraud and the global economic crisis

## A criminological analysis

**Tomson H. Nguyen**
*University of Houston—Downtown*

**Henry N. Pontell**
*University of California, Irvine*

## Research Summary

*The study outlined in this article analyzed the responses of 23 subjects previously and currently employed in the subprime lending industry to understand the implications and role of white-collar crime in the contemporary subprime mortgage crisis and to document the rationalizations that offenders use to explain their involvement in mortgage-related crimes. The subjects represented five sectors of the primary mortgage market, including brokerage, lender, escrow, title, and appraisal offices. Secondary sources of data for the study included media accounts, government reports, and industry studies. The research findings detail accounts of mortgage frauds in the subprime lending industry that resulted from inadequate regulation, the indiscriminate use of alternative loan products, and the lack of accountability in the industry.*

## Policy Implications

*The study results suggest that the problem of mortgage origination fraud would be prevented best by major reform of financial policies and lending practices that characterize the subprime mortgage industry. Several broad recommendations are proposed in this article that highlight the need to recognize the potential for insider fraud, to enhance government regulation*

Direct correspondence to Tomson H. Nguyen, University of Houston—Downtown, Department of Criminal Justice, One Main Street, Suite 330.F, Houston, TX 77004 (e-mail: nguyento@uhd.edu); Henry N. Pontell, Department of Criminology, Law, and Society, School of Social Ecology, University of California, Irvine, CA 92697. (e-mail: pontell@uci.edu).

*and oversight, to tighten loan qualification requirements, and to increase standards of underwriting. Observations are offered concerning the need to highlight white-collar crime in understanding the global financial crisis and to preventing future debacles.*

## Keywords

*mortgage fraud, subprime mortgage crisis, white-collar crime, fraud, subprime*

In early 2008, former Federal Reserve Board Chairman Alan Greenspan wrote, "The current financial crisis in the U.S. is likely to be judged in retrospect as the most wrenching since the end of the Second World War." By the end of 2008, the financial losses from the global economic meltdown had outgrown that of the savings and loan bailout in the 1980s and 1990s. "By some estimates, it has made that costly debacle look like chump change" (Schmitt, 2008). In a report compiled for the 2007 U.S. Conference of Mayors and the Council for the New American City, it was stated, "The wave of foreclosures that has rippled across the U.S. has already battered some of our largest financial institutions, created ghost towns of once vibrant neighborhoods—and it's not over yet" (Global Insight, 2007: 6).

One important question regarding the current financial crisis that has both theoretical and practical ramifications is whether the subprime mortgage crisis—a real-estate and financial disaster marked by an unprecedented rate of mortgage delinquencies and foreclosures brought on by factors that include lax lending policies, poor underwriting standards, inadequate regulatory structure, and government oversight—entails significant amounts of fraud at various institutional levels. As noted by some white-collar criminologists regarding earlier financial debacles, material fraud built into financial markets could remain virtually undetected until its consequences reach epic proportions (Black, 2005; Rosoff, Pontell, and Tillman, 2010). This situation was a difficult and seemingly yet-to-be-learned lesson of the savings and loan crisis in the 1980s, as demonstrated in several detailed empirical studies (Black, Calavita, and Pontell, 1995; Pontell, Calavita, and Tillman, 1994; Tillman and Pontell, 1995). In the current crisis, economists and other financial experts have failed to observe or, in some cases, have failed to accept, the reality that a significant undercurrent of financial crime exists, particularly mortgage fraud or "the material misstatement, misrepresentation, or omission by an applicant or other interested parties, relied upon by an underwriter or lender to fund, purchase or insure a loan" (Federal Bureau of Investigations [FBI], 2007: 2).

As the housing crisis unraveled beginning in late 2007, the number of reports of mortgage fraud investigations and indictments relating to the financial crisis increased. In January 2008, the FBI stated that it was investigating 14 corporations as part of its Subprime Mortgage Industry Fraud Initiative launched the previous year. Six months later, the FBI reported that more than 400 individuals were charged in a nationwide investigation that included the arrest of two Bear Stearns fund managers (Schmitt, 2008). The report noted that lending fraud involved "mortgage transactions based on gross fraudulent misrepresentations about the borrowers' financial status, such as overstating income or assets, using false or fictitious employment records or inflating property values" (FBI, 2008).

Recently, mortgage fraud has emerged as a major problem in the United States. In 2006 alone, it was estimated that fraud cost the mortgage industry between $946 million and $4.2 billion (Mortgage Bankers Association, 2007). The federal Financial Crimes Enforcement Network (FinCEN) reported similar findings from data collected in the form of mortgage-related suspicious activity reports (SARs). According to FinCEN, the number of SARs filed in the first quarter of 2006 pertaining to mortgage loan fraud increased 35% during the same period in 2005. This follows a 29 percent increase from 2004 to 2005, and an almost 100 percent increase from 2003 to 2004" (FinCEN, 2006). Large mortgage lenders such as New Century Financial Corporation—once the second-largest U.S. subprime mortgage lender—were found to have "engaged in a significant number of highly improper and imprudent practices related to its loan originations, operations, accounting and financial reporting processes" (Kary, 2008). Smaller mortgage broker offices also were under criminal investigation by the FBI: "The question of fraud goes to the entire process—where the loans were created, whether there was fraud in their creation, or misrepresentation as to the quality of the loans in the sales process" (Sasseen, 2008).

Mortgage fraud has been a major topic of concern of social scientists and economists since the beginning of the 2008 economic downturn. Economist James Galbraith (2009), for example, has been an outspoken critic of the government's response to the banking credit and liquidity crisis resulting from the tremendous losses from home foreclosures. Galbraith repeatedly has noted a need for the government to "review loan tapes" before blindly buying these "toxics assets," arguing that such inspections would "reveal a very high proportion of missing documentation, inflated appraisals, and other evidence of fraud" (2009). Former regulator and criminologist, William Black, voiced similar concerns regarding the role of mortgage fraud as underlying the global financial crisis. Lenders should have a large stake in addressing the problem of mortgage fraud; yet according to Black, they were not the principal filers of suspicious fraudulent complaints. The underreporting of frauds discovered in subprime mortgage loans—loan products intended for borrowers with poor-to-average credit worthiness and characterized by higher interest rates, higher fees, higher risk of default, and difficult terms and conditions—by financial institutions does not come as a surprise because those culpable include the lenders themselves. "One only spots mortgage fraud if one conducts underwriting (and accounting control frauds abhor it), and the last thing a control fraud wants is to invite the FBI's attention" (Black, 2008). He noted that fraud incidents found in file reviews indicate that the amount of loans originated that contained fraud in fiscal year 2007 was 1 million, which is a much higher estimate than the actual mortgage fraud suspicious activities incidents filed by federally regulated lenders.

## Theoretical Underpinning

The aim of the study outlined in this article was to enhance our understanding of the impact and role of mortgage fraud in major financial debacles and the criminal acts, motives, and subjective experiences of those who are part of the industry. The criminological literature on white-collar crime in major financial debacles, particularly the savings and loan crisis, identified industry and organizational factors linked to white-collar crime (Calavita, and Pontell, 1990; Calavita, Tillman, and Pontell, 1997; Pontell and Calavita, 1993; Tillman and Pontell, 1995). These studies examined the criminogenic impact that competition—unleashed by financial deregulation in the 1980s—inadequate regulations, and weak regulatory enforcement had on the prevalence and forms of white-collar and corporate crime during that period. The research on the savings and loan crisis, for example, which identified links between various types of financial crimes and the structural policies and practices that characterized the thrift industry in the 1980s, has allowed for a general understanding of fraud and the current subprime mortgage crisis because both financial crises involved deregulatory policies that loosened financial restrictions, provided inadequate oversight, and required no accountability. The study detailed here explored the link between mortgage fraud and its role in the current economic debacle by examining detailed accounts by insiders concerning various types of mortgage frauds and the underlying motivations behind their crimes in the context of structural policies and lending practices of the subprime industry.

The detailed accounts document the decision-making processes of those persons involved in mortgage fraud. The notable work on the decision making of white-collar offenders conducted by Benson (1985) was founded on the groundbreaking theoretical framework provided by Sykes and Matza (1957) on "neutralization techniques," or a priori rationalizations that free persons to engage in deviant acts by redefining their behaviors in ways that allow them to maintain positive self-images. Subsequent studies on white-collar offenders have found similar patterns regarding the manner in which criminal acts are redefined to alleviate or eliminate culpability (Coleman, 2002; Conklin, 2004; Jesilow, Pontell, and Geis, 1993; Shover and Hunter, 2010). These studies have found consistent evidence that white-collar criminals explain their actions within the context of both legal and ordinary occupational activities, which makes identifying the illegal activities difficult. For example, Shover and Coffey's (2002: 15) work on telemarketing fraud found that most "subjects have a disinclination to see telemarketing as a crime . . . most deny engaging in criminal decision making at all. They are sustained in this moral stance by blaming their victims and also by the way their work is structured and carried out. They believe that they need do nothing more than comply with business regulation." A major goal of this study was to expand our understanding of the reasons for how and why most white-collar criminals successfully can denounce their criminality.

The findings presented here are informed by rational choice theory, a predominant explanatory model historically used to understand the decision-making processes of street offenders. Recent research on the "crime-as-choice" theory for understanding and controlling white-collar crimes has provided a useful framework from which to understand subprime mortgage fraud.

Shover and Hochstetler's (2006: xvi) model of "lure, oversight, and the supply of tempted and predisposed, concepts at the heart of crime-as-choice theory," will be a useful paradigm for understanding the factors that lead to criminal decision making. The following sections discuss basic relevant background information concerning mortgage fraud and the complex nature of the loan origination process. This discussion will allow for a better understanding of the complex nature of mortgage fraud and its role in the subprime mortgage crisis.

## Mortgage Fraud

Mortgage fraud traditionally has been viewed by researchers, government authorities, and industry organizations as either fraud for property or fraud for profit:

> Fraud for property/housing entails minor misrepresentations by the applicant solely for the purpose of purchasing a property for a primary residence. This scheme usually involves a single loan. Although applicants may embellish income and conceal debt, their intent is to repay the loan. Fraud for profit, however, often involves multiple loans and elaborate schemes perpetrated to gain illicit proceeds from property sales. Gross misrepresentations concerning appraisals and loan documents are common in fraud for profit schemes and participants are frequently paid for their participation (FBI, 2007: 2).

Between the two categories of mortgage crimes, the one that "is the most concern to law enforcement and the mortgage industry" is fraud for profit (ibid). This offense category usually involves fraudsters who are mortgage professionals and who have extensive experience in the real-estate industry. According to the FBI (2007), a proliferation of fraud-for-profit schemes could be so costly as to have had devastating implications for the entire U.S. economy.

As with most other forms of white-collar crime, a thin line between actual "crime" (e.g., mortgage fraud) and "unethical or risky practices" (e.g., predatory lending) exists. Without proactive enforcement, it is often difficult if not impossible to distinguish between the two. According to the Mortgage Bankers Association (2007), predatory lending involves a range of unethical loan origination practices that have detrimental effects on borrowers. Such practices might be financially or racially motivated and can be costly to an unsuspecting borrower. For example, borrowers unknowingly might be steered into a subprime mortgage, which will have higher fees and interest rates, when they actually might qualify for a prime mortgage at lower rates. Similarly, lenders might sell loans with attractive introductory terms and conditions under the pretense that such conditions are fixed throughout the term of the loan when, in fact, they are not. Although predatory lending might be harmful and widespread, it is also legal in most cases (Schloemer, Ernst, and Keest, 2006). Yet, under certain circumstances, such practices can cross the legal threshold of criminality. A loan agent might engage in both predatory lending and fraud in the origination of a single loan, as in the case in which a mortgage broker steers his client into a high-cost loan (predatory lending) while intentionally misstating financial information to qualify the borrower (fraud).

*The Growth of Mortgage Fraud*

According to a 2006 report by the FinCEN Office of Regulatory Analysis, mortgage-related fraudulent SARs filed by participating financial institutions increased by 1,411% between 1997 and 2005. Several important findings were discovered in the FinCEN report. First, 66% of the sample involved material misrepresentation or false documents including: (a) altered bank statements, W-2s, credit scores, and tax returns; (b) fabricated letters of gift and letters of credit; (c) invalid social security numbers; and (d) false employment. "The most commonly reported misrepresentation (81 percent) was occupancy fraud" (FinCEN, 2006). Second, reports of SARs among mortgage broker originated loans—which accounted for more than two thirds of loans as of 2006—greatly increased between 1996 and 2006, which coincided with the unprecedented growth of mortgage brokers in the United States since the 1990s.

In April 2006, a report on mortgage fraud by the Mortgage Asset Research Institute identified several forms of mortgage-related crimes, including fraud in applications, tax and financial statements, verifications of deposits (VODs), appraisals/valuations, verifications of employment, escrow/closing, and credit reports. Incidents of fraud reported among mortgage applications were the most common type, followed by tax and financial statements. Of the six identified frauds, four fraud types, or more than 80% of the frauds, involved information gathering and verification that take place during the application process (Sharick, Omba, Larson, and Croft, 2006). Material misrepresentation was prevalent among loan products that required little scrutiny of the borrowers' financial disposition. BasePoint Analytics, a consulting firm that specializes in fraud detection software, analyzed more than 3 million loans and found that "as much as 70 percent of recent early payment defaults (EPDs) had fraudulent misrepresentations on their original loan applications; applications that contained misrepresentations were also five times as likely to go into default" (2007: 1–2). The study also found that frauds included income inflated by as much as 500%, appraisals that overvalued the property by 50% or more, fictitious employers, and falsified tax returns.

The growth of alternative loan products such as no-documentation/low-documentation loans, otherwise known as "liar loans," were much more likely to be open invitations to fraudsters. In a Bill Moyers interview, Black (2009) noted, "Liars' loans mean that we don't check. You tell us what your income is, what your job is, and what your assets are and we agree to believe you. We won't check on any of those things. And by the way, you get a better deal if you inflate your income and your job history and your assets." "When the stated incomes were compared to the IRS figures, the resulting differences were dramatic—ninety percent of the stated income loans contained financial information that was exaggerated by 5 percent or more; almost 60 percent of the loans were exaggerated by more than 50 percent" (Sharick et al., 2006: 12).

The growth of the broker system, which has complicated the loan origination process and drastically reduced accountability in the origination process, has aggravated the problem of mortgage fraud within the subprime lending industry. Under the dominant fragmented system, as many as five self-interested independent agencies (broker, lender, appraiser, escrow, and title) work together on a single loan. Currently, no national standards are in place for licensing and oversight of mortgage brokers. Some states license mortgage brokerage offices but not individuals; 24 states have no specific educational or experience requirements for mortgage brokers, and only a few states require criminal background checks on mortgage brokers; making it possible for unethical individuals to move from one mortgage brokerage firm to another (FinCEN, 2006).

To understand the relationship between mortgage fraud and the global economic crisis better, it is instructive to consider other financial debacles in the postindustrial period. Examining the role of white-collar crime in past major financial debacles, such as the savings and loan crisis, provides insight into underlying structural factors that allow for crime-facilitative environments to develop, as well as a criminological context for analyzing the current financial meltdown.

## Mortgage Origination Process

The process of a obtaining a mortgage involves interacting with several agents from the initial application to the eventual funding of the loan. To understand the sometimes complicated and convoluted nature of loan origination and funding, it is necessary to describe the roles of the key actors in the mortgage business. Five key players are involved in this process: the borrower, the broker, the lender, the escrow and title agents, and the appraiser. It is important to note this applies only to the "primary mortgage market" (where lenders and banks originated and provide loans to borrowers) and does not include the secondary mortgage market (the business enterprise of managing loans originated in the primary mortgage market).

The mortgage origination process begins when an applicant, or borrower, applies for a mortgage loan. At this initial stage, the borrower has several options that include using a traditional retail bank or using a third-party source such as a mortgage broker. We focus here on the third-party agent or mortgage broker system—or what we term "fragmented loan origination system"—because it has become the main source of subprime origination during the last decade, which ended in approximately October 2007. Once the borrower completes an application, including basic loan documents, a credit check, and employment and financial verification with a mortgage broker, the agent then uses an available network of approved mortgage lenders, appraisers, and escrow and title companies to seek a loan with the most "favorable" or suitable terms and conditions. The broker plays a crucial role in the overall mortgage origination process and is the "go-to" person between the borrower and all other agencies (lender, appraiser, escrow, and title). Once a suitable lender has been selected, the application then is submitted by the broker on behalf of the borrower. The broker often will recommend that the borrower use the agent's own real-estate appraiser and escrow and title companies because they provide the broker with discounted rates. All correspondence between the borrower and the lender, appraiser, escrow, and title company must go through the mortgage broker. For example, once the lender underwrites the loan application and establishes loan approval conditions (e.g., proof of income, employment, and financial assets), the lender forwards these materials to the broker. The mortgage broker then will attempt to obtain the documentation from the borrower. Once conditions established by the lender have been cleared, the loan is funded, thereby completing the process.

The appraiser, an "objectively independent" valuator of real-estate property, plays a crucial role in this process—to determine the value of the property in the transaction. A particular property value is always a condition of a lender's loan approval. The escrow company is responsible for the equitable and legal exchange of monies as determined by the conditions of the transaction, and the title company is responsible for all matters relating to legal ownership records.

For the purposes of this study, the broker system is referred to as a "fragmented loan origination system" because of the inherent problems that prevent such a system from being independently and objectively viable. These agencies are designed to be independent and objective from each other; yet their profitability is predicated upon their willingness to "bend the rules" to please their broker. For example, a mortgage broker might continue to use an appraiser whose property valuations fall, not within the actual range of a given market, but rather are in line with the broker's business agenda—which includes getting the highest value for each property as possible. Appraisers who are unwilling to bend the rules to obtain the "broker's value" quickly find themselves out of business, as few brokers will use them. The same applies to escrow and title companies, the success of which depends on the business provided by mortgage brokers.

Understanding the process of loan origination and the roles of key participants is necessary for comprehending the complex nature of mortgage fraud and its significance in the subprime mortgage crisis. By doing so, an interesting aspect of the third-party broker system is revealed that is in contravention to the accepted financial industry dogma regarding the importance of independent agency, fairness of competition, and the law—the key players involved in originating a loan are extremely dependent on each other for profitability, and those who are willing to "bend the rules" often are rewarded with continued business and success.

## Methods and Data

Compared with the rest of the country, southern California is ranked among the most active areas in terms property value fluctuation, rate of foreclosures, and lending activity. It is, therefore, no surprise that California is also home to the largest number of subprime mortgage lenders whose activities contributed to the current global economic meltdown. A recent study that analyzed $1.38 trillion worth of subprime mortgages originated between 2005 and 2007 found that approximately 56% of the loans were originated by 15 lenders from California (Abate, 2009). California, thus, represented a suitable site for the selection of respondents in this study.

The primary goal was to locate and identify a pool of potential subjects who (a) had working experience in the subprime lending industry and (b) represented the five sectors of the primary mortgage market (brokerage, lenders, escrow, title, and appraisal). The selection process and access to interviewees were made more manageable as a result of the primary author's previous work experience in the mortgage industry as a mortgage broker. (Between March 2005 and 2007, the lead author worked in the mortgage industry. Although his short tenure in the industry in no way qualifies him as an expert on the topic of fraud, the established business relationships and connections were used as one means of locating and targeting potential research subjects.) Using business solicitation e-mails, business cards, existing loan applications, and lender lists, 56 industry agents were contacted, including brokers, account executives, underwriters, and appraisers. Of the 56 loan agents, 37 were reached, and 17 offered verbal consent over the phone to participate in the study. Six additional subjects were referred later by the original 17 subjects.

### Interviews

All interviews were conducted in person with a total of 23 ($N = 23$) subjects from 2008 to 2009. All interviews took place in a one-on-one context with the exception of two, which were conducted in a group setting. These two interviews involved research subjects who had an established a working relationship with each other and who had agreed to be interviewed together.

A decision not to use a digital voice recorder for the interviews eliminated concern among interviewees about voice recognition. Instead, written notes were taken on a notepad, which led the subjects to feel more comfortable. They were advised to avoid using any identifiers (names, dates, locations, and times) verbally; however, it was common for subjects to speak openly and, in the process, possibly reveal names of persons and places. In such instances, a pseudonym replaced the identifier. No one was allowed to enter or leave the research location during the interview. Once the interview was completed, the data were placed in a locked file.

The interviews were conducted using an elite interview method that allowed the subjects with specialized knowledge of mortgage lending practices and procedures to relate them during the conversation (Dexter, 1970; Lofland and Lofland, 1971). The method followed that used by Pontell, Calavita, and Tillman (1994), who suggested that "the best way to conduct elite interviews is to understand the situation and make full use of the opportunity to extract information from the research situation" (1994: 387). The interviews were semi-structured, which facilitates capturing the subjects' emotions and perspectives. This approach also allowed the subjects to provide information and insight into situations and circumstances that might have been overlooked completely if a predesigned series of questions had been asked. Although structured interviews might benefit the less skilled researcher because they employ a set series of fixed questions, they also necessarily narrow conversations that can omit valuable data.

The discussions with interviewees included topics such as day-to-day mortgage practices and sensitive information, including potentially illegitimate loan origination acts, corporate pressures, and incentives and motivations for fraud. The research questions focused on several broad and specific themes. These themes are personal background and demographic information, employment background and experience in the mortgage industry, understanding of company policies and practices, and employee training. More specific areas focused on the work environment, duties, and responsibilities of the subjects, including common loan origination practices (legal or illegal), organizational pressures, priorities, expectations, financial incentives, and business relationships. Knowledge of the subjects' identities and their actions required extra precautionary measures to ensure that identifiers were not recorded. Subjects were offered the option of giving written consent or waiving written consent. Interviews with each subject lasted between 1 and 2 hours. None required a follow-up interview.

### TABLE 1

### Research Subjects

| Mortgage Sector | Position | n |
|---|---|---|
| **Broker Office** | Mortgage broker | 3 |
| | Loan processor | 2 |
| | Loan officer | 4 |
| **Lender** | Underwriter | 2 |
| | Loan representative | 2 |
| | Account manager | 3 |
| **Appraisal** | Appraisers | 2 |
| **Escrow** | Escrow officer | 2 |
| **Title** | Title officer | 0 |
| **Borrower** | Not applicable | 3 |
| *N* | | 23 |

*Research Subjects*

Table 1 presents the characteristics of the research subjects. To supplement information provided by loan agents, interviewees also included three borrowers who obtained a subprime mortgage. It is important to note that of the three borrowers, two had lost their home because of foreclosure. These borrowers provided input about their experiences in obtaining a subprime loan and their knowledge, or lack thereof, of questionable practices during the loan origination process.

Access was available to loan practitioners who represented a wide spectrum of mortgage industry players. For example, two of the three account managers and both loan representatives in the study were employed by three of the top ten largest subprime mortgage lenders in the United States. Of the four loan officers interviewed, two were employed by small mortgage brokers with ten or fewer employees. Of the 20 loan agents interviewed, 16 worked in a company of 25 or fewer. It is important to note that, although the subjects did not necessarily constitute a representative sample of loan agents in the subprime mortgage industry because they all resided in southern California, all subjects originated loans both inside and outside of the state.

The research subjects' backgrounds varied considerably. The ages ranged from 20 to 46 years with a mean age of 28. Fourteen were male. Of the 23 subjects, all had completed high school, 14 had an educational background that included some college, and 6 had completed a bachelor's degree. None of the subjects had a postgraduate education. Nineteen had no prior experience or training before entering the mortgage industry; most subjects were trained by their employer. Six subjects entered the mortgage industry with related financial background experience, and all had experience in the retail banking industry.

Nguyen, Pontell

### Secondary Data Sources

This research project began in late 2007, only months into the contemporary subprime mortgage crisis. Daily news media accounts, reports, and coverage related to the mortgage crisis were, thus, an invaluable source of data. These sources of information can provide invaluable insight regarding our world (Larson, 2005). As the financial crisis was unraveling, it was imperative to use data sources such as the *Wall Street Journal*, Bloomberg, and the *Financial Times*, to provide the latest information on the subprime fallout and the responsive actions taken by local and federal agencies.

Another crucial source of data was government reports, such as Senate and Congressional hearings, which addressed mortgage-related fraud or problems relating to the housing crisis. Various reports by agencies, such as the U.S. General Accounting Office, the U.S. Federal Housing Administration, and the U.S. Department of Housing and Urban Development, were examined to determine the government's role and response to mortgage-related crimes. Other government sources of data included published reports of the Joint Hearings by the U.S. Senate on predatory lending and the Congressional hearing on mortgage fraud and its impact on mortgage lenders. State and federal law-enforcement information was another data source. The Department of Justice and the FBI disseminated information on mortgage fraud, such as current investigations, mortgage-related crime rates, and trends.

Industry organizations, such as the National Association of Realtors, the Center for Responsible Lending, the Mortgage Bankers Association, and the National Association of Mortgage Brokers, provided additional data. These agencies collect and disseminate housing data, including real-estate values, homeownership rates, and sales projections. The real-estate and finance organizations also conduct studies and release data on mortgage fraud.

## Results

### Mortgage Origination Fraud

Perpetrators commonly perceive many acts of mortgage origination fraud as inseparable from conventional lending practices that are necessary in any "successful" *legitimate* subprime business. As noted, the denial of crime is not a new phenomenon among white-collar criminals (see, for example, Benson, 1985; Jesilow, Pontell, and Geis, 1993; Shover and Coffey, 2002, Shover and Hunter, 2010 Sutherland, 1983). For example, research on telemarketing fraud found that most subjects "rejected the label *criminal* and *crime* as fitting descriptions of them and their activities" (Shover and Coffey, 2002: 13). In the current case, it boils down to different manifestations of a common theme: "We are simply doing our jobs and getting our clients what they want. They are usually happy I got the loan for them." An example is illustrated by the following statement from a loan officer:

> When I get an A paper (good credit) client who wants a 30-year fixed loan but does not make enough, all my brokers told me to put them in stated loan program where I can just state whatever is needed to get the loan. Everyone in the offices I

have worked in would offer stated-loans if the clients didn't make enough money or have enough money in the bank. I have had brokers tell me to state the income much higher on an application just to make sure we get the loan, since we can't restate the income. I have been at many broker offices—this type of stuff is normal in the mortgage industry.

In this particular instance, the perpetrator completely diffused responsibility by redefining the situation so that the blame was placed on the authority figure—the broker. One also can perceive this statement as an appeal to a higher authority, which in this case is the business or corporation s/he works for. Loan agents, especially those who are employed by large organizations, often use this type of rationalization to suborn internal and external controls by contextualizing their actions as consistent with the ethos of the organization to which s/he belongs. When illegitimate loan origination practices are condoned within a working environment—and even promoted by clients, colleagues, and superiors—constraints on unethical and illegal behaviors easily can become suppressed. An important point to keep in mind regarding the statement is the subjects' reference to stated-loans and its relation to fraud, which will be examined in the following section.

Certain types of frauds are not only perceived by loan agents as acceptable mortgage lending practice, but also are considered "good for business." Business leaders might ascribe to the means necessary to make a profit, even if such methods violate the law. Benson (1985: 593) argued that business rules govern profit making and survival in a competitive capitalist environment, thereby superseding legislation and governance. Illustrating business reality's rule of "good business practice," another loan officer stated:

> I work with my clients and let them know right off the bat what income they need to have for the loan. Most of my clients don't make enough so I put them in a stated product where I can state the income that is needed to get the loan. It's hard sometimes to make it (financial information) look legitimate, but most of the time you can find a lender to approve the loan. I took care of my borrowers and gave them what they wanted. They all knew that they can get a loan anywhere, so I have to take good care of them if I want to make money. A lot of my business is repeat business. I have borrowers who have refinanced their one home with me three times.

This is an example of a loan agent who committed both fraud and predatory lending simultaneously. In this case, the agent had prior knowledge that the borrower did not have the ability to pay the monthly mortgage and yet steered the borrower into a particular loan for which it was relatively easy to provide false financial information.

A common theme among our interviewees was the accessibility to fraud. Subjects often referred to the importance of a "willing lender," a specific loan product, or a cooperative borrower in the successful outcome of a loan originated by illegitimate means. For example, having an appraiser willing to "bend the rules" to maximize the value of the property in question is a crucial part of any loan. It was common for interviewees to express that, during the real-estate boom, it was relatively easy to justify appraisal values that exceeded the actual value of a property. Appraisers could avoid taking pictures that showed damage to the property or could use nearby properties with greater appreciation as comparable, for example. One interviewee said all that had to be done was "not reveal anything that would reduce the value of the property." For example, if a garage was converted into a bedroom without a permit, then the appraiser would include only an exterior picture. In the 1990s, the extraordinary increase in real-estate values made the practice of inflating home prices relatively easy and very lucrative for appraisers. This development is an important aspect of understanding mortgage origination fraud as it directly relates to the overarching theme of alternative loan products, poor underwriting standards, absent accountability, and fraud.

Subjects often described actions such as overstating a borrower's income and assets, post-dating documents, file stuffing, and altering employment title as a financial skill rather than as a criminal act, which requires a "creative touch" to get a loan funded. These loan agents were proud of their abilities and often would engage in self-admiration. When two or more of these types are present within an organization, competition for status between the agents can occur. Some might perceive themselves to be invaluable to the loan business. Remarks by a loan representative and a broker that "I had many clients who couldn't get a loan anywhere before they came to me" and "I closed loans using my toolkit when they had nowhere else to go" are some examples of this justification. Although this behavior is an uncommon self-preservation strategy, it can be successful in maintaining one's positive image. For example, a loan representative remarked that:

> Every month we would check to see who closed the most deals, and it was always between me and two other reps. I had one of the highest funding ratios in the company. I funded a minimum of a couple million dollars a month. I try not to deny any loan, if possible. There is always a way to make a loan work—you just have to find the angle.

The following description from a loan officer is another example of this viewpoint:

> You can get anyone a loan if you are good. You have to work with what your client has. If he has a crappy job, change his title so you can state a higher income. If the income is still not enough, give him another job. There is a lot you can do to qualify someone. Go stated, make him pay off debts, change the loan amount, change his job title, add someone to the loan. If he doesn't have enough money in the bank, for example, put his name on another person's account and get a VOD of that account.

The involvement of the borrower in the fraud was described by subjects as much more commonplace and widespread than traditionally understood. Borrowers are well aware that they lack certain qualifications for a loan and depend on their loan agent to qualify them. Illustrating this point, a loan officer stated the following:

> When my clients do not make enough money to get a certain loan or a certain rate they want, I get them a stated loan. You can put down anything for their income or assets as long as it sounds reasonable to the lender. They want the loan, so even though they know that my client can't possibly make what I put down, it's a stated loan. My lenders don't really make an issue about the income I state unless it doesn't make sense at all. So I just work the employment title and that's it. Borrowers are usually grateful that I got them the loan. They don't care that I stated in the application that they make this amount of money when they really didn't. They are just happy I got them the loan.

In this instance, the perpetrator used a classic neutralization technique—denial of victim. Everyone involved in this transaction serves to benefit; the borrower gets the loan, and the remaining parties (loan officer, broker, and lender) get the business. In a period when home values continued to skyrocket and mortgages were paid on time, everyone stood to benefit. It was only when the housing crisis began that the true victims emerged.

In discussing the role of fraud among loan originators and borrowers, Black (2008: 6) noted that "mortgage origination personnel, not borrowers, overwhelmingly took the lead in mortgage fraud—even when the borrowers shared culpability because they knew that the representations the lender recommended were false. It is, therefore, extremely difficult to determine not only the true incidence of frauds but also the true number of borrowers that obtain loans with the knowledge that their financial representations were false." The most common forms of financial misrepresentations that occur in loan applications are the borrower's income and assets, both of which are clearly visible on the loan application. A borrower seeking a mortgage usually finds out early in the process the potential factors (e.g., insufficient credit, income, assets, or mortgage history) that might led to denial of the loan. For example, one borrower stated the following:

> I tried getting a loan but was unable to for like 2 months. Then my broker told me that I was rejected for a loan, and so we needed to go to different lenders. I don't remember exactly, but I think it was because I didn't make enough or that my credit wasn't that great. He had to submit my loan to several banks, and on the loan application, we had to put that I made $14,000 a month, which was obviously not true, but he got me the refinance I wanted so I was happy.

As a result, the loan agents and borrowers in this study each stipulated that a fully informed and cooperative relationship was mutually beneficial to the successful outcome of a loan origination. Loan originators commonly expressed the importance of being straightforward and honest with their clients, despite the legitimacy of the loan. Inconsistent information and poor cooperation between the loan agent and the client can lead to problems should the lender conduct a thorough underwriting of the loan. The following comment made by a mortgage broker illustrates the denial of a victim and the diffusion of responsibility:

> Everyone thinks that borrowers are victims when they know about what is needed to get them approved. I tell my borrowers if they don't make enough or don't have enough money and tell them this is what we have to do or no one will give them a loan. They all know and have to agree or we don't even try to submit the loan to the lender. They have to work with us if they want the loan.

Once the loan application has been submitted to a prospective lender, it is managed by an account manager or an underwriter. These loan agents are critical to the successful outcome or funding of a loan and to the detection of fraud. They work directly with brokers, loan officers, and processors on a regular basis, and it is not uncommon for them to coach their clients on how to structure a loan or document to avoid red flags from their lender. In this stage of the loan origination process, the most common forms of fraud are directly associated with poor underwriting practices:

> Most of my brokers were good. They knew what they were doing, but some brokers came into the industry and didn't know the difference between a 1003 (uniform residential loan application) and a 1008 (transmittal summary). When my bad brokers submitted a loan that obviously didn't work, I would send it back and tell them what to change. Many times, they still wouldn't get it, and I have to go back and forth several times with them. Sometimes, I just tell them to submit the loan somewhere else because it got too fishy. My good brokers knew better. They made sure everything was clean by the time I got the file.

Account managers and underwriters are responsible for approving loan conditions once they have verified the information. For example, a loan approval might be predicated on verification of conditions such as an applicant's employment and assets. It is common for these loan agents to overlook questionable information or to approve a condition of a loan without verification. Funders and appraisal reviewers also commonly overlook questionable information, such as an appraisal that lacks the required comparisons to justify the value of the property in question.

It should be noted that the subjects interviewed in this study stipulated that fraudulent acts were uncommon among escrow and title company agents. Although rare, acts of concerted ignorance sometimes occur among escrow agents, such as intentionally ignoring or leaving out the "yield spread premium" (i.e., the money or rebate that is paid to the mortgage broker by the lender for selling a higher interest loan than what the borrower qualifies) on the final legal disclosure statement. This oversight allows a mortgage broker to conceal from the borrower how much money or "kickback" was paid by the lender. Such a practice by an escrow company is a violation of the Real Estate and Settlement Procedures Act (1974).

Levi (1984: 322) stated, "It is extraordinary difficult to distinguish white-collar crime from ordinary business transactions." The complex nature of financial transactions made it "difficult to disentangle victim from criminal and crime from business as usual" (Lloyd, 2006: k–2). In the mortgage industry, an intricate collaboration must exist among loan agents, borrowers, and lenders (account managers, reps, underwriters, and funders) to originate a loan and get it funded. Information on a loan application must undergo numerous levels of scrutiny and verification by different parties for a loan to be approved. The problem, however, was the widespread culture of maximizing profit margins and achieving financial targets over ethical practices. These detailed accounts provided by loan agents who currently are employed and who previously were employed in the subprime lending industry provide insight into central aspects of mortgage origination fraud. Besides documenting the a priori rationalizations offenders used to excuse their actions, a primary purpose of the accounts was to provide a deeper understanding of the types and patterns of fraud that led to the global economic crisis and to apply this understanding to effective preventative policy.

## Conclusion and Policy Implications

To prevent mortgage origination fraud effectively, one must first understand the crime-facilitative environment (Needleman and Needleman, 1979; Shover and Hochstetler, 2006) that naturally led to such practices and, thus, consider strategies that address problematic lending policies and practices in general. As of early 2010, the subprime lending industry held a much smaller market share of the overall mortgage industry because of the massive number of subprime-related mortgage defaults and out-of-business subprime lenders. The subprime lending system, which held a large share of total mortgage originations until the end of 2007, rewarded mortgage brokers for placing borrowers in higher cost loans, which is in contrast to a loan agent's fiduciary responsibilities, making the lender–broker reward system a fiduciary conundrum. A holistic approach to addressing the problem of mortgage fraud requires a consideration of policies that not only directly address offending but also reduce and effectively monitor potential conflicts of interest in the home-lending system itself. What follows are general recommendations aimed at (a) addressing policies and lending practices that provide major opportunities and incentives for engaging in mortgage fraud and (b) eliminating the sources of the justifications loan agents use for their illegal behaviors.

The poor underwriting standards and practices associated with the subprime lending industry are major contributors to fraud. Lenders need to incorporate additional layers of verification regarding sensitive financial data and documents. For example, a separate and independent entity or department can be established by the lender to scrutinize every loan immediately prior to funding. Lenders also might consider the option of an off-site and unbiased independent reviewer. Certain alternative loan products such as stated ("liar") loans either should be abolished or modified into a hybrid loan product that can be an amalgam of stated and verified, whereas fully stated loan products need to be eliminated altogether. Such hybrid loan programs should be combined with strict underwriting standards and procedures that enhance the verification of financial information not only to ensure the accuracy and authenticity of sensitive information but also to verify that the borrower can afford the loan.

Deregulation in the banking industry driven by neoclassical policies has circumvented legal and social constraints, ethics, and accountability in a period of subprime lending expansion where increased government supervision and oversight was paramount. The government protections and internal controls offered by the Community Reinvestment Act (1977), for example, need to be extended over all lending organizations to reconcile the perverse growth of alternative mortgage products, loose underwriting standards, and no accountability—which currently characterize the subprime industry.

The dominant, fragmented broker system that involves as many as four different independent entities (mortgage broker, appraiser, lender, and escrow and title) in the loan origination process has reduced the accountability of loan agents involved in the process greatly. Although benefits exist to this system (e.g., the convenience of shopping multiple lenders), the self-interested motivations of those involved raise questions of a contradictory nature regarding ethics and the goals of finance capitalism. A mortgage broker, for example, should serve the best interests of their client; however, brokers will make more money if they charge clients higher upfront fees, higher interest rates, hidden prepayment penalties, and sell loans that contain difficult terms and conditions. The mortgage industry needs to reconsider this compensation system and, instead, to take a commission or bonus-for-quality approach to rewarding their employees. Employees who are rewarded based on loans that are performing likely will take into account the ability of their client to repay. One approach, for example, is a bonus system that rewards quality screening of applicants rather than how many loans an employee can secure each month. Lenders should consider rewarding employees once a loan has been in good standing for 6 months to 1 year rather than immediately after the loan is funded. Lenders should adopt compensating brokers a flat fee for each loan, which would eliminate the motivation of placing borrowers in loans that contain hidden interest rate charges and fees. Although these recommendations do not address the problem of fraud directly, they aim to correct the poor lending practices that have contributed to the overall problems—including fraud—that characterize the subprime lending industry.

The passage of Bill H.R. 1728, the Mortgage Reform and Anti-Predatory Lending Act of 2009, in the House of Representatives signifies a major step in the right direction by the federal government. The new law, if passed in the Senate, will mandate new restrictions on lending activities and increased standards regarding consumer protection notification and disclosure in the loan origination process. According to the Bill, mortgage originators, creditors, and lenders will be prohibited from charging certain prepayment penalties, must make a good-faith determination regarding their clients' reasonable ability to repay a loan, and must establish that a concrete net benefit to the borrower exists for all mortgage refinances. The rationale behind these reforms is to ensure that the creditor is acting in the best interest of the borrower. The Bill also improves on existing regulatory inadequacies that have allowed loan originators or creditors to escape accountability for their actions. Under the proposed Bill, creditors will maintain a portion of the risk on subprime loans that they sell to investors, and consumers will be allowed to "obtain redress directly from firms involved in securitizing mortgages" (House Committee on Financial Services, 2009).

Policies that focus on the perpetrator might include techniques that confront the neutralizations that are commonly used by perpetrators, which can be effective at an organizational level. Mortgage companies should be required to provide continued training and legal awareness programs as a condition of operation. These programs could focus on delegitimizing excuses, identifying criminal violations and sanctions of such actions regardless of seriousness, pinpointing victims, and promoting ethical standards. By attacking the belief systems or by blocking the justifications that inhibit the perpetrators' guilt levels, loan agents might be less likely to normalize their actions within the context of their organization. Organizational leaders also can educate their lower level employees of the common lending practices that might be construed as legal when, in fact, they are criminal violations. These measures would make it very difficult for loan agents to justify illegal behavior. For those offenders who "acknowledge the immorality of their conduct," the use of reintegrative shaming might serve as a viable solution (Shover and Coffey, 2002: 21). Such an approach would "try to impress on the offenders the harm they have done to the persons they have victimized, and yet treat them so that they do not find themselves isolated from the support that might set them on another and law-abiding vocational path" (Doocy et al., 2001: 22).

The preceding recommendations have major domestic and global implications, of which financial institutions should observe. An important step in the recovery process will be the need to accept, observe, and understand the role of fraud in the global crisis. This study has examined the "bottom level" offending that provided the foundation for the global financial crisis. Subprime loans, which were packaged and sold worldwide, provided the "toxic assets" that poisoned the international banking system through a complex structuring of derivatives and other financial instruments. Through future investigation, it is likely to be found that fraud played a significant role in other aspects of the crisis as well. The savings and loans debacle should have taught us the dangers of poor regulatory oversight and enforcement, loose lending policies, lack of accountability, and underwriting standards that allow fraud to flourish.

The findings in this study also present major theoretical implications for understanding the causes of white-collar crime, albeit outside the economic perspective. Recent application of crime-as-choice theory—a criminological perspective historically used to understand traditional street level crimes—as a model for understanding white-collar crimes provides tremendous insight into mortgage frauds and the perpetrators who commit them. Shover and Hochstetler's (2006: xvi) paradigm of "lure, oversight, and the supply of the tempted or predisposed" illustrates the various temptations (i.e., vulnerable and unsuspecting borrowers eager to obtain a loan and loose lending policies that make it effortless to overcharge borrowers and manipulate financial data) present in the structure of the subprime lending industry, and also highlights the criminal implications of these factors in the absence of credible oversight. White-collar "lure is not criminal opportunity, but in the absence of credible oversight it is" (Shover and

Hochstetler, 2006: 28); couple these factors with a motivated offender and the outcome likely is criminal decision making. The findings in the study illustrate that loan agents—traditionally law-abiding members of society—often face situations (e.g., organization culture that promotes and encourages fraud or management that focuses on profit margins more than ethical standards) in the industry that compromise or threaten their self-restraint (a primary defense mechanism against criminal decision making), thus rendering them criminally predisposed (Shover and Hochstetler, 2006). The results presented here point to the need for more scientific inquiry into choice theory as an explanatory model for mortgage frauds in the subprime lending industry and for understanding white-collar crime more generally.

## References

Abate, Tom. 2009. California had most subprime loans, study says. *San Francisco Chronicle*. Retrieved July 21, 2009 from sfgate.com/cgi-&bin/article.cgi?f=/c/a/2009/05/07/MNF417FUBR.DTL&type=business.

BasePoint Analytics. 2007. *New Early Payment Default: Links to Fraud and Impact on Mortgage Lenders and Investment Banks*. White paper. Carlsbad, CA: BasePoint Analytics.

Benson, Michael L. 1985. Denying the guilty mind: Accounting for involvement in white-collar crime. *Criminology*, 23: 583–608.

Black, William K. 2005. *The Best Way to Rob a Bank is to Own One: How Corporate Executives and Politicians Looted the S&L Industry*. Austin, TX: University of Texas Press.

Black, William K. 2008. *Why Greenspan's & Bush's Regulatory Failures Allowed a "Criminogenic Environment."* Paper presented at the Levy Institute's Minsky Conference, Annandale-on-Hudson, NY.

Black, William K. 2009. Bill Moyer's journal. *PBS.org*. Retrieved June 2, 2009 from pbs.org/moyers/journal/04032009/transcript1.html.

Black, William K, Kitty Calavita, and Henry N. Pontell. 1995. The savings and loan debacle of the 1980s: White-collar crime or risky business? *Law and Policy*, 17: 23–55.

Calavita, Kitty and Henry N. Pontell. 1990. Heads I win, tails you lose: Deregulation, crime, and crisis in the savings and loan industry. *Crime & Delinquency*, 36: 309–341.

Calavita, Kitty, Robert Tillman, and Henry N. Pontell. 1997. The savings and loan debacle, financial crime, and the state. *Annual Review of Sociology*, 23: 19–38.

Coleman, James W. 2002. *The Criminal Elite: The Sociology of White-Collar Crime*, 5th edition. New York: St. Martin's.

Conklin, John E. 2004. *Criminology*, 8th edition. Boston, MA: Pearson.

Department of Justice. 2008. *Federal Authorities Announce Significant Regional Federal Mortgage Fraud Investigations and Prosecutions Coinciding with Nationwide "Operation Malicious Mortgage" Takedown*. Department of Justice Press Release. Retrieved January 3, 2009 from sacramento.fbi.gov/dojpressrel/pressrel08/sc061908a.htm.

Dexter, Lewis A. 1970. *Elite and Specialized Interviewing*. Evanston, IL: Northwestern University Press.

Doocy, Jeffrey, David Shichor, Dale Secrest, and Gilbert Geis. 2001. Telemarketing fraud: Who are the tricksters and what makes them tick? *Security Journal*, 14: 7–26.

Federal Bureau of Investigation. 2003. *Financial Crimes Section: Financial Institution Fraud Unit, Mortgage Fraud: A Guide for Investigators*. Washington, DC: Author.

Federal Bureau of Investigation. 2007. *2006 Mortgage Fraud Report*. Retrieved August 21, 2009 from fbi.gov/publications/fraud/mortgage_fraud06.htm.

Financial Crimes Enforcement Network (FinCEN). 2006. *Mortgage Loan Fraud: An Industry Assessment Based upon Suspicious Activity Report Analysis*. Retrieved August 8, 2008 from fincen.gov/news_room/rp/reports/pdf/mortgage_fraud112006.pdf.

Financial Crimes Enforcement Network (FinCEN). 2007. The *SAR Activity Review—By the Numbers*. Retrieved June 3, 2008 from fincen.gov/news_room/rp/files/sar_by_numb_09.pdf.

Financial Crimes Enforcement Network (FinCEN), Regulatory Policy and Programs Division. 2006. *Mortgage Loan Fraud Connections with Other Financial Crime: An Evaluation of Filed by Money Services Businesses, Securities and Futures Firms, Insurance Companies and Casinos*. Report analysis. Washington, DC: U.S. Department of Treasury.

Galbraith, James. 2009. No return to normal: Why the economic crisis, and its solution, are bigger than you think. *Washington Monthly*. Retrieved July 26, 2009 from washingtonmonthly.com/features/2009/0903.galbraith.html.

Global Insight. 2007. *U.S. Metro Economies: The Mortgage Crisis*. Retrieved June 2, 2009 from usmayors.org/metroeconomies/1107/report.pdf.

Greenspan, Alan. 2008. We will never have a perfect model of risk. *Financial Times*. Retrieved January 3, 2009 from ft.com/cms/s/0/edbdbcf6-f360-11dc-b6bc-0000779fd2ac.html?nclick_check=1.

House Committee on Financial Services. 2009. *Press Release: March 26, 2009. Miller, Watt and Frank Introduce National Mortgage Reform and Anti-Predatory Lending Bill*. Retrieved December 20, 2009 from house.gov/apps/list/press/financialsvcs_dem/press0326098.shtml.

Jesilow, Paul, Henry N. Pontell, and Gilbert Geis. 1993. *Prescription for Profit: How Doctors Defraud Medicaid*. Berkeley: University of California Press.

Kary, Tiffany. 2008. New Century bankruptcy examiner says KPMG aided fraud. *Bloomberg*, Update4. Retrieved August 28, 2008 from bloomberg.com/apps/news?pid=20601103&sid=aXebBOZ3eBjQ&refer=news.

Larson, Stephanie G. 2005. *Media and Minorities: The Politics of Race in the News and Entertainment Media*. Lanham, MD: Rowman & Littlefield.

Levi, Michael. 1984. Giving creditors the business: The criminal law in inaction. *International Journal of the Sociology of Law*, 12: 321–333.

Lloyd, Carol. 2006. Mortgage fraud—The worst crime no ones heard of. *San Francisco Chronicle*, p. K-2.

Lofland, John and Lyn Loftland. 1971. *Analyzing Social Settings: A Guide to Qualitative Observation and Analysis*. Belmont, CA: Wadsworth.

Mortgage Bankers Association. 2007. *Mortgage Fraud: Strengthening Federal and State Fraud Prevention Efforts.* Retrieved June 3, 2008 from mortgagebankers.org/files/News/InternalResource/57274_Study.pdf.

Needleman, Martin L. and Carolyn Needleman. 1979. Organizational crime: Two models of criminogenesis. *The Sociological Quarterly*, 20: 517–528.

Pontell, Henry N. and Kitty Calavita. 1993. Organizational crime in the savings and loan industry. In (Michael H. Tonry and Albert J. Reiss, Jr., eds.), *Beyond the Law: Crime in Complex Organizations*. Chicago, IL: University of Chicago Press.

Pontell, Henry N., Kitty Calavita, and Robert Tillman. 1994. Corporate crime and criminal justice system capacity: Government response to financial institutions fraud. *Justice Quarterly*, 11: 383–410.

Rosoff, Stephen M., Henry N. Pontell, and Robert Tillman. 2010. *Profit without Honor: White-Collar Crime and the Looting of America*, 5th edition. Upper Saddle River, NJ: Pearson Prentice Hall.

Sasseen, Jane. 2008. FBI widens net around subprime industry. *Times Online*. Retrieved July 24, 2009 from business.timesonline.co.uk/tol/business/markets/united_states/article3275102.ece.

Schloemer, Ellen, Keith Ernst, and Kathleen Keest. 2006. Losing Group: Foreclosures in the subprime market and their cost to homeowners. Center for Responsible Lending. Retrieved January 4, 2009 from responsiblelending.org/mortgage-lending/research-analysis/foreclosure-paper-report-2-17.pdf3.

Schmitt, Richard B. 2008. Federal sweep triggered by mortgage crisis nets over 400 for alleged scams. *Los Angeles Times*. Retrieved December 2, 2009 from articles.latimes.com/2008/jun/20/business/fi-mortgage20.

Sharick, Merle, Erin E. Omba, Nick Larson, and James D. Croft. 2006. *Eighth Periodic Mortgage Fraud Case.* Report to the Mortgage Bankers Association. Reston, VA: Mortgage Asset Research Institute.

Shover, Neal and Glenn S. Coffey. 2002. *Origins, Pursuits, and Careers of Telemarketing Predators.* Final Report to NIJ. Grant 00-IJ-CX-0028.

Shover, Neal and Andy Hochstetler. 2006. *Choosing White-Collar Crime*. Cambridge, MA: Cambridge University Press.

Shover, Neal and Ben W. Hunter. 2010. Blue-collar, white-collar: Crimes and mistake. In (Win Bernasco, ed.), *Offenders on Offending: Learning about Crime from Criminals*. Cullompton, U.K.: Willan.

Sutherland, Edwin H. 1983 [1949]. *White-Collar Crime: The Uncut Version*. New Haven, CT: Yale University Press.

Sykes, Gresbam and David Matza. 1957. Techniques of neutralization: A theory of delinquency. *American Sociological Review* 22: 667–670.

Tillman, Robert and Henry N. Pontell. 1995. Organizations and fraud in the savings and loan industry. *Social Forces*, 73: 1439–1463.

**Statutes Cited**

Community Reinvestment Act, 12 U.S.C. § 2901 (1977).

Mortgage Reform and Anti-Predatory Lending Act, 15 U.S.C. § 1641 (2009).

Real Estate and Settlement Procedures Act, 12 U.S.C. § 2601 (1974).

---

**Tomson H. Nguyen** is an assistant professor of criminal justice at the University of Houston—Downtown. His academic awards include the Western Society of Criminology *Student Paper Award*, the Academy of Criminal Justice Sciences *Student Paper Award*, and the *Minority Fellowship Award* from the American Society of Criminology. His research has appeared in *Deviant Behavior* and the *Journal of Asian Americans and Pacific Islander Nexus: Policy, Practice and Community*. He received his Ph.D. in criminology, law, and society from the University of California, Irvine in 2009.

**Henry N. Pontell** is a professor of criminology, law, and society at the University of California, Irvine. He has written broadly on white-collar and corporate crime, particularly in the areas of health care and financial frauds. More recently, his work has focused on the role of white-collar crime in major financial debacles, identity theft, economic crime in the gambling industry, and comparative studies of corporate crime in Asia. He is a former vice president and fellow of the American Society of Criminology and is co-author (with Stephen Rosoff and Robert Tillman) of *Profit Without Honor: White-Collar Crime and the Looting of America,* 5th Edition (Pearson Prentice Hall, 2010).

# [12]

# ODIOUS DEBT, ODIOUS CREDIT, ECONOMIC DEVELOPMENT, AND DEMOCRATIZATION

TOM GINSBURG*

THOMAS S. ULEN**

## I

## INTRODUCTION

Consider an all-too-common story. A dictator of a poor country borrows liberally from international donors, nominally to fund development projects. Some fraction goes to development projects, but a larger share ends up in the hands of the elites who are part of the dictator's governing coalition or in the dictator's Swiss bank account. At the same time, the dictator is misgoverning the country, not undertaking health and educational expenditures that could enhance the well-being of the citizens of the country, further enriching himself and his supporters from domestic sources. As the foreign debt and the dictator's personal riches add up, it increasingly looks as if the debt cannot be paid. Lending stops, the dictator's government collapses, and the country struggles to establish new democratic institutions. The new democracy tries to make the debt payments but finds that they draw away from necessary spending on social services to meet pent-up demands. The government becomes unstable; the democracy waivers and eventually collapses.

In this story, the dictator has taken not just the present but also the future, dooming the country's democratic institutions in their infancy. Why then should the new democratic government pay the dictator's debts, even those made in the name of the nation? To put it in more concrete terms, why should the citizens of Zaire be saddled with the debt of Mobutu Sese Seko, under whom the country accumulated over $12 billion in sovereign debt, while Mobutu's personal assets reached $4 billion? Why should Filipinos today be responsible for the $28 billion in sovereign debt left by Ferdinand Marcos, who left his heirs a personal fortune of $10 billion?

This article is also available at http://law.duke.edu/journals/lcp.

\* Professor of Law, University of Illinois College of Law, and Director, Illinois Program on Asian Law, Politics, and Society.

\*\* Swanlund Chair, University of Illinois at Urbana-Champaign, and Professor of Law, University of Illinois College of Law, and Director, Illinois Program on Law and Economics. The authors would like to thank Amber Danielle Evans for excellent research assistance.

The standard international-law response is that states, not governments, are responsible entities.[1] So, for instance, when a country signs an international treaty, it is not the government but the state that is bound, and the obligation will stand until a subsequent government formally exits the treaty. Exit is presumed to be costly: a government that "repudiates" earlier treaty obligations will suffer reputational harm in its international relations.[2] This general background norm of international law applies as well to debt: a government can announce that it is renouncing debt, but it will suffer severe reputational harm in the debt marketplace, much as a government that repudiates public international law obligations suffers a reputational harm. In addition, assets of the repudiating state can be seized abroad, so there will be real enforcement of the obligation. There is, as yet, no form of sovereign bankruptcy to allow debtor nations to escape obligations.[3]

## A. The Odious Debt Problem

At times, major powers—invoking what has come to be known as the doctrine of "odious debt"—have argued that new regimes should not be responsible for debts incurred by old ones. After the Spanish-American War, for example, the United States argued that neither Cuba nor the United States should be responsible for debt incurred by the colonial Spanish government. In the famous Tinoco Arbitration of 1923, the panel suggested that credits knowingly extended to a country for a dictator who used the money for his personal purposes should not be recoverable.[4] Recently, the fall of Saddam Hussein in Iraq has prompted renewed calls for reviving this doctrine and creating an odious debt exception to state succession.[5] Despite these incidents,

---

1. *See generally* IAN BROWNLIE, PRINCIPLES OF PUBLIC INTERNATIONAL LAW (6th ed. 2003).

2. One example is the Argentinean experience with reneging on international debt obligations. PAUL BLUSTEIN, AND THE MONEY KEPT ROLLING OUT (AND IN) (2006).

3. *See generally* Conference, *Sovereign Debt Restructuring: The View from the Legal Academy*, 53 EMORY L.J. 657, 657–1218 (2004) (examining potential methods of sovereign-debt restructuring); Andrew T. Guzman, *Colloquy: International Bankruptcy: In Defense of Universalism*, 98 MICH. L. REV. 2177 (2000) (evaluating universal and territorial approaches to the adjudication of international insolvencies).

4. *Arbitration Between Great Britain and Costa Rica*, 1 U.N. REP. INT'L. ARB. AWARDS 369, 375–76 (1923), *reprinted in* 18 AM. J. INT'L L. 147, 148 (1924).

5. For some of the recent literature, see generally PATRICIA ADAMS, ODIOUS DEBTS: LOOSE LENDING, CORRUPTION AND THE THIRD WORLD'S ENVIRONMENTAL LEGACY (1991) (reviewing the history of odious lending); Joseph Hanlon, *"Illegitimate Debt": When Creditors Should be Liable for Improper Loans, in* SOVEREIGN DEBT AT THE CROSSROADS 109 (Chris Jochnick & Fraser A. Preston eds., 2006) (focusing on the odiousness of lending regardless of the status of the borrower); Anna Gelpern, *What Iraq and Argentina Might Learn from Each Other*, 6 CHI. J. INT'L L. 391 (2005) (analyzing sovereign debt in Iraq and Argentina); Seema Jayachandran & Michael Kremer, *Odious Debt*, 96 AM. ECON. REV. 82 (2006) (arguing that loan sanctions, unlike trade sanctions, may prevent odious debt); Ashfaq Khalfan, Jeff King & Bryan Thomas, *Advancing the Odious Debt Doctrine* (Ctr. for Int'l Sustainable Dev. Law, Working Paper, 2003), *available at* http://www.odiousdebts.org/odiousdebts/publications/Advancing_the_Odious_Debt_Doctrine.pdf (defining odious debt and arguing for cancellation of odious debt under international law); *see also* FOREIGN POLICY, *Ranking the Rich*, FOREIGN POLICY, Sept.–Oct. 2006, at 68, 70 (discussing Iraqi and Nigerian loan write-offs);

the international community has not yet adopted a general doctrine of excusing odious debts. Rather, the default rule is that sovereign debt is to be repaid, regardless of the circumstances under which it was contracted or for which the debt was used. Whereas international powers may act in an ad hoc way to assume or restructure sovereign debt of favored countries, no general off-the-shelf doctrine is available to be applied in a neutral manner across cases.[6]

## B. Three Responses

Scholars who have recognized the odious debt problem have proposed several creative solutions. Of these, three general forms of proposed solutions can be identified.

### 1. The "Do Nothing" Approach

The most elemental of the proposed solutions to the problem of odious debt—one to which very few tie their flags—is simply to do nothing.[7] An alternative way of stating much the same position is to hold that sovereign debt is always to be enforced.[8] If that is the clear rule governing these matters, then all parties in this market are on notice and can make their own calculations of expected cost and benefit. The market for international debt is a sophisticated and ongoing competitive market. There is no obvious source of market failure that calls for correction. In essence, this position holds that odious debt presents no systematic problem in international law and relations requiring a novel institutional, policy, or legal solution.

An argument in favor of a clear rule for the enforceability of sovereign debt begins with the observation that the parties involved in lending and borrowing money in international debt markets are sophisticated. They understand how to evaluate risk, including the risk of default; how to use contractual language and legal processes to protect themselves; and how to appeal to public bodies for relief if the law is unavailing. As a result, lenders who extend credit to nations ruled by despots whose successors might seek to repudiate the debt can hardly

---

Lee. C. Buchheit, G. Mitu Gulati & Robert B. Thompson, *The Dilemma of Odious Debts*, 56 DUKE L.J. 1201, 1208–24 (2007) (addressing the taxonomy of sovereign debt).

6. Odious debt can be seen as a special case of the more general problem of debt relief, which is an issue raised by many developing countries that cannot meet their debt burden. *See, e.g.*, Ellen Johnson Sirleaf & Paul Wolfowitz, *Lift Liberia's Debt Burden*, WALL ST. J., Feb. 13, 2007, at A25.

7. *See generally* Albert H. Choi & Eric A. Posner, *A Critique of the Odious Debt Doctrine*, 70 LAW & CONTEMP. PROBS. 33 (Summer 2007) (suggesting that the overall effect of the application of the current odious debt doctrine could potentially be negative and stating a need for more empirical work before instituting the doctrine).

8. One might argue that the opposite rule—that sovereign debt is never enforceable—would also, under the appropriate assumptions, lead to an optimal state of affairs. This is simply an exercise in the application of the Coase Theorem, which examines economic efficiency through the allocation of property rights and considerations of transaction costs. Note, though, that there is some evidence that enforceability of sovereign debt played a key role in early capitalism, underpinning the industrial revolution. *See, e.g.*, Douglass C. North & Barry R. Weingast, *Constitutions and Commitment: The Evolution of Institutions Governing Public Choice in Seventeenth-Century England*, 49 J. ECON. HISTORY 803 (1989).

complain that they were unfairly surprised by this turn of events. Rather, those lenders could plausibly be thought to have willingly assumed the risk of non-payment: they assessed the likelihood of a default's occurring and took (or could have easily taken) steps—such as self- or market-insurance—to protect themselves from loss.

Despots seeking loans are equally adept at assessing their market opportunities and, no doubt, seek the best deal that they can, subject to the obvious fact that lenders want to be repaid. If a despot repeatedly uses loans for purposes other than those for which it was loaned, his access to international debt markets might be compromised. To the extent that despots are repeat players in the international debt market, they have an incentive to be reasonably truthful and relatively transparent to the lending community.

If the market for international debt "works" in the sense that all relevant information is available, all parties are well informed, and there are no obvious market imperfections, then there is no particularly compelling case for third-party intervention.

However, there might be an external cost to a despot's loans taken out in the name of his country—a cost born by the citizens who may be obliged to repay the loans after the despot's departure. Those citizens cannot be fairly inferred to have approved of the despot's loans—unless, of course, those loans were used for public projects. That is, if the despot's loans were incurred, as in some of the examples above, to enrich the despot or for the furtherance of some folly—uses for which a democratically elected government would have been extremely unlikely to have incurred international debt—then there is no principled argument (other than that laid out in Part II) for the nation's citizens to be held responsible for those debts. They could not meaningfully (as through election, public pressure on legislators, or expressions of displeasure in public fora) have prevented the loans from being incurred. And it is unlikely to be the case that the dictator's loan activity is a triggering action for regime change. Dissatisfaction with that aspect of a despot's rule might have been relatively minor in the list of complaints—that is, perhaps not enough of a dissatisfaction to warrant armed rebellion. So, the citizens are simply stuck with responsibility for a despot's debts incurred in the name of the nation, or hopeful of simply reneging on the loans without damaging the nation's access to credit.

At first blush, this externality argument might seem to defeat the "do nothing" solution in favor of some internationally mediated, institutional method of dealing with odious debt. But further consideration might suggest that even the presence of unfairly burdened citizens is not really a cause for an international institutional solution; it might be the case that international donors, organizations, or nations might step in to relieve unfairly burdened citizens of responsibility for sovereign debt incurred by a former dictator.

Consider this scenario. Saddam Hussein, while the dictator of Iraq, incurs billions of dollars in loans, ostensibly for legitimate public purposes but, in reality, for unsupportable purposes. He is toppled by a U.S. invasion, and an unstable but roughly democratic government takes over administration of the country. The "do nothing" solution would argue in favor of this new government's assuming the debt obligations of the Hussein government. And naturally the lenders who are owed millions argue that the new government has the resources to discharge these obligations. For example, in theory the new government can now sell oil freely to international buyers, something that the Hussein government could not legitimately do because of United Nations sanctions. But, just as naturally, the new democratic government argues that it should not have to discharge these obligations. It has obligations to rebuild the country from the invasion and from years of neglect under Hussein; to build or reconstruct schools, roads, hospitals, water and sewerage infrastructure; and so on. If the new, democratically elected government were obliged to discharge Hussein's debts, it would have much less revenue left to undertake the nation-building that will make the democratic government more stable.

Suppose that there are some extraordinarily large international private enterprises that believe that if Iraq is stabilized, significantly profitable economic opportunities will result. They might therefore be willing to extend loans to the new Iraqi government on very favorable terms, independent of what is done about the problem of Hussein's odious debt. Moreover, these international private enterprises might have sufficient political capital to persuade the lenders, who are expecting to be repaid, either to refinance or forgive portions of the outstanding debt or to persuade their home country governments to find some method of relieving the new government of the burden of Hussein's debt.

The general lesson of this brief scenario is that the possibility of future economic profit in a newly democratic nation and the exertion of international political power might relieve the unfairly burdened citizens of a national obligation to repay sovereign debt. One might further predict that these forces will come into play in precisely the circumstances in which the burden of odious debt would be most likely to harm the prospects of a new government.[9]

2.  The Ex Ante Approach

The second class of solutions to the problem of odious debt is to try to identify and deal with the problem ex ante through a formal mechanism.[10] In general, this would provide some method of identifying portions of new

---

9.  This is a variant on the position for which we shall ultimately be arguing. To foreshadow that position, we find some attraction in the scenario we have just painted—that is, one in which there are forces compelling the relief of the burden of odious debt in those circumstances in which holding a nation to sovereign obligations threatens a democratic government. But we are not sufficiently sanguine about this possibility to leave these matters to chance. Efforts to provide relief in this manner may be subject to collective action problems among those seeking to do so. So, we argue in favor of a more explicit relationship between forgiveness of odious debt and the process of democratization.

10.  *See, e.g.*, Jayachandran & Kremer, *supra* note 5, at 1.

sovereign debt that would (and those that would not) survive a regime change.[11] Because the borrower—in this instance, a despot—would not have the appropriate incentives to reveal his true intentions for the loan, identifying the points of bargaining could not be left to the parties. Rather, some neutral third party (or tribunal)[12] would have to identify which fraction of the loan was odious debt and which was not, or which regimes would be characterized as presumptively odious. This would have to be done early enough in the bargaining process between lender and borrower that the terms and conditions of the loan—say, its interest rate—could be adjusted in light of the tribunal's findings. The theory is that by identifying odious debt ex ante, there will be not only a chilling effect on both lenders and borrows in extending odious debt, but also fewer grounds for dispute later on.

One interesting question is when a regime should be labeled as odious.[13] On the one hand, labeling a regime as odious early in its tenure is likely to minimize damage from the regime's bad performance. On the other hand, waiting will reduce the risk of mislabeling a regime, as more information on odiousness becomes available. Furthermore, waiting will make international consensus easier to develop and will minimize market uncertainties. There is also the problem of regime behavior shifting over time. It is likely that rulers with shorter time horizons will be more prone to looting their countries. This complicates the time calculation for assessing odious debts.

Although it is not impossible that this ex ante certification scheme could develop into a viable method of dealing with the problem of odious debt, its effectiveness is doubtful. The evidentiary basis on which to designate portions of a loan package as odious ex ante is not at all obvious. There are several reasons for this belief.

First, no borrower, despotic or otherwise, is going to reveal in complete candor what he intends to do with the proceeds of an international loan, and he will certainly be wise enough not to reveal odious aspects of the loan. Even Saddam Hussein was able to convince U.N. inspectors that he was using sequestered oil sale revenues for humanitarian purposes, a claim now known to be very wide of the truth.[14] Surely the borrower will be able to manufacture all sorts of attractive public projects for which he needs international loans, while concealing the real plans for the money. And it is unlikely to be easy for lenders to make inquiries that will reveal the true plans for the funds.

The second reason that evaluating debt packages ex ante is so difficult is the absence of any metric by which the rule can realistically or should in theory be

---

11. In current practice, either all of a sovereign debt is deemed odious or none of it is. For the purposes of this article, however, the assumption will be made that fractions of debt can be designated odious and nonodious.

12. *See* Jayachandran & Kremer, *infra* note 15 (proposing a tribunal for this purpose).

13. Stephania Bonilla, A Law-and-Economics Approach to Odious Debts 20–22 (paper prepared for 23rd EALE Conference, Madrid, Spain, 2006, on file with authors).

14. *See* JEFFREY A. MEYER & MARK G. CALIFANO, GOOD INTENTIONS CORRUPTED: THE OIL FOR FOOD SCANDAL AND THE THREAT TO THE U.N. (2006).

applied. Will (or should) the tribunal give an overall odious score to the loan on, say, a one-to-ten scale? Will (or should) it be the case that if some portion of a loan package is deemed odious, then the entire package should be deemed odious? And what would or should the threshold be for determining what proportion of a loan package's odious provisions deems the entire package odious—twenty percent by value, thirty-three percent, fifty percent?

Furthermore, even if the tribunal did succeed in designating a particular debt offering as "odious," it is doubtful that this would estop subsequent disputes between the lenders and the country if there were regime change. Indeed, litigation galore about such matters as whether the tribunal adequately considered all the evidence or whether the assertions of the despot-borrower were treated skeptically enough would likely ensue. These ex post disputes are all the more likely in view of lenders' limited opportunities to monitor the borrower's behavior during the course of the loan. So, if odious uses of a loan come to light, they are only likely to be revealed after the despot has left the scene, and by the efforts of the successor government.

### 3. The Ex Post Approach

The third and final class of solutions to the problem of odious debt is to deal with the problem ex post. The most frequent suggestion of this sort is to create an international tribunal to adjudicate between lenders and nations regarding whether the unpaid sovereign debt is odious.[15] Just as the ex ante designation of all or part of sovereign debt as odious is fraught with problems of administrability, so, too, is the ex post adjudication of sovereign debt as odious and, therefore, excusable. No doubt interest rates would increase because of the risk of being declared odious in the future or of being mistakenly labeled "nonodious." Whereas interest rates would increase more steeply for the authoritarian regimes that had the potential to be labeled odious, all borrowers would have to pay increased rates. Ironically, this effect might be hardest on poorer countries, for which the marginal cost of interest rate increases is higher. It is possible, however, that the administration costs of this ex post demonstration would be less than those of the ex ante designation. The central claim would likely be that the loans had been acquired under fraudulent pretenses—an allegation that is reasonably easy to demonstrate—as opposed to the exceedingly difficult ex ante demonstration that the loans were not those that a duly elected democratic government would have entered into in the first place.

---

15. Michael Kremer & Seema Jayachandran, *Odious Debt*, BROOKINGS INSTITUTION POLICY BRIEF #103 (July 2002) (calling for a third-party adjudicator to determine whether debt is odious), http://www.brookings.edu/comm/policybriefs/pb103.htm; Patrick Bolton & David Skeel, *Odious Debts or Odious Regimes?* 70 LAW & CONTEMP. PROBS. (forthcoming Autumn 2007).

4. An Alternative Approach: The Roles of the "Odious Creditor" and of Economic Development and Democratization

Unfortunately, none of these proposals for dealing with indefensible sovereign debt has commanded, or is likely to command, a majority scholarly or public following. Odious debt is still a major policy problem, and this article proposes alternative mechanisms for finding a solution.

This article recognizes two dimensions of the odious debt problem that have received too little attention—the potential role of the "odious creditor" and the connection between obligations to repay sovereign debt and the process of economic development and democratization. First, consider the role of "odious creditors," which we define as government creditors willing to make loans to despots as part of a calculated strategy of national politics. One example is the Chinese government's support for the regimes in the Sudan, which itself is associated with the ongoing genocide in Darfur. China has extended billions of dollars in loans to the Sudanese government in an effort to secure a favored position as a buyer of natural resources. Needless to say, China would be unlikely to support debt forgiveness should a democratic regime ever emerge in the Sudan. The odious creditor complicates the development of solutions to the problem of odious debt. Recognizing this connection between international relations and the problem of odious debt casts doubt on the workability of the ex ante and ex post structural solutions discussed above.

Second, there is an explicit connection between the problem of odious debt and the related processes of economic development and democratization. The arguments in favor of furthering economic development are so obvious and those in favor of democratization are so compelling that a sensible solution to the issue of odious debt should explicitly consider the extent to which forgiveness of odious debt can significantly further these objectives.

The arguments for approaching the odious debt problem are made here in several stages. Considered first, as a threshold point, is the quasi-constitutional issue of why state succession makes sense in international law and how carving out an exception to this doctrine affects the development and democratization of debtor nations. Second, this article briefly examines the arguments in favor of economic development and the role of democratization in development. Third, the article discusses the odious creditor problem and argues that it is unlikely that international law will ever acknowledge an odious debt doctrine as a general matter. We also express skepticism about the United Nations as a forum for addressing the issue. Fourth, this article elaborates on what we believe is a workable solution that relies on existing institutions and avoids the problem of the odious creditor. A concluding section summarizes.

II

WHY STATE SUCCESSION TO INTERNATIONAL OBLIGATIONS IS NECESSARY

A threshold question in the odious debt debate is why states ought to be responsible at all for debts incurred previously. That is, why should today's citizens *ever* be responsible for earlier debts incurred by their political predecessors? Mitu Gulati and his co-authors deal with this issue in their article on the taxonomy of debt, pointing out that one reason to support successor liability is that the successors have benefited from the earlier investments.[16] This presents a morally unproblematic case. In other cases, such as the kind of debt labeled odious, it is not so obvious why the successors should be obligated. They have not, after all, benefited at all from the money, nor did they have a role in choosing the rulers who made the decision to borrow. Rather, they simply had the bad luck of succeeding bad rulers, and their populations the misfortune of having been "born under a bad sign."

One needs, then, a broader theory of how state succession relates to democracy. An initial argument is that state succession facilitates international exchange and domestic state-building by facilitating credible commitments.[17] The intuition is simple: a promise at Time 1 has value only if the promisee believes that it will be obeyed at Time 2. For governments that enter into treaty commitments, their counterparts may be unwilling to count on the obligation's being upheld if subsequent governments might not perform the promise. This problem is particularly acute when the promising state actors are uncertain about the incentives they, themselves, will face in the future.[18] If costs and benefits vary in unpredictable ways, a politician's promise to behave in a specified way may be less believable. A doctrine of state succession facilitates international cooperation by making the promises of all states more believable to other states.[19]

Note that the function of state succession is more important for democracies than for dictatorships. Democracies are by definition characterized by governments that come and go. Dictators do go but typically have a longer time horizon than democratic governments. For example, the Chinese Communist Party has been able to make sufficiently credible promises to attract massive amounts of foreign investment even in the absence of an independent legal system. Investors understand that the Party, like the House of Saud and other institutionalized authoritarian regimes, has a long time horizon. If the doctrine

---

16. Buchheit et al., *supra* note 5, at 6–21 (addressing the taxonomy of sovereign debt).

17. For scholars making this argument, see, e.g., JON ELSTER, ULYSSES AND THE SIRENS: STUDIES IN RATIONALITY AND IRRATIONALITY 36–111 (1979); JON ELSTER, ULYSSES UNBOUND: STUDIES IN RATIONALITY, PRECOMMITMENT AND CONSTRAINTS 129–41, 157–61 (2000); STEPHEN HOLMES, PASSIONS AND CONSTRAINT: ON THE THEORY OF LIBERAL DEMOCRACY 134–77 (1995); Stephen Holmes, *Precommitment and the Paradox of Democracy, in* CONSTITUTIONALISM AND DEMOCRACY 195–240 (Jon Elster & Rune Slagstad eds., 1988). *But see* JEREMY WALDRON, LAW AND DISAGREEMENT (1998) (arguing that disagreements should be solved by decisionmaking between right-holders); Jeremy Waldron, *Precommitment and Disagreement, in* CONSTITUTIONALISM 271–99 (Larry Alexander ed., 1998) (criticizing Holmes and Elster).

18. *See generally* GEORGE W. DOWNS & DAVID M. ROCKE, OPTIMAL IMPERFECTION? DOMESTIC UNCERTAINTY AND INSTITUTIONS IN INTERNATIONAL RELATIONS (1995) (exploring domestic uncertainty through information games and game theory).

19. Of course subsequent governments can exit the obligations by withdrawing from or denouncing the treaties that contain the commitments. Doing so, however, entails political costs. *See* Laurence R. Helfer, *Exiting Treaties*, 91 VA. L. REV. 1579 (2005).

of state succession did not exist, then democracies would be at a disadvantage in the international sphere because contractual counterparts would be less willing to trust that the successor governments would uphold the obligation.

An underappreciated dimension of state-succession doctrine is that it not only facilitates commitment to international audiences, but also to domestic ones. That is, politicians may in some circumstances choose to convey promises to domestic constituents in international instruments rather than in domestic ones. Consider this negative example: by joining the World Trade Organization, politicians signal to domestic constituents their inability to enact special protections for domestic producers against foreign competitors. In this sense, some international agreements parallel national constitutional structures.[20] International obligations are particularly attractive in some circumstances *precisely because* of state succession to obligations. Political actors who have trouble making credible commitments in the domestic sphere may prefer to make promises through an international obligation. This feature is, however, particularly crucial for new democracies and new states that have few other means of making credible promises.[21] Thus, state succession to international obligations helps increase the power of those commitments that states do enter into, facilitating both international cooperation and domestic constitutionalism.

This form of commitment beyond the state is particularly useful for new democracies. Imagine a newly democratic government that emerges after an authoritarian regime and promises to protect the human rights of its own citizens. The citizens might believe the government, but they might also be concerned that the promise will not be kept by the new government's successors. The government can make its promise more credible by embedding it in an international treaty to respect human rights. Any future government that violates the human rights of its citizens will suffer some form of sanction, either as an effect on its international reputation or possibly even as formal enforcement mechanisms. This helps explain why new democracies are particularly prone to include provisions for international obligations in their constitutions: state succession facilitates democratic commitments.

---

20. CASS SUNSTEIN, WHAT CONSTITUTIONS DO 241 (2001) ("Democratic constitutions operate as 'precommitment strategies' in which nations, aware of problems that are likely to arise, take steps to ensure that those problems will not arise or that they will produce minimal damage if they do."); *see also* FRIEDRICH A. HAYEK, THE CONSTITUTION OF LIBERTY 179 (1960) ("[The reason for constitutions] is that all men in the pursuit of immediate aims are apt—or, because of the limitation of their intellect, in fact bound—to violate rules of conduct which they would nevertheless wish to see generally observed. Because of the restricted capacity of our minds, our immediate purposes will always loom large, and we will tend to sacrifice long-term advantages to them."); STEPHEN HOLMES, PASSIONS AND CONSTRAINT: ON THE THEORY OF LIBERAL DEMOCRACY 135 (1995) (arguing that constitutional restraints facilitate democracy and that liberal theory provides a foundation for democratic government); A.C. Pritchard & Todd J. Zywicki, *Finding The Constitution: An Economic Analysis Of Tradition's Role In Constitutional Interpretation*, 77 N.C. L. REV. 409, 447–49 (1999) (discussing the efficiency purposes of constitutionalism, including precommitment).

21. Tom Ginsburg, *Locking in Democracy: Constitutions, Commitment and International Law*, 38 NYU J. INT'L L. & POLITICS 707 (2006).

One could, of course, carve out a category of international obligations that should not be honored. But such a carve-out would undercut the making of commitments by those states most in need of credibility, namely new democracies. These states will find that their credibility for both domestic and international audiences is more enhanced if there are fewer carve-outs that are more rarely invoked.[22]

Furthermore, as previously mentioned, a carve-out creates administrative problems—mainly those of developing a principled set of criteria for distinguishing odious from nonodious debt. After all, odious debts can be "laundered" by international financial institutions (IFIs), as in the case of the Congo after dictator Mobutu Sese Seko left the country in arrears to the International Monetary Fund (IMF).[23] Several governments gave the Congo bridging loans to repay the IMF, which then extended new credit for the Congo to repay the donating countries for the bridging loans.[24]

In short, state succession is a useful doctrine, not just for promisees but also for promisors. Credibility helps precisely those countries that lack other mechanisms for making promises believable, both to international and domestic audiences. Efforts to create a carve-out regime are noble, but have substantial line-drawing problems. Furthermore, any plausible and administrable carve-out will likely increase the price of debt for all countries because it introduces additional uncertainty in the debt market.

## III

### ECONOMIC DEVELOPMENT AND DEMOCRATIZATION

Because economic development and democratization are necessary criteria for dealing with the doctrine of odious debt, it is worthwhile, very briefly, to make the case for development and democracy and the link between them. In *Integrating a Theory of the State and Sovereign Debt Restructuring*,[25] Robert Rasmussen identified the necessary connection between a nation's governance system and the desirability of restructuring the nation's debt when there is distress from sovereign-debt service. That analysis can be extended to the particular problems associated with economic development and odious debt.

The case in favor of economic development is almost too obvious to need elaboration.[26] Nonetheless, briefly put, there are a significant number of people whose lives would be greatly improved by additional income and wealth. The

---

22. An unintended consequence of any carve-out regime is that it will increase debt prices for all, odious or not.

23. Joseph Hanlon, *'Illegitimate' Loans: Lenders, Not Borrowers, Are Responsible*, 27 THIRD WORLD Q. 211 (2006); Hanlon, *supra* note 5, at 123.

24. *Id.*

25. *See* Robert Rasmussen, *Integrating a Theory of the State and Sovereign Debt Restructuring*, 53 EMORY L.J. 1159 (2004).

26. *See* The World Bank, PovertyNet Overview, http://web.worldbank.org/WBSITE/EXTERNAL/ TOPICS/EXTPOVERTY/0,,contentMDK:20153855~menuPK:373757~pagePK:148956~piPK:216618~t heSitePK:336992,00.html (last visited May 22, 2007).

World Bank has established two threshold measures of poverty—living on one dollar or two dollars per day—and reports that nearly half of the earth's population is living at or below the latter level. The costs of poverty itself are daunting, from dramatically high rates of infant mortality and illness[27] to dramatically low life expectancies.[28] And yet, amazingly, it is trivially inexpensive to address most of the issues—infant mortality, disease, and malnutrition—resulting from extreme poverty.[29] At a minimum, being wealthier means being healthier. To put this dramatically, a study by Lant Pritchett and Larry Summers found that "the deaths of about half a million children in 1990 would have been averted if Africa and Latin America's growth in the 1980s had been 1.5 percentage points higher."[30]

Not only is economic development better in terms of eradicating the effects of poverty, but development is better for citizens' psyches. The evidence is accumulating on the relationship between self-reported happiness and per

---

27. William Easterly makes a compelling case for why poverty is to be avoided: "The typical rate of infant mortality in the richest fifth of countries is 4 out of every 1,000 births; in the poorest fifth of countries, it is 200 out of every 1,000 births. Parents in the poorest countries are fifty times more likely than in the richest countries to know grief rather than joy from the birth of a child. . . . The higher rates of babies dying in the poorest countries reflect in part the higher rates of communicable and often easily preventable diseases such as tuberculosis, syphilis, diarrhea, polio, measles, tetanus, meningitis, hepatitis, sleeping sickness, schistosomiasis, river blindness, leprosy, trachoma, intestinal worms, and lower respiratory infections. At low incomes, disease is more dangerous because of lower medical knowledge, lower nutrition, and lower access to medical care. WILLIAM EASTERLY, THE ELUSIVE QUEST FOR GROWTH: ECONOMISTS' ADVENTURES AND MISADVENTURES IN THE TROPICS 8–9 (2001).

28. Statistics from the HUMAN DEVELOPMENT REPORT 2003 indicate differences in life expectancies vary dramatically across regions and countries: life expectancy at birth in Sierra Leone today is 34.5 years, whereas it is 81.3 years in Japan. U.N. DEVELOPMENT PROGRAMME, HUMAN DEVELOPMENT REPORT 2003: MILLENNIUM DEVELOPMENT GOALS: A COMPACT AMONG NATIONS TO END HUMAN POVERTY 237, 240, *available at* http://hdr.undp.org/reports/global/2003/. Another measure of this can be found in our own history. In 1900 the combined average life expectancy for men and women in the United States was 47.3 years. CENTERS FOR DISEASE CONTROL AND PREVENTION, HEALTH, UNITED STATES 2006 176, *available at* www.cdc.gov/nchs/data/hus/hus06.pdf#027. Approximately one hundred years later, in 2001, the average life expectancy for males was seventy-four years and for women, eighty years. *Id.* at 310. And it is said that a female baby born today in Japan or France has a fifty percent change of living to one hundred. *See* Jim Oeppen & James W. Vaupel, *Broken Limits to Life Expectancy*, 296 SCI. 1029 (2002); James Meek, *Health Crisis Looms as Life Expectancy Soars*, GUARDIAN, May 10, 2002, *available at* http://www.guardian.co.uk/medicine/story/0%2C11381%2C713141%2C00.html (explaining Vaupel's extrapolated findings).

29. Oral-rehydration therapy, which would address the issues of dehydration caused by, among other things, diarrhea, costs less than ten cents per dose. Rehydration Project, Oral Rehydration Salts, http://rehydrate.org/ors/index.html (last visited May 22, 2007). Vaccinations against a range of debilitating diseases—pertussis, polio, diphtheria, measles, and tetanus—cost between twenty and thirty dollars per child. UNICEF, Facts on Children: Immunization, http://www.unicef.org/media/media_9479.html (last visited May 22, 2007). Vitamin A capsules cost about two cents each. UNITED NATIONS CHILDRENS FUND, WORLDMUN ISTANBUL 2001 at 5, *available at* http://www.worldmun.org/2006/archives/01/xcomunicef.pdf. Iodizing salt supplies cost about five cents per affected person per year. ASIAN DEVELOPMENT BANK, ASIAN DEVELOPMENT BANK REVIEW 2005, *available at http://www.adb.org/Documents/Periodicals/ADB_Review/2005/vol37-4/simple-solutions.asp* (last visited May 22, 2007). And intestinal parasites can be cured with inexpensive drugs.

30. Lant Pritchett & Lawrence Summers, *Wealthier is Healthier* (World Development Report, Working Paper No. 36, 1993), *available at* http://www-wds.worldbank.org/servlet/WDSContentServer/WDSP/IB/1993/06/01/000009265_3961004215604/Rendered/PDF/multi0page.pdf.

capita income. The World Values Survey of over 100,000 people in over ninety countries, including developing countries, found a robust correlation between increases in per capita income and self-reported happiness.[31] Somewhat less obvious is the connection between economic development and democratization. There is a consensus among students of economic growth—a belief known as the "Lipset hypothesis"—that democratization is not a precondition for the early stages of development.[32] Indeed, there is some evidence that democracy may make the early stages of growth faltering and messy.[33] Powerful individuals and interest groups may use the nascent democratic process to their advantage, while the ability of the government to implement public-spirited reforms may be severely limited. So, in the early stages of growth, it may well be the case that an enlightened despotism is more efficient than a new democracy.

Eventually, however, democracy may be necessary for sustained economic growth. This may be the case when the government has become more mature in its ability to resist blandishments from powerful individuals and interest groups or when corruption has been brought under control. An additional virtue of democracy at a later stage is that a large enough number of interest groups may have formed so that politics can provide a competitive arena in which no one group or coalition is able to dominate the governmental structure. Some theorists claim that an example of this in a developing society is when an urban commercial class becomes strong enough to grab a share of democratic power away from the landed interests who controlled the society before development began in earnest.[34]

---

31. *See* WORLD VALUES SURVEY, EUROPEAN AND WORLD VALUES SURVEYS FOUR-WAIVE INTEGRATED DATA FILE 1981–2004 (2006), *available at* www.worldvaluessurvey.org (follow "Findings" link, then "Collection of Graphs Presenting WVS Data" link to the tenth chart); *see generally* BRUNO S. FREY & ALOIS STUTZER, HAPPINESS AND ECONOMICS: HOW THE ECONOMY AND INSTITUTIONS AFFECT HUMAN WELL-BEING (2001). The correlation is robust only up to an annual income of approximately $15,000. Beyond that figure there is still an increase in reported well-being that comes from additional income, but those increases come at a steeply diminishing rate. *Id.* at 83.

32. *See* Tom Ginsburg, *Democracy, Markets and Doomsaying: Is Ethnic Conflict Inevitable?* BERKELEY J. INT'L L., 310 (2004) (reviewing AMY CHUA, WORLD ON FIRE: HOW EXPORTING FREE MARKET DEMOCRACY BREEDS ETHNIC HATRED AND GLOBAL INSTABILITY (2003)). On the history and theory of democracy, see generally JOHN DUNN, SETTING THE PEOPLE FREE: THE STORY OF DEMOCRACY (2005).

33. *See, e.g.*, ADAM PRZEWORSKI, MICHAEL E. ALVAREZ, JOSE ANTONIO CHEIBUB & FERNANDO LIMONGI, DEMOCRACY AND DEVELOPMENT: POLITICAL INSTITUTIONS AND WELL-BEING IN THE WORLD, 1950–1990, 142–86 (2000) (discussing political regimes and economic growth).

34. *See, e.g.*, KARL DE SCHWEINITZ JR., INDUSTRIALIZATION AND DEMOCRACY (1964) (arguing that historically democracy developed through economic gains of the commercial class and their subsequent demands for a larger share of political power); *see generally* Kenneth A. Bollen, *Political Democracy and the Timing of Development*, 44 AM. SOC. REV. 572 (1979) (arguing that greater state control of the economic system leads to lower levels of democracy in the political system); LARRY J. DIAMOND, JUAN J. LINZ & SEYMOUR MARTIN LIPSET, *Introduction: Comparing Experience with Democracy,* in POLITICS IN DEVELOPING COUNTRIES: COMPARING EXPERIENCES WITH DEMOCRACY 1 (Larry J. Diamond et al. eds., 1990) (exploring links between politics and democracy in the developing world).

The purpose in summarizing even these few studies on economic development and democracy is to invoke those goals as criteria for a principled approach to managing odious debt. Both development and democratization are valuable, and both of these goals are likely to be at issue in each instance in which a nation seeks to be excused from some portion of its sovereign debt. That is, odious debt is most likely to be an issue for developing countries that have recently shifted their regime from one of despotism to democracy.

IV

THE PROBLEM OF THE ODIOUS CREDITOR

Proposals for solving the odious debt problem should be seen not as purely legal doctrine, but as attempts to achieve admirable foreign policy goals related to development and democratization. It follows that international relations matter a good deal for understanding the feasibility of potential solutions: one must consider the incentives for major international players that would have to acquiesce to the formation and implementation of a new doctrine of odious debt. A particularly significant problem in this regard—one of increasing importance in the current international debate—is the problem of the "odious creditor": states that have no interest in advancing democratization goals but that are significant lenders to other states.

After much optimism in the 1990s about the spread of democracy, it is clear that dictatorships are playing an increasingly important role in the global political economy. China is a crucial player in that Chinese decisions to finance American debt enable American profligate macroeconomic policy to continue, in turn generating demand for Chinese goods. China now sits on $1.1 trillion of U.S. dollar reserves and is using this to finance regimes that have trouble obtaining credit from the International Monetary Fund and other multilateral sources.[35]

Rich authoritarians are unlikely to acquiesce to a doctrine that penalizes other authoritarians. China has shown itself to be generally unconcerned about the character of regimes it deals with in its insatiable demand for raw resources. China is the single biggest supporter of the Sudanese government, which is enabling genocide in Darfur. Even if the democratic nations on the U.N. Security Council wished to move forward with aggressive sanctions against Sudan, the Chinese would likely block them.[36] Another example is the Chinese support for the regime in Angola, which is Africa's second largest producer of oil after Nigeria and has been described as "one of the most corrupt and

35. Moises Naim, *Rogue Aid*, FOREIGN POLICY, Mar.–Apr. 2007, at 96.

36. *See China, Russia Bar Sudan Sanctions*, BBC NEWS, Apr. 18, 2006, *available at* http://news/.bbc.co.uk/2/hi/africa/4917970.stm (discussing China's refusal to impose sanctions on Sudanese officers); John Prendergast & Colin Thomas-Jensen, *Blowing the Horn*, FOREIGN AFFAIRS, Mar.–Apr. 2007, at 59, 73 (explaining Beijing's reluctance to lean on Khartoum).

impoverished countries in the world."[37] Corruption and transparency concerns led the International Monetary Fund to cease lending to the government, but China stepped in to provide finances, secured by Angola's oil reserves.[38] China also recently hosted a summit for 1,500 leaders and forty-eight heads of state from of the African continent, including such luminaries as Zimbabwe's Robert Mugabe.[39] China is the primary sponsor of the government in Myanmar,[40] significantly hindering two decades of American attempts to turn that government into a pariah. China is thus an ally of many of the regimes that might be declared odious under current proposals, and it is in a particularly favorable position to extend credit to those regimes.

China is not the only autocracy in such a position. While less significant on a global scale, smaller countries such as Venezuela and Iran have emerged as regional powers whose coffers are filled with oil monies and who have limited interest in democratization at home. Venezuela's oil surpluses have been recycled to Cuba, providing much-needed hard currency that sustains the regime two decades after the end of the Soviet Union.[41] The boom in oil and other "point-source" natural resources—those drawn from a narrow geographic area, which tend to be associated with negative governance outcomes like civil war and corruption—has empowered all kinds of governments and encouraged

---

37. John Reed, *Angolan Oil Loan Likely to Raise Transparency Issues*, FIN. TIMES, Oct. 11, 2005, at 13 (quoting the non-governmental organization Global Witness).

38. *Id.*; *Angola: Oil Backed Loan Will Finance Recovery*, IRIN Africa, Mar. 5, 2007, *available at* http://www.irinnews.org/report.aspx?reportid=53112. *See generally* Steve Kibble, *Angola: Can the Politics of Disorder Become the Politics of Democratisation & Development?*, 109 REV. AFRICAN POL. ECON. 525, 528–29 (2006) (describing Chinese loans as undermining international leverage, undercutting civil society, and serving as core obstacles to development). We are grateful to our colleague Pat Keenan for drawing this issue to our attention and for providing extensive documentation.

39. *See* Simon Elegant, *Beijing Hosts Africa's Leaders: Just Don't Mention Darfur*, TIME.com, Nov. 3, 2006; *see also* Luis Ramirez, *China Defends Decision to Invite Sudan, Zimbabwe to Africa Summit*, VOICE OF AM., Nov. 3, 2006, *available at* http://www.voanews.com/tibetan/archive/2006-11/2006-11-03-voal.cfm.

40. *See generally UN Votes to Put Burma on Agenda*, BBC News, Sept. 16, 2006 (discussing China's opposition to the U.S.-backed placement of Burma on the Security council agenda), *available at* http://news.bbc.co.uk/2/hi/asia-pacific/5351246.stm; *see also* U.S. – CHINA ECONOMIC AND SECURITY REVIEW COMMISSION, 2006 REPORT TO CONGRESS, 78, 109th Cong. (2006), *available at* http://www.uscc.gov/annual_report/2006/annual_report_full_06.pdf (equating the strong economic relationship between China and Burma with "keeping the Burmese economy afloat in the face of international sanctions.").

41. *See generally* Michael Ross, *Does Oil Hinder Democracy?*, 53 WORLD POLITICS 325, 356 (Apr. 2001) (concluding there is a negative correlation between a country with large number of oil reserves and democratic governance); CENTER FOR ADVANCED DEFENSE STUDIES [CADS], VENEZUELA'S GROWING APPETITE FOR REGIONAL POWER (2006), *available at* http://www.isn.ethz.ch/pubs/ph/details.cfm?lng=en&id=26991; John Simpson, *Iran's Growing Regional Influence*, BBC WORLD NEWS, Sept. 20, 2006, *available at* http://news.bbc.co.uk/2/hi/programmes/5363098.stm; *see also* CUBA TRANSITION PROJECT, HOW VENEZUELA SUBSIDIZES THE CASTRO REGIME, Issue 10 (2005), *available at* http://ctp.iccas.miami.edu/FACTS_Web/Cuba%20Facts%20Issue%2010%20April%202005.htm (estimating Cuba's total value of imported Subsidized Oil from Venezuela at $940 million in 2004).

odiousness.[42] A distinctive characteristic of such resources is that they have a relatively low elasticity of demand, which means that the quantity demanded of those resources is relatively insensitive to changes in prices. As a result, regimes with oil (or diamonds, for example) have poor human rights records and are relatively insulated from international criticism and condemnation.[43]

There is no reason to think that any of these countries would support the emergence of an odious debt doctrine. China's foreign policy is based on longstanding concerns of sovereignty and noninterference in the internal affairs of other states.[44] This matters a good deal, since, as a permanent member of the U.N. Security Council, China is in a position to block or slow the emergence of international legal doctrines that seek to punish regimes of any particular character. We think this fact poses a fatal objection to the proposal put forward by Professors Bolton and Skeel.[45] Bolton and Skeel believe the United Nations Security Council can provide an effective forum for identifying and regulating odious regimes. They recognize that there will be some "false negatives" in the form of odious regimes not declared as such because of political considerations.[46] In our view, however, the real issue is whether there will be any "true positives." The Security Council is not an exclusively cooperative institution, but rather a complex arena of political competition and cooperation. One needs to make a strong affirmative case based on the incentives of its members to demonstrate that the Security Council can be an effective forum for advancing the odious debt proposal.

Even beyond political obstacles, the odious debt doctrine may strengthen the position of China and other odious creditors vis-à-vis authoritarian regimes. Dictators will seek to borrow from relatively benign creditors rather than risk non-recovery from Western sources with their moral agendas. And if Western powers stopped lending to such countries, China would be able to fill the void and gain significant political leverage over other autocracies. Lending from other governments can be crucial in maintaining odious regimes—in the case of Saddam's Iraq, only a small proportion of debt was held by private creditors.[47]

There is already some evidence that a club of autocracies is emerging. In Asia, the Shanghai Cooperation Organization, founded in 2001, brings together Russia, China, and various central Asian dictatorships to talk about common

---

42. Jonathan Isham et al., *The Varieties of Resource Experience: How Natural Resource Export Structures Affect the Political Economy of Economic Growth* (Middlebury College Discussion Paper No. 2003-08, Apr. 2003), *available at* http://papers.ssrn.com/sol3/papers.cfm?abstract_id=410364.

43. *Id.*; *See, e.g.*, HUMAN RIGHTS WATCH, SUDAN, OIL AND HUMAN RIGHTS (2003), *available at* http://www.reliefweb.int/library/documents/2003/hrw-sud-25nov.pdf (exploring how Sudan's poor human rights record was partially driven by the desire to control oilfields, and criticizing foreign government support throughout the human rights abuses).

44. Samuel S. Kim, *The Development of International Law in Post-Mao China: Change & Continuity*, 1 J. CHINESE L. 117, 148–49 (1987) (describing the Five Principles of Peaceful Coexistence).

45. *See* Bolton & Skeel, *supra* note 15.

46. *Id.*

47. Patricia Adams, *Iraq's Odious Debts*, Cato Institute Policy Analysis No. 526 (Sept. 2004) at 5, *available at* http://www.cato.org/pubs/pas/pa-526es.html.

views and to participate in military cooperation.[48] If, for example, Uzbekistan were declared an odious regime such that credits extended to it might not have to be repaid in the event the government fell, the regime would certainly still be able to attract capital and development assistance from Russia, China, and another potential member, Iran. The odious debt doctrine, perversely, could strengthen autocracies and contribute to their economic integration as a counterbalance to the industrial West.

The problem of the odious creditor ought to trouble those who are committed to the odious debt doctrine. Because China will likely block the formal emergence of universal norms against the collectability of odious debt, the doctrine will likely emerge only among a subset of countries, the industrial democracies, which no longer dictate the price of sovereign debt. To the degree the industrial democracies remove themselves from the global lending picture, they increase the incentives of a "rogue creditor" with deep pockets, such as China, to enhance its geopolitical and economic influence. The Washington Consensus may be giving way to a "Beijing Consensus."[49] Whatever this means for economic well-being, this shift can hardly help the long-term cause of democracy.

## V

### A MODEST SOLUTION TO THE PROBLEM OF ODIOUS DEBT

So far we have argued that the odious debt proposal is best understood as part of the broader foreign policy objectives of economic development and democratization. Although a policy that would make odious debt uncollectible would, according to proponents, raise the cost of capital for authoritarians and prevent new democratic regimes from being burdened with heavy debt, it is unclear whether such a new legal doctrine can be created in a world of "odious creditors."

Even so, the modest proposal presented here could help advance some of the goals of the odious debt proposal without encountering some of the severe challenges to administrability raised above. Suppose that the international community identifies foreign debt as a crucial barrier to the democratization of a post-dictatorial regime—say, Iraq. Two distinct problems have to be faced: First, how can friends of development and democracy ensure that the country maintains a solid credit rating in the event that it defaults on its debt? One possibility would be for those friends to take over the debt directly through the

---

48. Charter members included China, Russia, Kazakhstan, Kyrgyzstan, Uzbekistan, and Tajikistan. Mutlaq Al-Qahtani, _The Shanghai Cooperation Organization and the Law of International Organizations_, 5 CHINESE J. INT'L L. 129, 130 (2006); _see also_ Frederick W. Stakelbeck, Jr., _The Shanghai Cooperation Organization_, FRONT PAGE MAGAZINE, Aug. 8, 2005, _available at_ http://www.frontpagemag.com/Articles//Printable.asp?ID=19041. _See generally_ Richard Komaiko, The Great Game (unpublished manuscript, on file with authors).

49. _See generally_ RANDALL P. PEERENBOOM, CHINA MODERNIZES: THREAT TO THE WEST OR MODEL FOR THE REST? 1 (2007).

IMF. Although this would relieve the new democracy of the burden of debt repayment, it does not address the second problem, the moral-hazard problem of prospective creditors. Those creditors would continue to extend credit to the authoritarian regime, even extending its lifespan, in confidence that the debt would be repaid after the regime fell.

To introduce real risk into the calculations of creditors, *effective* repudiation of the odious debt is needed—not merely transferring the debt to parties with pockets sufficiently deep to pay it off. Here, the best approach is not to set up an unwieldy new doctrine in international law, but simply to provide incentives in the marketplace to reduce the harm to poor countries that repudiate odious debts.

Modest steps can be taken to encourage selected, carefully identified recipient countries to repudiate the debt. The IMF or World Bank could offer insurance on future loans to be extended to the country after repudiation, thus reducing the interest-rate penalty the country will suffer as a consequence of reputational harm. A useful parallel can be found in the World Bank's Multilateral Investment Guarantee Agency (MIGA), established after several decades of discussion in 1986.[50] MIGA is designed to facilitate private investment in developing countries by offering investment insurance against a variety of "political" risks.[51] An American equivalent is the Overseas Private Investment Corporation, an independent agency of the U.S. government that also offers insurance against the expropriation of invested capital by foreign governments. The proposal offered here, however, would be more limited, focusing on sovereign debt rather than on private-investment capital. The World Bank or IMF could set up an agency that would in essence guarantee debt repayment by selected sovereign borrowers. This debt insurance program would be applied only to very particular regimes emerging from particularly odious dictatorships. It does not require general legal criteria but rather specific political decisions within the context of multilateral lending agencies, and it compensates for reputational losses associated with repudiation. Decisions could be made relying on many of the criteria put forward in other proposals related to odious debt, voted on by a majority vote of international financial institution (IFI) shareholders.[52]

The insurance that would be offered would be designed to compensate for reputational losses associated with repudiation by new democracies emerging from odious dictatorships. It would apply only to new lending directed to those countries and would be designed to reduce the spread between interest rates demanded by creditors and those prevailing under market conditions. Because

---

50. Alex Khachaturian, Note: *"Are We In Good Hands?" The Adequacy Of American and Multilateral Political Risk Insurance Programs In Fostering International Development*, 38 U. CONN. L. REV. 1041, 1050 (2006).

51. These include currency inconvertibility, expropriation, and political violence. *Id.*

52. For a description of the criteria that might be used to define Odious Regimes, see Bolton & Skeel, *supra* note 15.

the new democracies will have recently repudiated all or some of the debt accumulated under the previous regime, we assume that lenders would demand higher interest rates on new lending. The proposed insurance scheme could either insure the entirety of the new loans, or simply target the additional interest rate so as to make the lender indifferent between lending to the new democracy or lending to another debtor in the marketplace.

One objection to our proposal is that of moral hazard. There is some risk under our proposal that new democracies may seek to incur "too much" new debt because of the implicit subsidy offered by the debt insurance. However, the IMF is already in a position to monitor debt levels as part of its mandate to manage balance of payments under the Articles of Incorporation. The World Bank is the body in the best position to monitor whether borrowing is being used for development purposes. Certainly there is no better-positioned set of institutions in the international arena than the IFIs to address the moral hazard concerns.

We believe the IMF and World Bank are better vehicles for addressing the odious debt problem than the United Nations.[53] Potentially odious creditors wield veto power in the United Nations Security Council; the United Nations General Assembly is a highly politicized body in which nondemocracies have a strong voice. It is unreasonable to expect non-democracies to endorse a policy that is designed to promote democratization. The IMF and World Bank, on the other hand, are governed by Boards of Governors with weighted voting based on subscriptions paid or shares held.[54] The largest five countries by voting weight in the IMF, for example, are the United States, Japan, Germany, the United Kingdom, and France.

Naturally, this proposal assumes that international institutions can effectively handle this set of goals. Currently, the articles of incorporation for both the IMF and World Bank do not include a mandate to encourage democratization. International financial institutions, and development assistance generally, create what might be called a "bilateral agency problem," involving citizens and governments in both donor and recipient countries.[55] Citizens in one country support foreign aid and development for a variety of reasons—altruistic, ideational, and pecuniary. Their representatives, through political institutions, translate these preferences into foreign aid policy. This involves the transfer of resources to foreign countries, through a mix of international, bilateral, and private institutions, for spending on behalf of citizens in the recipient country.

An agency framework illuminates one feature of foreign aid, namely that it is given almost exclusively by democracies. The top aid-giving countries by

---

53. *Cf. id.*

54. International Bank for Reconstruction and Development Articles of Agreement, art. V.3; International Monetary Fund Articles of Agreement, art. XII.5.

55. *See* Peter Murrell, *The Interaction of Donors, Contractors and Recipients, in* THE INSTITUTIONAL ECONOMICS OF FOREIGN AID (Bertin Martens et al. eds., 2002).

absolute dollars are the United States, Japan, the United Kingdom, Germany, and France;[56] the top by percentage of Gross Domestic Product is Norway.[57] Traditionally, and in contrast to the democratic nature of the donors, recipients have been selected without regard to the governmental structure of their regimes.[58] Some of the biggest recipients of American foreign aid, for example, include Egypt and Pakistan.[59]

This asymmetry between donors and recipients—of democracies giving and lending money to non-democracies—matters for thinking about the odious debt problem. International financial institutions have not explicitly incorporated democracy into their decisionmaking criteria or goals. International financial institutions are ultimately creatures of their member governments, but they are several steps removed from the preferences of national citizens in donor countries. These institutions have their own structures and sets of incentives; as in any bureaucracy, individual incentives may not align with the nominal purpose of the institution. There are many concerns about the accountability of international bureaucracies, many of which have ultimately not been answered.[60]

---

56. *See* ORGANIZATION FOR ECONOMIC CO-OPERATION AND DEVELOPMENT, OFFICIAL DEVELOPMENT ASSISTANCE DATA FOR 2005 3, *available at* http://www.oecd.org/dataoecd/52/18/37790990.pdf.

57. *See* Sanjeev Gupta, Catherine Patillo & Smita Wagh, *Are Donor Countries Giving More or Less Aid?* 5 (IMF Working Paper No. 06/1, 2006), *available at* https://www.imf.org/external/pubs/ft/wp/2006/wp0601.pdf.

58. To be fair, however, thinking about foreign aid as a bilateral agency problem illustrates the *similarity* across recipient regimes. No doubt the governing coalitions in all countries, both democratic and authoritarian, take at least a portion of the foreign aid for their own benefit and in order to keep together the governing coalition. But nations differ in the degree to which the aid is skimmed off. Probably there is less skimming in democracies than autocracies, although this is not categorically true. There are examples of developmental state autocracies that were, in fact, quite clean. Democracies suffer legion problems of interest-group politics, too; so one cannot simply assume that autocracies are worse. Autocracies, however, have greater variance. The main point is that the spending and borrowing in any recipient country is likely to be greater than the benefit received by the citizenry. This creates an agency problem endemic in the world of all foreign aid.

59. The top recipients in 2005 in order are Israel, Egypt, Afghanistan, Pakistan, Colombia, Sudan, Jordan, Uganda, Kenya, and Ethiopia. Afghanistan and Israel are the only democracies on the list. CONGRESSIONAL RESEARCH SERVICE REPORT: FOREIGN AID: AN INTRODUCTORY OVERVIEW OF U.S. PROGRAMS AND POLICY 18 (Jan. 19, 2005), *available at* http://www.italy.usembassy.gov/pdf/other/98-916.pdf.

60. *Cf.* Anne-Marie Slaughter, *The Accountability of Government Networks*, 8 IND. J. GLOBAL LEGAL STUD. 347 (2000–2001). One particular problem is the threat of "negative net transfers." This idea draws on the fact that when international development lending institutions extend loans, the loans must eventually be paid back. In the early years of operating in a country, the amount of money going in will exceed the amount being paid back. As the country develops however, the recipient becomes more able to pay the money back and is less in need of new credits. When funds are extended across many countries, a development-lending institution may eventually have more funds coming in than going out in new loans. And this would mean that the institution was a net drain on the resources of developing countries. An international development institution drawing capital out of developing countries is unlikely to earn the support of the citizens of rich countries. Thus, IFIs are in continuous need of finding new targets for loan programs. *See* Paul Mosley, AID AND POWER: THE WORLD BANK AND POLICY-BASED LENDING 47 (2d ed. 1995).

The odious debt problem thus focuses attention not only on the justice of having borrowers pay back lenders but also on the agency problem between rich world citizens and development institutions—a point that has been underappreciated in many odious debt discussions. Structuring less perverse incentives for development institutions will improve their role of monitoring the use of rich country citizen funds spent abroad.

In recent years, donors have begun to pay attention to the agency problems involved in giving foreign aid to nondemocracies. Most of the United States' increase in development aid in the past few years has gone into the Millennium Challenge Account ("MCA"), the Bush Administration's innovation in foreign aid. The Millennium Challenge Account Framework is designed to introduce a form of conditionality to the modern aid situation.[61] Aid is targeted especially at countries that have already democratized somewhat and have made progress in such areas as corruption control, political rights, civil liberties, rule of law, voice, and accountability—governance criteria relevant to effective use of the aid dollar.[62]

The MCA has been criticized in some quarters, and funds have been slow to flow under it. Nevertheless, the concept of aligning incentives among rich country citizens, development-institution bureaucrats, and citizens in recipient countries seems to have great promise. International financial institutions ought to consider the democratic prospects of recipient countries as well as those countries' development prospects in structuring policies. Setting up an institutional structure to facilitate selective repudiation of particularly odious debt by subsidizing future loans to the repudiating country will ultimately help the cause of democracy, advancing foreign policy as well as development goals.

Although odious debt comes in many forms, the presence of IFIs significantly changes market incentives, creating a moral hazard that might lead private banks to loan money to countries expecting an international bailout.[63] The institutional incentives of the IFIs must be addressed in thinking about odious debt. The approach described in this article is more advantageous in that it focuses on the entities that have some control over debtor-state actions.[64] And it does so in a way that enhances democratic accountability in rich countries as well as poor ones.

## VI

### CONCLUSION

Consideration of odious debt should focus on three features of the international context. First, the odious debt doctrine should be seen as part of

61. *See, e.g.*, President George W. Bush, Remarks on Global Development at the Inter-American Development Bank (Mar. 14, 2002), *available at* http://www.whitehouse.gov/news/releases/2002/03/20020314-7.html.

62. The MCA also considers metrics on basic health and human services and economic freedom.

63. Kremer & Jayachandran, *supra* note 15, at 3.

64. Rasmussen, *supra* note 25.

an overall foreign-policy goal of democratization. Second, this focus calls into sharp relief the contrast between the behavior of democracies such as the United States and other major actors in the international sphere who have been only too happy to support the most odious of regimes. The problem of the "odious creditor" will be an increasingly important challenge as China becomes a major player in international financial markets. Achieving the goals of odious debt proponents requires consideration of this issue. Finally, a third feature of the international environment is the incentive structure of IFIs, whose presence creates a moral hazard for creditors.

Advancing the goals of the odious debt doctrine requires making democracy an element of lending decisions by IFIs. International financial institutions are, by their charter, politically neutral institutions, but they are not subject to conventional market discipline. In recent years, the World Bank has become extensively involved in governance-promotion activities, notwithstanding its mandate to avoid politics. In practice, IFIs ought to help advance the foreign-policy objectives of their ultimate principals, the citizens of rich countries whose national budgets contribute to the overwhelming majority of funds given to IFIs. Making IFIs take democracy seriously will both enhance democracy in the developing world and alleviate the agency problem in donor countries.

A special fund designed to subsidize new lending by countries burdened with odious debt can help alleviate in a modest way some of the problems associated with earlier proposals. The ultimate decision to repudiate debt would still be made by the new democracy, but the costs of such repudiation would be reduced. Knowing this, creditors would think twice about lending to odious dictatorships, being less confident that a bailout would occur and having to consider the possibility of repudiation. No doubt the proposal will leave some moral hazard in place. Some creditors will take the risk, and odious dictators will continue to find sources of capital. At the margin, however, getting IFIs to better structure the incentives for new democracies will advance some of the goals of those who wish to deal with the odious debt problem.

# [13]

# Defence Expenditures, Arms Procurement and Corruption in Sub-Saharan Africa

*Susan Willett*

In November 2007, the UK Department for International Development (DFID) launched its 'Transparency in Defence Expenditure', or TIDE, initiative, designed to fight corruption in military expenditures and arms procurement. Its initial focus was on sub-Saharan Africa (SSA), a region regarded as the most corrupt in the world. By focusing solely on the bribe-takers in SSA while studiously avoiding reference to the bribe-makers, DFID has opened itself up to accusations of double standards and hypocrisy. Corruption in arms procurement in SSA represents a small segment of a complex global pipeline that links Western arms firms and licensing governments to corrupt foreign officials and offshore financial institutions; tackling this web of corruption requires major reforms at the level of global governance, not just in governance procedures in SSA. With an analysis limited by inappropriate neoliberal methodologies and tainted by the alleged corrupt practices of British arms firms operating within SSA, DFID has been forced to put its TIDE initiative on the back burner.

## Introduction

Within neoliberal discourse, corruption, understood as the 'misuse of public power for private or political gain', has been identified as a major obstacle to development in that it reduces domestic investment, discourages foreign direct investment (FDI), inflates government expenditures and distorts public spending by shifting resources from education, health and infrastructural investment into sectors more malleable to corruption, such as the security sector.

In its 2006 *Development White Paper*, DFID committed itself to scrutinising public spending and procurement in the defence sector in developing countries as part of its broader anti-corruption campaign and as an extension of its work on security sector reform. The goal was to improve transparency and accountability in military budgeting and arms procurement in developing countries. In November 2007, DFID tentatively launched its Transparency in Defence Expenditures (TIDE) initiative. The stimulus for this initiative was inspired by a paper produced by the IMF economists Gupta *et al.* (2000), who hypothesised that corruption is highly correlated with (1) high shares of military expenditure in both GDP and overall government expenditure; and (2) high levels of military procurement spending in relation to both GDP and total government spending. Without evaluating the suitability of their methodology to the context of sub-Saharan Africa (SSA), DFID officials commissioned a series of consultancy papers from defence economic 'experts' to explore the extent of corruption in military expenditures and arms procurement in sub-Saharan Africa, using the quantitative methodologies favoured by Gupta *et al.* (2000).

This article attempts to show that DFID's neoliberal assumptions about the nature of corruption in arms procurement are highly biased, and that studies based on neoliberal methodologies produce a prejudicial picture of the nature of corruption in military procurement in SSA. In much of the development literature, corruption in the security sector has been treated as though it was exclusive to emerging market economies and poorer developing economies. However, there is a growing body of evidence which suggests that misgovernance and corruption in the security sector are more widespread (Kaufman 2004) than the neoliberal institutions have been willing to acknowledge. Multinational companies, including British-based companies operating outside the OECD region, have been implicated in providing lucrative bribes to government officials in developing countries, in gross violation of the OECD Anti-Bribery Convention. A number of high-profile arms procurement corruption cases in SSA highlight the role that multinational companies have played in arms corruption on the continent, strongly suggesting that corruption in arms procurement is far more complex and more common than DFID is willing to acknowledge.

Furthermore, for corruption in arms procurement to thrive, there have to be financial institutions willing to launder the ill-gotten gains of graft. This implies that a web of transnational corruption exists that links transnational arms companies to corrupt foreign officials and global financial institutions. Given this global pipeline of corruption, a focus that seeks solely to demonise political and military elites in the developing countries can only provide a very partial picture of what is actually going on in the world of corrupt arms transactions. Such partiality leaves donors open to accusations of hypocrisy and discrimination, thus undermining the supposed solidity and consistency of their good governance, anti-corruption and security-sector reform programmes.

## The Challenge of Measuring Military Expenditures and Corruption in SSA

The *IMF Working Paper* produced by Gupta *et al.* (2000) relies on the elegant algorithms of econometric analysis that seek observable patterns in quantitative data in order to reveal significant statistical correlations. The models are built upon probabilistic assumptions, e.g. when $x$ occurs, $y$ will follow. Gupta *et al.* hypothesised that corruption is correlated with high shares of military expenditure in both GDP and overall government expenditure, as well as with high levels of military procurement spending in relation to both GDP and total government spending. To be able to test this hypothesis in the sub-Saharan African context, reliable statistical data on military expenditures and arms procurement in SSA needed to exist, but as Hartley (2007) revealed, statistics on defence expenditure and arms procurement in sub-Saharan Africa are weak and, in some cases, non-existent. Datasets on military expenditures in SSA, while being available from a number of sources including the Stockholm International Peace Research Institute (SIPRI), the Congressional Research Service (CRS) and the United Nations Office of Disarmament Affairs (UNODA), are often incomplete, rarely correspond with each other and, as the collators of the data admit, are often unreliable, as transparency and accountability in military budgeting in SSA are notoriously poor.

Currently, the most reliable and consistent time series data on military expenditures in SSA is supplied by SIPRI, whose data suggest that formal military expenditures and arms procurement levels in SSA are well below the international average. In 2006, total military expenditure for sub-Saharan Africa amounted to just under US$9 billion, or some 0.8 per cent of global military spending (SIPRI military expenditure database 2007). The average military burden – military expenditure measured as a percentage of GDP – for the 30 SSA countries for which SIPRI had data in 2005 was only 1.5 per cent, less than half the average military burden during the height of the Cold War, when SSA military expenditure averaged between 4–5 per cent of GDP. This implies that military expenditure in the region is relatively low. However, reference to regional averages masks the wide variation in country-level military expenditures across the continent. For example, between 1998 and 2004, Gambia averaged a very low rate of military expenditure at 0.6 per cent of GDP, while Eritrea, engaged in a border war with Ethiopia, expended an average of 30 per cent of GDP during this same period. Moreover, there is a marked disparity in absolute levels of military spending. South Africa, for example, spent only 1.5 per cent of its GDP on defence in 2005, but with a budget of US$3.6 billion accounted for over one-third of total military expenditure in sub-Saharan Africa. Compare South Africa with Mali, with a budget of only US$33.6 million, but which spent 2.3 per cent of GDP on military expenditure, and the scale of disparity becomes apparent. This lack of correspondence draws attention to the wide differences on the continent, and cautions against making over-hasty assumptions about cross-country comparisons or correlations between high military expenditures and other variables.

Above all, there is a problem with the reliability of existing country-specific data on military expenditures. Omitoogun and Hutchful (2006, p. 2) conducted a series of case studies on military budgets in SSA and noted that 'data on military expenditure ... were very weak and needed improvement'. Most of their sample countries 'have been known to engage in collusion to hide the cost of military activities from the general public and donors of economic assistance ... who make aid conditional on low military budgets' (Omitoogun and Hutchful 2006, p. 242). By way of illustration, it would be expected that African states involved in conflict, or having recently emerged from conflict, would record higher levels of military expenditure as a proportion of GDP than those countries not at war. While this assumption certainly holds for the majority of conflict states, as the figures in Table 1 illustrate, certain conflict-bound states, including Chad, DRC, Ethiopia, Nigeria, Sierra Leone and Sudan, record official levels of military expenditure well below 2 per cent of GDP. If we change tack and examine the Corruption Perception Index ranking for SSA states that is produced by Transparency International (Table 2), it is apparent that these same states have a very poor record on corruption, all being listed as among the most corrupt states in the world.

The military burdens of those SSA countries listed by Transparency International (TI) as the least corrupt are recorded in Table 3. Despite lower levels of corruption than most SSA states, Botswana, Namibia and Lesotho have relatively high military burdens. Indeed, they appear to have spent a higher proportion of their GDP on defence than conflict-prone states such as the DRC, Chad, Congo and Nigeria listed in Table 1. How can this phenomenon be explained? The fact that less corrupt countries have a higher military burden may be attributable to the fact that the governments of these countries are committed to greater transparency and accountability in their military budgets than the afore-mentioned fragile states. If this is indeed the case, the whole notion of using the military burden as a benchmark to judge the 'excessiveness'

**Table 1.** Military Burden (ME/GDP) of SSA Countries in Conflict 1998–2005

| Country | 1998 | 1999 | 2000 | 2001 | 2002 | 2003 | 2004 | 2005 |
|---|---|---|---|---|---|---|---|---|
| Angola | (5.2) | (9.9) | (2.21) | (1.4) | (1.8) | (2.2) | (4.0) | (5.7) |
| Burundi | 6.6 | 6.3 | 6.0 | 8.0 | 7.2 | 7.3 | 6.6 | 6.2 |
| CAR | | | | | 14.8 | 16.7 | 15.6 | 15.4 |
| Chad | 1.2 | 1.7 | 1.9 | 1.8 | 1.7 | 1.5 | 1.1 | 1.0 |
| Congo Republic | – | – | – | 1.4 | 1.7 | 1.9 | 1.7 | 1.4 |
| DRC | 1.2 | 1.7 | 1.9 | 1.8 | 1.7 | 1.5 | 1.1 | 1.0 |
| Djibouti | 4.4 | 4.2 | 4.0 | 3.9 | 4.2 | – | – | – |
| Eritrea | 35.3 | 37.4 | 36.3 | 24.7 | 23.7. | 24.1 | – | – |
| Ethiopia | 6.7 | 10.7 | 9.6 | 5.0 | 3.9 | 2.9 | 2.8 | 2.6 |
| Nigeria | 0.9 | 1.4 | 0.8 | 1.3 | 1.9 | 1.1 | 1.8 | 0.8 |
| Rwanda | 4.4 | 4.2 | 3.4 | 3.3 | 2.9 | 2.5 | 2.3 | 2.9 |
| Sierra Leone | – | – | 4.1 | 2.4 | 1.7 | 1.8 | 1.2 | 1.0 |
| Sudan | 2.4 | 4.1 | 4.8 | 2.9 | 3.2 | 2.3 | – | – |

Note: there are no available figures for Somalia or Côte d'Ivoire, and the figures for Angola should be seen in the context of highly uncertain economic statistics, due to the impact of war on the Angolan economy.
Source: SIPRI Military Expenditure Database 2007.

**Table 2.** Corruption Perception Index for Sub-Saharan Africa

| Country | Global ranking in corruption | Country | Global ranking in corruption |
|---|---|---|---|
| Botswana | 31 | Guyana | 123 |
| South Africa | 43 | Mauritania | 123 |
| Cape Verde | 49 | Niger | 123 |
| Mauritius | 53 | Zambia | 123 |
| Namibia | 57 | Burundi | 131 |
| Seychelles | 57 | Cameroon | 138 |
| Ghana | 69 | Ethiopia | 138 |
| Senegal | 71 | Gambia | 143 |
| Gabon | 84 | Togo | 143 |
| Lesotho | 84 | Guinea-Bissau | 147 |
| Swaziland | 84 | Nigeria | 147 |
| Madagascar | 94 | Congo Republic | 150 |
| Tanzania | 94 | Côte d'Ivoire | 150 |
| Burkina Faso | 105 | Kenya | 150 |
| Djibouti | 105 | Liberia | 150 |
| Eritrea | 111 | Sierra Leone | 150 |
| Mozambique | 111 | Zimbabwe | 150 |
| Rwanda | 111 | CAR | 162 |
| Uganda | 111 | DRC | 168 |
| Benin | 118 | Equatorial Guinea | 168 |
| Malawi | 118 | Chad | 172 |
| Mali | 118 | Sudan | 172 |
| São Tomé and Principe | 118 | Somalia | 179 |
| Comoros | 123 | | |

Source: Transparency International Corruption Perceptions Index (CPI) 2007
Available from: http://www.transparency.org/policy_research/surveys_indices/cpi

**Table 3.** Least corrupt countries in SSA and military expenditure levels (US$ 2005)

| Country | Military expenditure (US$ millions) 2005 | Average military expenditure/GDP 1998–2005 | CPI score | CPI global rank |
|---|---|---|---|---|
| Botswana | 313.0 | 3.5 | 5.4 | 31 |
| South Africa | 3,568.0 | 1.4 | 5.1 | 43 |
| Mauritius | 12.3 | 0.2 | 4.0 | 53 |
| Namibia | 187.0 | 2.9 | 4.5. | 57 |
| Ghana | 80.0 | 0.75 | 3.7 | 69 |
| Senegal | 124.1 | 1.4 | 3.6 | 71 |
| Gabon[1] | 110.0 | 1.8 | 3.3 | 84 |
| Lesotho | 33.6 | 2.9 | 3.3 | 84 |
| Swaziland | (48.8) | 1.7 | 3.3 | 84 |
| Madagascar | 54.0 | 1.2 | 3.2 | 94 |
| Tanzania | 135.0 | 1.5 | 3.2 | 94 |
| Burkina Faso | 76.2 | 1.3 | 2.9 | 105 |

Note: Military expenditure figures for Gabon are for the years 2000–2005.
Source: SIPRI Military Expenditure Database 2007 and Transparency International's Corruption Perception Index 2007.

of military expenditures is called into question, as is the supposed correlation between military expenditures and corruption.

Data on the share of defence spending in government expenditure are even less readily available. *World Military Expenditures and Arms Transfers* (WMEAT), produced by the US Department of State, provides the only reliable source of time series data on the defence share of government expenditures in SSA. However, collection of these data ended in 2002, and the latest available set are for the year 2000. The WMEAT data reveal some dramatic differences between SSA nations, as Table 4 shows. For 1999, the median share was some 8 per cent, with the highest shares in Eritrea (51.1 per cent) and Sudan (46.8 per cent), and the lowest shares for Cape Verde (2.2 per cent) and Mauritius (0.9 per cent).

The weakness and unreliability of existing data on military expenditure in SSA suggest that the quantitative approach adopted by DFID, and Gupta *et al.* have limited utility in the SSA context. If the Gupta hypothesis of the relationship between military expenditures and corruption is accepted, it would have to be assumed, on the basis of existing statistical data, that corruption in military affairs in SSA was on the decline. However, the qualitative studies commissioned by SIPRI on the military budget process in selected SSA countries suggest that this is far from the case (Omitoogun 2003, Omitoogun and Hutchful 2006). These studies strongly suggest that corruption in the security sector is increasing, and that this trend appears to be proportional to the amount of military expenditure which has gone 'off-budget'.

## Donors and Defence Budgets in SSA

During the 1990s, multilateral and bilateral donors attempted to control 'excessive' levels of military expenditure in aid-dependent countries, using a 'benchmark' of 2 per cent of GDP. According to Omitoogun and Hutchful (2006), this had the unintended consequence of increasing secrecy surrounding military budgets in many

**Table 4.** Defence share of government spending (%), 1990–1999

| Country | 1990 | 1999 | Country | 1990 | 1999 |
|---|---|---|---|---|---|
| Angola | 39.8 | 41.1 | Kenya | 9.8 | 7.1 |
| Benin | (19.4) | 8.3 | Lesotho | 17.1 | 6.5 |
| Botswana | 10.8 | 9.8 | Liberia | NA | 8.3 |
| Burkina Faso | 17.5 | 5.9 | Madagascar | 6.9 | 7.4 |
| Burundi | 12.7 | 26.7 | Malawi | 4.8 | 2.2 |
| Cameroon | 8.1 | 10.6 | Mali | (8.6) | 8.7 |
| Cape Verde | (2.8) | 2.2 | Mauritania | 12.3 | 18.9 |
| CAR | (6.6) | 15.4 | Mauritius | 1.5 | 0.9 |
| Chad | 16.5 | 12.7 | Mozambique | NA | 9.1 |
| DRC | (16.1) | NA | Namibia | 5.9 | 7.2 |
| Republic of Congo | 11.1 | 8.4 | Niger | (8.4) | 6.4 |
| Dijibouti | 20.1 | 12.7 | Nigeria | 7.6 | 8.1 |
| Equatorial Guinea | NA | 16.5 | Rwanda | 19.8 | 22.7 |
| Eritrea | (34.6) | (51.1) | Senegal | (6.3) | 8.2 |
| Ethiopia | 39.8 | 29.1 | Sierra Leone | 20.8 | 13.5 |
| Gabon | 13.7 | 7.3 | Somalia | NA | NA |
| Gambia | 5.1 | 5.4 | South Africa | 12.6 | 5.0 |
| Ghana | 3.4 | 3.1 | Sudan | (61.5) | 46.8 |
| Guinea | 5.0 | 7.4 | Swaziland | 6.6 | 4.6 |
| Guinea-Bissau | (4.0) | 6.1 | Tanzania | 8.7 | 10.1 |
| Côte d'Ivoire | (3.9) | 3.4 | Togo | 14.0 | 9.4 |
| | | | Uganda | 25.9 | 13.9 |

Source: WMEAT (2002).
Note: NA = not available: figures in brackets are for nearest year to 1990 (e.g. 1989 or 1991).

SSA countries. One of the reasons for this was that donors had failed to take into account the legitimate security needs of recipient countries. The net effect was that an increasing amount of military spending was pushed 'off budget', thus reducing the reliability of military data upon which donor judgements are based.

The case of Uganda is illustrative of the inability of the state to provide basic security under donor terms of conditionality, which forced it to fund military campaigns with off-budget sources of income. In the 1990s, Museveni's Government, facing the costly task of attempting to contain the Lord's Resistance Army (LRA), was unable to realistically bring its military budget to below 2 per cent of GDP, given the manpower, logistical and arms expenditure needs required to conduct a campaign on its northern border. At the time, President Museveni's Government was dependent for more than 60 per cent of its expenditures on international aid, and was thus under considerable donor pressure to rein in military spending. In 1998–99 Museveni exceeded the 2 per cent benchmark. The donors, led by the IFIs, suspended aid to Uganda, and only resumed lending when the government returned military expenditure to the 2 per cent 'acceptable level'. Faced with these intractable demands Museveni implemented several creative accounting techniques to enable him to allocate sufficient resources to his military campaign, while allowing him to keep official military expenditures below the 2 per cent benchmark. Resources earmarked for other government departments were diverted to the Ministry of Defence. In 2001 Museveni openly asked the donors to lift the 2 per cent ceiling, and requested permission to spend twice what the government had officially allocated to the military in 2000. In effect, the request was merely an attempt to gain permission to officially spend what was already being allocated to the military. Reluctantly, and in the face of international pressure to find some kind of solution to the human rights violations perpetuated by the LRA, the donors agreed. Since then, there has been a steady rise in official military expenditures. Under sustained military pressure from the Uganda People's Defence Force (UPDF), the LRA has to all intents and purposes been defeated. Peace negotiations are under way at the time of writing.

Where budgets have been kept within donor-defined levels of acceptability, military forces have suffered from chronic under-funding, which is reflected in low pay and allowances, inadequate training, poor living and working conditions, a lack of medical services and an absence of basic equipment (Henke and Rupiya 2001, Omitoogun 2003). In certain circumstances, this state of affairs has proved destabilising on two counts:

- resources are insufficient to sustain effective military capabilities, which limits the capacity of the state to provide basic security; and
- low pay and poor working conditions can lead to severe grievances and even mutiny amongst military personnel which, in extreme cases, can result in full-scale military coups, as in the case of Côte d'Ivoire in 2002.

The experience of Uganda, and to a lesser extent Côte d'Ivoire, forced a realisation among donors that their policy on excessive military expenditures had considerable shortcomings. Donors began to reformulate their policies towards military expenditures in early 2000. The new policy approach, largely formulated by DFID, placed emphasis on the 'process' or 'good governance' approach to military budgeting. New weight was given to applying sound financial management principles to the military sector (Ball and Fayemi 2004). On paper these reforms sound very plausible, however, as Omitoogun and Hutchful (2006) have noted, a number of serious structural obstacles need to be overcome before sound financial management principles can be applied to the military sector in most SSA countries.

First, there is a general lack of qualified accountants. The systematic downsizing of the civil service, and reductions in public sector pay under the terms of IMF-imposed structural adjustment programmes during the 1980s and 1990s, resulted in a widespread exodus of skilled professionals from public sector employment across Africa, which meant there was an acute shortage of personnel able to audit and reconcile accounts. The outcome has been that, all too often, unqualified personnel perform budget preparation and the reconciliation of accounts. Unless efforts are made to recruit and pay accountants a decent salary, sound financial management of government accounts, including defence budgets, will remain unattainable.

Second, there is a need to introduce integrated defence planning systems. The majority of African states lack the capacity and skills to design and implement defence planning procedures and military budgeting processes. As a consequence, military budgeting is extremely ad hoc and inefficient, often rendering security forces bereft of even the most basic of equipment, such as uniforms and boots, let alone any military equipment.

Finally, the necessary legal and institutional mechanisms that ensure and enforce accountability tend to be weak in almost all SSA countries. Oversight of the military budget is plagued by weak control by the ministry of defence, a lack of coherent defence policy, weak parliamentary control and limited involvement of civil society.

Even where institutional arrangements for accountability and public scrutiny exist, they are often bypassed under the rubric of national security (Adekanye 1999, Omitoogun and Hutchful 2006). The general absence of transparency and accountability mechanisms in the defence budgetary process allows for the systematic manipulation of military data by corrupt officials. The manipulation of military accounts, and the secrecy that surrounds this, have arisen to hide graft and the mismanagement of resources from public scrutiny, but also to deceive donors about the true cost of military activities.

## 'Off-budget' Military Funding and Corruption

As already noted, a significant proportion of arms procurement transactions in SSA occur 'off budget'. The secret and shadowy nature of 'off-budget' funding creates ample opportunity for malfeasance. A variety of highly innovative off-budget mechanisms that enable the funding of procurement and other military 'excesses' have evolved in Africa.

- *Asset transfers*: The redistribution of existing assets to the benefit of the armed forces that may involve the reallocation of resources from other budgetary headings or state revenues. Examples include the Ugandan Government's initial allocation of resources to the police budget, later redirected to the military, to augment the costs of the campaign against the Lord's Resistance Army in the North of Uganda (Omitoogun 2003). During the border war between Eritrea and Ethiopia (1998–2000), Ethiopia diverted the proceeds of the privatisation of state companies to fund its war effort, in particular the US$300 million purchase of Sukhoi Su-27s from the Russians (*Africa Confidential* 1999).
- *Natural resource predation*: The pillage of natural resources such as diamonds, copper, coltan, oil and timber, and the use of revenues for arms procurement and the personal gain of warlords and generals alike, is well documented in the DRC, Liberia, Sierra Leone and Angola (Renton *et al.* 2007, Global Witness various, UN Security Council 2003). In Nigeria, the notoriously corrupt cash-call system that operated in the state-owned oil industry is thought to have funded Nigeria's role in the ECOMOG operations in Liberia and Sierra Leone between1990 and 1999. The figures for these 'peace' operations did not appear in Nigeria's defence accounts, but are thought to have cost an estimated US$12 billion (Adekanye 1999). In Angola, it has been estimated that as much as US$1 billion a year of state oil revenues have been siphoned off into shell companies for use in a tangled web of corruption and backroom arms deals (Global Witness 2004). In the DRC, a total of US$80 million was appropriated from the state-owned diamond mining company (MIBA), of which US$20 million is thought to have been used to buy weapons from Ukrainian and Czech arms suppliers (*Africa Confidential* 2004).
- *Taxes and levies*: Soldiers and rebel groups often augment their wages and raise money for weapons through the imposition of informal taxes and levies, and other illegal activities. Warlords in Somalia organised 'tax zones' to raise resources to prosecute their clan wars. In Burundi, soldiers augment their wages by imposing taxes on farmers' crops and levies on border trade (Nimubona and Sebudadi 2007). Soldiers employ road blocks all over Africa to extract payments to embellish their paltry wages.
- *Shadow trade*: In the Niger Delta, officers in the Joint Task Force are reportedly involved in the criminal gangs that are engaged in the illegal bunkering of oil (*Africa Confidential* 2007). Some 30,000–100,000 barrels of oil are stolen each day; the revenue from oil is thought to buy arms for the militias (*Africa Confidential*

2006). West Africa has become a major exporter of cocaine. It is not produced in the region, but the networks linking Colombian and Venezuelan drug barons with their West African business partners, which include senior military officers and government officials, have established complex and lucrative transshipment operations along the West African seaboard. The president and senior military officers in Guinea-Bissau are thought to be at the centre of the cocaine trade in West Africa (*Africa Confidential* 2007).

- *The diversion of humanitarian assistance and aid*: Humanitarian relief for the victims of armed conflict in SSA opened up opportunities for new income streams for both the military and rebel groups. In Liberia, the widespread diversion of relief supplies and assets was believed to have significantly assisted those involved in the fighting (Atkinson and Leader 2000, Savage 2007). In southern Sudan, the fraudulent 'redeeming' or buying-back of slaves, a campaign that raised millions of dollars in charity in the US and other developed countries, enabled the Sudan People's Liberation Army to use the diverted funds to buy arms and ammunition (Harker 2000). Ethiopia is thought to have diverted humanitarian aid to procure weapons in the build-up to its border war with Eritrea (Cooper & Kyzer 2003).

- *External military assistance*: After years of ignoring Africa, the US has dramatically increased military assistance to the region. The total amount of US military sales to, and financing and training expenditures for, eight African countries considered strategic partners in the 'war on terror' has increased from about US$40 million over the five-year period 1997–2001, to over US$130 million between 2002–2006 (LeMelle 2008). Under the Trans-Saharan Counter-Terrorism Initiative (TSCTI), the Pentagon supplied US$500 million to increase border security and counter-terrorism capacities in Mali, Chad, Niger and Mauritania. The African Contingency Operations Training and Assistance programme (ACOTA) has provided small arms and training for peacekeeping operations to Benin, Botswana, Côte d'Ivoire, Ethiopia, Gabon, Ghana, Kenya, Malawi, Mozambique, Nigeria, Senegal, South Africa, Uganda and Zambia. Another source of external support is derived from neighbouring African states. They may supply arms or other forms of military assistance to rebel groups, or state forces, involved in conflict. For example, in the civil war in the Republic of Congo 1993–2002, Angola and Chad provided military assistance to President Sassou-Nguesso. In the DRC, Laurent Kabila received military assistance in the form of arms, training and supplies from neighbouring states, including Zimbabwe, Angola, Namibia and, in the early days of the war, Rwanda and Uganda.

- *Diaspora contributions*: Funds raised from diasporas are another means of augmenting 'off-budgetary' resources. Eritrea was reported to have raised US$400 million for its war effort in the form of donations from the Eritrean diaspora (*The Economist* 1999). These funds are thought to have been used to purchase MiG-29s from the Ukrainians.

- *Peacekeeping*: Volunteering soldiers for UN or African Union peacekeeping operations (PKOs) is another means of generating extra funds. Ethiopia, Ghana, Nigeria, Kenya, Mozambique, Namibia, Senegal, South Africa, Uganda and Zimbabwe are among those countries that have volunteered for PKOs. Rarely do UN payments for these forces appear in annual military budgets. The failure to declare payments offers opportunities for malfeasance. In certain cases, corrupt military officers have banked soldiers' pay (Hutchful 2003). During Nigeria's involvement in ECOMOG missions in West Africa, generals benefited from revenues written off as expenses (Adebayo 2002). Millions of dollars were diverted into private bank accounts as part of this ruse.

- *Prolonged conflict*: Many conflicts in Africa are purposely prolonged by the military and rebel groups, because the conditions of instability enable warlords and generals to rob their nations of resources and funds. Plundered resources provide the income with which militias and the armed forces are able to purchase arms so that they can continue to prosecute war.

- The diversity and opacity of these resources makes it almost impossible to monitor off-budgetary procurement trends. Subsequently, little is known about the nature of the arms being procured, how much is being spent, the scale of bribes and kickbacks involved, or where and how the ill-gotten gains from corrupt practices in this form of procurement are laundered.

## Arms Procurement and Opportunities for Corruption

Even in the context of 'best practice' in defence procurement, i.e. with proper systems of public accountability and transparency in decision making and auditing, the large and technically complex nature of defence contracts makes it hard for civilian authorities to fully comprehend and assess whether or not a contract is necessary, appropriate or indeed 'value for money'. Challenging equipment specifications is a highly technical process and one that requires a combination of strategic, engineering and accounting expertise. In South Africa, where most of these skills exist and parliamentary oversight mechanisms and auditing procedures have acquired a considerable degree of sophistication, the size and complexity of the recent 'Strategic Procurement Package' created an ideal environment for corruption to flourish.

In the 1995 *Defence White Paper*, the South African Ministry of Defence highlighted the need to re-equip the South Africa National Defence Force (SANDF) to meet the national security needs of the new democracy. This resulted in the Strategic Arms Procurement Package, which was signed off in December 1999, costing the South African taxpayer US$4.8 billion. The South African Government claimed that the package would pay for itself in the long run, through counter-trade and offset agreements. There was a huge public outcry about this allocation of scarce public expenditure resources at a time when the Reconstruction and Development Programme, designed to lift poor black people out of poverty, had been abandoned.

Controversy associated with the 'Arms Deal', as it has become known, spread, as irregularities in the tendering process and general lack of transparency came to light. Several high level investigations have been conducted into accusations of corruption involving bribe-takers – African Defence Systems (ADS) and senior figures within the ANC, including former Defence Minister Joe Modise, Tony Yengeni, ANC Chief Whip and former chairman of the Parliamentary Defence Committee, and brothers Shamin and Shabir Sheik, who have links to senior ANC officials. Bribe-payers, notably BAE Systems, the European Aeronautic Defence and Space Company (EADS) and Thales/Thompson, have also been implicated. Despite substantial evidence of widespread corruption in the deal, the major players have not been prosecuted to date, and the various phases of the US$4 billion arms deal continue unabated.

The sheer size of 'Arms Deal', the South African Department of Defence's ill-preparedness to manage the simultaneous acquisitions, SANDF's questionable ability to absorb the state-of-the-art equipment, the choice of expensive, offensive weapon platforms such as the new Gripen JAS 39 fighter aircraft, at a time when the southern African regional security environment has achieved relative stability, all point to a government agenda quite divorced from its stated objective of re-equipping the country's navy and air force.

Given the resource constraints of most African buyers, including South Africa, a number of non-currency methods of payment for arms procurement have evolved, including counter-trade and offsets. Trading prospects are enhanced, both for suppliers and recipients, as trade is facilitated through a cashless, mutual exchange of needs. Offsets are industrial or commercial compensation practices required as a condition of purchase of defence articles and/or services. They include co-production arrangements, licensed production, sub-contractor production and overseas investment or technology transfer. As offset arrangements tend to favour countries that have attained a degree of industrialisation, few arms deals involving sub-Saharan countries involve offset agreements. South Africa is an exception to this rule.

Offset agreements are outlawed in all other forms of government procurement by Article XVI of the WTO plurilateral Agreement on Government Procurement, but are often the decider in defence deals because of their anticipated economic benefits. However, as Dunne and Haines (2006, p. 43) have shown in the South African case, offset deals often have questionable economic benefits. The prices of the new weapons systems appear to have been inflated by the offset arrangement. Hidden costs include unanticipated capital expenditure on imported equipment, which has had a detrimental effect on the balance of payments; an increase in state expenditure on R&D in order to realise technology transfers; and the downward revision of anticipated job creation. Overall, the economic benefits to the South African economy remain unclear and there may even be considerable opportunity costs in the long run. Finally, in the non-competitive and non-transparent arrangements that surrounded South Africa's offset arrangements, the potential for corruption was extensive.

Counter-trade is far more common in arms transactions in SSA. This type of transaction takes various forms, including barter and counter-purchase arrangements. Barter refers to the direct exchange of goods-for-goods where no cash is involved. Although barter is as old as trade itself, contemporary barter deals are more common than is often realised. State-to-state transactions between African governments often involve barter. For example, Zimbabwe Defence Industries supplied the DRC armed forces with light weapons in exchange for mineral concessions. Angola was also thought to benefit from mineral concessions extended by President Laurent Kabila in exchange for military assistance. Counter-purchase, on the other hand, is a form of exchange that commits the arms seller to purchase a compensatory amount of commodities. In the context of developing countries this normally involves primary commodities. The arms contractor can either market these counter-purchased goods themselves or employ a specialist commodity broker to do the job for them. On the whole, defence firms try to avoid counter-purchases because they inevitably incur extra transaction costs.

Offsets and counter-trade are notoriously difficult to monitor and audit, because the deals are complex, multi-layered, take a long time to negotiate and are subject to fluctuating currency rates and/or commodity prices. This ambivalence provides ample opportunity to inflate deals with bogus expense claims, 'bonuses', 'incentives' and commissions.

## The Bribe-makers

The main focus of DFID's concern with corruption in military expenditures and arms procurement is on the demand side of corruption dynamics, namely, on the corrupt role of political and military elites in SSA. But for bribe-takers to exist there have to be bribe-makers. Transparency International (2007) has noted that the arms market is one of the most corrupt sectors in the world. Despite accounting for less than 1 per cent of total world trade, the arms trade accounts for around 50 per cent of all corrupt transactions, according to a report issued by the US Government (US Department of Commerce 2000, p. 11). A 2006 survey revealed that approximately one-third of all defence companies claimed that they had lost defence contracts because competitors had offered bribes to secure sales (Control Risks 2006).

The payment of large 'commissions' by arms companies to individual officials in defence procurement deals can provide an incentive for the recipient to increase the technical specification of the weapons and even to persuade governments of the need to purchase entire systems, often entirely unnecessarily. The helicopter scandal in Uganda is a case in point. In 1998 the Ugandan Government purchased four second-hand Mi-24 helicopters from the Republic of Belarus at an inflated price of US$12.3 million (Ochieng 1998). The helicopters were not airworthy. Reportedly, Museveni's brother, Major General Salim Saleh, received an US$800,000 'incentive' to seal the deal. In 1998, the South African Government's last-minute decision to switch from the Italian Aermacchi MB-339 trainer aircraft, the preferred option of the South African Air Force, to the more expensive BAE Systems-built Hawk 100 trainer, is thought to have occurred as a result of substantial sweeteners offered by BAE Systems to the late Joe Modise, then Minister of Defence, and his aide Fana Hlongwane (Roeber 2004, p. 61, Groenink 2007).

The sums involved in bribes are often life-changing for the individuals involved. Payments come in a number of forms, and are made through a variety of channels such as the brown envelope or the Swiss bank account, and take the form of luxury commodities such as cars, villas, private jets and access to private clubs. The scale of 'commissions' and bribes is unknown, and varies from sale to sale. A conservative estimate made by TI UK has put it at 10 per cent of a contract's value (TI UK 2002). However, findings by the UK Special Fraud Office inquiry into the 2006 Tanzania arms scandal found that commissions of 29 per cent were paid, and suggests that bribes may be significantly higher than TI's estimates (Leigh 2006, McGreal 2007). Estimating the total cost of corruption in the arms trade is fraught with challenges, but extrapolating from World Bank figures on global rates of corruption, Transparency International's defence team has conservatively estimated that corruption within the global defence sector averages around US$20 billion per annum (TI UK 2002).

The firms and the government officials who facilitate arms sales often refer to bribes as 'commissions' or 'incentives'. European arms manufacturers in stiff competition with each other, and with US defence giants, like to think that their commissions and 'incentive packages' create a 'level playing field' in a highly competitive defence market. Before the OECD Anti-Bribery Convention was introduced in 1997, these incentives were seen as legitimate practice in defence sales, notably when the payments were made abroad. Since the introduction of the OECD Convention, it is illegal for corporations from OECD countries to offer bribes to foreign officials; however, evidence from recent investigations into arms scandals suggest that the paying of bribes to secure arms sales continues to be widely practised outside the OECD region.

The Bribery Payers Index 2006 (BPI) produced by Transparency International found that Northern companies tend to offer more bribes in Africa than in any other region of the world (TI 2006, p. 8). Of this trend, TI has observed that:

*It would seem that many foreign companies do not resort to bribery while operating in the 'developed' world, where institutions are strong and there is a significant threat of legal retribution for illegal activities. However, in less developed countries (many of which are characterised by poor governance and ineffective legal systems for dealing with corruption), it appears that many companies continue to engage in corrupt practices. The result is that the countries least equipped to deal with corruption are hardest hit, as their anti-corruption initiatives are undermined.* (TI 2006, p. 10)

A number of factors have contributed to the rise in corruption in the arms trade sector during the last decade. On the supply side, the end of the Cold War simultaneously dampened demand for weapons systems and increased competition between arms suppliers. Arms manufacturers responded by aggressively marketing their wares, often resorting to bribes to secure deals (Gupta *et al.* 2000). On the demand side, opportunities for rent-seeking increased with the growing opacity of military procurement and with a reduction in the number of suppliers due to increasing levels of consolidation and concentration in the global defence industry.

The arms industry is 'hard-wired for corruption', mainly because of both the special treatment it receives from governments and the secrecy that sanctions every aspect of its transactions. Arms companies from the rich West bribe the political and military elites of poor countries to purchase weapons they cannot afford, and often do not need. These sales are justified on the basis of the national economic, employment and security interests of rich Western states, but there is a high cost to such deals, which contribute to the burden of national debt in poor countries, divert scarce national resources from social spending, and often contribute to the undermining of the security of nations through the purchase of expensive and inappropriate equipment.

## The Role of the International Financial Institutions

Every single corrupt arms deal involves a financial pipeline that enables bribery to take place. It is not just the corrupt African elites, or the arms companies and their agents, that are prepared to pay bribes and mask their shadowy deals. There are other less visible players – including banks, offshore shell companies, accountants and lawyers – who facilitate the funding of arms deals and help to launder ill-gotten gains.

In laundering money, large amounts of cash are usually spread among many different accounts – such as in free-trade zones, financial offshore centres, and tax havens – where they are converted into financial instruments such as money orders, bonds, investments in trusts or charities, or into shell companies. The money is then transferred to other locations, sometimes in the form of payments for bogus 'goods and services' issued by holding companies owned by lawyers or accountants on behalf of unnamed beneficiaries. The funds are then wired back to their originators as part of the earnings of a legitimate business. It is a relatively simple process that leaves either no paper trail, or one that is so complicated that it is difficult to trace. Because the objective of money laundering is to return the illegal funds in a legal form to the individual who generated them, launderers prefer to move funds through stable financial systems – hence the central role of banks in the money laundering process.

A few examples reveal how global and widespread the money laundering of illegal arms receipts is. In 2006, *Africa Confidential* reported that Kenyan banks had been involved in the laundering of the ill-gotten gains of Nigeria's military and political elites in the late 1990s (*Africa Confidential* 2005). Extensive investigations into the 'Angolagate' scandal, involving illicit arms transfers to Angola worth US$790 billion orchestrated by key members of the French political elite, have revealed that a number of Portuguese banks were involved in transferring illegal commissions. In total, some 70 transfers took place, totalling US$54 billion. Fifty of these transfers, to a total value of US$21 million, were deposited in Portuguese banks. The largest transfers were to the state-run Caixa Geral de Depositos (CDG) and the Banco Comercial Português (BCP), the country's two largest banks. The Nacional de Crédito, Nacional Ultramarino, Comercio e Industria, Totta and Açores, Pinto and Sotto Mayor banks, and the Portuguese branches of Spain's Banco Bilbao and Britain's Barclays, are also on the list of institutions contained in the indictment (Inter Press Service 27 January 2009).

Until relatively recently, the bribes or incentives involved in arms deals were not considered illegal, and banks readily complied with their clients' need to launder their ill-gotten gains. Since 9/11, anti-money-laundering legislation and practice have been tightened up. More than 150 countries promised to cooperate with the US in its fight against the financing of terrorism, 81 of which (including the Bahamas, Argentina, Kuwait, Indonesia, Pakistan, Switzerland and the EU) actually froze assets of suspicious individuals, suspect charities and dubious firms, or passed new anti-money-laundering laws and stricter regulations (the Philippines, the UK, Germany). Nevertheless, 19 'black holes', or poorly regulated financial services and offshore banking facilities, still persist in Russia, Indonesia and Israel, to name the most prominent.

Money launderers are resilient. They adapt fast to changing circumstances. Alternative banking systems are being established beyond the bounds of the West's financial regulation and jurisdiction. Defunct banks in territories with corrupt politicians, lax regulation and porous tax regimes are being purchased. The cash-hungry countries of Montenegro, Serbia, Macedonia, Ukraine, Belarus and Albania are proving willing participants.

## Hypocrisy and Discrimination

In December 2006, in response to political pressure from the highest levels in the British Government, the Director of the Serious Fraud Office announced his decision to terminate the investigation into accusations of BAE corruption in the al-Yamamah deal. By failing to conduct full investigations into arms trade scandals, the British Government exposed itself to accusations of hypocrisy and discrimination. It was a major setback in the campaign to control corruption in the transnational arms industry.

In July 2007, Jacob Zuma, himself implicated in corrupt arms dealing in South Africa, accused the British Government of double standards, and posed a pertinent question to the *Newsnight* investigator Peter Marshall: 'Why should the rulers (of the West) be allowed to pick and choose on matters that relate to the application of law?' (*Newsnight* 28 May 2007). Whatever his own culpability, Jacob Zuma has a point. DFID and other donors are hardly in a position to impose yet more levels of pernicious conditionality on development aid when their own governments are implicated in diverting scarce resources towards expensive and corrupt arms deals and in repressing enquiries into corruption. This state of affairs not only makes a mockery of DFID's good-governance and anti-corruption programmes, but also undermines its security-sector reform agenda, which is a critical component of its post-conflict work.

If the British Government hoped that UK involvement in arms scandals could be covered up and would quietly disappear, they have had a nasty shock, as the US Department of Justice has decided to prosecute BAE Systems for its prominent role in corruption in the global arms trade. The US appears to be the only country currently willing to impose the ethical and legal principles governing the arms trade and embodied within international law. Cynics may argue that they are motivated by their own national interests in preserving the dominance of US arms companies within the international arms market. While there may be some truth to this accusation, if the US Department of Justice can help to regulate the ruthless and corrupt transnational arms industry, whatever its motivation, this may open up opportunities for challenging corruption in the military sector in SSA.

## Conclusion

DFID's cautious attempt to tackle corruption in arms procurement through its TIDE programme has been put on the back burner. Not only did the neoliberal methodologies employed to analyse the problem prove inadequate to the task in the SSA context, but it became increasingly apparent to DFID officials that British companies and, by implication, the British Government which had sanctioned and supported British defence companies' sales abroad, were heavily implicated in arms procurement scandals. Given DFID's past record of attempting to control excessive military expenditures, and its more recent attempts to improve transparency and accountability in defence budgeting, it appears to be hopelessly out of touch with the reality of Africa's military and security environment. It should therefore come as little surprise that its endeavour to design an anti-corruption policy for arms procurement and expenditures in SSA has failed to take off.

Corruption in the arms trade is a phenomenon that can only be controlled when it is identified as a 'global governance' problem, one in which the rule of law and, in particular, anti-corruption legislation, has to apply to all parties engaged in corruption. These actors include Western politicians who promote arms sales, civil servants who oversee the licensing of arms exports, export credit guarantee services, arms company salesmen and executives, 'independent agents', political and military elites in recipient countries and the offshore banks who launder the ill-gotten gains. Only then can the global pipeline of covert deals, bribery, kickbacks, money laundering and secrecy be overturned, and ethical and legal principles upheld.

As a first step in regaining moral authority, Western governments need to adhere to, and actively enforce, the 1997 OECD Anti-Bribery Convention. This requires the provision of adequate resources to empower the OECD Anti-Corruption Committee to effectively investigate and prosecute those arms companies engaged in corruption in the developing world. A second step should be to impose conditions on export licences to ensure that companies comply with anti-corruption legislation and practice. Scrutiny of individual arms export licences should also be undertaken by government committees, to ensure both greater transparency in the licensing process, and increased company compliance with anti-corruption legislation. To complement these measures, arms companies should be made to adopt internal auditing systems capable of detecting corruption and the payment of bribes. Finally, government support for the domestic arms industry through the supply of export credit guarantees should be conditional upon anti-corruption compliance. Once the West has put its own house in order, it will be in a stronger position to start tackling the complex and challenging nature of security sector corruption in the developing world. To lead by the example of 'best practice' is a first and necessary step in the challenging task of dismantling the transnational web of corruption in arms procurement and the arms trade.

**Susan Willett** is a freelance consultant specialising in security and development issues and a Fellow of Economists for Peace and Security, Levy Institute, New York State, USA. In addition, she serves as a Board Member of the Verification Information and Training Council (VERTIC). Email: swillett@easynet.co.uk

## References

**Adebayo, A.** (2002), *Building peace in West Africa: Liberia, Sierra Leone and Guinea-Bissau*, Boulder, CO: Lynne Rienner.

**Adekanye, J.B.** (1999), *The retired military and emergent power factor in Nigeria*, Ibadan: Heinemann Educational Books.

**Africa Confidential.** (1999), 'Ceasefire under threat. 40, (22), 5 November.

 (2005), 'Nigeria: the net widens. 46, (15), 22 July.

 (2006), 'Breaking the arms embargo. 47, (23), 17 November.

 (2007), 'Nigeria: a tale of two cities. 48, (18), 7 September.

**Atkinson, P. & N. Leader** (2000), *The joint policy operations and the principles and protocols of humanitarian operations in Liberia*, HPG Report No. 3, London: ODI, Humanitarian Policy Group.

**Ball, N. & K. Fayemi**, (eds.) (2004), *Security sector governance in Africa: a handbook*, Lagos: Centre for Democracy and Development.

**Control Risks.** (2006), *International business attitudes to corruption survey 2006*, Simmons and Simmons. Available from: www.controlrisks.com/pdf/corruption_survey_2006_V3.pdf

**Cooper, T. & J. Kyzer** (2003), *II Ethiopian Eritrean war, 1998–2000*, Air Combat Information Group, 2 September. Available from: www.acig.org/artman/publish/article_189.shtml

**Dunne, P. & R. Haines** (2006), 'The making of arms in South Africa', *The economics of peace and security journal*, 1, (1), pp. 39–48.

**The Economist.** (1999), 'Carnage on the plain. 17–23 April.

**Global Witness.** (2002), *All the Presidents' men*, Washington DC: Global Witness, March.

 (2004), *Rich man, poor man – development diamonds and poverty diamonds*, Washington DC: Global Witness, October.

 (2005), *Extracting transparency*, Washington DC: Global Witness, September.

 (2005), *The riddle of the Sphinx: where has Congo's oil money gone?*, Washington DC: Global Witness, December.

 (2005), *Timber, taylor, soldier, spy*, Washington DC: Global Witness, June.

 (2007), *Oil revenue transparency: a strategic component of US energy security and anti-corruption policy*, Washington DC: Global Witness, March.

**Groenink, E.** (2007), 'Arms deal: who got R1bn in pay-offs?', *Mail & Guardian Online*, Available from: www.mg.co.za/article/2007-01-12-arms-deal-who-got-r1bn-in-pay-offs

**Gupta, S., L. de Mello & R. Sharon** (2000), *Corruption and military spending*, IMF Working Paper No. 60/23, Washington DC: World Bank, 1 February.

**Harker, J.** (2000), *The Harker Report: human security in Sudan: the report of a Canadian Assessment Mission*, Prepared for the Ministry of Foreign Affairs Ottawa, February.

**Hartley, K.** (2007), *Military expenditure data for SSA nations: Report for DFID*, Monograph, York, Canada: Centre for Defence Economics, University of York.

**Henk, D. & M. Rupiya** (2001), *Funding defence: challenges of buying military capability in sub-Saharan Africa*, Strategic Studies Institute (SSI) monograph. Available at: http://www.strategicstudiesinstitute.army.mil/pubs/display.cfm?pubID=198

**Hutchful, E.** (2003), 'Ghana', in W. Omitoogun (ed.), *Military expenditure data in Africa: a survey*

*of Cameroon, Ethiopia, Ghana, Kenya, Nigeria and Uganda*, Oxford: University Press of SIPRI.

**Inter Press Service** (2009), *Portugal 'Angolagate' tribes in local banks*, Lisbon 27 January. Available at: http://www.humanrights-geveva_info?portugal-angolagate-bribes-in,3676

**Kauffman, D.** (2004), *Corruption, governance and security: challenges for the rich countries and the world*. Available at: http://ssrn.com/abstract=605801

**Leigh, D.** (2006), 'Fraud Office inquiry into BAE Tanzanian deal', *The Guardian*, 13 November 2006. Available from: http://www.guardian.co.uk/politics/2006/nov/13/armstrade.foreignpolicy

**LeMelle, G.** (2008), *African Policy Outlook 2008*, Washington, DC: Foreign Policy in Focus, 7 February.

**McGreal, C.** (2007), 'Arms deal investigation probe BAE payment to South African', *The Guardian*, 6 January. Available from: http://www.guardian.co.uk/world/2007/jan/06/bae.armstrade

*Newsnight*. (2007), 'David Marshall interview with Jacob Zuma', London: British Broadcasting Corporation, July.

**Nimubona, J. & C. Sebudadi** (2007), *Le phénomène de la corruption au Burundi: révolte silencieuse et résignation*, Bujumbura: International Alert, March. Available from: http://www.eurac-network.org/web/uploads/documents/20070504_9136.doc

**Ochieng, L.** (1998), 'Military copters condemned by S. African firm', *The East African*, 3 September.

**Omitoogun, W.** (2003), *Military expenditure data in Africa: a survey of Cameroon, Ethiopia, Ghana, Kenya, Nigeria and Uganda*, Oxford: Oxford University Press for SIPRI.

**Omitoogun, W. & E. Hutchful,** (eds.) (2006), *Budgeting for the military sector in Africa: the process and mechanisms of control*, Oxford: Oxford University Press for SIPRI.

**Renton, D., D. Seddon & L. Zeilig** (2007), *The Congo: plunder and resistance*, London: Zed Books.

**Roeber, J.** (2004), 'The politics of corruption in the arms trade: South Africa's arms trade scandal and the Elf affair', in: *Transparency International global corruption report 2004: political corruption*, London: Pluto Press for Transparency International, 59–67.

**Savage, K., M. Jackollie, D. Kumeh & E. Dorbor** (2007), *Corruption perceptions and risks in humanitarian assistance: a Liberia case study*, Humanitarian Policy Group Background Paper, London: ODI, April.

**SIPRI Military Expenditure Database.**, Available from: http://www.sipri.org/contents/milap/milex/mex_database1.html

**Transparency International.** (2006), *Bribery payers index 2006 analysis report*, Available from: www.transparency.org/policy_research/surveys_indices/bpi/bpi_2006

**Transparency International.** (2007), *Addressing corruption and building integrity in defence establishments*, Working Paper No. 2, London: Transparency International.

**Transparency International UK** (2002), *Corruption in the official arms trade*, Policy Research Paper 001, London: Transparency International UK.

**UN Security Council.** (2003), *Panel of experts on the illegal exploitation of natural resources and other forms of wealth of the DRC*, 5/2003/027, 23 October, New York: United Nations.

**US Department of Commerce.** (2000), *The National Export Strategy Trade Promotion Coordinating Committee Report*, Washington DC, March.

**WMEAT.** (2002), *World Military Expenditures and Arms Transfers 1999–2000*, Washington DC: US Department of State.

# [14]

# WHY DO SO MANY ANTI-CORRUPTION EFFORTS FAIL?

*MICHAEL JOHNSTON**

## I.
## INTRODUCTION

Anti-corruption efforts are usually launched with high hopes, considerable fanfare and, at times, genuine political backing by top-level leadership. But success has been elusive at best: even where agencies are part of bona fide reform efforts, there are very few success stories to report. Improvements in specific programs and agencies tend to be short-lived, difficult to demonstrate, and hard to generalize to broader segments of government. Why is corruption so tenacious? I suggest several main difficulties, some of them inherent in the nature of corruption control and others coming in the form of avoidable strategic mistakes. Among the main issues is an overly-narrow analysis of corruption that reduces it to a law-enforcement issue and/or to one of unbalanced incentives, without considering deeper causes or variations in kind among cases. Another is a tendency to conceive of reform as a public good—"better

---

* Charles A. Dana Professor of Political Science, Colgate University.

government for all"—without paying close attention to collective-action problems and the range of incentives needed to overcome them. These and other difficulties weaken the credibility of and support for reform; all must be addressed in systematic ways if anti-corruption agencies are to improve their track records.

Corruption control has enjoyed broad-based support over the past generation, and has taken on increasingly sophisticated forms. The issue figures prominently, not only in discussions of economic development and democratization,[1] but also (for example) in analyses of the current upheavals in the Middle East[2] and the terror attacks at Domodedovo airport in Moscow.[3] During the summer of 2011, a broad-based anti-corruption movement energized by Anna Hazare's widely publicized hunger strike threatened, at times, to convulse Indian politics.[4] Many smart, committed, and often courageous individuals, backed by resources and official support that would have been difficult to imagine a generation ago, have energized reform and research.

Clear-cut success stories, however, have been scarce.[5] Given the difficulties in measuring corruption, any such judgment is impressionistic: most corrupt activities are clandestine and go unreported because they lack an immediate victim, while those in the know often share an interest in secrecy. Tracing trends is even more difficult. Furthermore, as I will suggest below, different societies have different kinds of corruption problems; just how much of one variety might equal or exceed another is anyone's guess. Some countries' anti-corruption agencies have had conspicuous success: Hong Kong and Singapore, both deeply corrupt in times past, are well-known examples.[6] But both are relatively small city-states in which

---

1. *See* Bo Rothstein, The Quality of Government: Corruption, Social Trust and Inequality in International Perspective 1–57 (2011).

2. *See* Issandr El Amrani, *Why Tunis, Why Cairo?*, London Rev. Books, Feb. 17, 2011, at 3–6, *available at* http://www.lrb.co.uk/v33/n04/issandr-elamrani/why-tunis-why-cairo; Sudarsan Raghavan, *In Tunisia, Luxurious Lifestyles of a Corrupt Government*, Wash. Post (Jan. 28, 2011, 3:09 PM), http://www.washingtonpost.com/wp-dyn/content/article/2011/01/28/AR2011012901921.html.

3. Simon Saradzhyan, Op-Ed., *From Toilet to Airport*, Moscow Times (Jan. 27, 2011), *available at* http://belfercenter.ksg.harvard.edu/publication/20688/from_toilet_to_airport.html.

4. *See, e.g.*, Maseeh Rahman, *Anna Hazare Ends Hunger Strike After Indian Government Backs Down*, Guardian (Aug. 28, 2011, 9:12 AM), http://www.guardian.co.uk/world/2011/aug/28/anna-hazare-ends-hunger-strike.

5. *See* Alina Mungiu-Pippidi, *Corruption: Diagnosis and Treatment*, 17 J. Democracy 86–99 (2006).

6. *See* Jon S. T. Quah, Curbing Corruption in Asian Countries: An Impossible Dream? 199–236 (2011) (Singapore); *id.* at 237–68 (Hong Kong).

undemocratic regimes could force extensive change, and in which the economic benefits of reduced corruption could rapidly become apparent. Botswana teaches us important lessons about the value of socially rooted leadership, but its population, spread over a large area, is a quarter of Hong Kong's.[7] Japan and Belgium have made steady progress, if corruption indices based upon perception data are any indication, but both already had relatively strong national institutions in place. Korea, Indonesia, Ghana and Taiwan, for examples, are promising cases worth watching in coming years.

Still, when it comes to lasting reductions in corruption in full-scale societies where it has been endemic, the results of a generation's pursuit of better government have not been encouraging.[8] The well-known corruption problems of Russia, China, and Thailand have been the focus of widely (and frequently) proclaimed concern and control efforts, but there are few if any credible claims of sustained reductions in abuses. Corrupt practices of tightly organized rings of elites in Argentina date back to the early decades of the 19th century and continue today.[9] Hopes are high among many in the Philippines that the government of President Benigno S. "Noy Noy" Aquino can stem tides of corrupt dealing that peaked during the recent Arroyo administration, but the track record of dozens of anti-corruption projects and key institutions over many years is disappointing.[10] Equally sobering, if less apparent based on corruption indices, are the periodic scandals in established market democracies like the United Kingdom, the United States, and Germany, where the Siemens conglomerate has been the center of at-

---

7. *See* Anne Pitcher, Mary H. Moran & Michael Johnston, *Rethinking Patrimonialism and Neopatrimonialism in Africa*, 52 AFR. STUD. REV. 125, 144–49 (2009).

8. *See, e.g.*, Anna Persson, Bo Rothstein & Jan Teorell, *The Failure of Anti-Corruption Policies: A Theoretical Mischaracterization of the Problem* (Göteborg Univ. Quality of Gov't Inst., QoG Working Paper Series, Paper No. 19, 2010), *available at* http://www.qog.pol.gu.se/working_papers/2010_19_Persson_Rothstein_Teorell. pdf (providing an overview of such failures, with particular emphasis on Kenya and Uganda).

9. An excellent analysis of long-term trends appears in Aranzazu Guillan-Montero, As if: The Fiction of Executive Accountability and the Persistence of Corruption Networks in Weakly Institutionalized Presidential Systems. Argentina (1989-2007) 12–25 (Aug. 5, 2011) (unpublished Ph.D. dissertation, Georgetown University), *available at* ProQuest Dissertations & Theses, Doc. ID 2466588931.

10. *Cf.* Jong-Sung You, Embedded Autonomy or Crony Capitalism? Explaining Corruption in South Korea, Relative to Taiwan and the Philippines, Focusing on the Role of Land Reform and Industrial Policy 7–10, 21–27 (unpublished) (2005), *available at* http://irps.ucsd.edu/assets/003/5292.pdf. *See generally* RONNIE V. AMORADO, KAKISTOCRACY 32–37, 42–53 (2011) (discussing several case histories involving intra-governmental betrayal and corrupt dealings in the Philippines).

tention.[11] Those nations' would-be reformers, critics might well contend, need to address their own societies' problems before venturing out into the wider world with schemes for "good governance."

At the same time, a longer view shows that even deeply entrenched corruption need not be a permanent condition. Had there been governance rankings in the Seventeenth Century, England would have been near the corrupt end of the scale. In the Nineteenth Century, the United States, and the United Kingdom with its "Old Corruption"—pervasive vote-buying, intimidation, and outright electoral fraud dominated by local landholders—would have received poor ratings.[12] At times during the Eighteenth Century, Denmark and Sweden were seen as extensively corrupt.[13] Australia's first seventy years were marked by frequent scandals, and its subsequent half-century featured a long struggle between politically connected interests and emerging advocates of reform.[14] Chile, Canada, Finland, and the Netherlands have had their periods of scan-

---

11. As just one spectacular example, consider the extensive bribery and kickback schemes associated with the activities of British Aerospace in Saudi Arabia, in which the U.K. government obstructed inquiries rather than risk lucrative export deals. *See* R. v. Dir. of the Serious Frauds Office, [2008] UKHL 60, [2009] 1 A.C. 756 (H.L) (appeal taken from Eng.), *available at* http://www.controlbae.org.uk/jr/Lords_judgment.pdf (affirming U.K. government's decision to halt investigations into dealings between British Aerospace and the government of Saudi Arabia); *see also The BAE Files*, GUARDIAN, http://www.guardian.co.uk/world/bae (last visited Nov. 15, 2011); *OECD Says UK's Dropping of BAE-Saudi Corruption Probe Symptom of Wider Problem*, FORBES (Mar. 14, 2007, 2:14 PM), http://www.forbes.com/feeds/afx/2007/03/14/afx3516213.html; Michael Peel et al., *UK 'Unlawfully' Scrapped BAE Probe*, FINANCIAL TIMES (Apr. 10, 2008), http://us.ft.com/ftgateway/superpage.ft?news_id=fto041120080448538287. In Germany, the Siemens conglomerate has been the center of attention. Siri Schubert & T. Christian Miller, *At Siemens, Bribery Was Just a Line Item*, N.Y. TIMES (Dec. 21, 2008), http://www.nytimes.com/2008/12/21/business/worldbusiness/21siemens.html.

12. *See* CORNELIUS O'LEARY, THE ELIMINATION OF CORRUPT PRACTICES IN BRITISH ELECTIONS 1868-1911, at 1–22 (1962); W.D. Rubinstein, *The End of "Old Corruption" in Britain 1780-1860*, 101 PAST & PRESENT 55 (1983).

13. *Introduction to Part I, in* POLITICAL CORRUPTION: CONCEPTS & CONTEXTS 4–5 (Arnold J. Heidenheimer & Michael Johnston, eds., 3d ed. 2002). On Scandinavia generally, see ROTHSTEIN, *supra* note 1, at 117–18, 126 (citing Mette Frisk Jensen, Korruption og embedsetik: dansk embedsmændskorruption i perioden 1800 til 1886 [Corruption and Official Ethics] (2008) (unpublished Ph.D. dissertation, Aalborg Univ.); Bo Rothstein, *Anti Corruption—A Big Bang Theory* 17–23 (Göteborg Univ. Quality of Gov't Inst., QoG Working Paper Series, Paper No. 3, 2007), *available at* http://www.qog.pol.gu.se/working_papers/2007_3_Rothstein.pdf.

14. Ross Curnow, *What's Past is Prologue: Administrative Corruption in Australia, in* THE HISTORY OF CORRUPTION IN CENTRAL GOVERNMENT 37, 39–49 (Seppo Tiihonen ed., 2003) [hereinafter HISTORY OF CORRUPTION].

dal and corruption.[15] All of those societies are generally regarded as well governed today and, for what such scores are worth, fare well on international corruption rankings.

In most such cases, progress, even when spurred by periods of relatively rapid legal innovation and changes in social expectations, grew out of fundamental conflicts over questions of power and accountability that took place over decades or more. Several of today's better-governed societies took major steps toward corruption control and more accountable government in the course of significant political contention.[16] Dedicated schemes of reform did, at times, push such processes in positive directions, but at least equally often it was various groups' efforts to defend themselves against exploitation that unleashed essential political energy and opened up space for reformers. If indeed corruption control has been an indirect consequence of contention and disagreement among interested parties, rather than solely a civic-minded quest for better government for all, and if local issues and groups have been critical to such processes, can we identify any common reasons for the indifferent record of the anti-corruption movement?

This paper offers two parallel arguments: first, that we need to view corruption control not only as an array of specific legal remedies and administrative controls, important though they are, but also as a long-term *political* process through which people defend themselves against abuses by others—or as Madison had it, through which they "*oblige* [government] to control itself."[17] The second is that the corruption problems of various societies differ in qualitative ways, in large part because divergent interests are taking advantage of contrasting opportunities and institutional weaknesses. Seen in that light, reform confronts us with a wide range of challenges

---

15. *See, e.g.,* SIMON COLLIER & WILLIAM F. SATER, A HISTORY OF CHILE: 1808-2002, 191–92 (2d ed. 2004) (describing electoral bribery in Chile in the late nineteenth and early twentieth centuries); Kenneth Kernaghan, *Corruption and Public Service in Canada: Conceptual and Practical Dimensions, in* HISTORY OF CORRUPTION, *supra* note 14, at 83, 87; Paula Tiihonen, *Good Governance and Corporation in Finland, in* HISTORY OF CORRUPTION, *supra* note 14, at 99, 104–12; Frits M. van der Meer & Jos C.N. Raadschelders, *Maladministration in the Netherlands in the 19th and 20th Centuries, in* HISTORY OF CORRUPTION, *supra* note 14, at 179, 186–93.

16. For example, Stuart England engaged in civil war over issues of royal privilege versus parliamentary autonomy and Sweden's dominant landholding and administrative classes had to make room for a new generation of educated citizens created by rising economic modernization. On the former, see LINDA LEVY PECK, COURT PATRONAGE AND CORRUPTION IN EARLY STUART ENGLAND (1990); for Sweden, see ROTHSTEIN, *supra* note 13, at 17–23.

17. THE FEDERALIST NO. 51, at 264 (James Madison) (Ian Shapiro ed., 2009) (emphasis added).

and with various starting points from which to attack them. Those variations are both marked and fundamental, meaning that while the anti-corruption movement has gained strength nearly everywhere it has had difficulty succeeding anywhere. To help explain the indifferent track record of those reform efforts, I will focus on two different families of problems: those inherent in the task of fighting corruption anywhere and those reflecting the contrasting forces shaping different sorts of cases.

## II.
## CHALLENGES INHERENT IN
## CHECKING CORRUPTION

### A.   *Corruption Eludes Precise Definition*

One basic, and universal, problem with controlling corruption in any society is that there is little agreement about the meaning of the term, or about what activity is or is not corrupt. The definitions debate is a hardy perennial in corruption analysis: reformers generally have proceeded on an "I-know-it-when-I-see-it" basis, reasoning that enough activity occurs that would be corrupt by *any* measure that we need not concern ourselves with parsing out details at the boundaries of the concept. In most societies it is hard to dispute that assessment. Still, a lack of settled definitions makes it more difficult to assess the seriousness of corruption and to track trends; further, in ways I will discuss below, typical conceptions of the term are based on individuals' or specific groups' behavior, and thus divert our attention from important aspects of the social and institutional setting that shape both corruption issues and prospects for reform. Understanding the political processes and conflicts that make precise definitions difficult may point to ways in which we can intensify and sustain demands for accountability and limits on official power and privileges.

### B.   *Corruption Undermines Collective Action for Reform*

Other inherent problems have to do with power, incentives, costs and benefits—in effect, with the political economy of corruption.[18] Corruption undermines the quality of government as well as its accountability to society at large. It disrupts fair and openly competitive economic and political processes, generally benefiting the "haves"—that is, the well-connected and their clients—at the ex-

---

18. *See generally* Susan Rose-Ackerman, Corruption and Government: Causes, Consequences, and Reform 9–88 (1999); Rothstein, *supra* note 1, at 77–163.

pense of the "have-nots," whose opportunities often depend more upon fair procedures and dependable rules. It can offer sizeable material gains while draining away resources and weakening the property and political rights of society at large. It is true that at times corrupt benefits trickle downward to broader segments of the population. But the long-term costs of accepting such benefits usually outweigh their immediate value, because the benefits are often used to control clients and buy off potential opponents, not for genuine help and assistance. It is hardly surprising that people with pressing needs and few immediate alternatives will agree to accept such benefits; in the larger context, however, it is safe to say that most corruption hurts most people most of the time.

It is tempting to think that with so many losing so much to corruption, it ought to be relatively easy to mobilize most people and groups against it. But the benefits of corruption are immediate, tangible, and often concentrated in relatively few hands; its costs tend to be widespread, long-term, and often intangible, or at least difficult to quantify. Those costs are no less real for being hard to assess, but this asymmetry reduces incentives for any one citizen to challenge corrupt figures at any one time, particularly where doing so is risky. Making the imbalance all the greater is the fact that corrupt leaders may be able to buy support, compromise the courts and law enforcement, intimidate the press, and divide the opposition.

As a result, reform must overcome significant collective action problems.[19] Collective action problems are particularly likely when, as is often the case, reformers justify the need to control corruption primarily in terms of the public interest. Even if reduced corruption could bring forth an era of rational, effective government and prosperity for all, why should I take on the hard work and risks of reform, which may well involve challenging some of society's most powerful people? And why should I give up the corrupt benefits I might now receive, when I stand to benefit from successful reform even if I stay on the sidelines? Further, as Ostrom and Rothstein point out, while it might be possible and desirable to reach agreements and build institutions that could reduce the risks and costs of actively pursuing reform, the task of building those sorts of foundations for reform itself presents a second-order collective action

---

19. The classic treatment is MANCUR OLSON, THE LOGIC OF COLLECTIVE ACTION: PUBLIC GOODS AND THE THEORY OF GROUPS 5–65 (1965). *See also* MARK IRVING LICHBACH, THE COOPERATOR'S DILEMMA 3–29 (1996); ROTHSTEIN, *supra* note 1, at 99–105.

problem.[20] Thus, even where a strong civil society is in place diverse and targeted incentives and appeals that evolve as situations change will be needed if we are to build active political support for reform.

Reform forces not only must contend with powerful, wealthy interests who are able and all too willing to defend their advantages and gains, but they also often do so in conditions of social fragmentation, distrust, and weak social and political institutions. In post-conflict societies, longstanding social divisions, as well as memories of more recent violence, may undermine social trust and spur suspicion and resentment of even the most ordinary aspects of governance. Those difficulties will be all the more pronounced where ineffective or compromised police forces struggle to confront illicit trafficking, gang activities, organized crime, and private armies. Adding to the instability and pervasive sense of personal insecurity often found in such situations is the fact that today's developing societies are far more exposed to global forces than were most affluent market democracies during their own emergent phases. While liberalization and integration into wider markets may limit corruption in some ways,[21] it creates new risks as well.[22]

---

20. ROTHSTEIN, *supra* note 1, at 100; Elinor Ostrom, *A Behavioral Approach to the Rational Choice Theory of Collective Action*, 92 AM. POL. SCI. REV. 1, 6–9 (1998); *see also* Jan Teorell, *Corruption as an Institution: Rethinking the Nature and Origins of the Grabbing Hand* 11–12 (Göteborg Univ. Quality of Gov't Inst., QoG Working Paper Series, Paper No. 5, 2007), *available at* http://www.qog.pol.gu.se/working_papers/2007_5_Teorell.pdf. Teorell notes that as institutions become more corrupt, "it becomes more profitable to be corrupt at the same time as the costs for auditing corrupt public officials increase," and that individuals in groups with corrupt reputations have little incentive to be honest themselves. *Id.* at 11–12.

21. *See, e.g.*, Juan-Jose Ganuza & Esther Hauk, *Economic Integration and Corruption*, 22 INT'L. J. INDUS. ORG. 1463, 1463–67, 1478–79 (2004) (positing that corrupt, isolated countries who have the most to gain from wider integration will constrain their corrupt practices because potential trading partners would otherwise exclude them); Daniel Triesman, *The Causes of Corruption: A Cross-National Study*, 76 J. PUB. ECON. 399, 440–42 (2000) (finding empirically that the process of economic development can limit corruption).

22. *See, e.g.*, CAROLYN M. WARNER, THE BEST SYSTEM MONEY CAN BUY: CORRUPTION IN THE EUROPEAN UNION (2007). In a competitive environment, the edge that can be gained via corruption is more valuable, *id.* at 33–53, while access to other markets broadens the range of profitable corrupt activity, *id.* at 54–83. *See also* Boliang Zhu, Economic Integration and Corruption: The Case of China (Nov. 2009) (unpublished manuscript), *available at* https://ncgg.princeton.edu/IPES/2009/papers/F120_paper2.pdf (claiming that economic integration can increase the levels of corruption in countries with limited market competition and weak domestic institutions).

## C.   Corruption Is a Transnational Problem

Modern corruption involves diverse and unpredictable techniques, respects no boundaries, feeds upon new technologies, and evolves far more rapidly than do our efforts to contain it. Governments of affluent democracies have until recently given their domestic corporations political cover and substantial incentives to bribe officials in the developing world.[23] Banks and markets in affluent countries can profit by offering safe havens for the proceeds of corruption in less secure societies. Many cases of corruption involve transnational corporate entities and their employees, corporations that are capable of doing business almost everywhere yet difficult to hold accountable anywhere. A recent U.S. investigation of the French communications giant Alcatel, which does business in over 130 countries, found that the firm had violated the U.S. Foreign Corrupt Practices Act through its Swiss-based subsidiary Alcatel Standard.[24] The subsidiary, whose primary activity seems to have been funneling money to public officials, had engaged in systematic bribery in Central America, Taiwan, and Malaysia between 1990 and 2006.[25] At present Alcatel is also under scrutiny for the activities of another subsidiary involved in major infrastructure projects in Australia.[26] While the U.S. investigation resulted in $137 million in fines for the parent corporation, other corrupt activities—notably, individual schemes in which some company officials received a portion of the corporate bribe funds in the form of kickbacks for themselves—have gone unpunished.[27]

## D.   Corruption is Systemically Embedded

Another fundamental problem is the embedded nature of serious corruption. It is one thing to refer to "systematic" and "systemic" corruption, as we commonly do, but grasping the full implications of those ideas is another thing. Many reform strategies

---

23. Before the advent of the OECD Anti-Bribery Convention in 1999, France and Germany were among a number of countries that not only allowed corporations to pay bribes abroad, but also allowed them to treat such payments as legitimate business expenses, reducing their tax liabilities. OECD, Update on Tax Legislation on the Tax Treatment of Bribes to Foreign Public Officials in Countries Parties to the OECD Anti Bribery Convention (June 16, 2011), http://www.oecd.org/dataoecd/58/10/41353070.pdf.

24. Ian Verrender, *Bribery, Corruption: A World of Deceit*, SYDNEY MORNING HERALD (Aug. 30, 2011), http://www.smh.com.au/business/bribery-corruption-a-world-of-deceit-20110829-1jicn.html.

25. *Id.*

26. *Id.*

27. *Id.*

still reflect a view of corruption as a form of deviance—as an exception, a transgression of legitimate and widely-accepted standards, as an illness (corruption-as-cancer is a popular though generally misleading metaphor), or as something that "happens to" a society, rather than as a part and product of long-term developments. Thinking of corruption as deviance leads us to overemphasize crime-prevention approaches that rely on penalties and law enforcement as the primary mechanisms of reform. These ineffective approaches are used even where police, the courts, and the broader legal system are deeply compromised and political pressure for better performance is lacking. In affluent market democracies corrupt actions may in fact deviate from legal and social norms. Crime-prevention approaches may seem to work well in those settings, although even there the laws benefit from a variety of other sorts of support, such as public expectations of government and business, and widespread disapproval of corrupt figures. But where the law has little credibility or serves the interests of corrupt figures, where corrupt practices are rewarded or merely regarded as inevitable, and where legitimate alternatives to corrupt dealings are scarce, crime-and-punishment strategies may have little success. In those situations, adding more penalties and law-enforcement reforms may not so much increase *risks* associated with corruption—if I do X I stand a strong chance of being punished—but rather add to *uncertainties*: the law says I cannot do X, but it is not well-enforced, I've heard lots of officials use that law just to put the squeeze on small businesses, another part of the law says something quite different, penalties vary widely, and the judge is a distant relative anyway, so why should I not go ahead with my scheme? Particularly when controls are poorly conceived or lack solid official and social support, bad law and enforcement in some sectors can undermine the credibility of good law in others. Such uncertainties can even increase the temptations to pay for positive outcomes and give venal officials and other operators added leverage over citizens and honest business people: in many countries "middlemen" and touts hang around the entrances to government offices, doing all they can to persuade citizens that without their help—for a price, of course—there is no way to predict what will happen when they go through the door.[28]

Because we do not pay sufficient attention to "embeddedness"—to the ways the social, political and economic contexts shape

---

28. *See, e.g.*, Jyoti Khanna & Michael Johnston, *India's Middlemen: Connecting by Corrupting?*, 48 CRIME L. & Soc. CHANGE 151 (2007).

corrupt dealings—we frequently view corruption as more or less the same wherever it occurs, varying in extent but not in nature. As implausible as that idea may seem when stated explicitly, our most widely employed corruption indices persist in ranking entire societies as single data points along one common dimension. The most widely used indices of that sort are the Transparency International Corruption Perception Index (CPI)[29] and, at a higher level of methodological sophistication, the "Control of Corruption" indicators included in the World Bank's Worldwide Governance Indicators (WGI).[30] Both generate intriguing worldwide standings in the corruption and reform leagues, and both—particularly the CPI—have helped focus public attention and pressure upon regimes whose leaders had rather we looked the other way. But those rely wholly or substantially on perceptions, which are not the same thing as corruption itself.[31] Worse yet, they apply one score to all levels, regions and sectors of a country, despite the fact that corruption exploits far more specific niches and vulnerabilities. Such one-dimensional indices, and models built with them, encourage us to think of the causes and consequences of corruption as being essentially uniform across the board.

Not surprisingly, therefore, our reform prescriptions are strikingly simple from one case to the next. Lack of nuance plagues our broader visions of what reform might look like: we frequently justify proposed changes, estimate the damage done by corruption, and gauge the success of reform by comparison to an efficient, rational, corruption-free state that does not actually exist anywhere. We then judge poorer and developing societies in terms of institutions, policies, and controls that they appear to lack by comparison to our own countries, an approach that diverts our attention from the forces that actually are at work in such settings, as well as from the corruption problems visible in affluent market democracies. In the end we do not consider the likelihood that many of the values and institutions checking corruption in generally well-governed societies today might be the *outcomes* of political struggles over accounta-

---

29. *Corruption Perceptions Index 2010 Results*, TRANSPARENCY INT'L (Oct. 26, 2010), http://www.transparency.org/policy_research/surveys_indices/cpi/2010. For indices from previous years, see *Corruption Perceptions Index*, TRANSPARENCY INT'L, http://www.transparency.org/policy_research/surveys_indices/cpi (last visited Nov. 16, 2011).

30. *See Worldwide Governance Indicators*, WORLD BANK, http://info.worldbank.org/governance/wgi/index.asp (last visited Nov. 16, 2011).

31. In many years past, international business people have been the most frequently surveyed, though in recent indices expert opinions and more diverse survey samples have been included.

ble government, not the initial causes of effective corruption control.

### E.  *The Most Urgent Reform Requires Extensive Institutional Change*

A final general concern has to do with the sorts of societies in which reform is most urgent. Not only are political and administrative foundations for reform weak or absent in many places; the regimes and societies themselves may be fundamentally fragile. In the worst cases corrupt networks become the *de facto* framework of politics and the economy, to the extent that anyone is in charge at all. They do not so much cripple the system of governance as they *become* the system. The resulting equilibrium of high corruption, low accountability, and delayed or distorted development can be a persistent state of affairs, not an advancing disease bringing society to the brink of collapse.

Societies facing such difficulties are not just "more corrupt" than others; they confront qualitatively different abuses and injustices, and the reforms they require may have little to do with "best practices" elsewhere. Weak and ineffective institutions, divided societies emerging from conflict or authoritarian rule, and low levels of trust in government and among citizens can make reform an empty promise. This is especially concerning because most mainstream corruption-control approaches—law enforcement, civil-society based efforts seeking to mobilize public resistance, transparency initiatives, efforts to reset the incentives affecting officials' and citizens' actions—assume institutional frameworks, commitments to rule of law, and levels of trust and security that are absent in fragile societies.

One-size-fits-all reforms are thus unlikely to be widely successful. But it is no more helpful to suggest that every society's corruption problems, and therefore its reform needs, are *sui generis*. In fact, the major variations in kinds of corruption problems, I argue, fall into identifiable patterns sharing their own commonalities. Understanding such variations and their implications is a first step toward knowing what we ought to do—and where we must exercise caution. The following section lays out the essential elements of a scheme for understanding those variations, and for mounting more appropriate and effective corruption controls.

## III.
## CONTRASTING CORRUPTION PROBLEMS: FOUR SYNDROMES

Corruption is not just a generic problem or a statistic like GDP per capita. It reflects real actions and choices by people responding to incentives, opportunities and constraints that can vary widely. As corruption often involves the illicit pursuit, use, and exchange of wealth and power, the most important contrasts arguably are found not in terms of specific practices—do we see bribery versus nepotism, for example—but rather at the deeper level of the political and economic opportunities available in a society and the quality of the institutions that sustain, restrain, and link the political and economic arenas. On that basis, I argue that it makes sense to think of four contrasting syndromes of corruption.[32]

### A.  Headlines: Recognize Anyone?

Consider the following cases, which are composites of actual events. They illustrate some of the diverse characteristics of corruption cases we might see in various settings:

• A firm seeking tax changes contributes to parties and political candidates; much of the money is spent on campaigns and disclosed legally, but some is used to "sweeten" bureaucrats while another portion vanishes.

• A general skims ten percent of military procurement contracts and shares the proceeds with friendly politicos, bureaucrats, the prime minister's sister, and media owners; part of the proceeds are used over time to buy off would-be opposition leaders.

• An entrepreneur's "wholly owned" judge issues writ enabling him to seize a large firm and its assets, based on fictitious delinquent debts; the order is enforced with police and mafia help.

• Protected by a dictator, state bank officers operate an import-export business using bank resources.

The four scenarios noted above are not specific corruption cases, but neither are they wholly hypothetical. All four have clearly

---

32. For a more extensive exploration of these four syndromes, see MICHAEL JOHNSTON, SYNDROMES OF CORRUPTION: WEALTH, POWER, AND DEMOCRACY (2005).

corrupt aspects, and all four also venture into gray areas, at least in terms of legalities and official processes. While none of the four scenarios describes the full extent of corrupt activities within a given society, they illustrate the diversity of complications reformers face in different settings.

The first case involves routine political finance pushed to an unacceptable degree. At stake are relatively specific benefits, in the form of amendments to the tax code; the bulk of the funds go to legal uses, but the part that is funneled to bureaucrats by political intermediaries, and that which vanishes, signal corrupt dealings. We need not assume that the firm eventually succeeds in getting its preferred changes, nor would success in itself necessarily signal corruption. At issue, rather, is influence marketing: political figures putting their connections and access out for rent, private interests seeking influence over specific decisions rather than undermining regimes or whole institutions, and the ways strong administrative institutions and competitive elections increase the value of access and contributions. While we can easily imagine that the political middlemen might take the initiative in such deals, we do not see a pattern in which powerful officials plunder the private sector. Violence, organized crime, and similar abuses likewise are of little significance here.

The second scenario features collusion among diverse elites. Self-enrichment is a prime motivation, and the take can be quite large; equally important, however, is maintaining power in the face of increasing challenges, in a setting where official institutions are only moderately strong. Those institutions make official positions worth hanging onto, and the resulting political hegemony is one reason why corrupt funds can be obtained in amounts large enough to finance elite networks. But institutions in such situations are usually too weak to produce well-regulated political or economic contention; indeed, elites might have good reason to think that once lost, their political and economic dominance might never return. Elite alliances not only help shore up positions of power; they also can be the basis of monopoly positions that make corruption all the more lucrative.

Our powerful and ambitious entrepreneur in the third scenario is playing a high-stakes, high-risk game using personal clients within the judiciary and law-enforcement to augment his economic empire. He is a major player in an arena where very large stakes are on the table and several factions contend in a setting of few effective rules or institutions. The threat of violence from both police and criminal elements is integral to the deal, both in the process of seizure and as a warning to others that they better look the other way. In a climate of pervasive risk and insecurity, few will play on such a level; those who do must reward their followers. Oligarchs thus need a continuing flow of large-scale rewards and incentives, making for more corruption, further weakening institutions, and intensifying insecurity for honest and corrupt operators alike. In such a setting, proposals to make or enforce anti-corruption laws and efforts to mobilize social opposition to the oligarchs may well amount to little.

In the fourth scenario, corrupt dealings and networks again pervade both the state and the economy and official and social institutions are very ineffective. But there is no doubt as to who is in charge and there is little to deter those top figures and their clients from engaging in corrupt schemes. Offices are little more than useful monopolies, held thanks to the patronage or mandates of top figures. Political loyalties and sources of power are personal—deriving, in this case, from a dictator, but in others from a ruling inner circle or accessible fragments of regime power. Corrupt operators enjoy a kind of impunity not found in our other three scenarios. The stakes of corruption come in many forms and there are likely few restrictions on what can be obtained by corrupt means. While most such societies are poor on aggregate, extractive industries, flows of aid and investment, and the revenue streams of the state itself can all be sufficient to make a few individuals and their minions very wealthy indeed.

## B.   Four Syndromes of Corruption

While it is tempting to classify corruption cases in terms of techniques—bribery, extortion, judicial corruption, violence—fundamentally, these scenarios are distinguished from one another by deeper factors. The balance between wealth and power opportunities will influence whether official clout is used for self-enrichment or wealth is deployed in pursuit of influence and power.[33] The strength of institutions—social, political, and economic as well as those of the state itself—will influence the available stakes and the rules—if any—that constrain contending interests. From those factors derive a variety of related characteristics of corruption problems, such as expectations, insecurity, the balance of power between corrupt operators and their potential opponents, and the opportunities reformers can safely put to use. Those underlying

---

33. *See* SAMUEL P. HUNTINGTON, POLITICAL ORDER IN CHANGING SOCIETIES 59–71 (1968).

factors create combinations of *participation*—the ways in which people pursue, use, and exchange wealth and power—and *institutions*.

A few years ago I explored those ideas in a book that proposed ways in which various countries' corruption problems might differ in kind.[34] Using statistical indicators and case studies, the book offered the argument that four major syndromes of corruption can be observed in countries around the world:

• *Influence Markets*: in a climate of active, well-institutionalized markets and democratic politics, private wealth interests seek influence over specific processes and decisions within strong public institutions, not only bribing officials directly but channeling funds to and through political figures who put their access and connections out for rent. The United States, Japan, and Germany were discussed as case studies.[35]

• *Elite Cartels*: in a setting of only moderately strong state institutions, colluding elites—political, bureaucratic, business, military, and so forth—build high-level networks by sharing corrupt benefits, and are able to stave off rising political and economic competition. Examples presented were Italy, South Korea, and Botswana.[36]

• *Oligarchs and Clans*: a small number of contentious elites backed by personal or family followings pursue wealth and power in a climate of very weak institutions, rapidly expanding opportunities, and pervasive insecurity, using bribes and connections where they can and violence where they must. Opponents of corruption, and of dominant parties and politicians, face major risks and uncertainties. Distinctions between public and private sectors, and between personal and official loyalties and agendas, are very weak in this syndrome. Case studies included Russia, the Philippines, and Mexico.[37]

• *Official Moguls*: powerful individuals and small groups, either dominating undemocratic regimes or enjoying the protection of those who do, use state and personal power—at times, a distinction of little importance—to enrich themselves with impunity. The primary loyalties and sources of power are personal or political, rather than official in nature; anti-corruption forces, like opposition to the regime generally, are very weak. In this final group China, Kenya, and Suharto's Indonesia were examined in detail.[38]

---

34. JOHNSTON, *supra* note 32, at 36–185.
35. *Id.* at 60–88.
36. *Id.* at 89–111.
37. *Id.* at 120–54.
38. *Id.* at 155–85.

These four syndromes are "ideal types" highlighting important similarities and contrasts, not full or deterministic accounts of any one country's corruption problems.[39] There are generic varieties such as police corruption that occur in every society. The syndromes are not "system types": countries that differ in important ways may be found within each group, a given society can move from one to another over time, and while they are meant to highlight a society's dominant corruption problems, we might find more than one syndrome at work in various regions, economic sectors, or levels of government. They do not embody a developmental sequence; in practice, change of several sorts is possible. Nor do they amount to a rediscovery of "high" versus "low," or "bad" versus "good" or "functional," corruption by other names: contrasts among the four syndromes are qualitative rather than matters of degree, and the Influence Market corruption seen in many affluent democracies with good corruption-index scores is definitely a problem worth worrying about. Table 1 summarizes these broad patterns:

---

39. *See* LEWIS A. COSER, MASTERS OF SOCIOLOGICAL THOUGHT: IDEAS IN HISTORICAL AND SOCIAL CONTEXT 223–34 (1971). "An *ideal type* is an analytical construct that serves the investigator as a measuring rod to ascertain similarities as well as deviations in concrete cases." *Id.* at 223.

TABLE 1: FOUR SYNDROMES OF CORRUPTION[40]

| Syndrome | Participation | | Institutions | | Examples |
|---|---|---|---|---|---|
| | Political Opportunities | Economic Opportunities | State/Society Capacity | Economic Institutions | (cases in **bold** were case studies in *Syndromes of Corruption*) |
| Influence Markets | **Mature democracies** Liberalized, steady competition and participation | **Mature markets** Liberalized, open; steady competition; affluent | Extensive | Strong | **United States, Japan, Germany,** Australia, France, UK, Uruguay |
| Elite Cartels | **Consolidating/ reforming democracies** Liberalized; growing competition and participation | **Reforming markets** Largely liberalized and open; growing competition; moderately affluent | Moderate | Medium | **Italy, South Korea, Botswana,** Argentina, Belgium, Brazil, Israel, Poland, Portugal, S. Africa, Zambia |
| Oligarchs and Clans | **Transitional regimes** Recent major liberalization; significant but poorly-structured competition | **New markets** Recent major liberalization; extensive inequality and poverty | Weak | Weak | **Russia, Philippines, Mexico,** Bangladesh, Bulgaria, Colombia, India, Malaysia, Niger, Senegal, Turkey |
| Official Moguls | **Undemocratic** Little liberalization or openness | **New markets** Recent major liberalization; extensive inequality and poverty | Weak | Weak | **China, Kenya, Indonesia,** Algeria, Chad, Haiti, Iran, Kuwait, Nigeria, Rwanda, Syria |

40. This table is adapted from JOHNSTON, *supra* note 32, at 40.

There is no magic in this list of four syndromes; a different categorization might be superior.[41] The main point for our purposes is that we must move beyond ranking whole countries on one-dimensional corruption indices and get to grips with the differing opportunities and vulnerabilities that shape various societies' corruption problems. Such cases confront reformers with contrasting challenges, opportunities, and sources of resistance. A successful reform or best practice in Country *A* may be impossible in Country *B*, irrelevant in Country *C*, and downright harmful in Country *D*. While it would not be entirely fair to describe current reform strategies as uniform, neither they nor our views of what successful reforms might look like, reflect enough attention to important qualitative contrasts in corruption problems.

## IV.
## SORTING OUT STRATEGIES

The difficulties outlined in the previous two sections make corruption control very difficult in any but the most favorable circumstances. Compounding those problems, however, have been a variety of strategic errors—notably, an overly restrictive view of corruption as an administrative rather than political issue, underestimating the incentives needed to sustain reforms, and treating corruption as nearly the same everywhere. These errors have resulted wasted resources, lost opportunities, and overlooked lessons from experience.

One way to think about the first problem—misunderstanding the political dimensions of corruption and reform—is to return to the definitions debate, which generally zeroes in on the question of what constitutes a corrupt act. I suggest we should ask a somewhat different question: how do corruption issues arise in the first place? The change in emphasis is subtle—corruption, as we shall see, is conceptualized here not as an attribute of an action or individual but rather as a systemic dilemma arising as people pursue, use, and exchange wealth and power, and as societies contend with—and over—the never-ending problems of how to restrain excesses in those activities.[42] The clashing interests, values, and traditions that make clear-cut definitions of a corrupt act so difficult should not be seen as problems to be resolved by devising better-worded definitions. Instead, they point to political conflicts *inherent in* the rise of

---

41. *See generally* JOHNSTON, *supra* note 32 (discussing the evidence and arguments underlying the various syndromes of corruption).

42. *Id.* at 1–35.

corruption issues, and in the mobilization of political energy essential to successful reform.

To illustrate this approach, consider a brief thought experiment. Instead of visualizing a society into which corruption intrudes as an unwelcome influence, imagine an absolute, utterly unchallenged autocrat. No rules, competitors, or countervailing forces restrain that ruler's actions. The right to rule, in this situation, is a matter of having the biggest army and personal following, a ruthless attitude toward others, claims of divine blessing, or—via hereditary succession—taking a lucky dip into the gene pool. In this imagined situation, limits upon power and notions of accountability to the public and its interests mean nothing. People and territory exist to be dominated and exploited.

That absolute autocrat cannot be "corrupt" in any contemporary sense of the term.[43] No rules restrain his actions; no one else's wellbeing matters. There are no collective principles of loyalty or accountability, and no de facto constraints. We might judge the dictator corrupt by our own standards, which he or she is free to ignore, or as morally corrupt in the eyes of God, a definitive judgment for some but not much of a practical restraint. Likewise, conceptions of corruption built upon checks and balances, duties of office—indeed, the basic idea of a *public* office itself—the public interest, or positions of trust have no meaning.

The case of our imaginary autocrat is a deliberate oversimplification. Its value lies in highlighting the *political* processes by which limits and accountability arise, and the political processes through which they acquire legitimacy and force. Political ethics and rules and institutions limiting official powers are not natural features of the political landscape, however much they seem to be, because of their legitimacy and basis in widely-shared values in well-governed societies. Limits on official powers arise when someone other than the rulers with the political resources to protect their interests demands them, and they exist because rulers find it advantageous to abide by them. That process, not surprisingly, can be contentious:

---

43. There are older "classical" conceptions of corruption as a collective state of being that might enable us to call our autocrat corrupt. For example, in ancient Athens, corruption amounted to the loss of the ruling order's ability to command or inspire loyalty. J. Patrick Dobel, *The Corruption of a State*, 72 Am. Pol. Sci. Rev. 958, 969–70 (1978). For ways in which such older modes of thinking retain relevance today, see generally Michael Johnston, *Keeping the Answers, Changing the Questions: Corruption Definitions Revisited*, 35 Politische Vierteljahresschrift Sonderhefte (Dimensionen Politischer Korruption) [Political Quarterly Special Issues (Dimensions of Political Corruption)] 61 (2005).

holders of great power and wealth rarely relinquish them voluntarily. To draw such limits, those "others" need a degree of space, in the form of basic security and a measure of liberty, and political resources they can call their own (wealth, a following, rhetorical gifts). Equally important, they need *a reason* to take a stand: an interest or people to protect, for example, or significant grievances and aspirations.[44]

Political contention and the clash of interests and outlooks—often seen not only as complicating our definitions, but also as a corrupting influence to be isolated from the administration and reforms—shape and reshape working meanings of "corruption" and drive the process of limiting power and insisting on accountability. In democratic societies we take it as given that public officials ought to serve interests above and beyond their own, and that taxpayers, business people, civic activists and other private parties will demand that they do so. Reform then becomes a matter of conceiving of effective institutions, rules, and systems of incentives. But even in those relatively settled systems, terms like *public, private,* and *abuse of power* have shifting and contentious meanings. Further complicating matters at a practical level is the fact that allegations of corruption and the moralizing language of reform can be a smokescreen for poorly-conceived or counterproductive controls, and for self-serving proposals.[45] Elsewhere—particularly where regimes lack credibility, institutions and are weak or widely distrusted, public-private boundaries are porous or meaningless, and a sense of common interest is not widely shared—new rules and demands for accountability may have little or no practical effect. Where do workable limits and boundaries originate, and what forces shape and reshape them over time?

---

44. For the record, I define corruption not as an attribute of an action or person, but a systemic dilemma of defining acceptable and unacceptable ways to pursue, use, and exchange wealth and power, and then as consisting of the abuse of public power or resources for private benefit, emphasizing immediately that the terms *abuse, public, private,* and even *benefit* can be politically contested, changing in their meaning, and rarely if ever delineated once and for all. Such terms, after all, refer to deeply political boundaries, distinctions, and relationships.

45. If I were sponsoring legislation to treble the salaries of academicians across this great land of ours, I would, of course, call it the Higher Education Reform Act of 2011.

## V.
## "DEEP DEMOCRATIZATION" AND
## CORRUPTION CONTROL

I suggest that the essence of sustainable corruption control is "deep democratization." That idea draws upon the same sorts of participatory and institutional dynamics that define the four syndromes discussed above. The goal is to encourage the development of free, fair, and openly competitive political and economic arenas, both sustained and restrained by a strong and legitimate framework of state, political, and social institutions, within which people can pursue their interests and protect themselves against abuses.[46] That system of order rests upon a dynamic balance among state and society, and includes both politics and the economy. Clear boundaries between public and private domains are essential, but they cannot be isolated from each other: legitimate communication between them is essential for accountability, as each domain can contribute to the vitality and restrain the excesses of the other. Competition and contention must be vigorous, open with respect to both participants and the range of possible outcomes, yet governed by legitimate rules and institutions. Although it may seem that this argument promotes American- or European-style systems as a universal ideal, affluent market democracies also fall short of these ideals in many ways. Even the most established democracies may be in need of democratic renewal to the extent that their political processes have lost credibility, citizens feel ignored by decision makers, and elections become exercises in collusion.

Democracy can hardly claim unique corruption-controlling abilities—far from it. Indeed, the "influence markets" syndrome illustrates the ways competitive elections, open institutions, incremental policy processes, strong civil liberties, and vigorous private markets—all presumably institutions most of us value greatly—can combine to create distinctive corruption hazards. At the very least, such abilities appear to depend upon a minimal level of economic development, understood not only in terms of resources and affluence but also as a process of institutional development.[47] Moreover, some societies, such as Pinochet's Chile, can claim to have reduced

---

46. *See generally* JOHNSTON, *supra* note 32, *passim.* "Strong institutions and balanced participation enable societies to respond to corrupt activities more effectively. They provide non-corrupt economic and political alternatives for citizens and firms and enable them to defend their interests." *Id.* at 199.

47. *See* Yan Sun & Michael Johnston, *Does Democracy Check Corruption?: Insights from China and India,* 42 COMP. POL. 1, 3–7 (2009) (analyzing the dynamic balance between economic and political factors and its effect on corruption).

corruption in strikingly undemocratic ways, while others—Botswana, for example—have done significantly better than might have been expected even though their democratic processes are still works in progress.[48] In still other settings, civil liberties sufficient to allow criticism of the regime, while falling well short of fully elaborated democracy, have effectively encouraged better government performance.[49] The driving factor here is not a veneer of formal democratic processes, but rather resources and opportunities to insist that our interests be taken into account by those who govern.[50]

Deep democratization is contentious: real interests must be at stake. But it cannot be solely a grudge match: principles and values can play a role as well. At times they provide the "vocabulary" through which challenges to established power can be justified; or, they help bond diverse resentments into a common cause. New principles too can emerge in the heat of contention, if only as useful clubs with which to belabor those on the other side. Later on such principles can be refined, and can draw broader support, not so much because they are good ideas in the abstract but *because they work* to protect and serve the interests of various groups. In many respects, the enterprise of checking corruption by seeking fairness and justice not as public goods but rather as valued rights and protections, *is* a process of deep democratization.

Years ago, Dankwart Rustow offered a fascinating argument that the factors *sustaining* democracy where it is strong, *e.g.*, literacy, affluence, multi-party politics, or a middle class, are not necessarily the same factors that created it.[51] He contended that the rise of democracy required "prolonged and inconclusive political struggle . . . . [T]he protagonists must represent well-entrenched forces . . . and the issues must have profound meaning to them."[52]

---

48. Pitcher et al., *supra* note 7, at 144–49.

49. Jonathan Isham, Daniel Kaufmann & Lant H. Pritchett, *Civil Liberties, Democracy, and the Performance of Government Projects*, 11 WORLD BANK ECON. REV. 219, 226–32 (1997). "The total effect of an improvement in civil liberties is positive, even accounting for the [i]nduced [democratic] political changes." *Id.* at 232.

50. "Environments that allow civil strife or unrest to occur also allow other mechanisms for expression of popular (dis)content with government performance[.] The availability and effectiveness of those mechanisms improve government efficacy." *Id.* at 234. *Compare* Fareed Zakaria, *The Rise of Illiberal Democracy*, FOREIGN AFF., Nov.–Dec. 1997, at 22 (discussing the ways in which outwardly democratic systems can be deeply illiberal).

51. *See* Dankwart A. Rustow, *Transitions to Democracy: Toward a Dynamic Model*, 2 COMP. POL. 337, 341–42 (1970).

52. *Id.* at 352.

In those struggles, "[d]emocracy was not the original or primary aim; it was sought as a means to some other end or it came as a fortuitous byproduct of the struggle."[53] Over time, political settlements among contending groups—even if grudgingly conceded and compromised in unsatisfying ways—could solidify into institutions made legitimate and durable because they served lasting interests.

An analogous argument can be made with respect to corruption control. Limits on power and mechanisms of accountability may be expressed in terms of enduring moral values. But they *came from somewhere*—broadly, from people and groups defending themselves from abuses by others. Independent judiciaries, conflict-of-interest rules, civil service restrictions upon patronage, and values of integrity are the culmination of political processes of reform, not their origin. Basic notions of accountability, effective institutional controls and safeguards, and the civic values through which we justify them, are as much the *outcomes* of corruption-checking political developments as their causes. Failing to appreciate that point, and expecting people to line up behind the banner of reform simply out of concern for the common good, leads to the sorts of collective-action problems sketched out earlier. So too will schemes for reform that excessively minimize political influence over processes of governing. Transparency means little if no one has a stake in "looking in." Best practices, no matter how effective they may be in one society, will accomplish little if they lack solid political foundations in the places where they are transplanted.

## A.  The Value of Politics and the State

Throughout the push for reform, we have misunderstood those political dynamics—not just during the past generation, but for well over a century throughout the world. Indeed, for many reformers, politics and government—the latter envisioned as an essentially technical administrative process—were opposing influences. The more recent notion of good governance has often been equally bloodless, with the state being regarded essentially as a referee in a liberalized economy. At best, the value of politics lay in civic processes of legitimation and consensus-building, and in providing useful feedback for the state's few essential functions. Occasionally, politics helped oust scoundrels once their misconduct had been revealed, but more often it was viewed as a parallel market, mirroring the economy. At worst, political processes and demands

---

53. *Id.* at 353.

were portrayed as a drag on governance and development because they introduced private-regarding demands into what ought to be rational, and minimal, processes of administration, creating incentives to enact costly, fraud-prone public benefits as a way of building popular support. A key critique of the State was that rent-seeking officials interfered in markets and distorted administrative processes in order to enrich themselves. While that critique was all too often right on target, its obverse—that with the government out of the economy, rationality and fairness would take the place of rent-seeking—remains unproven. More often, "rolling back" government has shifted important questions of equity and justice out of the public arena and into more private settings, where rules and enforcement are weaker and accountability is far more selectively applied.

In the deep democratization view, however, the state is not just the referee, politics is not just another kind of market, and democratic governance is not just a bundle of sound administrative processes. Instead, critical questions of power, authority, and justice are at stake. Bukovansky has argued persuasively that basic normative principles inherent in the notion of corruption have been strikingly absent from the past generation's conversations about governance, administration, and reform.[54] Reformers would do well to revisit basic ideas of republican political thought, she contends, which at the very least would remind us that political change is not an impersonal process of progress or rational modernization but rather is rooted in the agency of real people dealing with normatively complicated dilemmas.[55]

Accordingly, reform is not a matter of persuading people to be good or to put self-interest aside. Nor should we expect political parties and interest groups to put civic goals first. As Van Biezen points out, too often we treat the political parties of emerging societies as though they were public utilities established to serve democracy as a grand civic project, rather than as forces that energize it by vying on behalf of real groups and interests.[56] If corruption control is a public good, most people will leave the hard work and risks to others. We may try to overcome that dilemma by calling for more political will, but corruption often reflects an *excess* of unchecked political will.

---

54. *See* Mlada Bukovansky, *The Hollowness of Anti-Corruption Discourse*, 13 REV. INT'L POL. ECON. 181 (2006).

55. *Id.* at 204.

56. Ingrid Van Biezen, *Political Parties as Public Utilities*, 10 PARTY POL. 701 (2004).

492        NYU ANNUAL SURVEY OF AMERICAN LAW      [Vol. 67:467

Deep democratization is a long-term process that will never be finished. There are no guarantees against backsliding. It inevitably involves conflict and thus will not satisfy anyone who seeks the dawn of reason in government, much less the final triumph of good over evil.[57] Moreover, it is in an *indirect* strategy—one in which we simulate the developments that led to the emergence of political forces in once-corrupt societies that brought the problem under control. Familiar and tempting reform tactics may have to be postponed while the social and political foundations they require are under construction. Citizen participation need not focus directly upon corruption; given the risks and collective action problems involved, it may be better to organize around more immediate concerns. A diverse range of benefits and gratifications—sociability, personal interests, and symbolic rewards are just a few examples—can be as important as those of a civic and purposive nature.[58] Hiking clubs, a Tuesday Music Society, and professional or occupational associations may seem to have little to do with reform, yet can still contribute to a fund of social capital[59] and higher levels of social trust— essential resources when opportunities for reform eventually appear.

In no way do open and competitive societies inevitably converge toward "the public interest" or a lasting political equilibrium, either through a superior state of harmony or the workings of some invisible hand. Leadership remains essential. Reform will involve many dead ends and reverses and bad or self-serving ideas will abound. But most of today's better-governed societies established systems of accountability, and the rules and values that restrain abuses of wealth and power, in equally roundabout ways while contending over other things.

### B.    What to Do—First, Next, and Not at All?

If we should not immediately bombard corruption with any good ideas that fall to hand, how should we make our choices and what sequence should we follow?

---

57. *See, e.g.*, Christian von Luebke, *The Politics of Reform: Political Scandals, Elite Resistance, and Presidential Leadership in Indonesia*, 29 J. CURRENT SE. ASIAN AFF. 79, 85–89 (2010) (discussing recent conflict within Indonesia's anti-corruption agency and resistance from the elite class).

58. Michael Johnston & Sahr J. Kpundeh, *Building a Clean Machine: Anti-Corruption Coalitions and Sustainable Reform* 8–15 (World Bank Inst. Working Paper Series, Paper No. 37208, 2002), *available at* http://siteresources.worldbank.org/WBI/Resources/wbi37208.pdf.

59. ROBERT D. PUTNAM, BOWLING ALONE: THE COLLAPSE AND REVIVAL OF THE AMERICAN COMMUNITY (2000).

Often we are told that corrupt societies are in a state of near-collapse, even where illicit power and spoils underwrite networks and alliances that can be very durable indeed. This sense of urgency, together with the assumption (or hope) that societies and institutions would be healthy and effective if we could just stop the corrupt behavior, encourages us to attack head-on. But deeper contrasts among syndromes of corruption and historical and situational differences among societies themselves mean that what might be a fine idea elsewhere can be irrelevant or harmful in the case at hand. Frontal assaults on corrupt behavior are tempting, but may in fact call down repression upon those who have suffered most.

The variations noted above make it quite risky to make generalizations about what to do first, later, and never. But I suggest that judiciously paced *structural strategies* must precede *political strategies*.[60] In Influence Market and Elite Cartel cases, structural developments are largely in place or have gathered significant momentum, and thus a focus on specific corruption controls may well make considerable sense. In Oligarch-and-Clan and Official Mogul cases, by contrast, those political foundations are weak or nonexistent, and rushing in with "best practices" evolved over long periods of time elsewhere may in fact make matters much worse. Knowing what *not* to do, or at least understanding why some good ideas must be deferred for a time, may be the most useful insights of all.

In Official Mogul cases the best anti-corrupt approach might be patient encouragement of basic civil liberties and the diffusion of political resources. Efforts to redefine power and authority as official and public, rather than as personal, may likewise be worthwhile; this latter strategy might revolve around education and changing expectations. Rushing to confront an Official Moguls regime by opposing corruption with anything less than overwhelming social backing, by contrast, may be very unwise: to the extent that such efforts threaten sources of wealth, repression may be an immediate response. To the extent that they actually threaten Moguls' power, the result may be voracious, hand-over-fist corruption as officials both high and low, no longer secure in their positions, steal as

---

60. Structural strategies include creating space for the growth of safe social and political activity, encouraging the emergence of multiple centers of power and types of political resources, and building a framework of institutions strong enough to withstand and sustain contention. Political strategies include formal checks and balances, competitive politics, mobilizing civil society, creating reform organizations, putting transparency to use, journalistic exposés, and the like.

much as they can as fast as they can take it.[61] Indeed, too much pressure applied too quickly might push an Official Moguls case over into an Oligarchs-and-Clans situation, with disastrous consequences, as arguably happened in Russia in the 1990s as aggressive economic and political liberalization were pursued in a setting of very weak institutions.[62]

Oligarch-and-Clan societies, by contrast, may have considerable or, indeed, excessive pluralism, but be too insecure and dangerous to allow most citizens to make political demands on their own behalf. There, the challenge is not diffusing power and resources, but rather institution-building. Predictable performance by law-enforcement and the courts is especially critical. Whichever syndrome we encounter, divided and post-conflict societies will present special challenges; the initial agenda might well revolve around re-establishing basic government services, on an even-handed basis, as a way of building trust and improving expectations.[63]

That point about basic services, mundane as it may seem, leads us to a final, but critical, challenge—that of measurement and assessment. How can reformers assess the scope of corruption problems? In light of the shortcomings of the existing country-level corruption indices,[64] how can they demonstrate the progress of reform—if any—to backers, citizens, and potential malefactors alike, in ways that are detailed and convincing? Measurement of corruption is the focus of a long-running debate over indices and statistical methodology.[65] None of the debaters is satisfied with existing

---

61. James C. Scott, Comparative Political Corruption 80–84 (1972).

62. Johnston, *supra* note 32, at 120–54.

63. *See* Michael Johnston, *First, Do No Harm—Then, Build Trust: Anti-Corruption Strategies in Fragile Situations*, World Dev. Rep. 2011 (World Bank), Sept. 2010, at 24–33, http://wdr2011.worldbank.org/sites/default/files/pdfs/WDRBackground Paper-Johnston_0.pdf. For discussions on what to do—and what *not* to do—in fragile situations, see Alask Orre & Harald W. Mathisen, *Corruption in Fragile States*, Fragile Situations Policy Briefs (Danish Inst. Int'l Studies, Oct. 2008), http://www.diis.dk/graphics/Publications/Briefs2008/PB2008_10_Corruption.pdf; Vinay Bhargava, *Practitioners Reflections: Making a Difference in High Corruption and Weak Governance Country Environments*, [2011] 1 U4 Practice Insight (Chr. Michelson Inst.), http://www.cmi.no/publications/file/3962-practitioners-reflections.pdf.

64. *See supra* notes 29–31 and accompanying text.

65. *See, e.g.*, Christine Arndt & Charles Oman, OECD Dev. Ctr., Uses and Abuses of Governance Indicators (2006), http://www.oecd-ilibrary.org/development/uses-and-abuses-of-governance-indicators_9789264026865-en (arguing that governance indicators based on observers' subjective perceptions lack transparency and comparability over time, suffer from selection bias, and are not well suited to help developing countries identify how to effectively improve the quality of local governance); Measuring Corruption (Charles Sampford, Arthur Shacklock, Carmel Connors & Fredrik Galtug eds., 2006) (discussing the reliability

perception-based indices, but consensus over a better approach has yet to emerge. Most suggest overly literal reliance upon such indices may not only waste scarce reform opportunities while giving reformers little guidance as to where to attack and what steps are (or are not) working, but may also stigmatize societies that take serious anti-corruption steps—and thereby put scandals, trials, and revelations of graft on page one. At the very least, many governments that have launched transparency initiatives find that even extensive efforts fail to "move the needle." A related criticism is that affluent market democracies—broadly speaking, our "influence markets" group—get a "pass" from existing indices since their legal frameworks and political systems are hospitable to wealthy interests who thus have less reason to engage in corruption.

One possible alternative is use indicators of government performance, benchmarked across comparable agencies and jurisdictions, to assess indirectly the effects of past corruption, the incentives and opportunities that sustain it, and trends in specific vulnerabilities. Those indicators can be "actionable," a clunky word meaning that they not only indicate where risks exist but also give strong signals as to what must be done. Better yet, they allow successful leaders, agency managers, and reformers to claim political credit for their efforts.[66] Such initiatives often draw strong resis-

---

and limitations of various measures of corruption); Marcus J. Kurtz & Andrew Schrank, *Growth and Governance: Models, Measures, and Mechanisms*, 69 J. POL. 538, 542–47 (2007) (arguing that divergent interests and cultural backgrounds of those surveyed, sampling error, and lack of direct knowledge by respondents introduce systemic errors into perception-based indices); M.A. Thomas, *What Do the Worldwide Governance Indicators Measure?*, 22 EUR. J. DEV. RES. 31 (2010) (considering the construct validity of the WGI and concluding that the indicators stand as an elaborate and unsupported hypothesis); Charles Kenny, *Measuring and Reducing the Impact of Corruption in Infrastructure* (World Bank Policy Research Working Paper No. 4099, 2006), *available at* http://ideas.repec.org/p/wbk/wbrwps/4099.html (arguing that, in the infrastructure sector, perception-based indices measure petty rather than grand corruption, a weak proxy for the true extent of corruption); Tina Søreide, *Is It Wrong to Rank? A Critical Assessment of Corruption Indices* (Chr. Michelsen Inst., Working Paper No. 1, 2006), *available at* http://www.cmi.no/publications/file/2120-is-it-wrong-to-rank.pdf (arguing, *inter alia*, that composite corruption rankings like Transparency International's CPI can blur the line between legal and illegal activities and rest on unreliable or systemically biased individual perceptions); Dilyan Donchev & Gergely Ujhelyi, What Do Corruption Indices Measure? (June 7, 2010) (unpublished manuscript), *available at* http://www.class.uh.edu/faculty/gujhelyi/corrmeasures.pdf (finding country-level corruption indices have received much attention from researchers, commentators, and policy-makers alike).

66. *See* Michael Johnston, *Components of Integrity: Data and Benchmarks for Tracking Trends in Government*, Global Forum on Public Governance (OECD, Apr. 27,

tance, and can be gamed by officials and misused by the public and critics. But particularly in the socially and politically fragile situations in which reform is the most difficult, publishing such indicators of government performance and opening them up for public discussion can be a way to demonstrate the credibility of government, build social and political trust, and link the quest for better governance to citizens' immediate needs and problems.

## VI.
## CONCLUSION

These arguments, taken together, set the bar quite high for reformers. But to think of reform in terms of the ability of citizens to advocate and defend their own interests and wellbeing is also to spell out a good working definition of *justice,* and to build reform on a base of lasting interests. Justice, in that view, is not just an abstract goal, a set of process standards, or a slogan. It is more than an instrumental sense that following rules *A, B,* and *C* will raise one's income or ward off crime. It is instead a sense of confidence that our rights, interests, outlooks, and security *matter,* and that others' do as well; that even the most powerful figures in politics and the economy must respect those values, and that they can be called to account if they do not. Justice is the linchpin between self-interest and one's obligations to fellow citizens and society. It requires, and over time can reinforce, a working level of mutual trust. It is precisely these values and linkages that corruption undermines, and that reform, if it is to be sustainable, must credibly promise to uphold.

---

2009), *available at* http://www.oecd.org/officialdocuments/displaydocumentpdf/?cote=GOV/PGC/GF(2009)2&doclanguage=en.

# [15]

## The Genesis of the BCCI Scandal

NIKOS PASSAS

By revealing how the political system [dys]functions, scandals have the potential to force debates over the norms regulating public conduct, the appropriate role of public officials, and the degree to which private and public spheres should be separated. Thus, scandals represent opportunities for reform. Yet, not all scandals lead to drastic measures or significant reform (if any) and not all revelations of deviant or corrupt practices actually produce scandals.

Exposure and punishment of repeated corporate misconduct[1] has not created scandals. Matters are handled with even higher discretion in the banking industry, in which the closure of an offending institution has been extremely rare even in cases of serious misconduct.[2]

When the Bank of Credit and Commerce International (BCCI) was closed down in July 1991, however, a global political scandal ensued as allegations of all manner of misdeeds affected government officials around the world. What was special about BCCI to cause both its closure and scandal? What does the BCCI case tell us about the conditions enabling the exposure and sanctioning of corrupt behaviour, about the creation of scandal, and about its political or legal consequences?

In contrast to conspiracy theories, I examine the social and political (external) as well as BCCI-related (internal) conditions that enabled controllers to prosecute and close down BCCI. In this way, I offer an alternative, structural theory of the genesis and development of the BCCI scandal and argue that the most important factor are geopolitical changes that robbed BCCI of its past instrumentality and usefulness to powerful interests and groups.

### THE BCCI AFFAIR

BCCI was established in 1972 with capital from the ruler of Abu Dhabi, Sheikh Zayed, and the Bank of America. This association lent BCCI the necessary credibility to grow and expand very fast. It gradually became a significant banking complex comprising a Luxembourg holding company, banks incorporated in Luxembourg and Grand Cayman, subsidiaries, branches, affiliates, and charitable organizations in seventy-two countries.

Yet, the bank was insolvent from the 1970s and its top managers had been manipulating the accounts concealing losses, keeping deposits off the books, hiding illegal BCCI investments in United States financial institutions, and generating false profits. Loans to the Gulf Group of shipping companies,[3] which were larger than BCCI's capital base, were not serviced causing unsustainable costs of over $1 billion in the 1980s. An additional $1 billion losses were incurred in BCCI's treasury department. As the liquidators suggested that several billion dollars were unaccounted for and investigations into BCCI's practices intensified and multiplied, an unparalleled international scandal was fuelled by press reports about BCCI's banking services to money launderers, drug traffickers, arms dealers, coffee smugglers, tax evaders, political offenders, dictators, and intelligence agencies around the globe.[4]

BCCI stood accused of systematically making questionable or illegal payments to world leaders, political figures and government officials in most countries where it operated, in order to obtain deposits, open banks, gain preferential treatment, handle a country's US commodity credits, or gain respectability.[5] When evidence and allegations of corruption and financial offences surfaced against BCCI, many wondered how did all this go undetected for so long.[6]

It must be stressed, however, that BCCI was an institution with powerful allies and friends. Despite a level of distrust and nasty rumours, by the early 1980s BCCI was doing business with powerful organizations and individuals around the world. It provided banking services, held accounts for, or was publicly associated with, heads or former heads of governments (James Callaghan,[7] Willy Brandt, Alan Garcia of Peru, Jimmy Carter, among many others), intelligence agencies and agents (for example, the CIA, Kamal Adham,[8] Richard Helms, William Casey)[9] international organizations (such as the United Nations) and public relations firms (Hill and Knowlton), ambassadors (for example, Andrew Young, Sergio da Costa of Brazil), high-level politicians (for example, United States Senator Orrin Hatch, former Senator John Culver – five British Tories, including Sir Julian Ridsdale, were BCCI consultants),[10] and influential business people and bankers (including Larry Romrell, Bob Magness – founder of TCI, the largest United States cable company – David Paul, Jackson Stephens, Alfred Hartmann, Yves Lamarche). The lawyers and lobbyists that represented BCCI in the United States of America included former Federal Reserve officials, federal prosecutors, and former high-level military officers, senators or government officials, including Clark Clifford, the counsel to Democratic Presidents from Truman to Carter.[11] BCCI's shareholders or nominees (for example, Saudi businessman Gaith Pharaon) had equally powerful associations of their own adding to the clout enjoyed by BCCI. BCCI and its friends were also contributors to politicians' campaigns and enjoyed their company at private and social events.

In addition, BCCI was a useful listening post for intelligence agencies wishing to obtain sensitive information such as to monitor international criminal networks and transactions concerning arms and technology. In some cases, bank managers collaborated with authorities offering critical information (such as to British intelligence on the Abu Nidal organization's account in London). The CIA held accounts at BCCI and its affiliates, but its role may have been far more important in shielding BCCI from its enemies – it has been suggested, for instance, that a deal was struck between the president of BCCI and the CIA in the early 1980s and that United States intelligence may have been involved in the creation of BCCI.[12] The international network offered by BCCI and its presence in secrecy jurisdictions made it attractive for the payment of intelligence agents around the world and the conduct of covert operations. For example, Iran-Contra transactions went through a number of BCCI branches; funds were provided to Afghani rebels; General Manuel Noriega, the former leader of Panama was paid at BCCI for his services to the CIA.[13] With numerous prominent clients of all sorts of origin and ideology, there was a common disincentive to disclose.[14]

Moreover, BCCI's empire was audited by the most respected accounting firms (Ernst and Whinney – now Ernst and Young – and Price Waterhouse). Finally, in 1991 BCCI was in a process of restructuring and recapitalization by the Abu Dhabi majority shareholders. This process was both known and encouraged by the Luxembourg and British bank regulators. It appeared that the bank could be saved quietly with a change of management and headquarters.

In this light, the question is why and how the BCCI-related misconduct was publicly revealed at all. Why did the scandal take place when it did? Why was BCCI not allowed to proceed in the usual way, that is, settle matters without admitting or denying guilt, pay a fine so as to 'avoid costly and prolonged litigation' over 'honest differences of opinion' regarding 'technical violations'? How did such a well-connected organization become vulnerable?

Some argue that had it not been for the action of a few committed individuals, the bank would still be operating today under new management.[15] Another theory is that the closure of BCCI was the result of a Western conspiracy against the Third World and its most important bank, a bank that gave a degree of independence to the South.[16] This theory has the difficulty that there was undeniable and devastating wrongdoing at the bank. Supporters of this theory counter that such misconduct is not uncommon at other banks and that money claimed to be lost is either not really lost or lost to Western (possibly, intelligence) causes. They add that it is only a few Middle Easterners or Pakistanis who have been severely sanctioned by the authorities so far, while the beneficiaries of most BCCI-related illicit activities have been left untouched. Although both George Bush and Bill Clinton 'were surrounded by people with ties to BCCI',[17] and plenty of Westerners were implicated in questionable practices and conflicts of interest, there has been no legal action against them nor any reform of the political/regulatory system that facilitates such practices. All that changed in the aftermath of the BCCI scandal was the law regulating foreign banks operating in the United States of America.

However important the role of some individuals in uncovering frauds and corruption, like all scandals, the BCCI affair is a socially constructed phenomenon,[18] exemplifying international competition for influence and power, and political conflicts.[19] At an abstract level, three general conditions must be met for a scandal to occur:

i)   incriminating information/allegations of misconduct must be shared with outsiders;
ii)  there must be channels through which this information can be disseminated; and
iii) there must be an audience responsive to this information, an audience that can be 'scandalized'.[20]

All three conditions were fulfilled long before the BCCI closure in 1991. Allegations against BCCI's practices, organizational structure, management, internal controls, and clients had been surfacing since the late 1970s. Disclosures had been made to the press, to regulatory authorities, while some of the information had been published in Europe and in the United States of America.[21] Moreover, legal action had been taken against BCCI's attempted take-over of an American bank in the late 1970s.[22]

The channels through which disclosures could be made public and disseminated existed since the creation of BCCI itself, especially in the United States where there are institutionalized means of exposure typical of a liberal democracy.[23] The press, State prosecutors and Congressional investigators enjoy a great deal of freedom and autonomy from central government, while competitive political parties have the incentives to provide compromising information about their opponents.

The audience that consumed reports on money laundering, terrorism, political corruption, prostitution, fraud, and other financial crimes was also there throughout BCCI's history. There is no reason to believe that public concern and interest in such matters simply increased in the 1990s.

So, the question of the causes and timing of the BCCI scandal remains unanswered. I argue that a key to understanding the underlying conditions of scandal is an analysis of the power struggles in which the various parties are involved. On the one hand, scandal reflects conflicts of interests and shifts in the balance of power among the protagonists; on the other hand, scandal itself shapes that balance usually to accentuate these shifts, unless the accuser takes it too far and those attacked are viewed as 'unfairly assailed'.[24] As Neckel put it, '[p]olitical scandal . . . is not only a method to control power, but also a method controlled by power'.[25] In order to better appreciate the power struggles, we need to look in some detail into the course of events leading up to BCCI's closure and changes that were taking place in what organization theorists would term its 'task environment'.[26]

## CONFLICTS OF INTEREST AND THE NORIEGA INVESTIGATION

Long before General Manuel Noriega became the Panamanian head of government, he worked for the CIA providing intelligence on Central and South American countries. He later assisted certain DEA operations targeting the drug traffic, for which he received letters of commendation.[27] He also provided many valuable services to the Contra guerrillas who were fighting the left-wing Sandinista government with both legal and illegal help from the United States of America in the 1980s.[28]

An exchange during Congressional hearings illustrates the climate in which Noriega and BCCI used to operate. When asked whether eyebrows would have been raised upon finding that Noriega was paid by BCCI cheques drawn on First American Bank (FAB), a former FAB director testified: 'No. That was in 1986. In 1987, the US Government was writing letters to Noriega telling him what a fine job he was doing. We wouldn't have reacted to that'.[29]

Given that Noriega offered his services to Republican administrations, political mileage could be made if this association were exposed in conjunction with the dictator's corruption, authoritarian rule, and role in drug trafficking enterprises.[30] Indeed, an investigation was initiated by the Democrat Senator Kerry's subcommittee on terrorism, narcotics and international operations, and probed Noriega's business affairs. In that context, a witness drew attention to Noriega's 'corrupt empire', a graphic representation of which included BCCI. This led to information and investigative leads about BCCI itself, which were later passed on to control agencies.

The Kerry investigation into the Noriega-BCCI relationship, did not proceed smoothly. M. Pillsbury, an aid to Republican Senator Hatch was advising BCCI on lobbying strategy and on how to deal with Kerry.[31] As indicated by BCCI lawyers' notes, Kerry's interest was not in BCCI by itself:

> [According to Pillsbury] Senator Kerry wants to be praised for what he has done on money laundering; especially by conservative Republicans. His only interest in BCCI is to get info re: Noriega and get credit for his work.[32]

In the face of opposition from various parties including within Kerry's own Committee on Foreign Relations, the section on BCCI was left out of the final report with only a recommendation of further investigation.[33]

These events point to the crucial role played by partisan politics in the generation of crucial information that fed subsequent prosecutorial actions. They also lend support to the thesis that clashes of interests in multi-party liberal democracies are an indispensable condition for the creation of scandals.[34]

## THE BCCI INDICTMENT FOR MONEY LAUNDERING

Parallel to Kerry's inquiry, there was an undercover operation code-named C-Chase which was led by the US Customs Service. This investigation culminated in charges of money laundering against BCCI and several of its managers. Following a bitter struggle, on the advice of its United States lawyers BCCI pleaded guilty in 1989. BCCI managers went to trial in Florida, only to be convicted and receive record penalties. The fact that this was the first time an international bank was convicted of money laundering was taken up by the international press and caused substantial injury to BCCI's reputation, loss of business, and lower morale among employees.

Partisan politics did not leave this investigation and prosecution unaffected. Line agents complained about the premature close-down of C-Chase suggesting that the timing was determined to coincide with the Presidential elections in 1988, enabling George Bush to argue that he was leading a winning war on drugs.[35] Yet, the Democratic side made sure that the press was also informed about Noriega's intimate relations with BCCI. Given that Bush was CIA director when Noriega was being paid for his intelligence services and pictures of the two men sitting together were available, Bush's ammunition got too wet to be used.

The money laundering conviction was a clear blow to BCCI. It added plausibility to the rumours about it being a dirty bank and created a public relations nightmare. BCCI was forced to close its Florida offices. These problems, however, were professionally handled by consultancy firms and BCCI's high profile representatives. A good deal of business returned to the bank and a big scandal was averted.

Nevertheless, the power struggles underlying the handling of the Congressional and Customs investigations continued. Critics' charges against the Department of Justice ranged from mismanagement to cover-up,[36] particularly in the aftermath of a plea bargain between BCCI and the federal prosecutors, who agreed not to charge BCCI in the Middle District of Florida with '. . . any other federal criminal offenses under investigation or known to the government at the time of the execution of this agreement or relating in any manner to the charges that were the subject of the instant prosecution . . .'.[37] Kerry and four other Senators wrote to the judge urging him to reject the agreement. Kerry drafted legislation mandating the closure of any bank convicted of money laundering as a corporate policy.[38]

Senator Hatch, on the other hand, took the Senate floor to oppose this bill, praise the Justice Department for its handling of the BCCI case, and offer kind words for BCCI itself. As was later found out, the speech was largely prepared by Hatch's personal friend Robert Altman, a prominent lawyer who at the same time was lawyer and registered lobbyist for BCCI. The bill was not passed at that point.

Costly as it was, this conviction alone was unable to bring down BCCI. As the Kerry inquiry was over and federal authorities were not enthusiastically following up evidence of wrongdoing, Senate investigator Jack Blum approached Robert Morgenthau, the Manhattan District Attorney in the hope of getting some action.

## THE NEW YORK INVESTIGATION

The available evidence was not solid, but there were enough leads and indications for Morgenthau to decide to begin an investigation into BCCI. It was essentially Morgenthau's indictment of the bank and its top management that precipitated the closure of BCCI. The DA's efforts, however, faced strong resistance and high obstacles. Collaboration was not forthcoming from the Justice Department or the Serious Fraud Office. Bank regulators in the United States and the United Kingdom offered no assistance in the early stages either, in a way typifying the clash of mandates given to the two kind of agencies. That is, New York prosecutors were treating everyone with suspicion and were keen to bring evidence into the open and sanction the culprits. Regulators, on the other hand, were operating largely within a culture of trust and preferred to manage the crisis, save the bank if possible, avoid systemic risks to the international financial network, and prevent losses to depositors.

In the end, Morgenthau was successful in his fight to bring down BCCI. The Bank of England was eventually forced to co-ordinate a global closure of BCCI just ahead of his devastating indictment. Without underestimating Morgenthau's power and influence, it is still remarkable that a State prosecutor would emerge victorious from a battlefield replete with federal agencies, prosecutors, regulators, and foreign governments. The question, thus, is what forces operated and shaped the outcome of this struggle; what conditions operated in favour of prosecutorial rather than regulatory approaches. What strengthened Morgenthau or what weakened BCCI's support? The answer, I believe, lies in two sets of factors, internal and external to BCCI.

## INTERNAL ORGANIZATIONAL FACTORS

BCCI's founder and charismatic leader, Agha Hassan Abedi suffered a heart attack in the beginning of 1988. He was thus incapacitated just before the Tampa indictment and during the Kerry inquiry. He later stated publicly that the Florida plea bargain was the decision 'of a weak man', but Abedi was unable to play a part.

The financial crisis, chronic as it was throughout BCCI's history, became unmanageable due to the Treasury losses, the non-performing loans, and the cost of financing the illegal investment in CCAH, the holding company of First American Bank. The injection of several billions US dollars in capital was now indispensable for the survival of the group.

There was no obvious successor who could lead BCCI's defence against the multi-front attack it was facing and who could keep the different parts of the group together. As a result, antagonisms, tensions, and infighting among managers from different regions (for example, Dubai and Abu Dhabi) and religious persuasions were no longer contained. Many of them were disgruntled, demoralized by the conviction in the United States of America, or defeated in the internal struggles over control of the BCCI group. As a result, some managers made extortionate demands threatening to disclose the false and deceitful accounting at BCCI. Others turned informants, providing vital information and evidence to auditors, investigators, and journalists.[39]

All this further undermined BCCI's stability and strength, making it vulnerable to outside threats. Although its inefficiency was getting out of control, Abu Dhabi was prepared to bail it out. Therefore, more central to BCCI's closure is its ineffectiveness in delivering the services that afforded it better protection in the past.

## EXTERNAL FACTORS

BCCI gained its strength, first by offering Westerners an entry into the oil-rich Gulf area, then because it performed key services to powerful people and institutions. However, it has always been insolvent and has always had its enemies. It grew very fast and became an important competitor to Western banks that gladly took over after BCCI's closure. BCCI and its unorthodox managers were not part of the Establishment and were always viewed with suspicion. By extending services to Third World countries, BCCI assisted them in avoiding restrictions imposed by the World Bank or the IMF. Even in Pakistan and the Arab world, BCCI faced antagonisms and conflicts. So, when its functionality eclipsed, when it became *ineffective* as well as inefficient, the protective shields practically dropped and investigators and enemies could act with more ease.

Geopolitical changes in the late 1980s played a crucial role in reducing BCCI's functionality to intelligence agencies, politicians, and businessmen. The collapse of the USSR brought with it the end of the civil war in Afghanistan, a war previously fuelled by covert US aid to the mujaheddin rebels through Pakistan, where BCCI had a dominant role. Pakistan itself lost part of its strategic importance (buffer against the communist frontier) and became a black sheep, as its efforts to obtain nuclear capability (aided by BCCI) received widespread publicity.

The Iran-Contra transactions were over and so was the Iran-Iraq war (both sides were secretly, illegally, or against overt foreign policy assisted by the United States of America, partly through BCCI). In addition, clients of BCCI such as Noriega, Duvalier, Somosa, Saddam Hussein were now overthrown or demonized by the West and the United States in particular. Ironically, such clients, who would have provided clout and enhanced BCCI's power in the past because they were allies and friends of the United States, increasingly became sources of weakness and vulnerability.

Consequently, both politically important and criminal customers would move their accounts to other banks better shielded against prying eyes. With reduced usefulness as a listening post and insecure for own use by intelligence services, BCCI was no longer valuable enough to keep open.

Geopolitical changes also created new poles of conflict. For example, weapons left behind in the Afghani war theatre were used by uncontrolled fundamentalists involved in the drug traffic in the North-West frontier. In an era of *détente* among the big global powers, the risk of conventional, chemical or even nuclear armament of Third World countries came to the fore. By assisting these countries, BCCI offered them a degree of secrecy and autonomy not particularly welcomed by Western secret services who were thereby losing control.

Blind eyes, therefore, could now regain their sight, also aided by the post-Cold War concern about 'organized crime'. Kerry conducted a series of public hearings on BCCI, emphasising that BCCI illustrated the growing threat on which public policy ought to concentrate.[40] The 'new world order' in which intelligence agencies are seeking new roles and grounds of legitimacy has rendered them more prone to highlight security risks caused by international criminal groups. In this context, old disincentives to blow the whistle on BCCI ceased to exist and BCCI's old Western friends were rushing to disassociate themselves from what was about to be labelled a 'criminal organization'.[41]

Evidence available to the Bank of England and other regulatory agencies could have justified the closure of BCCI much earlier than they did. Yet, BCCI could not be attacked before the end of the Gulf War. By 1991, however, Iraq was defeated by an alliance that depended heavily on the Arab support. It would be unlikely for regulatory agencies to engage in actions that could jeopardise the alliance by embarrassing or antagonizing the owners of BCCI, the authorities of Abu Dhabi.[42] Action that risked damaging the relations with the ruling élites in Abu Dhabi or Saudi Arabia[43] – wealthy and eager backers of anti-communist activities – would have been blocked by foreign policy makers during the Cold or the Gulf Wars. *The Financial Times* argued that earlier action against BCCI 'would scarcely have pleased the Foreign Office'.[44]

The recovery of controllers' eyesight, however, turned out to be only partial. Investigations around the world contributed juicy information and kept the scandal going for many months. Given that scandal is an opportunity for reform,[45] one might expect some change in the way political campaigns, the revolving door, conflicts of interest, business activities of politicians, or intelligence operations are regulated. Yet, the only reform that took place dealt with foreign banks operating in the United States of America.[46] How are we to understand this beyond conspiratorial thinking?

## FACTORS LIMITING REFORM

Firstly, the bipartisan nature of the scandal generated a dynamic discouraging investigation and press reports coming from either side of the political spectrum. This did not necessarily happen through open or discretionary blocking of inquiries. Rather, the containment of the scandal occurred through partisan (that is, biased or one-sided) investigations of particular aspects of the BCCI affair and selective reporting of findings. For example, as Democrats in Congress headed inquiries into BCCI (Senator Kerry, Henry Gonzalez in the House Banking Committee and Charles Schumer in the House Judiciary Subcommittee in Crime and Criminal Justice), so did Republicans (the minority House Banking Committee issued a report on Democrats Clifford and Altman). As evidence about possible conflicts of interest by Orrin Hatch came out, information on Democratic fund-raiser David Paul's relations with BCCI was fed to the press. Information about the Bush family and BCCI parties was effectively countered with stories about the Clintons and BCCI. Arkansas financier Jackson Stephens, an important middle-man who brokered the secret sale of the United States bank to BCCI, had relations with, and contributed to the campaigns of both Bush and Clinton. Effectively, each side showed enough of its hand to the opponents to put a brake on their respective investigations. Murder-suicide scenarios are not very likely in the political game. Thus, it is overseas participants in BCCI's affairs who have shouldered the blame and criminal sanctions (at least so far).

Secondly, resistance came from editorial control and cultural barriers to scandalous stories. The media normally 'ride' on scandal once misconduct is discovered and exposed. Few journalists do anything before action is taken by the authorities. Once the cat is out of the bag, they all compete to find new angles on the story, occasionally distorting or decontextualizing events.[47]

During a conference debating the media coverage of the BCCI and savings and loan disasters, a reporter pointed out that the 'élite world of good journalism . . . [has] become too much embedded in the establishment' and that 'it's very hard to convince editors who are having dinner with White House family members that [the S&L problem] is a good story.' Peter Truell, the *Wall Street Journal* correspondent who covered the BCCI affair, noted 'the corruption which is endemic to Washington . . . and the complete . . . reluctance of the press and many other people to point to these kinds of conflicts'. He also pointed out that members of the media establishment socialized with major players in the BCCI affair and that 'individuals implicated in the BCCI scandal have served on various corporate boards with directors of media companies'.[48]

Thirdly, there were numerous crimes to pursue in the BCCI affair, beyond the possible misconduct of 'powerful resisters'. In this way, both media and government investigators could continue busily to explore, expose, and punish serious offences without being accused of, or feeling that they were only dealing with trivial or marginal criminality.

Fourthly, unambiguous, easily comprehensible crimes or crimes related to domestic problems were often perpetrated by the overseas criminal cast, while the domestic cast was involved in more obscure, financial offences or conflicts of interest. 'Juicy' crimes, such as providing prostitutes for important clients or BCCI's assistance to drug traffickers and money launderers, helped draw the attention of a wider audience to the scandal.

Frauds, account manipulations, and distinctions between bribes and non-recourse loans did not find a very receptive audience nor could the label 'stick' as easily. This is illustrated by the New York case of BCCI lawyers Clifford and Altman. Beyond their conflicts of interests noted above, the two lawyers received risk-free loans from BCCI to purchase First American Bank shares. They later sold most of them to Mohammed Hammoud, a BCCI nominee shareholder, who received a loan against these shares from BCCI. Clifford and Altman paid back their loans and interest and made a profit of about $10 million between them. Criminal charges against Clifford were dropped on ill-health grounds, while Altman was acquitted of charges that these transactions and millions of dollars in legal fees were essentially bribes for assisting BCCI in its illegal control of United States institutions. Notwithstanding ongoing legal action, this was because many of these transactions (for example, non-recourse loans) are not criminal. So, despite the multiple hats the lawyers wore,[49] they could still argue that they did not know about the deception they were effectively aiding and abetting.

Finally, legal formalism regarding lobbying and political financing practices prevents controllers from taking action often because many questionable or unethical practices they encounter are not illegal. The status quo was both well served by BCCI and preserved by the formalism in United States responses to conflicts of interest and corruption. The legal framework allows the institutionalization of improper practices by encouraging the belief that anything not expressly prohibited is allowed.[50] This, in turn, promotes an attitude that disclosure of an interest resolves any conflicts. In a case in point, Hatch admitted that he contacted BCCI after his Senate speech for a loan on behalf of a business associate who managed a trust fund for him. He then stated:

> In 1988 I invested $10,000 in that trust and have *filed the appropriate public disclosure documents* on the property with the Senate Ethics Committee every year since I've been involved with the trust. *The Ethics Committee has never raised concerns about my involvement in the trust. It was fully disclosed.*[51]

That the United States audience was probably unreceptive to such unclear political corruption can also be attributed to a media-fuelled cynicism about the class of politicians.[52] There would be little there to scandalize the public.

## CONCLUSIONS

At a general level, the view that people get weakened by scandal may need qualification. In the course of battles that make up scandals, the balance of power is undoubtedly altered. However, the BCCI affair evolved like a river: the scandal followed the path of least resistance. The BCCI case suggests that those vulnerable to scandal are those already weakened by other forces. At least in some cases, therefore, scandal merely speeds up or intensifies a pre-existing crisis.

Further, the BCCI scandal has had some cathartic effects à la Durkheim while leaving many troublesome practices out of mainstream debate and scrutiny. Some drew reassuring conclusions that the 'system worked'. A Federal Reserve official, for example, argued that, despite the tremendous complexity of BCCI arrangements and attempts to hide illegal activities, 'we got them; and the message to anybody else who thinks they are going to play this game will be aloud and clear: we'll get you too'.[53] So, we reach a Hollywood-like happy ending and glorification of the United States of America, its law enforcement and regulatory heroes. At the same time evil and blame were externalized. Just like in earlier debates on 'organized crime', foreigners were demonized[54] – Pakistanis and Arabs, corrupt Third-World politicians and bankers are regarded as the chief cause of problems.

In the West, thus, there has been some catharsis. In the South, however, where many were prepared to believe in a Western conspiracy against BCCI and the Muslim world, the effect there has been anything but cathartic. People (not only there) were left wondering what exactly was hidden behind the CIA's non-co-operation with Kerry and the classified Appendix 8 to the Bingham report. Without some sort of Western *glasnost*, we will never learn about the precise extent and role intelligence agencies played in this case.

Moreover, a host of insiders and influential Westerners took part in complex networks of business relationships.[55] Most, if not all, of those implicated in the BCCI scandal argue that they were deceived and were unaware of any unlawful practices. Unconvinced observers, however, argue that it is hardly believable that such a large number of intelligence-connected, astute, and well-informed individuals and agencies would not have known. After all, a number of clear and public warning signals had been given over the years about BCCI. For instance, Singapore authorities did not allow BCCI to operate there; the Federal Reserve disallowed BCCI's open entry into the United States banking industry; in the United Kingdom, BCCI had only the status of licensed deposit taking institution, rather than that of a fully licensed bank until the 1987 Banking Act; in addition, when BCCI moved into Canada, the Canadian Bankers' Association voiced concerns and opposition, and most United Kingdom merchant and retail bankers would have no dealings with it. The reasons for this treatment were BCCI's tarnished reputation, unclear ownership, lack of lender of last resort, and absence of consolidated supervision. In 1988, we had the Florida money laundering case. BCCI's heavy losses, imprudent concentration of risk, and the existence of substantial inside loans were known to auditors, regulators, directors, and shareholders in the mid-1980s.

Uncomplimentary rumours about BCCI, its practices and its clients had always been circulating in banking milieux. Some rumours may have been untrue, racially motivated or mere envy talk. Yet, the point is that powerful actors decided to represent BCCI or continued to do so despite this public knowledge and commentary. In several instances, these actors lobbied openly or behind the scenes on behalf of BCCI, trying to convince the authorities that such rumours and evidence were baseless or exaggerated.

The most benign interpretation is that they were unable to find out the massive fraud and deceptions going on for more than a decade behind their backs.[56] If so many experienced Westerners can be fooled for so long, about so many things, and most of the time, what does this tell us about the possibility of scores of examples of BCCI-type of misconduct lurking around, especially in view of the huge demand for the sort of illegal goods and services offered by BCCI?[57] Alternatively, some of them knew what was going on.[58]

The above analysis allows for at least partial knowledge of the participants while providing a non-conspiratorial theory of the development of the BCCI scandal in the United States of America. The whole affair exposes such structural problems and conflicts of interests inherent to the United States and international political arena that the problem is far more difficult than what a conspiracy theory allows.

First, accounts labelled as 'conspiracy theories' – even if true – are easily discredited in public discourse, become fictionalized in commercial books, and thus have no real impact. Secondly, they imply a bad apple theory – consistent with the United States culture of individualism and attribution of both success and failure to particular people – which clouds the systemic risk of similar disasters in the future. So, if we can catch the 'bad guys', the problem is considered solved and structural conflicts are overlooked.

My analysis, by contrast, suggests that the system in place has been badly malfunctioning. This case demonstrates why we can be nearly certain that such misconduct is common.[59] Instead of believing that we can litigate our way out of problems highlighted by the BCCI affair, we need to promote structural reforms at home.

My last point is that transparency is necessary and can achieve short- and medium-term goals. Yet, it is foolhardy to think that it is sufficient to prevent corrupt and unethical conduct. The implicit change-behaviour-not-attitude approach has certain immediate advantages, but also carries the risk of acquiescence. If no effort is made to affect attitudes and culture in the long term, the tension between what people believe and think on the one hand, and what they must do or appear to do will remain.

Another risk might lie in a cultivated self-righteousness, because much of what is done in the business and political spheres is open to the public. One still needs an enormous amount of 'digging'[60] and analysis to put together mind-boggling potential conflicts of interest in the context of a revolving door justified by the rhetoric of free market and democracy. The latter is ironically undermined by the very existence of the revolving door. Not everyone has the resources to collect the 'public' information nor equal power to do something about it.

Sunlight is a good doctor, but additional policies are required to lessen the need for a doctor in the first place – policies which lower tolerance of what many who looked into the BCCI affair in Washington saw as confirmation of a pervasive corrupt environment.

## NOTES AND REFERENCES

1   M.B. Clinard and P. Yeager, *Corporate Crime* (1980); M. Levi, 'Fraudulent Justice? Sentencing the Business Criminal' in *Paying for Crime*, eds. P. Carlen and D. Cook (1989) 86; E.H. Sutherland, *White Collar Crime: The Uncut Version* (1983).

2   R.A. Hutchison, *Off the Books: Citibank and the World's Biggest Money Game* (1986); P. Lernoux, *In Banks We Trust* (1984); R.T. Naylor, *Hot Money and the Politics of Debt* (1987).

3   Owned by the Gokal brothers.

4   N. Passas, 'I Cheat, Therefore I Exist? The BCCI Scandal in Context' in *Emerging Global Business Ethics*, eds. W.M. Hoffman et al. (1994) 69.

5   Kerry Report, *The BCCI Affair*, Report to the Senate Foreign Relations Committee. Subcommittee on Terrorism, Narcotics, and International Operations (1992); T. Sebastian, 'Big Cheques From Conmen Investigated' *Mail on Sunday*, 6 November 1994, Night and Day section, 8; P. Truell and L. Gurwin, *False Profits* (1992).

6   'Part of the history of any scandal is why and how the disclosure came about, and often why, especially, it was for so long delayed.' G.C. Moodie, 'On Political Scandals and Corruption' in *Political Corruption: A Handbook*, ed. A.J. Heidenheimer et al. (1989) 880.

7   A letter from Callaghan to a BCCI official on 1 February 1988 concluded by saying: 'I am at your service'; it was printed on a House of Lords letterhead.

8   Former head of the Saudi intelligence and reported facilitator of the Camp David Accord.

9   Former directors of the CIA.

10  K. Cahill, 'Superman Arrives to Sort Out the Conservative Party Finances and the £200m Slush Fund' *Business Age*, February 1993, 41.

11  Kerry, op. cit., n. 5; N. Passas, 'The Mirror of Global Evils: A Review Essay on the BCCI Affair' (1995) 12 *Justice Q.* 801; Truell and Gurwin, op. cit., n. 5.

12  Kerry, id.; Truell and Gurwin, id.

13  P.D. Scott and J. Marshall, *Cocaine Politics: Drugs, Armies, and the CIA in Central America* (1991).

14  N. Passas, 'Structural Sources of International Crime: Policy Lessons from the BCCI Affair' (1993) 20 *Crime, Law and Social Change* 293.

15  'It was only through the efforts of a handful of dedicated people . . . that BCCI's criminal rampage was finally ended. If it were not for these men, the bank might still be in business

today, laundering criminal money, stealing deposits, and corrupting governments' (Truell and Gurwin, op. cit., n. 5, p. 434).

16 'BCCI A Victim of Operation Overkill by West, Claims Businessman Adham' *Moneyclips*, 20 January 1992.

17 Truell and Gurwin, op. cit., n. 5, p. 427.

18 '. . . the making of almost any scandal seems to be far more deliberate than accidental. Scandals do not just happen; they are socially constructed phenomena involving the co-operation and conflict of many people' (L.W. Sherman, *Scandal and Reform* (1978) 59).

19 'Scandals are context-bound events and can only be understood against the background of the typical conflicts, opportunities for power and normative patterns of the field of society in which they occur' (S. Neckel, 'Power and Legitimacy in Political Scandal: Comments on a Theoretical Framework for the Study of Political Scandals' (1989) 4 *Corruption and Reform* 153.

20 Moodie, op. cit., n. 6.

21 L. Gurwin, 'Who Really Owns First American' *Regardie's*, May 1980, 66; *Private Eye*, 31 March 1978, 19.

22 BCCI's efforts to control illegally that bank, later named First American Bank, was successful in the 1980s.

23 T. J. Lowi, 'Foreword' in *The Politics of Scandal: Power and Process in Liberal Democracies*, eds. A.S. Markovits and M. Silverstein (1988) vii.

24 M. Gluckman, 'Gossip and Scandal' (1963) 4 *Current Anthropology* 313.

25 Neckel, op. cit., n. 19, p. 154.

26 D.C. Smith, 'Some Things That May Be More Important to Understand About Organized Crime Than Cosa Nostra' in *Organized Crime*, ed. N. Passas (1995) ch. 3.

27 US Senate Committee on Foreign Relations, *Drugs, Law Enforcement and Foreign Policy*, hearings before the Subcommittee on Terrorism, Narcotics and International Operations (1988) part 2, 391.

28 Scott and Marshall, op. cit., n. 13.

29 US House of Representatives Committee on Banking, Finance and Urban Affairs, *BCCI Investigation – Part 3* (1992) 68.

30 This role led to his indictment and conviction in Florida, following the invasion of Panama.

31 He also advised on the defence strategy against the money laundering charges BCCI faced in Florida; see below.

32 Kerry, op. cit., n. 5, p. 509.

33 id., pp. 504–5.

34 Lowi, op. cit., n. 23.

35 J. Adams and D. Frantz, *The Full Service Bank* (1992).

36 N. Passas and R.B. Groskin, 'BCCI and the Federal Authorities: Regulatory Anesthesia and the Limits of Criminal Law', paper given at Society for the Study of Social Problems annual meeting, 1993; US House Judiciary Committee, *Federal Law Enforcement's Handling of Allegations Involving the Bank of Credit and Commerce International*, staff report by the Subcommittee on Crime and Criminal Justice (1991); US Senate Committee on Foreign Relations, *The BCCI Affair*, hearings before the Subcommittee on Terrorism, Narcotics, and International Operations (1992) parts 1 and 3.

37 Plea agreement, 1.16.90, 1[f].

38 An interesting question is how one would interpret 'corporate policy' and what use would be made of such a provision, given the discretionary powers of United States prosecutors.

39 Culminating to the most crucial one, when BCCI's former chief finance officer gave evidence to Morgenthau.

40 'BCCI cannot be taken as an isolated example of a rogue bank, but a case study of the vulnerability of the world to international crime on a global scope that is beyond the current ability of governments to control' (Kerry, op. cit., n. 5, p. 17).

41 News release of Morgenthau's office, 29 July 1991.

42 *Inquiry into the Supervision of the Bank of Credit and Commerce International* (1992; Cm.

71

198; Chair, Lord Justice Bingham).

43  Influential Saudi businessmen like Kamal Adham, Gaith Pharaon, and Adnan Khashoggi were important shareholders, nominees or clients of BCCI.

44  *Financial Times*, 22 July 1991, 12.

45  M. Johnston, 'Corruption, Inequality and Change' in *Corruption, Development and Inequality*, ed. P.M. Ward (1989) 13.

46  Interestingly, it was this law that provided the legal grounds for ordering Daiwa to close down its United States operations.

47  Thus, it is no wonder the last book on BCCI was also the worst; Passas, op. cit., n. 11; see also M. Levi and A. Pithouse, *Victims of White Collar Crime* (forthcoming, 1996).

48  D. McKean, *Why the News Media Took So Long to Focus on the Savings and Loan and BCCI Crises* (1993) 11.

49  Altman, for example, has been a lawyer for the (nominee) investors in FAB, for FAB and related entities, president and director of FAB and related entities, lawyer and registered lobbying for BCCI.

50  M. M. Atkinson and M. Mancuso, 'Edicts and Etiquette: Regulating Conflict of Interest in Congress and the House of Commons' (1992) 7 *Corruption and Reform*, 1.

51  Statement of Orrin G. Hatch on the NBC News report, 27 November 1991; emphasis added.

52  'Worried that the people who represent you in Congress are taking care of themselves and their friends at your expense? You are right. Keep worrying.' (D.L. Bartlett and J.B. Steele, *America: What Went Wrong* (1992 ) 2.)

53  PBS *Newshour*, 15 August 1991.

54  D.C. Smith, *The Mafia Mystique* (1990).

55  Kerry, op. cit., n. 5; Passas, op. cit., n. 11; Truell and Gurwin, op. cit., n. 5.

56  In this case, they are grossly incompetent and unworthy of their high fees, unless it is other services for which they are paid.

57  Passas, op. cit., n. 4.

58  Hammoud, the buyer of FAB shares from BCCI's lawyers, told a friend hours before his reported death: 'If anybody knew how dirty the Americans are in this BCCI business, they'd be surprised – they're dirtier than the Pakistanis.' (Truell and Gurwin, op. cit., n. 5, p. 381.)

59  Passas, op. cit., n. 11.

60  Through Freedom of Information Act requests, for instance.

# [16]

# Organized fraud and organizing frauds:
## *Unpacking research on networks and organization*

MICHAEL LEVI[1]
Cardiff University, UK.

## Abstract

This article examines the settings for frauds in the context of crime networks, fraud opportunities and of a victim-centric typology of fraud. It demonstrates the variety of actors, settings and the variable need for knowing collaboration between co-offenders in frauds of different types. It explores what is known about those involved in the organization of some forms of frauds; how they find both co-offenders and victims in face-to-face and remote settings; and the barriers to growth of the 'fraud business'. It concludes that the globalization of crime is part of contingent relationships between settings, with their rich and varied opportunities (reflecting patterns of business, consumer and investment activities), the variable abilities of would-be perpetrators to recognize and act on those opportunities (the 'crime scripts' perspective), and their interactions with controls (including, but not restricted to, law enforcement). Constructs of 'organized crime' are becoming less obsessed with the structure of groups than with what people need from the largely illicit and largely licit worlds before they commit fraud. Although some frauds are committed by generic transnational 'organized crime' networks, others are merely mobile small groups or individuals who can transplant techniques wherever they go; and others still commit very large one-off frauds without a need for long-term or any involvement in 'organized crime'.

## Key Words

crime and ethnicity • cross-border crime • identity fraud • organized crime • policing • white-collar crime

## Introduction

The analytical and research literature on fraud is much sparser than that on organized crime generally or drugs trafficking in particular.[2] This partly reflects its relatively low political valuation as a non-core part of 'the crime problem', which in turn affects research funding. But the relative (in)accessibility of fraud networks to outsiders is also a factor, since frauds (and other crimes) differ in the way that they are open for marketing, and in the interaction between the parties. In this article, we examine the settings for frauds, which both frames and reflects networks, in the context of fraud opportunities and of a victim-centric typology (Table 1, adapted from Levi and Burrows, 2008). This demonstrates the variety of actors, settings and (less clearly) need for collaboration in frauds of different types. In the process, we explore what is known about those involved in the organization of frauds, though the space available (as well as our knowledge) constrains the number of fraud types that can be discussed.

## Organizing frauds

Two important themes in analysing the extent to which crimes are loosely or tightly organized are (1) the ease with which willing criminals find the co-offenders necessary or helpful for any given set of offences; and (2) the breaking down of the elements of criminal organization into its component parts (i.e. what is termed 'script analysis'[3] by Cornish, 1994; Cornish and Clarke, 2002). These themes also reflect the tension (in this article and more generally—see Levi, 2007) between writing about the personnel involved in frauds (the networks) and what it takes to commit frauds (the scripts). It is helpful to think of the tasks that need to be performed to commit serious frauds (and other crimes) and the range of places where they need to be and are performed. (For all the talk about 'the' globalization of 'crime', some of these tasks are as easily accomplished at a local or regional level as they are transnationally, at least in some jurisdictions.) A higher level 'script analysis' of crime for gain might look like the following, with more specific frauds having their own 'scripts' and variable necessities to find co-offenders.

When analysing the dynamics of particular crimes and/or criminal careers, these procedural elements can be broken down further into much more concrete steps and the relationships between their criminal participants analysed (see e.g. Morselli, 2005; Morselli and Roy, 2008 for some advanced empirical efforts). These steps are not necessarily sequential: for example, we may see a financial crime[4] opportunity only when we meet accountants or lawyers who are able to facilitate it, or we may already have in place all the steps as part of our ongoing 'criminal enterprise'. Criminal finance, some or all criminal personnel or the 'tools of crime' (from non-transparent companies to credit cards) may come from or go to another country, constituting 'transnational' crimes; or else remain within one country, constituting 'national'

**Table 1.** A typology of fraud by victim category and form of activity

| Victim sector | Victim sub-sector | Examples of fraud |
|---|---|---|
| Private | Financial Services | Cheque fraud<br>Counterfeit intellectual property and products sold as genuine<br>Counterfeit money<br>Data-compromise fraud<br>Embezzlement<br>Insider dealing/market abuse<br>Insurance fraud<br>Lending fraud<br>Payment card fraud<br>Procurement fraud |
| | Non-financial services | Cheque fraud<br>Counterfeit intellectual property and products sold as genuine<br>Counterfeit money<br>Data-compromise fraud<br>Embezzlement<br>Gaming fraud<br>Lending fraud<br>Payment card fraud<br>Procurement fraud |
| | Individuals | Charity fraud<br>Consumer fraud<br>Counterfeit intellectual property and products sold as genuine<br>Counterfeit money<br>Investment fraud<br>Pension-type fraud |
| Public | National bodies | Benefit fraud<br>Embezzlement<br>Procurement fraud<br>Tax fraud |
| | Local bodies | Embezzlement<br>Frauds on Council taxes<br>Procurement fraud |
| | International (but affecting public) | Procurement fraud (by national against other—mainly but not always foreign—companies to obtain foreign contracts)<br>EU funds fraud |

*Note:* See Levi and Burrows (2008, Box 1) for a glossary of common fraud types. The counterfeiting of intellectual property counts as fraud only if the vendor represents it as being the genuine manufacturer's product (or, arguably, if the purchaser believes it to be genuine). Otherwise it may be a loss of the manufacturer's property rights, but no-one is defrauded: the manufacturer loses principally if the purchaser would have bought the legitimate product at the price offered for it, but also if there is collateral damage to the product's reputation.

crimes.[5] In the case of fraud, offenders may start with differential access to local, national or international resources, but the exploitation of inter-state and international regulatory and criminal justice asymmetries—e.g. different levels of enforcement in the states or countries in which the fraudsters operate—represents a positive advantage for fraud compared with most other crimes. In this article, I shall seek to combine the scripts with a brief analysis of the sorts of networks involved in them.

Applying the sort of script found in Box 1, would-be fraudsters have to find 'marks' to target with their schemes,[6] and develop techniques for getting them to part with their money voluntarily: the hallmark of fraud. Some such offences occur (at least in part) face to face; others are done remotely; while others still may start technologically (with a letter or an e-mail) and end with some interpersonal contact. Let us take as an example of the latter '419 frauds', so called after section 419 of the Nigerian criminal code. There are few e-mail users who have never encountered scam e-mails—which usually arrive from a yahoo or hotmail address—offering them vast wealth if only they will help their previously unacquainted banker/relative

**Box 1.** The process of fraud and other crimes for gain

---

1. See a situation as a 'financial crime opportunity'
2. Obtain whatever finance is needed for the crime
3. Find people willing and able to offend (if necessary for the crimes contemplated) and who are controllable and reliable
4. Obtain any equipment/data needed to offend
5. Carry out offences in domestic and/or overseas locations with or without physical presence in jurisdiction(s). This will usually involve manipulating—with varied degrees of complexity, technology and interpersonal communication skills—victims' perceptions of 'what is happening'
6. Minimize immediate enforcement/operational risks. Especially if planning to repeat frauds, neutralize law enforcement by technical skill, by corruption, and/or by legal arbitrage, using legal obstacles to enforcement operations and prosecutions which vary between States
7. Convert, where necessary (e.g. where goods rather than money are obtained on credit), products of crime into money or other usable assets
8. Find people and places willing to store proceeds (and perhaps transmit and conceal their origin)
9. Decide which jurisdiction(s) offers the optimal balance between social/physical comfort and the risk of asset forfeiture/criminal justice sanctions. Indifference in any one State or sub-state arena may suffice to neutralize an investigation, and staffing inadequacies as well as corruption may be the cause of official inaction.

of a deceased corrupt dictator put their 'dormant account' or 'unknown to the authorities but at risk' money into their own account for 25–40 per cent of the 'take' (usually $25 billion). Some data can be harvested for 'identity fraud' but the victim is often persuaded to pay 'advance fees' to remove blockages in the funds transfers, and may even be lured to Nigeria or some other country to pay out more. One of the ironies is that Nigerians are utilizing their stereotype of corruption in order to make the proposition more plausible to their intended 'marks'. Such propositions used to be made by letter (sometimes using counterfeit stamps to reduce operating costs) but are now more often made by e-mail, which is almost free. By contrast, other frauds such as lottery scams may have quite elaborate and convincing paperwork delivered by bulk mail, often from Spain: although the authorities may be able to identify such scam letters prior to delivery, legal prohibitions on interference with the mail (plus commercial interests insofar as they are paid by the distributors) prevent them from stopping distribution unless the stamps themselves are counterfeit. Such lottery scams (whether by mail or e-mail) seldom involve interpersonal contact.

We can see from the Box 1 process map (or 'script') one important difference between frauds and most traditional crimes that have victims: at the time when the offence is committed (which, in contrast with other property offences, may happen undetected continuously over years), the fraudster can be but does not normally need to be in the same place or even the same continent as the victims or their property. However, few frauds need to be executed on an international basis, and some fraudsters (like gangsters) have their domestic geographic comfort zones, even to the level of the shops in which they prefer to use stolen cards and those they avoid (Levi, 2003[p1]). It is quicker for a credit card fraudster or telemarketer to get a train from London to Paris than from London to Liverpool, and that can be important when the rate of fraud upon a stolen or counterfeited card is time-critical. Rising fuel costs notwithstanding, it is easy and relatively cheap to fly to many parts of the world, even if one is buying the ticket with a genuine credit card or cash (which may be the proceeds of past crimes). However in many other cases, speed of action is unimportant because there is a long elapsed time between the commission of fraud and its detection by the victim or by a third party: the latter includes American Express, Visa or MasterCard (for payment card frauds); Dun and Bradstreet or Experian (for personal and commercial credit frauds); and the UK Financial Services Authority, Office of Fair Trading and other regulators (for investment frauds, 'market abuse' and consumer scams). Choice of offender or victim location is determined by other factors (such as the large number of relatively wealthy but still anxious elderly people in Florida or the south-east of England). In the larger cases, professional intermediaries and bank accounts are necessary components in presenting a plausible front and in obtaining and laundering the funds; in others, cash may be wired via money service bureaux (like Western Union) or by 'underground banking' (Passas, 2005) to foreign or sometimes domestic locations.

What is different about frauds compared with other crimes? First, as researchers since Cressey (1955) have shown, most professionals are already in a position to commit major frauds such as embezzlement by virtue of their legitimate jobs. (One may add to Cressey's rather individual-oriented approach that few finance directors and CEOs will have their 'instructions to pay' questioned by subordinates: so they too do not need active conspirators—merely that the ciphers they have appointed follow orders.) Second, whether as (i) individuals and/or as (ii) corporate actors, they are less likely to be suspected as being 'out of place'—as Felson (2002, 2006) might put it, their camouflage is already there—both as transactors in the business deal and as movers of illicit funds after the fact. The latter is connected to the third point, which is that most (but not all) frauds obtain money in electronic form, and therefore have less need to deposit and transfer large cash sums, which more readily arouse suspicions among the ever-larger number of bodies (not just banks and building societies but also now antique dealers, car dealers, estate agents, and jewellers), who have a criminal law obligation to report to a Financial Intelligence Unit (SOCA in the UK) 'suspicious transactions'.[7] The imagery of cash and drugs trafficking still predominates in the anti-money laundering arena, despite the expansion of the legal mandate to include all crimes. (See further, Levi and Reuter 2006, 2008.)

One more point is noteworthy. There is a temptation—especially in work on 'organized crime'—to see the stages above as being part of a conscious plan: a preconceived strategy of deception (thus replicating the process of 'case construction' by police and prosecutors when preparing for court). However this can be a mistake. In *The Phantom Capitalists* (Levi, 2008a, originally 1981), I suggested the utility of looking at bankruptcy and other frauds in terms of a threefold typology:

(1) pre-planned frauds, in which the business scheme is set up from the start as a way of defrauding victims (businesses, public sector and/or individuals)
(2) intermediate frauds, in which people started out obeying the law but consciously turned to fraud later; and
(3) slippery-slope frauds, in which deceptions spiralled, often in the context of trying—however absurdly and over-optimistically—to rescue an insolvent business or set of businesses that in reality had no hope of repaying its debts in the future.

In short, motivation to defraud can be heterogeneous rather than a single phenomenon; and (where physical identification is not an issue) planned fraudsters have an interest in pretending to be slippery-slopers or honest-but-unlucky, to minimize the chances of prosecution, conviction and imprisonment, thus reversing prosecutors' case constructions. As with Cressey's embezzlers, existing business people have comparatively little problem in organizing funds transfers out of the company and/or bankruptcy fraud (although the disposal of large amounts of goods very quickly may be difficult—one may need an apparently legitimate or large scale illegitimate trader to perform a brokerage role in disposal).[8] Once people are willing to risk whatever ethical and social sanctions might be expected,[9] the key practical problem is organizing the escape from criminal sanctions and proceeds of crime recovery by creditors or state. These measures may involve willing collaborators and/or innocent third parties, or a combination (including the coalition of the willing pretending to be innocent and often remaining unchallenged). People can use corporations or professions as a means to attain fraudulent ends, and can do so either at the start (pre-planned fraud) or as an afterthought in a changed situation. The corporations can be substantive and real or mere fronts or shells for the perpetration of fraud. But people can also commit frauds against companies and the government as outsiders or from more junior positions. An example follows:

> Jagmeet Channa, a charity volunteer from a middle-class family and with no previous criminal convictions, who had been employed at HSBC headquarters first on a short term contract 10 months earlier, was sentenced to nine years in prison for attempting to steal £72 million from HSBC in April 2008. One Friday, Channa authorized two seemingly straightforward transactions in transfers to accounts at Barclays in Manchester and Société Générale in Casablanca, using passwords stolen from colleagues. Transcripts of telephone calls made from his HSBC landline that evening reveal a series of calls informing several people that the fraud was a triumph. Attempts to uncover their identities proved fruitless because they were using pay-as-you-go handsets, which were not already being monitored. Just after lunchtime on the Sunday, Channa's plan fell apart. Banking security officials in Malaysia had noted a double transaction, prompting 'cause for concern'. Channa had used a global financial holding account where vast amounts are paid in and then removed. At the close of daily trading, the account should register zero, but Channa had inexplicably forgotten to change it and his holding account was showing a massive debt. It was an elementary error that, if Channa had avoided it, might have allowed him to pull off his record-breaking crime.[10] Channa's decision to execute the crime on a Friday had compounded his mistake. With trading frozen over weekends, security officials find it much easier to detect anomalies. Had Channa committed the fraud during the working week, his scam might have remained undetected for long enough to allow his partners to empty the £72m from the accounts in Manchester and Morocco. The £72m was frozen and returned to HSBC.
> (Summarized from *The Observer* and other UK newspapers 13 July 2008 and from the author's interviews with bankers 2008.)

It is not currently known whether Channa was 'planted' at HSBC or was targeted by others after his arrival, but—were it not for the evidence of his phone calls to conspirators—it might have been possible for him to carry out all these things alone or with one or two conspirators rather than as a component of an ongoing 'organized crime group'. As I write, the other crime involvements—if any—of the other parties are unknown. (The sort of analysis conducted by Morselli and Roy, 2008, depends on long-term surveillance of the networks of people already suspected of serious crime.) This emphasizes the point that fraud permits a variety of offender organizational permutations.

As for the persistence of crime techniques over time, those businesses that during the 1960s and 1970s deceived their creditors, on the basis that they needed larger orders to supply their expanding 'mail order' trade, would now do the same on the basis that they have a booming internet-based sales business, especially prior to Christmas (Levi, 2008a). In the era of the credit card, dishonest merchants might pass large quantities of (i) fake or (ii) genuine (but on stolen card) transactions through their commercial accounts, claim (as is normal with traders) advance reimbursement from merchant acquirer card companies, and then disappear before the card issuer, merchant acquirer or cardholder realizes there has been a fraud at all.[11] Looking more at individual 'purchasers' than businesses, payment cards were rare during the 1970s, but fraudsters can now use credit card numbers skimmed from unsuspecting cardholders to order hundreds of computers on the net from different suppliers, have them delivered to 'drop addresses' in the UK or the US, and then forwarded to addresses elsewhere for resale: all of this before the cardholder or card issuer becomes aware there is anything wrong. (The limited availability of such 'drops' serves as a brake on the exploitation of these and other 'identity fraud' opportunities.) This and other cyberfraud techniques reflect a comparative criminal advantage arising from the combination of high technological skills and high motivation because of poor opportunities in their home countries. There are also large-scale credit card and loan 'bust outs' using people's own and stolen identities to obtain goods and money.

The illustrations above show that behaviour of victims-to-be and 'capable guardians' has to be considered as part of the organization of crime. Some suppliers of goods on credit simply make assumptions about creditworthiness without asking for references (or are satisfied by references from members of the credit applicant's family who had no plausible business dealings with the firm). They may check out the companies on telephone/trade directories such as yell.com or BT and, if they are there, may assume the entries reflect genuine trading, not realizing that they too may have been 'fixed'. If the fraudsters—as companies or as individuals—are buying electronic goods, the sales pressures on telecoms and computer firms are extreme, especially in a global next-day service culture, and the rewards for salespeople are often based on what they sell, irrespective of whether or not it is paid for, though some companies do claw back commission on fraudulent sales, which may act as a brake on enthusiasm or wilful blindness. Creditors in highly competitive industries are reluctant to share their fraud losses with other firms and are afraid publicity may make them more attractive to other fraudsters (author interviews with companies): whether the latter fear is reasonable is unverified. Sharing information anonymously via third parties such as trade reference agencies represents one route to learning from experience. These third parties might be viewed as 'capable guardians', but what they may see or construct out of their partly automated analytical methods are suspicions of fraud rather than undisputed crimes they have witnessed.

At the *individual* level, prior to the 1960s (as now in faith and other close communities), credit was seen more as a personal trust than as an impersonal risk judgement made by professionals. This is one reason some fraudsters target religious affinity groups, because the approach for investment is then seen as coming from a friend rather than a stranger, where trust norms may not apply (or not to the same extent). Often today, the granting (or refusal) of credit to individuals is driven largely by reports from agencies such as Experian and Equifax (internationally) and—in the UK—Callcredit. These reports incorporate large amounts of prior credit behaviour, as well as county court judgements and bankruptcy/Individual Voluntary Agreement records. To these are added financial institutions' proprietary credit scoring—statistical analysis of aggregate data on past loan experiences ('goods' and 'bads')—and the 'risk appetite' of the lenders, which in the decade before the 'credit crunch' in 2007 was high, due to the relative cheapness of money and the need to find outlets for funds held on deposit if they were to make a profit.

The role of criminal justice in the control of first party credit fraud—where borrowers themselves commit fraud rather than have others steal their details or their cards—is relatively unimportant. Unless the bad debtors change their names and evade indirect identification, credit reference agencies can still incapacitate future credit opportunities, irrespective of whether people have been convicted, discharged from bankruptcy or indeed have avoided going 'bust'. Electronic footprints on individual adults are quite pervasive (especially in the UK and North America, far less so in Asia, Africa and Eastern Europe), and attempts to sidestep these controls on identity thefts and cloning are a key battleground against fraud today. Licit and illicit migration flows generate particular difficulties and asymmetries in the validation of credit histories. For example. the birth registers and other personal identifiers are absent from centralized records in many African and Asian countries, so cannot readily be checked, and certainly not electronically. Many of the features of late modernity upon which 'identity validation' rests are not uniformly available.

## Fraud networks: between the opportunity and the criminal act

Tremblay (1993) argued that the likelihood of crime commission is a function of co-offender accessibility and suitability, and Felson (2003) stressed that offender convergence settings 'help likely co-offenders discover one another in the context of their routine activities. Such settings provide an ongoing structure for criminal co-operation, even as participants change. This makes possible a local process of accomplice regeneration, leading to sustainable criminal behaviour'. Morselli and Roy (2008) note that both script analysis and social embeddedness emphasize purposive social action, but differ inasmuch as the social embeddedness perspective places the social network as the force driving such action, whereas, following Cornish and Clarke (2002: 53), the script approach maintains that 'the shape of criminal organization emerges from the requirements of crime commission', the network being only one of these requirements. The evidence does not enable us to determine whether context or existing networks drive organization. Morselli and Roy argue (p. 77) that the 'main objective of a network analysis of crime scripts ... should be to untangle how some participants contribute in varying degrees to keeping the inherent channels of a [crime]script in place' (see p. 83 in their work for a car ringing 'script').

A priori, it would appear that different skill sets and statuses will be needed for different fraud offences, and the barriers to entry depend on the starting point of any given individual or network in relation to the practical opportunity and criminal justice obstacles confronting them.[12] In most countries of the world, a distinction is made between 'laissez faire' opportunities to set up and work in commerce[13] and some restrictions applied to people who want to open or work in the financial services sector, largely on the grounds that the latter can directly steal funds from the public. It is important to understand such restrictions in a global context rather than the traditional nation-state perspective of regulation and criminal justice: Nick Leeson (1997) was refused a licence by the predecessor of the Financial Services Authority because he had failed to declare to it a county court judgement against him on a debt; but Barings gave him a job in the far less controlled atmosphere of Singapore, where—though it is very doubtful he started out with that intent or with a concrete fraudulent plan—he was able to conduct trades that brought down the entire bank. One possibility for 'underworld' offenders is to obtain co-operation from or to put pressure on people in respectable positions in order to use them as tools of fraud (see the Channa example earlier, but also people in much more senior positions). Once they have committed one offence (or legal act that would be seen as highly disreputable), they may find blackmail makes exit difficult. Some frauds can be perpetrated most readily by licensed securities dealers, and persons who are part of or suspected of being connected to a conventional 'organized crime group' would have great difficulty passing the examinations and the 'fit and proper person' test for admission. (This would also require substantial elapsed time to acquire the knowledge, and a longer 'investment' than is normal.) Therefore, one port of entry is to 'do a deal' with existing brokers, as the younger members of New York Mafia families did with some Russian American brokers during the 1990s, against the advice of their elders, who thought it too dangerous to move outside 'the family', whom they could control via ties of mutual obligation (Diih, 2005).[14] Such intergenerational tensions are part of the response to declining market position for traditional 'organized crime', eroded as it was by the undercover infiltration and electronic surveillance, followed by prosecutions under the Racketeer Influenced Corrupt Organization (RICO) legislation. They chose Russian American brokers because they judged that people of that background were more likely than others to find an approach from 'the Mob' attractive: an example of the irony that a 'bad reputation' can bring in business opportunities.

To illuminate such issues, we must first consider what sorts of networks are needed for different offences, and the extent to which their contacts and skill sets enable them to commit a variety of fraud (and non-fraud offences). For price-fixing cartels, for example, what is needed is an ability to pose as a legitimate bidder (which will usually require them to have experience in a relevant area of business) and trust between 'repeat players' that if they overbid for contracts, the winner this time will overbid later to enable them to win. This is easier within a homogeneous elite—the 'good old boys' (a term that originated in the Southern States of the US)—than among comparative strangers, but such elites can be transnational businesspeople as well as locals. (See Harding, 2007, for a contemporary review.) In more competitive markets, the alternative may be corruption of the contract-giver, perhaps even at the specification stage where the 'spec' can be devised in order to give one party an inbuilt advantage. Cartels use their own corporate and individual identities for contracts (though not necessarily for the secret meetings that precede the bids) and would seldom need any false corporate fronts for money laundering purposes since no illicit money changes hands; but bribe-payers might need some false or genuine trading fronts in order to channel payments to the corrupt public official or private sector beneficiary.

Sometimes what is needed for the accomplishment of fraud is compliant people who do not ask critical questions: this was the case with Nick Leeson and Barings Bank, where as a leading trader, Leeson was surrounded by Singaporean subordinates and colleagues who were passive and with British superiors who understood little about trading and were content to take the results he fed them that fed their own large bonuses (Leeson, 1997). Some corporate fraudsters—such as the late Robert Maxwell and the chiefs of Enron—appoint staff on much higher than normal market salaries to ensure their loyalty or wilful blindness when facing alternative employment on much lower salaries. The circle of conspirators at Enron was larger, but for the main part, they had bankers and lawyers who constructed large numbers of offshore Special Purpose Vehicles, and bright, well paid staff whose jobs would have been imperilled by asking critical questions. Rogue trader Jerome Kerviel of French bank Société Générale may have had an occasional accomplice (as is alleged in 2008), but managed to rack up trading losses of billions in 2007 without the aid of an 'organized crime group', taking advantage of weaknesses in supervision which required the resignation of senior management. All of the above should be borne in mind when thinking about fraud and organized networks: there may be no need for conscious co-conspirators, depending on the chain of authority within large corporate or governmental settings and their competence. What some offenders are able to do is simply deploy the range of global corporate mechanisms available in a free enterprise society where there are (perhaps tautologically) insufficient 'capable guardians' to stop them misusing the disguises offered by the corporate form or the authority and power of a corporate role. Let us take as an example the career of Robert Vesco (Hertzog, 2003), who died in May 2008, to less than flattering obituaries around the globe.

### Robert Vesco

A high school dropout from Detroit, Vesco lied about his age to get a job on a car assembly line. In 1965, Vesco hustled control of a small, failing New Jersey valve-making company in return for a five-year $50,000 IOU. A year later he swapped its assets for control of a defunct stock market-listed company he renamed International Controls Corporation, which rose in the 1960s Wall Street boom. Exploiting heavy borrowing and creative accounting, Vesco used ICC shares to buy bigger companies. But he had to keep doing deals to pay interest and boost the share price. By the age of 30, Mr. Vesco was a millionaire.

He later became involved in a Swiss-based mutual fund company, Investment Overseas Services (I.O.S.), run by a swindler called Bernie Cornfeld (Raw et al., 1971). When I.O.S. ran into trouble, Mr. Vesco offered to rescue the company and was embraced by investors terrified of losing their savings. He bought I.O.S. in 1970 for less than $5 million, gaining control of an estimated $400 million in funds. The accounting at the company had been so chaotic that Vesco was able to plunder its holdings at will. After numerous complaints, the US Securities and Exchange Commission charged him and others in a civil suit with stealing more than $224 million. But he had already fled, first to the Bahamas and then to Costa Rica. There, he established a close friendship with President José Figueres, ploughing some $11 million into his adopted country, especially into a company founded by Figueres, who passed a law to guarantee Vesco would not be extradited. He also befriended a nephew of President Nixon, and gave $200,000 to the Nixon campaign (which allegedly helped fund the Watergate burglary) in the hope that the president would help quash the investigation against him. Eventually, a scandal following one of his high-tech brainstorms—a factory to make machine guns, which included President Figueres's son as a partner—led to his flight to the Bahamas, where he invested in the then Prime Minister. He was welcomed in Antigua and Nicaragua, before Cuba finally accepted him for 'humanitarian' reasons: of course there was no extradition from there to the US. Vesco eventually upset the Castro government with a scheme to produce a wonder drug that supposedly cured cancer, AIDS, arthritis and even the common cold. He was jailed for 13 years for defrauding a state-run biotechnology laboratory run by Fidel Castro's nephew, Antonio Fraga Castro. If we examine this remarkable life—and the lives of other transcontinental fraudsters (Block, 1991; Block and Weaver, 2004)—we can see that the tools of Vesco's trade—and his network—were his charisma, accountants and lawyers willing to create legal entities to serve his interests (especially in a period before money-laundering legislation imposed greater due diligence requirements on them), a level of wealth that enabled others to 'party' at his expense, and his ability to hone in on corruptible people who could offer him protection from other governments and creditors pursuing him through the civil courts.

### Enron

In the last year at Enron Global Finance group, managers were sometimes handed a list of Enron assets and instructed to go out and sell some to the Special Purpose Vehicles. A manager would pick something, from a plant to stock to a piece of a start-up company, then discuss the deal with a team of internal lawyers and auditors. A bank or other investor lent money to the newly created company to finance the purchase. The new company, in turn, paid the money to Enron. The use of an intermediary was to make the loan belong to the new company, not Enron, and thus not to count as a debt on Enron's financial statement.

Instead, it counted as income to Enron when the new company passed on the proceeds.

Less debt and more income assured Enron would keep its high credit rating (making borrowing cheaper) and would keep the stock price up.

Top graduate school employees told the *Houston Chronicle* (20 January 2002)[p3] there were many uses for the vehicles they considered legitimate, such as bringing in outside partners to share the risks of a particular venture: but there was little question, especially toward the end, that many had no real 'business purpose' other than improving financial appearances. Say the asset was 100 shares of IBM stock. Enron would divide each share into two parts, one called a 'control interest' and one called an 'economic interest'. Then it would sell the economic interest to a newly created Special Purpose Vehicle. The asset was rarely as simple as 100 shares of another company's stock. So Enron had to put a value on it. Because there was no real outside buyer, it decided the price itself and had that number approved by its auditor, Arthur Andersen.

The deal was placed with a bank, insurance company or other major lender, which put up 97 per cent of the money. Sometimes the promise of Enron stock would be put up to guarantee the loan, although Enron stockholders were never told of the risk that their shares could be diluted if such new shares had to be issued. To qualify as 'independent' from Enron for accounting purposes, a Special Purpose Vehicle had to be owned by someone else. So an outside entity would be brought in to make the required investment, perhaps a tiny percentage of the SPV's total start-up cash, sometimes illicitly lent by Enron itself. An employee told the *Houston Chronicle* (20 January 2002):

> Enron no longer owned the economic interest in the asset, but it did own control over it. In the sales contract with the vehicle, Enron promised always to act in the interest of the SPV. Lawyers and auditors said all this was OK.

As the asset made money for the SPV—if it did, and many didn't—it made principal and interest payments to the lender and issued dividends to the outside equity partners, just like in a normal company.

Enron got to report the proceeds of the sale of the asset as earnings. It had to repay the loan ... but the debt didn't show up on Enron's financial statements.

'Investors don't like to hear you say, "Oh, I was wrong." So you start having a yard sale to boost CFO (cash flow from operations) and net income,' the employee said.

As the Enron indictments showed, there were plenty of accountants, bankers and lawyers as well as some senior management willing to participate in criminal or marginal operations. But they had nothing to do with any criminal subcultures as conventionally defined. Likewise, the many works on the savings and loans 'failures' (Black, 2005; Calavita and Pontell, 1993) and on accounting frauds (Tillman and Indergaard, 2005, 2007a, 2007b), which emphasize—sometimes over-emphasize—elite networks rather than socio-economically marginal firms (Shapiro, 1984), whereas there is no logical reason why both sets (plus 'full-time criminals') cannot be involved in frauds and money laundering.

## Identity frauds and telemarketing scams

By contrast with notable criminal and 'close to the wind' entrepreneurs operating under their own personal names discussed above (though sometimes using many corporate and trust vehicles), other frauds may depend on false identities—wholly fictitious or 'borrowed' from real people—either for their commission or for the laundering process. Thus a senior executive or junior in the finance department might create a company or individual to receive payments, otherwise resting on their ability to make transfers without question: how elaborate the rest of the process is depends on how anxious they are to avoid suspicion and conviction. If the aim is to flee, then they may need false identities and that would usually involve others who can supply them consciously. If the aim is to stay and deceive, then it may involve others able to create a smokescreen of activities.

People other than insiders selling financial products need to find targets to approach and develop persuasive methods of getting them to part with funds. One way of doing so is to pretend to be someone else who is creditworthy. In the past, a simple method was to steal someone's credit card and (in the absence of photos on cards) look sufficiently plausible that a normally ill-motivated (in)capable guardian (in routine activities terminology) such as a shop assistant would sell goods to them or—a stiffer but still possible test—give them money at a bank counter. When Chip and PIN was introduced, this became much harder in the UK and in some terminals overseas, and the locus of fraud shifted to technological efforts to capture both, or to the use of cards and duplicate cards abroad, with UK-issued card losses overseas doubling between 2006 and 2007, after remaining fairly stable or falling over the previous six years.[15] Chip and PIN necessitated a change in the organization of fraud to greater internationalization of conspirators: electronic details copied from cards (a particular speciality of Sri Lankans working in UK petrol stations) could be sent to confederates abroad.[16] Though this had happened before, it accelerated as a result of the improvement of protection against fraud on lost and stolen cards (Levi, 2008b). Likewise, the cruder forms of bankruptcy fraud in which new companies were created by people using false names and paid for the first few orders before accelerating credit massively, selling the goods off and disappearing, were frustrated by enhancements in commercial credit control and pattern analysis, necessitating either wider transnational frauds or 'less organized' frauds in the sense of fewer scammers operating in tandem (Levi, 2008a). A key point here is the interaction between changes in the technology and organization of crime prevention and changes in the levels and organization of fraud. (See McIntosh, 1971; for an influential early exercise along these lines.) Alternatively, 'identity thieves' can try to bypass the control systems by applying for new credit facilities in the names of their victims, using a variety of techniques to get around the change of address (easier in highly mobile societies like the US) or even diverting the victim's mail to their own address for a period. (See Copes and Vieraitis, 2007, 2008 for an interesting research study of identity theft: a more heterogeneous term than the phrase might suggest.)

Much of the 'criminal (auto)biography' literature is devoted to individual con artists whose lives—though highly entertaining (if one is not a victim) and glamorous (if one is wedded, as they mostly are, to the culture of consumption)—are not embedded in crime networks to any significant extent (see e.g. Forsyth and Castro, 2007; Redding and Abagnale, 2003). The seemingly endless biographies and ghosted autobiographies of the Kray brothers and their entourage focus on the violence and extortion rather than the frauds that helped sustain their London 'empire' in the 1960s. This applies also to the Jake Arnott fictional trilogy, where even The Long Firm—which from the title should be about bankruptcy frauds (Levi, 2008a)—is almost all about sex and violence. The main fraud work that focuses us on networks is David Maurer's classic anthropological book *The Big Con* (2000, originally 1940). There, the assistant grifters were drawn from the world of (white) professional thieves about whom Sutherland (1937) wrote, while the principals were specialist confidence men. Maurer describes evocatively the way in which the fraudsters set up their 'marks' (targets) in both short and long cons, and the sometimes elaborate storefronts they used for their scams (as seen in the movie The Sting, which was based on the book).

The contemporary equivalents of these are telemarketing fraudsters: 'boiler room' operators, who in one recent case (author interview with police) worked in a room with a tape continuously playing in the background to simulate a busy stock brokerage; and the '419' advance fee fraudsters who may hire or 'borrow' rooms when they know the legitimate users are away to use as props in their stings. In some investment scams involving wines and spirits, or ostriches, the operators do have some real products on show, but vastly fewer than those 'purchased' by the victims.

How do they find their targets? This can be through random dialling of telephone directory entries; through share registers of public companies; through perusal of advertisements in personal columns, articles about wealthy people in the media; and through the use/purchase of existing 'sucker lists' (which, except for serial fraudsters reusing their old lists, is the only method that would require contact with other offenders). Shover et al. (2003) note that fraudulent firms employ sales agents who work from 'lead', or 'mooch', lists purchased from any of dozens of businesses that compile and sell information on consumer behaviour and preferences. My interviews with investigators in several countries (2008) suggest that exchanges of 'mooch lists' are extensive and rapid—once someone has subscribed to one lottery or other product by internet, post or telephone, they soon experience allied scam 'offers' from other fraudsters, suggesting that there is a sufficiently broad scope for fraudsters to be non-competitive.

Holtfreter et al. (2008) conducted an interesting study in Florida to examine whether low self-control was related to consumer fraud victimization. They distinguished between the targeting and actual victimization of the public and demonstrated that male consumers had a higher risk of being targeted (as in a previous case study of Ponzi investment fraud by Trahan et al., 2005), noting that since it is difficult for outsiders to judge whether people they do not know will engage in risky behaviour, demographic correlates or targeting are difficult to specify. They showed that fraud victimization was not a random event because, although the net may be cast at random, the financial behaviour of consumers was key. Traditional indicators of victimization such as going to bars at night were unrelated to fraud targeting and fraud victimization risk. So reducing financial risk-taking specifically might reduce the extent to which people with low self-control might become victims of fraud, though it would not have an impact on other forms of victimization risk. They conclude (2005: 209) that:

> Perpetrators choose potential victims based on obvious indicators of vulnerability .... Financial risk-taking ... is not an easily recognizable manifestation of low self-control that fraudsters can observe and use to target potential victims. On the other hand, the routine activities of consumers such as remote purchasing methods, are detected more easily by perpetrators of fraud.

This leads to targeting of people irrespective of their levels of self-control.

How are telemarketing fraudsters organized? Some fraudulent telemarketing organizations consist of two or three persons who operate in a community for only a few days or weeks before moving on. These 'rip and tear' operators depend on the months-long lapse between the time they begin operating and the time law enforcement and consumer protection agencies become aware of and target them. Somewhat larger 'boiler rooms' feature extensive telephone banks and large numbers of sales agents. Larger telemarketing operations commonly take on the characteristics of formal organizations, with hierarchies, a division of labour, graduated pay and advancement opportunities. Those who are ill-suited to cold call selling or who develop moral qualms simply leave the business.

In terms of 'scripts', if they wanted to commit a 'boiler room' fraud without being licensed, then all they would need is an office, a good telephone system and salespeople willing and able to persuade 'punters' to buy shares for more than they were worth. Unlike the cons described by Maurer—which are pure artifices and therefore must hire willing conspirators—the investment scams can hire junior personnel through advertisements and agencies who may be quite ignorant of the true rationale of the business. Only the originators may be active criminals. Some telephone salespeople may be experienced multi-scam participants (Stevenson, 1998; Shover et al., 2003, 2004), but others may simply have the (wilful or not) ethical blindness of commission-based income-generators: the sort of people responsible not just for telemarketing frauds but for financial services industry 'misselling' when working for major banks and insurance firms, leading to payments of hundreds of millions of pounds in compensation by the companies.[17] Some of those interviewed by Shover et al. (2003) had previous sales experience before beginning the work, but most did not: they either responded to ads in the newspaper or were recruited by acquaintances who boasted about the money they were making. Many were not succeeding at conventional careers, and telemarketing came along at a time when they needed to show that they could make something of themselves. They believed they were outstanding salespersons, who could sell over the telephone despite resistance from those they contacted; and they got a 'high' from doing so (see Katz, 1990; and Levi, 2008a for the emotional rewards from crime commission). These salespeople are unlikely to come from the 'general criminal classes' but rather from people with persuasive skills (some of whom may be 'shaken out' from financial services firms in recession), recruited by advertisement and via agencies, and incentivized by high commission and low basic pay. Such generic persuasion techniques are discussed by Cialdini (2007).

Shover et al. (2003) state that the sales agent generally works from a script that lays out successful sales approaches and responses. Promising contacts are turned over to a 'closer', a more experienced and better-paid sales agent. The hierarchy of the firms and the routine of turning prospects over to more experienced closers explain why victims typically report contact with multiple salespersons.

What factors influence the choice of venue for boiler rooms and their modus operandi? From UK cases examined, boiler rooms are commonly based abroad (e.g. in Spain, where police interest is low), never seek authorization by the Financial Services Authority (FSA)—which is a legal requirement to sell securities in the UK—and use high pressure sales and telephone techniques (author interviews with UK officials and police). One more sophisticated technique is to approach a small UK company not listed on the Stock Exchange and propose to raise capital by selling £100,000 worth of shares in that company on their behalf. Of this £100,000, the boiler room would agree to take 60 per cent as its fee, leaving the small company with £40,000 capital. In reality, the boiler room will 'cold call' UK investors to sell the shares at up to 100 per cent over the agreed price, take their fee and vanish. The small companies involved may become liable to refund investors the full price paid for their shares. There are several variations on the method of committing the crime:

- complete con, where there are no shares in existence;
- different instruments used—stock, currency options (and even bull sperm);
- restricted (e.g. US 'Regulation S'), worthless or over-priced shares;
- purported involvement in raising capital for companies;
- market manipulation where there are shares in existence and a (limited) market;
- deceptive share promotion via bulletin boards.

If the fraudsters have sufficient nerve, they can seek to become regulated in one EU country and obtain a 'passport' to operate in another under EU single market regulations, using that as a base for fraud and making it difficult for local regulators to intervene to close them down. In all of these cases, what the boiler room is really selling is deceptive and worthless expectations.

The growth in cross-border consumer fraud operations can be illustrated by data from the US. (No equivalent data are yet available for the UK.) During the calendar year 2007, the US multi-agency Consumer Sentinel (which acts as a one-stop shop for complaints) received over 835,000 complaints—258,000 identity theft and 577,000 fraud-related complaints: the latter rose from 428,000 in 2006. Fifteen percent of the fraud-related complaints were cross-border fraud-related, down as a percentage (rather than as a number) from 23 per cent in 2006, reflecting the growth in fraud complaints rather than the number of cross-border cases.[18]

Foreign Money Offers was the leading product/service category in US consumers' cross-border complaints (12%), followed by Prizes/Sweepstakes/Gifts (11%), Shop-at-Home/Catalogue Sales (8%), Lotteries/Lottery Ticket Buying Clubs (7%), and Internet Auction (5%). Internet-related complaints comprised 59 per cent (50,907) of the total cross-border fraud complaints (86,074) received during calendar year 2007. To give some idea of the distribution of complaints (which includes reports from Australian, British and Canadian authorities), table 2 below tracks changes over time (Federal Trade Commission, 2008):

Although complaints about overseas businesses may not reflect nationality of the perpetrators, it may also illuminate to consider the amounts of money at stake ($194 million—around £100 million in 2007) see table 3,

**Table 2.** Cross-border fraud complaints by consumer and company location[a] (calendar years 2005–2007)

| CY | US consumers against companies located in Canada (%) | US consumers against companies located in other foreign countries (%) | Canadian consumers against companies located in the US (%) | Canadian consumers against companies located in other foreign countries (%) | Foreign consumers against companies located in the US or Canada (%) |
|----|----|----|----|----|----|
| 2005 | 21 | 64 | 5 | 4 | 6 |
| 2006 | 26 | 59 | 5 | 4 | 6 |
| 2007 | 21 | 62 | 6 | 5 | 6 |

*Note*: [a]Percentages are based on the total number of cross-border fraud complaints for each calendar year: CY-2005 = 87,193; CY-2006 = 97,034 and CY-2007 = 86,074.

from which should be deducted business costs to fraudsters. These may be fairly modest, even assuming they pay for their communications.

In a longer work it would be possible to draw parallels, in terms of the dynamics between setting and criminal act, in relation to a broader range of identity and other frauds: for example, application frauds and insurance frauds. If we take mortgage frauds, for example, fraud typically takes two forms: customers lying about their own means—i.e., exaggerating their income—and/or falsifying documents, such as creating fake payslips that show they earn an amount large enough to justify the mortgage they need, even if it is a multiple of their real income. This can be done simply by printing fake payslips, if necessary on a colour printer. Self-certificated mortgages (at higher interest rates) were allowed to cater for the increasing number of self-employed persons who could not produce genuine pay slips. (They might also include their 'off the books' income!) One incentive for mortgage introducers is that they are paid commission; one incentive for lenders is that they have sales targets to hit and performance bonuses to get, and non-payment usually comes much later. In some cases, the borrower is told there is no way they are going to get the mortgage they want with their income, and that they should leave that part of the mortgage application form blank. After they have gone, the broker inserts the false income. In the US particularly, there have been widespread scandals relating to commission-hungry brokers lying to purchasers about the affordability of mortgages, which they discover only when the initial low rates expire. In other cases, the would-be purchaser colludes with the broker. In other cases still, the broker (or lawyer) purchases the properties for themselves as beneficial owner, using the names and real or fictitious income details of clients. In a rising market, where there is demand (for example from students) for rental properties, fraudulent purchasers see little downside risk. In some cases,

**Table 3.** Fraud complaints and amount paid by US consumers against companies located in other foreign countries (calendar years 2005–2007)

| CY | Total no. of complaints | Complaints reporting amount paid | Percentage of complaints reporting amount paid | Amount paid reported | Average amount paid | Median amount paid |
|---|---|---|---|---|---|---|
| 2005 | 55,474 | 28,729 | 52 | US$136,649,579 | US$4757 | US$1304 |
| 2006 | 57,644 | 50,471 | 88 | US$142,457,801 | US$2823 | US$1050 |
| 2007 | 53,629 | 47,388 | 88 | US$194,032,819 | US$4095 | US$750 |

valuers from a restricted panel are aware that the lenders need to lend and their judgment is swayed by this to give the valuation required to enable the mortgage to be granted: this is especially so where all the parties' desires are in the same direction (author interviews with surveyors, 1980s and 2008). However when the market turns, as it did in 2007 (and earlier in the US), these frauds are shaken out as people cannot keep up with repayments.

## Ethnicity, nationality and the supply of offenders

The conventional way in which Organised Crime Situation Reports or their recent variant threat assessments have worked (see Edwards and Levi, this volume) has been to identify national or ethnic groups involved in serious crimes for gain. To some extent those chosen for this association reflect those groups law enforcement and intelligence agencies have access to, and are self-justifying in 'intelligence-led policing'.[19] Many national and religious groups have occupied places in the demonology of crime, but in the particular case of fraud, the two most common demons are Jews and Nigerians. Ichheiser (1944), reviewing the social psychology of anti-Semitism, argued that

> 'Gangsters' and 'swindlers' may be considered ... as two *personified symbols* of ... fundamental forms of danger in social life .... Especially, in times like our own, characterized by deep economic insecurities, ideological confusion, fluidity and impenetrability of intricate social processes, by propaganda, advertising, adulteration of goods, the man in the street feels himself far more deeply threatened by those rather 'invisible' social dangers than by overt coercion and violence. And he is getting more and more suspicious that those invisible processes by which he is threatened are intentionally, and for someone's advantage, manipulated by some kind of swindlers 'behind the scenes.' Consequently the swindler ... *becomes the main symbol of the predominant fear.*

There is no need here to review the history of imagery that associated Jews with swindling, but it remains a much more restrained sub-text in the post-Hitler period, which understandably generates caution in its treatment in criminological and media circles. I have made a decision here to include this aspect of 'the supply of fraudsters' to fraud networks because it is a popular financial services industry and law enforcement theme. Analysis of prosecution cases cannot but reflect any criteria that underlie the reporting, investigation and prosecution processes, and so factors in the above that protect social elites (such as those involved in Enron or in price-fixing cartels) might lead to their under-representation compared with social outsiders. Likewise, negative social stereotypes (for example about who 'dangerous criminals' are) that affected these processes will lead to over-representation.

The analysis of white-collar offenders in the US Federal courts by Weisburd et al. (1991)—using data largely drawn from the 1970s—showed that two thirds had no previous convictions but of those who had, only one in five had previously been convicted of white-collar crime. The ethnicity of offenders varies by offence type: anti-trust and securities offenders were 99 per cent white; but around a quarter of credit card fraud, mail fraud and bank embezzlers were non-white. Jews were significantly over-represented among securities offenders (though not compared with their numbers in the general securities industry); but not among other white-collar offences. Although the research on this issue has not been intensive, by inspection similar remarks might be made about the UK in the initial years of the Serious Fraud Office, but not subsequently. Thus all four convicted (but none of those acquitted) in the Guinness case (Levi, 1991) were Jewish in origin (though CEO Ernest Saunders had converted to Christianity). However overall, neither Jews nor Asians nor any other religious, ethnic or national group are significantly over-represented in UK SFO cases, taking account of their numbers in the corporate and financial services industries. Of course one needs no 'racial' theories about these connections, for they are often relationships of propinquity and mutual trust. By volume, most fraudsters are blue-collar rather than white-collar in background (Weisburd et al., 2001; Piquero and Benson, 2004), and some sub-sets of American offenders (for example 'identity fraudsters') are disproportionately black or Hispanic (Copes and Vieraitis, 2007). This merely reflects the fact that some types of fraud can be accomplished by 'ordinary' offenders, and there is a ready supply of willing offenders from poorer communities who would commit fraud if they had the technical and social skills required and the confidence to engage in such crimes. Whether many such persons would have the verbal skills to commit securities frauds—even 'boiler room' and suchlike that do not require formal qualifications—is more doubtful, but payment card and social security frauds are relatively low-skilled.

Discussions about 'fraud' with bankers in many parts of the world immediately throw up the word 'Nigerians' (author interviews; see also Peel, 2006 and Glenny, 2008). As with many areas of 'organized crime', international Diasporas have become a common focus of risk discourses, and Nigerians represent a nationality whose Diasporas—whether in Nigeria itself or in Australia, Ghana, Ireland, the Netherlands, North America,

Russia, South Africa or the UK (to mention only some countries where Nigerian fraud networks have been observed)—are more visibly active than most in the sphere of fraud. See also Aning, 2007; Smith, 2007 and United Nations, 2005. Peel (2006) has demonstrated that some areas and tribes are more likely than others to be involved in such frauds, and they tend to be loose confederations rather than a tight hierarchy of offenders. He notes (pp. 22–23) that fraudsters buy respectability and even adoration if they channel some of their money back to their impoverished home towns. As Mertonian strain theory might lead us to expect, locals recognize what they have gained while displaying little interest in how they have obtained it. The explanations for heavy involvement in financial crime of Igbo people from the country's east include

(1) The social and economic marginalization (and exclusion from government patronage) both before the 1967–70 civil war and since.
(2) Policing is particularly poor there and in Lagos and Delta state, which are also rich sources of financial crime.
(3) The east has the kind of entrepreneurial commercial centres around which this type of crime will tend to be found. In Northern Nigeria, by contrast, there is a much smaller private sector and more government-based corruption. In Yorubaland in the west, scams are often linked directly to the accounting, banking and legal professions, which traditionally attract many Yoruba.

One might add that from the point of view of the Nigerian people themselves, these 419 frauds are far less harmful than the networks of corruption and patronage among military and civilian leaders who—especially but far from exclusively under military dictatorships—have stolen billions of dollars of income from the Nigerian oil production and from contracts, and who have converted these funds for their own use: the so-called 'curse of oil'. Between the British police and the Nigerian Economic and Financial Crime Commission during the time of President Obasanjo,[20] four Nigerian state governors were charged with money laundering and/or fraud. But the 419s and other 'advance fee' scams—called because people, once hooked, usually become trapped into paying fees to advance the payment of 'their' money—are the 'outward-facing' side of Nigerian fraud and involve losses to Westerners.

More generally in cybercrimes for gain (including payment card fraud), though there are plenty of indigenous fraudsters in the UK and the US, Eastern Europeans have developed a reputation for technical skill and cross-border operations. There is nothing exclusive about these nationalities, but in identified American and British cases (which are only partly the product of what law enforcement choose to pursue), Lithuanians, Rumanians and Russians predominate in such forms of fraud, though Brazilians are playing an increasing role. Rumanians also have played a significant role in the use in the UK of technical devices on ATMs (such as the Lebanese Loop—first developed by Lebanese crime groups and now in decline due to technical prevention improvements) to capture payment card

PINs. However it is less obvious what the analytical value is of such ethnic and national identifiers, which unintentionally scapegoat large classes of individuals who may be largely innocent of involvement in crime.

Trahan et al. (2005) link fraud victim behaviour to 'the American dream', applying interestingly the more general criminological analysis of Messner and Rosenfeld (2001). Yet it is not obvious how specific to America this dream (or nightmare) is. Where people have some IT education and intelligence but few legitimate opportunities in their home areas, they often seek opportunities elsewhere. Especially given legal migration and employment controls (supplemented perhaps by discrimination)—or fewer good jobs available for anyone in their place of emigration than they expected—they may be tempted by offers from others seeking co-offenders or they may develop their own fraud schemes. This was what drove the emigration of (non-Jewish) Germans to London in the mid-19th century, whereupon some of them turned to bankruptcy fraud, often against German companies (Levi, 2008a). Thus it is unsurprising that irrespective of any prejudices among social control agencies, we get clusters of offenders with similar backgrounds: colour, language (which also shelters from surveillance), and geography (people sharing ethnicities, nationality and religion often live close to each other) all contribute.

## Conclusion

Globalization of crime is part of contingent relationships between settings, with their rich and varied opportunities (reflecting patterns of business, consumer and investment activities), the abilities of would-be perpetrators to recognize and act on those opportunities (the 'crime scripts' perspective), and their interactions with controls, including law enforcement (touched only lightly upon here). Constructs of 'organized crime' should be (and are becoming) less obsessed with the structure of groups than with what people need from the largely illicit and largely licit worlds to go about the business of fraud. In other words, analysis of 'organized-ness' is becoming decentred and re-understood as much in terms of the settings in which offending and its precursors can take place as in terms of the acts themselves.

Such observations or claims about the contested and shifting nature of analysis over time complicate the already difficult question of whether fraud 'itself' has changed over the years. It seems reasonable to reflect on two 'historical' questions:

(1) In what respects has fraudulent activity changed, in terms of the sorts of techniques and organization that are or can be used, in relation to the efforts made (intentionally or not) to prevent frauds? And

(2) In what respects has the world of fraud changed and what would the sort of people with the sort of skill sets/networks who committed frauds in the 1960s and 1970s have contemplated doing today?

In relation to the first question, although the basic techniques used by fraudsters in the 1960s are still available today, especially against those investors and trade creditors who make only modest enquiries, the professionalization of investor protection and credit management in the UK, as well as consumer media interest, makes the commission of such frauds harder. E-commerce, the growth of lightweight, high value electronic products, and the technology of rapid delivery anywhere in the world have cut down decision times and opened up domestic and foreign markets to fraudsters within and outside the UK. At the high end of insolvency frauds, it seems doubtful whether the more skilful abuses of insolvency by those who, for example, establish beneficially owned corporate fronts offshore and then create artificial debts to them which enable them to vote in friendly liquidators or administrators, are any harder to commit or are any more likely to be punished today than they were 30 years ago. Formal social control—the police and criminal courts—has not been particularly interested in frauds other than the more visibly harmful 'widows and orphans' cases. There has been a growth in 'civil recovery' regimes, applying financial investigation and asset forfeiture (irrespective of criminal conviction) to supplement the post-conviction confiscation remedies that have replaced the Criminal Bankruptcy Orders. However even if they have substantial confiscatable savings rather than (as did the high-spending long-firm fraudsters interviewed by Levi, 2008 and the telemarketers interviewed by Shover et al., 2003, for example) spending 'their' proceeds as they went along, few fraudsters are high profile career criminals of a seriousness level that would interest the Serious and Organised Crime Agency. This question is connected to the second.

What forms of fraud constitute a 'rational choice' depends on the confidence, skills and contact set of any given individual offenders. The presence or absence of 'crime networks' known to and trusted by the willing offender makes a difference to 'crime capacitation': an issue often neglected in individualized explanations of involvement in crime. Choice of crime type might also be affected by age. Those offenders who were in their 50s and over might not be attracted towards the technological challenges of cyber-activities, and—except via close encounters on porn sites, in night clubs, or in prisons—the age gap might apply to co-criminality as it does to other features of contemporary life. So today's new generation fraudsters might gravitate towards more 'techie' forms of fraud, whereas if they were in late career, it might seem too risky to adapt in unfamiliar territory unless they could find someone younger to collaborate with. This is a general proposition about the relationship between age and risk-taking/innovation. Some fraudsters display a remarkable aptitude for creativity and constant testing out of commercial systems and private individuals for signs of weakness. This focus on 'criminal transferable skills'—the set of aptitudes including social networking individual/sets of offenders have—concentrates our attention on offender creativity, energy and social networking skills in finding co-offenders (or 'turning' non-offenders into co-offenders) and in adapting techniques: many offenders (and non-offenders) lack one or all of these qualities.

Objectively, there are far more opportunities for disintermediated crime in late modernity than in the post-war decades. With only modest sophistication, the internet and social constructions of what is normal have made it easier for foreign natural and legal persons to defraud consumers and suppliers, for example via counterfeited or cloned payment cards. Fraudsters could be involved in the theft of personal data from garbage ('bin raiding') or by hacking into data storage facilities; or account manipulation by insiders, whether in call centres or elsewhere. (The offshoring of call centres led to periodic media alarm stories about blackmail and corruption in India: but it is nonsensical to think that this cannot happen in the UK, with badly paid staff and high turnover ratios. Indeed, there may be tougher regimes in Indian call centres—staff searches and prohibitions on mobile phones in the premises—than might be allowed in the UK.) Rings of staged accidents with claims for hard-to-falsify personal injuries would be within the skill set of some (once they worked out what to do), as would organized benefit fraud and—especially—the sale of counterfeit products, whose quality digital technology has done so much to improve, despite the best efforts of the anti-counterfeiting coalitions. For the more adventurous, scams can involve some currently fashionable musical or sporting events, or a social cause such as 'renewable energy'. One may expect some future scams involving carbon trading. The underlying concepts were available to investors at the time of the South Sea Bubble, but some investors in each subsequent generation and/or country have to learn the lessons for themselves. Arguably, as evidenced by declining savings ratios and the willingness to borrow against the legal security of homes in the UK and elsewhere, there has been a step change in people's expectations of steady state or rising affluence, and resistance to personal financial decline. When times get hard as they have done in the period 2007-09, people may take more risks to avoid downward socio-economic mobility, and this offers opportunities to fraudsters. At a policy level, this means that a focus on 'regulating' rather than 'eliminating' frauds is sensible: what constitutes an acceptable level of fraud may depend on who the victims are, how much they can afford to lose, and the collateral damage caused.

## Notes

1 Professor of Criminology, Cardiff University. Contact details Levi@ Cardiff.ac.uk. The author is grateful for the ESRC Professorial Fellowship RES-051–27–0208, under whose auspices this research was conducted. I also thank Nicholas Dorn for comments on an earlier version of this article.
2 Though one would not overstate the strength in depth of quality research on the organization of any crimes.

3  This is a technical neologism rather than the common language sense of 'script'.

4  There is an ongoing debate, which we bypass here, about terminology in the white-collar and corporate crime arenas (see e.g. Levi, 2008a). Financial crime (more commonly 'economic crime' in Europe) is a term broader than fraud, which also includes corruption and money-laundering.

5  Consider this in relation to the UK and the European National Intelligence Model, in which Level 1 refers to crimes within a police force area; Level 2 to crimes within the UK but involving more than one force area; and level 3 refers to international crimes. Does the mere fact that money is transferred overseas or credit cards are used fraudulently overseas make them level 3 crimes?

6  In some cases, they may encounter people (or companies) they consider to be potential suckers and then develop ways of fleecing them. There is a flexibility here that is poorly captured in the term 'organized crime'.

7  Rather than 'suspicious activities' or 'suspicious transactions', as is the official terminology, I consider it more analytically accurate to term them suspected transactions. Electronic transfers create a clearer audit trail if and when identified and followed than do cash movements.

8  I interviewed one offender who would have had difficulty in disposing of a truckload of yoghurt, had he not been arrested before he dealt with the dilemma. One 19th century fraudster obtained from Germany a gross (144) of artificial glass eyes which he was unable to sell and in the end, he had to dispose of for the price of the postage it cost to obtain them (Levi, 2008a).

9  The sanctions would have to be significant in terms of their own values in the 'communities' (if any) they inhabit. Cultural variations in legitimacy can be quite broad.

10  This echoes other practical failures in the fraud attempts of others, like taking too long a lunch break and therefore not being in the office when the bank rang to verify that the £25 million transfer request to a new account was intentional. These also give willing future offenders some useful tips to avoid!

11  Unless the purchases on 'borrowed' card data are picked up by the sophisticated electronic systems that model customer transaction patterns and contact customers proactively if there are transactions that do not fit their profiles.

12  The longer and more intensive an investigation, the more likely it is that surveillance will generate an accurate model of interactions between players in the network. Morselli and Roy correctly argue that when combined with an understanding of the roles that are hard to substitute, Social Network Analysis gives a better idea of the impact of enforcement interventions against central players. Sometimes one only learns impact after the operation/arrests, and in my view, one key question is whether in practice investigations do continue to test the disruptive effects: this might be hard to justify both legally (in terms of criteria for surveillance authorization) and financially (given severe constraints on police finances – someone has to be paid to listen, and this is especially expensive in foreign languages). Boundary assessments for determining the limits of social networks may be harder in fraud than in some other networks.

13  Though in some European countries, for example, people with criminal records are not allowed to become company directors.

14  This is not a recent issue. Lefkowitz (1963: 51) notes: 'In recent years, persons with criminal records have attempted by various guises to infiltrate the securities market, posing major problems for governmental regulatory agencies in the securities field. New York State has attempted by statute to eliminate persons with felony convictions from engaging in the securities business. Another problem in New York was high-pressure "boiler room" operations. A New York statute now requires registration of securities salesmen, in an effort to alleviate that problem. The gangster element has found it increasingly difficult to conduct business in New York under these enactments.'

15  Between 2000 and 2007, 'card not present' losses on UK-issued cards rose from £72.9 million to £290.5 million. In 2007, there were over 2 million 'card not present' frauds in England and Wales, a rise of 58 per cent by volume. However while the frauds of this kind quadrupled 2000–2007, online shopping increased tenfold to £34 billion. So the rise in fraud was modest compared with the growth in this form of consumer behaviour.

16  Hence some connection between payment card fraud and the financing of the Tamil Tigers (LTTE): but what proportion even of Sri Lankan card fraud went to finance terrorism rather than to sustain impoverished people or make some foreigners wealthy remains unknown—another example of the loose conceptualization of the link between organized crime and terrorism.

17  The distinction between mis-selling and fraud can be a fine one at times. The UK Financial Services Authority has set out criteria for judging mis-selling (http://www.fsa.gov.uk/pages/Library/Communication/PR/2003/052.shtml), stating 'it is the suitability of the recommendation for the consumer, not the investment performance of the product that matters. As long as suitability was established at the time of sale, and the required explanation of risk made, then consumer dissatisfaction about investment returns achieved gives no basis for an allegation of mis-selling. Investment performance may be relevant in assessing redress due where mis-selling is shown to have occurred.'

18  A fraud complaint is 'cross-border' if: (1) a US consumer complained about a company located in Canada or another foreign country; (2) a Canadian consumer complained about a company located in the US or another foreign country; or (3) a consumer from a foreign country (e.g. the UK or Australia) complained about a company located in the US or Canada. Company location is based on addresses reported by the complaining consumers and, thus, likely understates the number of cross-border complaints. In some instances the company address provided by the consumer actually may be a mail drop in the consumer's country rather than the physical location of the company in a foreign country, and in other cases, the consumer does not know whether the location is in the US or abroad.

19  'There is a well-justified fear that raids [by the UK Borders and Immigration Agency] have focused on ethnic minority businesses. The list provided on the Home Office website shows that 95% of those targeted

have been Indian, Bangladeshi, Chinese, Vietnamese and Turkish-run.' Such businesses are the easiest 'low hanging fruit' to fulfil organizational targets, compared with other workers in the hotel and food picking/production trades. (http://www.guardian.co.uk/commentisfree/2008/jul/16/humanrights.immi grationpolicy.)

20  After Obasanjo's departure from office, the head and then the acting head of the EFCC were replaced in 2008, suggesting to some the view of the new regime that they had become over-active in combating elites. Action against 419 fraudsters was more acceptable, since these were not usually connected to government elites (interviews with police and other officials, 2008). Despite the reputational damage 419 frauds and governmental corruption were causing to Nigeria, it seems unlikely that much of this policing activity in Nigeria would have taken place had the country not been 'blacklisted' by the Financial Action Task Force for inadequate anti-money laundering processes.

## References

Aning; Kwesi (2007) 'Are there Emerging West African Criminal Networks? The Case of Ghana' *Global Crime* 8(3): 193–212.

Black, William (2005) *The Best Way to Rob a Bank is to Own One*. Austin, TX: University of Texas Press.

Block, Alan (1991) *Masters of Paradise: Organized Crime and the Internal Revenue Service in the Bahamas*. New Jersey: Transaction.

Block, Alan and Constance Weaver (2004) *All is Clouded by Desire*. New York: Praeger.

Calavita, Kitty and Henry Pontell (1993) 'Savings and Loan Fraud as Organized Crime: Toward a Conceptual Typology of Corporate Illegality', *Criminology* 31(4): 519–48.

Cialdini, Robert (2007) *Influence: the Psychology of Persuasion*, 2nd edn. New York: HarperCollins.

Copes, Heith and Lynne Vieraitis (2007) 'Identity Theft: Assessing Offenders' Strategies and Perceptions of Risk'. Technical Report for National Institute of Justice. NCJ 219122. NIJ Grant No. 2005-IJ-CX-0012.

Copes, Heith and Lynne Vieraitis (2008) 'Stealing Identities: The Risks, Rewards and Strategies of Identity Theft', in Megan McNally and Graham Newman (eds). *Perspectives on Identity Theft*. New York: Criminal Justice Press.

Cornish, Derek (1994) 'The Procedural Analysis of Offending and its Relevance for Situational Prevention', in Ron Clarke (ed.), *Crime Prevention Studies*, vol. 3. Monsey, NY: Criminal Justice Press.

Cornish, Derek and Ron Clarke (2002) 'Analyzing Organized Crimes', in Alexis Piquero and Stephen Tibbetts (eds) *Rational Choice and Criminal Behaviour*. London: Routledge.

Cressey, Don (1955) *Other People's Money*. New York: Free Press.

Diih, Sorle (2005) *The Infiltration of the New York's Financial Market by Organised Crime: Pressures and Controls*, unpublished Ph.D. thesis, Cardiff University.

Federal Trade Commission (2008) Consumer Fraud and Identity Theft Complaint Data January–December 2007. Online: http://www.ftc.gov/sentinel/reports/sentinel-annual-reports/sentinel-cy2007.pdf.

Felson, Marcus (2002) *Crime and Everyday Life*. Thousand Oaks CA: Sage.

Felson, Marcus (2003) 'The Process of Co-offending', in Martha Smith and Derek Cornish (eds) *Theory for Practice in Situational Crime Prevention, Crime Prevention Studies* vol. 16, pp. 149– 67. Mounsey, NJ: Criminal Justice Press.

Felson, Marcus (2006) *Crime and Nature*, Thousand Oaks CA: Sage.

Forsyth, Neil and Castro, Elliott (2007) *Other People's Money: The Rise and Fall of Britain's Most Audacious Fraudster*. London: Sidgwick and Jackson.

Glenny, Misha (2008) *McMafia: Crime without Frontiers*. London: Random House.

Harding, Chris (2007) *Criminal Enterprise: Individuals, Organisations and Criminal Responsibility*. Cullompton: Willan.

Hertzog, Arthur (2003) *Vesco: From Wall Street to Castro's Cuba*. New York: Universe.

Holtfreter, Kristy, Michael Reisig and Travis Pratt (2008) 'Low self-Control, Routine Activities and Fraud Victimization', *Criminology* 46(1): 189–220.

Ichheiser, Gustav (1944) 'Fear of Violence and Fear of Fraud: With Some Remarks on the Social Psychology of Antisemitism', *Sociometry* 7(4): 376–83.

Katz, Jack (1990) *Seductions of Crime*. New York: Basic Books.

Leeson, Nick (1997) *Rogue Trader*. London: Time Warner.

Lefkowitz, Louis (1963) 'New York Criminal Infiltration of the Securities Industry', *The Annals of the American Academy of Political and Social Science* 347(1): 51–7.

Levi, Michael (1991) 'Sentencing white-collar Crime in the Dark? Reflections on the Guinness Four', *The Howard Journal of Criminal Justice* 30(4): 257–79.

Levi, Michael (2003) 'Organising and controlling payment card fraud: fraudsters and their operational environment', *Security Journal*, (16)2, pp. 21–30.

Levi, Michael (2008a) *The Phantom Capitalists: the Organisation and Control of Long-Firm Fraud*, 2nd edn. Aldershot: Ashgate.

Levi, Michael (2008b) 'Combating Identity and Other Forms of Payment Fraud in the UK: An Analytical History', in Megan McNally and Graham Newman (eds) *Perspectives on Identity Theft*. Monsey, NJ: Criminal Justice Press.

Levi, Michael, John Burrows, Matthew Fleming, and Matt Hopkins, with the assistance of Kent Matthews (2007) *The Nature, Extent and Economic Impact of Fraud in the UK*. London: Association of Chief Police Officers. Online: http://www.acpo.police.uk/asp/policies/Data/Fraud%20in%20the%20UK.pdf

Levi, Michael and John Burrows (2008) 'Measuring the Impact of Fraud in the UK: A Conceptual and Empirical Journey', *British Journal of Criminology* 48(3): 293–318.

Levi, Michael and Peter Reuter (2006) 'Money Laundering', in Michael Tonry (ed.) *Crime and Justice: A Review of Research*, vol. 34, pp. 289–375. Chicago: Chicago University Press.

Levi, Michael and Peter Reuter (2008) 'Money Laundering', in Michael Tonry (ed.) *Handbook of Crime and Public Policy*. New York: Oxford University Press.

McIntosh, Mary (1971) 'Changes in the organisation of thieving', in Stan Cohen (ed.) *Images of Deviance*. London: Penguin.

Messner, Steven and Richard Rosenfield (2001) *Crime and the American Dream*. Belmont CA: Wadsworth.

Morselli, Carlo (2005) *Contacts, Opportunities and Criminal Enterprise*. Toronto: University of Toronto Press.

Morselli, Carlo and Julie Roy (2008) 'Brokerage Qualifications in Ringing Operations', *Criminology* 46(1): 71–98.

Passas, Nikos (2005) Informal Value Transfer Systems, Terrorism and Money Laundering. Online: http://www.ncjrs.org/pdffiles1/nij/grants/208301.pdf

Peel, Michael (2006) *Nigeria-Related Financial Crime and its Links with Britain*, London: Chatham House.

Piquero, Nicole Leeper and Michael Benson (2004) 'White-Collar Crime and Criminal Careers: Specifying a Trajectory of Punctuated Situational Offending', *Journal of Contemporary Criminal Justice* 20(2): 148–65.

Raw, Charles, Geoffrey Hodgson, and Bruce Page (1971) *Do You Sincerely Want to be Rich?*. New York: Viking.

Redding, Stan and Frank Abagnale (2003) *Catch Me If You Can: The True Story of a Real Fake*. London: Mainstream.

Shapiro, Susan (1984) *Wayward Capitalists*, New Haven: Yale University Press.

Shover, Neal, Glenn S. Coffey and Dick Hobbs (2003) 'Crime on the line: Telemarketing and the Changing Nature of Professional crime,' *British Journal of Criminology* 43(7): 489–505.

Shover, Neal, Glenn S. Coffey and Clinton R. Sanders (2004) [p4] 'Dialing for Dollars: Opportunities, Justifications, and Telemarketing Fraud', *Qualitative Sociology* 27(1): 59–75.

Smith, Daniel (2007) *A Culture of Corruption* Princeton, NJ: Prince University Press.

Stevenson, Robert (1998) *The Boiler Room and Other Telephone Sales Scams*. Urbana: University of Illinois Press.

Sutherland, Edwin (1937) *The Professional Thief*. Chicago: University of Chicago Press.

Tillman, Robert and Michael Indergaard (2005) *Pump and Dump: The Rancid Rules of the New Economy*. New Brunswick, NJ: Rutgers University Press.

Tillman, Robert and Michael Indergaard (2007a) 'Corporate Corruption in the New Economy,' in Henry Pontell and Gilbert Geis (eds) *International Handbook of White-Collar and Corporate Crime*. New York: Springer.

Tillman, Robert and Michael Indergaard (2007b) Control Overrides in Financial Statement Fraud, Report for the Institute of Fraud Prevention. Online: http://www.theifp.org/research%20grants/tillman%20final%20report_revised_mac-orginal-EDITED.pdf

Trahan, Adam, James Marquart and Janet Mullings (2005) 'Fraud and the American Dream: Towards an Understanding of Fraud Victimization', *Deviant Behavior* 26: 601–20.

Tremblay, Pierre (1993) 'Searching for Suitable co-offenders', in Ron Clarke and Marcus Elson (eds) *Routine Activity and Rational Choice*, Edison, NJ: Transaction.

United Nations (2005) Transnational Organized Crime in the West African Region, United Nations, New York.

Weisburd, David, Stanton Wheeler and Elin Waring (1991) *Crimes of the Middle Classes: White Collar Offenders in the Federal Courts*. Princeton: Yale University Press.

Weisburd, David, Elin Waring and Ellen Chayet (2001) *White-Collar Crime and Criminal Careers*. Cambridge: Cambridge University Press.

# Erratum

*Criminology & Criminal Justice* 8(4)
Organized fraud and organizing frauds: Unpacking research on networks and organization
Original article DOI: 10.1177/1748895808096470

In this article, the author's affiliation on p. 389 should have appeared as Cardiff University, UK.

The author's biography on p. 419 should have appeared as follows:

DR. MICHAEL LEVI has been Professor of Criminology at Cardiff University since 1991. In 2007, he began a 3-year ESRC Professorial Fellowship (RES-051–27–0208) to develop research on financial crime networks, transnational economic and organised crimes and responses to them. Recent publications include *The Phantom Capitalists* (2008); 'Organised crime and terrorism', in *The Oxford Handbook of Criminology* (2007); 'Measuring the impact of fraud in the UK: a conceptual and empirical journey', *B. J. Crim.* (2008); and 'Suite revenge? The shaping of folk devils and moral panics about white-collar crimes', *B. J. Crim.* (2009).

SAGE would like to offer its apologies for publishing the errors corrected above.

# [17]

## CRIME ON THE LINE

### *Telemarketing and the Changing Nature of Professional Crime*

NEAL SHOVER, GLENN S. COFFEY and DICK HOBBS*

*New opportunities for crimes of acquisition grew significantly in the second half of the twentieth century, but the criminological consequences of this development are poorly charted. We examine offenders who have stepped forward to exploit one category of the new opportunities. Drawing from interviews with 47 criminal telemarketers, we present a picture and interpretation of them, their pursuits and their lifestyles. As vocational predators, they share several important characteristics with the professional thieves sketched by earlier generations of investigators. Like the latter, they pursue a hedonistic lifestyle featuring illicit drugs and conspicuous consumption, and they acquire and employ an ideology of legitimation and defence that insulates them from moral rejection. Unlike professional thieves, however, telemarketing criminals disproportionately are drawn from middle-class, entrepreneurial backgrounds. They are markedly individualistic in their dealings with one another and with law enforcement. Finally, their work organizations are more permanent and conventional in outward appearance than the criminal organizations created by blue-collar offenders, which were grounded in the culture of the industrial proletariat. Our findings show how the backgrounds and pursuits of vocational predators reflect the qualities and challenges of contemporary lucrative criminal opportunities. Like the markets that they seek to manipulate and plunder, the enacted environments of professional criminals embrace infinite variations, and are largely indistinguishable from the arenas that capacitate legitimate entrepreneurial pursuits.*

Writing at the dawn of the twentieth century, E. A. Ross (1907: 3) was one of the first sociologists to call attention to the fact that crime 'changes its quality as society develops.' Ross focused specifically on growing social and economic interdependence and the variety of ways this permits both exploitation of trust and the commission of crime at a distance from victims. The transformative social and economic changes he noted only gained speed as the century progressed. In the United States and other Western nations, the middle decades of the century saw the emergence or the expansion of state policies and corporate practices with enormous criminological significance. These include a fundamental shift in the state's public welfare functions, which had the effect of expanding programmes and subsidies for citizens across the income spectrum. One measure of this is the fact that by 1992, 51.7 per cent of American families received some form of federal payments, ranging from social security, Medicare and military retirement benefits to agricultural subsidies (Samuelson 1995: 158).

* Neal Shover, University of Tennessee, USA; Glenn S. Coffey, University of North Florida, USA; Dick Hobbs, University of Durham, UK. The materials presented here are based upon research supported by grant No. 00–7185-TN-IJ from the US Department of Justice, National Institute of Justice. Points of view or opinions expressed here do not necessarily reflect the official position or policies of the Department of Justice. An earlier and much different version of this paper was presented at the Economic Crime Summit, Los Angeles, CA, 7–9 May, 2001. We thank Peter Grabosky, Andy Hochstetler, Richard Lundman, Declan Roche and Richard T. Wright for critical comments on that draft.

In addition, the years following World War II witnessed a rapid growth of the domestic economy, which made available goods that either were unknown or were unattainable by most citizens just a decade earlier. Houses, automobiles, refrigerators, television sets and a host of other commodities now were within the reach of a growing segment of the population. The disposable income available to the new owners of these commodities allowed them also to purchase the new comprehensive insurance policies offered by insurance underwriters. Increasingly, the middle-class family now was insured against not only major hazards to life, home and business but also loss of or damage to household items (Clarke 1990).

As the century drew to a close, there were fundamental changes also in the structure and dynamics of economic relationships and in communications technology (Adler 1992; Lash and Urry 1994). Most important, widespread use of telecommunications (Batty and Barr 1994; Turkle 1995), electronic financial transactions and consumer credit (Tickell 1996) presage a depersonalized, cashless economy. Electronic financial transfers among banks and businesses, automatic teller machines (Hirschhorn 1985) and home banking increasingly are used across the globe (Silverstone 1991). In the new world of personal computers and virtual identities, individuals and organizations conduct business with remote others whose credentials and intentions cannot be easily determined.

The net result of these political and economic developments is a cornucopia of new criminal opportunities (Grabosky *et al.* 2001; Taylor 1999). Federally funded health care programmes, for example, have given physicians and hospitals access to new pools of tax revenue for which oversight is so weak that it has been called a 'licence to steal' (Sparrow 1996). The growth of health insurance fraud, therefore, can be seen as 'emblematic of the emerging forms of . . . crime that reflect the changing economy of the late twentieth century' (Tillman 1998: 197). The new criminal opportunities extend far beyond health care, however.

The changing landscape of criminal opportunities is strikingly apparent in crimes of fraud. Fraud is committed when misrepresentation or deception is used to secure unfair or unlawful gain, typically by perpetrators who create and exploit the appearance of a routine transaction. Fraud violates trust, it is non-confrontational, and it can be carried out over long distance. In organizational complexity and reach, it ranges from itinerant vinyl siding scamsters to international banking crimes that can destabilize national economies. The number of Americans victimized by it is large and substantially exceeds the number victimized by serious street crime (Rebovich and Layne 2000; Titus 2001). A 1991 survey of US households found that compared to crimes of burglary, robbery, assault and theft, fraud 'appears to be very common' (Titus *et al.* 1995: 65). Although a number of methodological shortcomings limit confidence in the findings of previous studies of fraud victimization, there seems little doubt that it is an increasingly common-place crime.

### Telemarketing and Fraud

The rapid growth of telemarketing is one of several consequential changes in the nature of economic relationships in recent decades. In 2000, telemarketing sales accounted for \$611.7bn in revenue in the United States, an increase of 167 per cent over comparable sales for 1995. Total annual sales from telephone marketing are expected to reach $939.5bn by the year 2005 (Direct Marketing Association 2001). The reasons for the growth of telemarketing are understood easily in context of the 'general acceleration of everyday life, characterized by increasingly complicated personal and domestic timetables' (Taylor 1999: 45). The daily schedule no longer permits either the pace or the style of shopping that were commonplace a few decades ago, and the need to coordinate personal schedules and to economize on time now drives many household activities. In the search for convenience, telemarketing sales have gained in popularity.

But while it has become an important part of the legitimate economy, criminals also have been quick to exploit the opportunities presented by telemarketing. Although it was nearly unheard of until recent decades, few adults today are unfamiliar with telemarketing fraud. There are countless variations on the basic scheme, but typically a consumer receives a phone call from a high-pressure salesperson who solicits funds or sells products based on untrue assertions or enticing claims. Callers offer an enormous variety of products and services, and often they use names that sound similar to bona fide charities or reputable organizations (US Senate 1993). Goods or services either are not delivered at all, or they are substantially inferior to what was promised. Telemarketing fraud touches the lives of many citizens. A 1992 poll of a national sample of Americans showed that 2 per cent of respondents had been victimized in the preceding six months (Harris 1992).

*Problem and Methods*

For individuals, exploitation of the new criminal opportunities doubtless springs from one or more of the familiar motivations of greed, lust and power (Grabosky *et al.* 2001). Autobiographical accounts, occasional media reports and research give reason to believe, however, that a significant proportion of those who have stepped forward to exploit them do so with a spirit of calling (e.g. Abagnale 1980; Francis 1988; Jackson 1994). Little is known about these vocational predators and how they compare with their predecessors of earlier eras (Glaser 1972). We partially redress this situation with analysis of data on criminal telemarketing and offenders. Our approach is both descriptive and interpretive. We first present a picture of one category of the new predators, their backgrounds, their criminal pursuits and their lifestyles. We then interpret our findings in the light of past research on professional theft.

Most of the data used for this report were gathered in semi-structured personal interviews with 47 telemarketing offenders convicted of federal crimes.[1] Since there are no lists of the names of criminal telemarketers, investigators interested in learning about them and their activities can not draw random samples for study. Improvisation is required. We began by examining major metropolitan newspapers for the past five years

---

[1] In addition to interviews and an examination of pre-sentence reports, we interviewed four acquaintances who formerly worked as telemarketers for short periods of time, two legitimate telemarketing professionals who once held office in telemarketing trade associations, four assistant US attorneys with extensive experience prosecuting telemarketing offenders, and four US probation officers who have supervised a large number of convicted telemarketers. Finally, we examined ten depositions of telemarketing victims made by law enforcement personnel and three voluminous criminal trial transcripts containing detailed descriptions of criminal telemarketing organizations and operations.

and an assortment of approximately 75 websites that contain information about telemarketing fraud as well as names of convicted offenders. These search processes yielded the names of 308 persons who were convicted of telemarketing fraud in the period 1996 through 2000. Subsequently, pre-sentence investigation reports prepared on some of our interview subjects yielded additional names, many of them co-defendants of individuals we identified using other methods.

Under terms of an agreement with the Federal Bureau of Prisons, names were submitted to personnel in their Office of Research and Evaluation, who reported to us the institutional locations of those currently incarcerated.[2] Institutional wardens then were made aware that we were interested in interviewing these inmates. The warden or the warden's designate then presented to the inmates our written description of the research and its objectives and then inquired if she or he was agreeable to meeting with us when we visited the institution. We later travelled to a number of institutions to meet with inmates who responded affirmatively, to describe and explain our research objectives and to interview those who elected to participate in the study. Twenty-five members of the sample were incarcerated when we interviewed them. They were confined in 12 federal prisons, from Oregon to Florida and Massachusetts to Arizona.

To ensure that our sample included ample numbers of persons with diverse telemarketing experience, we also interviewed 22 offenders under federal probation supervision. We reasoned that their involvement in telemarketing fraud probably was not as lengthy or as serious as was the case with the incarcerated subjects. Fifteen of the probationers were interviewed in Las Vegas, Nevada, and the remaining seven were interviewed in other cities. Las Vegas was an early hotbed of criminal telemarketing, and it continues as home base for many operations. We acknowledge that the precise relationship of our sample to larger populations of theoretical and substantive interest is unknown, although it does capture persistent fraud offenders, the object of considerable public and official concern.

All interviews followed an interview guide, which was revised as data collection progressed and analytic insights were developed and tested. The interviews explored a range of topics, including subjects' background and criminal history, their employment history, and the nature and circumstances of their initial and subsequent participation in telemarketing fraud. Interviews were tape recorded and later transcribed for analysis using *NVivo*, a software package for text-based data (Richards 1999).

In addition to interviews with convicted telemarketing offenders, we also had access to pre-sentence investigation reports for 37 of the 47 subjects. Examination of these served not only as an independent check on the validity of information elicited during the interviews but also gave us a more complete picture of the subjects' backgrounds, lives and circumstances. Generally, we found the subjects to be forthcoming about their backgrounds although they were less candid when reporting on the extent of their knowledge of criminal operations and the nature of their participation.

---

[2] For reasons that never became clear to us, the proportion of names we were able to match with incarcerated inmates was much lower than we had expected. Of the 308 names submitted to the Office of Research and Evaluation, only 74 were returned to us with indication they were confined in Bureau of Prisons institutions. We completed interviews with 25 of these. Twenty-six elected not to meet with us, two declined to be interviewed after hearing our presentation of research objectives and methods, and seven had been released prior to our institutional visit. We did not attempt to contact or interview the remaining 14, principally because there were no other telemarketing offenders incarcerated in the institutions where they were confined, and it would not have been cost effective to travel there in hopes of securing only one interview.

## Findings

Of all who begin employment in criminal telemarketing, some quickly discover it is not their cup of tea; they dislike it or they do not perform well. Others find the work attractive and rewarding but see it only as a means to other life and career goals. Most, therefore, pursue it only temporarily. Others, however, discover they are good at fraudulent telephone sales, and they are drawn to the income and the lifestyle it can provide. On average, the members of our interview sample were employed in these endeavours for 8.25 years. Their ages when interviewed range from 26 to 69, with a mean of 42.4 years. Their ranks include 38 white males, three African American males, and six white females. Nearly all have been married at least once, and most have children.

### Organization and routine

Like its legitimate forms, criminal telemarketing is a productive enterprise that requires the coordinated efforts of two or more individuals. To work in it, therefore, is to work in an organizational setting (Francis 1988; Schulte 1995; Stevenson 2000). The size of criminal telemarketing organizations can vary substantially. Some are very small, consisting of only two or three persons, but others are considerably larger (e.g. *Atlanta Journal-Constitution* 2000). Their permanence and mobility vary also, ranging from those that operate and remain in one locale for a year or more to others that may set up and operate for only a few weeks before moving on. These 'rip and tear' operators count on the fact that up to six months' time may pass before law enforcement agencies become aware of and targets them. 'Boiler rooms', operations featuring extensive telephone banks and large numbers of sales agents, have become less common in the United States in recent years, largely because of the law-enforcement interest they attract. There is reason to believe, however, that criminal telemarketers increasingly are locating them in countries with weak laws and oversight and operating across international borders (e.g. Australian Broadcasting Corporation 2001).

Larger telemarketing operations commonly take on the characteristics and dynamics of formal organizations; they are hierarchical, with a division of labour, graduated pay and advancement opportunities. Established by individuals with previous experience in fraudulent sales, they generally employ commissioned sales agents to call potential customers, to make the initial pitch, and to weed out the cautious and the steadfastly disinterested. We took steps to insure that our offender interview sample included persons who formerly held a variety of positions in criminal telemarketing firms. It includes 22 owners, eight managers, and 17 sales agents.

Experienced telemarketers generally do not call individuals randomly but work instead from 'lead lists' (also known as 'mooch lists'). These are purchased from any of dozens of businesses that compile and sell information on consumer behaviour and expressed preferences. Individuals whose names appear on lead lists typically are distinguished by past demonstrated interest or participation in promotions of one kind or another. When a person is contacted by telephone, the sales agent generally works from a script. Scripts are written materials that lay out both successful sales approaches and responses to whatever reception sales agents meet with from those they reach by phone. Promising contacts are turned over to a 'closer', a more experienced and better paid sales agent. 'Reloaders' are the most effective closers; much like account executives in legitimate businesses, they maintain contacts with individuals who previously sent money to the company (i.e. 'purchased' from it) in hopes of persuading them to send more. As one subject told us: 'I had it so perfected that I could get these customers to buy again . . . I made sure they were happy so I could sell them again. It didn't do me—I didn't want the one time, I didn't want the two-timer. I wanted to sell these people ten times.'[3] The organization of larger telemarketing firms and the routine employees follow when handling promising calls explains why those who 'buy' from them typically report contact with multiple 'salespersons' (American Association of Retired Persons 1996).

The products and services offered by criminal telemarketers span a wide gamut. In one scam, subjects identified and located unaware owners of vacant property, led them to believe that buyers for the property could be found easily, and then charged high fees to advertise it. Other schemes we encountered included collection for charities, drug education programmes, and sale of 'private' stocks. One subject sold inexpensive gemstones with fraudulent certificates of grossly inflated value and authenticity. The stones were sealed in display cases such that purchasers would have difficulty getting them appraised, particularly since they were told that if they broke the seal, the value of the stones would decrease and the certificate of authenticity would become invalid. 'Private stocks', by definition are not listed or traded on a stock exchange, but telemarketers are able to entice investors with smooth talk and promising prospectives. Dependent upon their salesmen for market reports, those who purchase soon discover that the non-existent stocks take a nose-dive, and they lose their investments. A high proportion of the companies represented by our interview subjects promised that those who purchased products from them were odds-on winners of a prize soon to be awarded once other matters were settled. Typically this required the customers to pay fees of one kind or another. Some of our subjects solicited money for nonexistent charities or legitimate organizations they did not represent. In the products they sell, criminal telemarketers clearly are limited only by the human imagination.

*Backgrounds and careers*

A substantial body of research into the lives and careers of street criminals has shown that many are products of disadvantaged and disorderly parental homes. We were interested in determining if the homes in which our subjects were reared reveal similar or functionally equivalent criminogenic characteristics. They do not. Overwhelmingly, the members of our sample describe their parents as conventional and hard working and family financial circumstances as secure if not comfortable. Their parental families were traditional in nature, with the father providing the main source of income. Nevertheless, one-half of the mothers also were employed outside the home. Although the fathers' reported occupations ranged from machinist to owner of a chain of retail stores, 32 were business owners or held managerial positions. A substantial proportion of our subjects were exposed to and acquired entrepreneurial perspectives and skills while young. Business ownership appealed to many of them: 'You're always pursuing more money,

---

[3] Criminal telemarketers unstintingly employ the rhetoric of legitimate business when describing their operations and activities. Their accounts are filled with references to 'customers', 'purchases', 'account executives', 'premiums' and such. Consequently, when this subject talks of customers who 'bought' from his establishment in the past, he is referring to victims who sent him money and who he hopes can be induced to make additional 'purchases' despite receiving little of value in return for earlier ones.

CRIME ON THE LINE

most of us are. We're raised that way, we are in this country. And that's the way I was raised. But I also wanted to do my own thing. I wanted to be in business for myself, I wanted the freedom that came with that.' Clearly, telemarketing criminals are not drawn from the demographic pools or locales that stock and replenish the ranks of street criminals. Although we questioned them at length about their early and adolescent years, their responses reveal little that distinguishes them from others of similar age and class background. Certainly, the disadvantages and pathologies commonplace in the early lives of most street criminals are in scant evidence here.

If our subjects' early years reveal few clues to their later criminality, there also are few signs that they distinguished themselves in conventional ways. Their educational careers, for example, are unremarkable; eight dropped out of high school, although most graduated. Twenty-one attended college, but on average they invested only two years in the quest for a degree. Five claimed a baccalaureate degree. When invited to reflect upon how they differ from their siblings or peers, many reported they were aware of an interest in money from an early age. One subject told us: 'I had certain goals when I was a teenager, you know. And I had a picture of a Mercedes convertible on my bedroom mirror for years.' Another said: 'You know, I do have a major addiction, and I don't think I'll ever lose it. And I don't think there's any classes [treatment] for it. And it's money, it's Ben Franklin.' He and others like him were aware also that there are ways of earning a good income that do not require hard work and subordination to others. Another subject said:

You know, I was, I've never been a firm believer [that] you got to work for a company for 30 years and get a retirement. Like my dad thinks. I'm all about going out [and] making that million and doing it, doing it very easily. And there's a lot of ways to do it.

Typically, they began working for pay while young and maintained employment throughout their adolescent years.

None of our subjects said that as children they aspired to a career in telemarketing, either legitimate or criminal. Some had previous sales experience before beginning the work, but most did not. Their introduction to it was both fortuitous and fateful; while still in high school or, more common, while in college, they either responded to attractive ads in the newspaper or were recruited by friends or acquaintances who boasted about the amount of money they were making.

[A former acquaintance] . . . looked me up, found me and said 'you gotta come out here . . . We're gonna make a ton of money.' I went out for three weeks—left my wife back home. And I got on the phones, and I was making a thousand dollars a week. I'm like, 'oh, my God, Jenni, pack the stuff, we're going to Arizona.' . . . He was like, 'man, you're, you're a pro at this shit.' And I just, I don't know what it was. I was number one . . . I don't know, I loved it.

The influence of others is remarkably similar to what is known about the criminal careers of street criminals, particularly those who go on to pursue crime with a high degree of skill and success (Hobbs 1995: ch. 2; Winlow 2001: 66–86).

For our subjects, many of whom were foundering on conventional paths, criminal telemarketing was a godsend; it came along at a time when they needed to show that they could make something of themselves. In the words of one of them, it was 'a salvation to me as a means of income. And being able to actually accomplish something without an education'. Criminal telemarketing was the reason some reported for dropping out of college:

[It] was just something I picked up as a part time job, when I was sixteen . . . When I was in college, my second year in college, [fellow students] were talking about finishing their four years of college and making $28,000 or $30,000 a year. And I was making $1,000 a week part time, you know . . . And I just couldn't see doing it. I mean, I wound up, after the end of my second year of college, I never went back. I was making too much money. It just seemed so easy.

New recruits generally start as sales agents, although most of our subjects later worked also as closers and reloaders. Employment mobility is common; individuals move from one firm to another, with some eventually taking managerial positions (Doocy *et al.* 2001).

After gaining experience, former managers told us, they were confident they knew enough about the business to strike out on their own. They did so expecting to increase their income substantially. As one put it: '[I]n my mind I believed I was smarter than the owners of these other companies that were making millions of dollars. And I just said, "I can do this on my own."' Typically, defectors lure productive personnel from their current employer with promises of more money, and on the way out they are not above plundering the business's files and lead lists: 'I downloaded every lead in his file. I took it all. I opened up . . . my own office, took all those people and said "now, watch me."' Based in part on the widely shared assumption that the market is never saturated, they generally open a company based on similar products and sales approaches.

What about the criminal histories of fraudulent telemarketers? Information elicited in the interviews and a review of information contained in pre-sentence investigation reports shows that 13 of our subjects had previous criminal records, seven for minor offences (e.g. petty theft and possession of marijuana) and six for felonies. Of the latter, three were convicted previously of telemarketing offences. Clearly, many of our subjects are not one-time or accidental violators; they have histories of multiple arrests and convictions.[3] Others have reported similar findings. Thirty per cent of 162 sales agents employed by a California-based fraudulent telemarketing firm, for example, had records of at least one criminal offence, and another 16.4 per cent had records of alcohol or drug offences (Doocy *et al.* 2001). For members of our sample who have previous arrests, the age of onset for criminal activity is considerably higher than for street criminals. Our data do show persuasively, however, that many appear to have recurrent trouble with the law and, like street criminals, they are persistent users of alcohol and other drugs. This picture is confirmed also by information contained in their pre-sentence reports.

*Attractions and lifestyles*

Overwhelmingly, our subjects told us they got into and persisted at telemarketing for 'the money'. How well does it pay? Only one subject reported earning less than $1,000 weekly, and most said their annual earnings were in the range of $100,000 to $250,000. Five told us their annual earnings exceeded $1m. The fact that they can make money quickly and do so without incurring restrictive responsibilities adds to the attractiveness of the work. They find appealing both the flexible hours and the fact that it requires neither extensive training nor advanced education. Few employers impose rigid rules or strictures;

CRIME ON THE LINE

generally there are neither dress codes nor uniforms. The work can be done in shorts and a tee shirt (Doocy *et al.* 2001).

As important as the income it yields and the casual approach to employment it permits, criminal telemarketing appeals to many who persist at it for reasons of career and identity. Despite class and parental expectations, most of our subjects had not previously settled upon promising or rewarding occupations. Asked what he 'liked about telemarketing', one subject's reply was typical: 'Well, obviously, it was the money.' Immediately, however, he added that 'it gave me a career, [and] to me it was my salvation.' As with him, criminal telemarketing enables others to own their own business despite their unimpressive educational background, their limited credentials and the absence of venture capital. As president of their own corporation, telemarketing provides both outward respectability and an income sufficient to maintain the good life.

Other aspects of the work are attractive as well. Its interpersonal and psychological challenge, for example,

has strong appeal to many salespersons. The ability to impose one's will upon another person—and to achieve a measurable financial reward for doing so—is highlighted in many of the reports of illegal telemarketing practices . . . Enforcement officials told us that sellers often have mirrors in the cubicles in which they work. They are told to look into the mirror and see the face of a hot-shot salesperson. Sometimes there will be a motto on the wall, such as: 'Each No gets me closer to the Yes I want.' Boiler room owners and managers . . . may put large bills on a bulletin board and say that the next sale or the highest total for the day will qualify for this extra reward. Often the sales people have to stand up when they consummate a transaction, so that the boss can note them and they can take pleasure in the achievement. (Doocy *et al.* 2001: 17)

Characteristically, our subjects believe they are outstanding salespersons; they are supremely confident of their ability to sell over the telephone despite resistance from those they contact. Doing so successfully is a high. One subject told us:

You could be selling a $10,000 ticket, you could be selling a $49.95 ticket. And it's the same principle, it's the same rules. It's the same game. I like to win. I like to win in all the games I play, you know. And the money is a reason to be there, and a reason to have that job. But winning is what I want to do. I want to beat everybody else in the office. I want to beat that person I am talking to on the phone.

His remarks were echoed by others:

[I] sold the first person I ever talked to on the phone. And it was just like that first shot of heroin, you know. I'm not a heroin addict . . . I've only done heroin a couple of times. But it was amazing. It was like, 'I can't believe I just did this!' It was incredible. It was never about the money after that . . . Yeah, it was about the money initially, but when I realized that I could do this everyday, it was no longer about the money. It was about the competition, you know. I wanted to be the best salesman, and I want to make the most money that day. And then it became just the sale. It wasn't the money. I didn't even add the figures in my head anymore. It was just whether or not I can turn this person around, you know, walk him down that mutual path of agreement, you know. That was exciting to me. It was power, you know; I can make people do what I wanted them to do. And they would do it.

It was the money, but it was [also] the ability to control people, to be able to say over the phone, 'John, go pick up your pen and write this down.' And you write it down! You do exactly like a robot—they would do exactly what they were told to do. And they would do it pleasingly, they would do it without hesitation, because, again, they had enough confidence and faith in you to believe that you were gonna do the right thing about it.

Another subject said simply that the work 'gives you power. It gives you power'. The importance of this dimension of the payoff from fraud has been commented on by others as well (e.g. Duffield and Grabosky 2001).

Criminal telemarketers generally distinguish between working hard and 'working smart'. When asked, therefore, how he viewed those who work hard for modest wages, one replied, 'I guess somebody's gotta do it.' By contrast, work weeks of 20–30 hours are common for them, and even for owners and managers, the need for close oversight of operations decreases substantially once things are up and running. The short work week and their ample income provides considerable latitude in the use of leisure time and in consumption patterns.

The lifestyles of telemarketing participants vary by age and the aspects of the work that employees find most appealing, but ostentatious consumption is common to all. The young, and those attracted to the work and leisure it permits, live life as party (Shover 1996). Use of cocaine and other illicit drugs is common among this segment of the criminal telemarketing workforce.

The hours were good. You'd work, sometimes, from about 9 to 2, 9 to 3, sometimes from 12 to 4. Basically, we set our own hours. It was freedom. The money was fantastic.... You got the best of the girls. For me, it wasn't really about the job, it was a way of life.... I had an alcohol problem at a young age, and to be able to support the alcohol and drug habit with the kind of money that we were making seems to go hand in hand. And then you've got the fast lifestyle, ... up all night, sleep all day, you know. So, everything kinda' coincided with that fast lifestyle, that addictive lifestyle.

Asked how he spent the money he made, another subject responded saying:

Houses, girls, just going out to nightclubs. And a lot of blow [cocaine] ... Lots and lots of blow, enormous amounts. And other than that, you know, I look back, I get sick when I think about how much we spent, where the hell I put it all. I'm making all this money [but] I don't have a whole hell of a lot to show for it, you know. That lifestyle didn't allow you to save.

Heavy gambling is commonplace. One subject said that they 'would go out to the casinos and blow two, three, four, five thousand dollars a night. That was nothing—to go spend five grand, you know, every weekend. And wake up broke!' Commenting on one of his employees, a subject who owned a telemarketing firm when he was arrested said that the man

had a Porsche Speedster after he sold his Porsche 911. He had a Dodge Viper, he had a Ferrari 348, he had a Lexus LS400, he had a BMW 850i, he had a Jeep Grand Cherokee. He liked his cars. Now, he didn't have all these at one time, but he ran through them, you know. He traded the Dodge Viper ... in for the Ferrari. He always had a Porsche.

What we learned about the lifestyles and spending habits of criminal telemarketers differs little from what is known about street criminals and other vocational predators. It also confirms what has been learned about the relationship between easy, unearned income and profligacy: 'The way money is acquired is a powerful determinant of how it is defined, husbanded, and spent' (Shover 1996: 104).

CRIME ON THE LINE

The lifestyles of telemarketers change somewhat as they get older and take on more conventional responsibilities:

I started to realize that, as I was getting older in the industry, it was affecting my children and my relationship with my wife. To the point that it wasn't what I wanted. I wanted more of a home-type of family, where I got home at six o'clock and have dinner and spend time with my wife and children. And with that industry, it doesn't really do that. My lifestyle? Play golf, go to the lake, you know. I had a family, but . . . I was also, you know, making good money. And I wanted to party and that kind of thing. So, I did that a lot. We got together and partied a lot and went here and there and went to, you know—nightlife—go out to clubs occasionally, But, when you're married and have kids, it's limited. It changes. It changed a lot over those years.

For older and more experienced telemarketers, the lifestyle centres around home and family and impressing others with signs of their apparent success:

I played some golf. [In the summer] water skiing, fishing. I'm real heavy into bass fishing, me and my dad and my brothers. Hunting. Doing things with my wife and kids. I spent a lot of time with them. Evenings, maybe just walking the golf course, or whatever. Watching the sunset.

Another subject told us that after he moved up in the telemarketing ranks: 'My partner and I played, we played a lot of golf. The office was right down from the golf course. We'd go to the golf course and play two or three times a week.' Save for the unrestrained hedonism of their lives when young and neophytes at criminal telemarketing, the broad outlines of their occupational careers, particularly for those who went on to form their own businesses, resemble the work careers of more conventional citizens.

*Legitimation and defence*

Doocy *et al.* (2001: 18) remark that the telemarketing offender they interviewed 'conveyed the assured appearance of a most respectable entrepreneur' and 'conveyed no hint that what he was doing might not be altogether legitimate'. Our subjects are no different. Notwithstanding the fact that all were convicted felons, most reject the labels *criminal* and *crime* as fitting descriptions of them and their activities. They instead employ a range of mitigating explanations and excuses for their offences, although claims of ignorance figure in most (Scott and Lyman 1968; Sykes and Matza 1957). Some former business owners told us, for example, that they set out to maintain a legitimate operation, emulated the operations of their previous employers and assumed, therefore, that their activities violated no laws. Others said they are guilty only of expanding their business so rapidly that they could not properly oversee day-to-day operations. Some said that indulgence in alcohol and illicit drugs caused them to become neglectful of or indifferent toward their businesses. Most claimed that the allure of money caused them to 'look the other way'. Those who owned or managed firms are prone also to blame rogue sales agents for any fraudulent or deceptive activities. As one put it: 'The owners are trying to do the right thing. They're just attracting the wrong people. It's the salesmen.' Another subject likewise suggested: 'I guess I let the business get too big and couldn't watch over all of the agents to prevent what they were doing.' For their part, sales agents charge that their owners and managers kept them in the dark about the business and its criminal nature.

Fraud offenders typically derive moral justification for their activities from the fact that their crimes cannot succeed without acquiescence or cooperation from their victims; unlike victims of burglary and robbery, those who fall prey to fraud usually are willing, if halting or confused, participants in their own victimization (Goffman 1952). Chief among the legitimating and defensive tenets of telemarketing criminals is belief that 'the mooch is going to send his money to someone, so it might as well be me' (Sanger 1999: 9). In other words, 'customers' are thought to be so greedy, ignorant, or incapable that it is only a matter of time before they throw away their money on something impossible. The tendency of fraud offenders to see their victims as deserving of what befalls them was noted by Maurer (1940) more than six decades ago, and it remains true of contemporary telemarketing criminals. One of our subjects told us, 'They know what they're doing. They're bargaining for something, and when they lose, they realize that they were at fault.' There is neither concern nor sympathy for them. Another subject said:

If these people can't read, so be it. Screw them, you know. It [doesn't say] *everybody's* gonna get the diamond and sapphire tennis bracelet. They're dumb enough not to read, dumb enough to send me the money, I really don't care, you know. I'm doing what I have to do to stay out of jail. They're doing what they have to do to fix their fix. They're promo junkies, and we're gonna find them and get them, and we're gonna keep getting them. And they're gonna keep buying. And, you know what I used to say, 'they're gonna blow their money in Vegas, they're gonna spend it *somewhere.* I want to be the one to get it.'

Telemarketing criminals selectively seize upon aspects of their victims' behaviour and point to these as justification or excuse for their crimes. They maintain that they were not victimizing their customers but engaging in a routine sales transaction, no different than a retail establishment selling a shirt that is marked up 1,000 per cent. Telemarketing fraud is therefore construed by its practitioners as perfectly in tune with mainstream commercial interactions: a 'subculture of business' (Ditton 1977: 173).

Ensconced in their outwardly respectable and self-indulgent lifestyles, our subjects professed belief that, so far as the law was concerned, they were risking nothing more severe than a fine, an adverse civil judgment or a requirement they make restitution. They claim the entire problem more appropriately was a 'civil matter' and 'should not be in criminal court.' As one put it: 'If you have people that are not satisfied, we would be happy to give their money back.'

### Interpretation

Our description of telemarketing crime and criminals is noteworthy for several reasons, but principally for what it reveals about the relationship between social change and the changing character of lucrative professional theft (Taylor 1999). Defined by cultural criteria rather than legal yardsticks (cf. Sykes 1978: 109), the concept of professional crime has become infused with contradiction and ambiguity by the evolution of this new kind of 'respectable' predator.

Sociological debate over the descriptive validity of professional theft has been carried out largely as a dialogue with the tradition of Sutherland (1937), who located a behaviour system of criminal specialists featuring technical skill, consensus via a shared ideology, differential association, status and, most importantly, informal organization grounded in a shared cultural identity. Subsequently, scholars presented alternative perspectives regarding crimes other than theft (Lemert 1958; Einstadter 1969). However, Shover (1973) perhaps came closest to Sutherland's original conception by locating the social organization of burglary based upon highly instrumental, and constantly evolving networks of dependency as the key variable. In his view, these networks continue to evolve due to innovative strategies in policing, security and technology, and telemarketing fraudsters resemble Shover's professional burglar, in their adaptive pragmatic organization.

Telemarketers also share many core characteristics with 'hustlers' (President's Commission 1966; Shover 1996), or 'rounders' (Letkemann 1973), offenders whose lack of commonality or consensus contradicts the notion of a cohesive tightly knit behaviour system (see also Holzman 1983; Polsky 1964; Roebuck and Johnson 1962). Yet Letkemann suggests that explicit commitment to criminal activity as a means of making a living is the best criterion for differentiating between professional and non-professional criminals, which also echoes Sutherland's classic work, and offers some support for the notion of an occupational group defined by their commitment to illegal economic activities (Becker 1960).

While the investigation of professional thieves and their pursuits has a long history in criminology, the canon is replete with portraits of offenders who have passed from the scene. However, for contemporary observers, 'fraud masters' (Jackson 1994) deservedly command more attention than 'cut purses' (Tobias 1967), 'cannons' (Maurer 1964) and 'good burglars' (Shover 1973). Economic and social change inevitably transform the worlds in which offenders entertain options and organize for pursuit of criminal income (Hobbs 1997; McIntosh 1975; Shover 1983). The classic criminal subcultures of shared practices and beliefs as the basis of criminal community, have met the same fate as blue-collar communities based upon traditional industries (Soja 1989). The new entrepreneurial milieu is an enabling environment for a great range and variety of money making schemes (Ruggiero and South 1997), and the perceptual templates of contemporary professional criminals feature cues that are geared to success in a sphere emptied out of anachronistic practice (Wright and Decker 1994).

Automobile theft and 'chop shops' were not found in ninetieth century society, for the obvious reason there were no automobiles to steal or sell. The shift to a post-industrial order inevitably changed selectively the human qualities and social capital requisite for successful exploitation of criminal opportunities. Traditional professional thieves hailed from locations in the class and social structure where the young generally do not acquire the human capital requisite to success in the world of well paid and respectable work. The blue-collar skills of an industrial society, however, are not equal to the challenge of exploiting contemporary, increasingly white-collar, criminal opportunities. The post-industrial service-oriented economy instead places a premium on entrepreneurial, interpersonal, communicative and organizational skills, and it is the children of the middle-class who are most likely to be exposed to and acquire these.

The knowledge and skills needed to exploit criminal opportunities vocationally and successfully do not differ greatly from those required for success in the legitimate world. Like the professional thief, the new and increasingly white-collar vocational predators commit planned violations of the law for profit (van Duyne 1996), but they do so in the style of the middle class. They take on and publicly espouse a belief system that defends against moral condemnation from outsiders, and they are dismissive of both the world of hourly employment and the lives of those confined to it. But while the professional

501

thieves of an earlier era publicly endorsed and were expected to adhere to norms of loyalty and integrity in dealings with one another (Maurer 1955. Shover 1973; Irwin 1970; Irwin and Cressey 1962; Cohen and Taylor 1972; McVicar 1982; Mason 1994; Taylor 1984), criminal telemarketers by contrast are extremely individualistic and self-centred in their contacts with criminal justice officials and agencies. Whether this is because of their privileged backgrounds or because the nature of criminal relationships has been 'transformed by the advent of a market culture', their illicit pursuits manifest qualities not only of entrepreneurial creativity but also independence and 'possessive individualism' (Taylor 1999).

Professional thieves of earlier eras found a measure of success in crime despite their humble beginnings, and much about what they made of themselves is understandable in the light of their blue-collar roots. The lives they constructed emphasized freedom to live 'life as party' (Shover and Honaker 1991) by 'earning and burning money' (Katz 1988: 215), to roam without restraint and to celebrate these achievements with others of similar perspective. The class origins of contemporary garden-variety white-collar criminals are more advantaged, but they live their lives in substantially similar fashion. Unlike the 'foot pads' of Elizabethan England, they generally do not gravitate to a criminal netherworld or a self-contained criminal fraternity. Nor do they confine their leisure pursuits to others of similar work. The proletarian underworld was an essential network for exchanging, controlling and disseminating information (McIntosh 1971; Hobbs 1995: 21–3), but the telemarketing fraudster depends on networks of information that are largely indistinguishable from those that underpin the non-criminal sector.

What Benney (1936: 263) called 'the fabulous underworld of bourgeois invention' ironically has been decimated by the embourgeoisement of crime. Criminals now emerge from the economic mainstream and engage both socially and pragmatically with derivations of normative economic activity. The acquisitive entrepreneurial ethic that underpins both legal and illegal performances within the post-industrial market place, thrives upon 'new technical, social, psychological and existential skills' (Bauman 1992: 98), which in turn are bordered by new configurations of cultural and technological capital.

While the old underworld was safely ensconced in the locales, occupational practices, leisure cultures and oppositional strategies of the industrial proletariat (Hobbs 1997; Samuel 1981), it is the bourgeois who have emerged with the education and ideological flexibility to engage with lucrative contemporary professional crime, which is located not within a proletarian outpost of traditional transgression, but within rhetorics that legitimate and enable the entire 'spectrum of legitimacy' (Albanese 1989: 101).

Telemarketing fraudsters should be seen as 'fluid sets of mobile marauders in the urban landscape, alert to institutional weakness in both legitimate and illegitimate spheres' (Block 1983: 245). These spheres are pliant and not territorially embedded (Chaney 1994: 149). Detached from an 'underworld' (Haller 1990: 228–9), contemporary professional crime has mutated from an overworld in which the bourgeoisie rather than blue-collar culture is sovereign. This helps explain why telemarketing fraudsters, unlike the professional thieves of previous generations, are likely to spend their weekends on the lake, playing golf, or having friends over for a barbeque. Still, they blow their earnings on drugs, gambling, fast living and conspicuous consumption. They earn a reasonably good return from crime, but like 'box men' of yore, few spend appreciable time in jails and prisons.

CRIME ON THE LINE

# REFERENCES

ABAGNALE, F. W. (1980), *Catch Me If You Can*. New York: Grosset and Dunlap.

ADLER, P. S. (1992), *Technology and the Future of Work*. New York: Oxford University Press.

ALBANESE, J. (1989), *Organised Crime in America*. Cincinnati: Anderson.

AMERICAN ASSOCIATION OF RETIRED PERSONS (1996), *Telemarketing Fraud and Older Americans: An AARP Survey*. New York: American Association of Retired Persons.

ATLANTA JOURNAL-CONSTITUTION (2000), 'Alleged Scam on Elderly by Telemarketers is Revealed', 6 September: B3.

AUSTRALIAN BROADCASTING CORPORATION (2001), 'Beyond the Boiler Room', 24 September, www.abc.net.au/4corners/.

BATTY, M. and BARR, B. (1994), 'The Electronic Frontier: Exploring and Mapping Cyberspace', *Futures*, 26/7: 699–712.

BECKER, H. (1960) 'Notes on the Concept of Commitment', *American Journal of Sociology*, 66: 32–40.

BAUMAN, Z. (1992), *Intimations of Modernity*. London: Routledge.

BENNEY, M. (1936/1981), *Low Company*. Sussex: Caliban Books.

BLOCK, A. (1983), *East Side-West Side: Organizing Crime in New York, 1930–1950*. Newark, NJ: Transaction.

CHANEY, D. (1994) *The Cultural Turn*. London: Routledge.

CLARKE, M. (1990), 'Control of Insurance Fraud: A Comparative View', *British Journal of Criminology*, 30: 1–23.

COHEN, S. and TAYLOR, L. (1972), *Psychological Survival*. Harmondsworth: Penguin.

DIRECT MARKETING ASSOCIATION (2001), www.the-dma.org.

DITTON, J. (1977) *Part Time Crime*. London: Macmillan.

DOOCY, J., SHICHOR, D. SECHREST, D. and GEIS, G. (2001), 'Telemarketing Fraud: Who Are the Tricksters and What Makes Them Trick?', *Securities Journal*, 14: 7–26.

DUFFIELD, G., and GRABOSKY, P. (2001), 'The Psychology of Fraud', Paper 199. Australian Institute of Criminology.

EINSTADTER, W. J. (1969), 'The Social Organization of Armed Robbery', *Social Problems*, 17: 54–83.

FRANCIS, D. (1988), *Contrepreneurs*. Toronto: Macmillan.

GLASER, D. (1972), *Adult Crime and Social Policy*. Englewood Cliffs, NJ: Prentice-Hall.

GRABOSKY, P. N., SMITH, R. G. and DEMPSEY, G. (2001), *Electronic Theft: Unlawful Acquisition in Cyberspace*. New York: Cambridge University Press.

GOFFMAN, E. (1952) 'On Cooling the Mark Out: Some Aspects of Adaptation to Failure', *Psychiatry*, 15: 451–63.

HALLER, M. (1990) 'Illegal Enterprise: A Theoretical and Historical Interpretation', *Criminology*, 28/2: 207–35.

HARRIS, L. *et al.* (1992), 'Telemarketing Fraud', University of North Carolina, Institute for Research in Social Science.

HIRSCHHORN, L. (1985), 'Information Technology and the New Services Game', in M. Castells, ed., *High Technology, Space and Society*, 172–90. Beverly Hills, CA.

HOBBS, R. (1995), *Bad Business: Professional Crime in Contemporary Britain*. Oxford: Oxford University Press.

——(1997), 'Professional Crime: Change, Continuity and the Enduring Myth of the Underworld', *Sociology* 31: 57–72.

HOLZMAN, H. (1983), 'The Serious Habitual Property Offender as Moonlighter: An Empirical Study of Labour Force Participation among Robbers and Burglars', *Journal of Criminal Law and Criminology*, 73: 1774–92.

SHOVER ET AL.

IRWIN, J. (1970), *The Felon*. Englewood Cliffs, NJ: Prentice-Hall.

IRWIN, J. and CRESSEY, D. (1962) 'Thieves, Convicts and the Inmate Culture', *Social Problems*, 10: 142–55.

JACKSON, J. (1994), 'Fraud Masters: Professional Credit Card Offenders and Crime', *Criminal Justice Review*, 19: 24–55.

JESILOW, P., PONTELL, H. and GEIS, G. (1993), *Prescription for Profit: How Doctors Defraud Medicaid*. Berkeley, CA: University of California Press.

KATZ, J. (1988) *Seductions of Crime*. New York: Basic Books.

LASH, S. and URRY, J. (1994) *Economies of Signs and Space*. London: Sage.

LEMERT, E. (1958) 'The Behaviour of the Systematic Check Forger', *Social Problems*, 6: 141–9.

LETKEMANN, P. (1973) *Crime as Work*, Englewood Cliffs, NJ: Prentice-Hall.

MASON, E. (1994) *Inside Story*. London: Pan.

MAURER, D. W. (1940), *The Big Con*. Indianapolis: Bobbs-Merrill.

——(1955/1964), *Whiz Mob*. New Haven, CT: College and University Press.

MCINTOSH, M. (1971), 'Changes in the Organisation of Thieving', in S. Cohen, ed., *Images of Deviance*. Harmondsworth: Penguin.

——(1975), *The Organization of Crime*. New York: Macmillan.

MCVICAR, J. (1982), 'Violence in Prisons', in P. Marsh and A. Campbell, eds., *Aggression and Violence*. Oxford: Blackwell.

POLSKY, N. (1964), 'The Hustler', *Social Problems*, 12: 3–15.

PRESIDENT'S COMMISSION ON LAW ENFORCEMENT AND ADMINISTRATION OF JUSTICE (1966), '*Professional Crime*', *Task Force Report*, ch. 7. Washington DC: US Government Printing Office.

REBOVICH, D. and LAYNE, J. with JIANDANI, J. and HAGE, S. (2000), *The National Public Survey on White Collar Crime*. National White Collar Crime Center.

RICHARDS, L. (1999), *Using NVivo in Qualitative Research*. London: Sage.

ROEBUCK, J. and JOHNSON, R. (1962), 'The Jack of All Trades Offender', *Crime and Delinquency*, 8: 172–81.

ROSS, E. A. (1907), *Sin and Society: An Analysis of Latter-Day Iniquity*. Boston: Houghton Mifflin.

RUGGIERO, V. and SOUTH, N. (1997), 'The Late Modern City as a Bazaar', *British Journal of Sociology*, 48: 54–70.

SAMUEL, R. (1981) *East End Underworld: The Life and Times of Arthur Harding*. London: Routledge and Kegan Paul.

SAMUELSON, R. J. (1995), *The Good Life and Its Discontents*. New York: Random House.

SANGER, D. (1999), 'Confessions of a Phone-Scam Artist', *Saturday Night*, 114: 86–98.

SCHULTE, F. (1995), *Fleeced! Telemarketing Rip-offs and How to Avoid Them*. Prometheus Books.

SCOTT, M. B. and STANFORD, M. L. (1968), 'Accounts', *American Sociological Review*, 33: 46–62.

SHICHOR, D., DOOCY, J. and GEIS, G. (1996), 'Anger, Disappointment and Disgust: Reactions of Victims of a Telephone Investment Scam', in C. Sumner, M. Israel, M. O'Connell and R. Sarre, eds., *International Victimology: Selected Papers from the 8th International Symposium*, 105–11. Australian Institute of Criminology.

SHOVER, N. (1973), 'The Social Organization of Burglary', *Social Problems*, 20: 499–514.

——(1983), 'Professional Crime: Major Offender', in Sanford H. Kadish, ed., *Encyclopedia of Crime and Justice*, 1263–71. New York: Macmillan.

——(1996), *Great Pretenders: Pursuits and Careers of Persistent Thieves*. Boulder, CO: Westview.

SHOVER, N. and HONAKER, D. (1991), 'The Socially Bounded Decision Making of Persistent Property Offenders', *The Howard Journal*, 31: 276–93.

CRIME ON THE LINE

SILVERSTONE, R. (1991), *Beneath the Bottom Line: Households and Information and Communication Technologies in the Age of the Consumer*. London: Brunel University Centre for Research on Innovation, Culture, and Technology.

SOJA, E. (1989). *Postmodern Geographies*. London: Verso.

SPARROW, M. K. (1996), *License to Steal: Why Fraud Plagues America's Health Care System*. Boulder, CO: Westview.

STEVENSON, R. J. (2000), *The Boiler Room and Other Telephone Sales Scams*. Urbana, IL: University of Illinois Press.

SUTHERLAND, E. H. (1937), *The Professional Thief*. Chicago, IL: University of Chicago Press.

——(1949/1983), *White-collar Crime: The Uncut Version*, with an introduction by Gilbert Geis and Colin Goff. New Haven, CT: Yale University Press.

SYKES, G. (1978) *Criminology*. New York: Harcourt Brace Jovanovitch.

SYKES, G. and MATZA, D. (1957), 'Techniques of Neutralization: A Theory of Delinquency', *American Sociological Review*, 22: 667–70.

TAYLOR, I. (1999), *Crime in Context: A Critical Criminology of Market Societies*. Boulder, CO: Westview.

TAYLOR, L. (1984), *In the Underworld*. Oxford: Blackwell.

TICKELL, A. (1996), 'Taking the Initiative: Leeds' Financial Centre', in G. Haughton and C. Williams, eds., *Corporate City? Partnerships Participation in Urban Development in Leeds*. Aldershot: Avebury.

TILLMAN, R. (1998), *Broken Promises: Fraud by Small Business Health Insurers*. Boston: Northeastern University Press.

TITUS, R. (2001), 'Personal Fraud and Its Victims', in N. Shover and J. P. Wright, eds., *Crimes of Privilege: Readings in White-Collar Crime*, 57–67. New York: Oxford University Press.

TITUS, R. M., HEINZELMANN, F. and BOYLE, J. M. (1995), 'Victimization of Persons by Fraud', *Crime and Delinquency*, 41: 54–72.

TOBIAS, J. J. (1967), *Crime and Industrial Society in the 19th Century*. London: Batsford.

TURKLE, S. (1995), *Life on the Screen: Identity in the Age of the Internet*. New York: Simon and Schuster.

US DEPARTMENT OF JUSTICE (1995), *Fraud Victimization—The Extent, the Targets, the Effects*. Washington, DC: National Institute of Justice.

——(2000), *Criminal Victimization in the United States (1995)*. Washington, DC: Bureau of Justice Statistics.

US SENATE, CONGRESS (1993), Hearing before the Subcommittee on Consumer of the Committee on Commerce, Science, and Transportation, *Telemarketing Fraud and S. 568, The Telemarketing and Consumer Fraud and Abuse Protection Act*. 103d Congress, 1st Session. Washington, DC: US Government Printing Office.

VAN DUYNE, P. (1996), 'The Phantom and Threat of Organized Crime', *Crime, Law and Social Change*, 21: 241–77.

WINLOW, S. (2001), *Badfellas*. Oxford: Berg.

WEISBURD, D., WHEELER, S., WARING, E. and BODE, N. (1991), *Crimes of the Middle Classes*. New Haven, CT: Yale University Press.

WEISBURD, D., WARING, E. and CHAYET, E. F. (2001), *White-Collar Crime and Criminal Careers*. New York: Cambridge University Press.

WRIGHT, R. and DECKER, S. (1994), *Burglars on the Job: Streetlife and Residential Break-ins*. Boston: Northeastern University Press.

# [18]

# The insurgent economy: Black market operations of guerrilla organizations

R.T. NAYLOR

*Department of Economics, McGill University, Montreal, Quebec, Canada H3A 2T7, USA*

**Abstract.** This paper is a study of the finances of insurgent groups. It takes the view that a "model" guerrilla movement evolves through three stages, with corresponding changes in both its expenditure responsibilities and its fundraising activities.

In the earliest stage it engages in hit-and-run operations against individual symbols of the state, either officials or isolated institutions like police stations and army outposts. At that stage, the group's expenditure requirements are relatively small and mainly military. Hence, it can rely on fundraising activities based on similarly sporadic and predatory actions such as bank robbery and kidnapping that closely approximate the activities of blue-collar criminals.

In the next stage the guerrilla movement begins openly disputing the political power of the state, mainly through the conduct of low intensity war against the infrastructure of the formal economy. The guerrilla group's expenditure obligations are not only much greater in absolute amounts, but also include a rising social security component, for the care of dependents of its militants, as well as providing some assistance to the population whose support it is attempting to win. Fundraising therefore shifts from once-for-all, predatory operations to parasitical ones that yield a steadier, more dependable flow of income at the expense of the formal economy. The most important will be the "revolutionary taxation" of income and wealth, an activity that more closely approximates that of an "organized" crime group.

In the final stage the guerrilla movement succeeds in implanting itself firmly on a piece of territory from which the state is effectively excluded. To its obligations for military operations and social security for dependents of militants are added those arising from the provision of social services to the general population of the controlled area and the building of the infrastructure necessary for the growth and development of a parallel economy. The most important sources of revenue come from indirect taxation – sales taxes on domestic commerce and/or export and import taxes on foreign trade along with "user fees" for the public services the insurgent group is providing. Fundraising thus ceases to be parasitical with respect to the formal economy controlled by the state and becomes symbiotic with the emerging parallel economy controlled by the guerrilla group.

Although at any point the guerrilla movement may find itself with a temporary surplus of operating funds, it is in the symbiotic stage, with regular revenue flows, that problems of asset management are likely to become significant. Therefore, at this stage, while fundraising activities take on increasingly overt and legitimate-looking forms in areas under the group's governance, fund-management activities require the guerrilla group to interface with the formal and international economy in much the same manner as "white collar" crime, seeking to hide and launder the returns from its fundraising.

14

## 1. Insurgent groups and the underground economy

Over the last two decades the formal institutions through which economic and political life have traditionally been organized have seen their influence steadily eroded. Corporations, unions, and, not least, governments have lost power to a host of new competitors vying for the economic and political loyalty of civil populations.

In the economic sphere this change has manifested itself most dramatically in the rise of the "underground economy – where economic activity evades scrutiny, regulation and taxation by the state. In many developing countries the underground sectors may have not only reached absolute dimensions that rival or exceed those of the legal, formal economy but are frequently found to be growing even faster.

In the political sphere there has been a parallel development – the discrediting of the normal methods through which political choices are registered. This popular disenchantment shows itself in political cynicism and low participation rates in elections, in growing support for fringe or "protest" political groups, and, at the most extreme, in violent anti-state actions ranging from isolated incidents of political terrorism to small-scale guerrilla warfare through to full-fledged armed insurrections.[1]

Whatever its precise form, modern underground politics shares with modern underground economics the basic perception that the formal state apparatus has lost (or never had) legitimacy. Poor participation rates in elections have as their economic counterpart massive evasion of taxes; "protest" political movements have as their economic counterpart the creation of parallel structures of production and distribution of (otherwise legal) goods and services over which the state can exercise no regulatory control; and insurgent groups follow the lead of criminal entrepreneurs into economic activities that are explicitly banned by the state.

However, insurgent groups are more than merely extensions of the criminal economy. Their outlaw economic activities are motivated by considerations of political advantage rather than of profit. While criminal organizations function in a parapolitical way, attempting to control and regulate in order to increase income, insurgent groups work in a reversed sequence, using their income to promote their activities as underground governments. Like the formal governments they challenge, insurgent groups have political programs; they have control over armed forces; and they compete with the formal apparatus of the state for territory, population and economic resources.

But political power, including military strength, ultimately rests on financial foundations. Insurgent movements face fiscal problems analogous to those of formal governments. To meet their political responsibilities, guerrilla groups must undertake a wide range of expenditures on both current and capital account, while at the same time combatting financial corruption among militants and overcoming fiscal resistance from the population at large.

## 2. Guerrilla finance: the expenditure side

The expenditure obligations of guerrilla groups are derivative from not merely the scale but also the form of the guerrilla struggle. In the earliest stages of an insurgency, the guerrilla group operates in, to use the terminology of El Salvador's Farabundo Marti Liberacion Nacional, "zones of contention". Here the rebel organization engages mainly in hit-and-run operations – assassinations and kidnappings of officials and raids on police and military barracks in order to politically discredit the government. In this stage – which urban guerrilla groups like Italy's Red Brigades or West Germany's Red Army Faction rarely advance beyond – the organization's expenditure requirements are overwhelmingly military and logistical.

As a guerrilla group matures, it gets more deeply entrenched in a society or in particular geographic areas (which the El Salvador FMNL calls "zones of expansion"). In zones of expansion the strategy switches to classical low intensity warfare where the main targets cease to be micro-political and become economic. The objective is not yet the capture of territory. Rather it is the destruction of basic infrastructure and the disruption of industry and commerce to cause investment to shrink, capital to flee, formal production to fall and unemployment and inflation to rise.

Following such principles, the UNITA guerrilla movement made the Angolan economy its principal military target – destroying, where possible, wheat and manioc crops destined for local consumption; attacking diamond mines and coffee plantations to undermine the country's foreign exchange earnings; and sabotaging the railway and road network.[2]

Similarly, Peru's Sendero Luminoso guerrillas target mines, the main (legal) source of the country's foreign exchange, through direct attacks and, more recently, politically-inspired strikes; bomb the factories and kidnap the executives of transnational corporations to provoke capital flight; and blow up the power lines both to hurt the formal economy and to deliver to the population at little risk a massive demonstration of the government's impotence.[3]

These kinds of tactics – replicated, among many others, by the Nicaraguan *contras,* the Mozambican National Resistance (RENAMO) and the Kampuchean Khmer Rouge – have as their fundamental rationale the fact that continued poverty and underdevelopment can, in the long term, be even more dangerous to the targetted government than direct military confrontation.

As the formal economy is progressively eroded, the population shifts increasingly to the informal for survival. This trend reinforces the success of the

16

guerrilla tactics in several ways. It further discredits the government in the eyes of the poorest sectors of the population who are most prone to accept the political message of the guerrilla movement; it directly shrinks the fiscal resources available to the government; and it expands the relative size of the black markets from which most guerrilla movements draw the bulk of their fiscal sustenance.

In this second stage, such sustenance is of growing importance. Military expenditures escalate, as the size and firepower of units increases along with the frequency and scale of operations. At this stage, too, the social service component of the guerrilla group's budget becomes significant. For the true insurgent movement – as distinct from one engaged purely in political terrorism (RENAMO, for example) – must replace at least partially the social services formerly provided by the government that is being progressively dislodged.

Finally, as a guerrilla movement becomes more secure in its hold on territory, it creates "zones of control".[4] Zones of control are politically useful in terms of conferring legitimacy on the guerrilla movement at the same time questioning that of the formal government. This was the motivation for the Afghan *mujihadeen* to waste so much manpower in the late 1980s in a bungled effort to seize the city of Jalalabad and declare it the capital of "free Afghanistan". Zones of control are also important militarily, forming, as in the case of the Eritrean People's Liberation Front, the base from which to shift from guerrilla warfare to a full-fledged insurrection capable of ousting the formal government.

In this third stage, with zones of control well established, on top of military and social service expenses, the guerrilla movement incurs capital expenditure obligations for the provision of infrastructure and for the development of an economy parallel to the official (and now largely displaced) one.

Thus, Peru's Sendero Luminoso, after taking control of an area and chasing out or killing officials of the old regime, abolishes markets and imposes planting quotas on the population to establish a new, cooperative rural society; while in the cities it organizes among the urban poor, the supply of the social services and infrastructure (electricity, water, soup kitchens etc.) the government will not or cannot provide.

Similarly, the Phillipines New People's Army[5], in the poorest rural areas, implements land reform – expropriating big landlords, seizing and redistributing agricultural equipment and livestock, and forcing smaller landlords to cut rents and merchants to improve the prices they pay farmers for their products. And it attempts to replace capitalist principles with a cooperative parallel economy involving all aspects of production and distribution, with marketting links stretching right into the cities where products of the parallel economy are sold on informal markets.

But in terms of creating a parallel political economy, no group has ever matched the accomplishments of the Lebanese Forces. It was not only the most powerful and best organized of all of Lebanon's myriad of militias, paramilitaries and guerrilla groups, it also came closest in its enclave (embracing East Beirut and territory to the North East) to reproducing almost all the functions of the formal state. Its armed forces were equipped with sophisticated modern equipment. It ran a well-trained police and intelligence force. It provided a host of social services to the population under its rule – housing, especially for Christian refugees from elsewhere in Lebanon; food subsidies; an elaborate propaganda apparatus in the form of newspapers and magazines, radio and television services; and a transportation system in the forms of both a ferry service to Cyprus and an internationally unrecognized airstrip to partly replace the official one under the control of a rival force.[6]

By the time a guerrilla group is sufficiently entrenched to convert a zone of expansion into a zone of control and assume all the attendant expenditure obligations, its fiscal needs have passed well beyond those that can be met through the occasional act of politically-motivated banditry. To meet those fiscal needs, the guerrilla movement can rely on contributions from outside sponsors, or it can tap the resources of the host economy. While these options are not necessarily exclusive of each other, they do pose quite distinct advantages and disadvantages.

### 3. External finance: dilemmas and opportunities

If a guerrilla group decides to seek funds from abroad it has several options.

It can rely on private supporters. Such outside sponsors are sometimes motivated by ideological solidarity – as with the impressive list of right-wing lobby groups, Christian fundamentalists and paramilitary thrill-seekers that stepped forward to aid the Nicaraguan *contras* after the US Congress cut off offical aid in 1982.[7] Or the outside sponsors can be motivated by religious or ethnic solidarity. In the early stages of its post-1969 campaign against the British in Northern Ireland, the Provisional Irish Republican Army's main source of income came from contributions raised among Irish-Americans, five times as numerous as the population of Ireland itself.[8]

Often such outside sponsorship skirts and even trespasses into the realm of illegality. Much of the Irish relief money, nominally destined for humanitarian aid and therefore tax deductible in the US, was diverted into black market arms purchases. And the earliest guilty pleas in the *Iran-contra* scandal in the US came from fundraisers for the National Endowment for the Preservation of Liberty who issued tax-deduction certificates for "charitable" donations that ended up in the Swiss bank accounts of prominent arms dealers.

Furthermore, such support need not be voluntary. The Secret Army for the Liberation of Armenia (ASALA) regularly extorts money from well-to-do Ar-

18

menians in Europe to fund arms purchases. So too do the Turkish Grey Wolves in Germany, the PKK (Kurdish Workers Party) in France and Croatian nationalist groups in North America from their respective emigré communities.[9]

Granted that for the majority of insurgencies in developing countries the exile population is likely to be, like the millions of Afghans who fled to Iran or Pakistan, too poor to be a source of financial support directly. Nonetheless even in such cases opportunities still exist. Much of the logistical needs of the various Somali milita groups are met by hijacking emergency food aid for the famine-stricken population and diverting it to Kenya where it is bartered for weapons and for the popular local narcotic, *qat*.[10]

In a somewhat more benign fashion, guerrilla groups – like the El Salvador FMLN and the Phillipines New People's Army – quietly influence the aid flowing into the country from Non-Governmental Organizations abroad to steer it into local projects that fit the guerrilla group's own development program. This permits the guerrilla group to not only score a propaganda coup but also to channel more of its limited budget into military operations.

Finally, the guerrilla group can rely on public sponsors, albeit with the aid usually laundered through an array of front organizations to assure that the sponsoring state maintains "plausible deniability". Indeed, it has been suggested that one of the reasons the US government has been relatively complacent about the amount of aid being embezzled by the Khmer Rouge from refugee camps for Cambodians in Thailand is that it permits the US to fund the notorious Khmer Rouge without the risk of public approbrium.[11]

For the guerrilla group there are two great advantages to assistance from a foreign government. One is that the funds are likely to be regularly supplied as long as the guerrilla movement is carrying out operations that fulfill the political objectives of the sponsor. The second, and even greater advantage, is that outside aid has traditionally served to solve the main logistical problem that insurgent forces long faced, the supply of heavy and sophisticated weapons.

In the early stages of an insurgency, local supplies – stolen or manufactured – usually suffice. The Sendero Luminoso of Peru derives all of its explosives by stealing dynamite from the country's many mines. The El Salvador FMLN, in its zones of control, established a string of underground factories making crude weapons. And in one of the boldest actions of the Uruguayan Tupamaros saw them donning naval uniforms, marching into a naval training school and looting it of a large assortment of light weapons and ammunition.

There is also the local black market, supplied especially by underpaid and disgruntled soldiers. The more weapons the US has poured into the hands of the Phillipines army, the greater the firepower the Moro National Liberation Army in Mindanao has been able to deploy against it.[12]

But at some point most successful guerrilla insurgencies are likely to reach the stage (certainly just before the final, decisive confrontation with the state) where local arms supplies are no longer adequate, either by reason of limited quantity or of lack of sophistication. At that point the advantages of outside sponsors are evident.

Thus, by the end of 1986, when the USSR announced its intention to pull out of Afghanistan, the US and its allies had already provided, nominally for the Afghan *mujihadeen* rebels, some $ 3 billion in military aid plus hundreds of millions more in humanitarian assistance for the refugee population in Pakistan. It was the largest insurgent-support operation in history and was calculated to be sufficient to equip with sophisticated weaponry a field force of 200,000–300,000 men.

At least, that was the theory. The reality was a little different. From one end of the supply chain to the other, diversion and theft was the rule. The arms suppliers inflated invoices and pilfered cargo before loading. The American Central Intelligence Agency diverted some of the weapons off to support other insurgencies, notably those in Nicaragua and Angola where the American Congress had officially banned all US aid. On disembarkation at the Pakistani port of Karachi, Pakistani military intelligence, which offically ran the Afghan aid operation, helped itself to a share of the remaining weaponry, partly for its own use and partly for black market sales. The residual weapons were then handed over to the Afghan resistance groups, not according to their military worth, but in proportion to their political influence. And the political leaders promptly diverted much of the equipment onto black market sales. A similar traffic characterized the humanitarian aid flows. The result was that, not only did international aid organizations have to scour the bazaars to buy back the diverted food, clothing, tents and medecine, but those Afghan rebel chiefs who actually did fight sometimes had to use the profits of the heroin traffic to buy weapons that had already been paid for on their behalf by the US and Saudi Arabia.

In the final analysis, somewhere between 60 and 85% of the aid flow was stolen en route and diverted not just onto the local but also the international arms black market from which all manner of other guerrilla groups and bandit gangs could draw their logistical requirements.[13]

Granted these advantages from relying on outside sponsors – guaranteed supplies of arms and regular flows of money – there are also evident disadvantages. If revealed, aid from foreign governments makes the recipient group appear to be a tool of outsiders. Even worse, outside aid comes with strings attached. It is to minimize those constraints that many guerrilla groups who do receive outside aid – UNITA or the Khmer Rouge, for example – make sure they have alternative and supplementary sources of money. And it is to avoid those political constraints altogether that others – the Sendero Luminoso guerrilla group in Peru or the New People's Army in the Phillipines, for example – rely strictly on what can be raised through local underground operations.

20

## 4. General principles of guerrilla finance

Guerrilla fundraising is, by definition, an outlaw activity using techniques that, at least in the early stages, closely approximate ordinary criminality. For both groups the choice of technique depends on the group's relationship to the broader society and its relative strength vis-a-vis the enforcement arm of the state.[14]

When criminals are confined to a limited territory and/or linked by only loose associations – in urban street gangs, for instance – their activities are essentially predatory with respect to formal society. Vulnerable to the law enforcement apparatus, they will concentrate on activities that minimize the length of their exposure and produce once-for-all returns. Crimes such as hijacking, bank robbery, and ransom kidnapping nicely fit the bill.

At a more advanced stage criminal activity might pass from the local to the regional or even the national in scope and from the predatory to the parasitical in nature. Thus, with a better supporting infrastructure, criminals will engage in such activities as embezzlement, protection rackets, illegal gambling and the retailing of "recreational" drugs – activities that impose an on-going, long-term drain on formal society.

At the most sophisticated, the actions of criminals move from being parasitic on to being symbiotic with polite society. In the symbiotic phase, territorial reach can extend beyond the national to the international: organizational forms approximate those of mainstream business; and the central focus of criminal enterprise becomes the provision of goods and services which may even be legal in themselves, but are illegal in terms of the methods with which they are produced and distributed. It is at this stage criminals might pass, for example, from illicit gambling conducted in back rooms of bars, to operating formal casinos owned by publicly traded companies, behind the veil of which skimming and money laundering occur. At this stage, too, criminal enterprises can supply to otherwise legitimate corporations a range of services, varying from union-busting to illegal waste-disposal, which those corporations cannot be seen supplying by themselves.

Similarly, when a guerrilla group exists in a pronounced stage of geographic or political insecurity in the face of determined opposition from the state (in "zones of contention"), it might finance itself in much the same way as a blue-collar criminal gang – engaging in essentially predatory economic activities such as armed robberies and ransom kidnappings. (Though it must be noted that some, genuinely popular groups might be able to skip this stage of funding altogether.)

Subsequently, when the guerrilla group has a better defined territorial base and more secure access to the economic resources of that territory ("zones of expansion"), and when, by the same token, the state is weak and unable to provide adequate protection to the more well-to-do population, fundraising activities will shift to the parasitical mode, particularly extortion or "revolutionary taxation". While the returns from predatory activity such as robbery or kidnapping are episodic, parasitical activity are more likely to yield steadier income at much less risk.

Finally, when the guerrilla group has secured virtually complete control of its target territory and population and has succeeded in marginalizing, if not eliminating, the formal presence of the state (in "zones of control"), it shifts to symbiotic forms of fundraising. The key difference may not be the actual action that raises money, so much as the way in which that action is conducted. "Taxation" might move from simply calling on a business and extorting money at gunpoint to having officials of the movement regularly contact businessmen in the zone of control to negotiate the amount due in exchange for services rendered. It is at this point where the analogy between criminal and guerrilla economic activity needs qualification.

In the symbiotic phase, criminals become an integral, functional part of the society off which they formerly preyed, and the distinction between illegal and legal activities starts to blur. Rather than their income and wealth being a direct deduction from that of legitimate, formal society, the income and wealth of both increase together as the criminal sector supplies goods and services which, for a variety of reasons, the formal society's legitimate enterprises cannot be seen providing.

This symbiosis goes beyond the merely economic. It is a commonplace observation that much of the covert funding for political parties in those democratic systems that impose limitations on campaign financing comes from or through underworld sources. Witness the recurrent scandals in Japan over *yakuza* financing of Liberal Democratic Party candidates. In some areas of Colombia campaign finance fluctuates with the state of marijuana crop. And in parts of Sicily the Christian Democratic Party operates as little more than a joint venture of the Vatican and the Mafia.

The links are more than financial. More overtly corrupt regimes (like the Kuomintang government of China in the 1920s and 1930s) can actually endorse the stranglehold of powerful criminal syndicates (in this instance the Green Gang of Shanghaii) on a wide range of businesses in return for those criminal groups deploying their muscle to keep political rivals of the government at bay.[15]

By contrast, guerrilla groups opposing the status quo political order set out, not to make their activities symbiotic with those of the formal society, but to create virtually parallel economies from the benefits of which the state and legitimate society are excluded.

Thus, when a guerrilla group has secured control of territory and population and has marginalized or excluded the formal state, it can then act as a surrogate

22

state, promoting certain economic activities in exchange for a share in the income. The most important sources of income will be from taxation of commerce and/or the exploitation of the natural resources of the area under the movement's control along with "user fees" for the social and economic services the guerrilla group is providing. Just as the state in the formal sectors of the economy relies on a mixture of public acceptance of its legitimacy and public fear of legal penalty to assure taxes are paid, so too in the informal sector the guerrilla group's revenues will depend on it establishing in the public mind some balance between the perceived legitimacy of the group's objectives and the preceived capacity of the group to enforce its will.

In this case the economic development of the area and the economic well-being of the population are dependent on the provision by the guerrilla group of security and infrastructure in the controlled area. But any growth of income and wealth in the guerrilla-controlled area represents a deduction from the economic resources available to, and therefore the political-military power exercised by, the formal state against which the guerrilla group is ranged.

It is on this point that there is an important distinction to be made between guerrilla groups operating in opposition to the state and paramilitary groups that operate in a way which parallels and reinforces the state. Frequently such paramilitary groups will be tolerated, or even encouraged by the authorities. For as nominally illegal entities they can carry out violent operations that the state cannot be caught performing by itself.

Such official tolerance or even covert encouragement differentiates, for example, the actions of the Colombian paramilitary units organized jointly by rogue elements in the army and the drug barons from the activities of the anti-state guerrilla forces. The objective of the paramilitary groups is to use the resources of the black market, particularly the drug trade, to defend the political status quo in the face of the guerrilla challenge, while taking the occasion to eliminate peasant or union leaders, nosy journalists or opposition judges en route. The objective of the guerrillas is to build a parallel economic system to support their assault on the political status quo, though, like their antagonists, they may have no moral or ideological objection to financing those activities by taxing the drug trade.

Hence, in their most sophisticated stage, the activities of anti-state guerrillas are indeed symbiotic, but symbiotic with the informal or underground economy rather than the official one. And the greater the growth of the underground economy, the less the percentage of society's income and wealth available to the state to sustain its legal functions.

An important conclusion follows from this distinction. Mature criminality is compatible with the continued existence of the formal state structure and can even be employed to defend it; mature insurgency threatens the overthrow of that formal state structure and, by definition, cannot comfortably coexist with it. This distinction was neatly summed up in South Viet Nam in the 1950s when the government basically ceded to the *Binh Xuyen* gang of river pirates control of the Saigon-Cholon vice rackets in exchange for them keeping the city free of Viet Cong activity.[16]

Granted any insurgency using the international black market to finance its activities inevitably forms mutually profitable, and likely quite durable relations with **international** criminal groups. This is the case in narcotics trafficking out of Burma, for example, where insurgent groups of the left, the right and of the merely ethnocentric all liaise freely with Hong Kong and Bangkok based heroin syndicates. But with these international crime syndicates the guerrilla group has no territorial or political dispute.

Granted, too, the early stages of an insurgency there may be cooperation with domestic and local criminal organizations based on the fact that both are social outcasts.[17] In Italy some of the plethora of urban terrorist groups in the 1970s engaged in joint operations with different mafia groups – robbing banks, holding up payrolls, stealing paintings and engaging in ransom kidnapping. At one point the Unity of Communist Combat group is even reputed to have joined the Calabrian 'Ndrangheta in a raid on a Club Med that netted $ 2 million worth of cash and jewels and 300 foreign passports.[18]

But there are many instances where these supposed alliances turn out to be fictional. Argentinian criminal kidnappers used to claim to be guerrillas because guerrilla groups, with better supporting infrastructure, could hold victims longer and therefore command a higher ransom. In Ireland some criminal bank robberies are followed by claims the IRA is responsible in order to throw the police off the scent. And in the Phillipines businessmen frequently face extortion demands from criminals claiming to be members of the New People's Army.[19]

Moreover, even in the short-term, the two groups have totally different objectives. The criminal group seeks a smooth getaway and post-operational secrecy, while the guerrilla group revels in noisy confrontations with the state and brags about its prowess in the aftermath.

Furthermore, whatever short-term tactical alliances of convenience may occasionally emerge between well-entrenched criminals and anti-regime guerrillas within a particular state, in the long run they will generally end up on opposite sides of the political and military barricades, inevitably so if the guerrilla group's ideology is explicitly anti-capitalist.

For the guerrilla group the underground economy, and the treasures it yields, are tools with which to carry out a political agenda; for the criminal organization the riches of the black market are an end in themselves. The Brazillian guerrilla theorist, Carlos Marighela, in a tract widely read in Latin America and Europe, pointed out that in order to differentiate the left-wing guerrilla's bank robbery from that of either the criminal or the right-wing revolutionary it was

24

necessary to avoid misguided violence or taking money or personal property from customers of the bank. At the same time, he advised, the guerrilla should conduct propaganda by handing out leaflets explaining the purpose of the raid or by writing slogans on the wall before leaving.[20]

Of course, the lure of quick wealth can on occasion cause a guerrilla organization, or at least some of its militants, to degenerate into unabashed criminality. Despite the purity of its Marxist rhetoric, when the Baader-Meinhof Gang in Germany started scoring big returns from bank robberies, it attracted a new type of recruit more concerned with making easy money than making difficult revolutions. The options were starkly drawn after the end of the Huk rebellion in the Phillipines when some elements of the insurgent army took to the hills to engage in social banditry, redistributing stolen wealth among the poor peasants, and others settled down near American military bases to collect rake-offs from the gambling and prostitution rackets and to sell themselves to local bosses as strikebreakers and security guards.[21]

The danger of criminalization of motive is particularly acute when individual militants are allowed to run their own enterprises in exchange for kicking back a certain sum to the group as a whole. The Provisional IRA is known to be tightly disciplined and its gunmen turn over to the organization almost everything they collect (on pain of being executed if they are caught holding back). By contrast, militants of the Ulster Defence Association, which was once the IRA's main paramilitary antagonist, used to display their committment to the Protestant ethic by routinely grabbing 70–80% of the take for themselves. These antics produced so much public approbrium and internal dissension that the group came close to collapse by the end of the 1980s, and had to be reorganized with a new, "clean" leadership.[22]

## 5. Predatory forms of fund-raising

In its predatory mode guerrilla fundraising most closely approximates simple blue-collar criminal activities. Some of these activities are highly ideosyncratic.

Maritime fraud in the form of cargo hijacking was, for reasons peculiar to Lebanon's political and physical geography, a speciality of some of its guerrilla groups who had taken control of small ports along the coast. Instead of organizing armed takeovers of ships at sea, these contemporary pirates arranged in advance with shipowners to divert cargos secretly to one of the Lebanese milita-run ports. The cargo would be either sold locally or mixed with the transit traffic to the Persian Gulf. The ship, if old, would be scuttled. The ship, if new, would be reported as lost at sea – though after one or a few hasty name changes, it would return to active service. In the meantime the shipowner collected both a percentage from the cargo sale and the insurance money on his "lost" ship –

while possibly still operating that ship under another name elsewhere in the world.[23]

Although far from commonplace, some guerrilla groups have participated in counterfeiting their antagonist's currency both as a means of fundraising and as an instrument of economic warfare. If used merely as a form of fundraising, it must be kept strictly secret, sacrificing political for financial gains. An IRA foray into using counterfeit US dollars to pay its militants' travel expenses ended ignominiously in 1987 with the seizure of $ 2 million in phony bills and subsequent arrest of an IRA member.[24] Only briefly more successful was an Australian-based counterfeiting operation of the Liberation Tigers of Tamil Eelam, several of whose militants passed off to the Australian public phony airline tickets, fake travellers checks and counterfeit cash to raise money to buy arms in Israel – until busted by the Australian federal police in 1991.[25]

More successfully used was the $ 20 million in counterfeit Afghan government currency given by the American Central Intelligence Agency to the Afghan *mujihadeen*. Here the objective was both the purchase of supplies and the discreditting of the government once the existence of the counterfeiting was revealed.[26] On the other side, radical righwing groups in the United States, like the Posse Comitatus, have counterfeited American currency – whose legality they refuse to recognize – both to finance insurgency training and to disrupt the "enemy" economy.[27]

Clearly it requires special circumstances for a guerrilla group to be able to profit from maritime fraud or even to engage in counterfeiting. But there are two traditional criminal rackets open to virtually all insurgent groups regardless of geographic location or technical capacity. Bank robbery and ransom kidnapping have provided almost the entire operating budget of urban guerrilla groups like the Italian Red Brigades as well as forming the core of the "launching fund" for the El Salvador FMNL guerrillas to shift from hit-and-run tactics to full-scale insurgency.

In his widely-read manual, Brazilian guerrilla theorist Carlos Marighela, not only explained the difference between guerrilla and criminal bank robbery, but also explicitly recommended bank robbery as the first stage of revolutionary action. This advice was followed, either consciously or not, by a wide variety of guerrilla groups. Indeed, decades before that manual was written, the group creditted with being the pioneer of modern political terrorism, the Zionist Irgun Zvai Leumi in Palestine,[28] supplemented support money and arms sent over by American mobsters with the proceeds of bank robbery.[29] And from its inception the Tamil Eelam Liberation Army (bitter rivals to the Tamil Tigers) specialized in robberies – its first major "guerrilla" operation was to loot $ 600,000 worth of cash, gold and diamonds from a Colombo bank.[30]

Nor are some of these political bank heists minor in scope or size. The Argentinian Ejicito de Revolucion Popular in 1972 achieved the distinction of having

26

pulled off the country's biggest-ever bank robbery when it relieved a state-owned development bank of all the cash in the vault. And the world record for a bank robbery was set in Beirut in 1976. Of the 11 banks in the financial district that were looted by various warring factions, the worst hit was the British Bank of the Middle East. From it the Democratic Front for the Liberation of Palestine withdrew $ 4.5 million in cash and travellers' checks in addition to grabbing from the safety deposit boxes a sum that has been variously estimated at between $ 20 million and $ 60 million in cash, bearer bonds, gold and jewelry.[31]

The robbing of banks and similar financial institutions has a number of advantages over looting supplies directly from stores and warehouses. Cash is obviously more flexible. And a major hold-up can also be a propaganda coup, provided it does not lead to any offsetting public approbrium. The money taken can be represented as belonging to the "financial class", especially since depositors (as distinct from holders of safety deposit boxes) rarely, if ever, lose anything directly in a bank robbery. During one of the major bank jobs of the Baader-Meinhof Gang one of the guerrillas menacingly advised the bank patrons, "Keep quiet and nothing will happen to you." And he reassuringly added, "After all, it's not your money."[32]

Furthermore the proceeds of the bank robbery can take the form not just of cash but also of politically damaging information. When, in 1969, the Uruguayan government responded to a strike by bank employees by a military decree ordering them back to work, it simultaneously created a network of inside informants the Tupamaros guerrillas could use to pull of a spectacular series of bank robberies. One of those robberies yielded, beside cash and negotiable securities, documents and bank account records that, once published, implicated 22 prominent citizens, including a serving cabinet minister, in tax fraud, illegal currency speculation and exchange control evasion.[33]

By contrast, ransom kidnapping was for a long time a strictly criminal enterprise. If a guerrilla group did engage in kidnapping, it was generally for political purposes – to make a propaganda coup or to secure the release of prisoners.

However, by the end of the 1960s the situation had changed. In the wake of Che Guevera's defeat in rural Bolivia and the general trend to urbanization of developing countries, guerrilla warfare was also becoming urbanized. The result was easier access to tempting targets. In addition, the logistical needs of some of the more ambitious groups were rising. And there was a growing public resentment across much of the developing world of the activities of both indigenous economic elites and transnational corporations. Together these factors precipitated, in the early 1970s, a wave of ransom kidnapping, particularly in Latin America, with wealthy landlords, businessmen and transnational corporation executives as the prime targets.

The advantages were many. Well-to-do individuals (at least in the early stages) were usually easier victims than banks with guards, safes and alarms.

Ransoms, too, could be tailored to fit the guerrilla movement's logistical and political needs. They might be demanded in the form of goods and services for the poor, in the shape of the settlement of labour disputes on terms favourable to the workers, or in cash. And the cash could be in local currency or, especially in the case of ransoms for transnational corporation executives, in hard currency – something particularly useful as access to the international arms black market became more desirable.

Argentina seems to have been the innovator in modern political kidnapping.[34] The pattern was set in 1971 when the Ejicito de Revolucion Popular nabbed the British head of the local Swift Company plant and freed him on payment of $ 62,500 in food for the poor. That was the beginning of a kidnapping campaign of such dimensions that, by the mid-1970s, the ERP bragged of a warchest (including proceeds of bank heists) of $ 30 million. And the ERP's success prompted other Argentinian guerrilla groups into the business, collecting the proceeds in cash, in food and medicine for poor, and in the settlement of labour disputes with wage hikes and the rehiring of dismissed workers.

There were also side-benefits to be reaped in the form of both economic and psychological warfare. Kidnapping business executives, especially transnational corporation executives, might help precipitate politically destabilizing disinvestment and capital flight. And kidnapping wealthy businessmen or rentiers allowed the guerrilla group to make even better anti-capitalist propaganda than hitting a bank; for it personalized the message rather than forcing the guerrilla group to rely on vague slogans about the "financial class".

Thus, Argentina's Monteneros set a world record for kidnap ransom. In the face of bitter opposition from the government, the Born family, owners of one of the world's largest grain dealing firms, ransomed from the Monteneros their kidnapped sons. The price – $ 60 million in "bail" plus "fines for exchange irregularities" to be paide to the Monteneros as "representatives of the national interest". In addition the Borns had to distribute $ 1.2 million in goods to the poor as punishment for "hoarding and creating shortages". Finally, they were required to place in their factories, busts of Juan and Eva Peron, in whose name the Monteneros claimed to be fighting.[35]

By the onset of the 1980s political ransom kidnapping was on the wane in Latin America – except in Colombia. Although firms specializing in corporate security were quick to claim credit for the decline in kidnapping, the real reasons likely have more to do with changes on both the political and financial fronts.

In the context of the 1980s, transnational corporations were no longer a popular bête noir in Latin America. During the great debt crisis and its attendant economic depression, that role had been usurped by international bankers who were effectively unreachable in their New York, London and Tokyo headquarters. And in any event many of the Latin American guerrilla groups had ma-

28

tured to the point where they had more reliable sources of funding than bank robbery and kidnapping.

Meanwhile, elsewhere in the world, ransom kidnapping was and is very much a part of various guerrilla groups' kit of revolutionary fundraising tools.

In the 1980s much attention in the Middle East was focussed on the antics of a few marginal factions in Lebanon, who, denied access to other rackets, engaged in some high-profile, but usually low-return kidnappings of foreigners. However, the real frontier for the prosecution of the kidnapping business was in Iraqi Kurdistan. In 1981 the Pesh Mergas guerrillas unleashed a major wave of kidnapping of foreign skilled workers and professionals in the oil business to raise money, publicize the cause and embarrass the Iraqi regime. The captives were smuggled across the Iraq-Iran border and placed in the custody of the Iranian Pasdaran (Revolutionary Guards) until the ransom (in either cash or in medical equipment) was met, the Pasdaran taking a cut of the proceeds.[36]

Further east, in Afghanistan, Pakistan and India, where ransom kidnapping used to be only a criminal activity, the increased availability of arms, the wealth of the drug trade and mounting political tensions resulting partly from the Afghan war and partly from increased pressure from ethnic separatists all across the subcontinent added a distinctly political dimension to the business. Indeed, by the end of the 1980s the practice was so widespread, parts of the subcontinent boasted of a veritable wholesale market for kidnap victims. They would be sold by their captors, sometimes for as little as 5% of the ultimate ransom, to other gangs and insurgent groups better positioned to wait until the final price reached an acceptable level.[37]

Although kidnapping as a tool for guerrilla fundraising still possesses its attractions, there are certain powerful disincentives of which better security is only one. More importantly, while in the heyday of anti-capitalist and anti-imperialist agitation, important political points could be scored with a well-targeted kidnap, in the 1980s the political environment shifted dramatically. Kidnapping could often produce a public relations disaster. That was the experience of the IRA when a series of kidnappings culminated in a botched effort to ransom a valuable racehorse and a disastrous attempt to collect from the employers of a business executive. The executive died in capitivity of a heart attack, producing no ransom, a 20 year jail term for one of the perpetrators and a wave of public criticism. It was the last major kidnap operation mounted directly by the IRA – which, in any event, by then had safer and surer ways of raising money.

## 6. Parasitical forms of fundraising

When a guerrilla group switches from relying on once-for-all activities like kid-

29

napping and robbery to drawing most of its income from on-going sources like embezzlment and extortion, it crosses the (often hazy) line from predatory to parasitical modes of fundraising. If predatory fundraising by guerrillas approximates simple, blue-collar crime, parasitical fundraising is more akin to the activities of "organized crime" syndicates. There are many possible examples. But nowhere is the analogy to "organized crime" activities clearer than in the construction and labour rackets run by the various Irish paramilitary groups.[38]

As part of its counterinsurgency campaign during the 1970s and 1980s, the British government poured more than a billion pounds into building public housing in burnt-out areas of Belfast. The potential take from the reconstruction program was sufficient for the IRA, the Protestant UDA and even the ultra-radical Irish National Liberation Army to meet periodically to carve up territory and fix schedules of payments to be demanded from the construction companies.

To encourage reconstruction, the British government instituted for small contractors for whom receipts come in irregularly, a tax deferral scheme. The result, pioneered by the Official IRA, was a booming market in stolen and forged tax-exemption certificates and a series of militia-run tax scams in which the final link in the deferral chain would be a ghost company that vanished when the tax money finally fell due.

On the actual building site, the paramilitary force acts as an employment agency, collecting a fee from workers and forcing employers to hire only those designated by the guerrilla group. Most of the building site workers hired also draw unemployment insurance. Not only does the threat of its revelation help to keep the workers quiet, if not loyal, but the unemployment insurance fraud also permits the paramilitary group to offer the workers' services to construction companies for less than market wages – for which the companies show their gratitude by paying the paramilitary a kickback.

As with the Lebanese militias' profiteering from maritime fraud, the Irish paramilitaries' use of construction rackets and similar parasitical actions[39] is the product of a unique conjuncture of political and business factors. However, virtually every guerrilla organization, in its parasitic mode, makes use of one form or another of "revolutionary taxes".

Although the term is sometimes used to describe activities that amount to little more than glorified highway robbery, "revolutionary taxation" (or its equivalent, "war taxes") usually connotes something more sophisticated and better institutionalized. And it can take many forms.

It can take the form of a de facto excise tax on a particular commodity. In much the same spirit as the Salerno mafia Family in New York, levies a concrete tax on the construction industry, the Frangieh family militia in northern Lebanon supplements its revenues with a tax on the output of the only major cement factory in a country where the actions of the many warring factions assured a

30

steadily growing demand. The business was sufficiently lucrative to prompt, in 1980, an abortive but bloody hostile takeover bid by the powerful Christian rival, the Lebanese Forces.

Revolutionary taxation can also take the form of a levy on the income or wealth of well-to-do individuals or businesses. While the Colombian M-19 group was an essentially urban guerrilla organization and therefore, like Italy's Red Brigades, relied on kidnapping and hold-ups, the other major Colombian groups are powerfully implanted in areas that contained, at peak, at least one-third of the country's arable land. They could therefore regularly shake down wealthy landlords, ranchers and planters, on pain of having crops ruined and livestock stolen. In a similar spirit, the Basque separatist Euskadi Ta Azkatasu-na (ETA) organization drew up "intelligence files" (most of them sloppy and based on rumour) about the resources of prominent Basque businessmen to determine what their proper rate of "revolutionary taxation" should be.[40]

Often taxation is applied to specific commodities, corresponding to the economic resources of the areas where most of the guerrilla operations occurred. Afghanistan produces the great bulk of the world's lapis lazuli as well as being an important producer of emeralds. This provided an important source of income – through a ten percent tax – to the Jaamiat-i-Islami *mujihadeen* faction which, for political reasons, received only a very small share of the American and Saudi aid going to the Afghan resistance.

Diamonds are even more tempting. In Angola the UNITA guerrilla movement inherited an apparatus organized in the mid-1970s by the Portuguese government to allow fleeing Portuguese colonists to send their wealth back home. Portugal passed a law permitting people to import diamonds into Portugal without revealing either their names or the origins of the stones. The result was the emergence of a cabal of clandestine dealers specialising in smuggling stones from Angola to Portugal and then reselling them in Antwerp. Once the Portuguese colonists had fled, the cabal put itself at the service of UNITA which then organized smuggling rings inside the mines. The success was sufficient to inspire the South West Africa People's Organization in Namibia to similarly exhort its supporters inside the diamond mines to smuggle out the stones for patriotism and profit, stones whose resale in Europe provided an important part of the SWAPO budget – and the practice may well have been one factor inducing the De Beers diamond cartel to sign a treaty of mutual recognition with SWAPO years before South Africa agreed to withdraw its forces from Namibia.[41]

Similarly smugglers busy draining off most of Colombia's gold production into black market sales in Brazil, are encouraged and protected, for a fee, by the Ejercito de Liberacion Nacional and the Fuerzas Armadas Revolucionarias de Colombia (FARC).[42] However, the ELN's take from taxing the gold trade is minimal compared to the returns from its trademark activity – petroterrorismo.

After denouncing the international oil companies for "stealing" Colombia's oil, the ELN faced the same kind of policy dilemma many groups around the world have had to resolve – to reconcile economic warfare with its own revenue needs. It could kidnap oil company executives and destroy the infrastructure to attack imperialism and deny the government a critical source of foreign exchange. Or it could "tax" the companies' operations to help finance the revolution. It found a viable compromise. The companies pay the *elenos* handsomely both in cash (the ELN claimed by 1991 to have a war chest of $ 50 million) and in the construction of roads, schools and hospitals for the surrounding countryside in return for freedom to produce oil. Meanwhile, between 1986 and 1990, the ELN hit the actual government-owned pipelines carrying the oil to port, 138 times, spilling 630,000 barrels and costing the government in repairs and lost sales some $ 725 million.[43]

As shown by the ELN's insistence on receiving part of its "taxes" from the oil companies in the form of social infrastructure built for the civil population in the ELN-dominated area, at a certain point "revolutionary taxes" cease to be solely or primarily a parasitical drain on the formal economy and pass over more into the domain of symbiotic. At that point they are used to support the growth of the infrastructure of a parallel economy under construction in the zones of control; they are administered by a formalized officialdom, rather than by armed shakedowns; and they can take a wide variety of forms. Though direct taxation of income and wealth is still possible, more often the guerrilla movement shifts to indirect taxation – levying retail, wholesale and international trade taxes.

### 7. Symbiotic forms of fundraising

That frontier between the parasitical and the symbiotic may well have been at least approached by the IRA in its capacity to profiteer, politically and financially, from the impact of its own military campaigns on the infrastructure of social life in Belfast.

To replace the many public houses (bars) burnt down in the 1970s riots, the IRA (both the Official and Provisional wings) created a network of Republican Social Clubs, originally unlicensed and selling cut-rate, often hijacked beer. Much the way the American mob reacted to the repeal of Prohibition by switching from operating "speakeasies" selling bootleg alcohol to running apparently legal bars and clubs, so too, following a police crackdown, did the IRA, taking the Social Clubs overground and securing proper licences. In them the beer sold is sometimes legitimate, sometimes stolen, and sometimes extorted from companies on pain of a bombing or a kidnapping. Only the income from the first needs be reported, the rest being skimmed off in cash. In those clubs,

32

too, are slot machines, some legal, most illegal from which the IRA collects the proceeds. And in addition, as with orthodox criminal enterprise, bars, with their large volume of cash trade, are ideal places through which to launder the proceeds of other rackets.[44]

If the IRA only just approached the frontier, it was certainly crossed by the Lebanese Forces who imposed on Marounistan, the Christian enclave comprising East Beirut and part of the adjoining hinterland, what was likely the world's most complex and thorough system of parallel taxation. There were taxes on "government" services. These included duties on ships unloading cargo in the pirate ports controlled by the militia; "visa fees" imposed at checkpoints on people travelling to other parts of Lebanon; and user fees for public beaches. They even included a fee charged to Italian waste-disposal companies to permit them to dump radioactive waste just off the coast. There were also real estate taxes on commercial buildings and a hearth tax on private homes. There were sales taxes on private services like movie tickets and restaurant meals, and on basic goods like tobacco and cooking oil. Gasoline was taxed three times – at the import, wholesale and retail levels.

While estimates of the annual take from taxation run as high as $ 300 million, there is a chance that the figures were deliberately exaggerated, both to bolster the apparent legitimacy of the Lebanese Forces as a substitute government and to cover for the amount of money being covertly gathered from more traditional rackets, drug trafficking possibly high among them.[45]

What was unique about the Lebanese Forces' tax structure, apart from its comprehensiveness, was that it relied much more on the taxation on internal commerce than of foreign trade, a fact reflecting Lebanon's historical role as a free-trading entrepot and the resulting political power of its merchant princes. By contrast, most systems of guerrilla taxation depend predominantly on the taxation of imports and exports to and from zones of control.

Frequently the territorial hold of the guerrilla group does not extend beyond a border strip and even then may be firm only at night. The frontier between the Irish Republic and Northern Ireland, for example, is a virtual no-man's-land, with the Provisional IRA striving to keep it free of the customs and security services of both jurisdictions. That facilitates smuggling which costs the Irish government annually an estimated 100 million pounds, some of the customs' revenues lost by the Irish government ending up as "war taxes" paid to the IRA.

Granted in such cases the territorial hold of the guerrilla group may be tenuous. But even partial control of such a frontier, and the revenues it can yield, may be a necessary first step for a guerrilla group to begin converting zones of expansion into zones of control.

It was precisely the opportunity to openly control the Iraq-Turkey border in

33

the wake of the Gulf War that permitted Iraqi Kurdish rebels to shift from dependence on unreliable outside sponsors (plus the proceeds of kidnapping) to tapping the commercial possibilities of their own territory. The Iraqi refineries that survived the Anglo-American bombing produce too much diesel and aviation fuel for Iraq's own use. Yet UN sanctions prevent the export of the excess via pipeline to Iraq's pre-war customers. Instead, much of the fuel is hauled by truck to Turkey via Kurdistan. The emerging Kurdish autonomous administration therefore charges transit fees, on both the fuel going out and the cargos of food and general consumer goods coming back. The funds are then used for such purposes as paying civil service salaries and buying arms.[46]

Similar road traffic, either across the Soviet-Afghan border or between Kabul and Karachi, long provided landlocked Afghanistan with much of its food and consumer goods. The result was the spectacle of two of the most powerful *mujihadeen* groups, the Jaamiat-i-Islami and the Hezbe-i-Islami, battling each other for the right to tax the truck convoys carrying Soviet and East Bloc supplies to the Communist-led government in Kabul.

Nowhere its the organization of foreign trade taxes as systematic and comprehensive as in Burma with its plethora of insurgent groups. The reasons lie in a mixture of economics, ethnicity and geography.[47]

The Burmese government in the early 1960s introduced a "socialist" economic development model based on tight government controls on foreign trade and agriculture. And it also attempted to "birmanize" the country in which nearly half of the population, concentrated in the resource-rich hinterland and the border areas, consists of non-Bhuddist, non-Birman minorities.

The planning mechanism produced thriving black markets. Out of the country to Thailand and China would go, apart from subsidized basic commodities like rice (whose price was three times as high in Thailand), a huge flow of Burmese luxury goods – teakwood, perfume essences, rubies, jade, antiquities, opium and heroin. Back in would come ordinary consumer goods, everything from sandals to VCRs, along with arms to keep the ethnic insurgencies supplied.

Wherever possible the ethnic insurgents would take control of an area producing one or more of the valuable export goods and levy taxes on the trade flows both ways. Thus, while the Karen National Liberation Army levies a 5% tax on all the commerce (rice, gems, tin ore and textiles) crossing its part of the Burma-Thai border, by far the most important part of the Karen parallel economy is (or was, until a recent Burmese army offensive) the teak trade. Burma contains 70% of the world's rapidly depleting teak forests. Not only did the Karens tax the clandestine export of Burmese teakwood to Thailand and China, but they definitively moved beyond the parasitical into the symbiotic mode by directly setting up some 200 sawmills, the output of which purchased not only consumer goods for their sub-economy but the arms to defend it.[48]

34

An even greater range of activity characterized the most powerful of the Burmese ethnic insurgent forces, the Kachin Independence Army. Apart from sporadic support from China (and, anomalously, from Taiwan and South Korea), it derives much of its revenue to support an impressive array of social services by taxing luxury commodities, especially jade. Burma produces the world's finest jade. And while the jade mines are nominally government controlled, the government's writ does not really run beyond the main town. In the hinterland the Kachins demonstrate the whole range of fundraising techniques: they steal from government owned mines (predatory); they protect and tax the smugglers (parasitical), and they run their own illegal mines (symbiotic). In other parts of their zones of control the Kachins similarly organize ruby mining.[49]

While Burma produces most of the world's finest blood-red rubies, the Kachins' success in tapping the trade seems to have inspired a competitor.

After being ousted from government by the Vietnamese in 1979, the Khmer Rouge returned to guerrilla activity, relying mainly on China for arms and on embezzled refugee relief aid for general supplies. But as the 1980s wore on, fears mounted that China would join the US in imposing on the Kampuchean civil war a settlement that would marginalize the political role of the Khmer Rouge. The Khmer Rouge therefore began relying more on its own rackets for funding. It was aided immeasurably by the devastated state of Cambodia economy and the fact that its zones of control included key border crossings, permitting the Khmer Rouge to offer smugglers (for a fee) guidance across the heavily mined border as well as taxing the trade each way. And it was aided by the fact that Kampuchea ranks second to Burma as a source of high-quality rubies and it still has unlogged teakwood forests.

Thousands of Thai miners cross into the Kampuchean ruby-mining area under Khmer Rouge control. Each miner is required to lease mining rights from the Khmer Rouge and pay a tax on the output. The rules are rigorously enforced, with Khmer Rouge officials routinely checking permits and punishing unlicensed miners. Similarly many Thai lumber companies pay the Khmer Rouge for rights to hack down teak and other valuable hardwoods in areas made accessible via roads built by slave labour under Khmer Rouge supervision. The profits from the teak and ruby trade (estimated by 1990 to have totalled $ 100 million) permit the Khmer Rouge to directly tap the Bangkok arms black market and therefore drastically reduce its dependence on China.[50]

In effect, the Khmer Rouge's moves into the ruby- and teakwood-producing areas, abolishing money and markets and permitting only those private operations that assist the organization's access to the international arms black market, converted part of the hinterland of Kampuchea into a de facto independent state. It became, in that sense, remarkably similar to the coca republic that the

Sendero Luminoso guerrillas are reputed to have created in Peru's Upper Huallaga Valley.

## 8. Narcoterrorism?

This supposed development in Peru, together with similar events in Colombia, led to a widespread view that the West was being haunted by the spectre of "narco-terrorism", that an array of left-wing guerrilla movements, armed by Moscow, were responsible for the deluge of "recreational" drugs sweeping the urban areas of North America and Western Europe. The factual basis of the thesis was very flimsy.

Certainly some guerrilla groups do partake of the profits of the world drug trade. Since drug trafficking in the 1980s may have been the richest single component of the world underground economy, since its basic raw materials originate in areas where insurgencies abound, and since it has a close familial relationship to the international traffic in arms, participation would be much too tempting for many guerrilla groups to pass up. In Lebanon, for example, it is hard to identify a major paramilitary or guerrilla group that has not at some point supplied itself in the cannibis traffic.

However, far from being the exclusive domain of the leftist insurgent, the drug trade, in the best of liberal capitalist traditions, has attracted the participation of all manner of guerrilla groups, regardless of race, colour, creed or political affiliation.

When the remnants of the Kuomintang armies, ousted from China in 1949, fell back on the northern Shan states of Burma, they lost little time in getting down to business. The late Kuomintang general, Tuan Shi-wen, eloquently explained: "We have to continue to fight the evil of Communism, and to fight it you need an army and an army must have guns, and to buy guns you must have money. In these mountains the only money is opium."[51]

The KMT not only collected taxes on all commerce in and out of the area, but forced local farmers to pay an annual tax in the form of a percentage of their crop. The opium thus collected was run by the KMT to the border and sold to Thai police. They, in turn, arranged its refinement into heroin and further sale, via Hong Kong-based crime syndicates, first on the local market for smoking-grade heroin and later, with the appropriate quality improvements, on the international market for injectable heroin.

There were two main rivals for the business. One was the Communist Party of Burma, encouraged by China to expand into the Shan states to counter the threat of the KMT. Initially the party relied on the profits from its monopoly of the supply of smuggled Chinese consumer goods in Burma for the bulk of its

36

funding. But as China liberalized its trade policy, the Burmese Communist Party lost most of its trade tax revenue. However, it managed to oust the KMT from some of the best opium-growing areas, securing an independent source of funds – until ethnic rivalry and the corrupting influence of the narcotics money caused the party to fracture in 1989.[52]

Yet even at its peak the role of the Burmese Communist Party paled compared to that of the Shan United Army. Originally given by the Burmese government permission to run the local opium trade in exchange for fighting the communists, the SUA subsequently joined the ranks of the ethnic insurgents battling the government. The SUA not only taxes opium (and almost everything else) but has fully diversified downstream into heroin refining. At peak it accounted for an estimated 80% of the drug production of the Shan states.[53]

Thus, contrary to the narco-communist conspiracy thesis, right-wing guerrillas and non-ideological ethnic insurgents have been as active as left-wing rebels in fattening off the South East Asian opium/heroin trade. Furthermore, South East Asia has had in recent years a strong competitor for the supply of the bulk of the world's heroin – the Afghanistan-Pakistan frontier where the traffic was always exclusively the domain of ethnic and religious insurgents on the political right.

In Afghanistan traditional landlords and religious leaders encourage their people to grow opium, which the *mujihadeen* military chiefs could tax. The opium was sent across the border into the autonomous Afridi tribal areas of Pakistan where, in exchange for payoffs to tribal leaders, consortia of Afghan rebel political leaders and Pakistani businessmen were allowed to establish many heroin refineries. The heroin was then transported as return cargo in the same military vehicles (which police and Customs were not allowed to open) in which Pakistani military intelligence shipped weapons up to the *mujihadeen*. And the heroin made its way to final market by several routes.

Some was shipped through the port of Karachi to trafficking organizations in Western Europe and North America. Some headed westward through Baluchistan, to Iran where corrupt members of the Pasdaran (Iranian Revolutionary Guards) passed it off to Kurdish guerrillas for further transit across Turkey to Istanbul where the *babas* of organized crime wholesale it to Europe and North America. Finally, some was snuck across the Indian border by smugglers sympathetic to or willing to pay off the Sikh separatist guerrillas, and sent to Bombay for further distribution.

The Afghan rebel traffic has produced in its wake an epidemic of heroin addiction across the Indian subcontinent. It has induced a veritable explosion in banditry and turned Pakistan's North West Frontier province into the world's premier arms and drugs bazaar.[54] Further afield it has rejuvenated the Sicilian mafia and financed a bloody campaign of intimidation and revenge against the Italian state. And it has fed the growth of urban property crime in

North America and Western Europe. But it is all for a good cause. In words remarkably reminiscent of the sentiments expressed twenty years before by Kuomintang general Tuan Shi-wen, one *mujihadeen* leader declared, "We must grow opium to fight our holy war against Russian non-believers."[55]

Nor is the evidence of some sort of narco-communist conspiracy any clearer in the centre of the world's cocaine trade. It is certainly true that Colombia's FARC entrenched itself in a jungle region where some of the biggest narco-barons used to have cocaine refineries. And FARC lost little time in taxing the refineries, along with all other businesses in the area. But the notion that there is a strategic alliance in which the guerrillas assist the narco-barons and are paid for their services in arms flies in the face of logic and evidence.

There is fundamental long-term incompatibility of objectives of the two groups. The narco-barons are insurgent capitalists, seeking to beat or buy their way into participation in a hitherto largely closed social system, while the guerrillas are insurgent communists, seeking to actual overthrow that system. The two groups are in frequent conflict over control of territory, while the narco-barons resent and resist the payment of "revolutionary taxes". Indeed, it was precisely such conflicts that helped prompt the cocaine traffickers to shift their plant to areas closer to Brazil where they would be free of guerrilla harassment and closer to a supply of precursor chemicals.[56]

There is a similar lack of evidence to support the notion of a long-term strategic alliance between cocaine traffickers and Peru's Sendero Luminoso guerrilla movement which, it has been claimed, is collecting anywhere from $ 30 million to an astronomical $ 550 million per annum from the coca trade.

Granted that in the Upper Huallaga valley where Sendero Luminoso is deeply entrenched the *senderistas* encourage the return to aboriginal agricultural traditions which include the growing of coca. Nonetheless, the guerrillas won popular support by organizing armed peasant coops that were able to stop the Colombian traffickers from brutalizing and exploiting the growers. The result is higher prices for the coca growers, part of which may accrue to Sendero Luminoso in the form of tax revenues. This is a development the cocaine traffickers could hardly be expected to welcome. Nor could they be pleased that the guerrillas demand from the traffickers, taxes on the import of chemicals and on the export of coca paste, along with fees for such services as the use of landing strips. Far from being a sign of a strategic alliance, these activities by the guerrillas put them on a long term collision course with the traffickers.

Furthermore, it is difficult to see how a guerrilla group so vehemently and violently opposed to money and markets could effect a close working relationship with the ultra free-enterprising cocaine traffickers. Nor is the *senderista* policy of destroying all infrastructure associated with the formal state – including the communications and financial system – something calculated to improve the traffickers' business prospects. And if Sendero Luminoso is really

38

earning so much money from the cocaine trade, it has produced neither any significant symptom of corruption nor any sign of modern, heavy weapons from the international black market. The group's arms are almost all taken or bought from the army and police; its explosives are stolen from the mines by the many miners who are supporters and/or members; and its medical and general supplies are contributed by adherents who "requisition" them from their places of work.[57]

Finally the notion that Sendero Luminoso could be collecting even the lower figure of $ 30 million per annum from servicing the coca economy command conflicts with a basic law of the economics of drug trafficking – namely that the returns per unit volume rise dramatically at each stage of production-distribution chain. Sendero Luminoso, like most guerrilla groups, occupies territory where only the lowest and most poorly paid stages of production take place. To collect truly impressive sums for the warchest, a guerrilla group would have to get directly involved at least with the export traffic in finished product, and it would do best if it could participate in the actual marketing of the refined material inside the countries of final destination.

There have been attempts to do so. Efforts by the Tamil Tigers to supplement their warchest by purchasing heroin in Bombay and reselling it in Europe date at least as far back as 1985 when an official of the organization was arrested in Rome with 22 kilos in his suitcase. But the real push began after 1987 when the Indian army occupied the Jaffna Penninsula, the Tiger's zone of control, forcing them to fall back into the jungle and stripping them of most of the income from their protection rackets. Benefitting from absolute dedication of the young militants who courier the drugs and a complimentary traffic in phony documents, the Tamil Tiger heroin rings have reputedly become a significant force in the wholesale market across Western Europe.

Another occasional participant in the drug trade is the IRA. Although the organization is fanatical about keeping Catholic areas of Ulster free at least of hard drugs, when it comes to international fundraising the puritanical zeal of its militants gets somewhat tempered. In 1986 the US government indicted a Boston-based group that had snuck into the US over a ton of marijuana to finance the purchase of American arms for the IRA. And two years later an IRA-Detroit mafia joint venture to ship Bolivian cocaine to Britain was exposed by an informant.[58]

However, the role of the Tamil Tigers and the IRA in international trafficking is trivial compared to that of the Nicaraguan *contras* during their anti-Sandinista crusade. Cocaine dealers paid for the use of *contra* bases and airstrips in Central America. They also gave the *contras* contributions in cash or supplies, including aircraft, to curry favour with US authorities and to head off prosecution in cases already under investigation. Furthermore, at one point a group of *contras* plotted to assassinate the former American ambassador to Colombia

39

and to arrange to have the assassination blamed on the Nicaraguan government in exchange for a reward of $ 1 million from a leading Colombian cocaine baron. *Contra* involvement in cocaine trafficking actually reached the point where money seized by the San Francisco police from a drug trafficking gang was returned to the leader of that gang after he presented the prosecutor with a letter stating the money was for "the reinstatement of democracy in Nicaragua".[59]

## 9. Revolutionary asset management

As those *contra* fundraisers discovered, the treasures of the black market present the guerrilla movement not only with opportunities, but also with challenges of financial management of the same sort faced by successful criminal organizations. Both criminal and guerrilla groups must make decisions regarding the collection of revenue, the hiding of the money and the investment of surpluses in such a way to assure they will be available to meet future needs.

However, a criminal organization, like any business, focusses, first, on earning income, and then on enjoying the resulting opportunities for expenditure. By contrast, a guerrilla group, like a government, is concerned, first, with anticipating future possible expenditures, and then tailoring its fundraising activities to meet those obligations.

The initial decision in revolutionary asset management is the selection of the medium of exchange in which the guerrilla group should be paid. That decision will reflect such factors as whether expenditures will be local (for example, for basic supplies) or international (noteably for heavy weapons). And in turn the choice of a medium of exchange will affect the selection of targets for fundraising activities.

The simplest form in which to collect revenues is basic commodities. In the earliest stage of an insurrection, the group might simply requisition directly supplies for immediate consumption. Colombia's FARC, at the start of its campaigns, called on ranchers and essentially begged handouts of food and clothing. Nor must such payments in kinds be reserved for the direct consumption of members of the group. During its highly successful early-1970s kidnapping campaign, the Argentinian ERP squeezed from the local Ford subsidiary $ 2 million worth of medicine, food, and school supplies for distribution to the poor.

One of the more useful forms of commodity payment is arms. Apart from staging dramatic weapons heists from military depots, the Argentinian ERP supplemented a host of successful kidnappings in 1974 by grabbing the Argentinian head of an Italian arms corporation and demanding a ransom in weapons. That is also the form in which Sikh separatists sometimes collect payment for

40

their assistance to smugglers moving drugs from the Afghan rebel-run heroin refineries in Pakistan's North West Frontier province across the border into India.[60]

Sometimes "revolutionary taxes" are collected in resaleable commodities. El Salvador's FMLN reputedly levies a coffee tax – nearly 400,000 kilograms in 1987 – on planters in its zones of control. And, of course, in Burma much of the taxation imposed on the Shan populations by the KMT, BCP and SUA alike is or was in the form of a percentage of the opium crop.

When bank loot, kidnap ransom and "tax" revenues are collected in kind, the other asset management decisions – hiding the proceeds and investing the surpluses – are taken care of more or less automatically as a problem merely of physical storage. Those decisions become more complicated when fundraising activities are conducted in cash or internationally traded luxury goods.

If the amount collected in local currency is relatively small, it likely poses little difficulty. But, just as with a drug trafficking ring in Europe or North America, a guerrilla group can be in danger of choking on its own success. When the Argentinian ERP forced Firestone to ransom its local president for $ 3 million worth of 500 peso notes, it was enough to fill the armoured car that the ERP thoughtfully provided. Kidnap ransom also poses another difficulty. Even in many developing countries ransom money can be more dangerous to handle and harder to launder than drug money, for the bills are almost invariably marked and/or their serial numbers recorded.

As to "war taxes" paid and held in local cash, one danger, that has come to pass on no less than three separate occasions since the Burmese ethnic insurrections began, is that the government could announce a sudden demonetization of all or part of the outstanding currency, generally the high denomination notes in which black market savings are often held.

The risk of local seizure, demonetization or even of severe exchange depreciation (possibly a consequence of the guerrilla group's own success in waging economic warfare) can obviously be minimized if the guerrilla group succeeds in having its assets converted into foreign currency form and stored abroad. If the currency in which income is "earned" is convertible, that should pose little difficulty. However even then the business of currency arbitrage is not entirely without its own risks. The IRA for a time used the services of a currency exchange house run by a disbarred lawyer. The firm specialized in picking up Irish punts from smugglers who had sold their goods in the Irish Republic, and converting them into the English pounds (the currency of Northern Ireland) at a better rate than the banks. Unfortunately, in 1988, the exchange house collapsed, leaving a hole in the books variously estimated at between 500,000 and 1.2 million pounds, of which a large amount belonged to the IRA.[61]

Unlike the IRA, most guerrilla groups operate in developing countries with soft currencies and tight exchange controls. Hence getting the money out of the country where it was earned can be a problem.

One way to solve it is to conduct fundraising activities in the form of valuable commodities that can be easily sold abroad. One excellent choice is diamonds, the vehicle of preference not just of UNITA and, for a time, SWAPO, but, more recently, the instrument through which the National Patriotic Front of Liberia has been funding its campaigns – though in this case it is through the military takeover of the diamond producing areas of neighbouring Sierra Leone.[62]

All manners of other valuable commodities will do quite well. UNITA also managed to slaughter over half of Angola's elephants, the poached ivory joining stolen diamonds and illegally cut hardwoods in barter deals for Israeli and South African arms.

Even more negotiable on international markets is drugs, the currency form in which various militia and guerrilla groups – from certain Afghan *mujihadeen* factions to the Burmese Communist Party – have taxed the populations under their control. Drugs can be sold for cash abroad, or even used in direct barter deals for weapons. Much of the Lebanese hashish crop used to be negotiated for sale in Cyprus to representatives of international syndicates who simultaneously arranged return cargos of weapons. During the Israeli occupation of Lebanon, the mechanics were even simpler. The rightist, pro-Israeli Christian forces exchanged hashish oil for heavy weapons with officers of Israeli military intelligence. And, while units of the Israeli army were busy in house-to-house searches, attempting to strip the occupied areas of their lethal arsenals, members of the leftist, anti-Israeli Lebanese National Resistance Front were bartering hashish and opium to individual Israeli soldiers in exchange for their guns and ammunition.

Yet another, even more direct approach is to request that payments of revolutionary taxes be made into foreign bank accounts. The Basque separatist group, Euskadi Ta Azkatasuna, used to finance operations by extorting money in pesetas from wealthy Basque businessmen on threat of assassination or destruction of their businesses. But when, in the late 1980s, support for ETA flagged and the Spanish police began interfering with its rackets, ETA shifted back to simple predatory activity, successfully kidnapping Spain's richest businessman and having the $ 5 million ransom deposited in ETA's French bank account.

Perhaps the most sophisticated example of the use of foreign banks is provided by the Phillipines' New People's Army. "Revolutionary taxes" from businesses seeking to operate in NPA-controlled territory along with donations from solidarity groups are paid straight into offshore accounts protected by Hong Kong and Singapore bank secrecy laws, and used to support a multimillion dollar international training and arms procurement operation based in Ja-

42

pan, Malaysia and Singapore. The transnational corporations that cooperated in providing much of the contents of the warchest seemed to feel that paying "revolutionary taxes" to the NPA was not much different from paying bribes to officials of the legal government.[63]

These offshore accounts are useful, not merely as means of financing immediate expenditure obligations but also for creating portfolios of income earning assets. Guerrilla groups, for obvious reasons, cannot engage in deficit financing and must meet their current expenditures solely out of current revenues. (The one exception, a *contra* issue of Nicaragua Freedom Bonds in the US, was a complete fiasco.) However, some of the older and wealthier guerrilla groups have been successful in exceeding their immediate funding targets. Like fiscally conservative states, they have, by running budget surpluses, been able to build up asset portfolios that serve to insulate the group's activities from fluctuations in their current revenues and allow them to fund expenditure obligations beyond those that their current revenues alone would support. It is precisely the PLO's portfolio of financial assets that has enabled it to transform itself from merely a successful guerrilla organization to a bona fide government-in exile.[64]

In its early days the PLO relied almost exclusively on outside sponsors, mainly the Arab states, who used their financial aid to try to manipulate the Palestinian national movement to their own political ends. Indeed, the first major quarrel the PLO had with a host government was when it was refused permission to independently tax the Palestinian population of Jordan.

By the early 1980s tax revenue and investment income was sufficient that the PLO itself was largely insulated from pressures from outside sponsors. Palestinians around the world, especially those employed in the oil states of the Gulf, were contributing 5–7% of their salaries, while income from assets – direct investment in factories, real estate holdings, plus stocks and bonds managed through the Swiss subsidiary of the Arab Bank of Amman – was running in excess of $ 1 billion a year. It was sufficient to support Diaspora schools and hospitals, a diplomatic corps in 90 countries, and a standing army of 14,000 in addition to allowing the PLO to run money by courier to assist the civil population of Occupied Palestine.[65]

While assets mean flexibility and independence, they also open a new window of vulnerability. In protecting their assets, guerrilla groups face the same problems as criminals, and more. For successful criminals are precisely those most desirous of a public front of respectability which simultaneously provides them with a means for disguising the origins of their income and wealth. By contrast, successful guerrillas seek notoriety in terms of public confrontation with the authorities, in which case identifiable assets are susceptible to counterattack by the state. These challenges are particularly intense now in the face of rapidly changing financial technology and the increasing commitment of national intelligence agencies to tracing and seizing their antagonists' funds.

43

Thus, when the PLO shifted from being a guerrilla organization to a government-in-exile for the refugee population, the requirement of fixed infrastructure exposed its assets to direct assault. In 1982 Israel invaded Lebanon in an effort to wipe out the economic foundations of the PLO's worldwide operations. During the course of the invasion the Israeli armed forces sought out and physically destroyed $ 400 million worth of PLO infrastructure and assets in the form of factories, offices, commercial real estate, hospitals and schools, as well as seizing bank records that might have permitted them to trace financial assets around the world. To this the PLO responded by liquidating most of its portfolio of stocks and bonds, and moving the money into short-term, money-market assets hidden behind the screen of ghost companies and nominee accounts. The PLO's skill in keeping its assets liquid and essentially intact has enabled it to survive further disasters like the cancellation during the Gulf War of the mandatory checkoff the Gulf State rulers used to impose on the PLO's behalf on the salaries of Palestinian workers.

Less prominent organizations can protect themselves to some degree by operating strictly in cash – as the IRA long did. But as IRA operations widened in geographic extent and broadened in scope, as the British authorities began paying closer attention to the income side of the guerrilla group's operations, and as the US became less hospitable to the IRA (and more inclined to cooperate with Britain), the financial tactics necessarily became more sophisticated, including sharing banks and courier services with American mafia figures. In 1984 the IRA instructed a victim company to deposit a multimillion dollar extortion payment directly into a Swiss bank. The money was then wired to the Manhattan branch of the Bank of Ireland. To break the trail, the money was subsequently picked up in cash and couriered across to Ireland for deposit in another branch of the same bank.

But it was all in vain. The next year the British government managed to trace the money and the Irish government impounded $ 2.5 million in the IRA account.[66]

Furthermore, even if a guerrilla group is successful in hiding its assets from an opposing government, there are other dangers with which to contend. In the hot money business those who seek secrecy, by definition, have something to hide. They are therefore without (legal) recourse in the event of defalcations by their financial agents. Thus, the wealth the Colombian M-19 had painstakingly accumulated from bank robbery and kidnapping was prudently stashed in a Panama bank, awaiting a time of need. When, in 1985 the M-19, facing an army offensive, tried to withdraw some of the $ 50 million, the bank's owner refused permission. So the M-19 staged another kidnapping – of the reluctant banker – and the money was released.[67]

Not so fortunate were the Argentinian Monteneros. Of the $ 60 million in cash collected from the ransom of the Born brothers, the Monteneros guerrillas

44

entrusted between $ 12 and $ 20 million to an Argentinian banker who was already running a capital flight business for leading Peronist politicians. The money was stashed in Uruguay, the most common destination for funds fleeing Argentina. Once a month the Monteneros would call at the banker's office with a suitcase to pick up $ 150,000 in interest payments. This happy arrangement came to an end during the 1975–6 crackdown by the Argentinian military. The banker fled the country, reportedly dying in a strange plane crash in Mexico and leaving behind a string of broken banks stretching from Argentina to Belgium to the US. One thing that was not left behind was the Monteneros's money.[68]

## 10. Insurgency's new frontiers

During the 1970s and 1980s, across continents and around the world, insurgencies abounded and civil wars raged. With the end of the Cold War, there is now widespread optimism that the pattern of terrorism leading to guerrilla warfare leading to full-fledged insurrection has been broken. Direct East-West tensions have not only abated, but have been replaced by a willingness to seek peaceful resolutions to many Third World political, ideological and military disputes.

Indeed, the current thaw suggests that the analogy between criminal groups and guerrilla organizations in their predatory, parasitical and symbiotic stages, can be carried one step further, to the stage of reintegration into formal society.

Criminals have often succeeded in achieving respectability through a combination of state amnesty and social amnesia. If the criminals are minor in importance, the criminals will explicitly agree to live by the rules of the state. If the criminals are sufficiently powerful, the state will implicitly agree to live by the rules of the criminal. No better example of the latter can be seen than in Kuomintang China in the 1930s. There, Huang Chih-jung, (aka Pock-Marked Huang), boss of the Shanghai underworld and of its opium and prostitution rackets, was chosen as chief of police of the French Concession, while his lieutenant and chief enforcer, Tu Yueh-sheng (aka big-Eared Tu) would take tea with President Chaing Kai-shek's sister and chat with her husband, the government's main financial advisor, about mutually profitable investments.[69]

Nor are such instances merely of historical interest. Currently more than ten percent of the members of the legislature of the Indian state of Bihar have criminal records, and they assure their continued wealth and power through heavily armed gangs whose activities, not surprisingly, the political authorities seem loath to curb.[70] Similarly in Lebanon, Walid Joumblatt, the leader of the Druze Progressive Socialist Party and its paramilitary arm, insisted it was necessary for all "progressive" groups to take part in the recent elections to prevent the heroin traffickers from taking control of the legislature.

In a similar way guerrilla groups can be amnestied, and evolve into respectable political parties. That has already happened with the M-19 in Colombia, and it remains the primary objective of the FMLN in El Salvador today. Or they can achieve victory, with even more spectacular results. Israel is unique, not in the fact that someone could climb to the country's highest elected office after a successful career in bank robbery, extortion and assassination – many heads of state have had such accomplishments on their curriculum vitae. Rather it is unique in the fact that not one but two recent Israeli prime ministers have so distinguished themselves.

The proven possibilities of amnesty and reintegration, then, seem to be further reasons for optimism that the worst is over. However, this optimism is likely unwarranted.

Granted that the Cold War did fan the flames of guerrilla and civil war in the 1970s and 1980s, on neither the ideological nor the financial-logistical levels could it be blamed for lighting the fires.

Apart from the fact that the most tenuous of leftwing guerrilla groups routinely denounced the Communist countries for betraying revolution, it was never clear that for most of these groups Marxism was really very high on their political agendas. While small, urban "terrorist" groups operating in ethnically homogenous societies might have found their sole ideological raison d'etre in some obsure passage in Marx, Lenin or Mao, serious popular insurgencies, be they in Peru, Ireland or Kampuchea, seemed to use Marxist ideology essentially as legitimation for the expression of much more fundamental ethnocultural alienation or tribal and religious animosities, not to mention its occasional usefulness as cover for simple criminality.

The politico-ideological veneer was always thin in the case of something like the Basque separatist ETA organization which invokes the notion of proletarian solidarity to justify the creation of an independent Basque homeland in a region of Spain where the great majority of the working class is made up of poor Spaniards from other provinces.[71] It was harder to penetrate in the case of the Burmese Communist Party where much effort was made to politically indoctrinate lower-level cadres. But inevitably the Burmese Communist Party succumbed to larger Burmese political realities – disintegrating in the face of a military rebellion by the ethnic rank-and-file against the aging Birman leadership. In retrospect it turned out that much of the enthusiasm with which the rank-and-file devoured the Maoist tracts passed out by the political leaders was the fact that the thin paper on which they were written was excellent for rolling cigarets.[72]

On the other side, once rhetoric gave way to action, the political programs of many "rightwing" rebel groups, too, seemed to have more to do with the desire to use their military muscle to concentrate power and wealth in the hands of an ethno-religious minority than to open their societies to notions of the free-market brotherhood of homo economicus. Despite repeated offers of power shar-

46

ing from the Angolan government accompanied by a major program of free-market reforms, the UNITA guerrilla group (which started off as a Marxist organization before ego and ethnicity got in the way) seems intent on the continuation of a military campaign whose ultimate objective appears to be the political division of Angola by tribal affiliation.

Furthermore the notion that the Soviet Union or the People's Republic of China were financially "behind" the former wave of guerrilla activity is simply false. Financial aid given by Communist countries to "leftwing" guerrilla groups in the 1970s and 1980s varied from minimal (like East Germany occasionally offering refuge to fleeing members of the Red Army Faction) to nonexistent. The Soviet Union covertly pumped money into the hands, not of insurgent groups, but of Communist parties willing to contest elections. And, following the death of Mao, China restricted its aid to the Burmese Communist Party and the Khmer Rouge in order to control events close to its own border. Overwhelmingly financing for "leftwing" insurgents came initially from predatory criminal activity, then from black market dealings, and finally from the tax base of their own zones of control.

This essential self-reliance by the "leftwing" insurgents is a stark contrast to the cornucopia of American, British, French and Saudi Arabian financial and military aid available to rightwing anti-government rebel forces. Yet even here their dependence on their sponsors was far from absolute. Be it the Afghan *mujihadeen* in heroin trafficking or the Angolan UNITA group in diamond smuggling and ivory poaching, any sensible insurgent group did its best to minimize the political constraints of outside aid by diversifying its funding sources.

Thus, far from assuming that the epidemic of insurgency is likely to diminish with the end of the Cold War, there are compelling reasons – on the level of both ideology and finance – for believing that the opposite is quite possibly true. Not only will "low intensity" conflicts of all sorts accelerate but their destructive power is likely to get much worse.

The end of the Cold War has succeeded in stripping the last constraints from the more primordial forms of ethnic and theological conflict. "Class enemies" who could be "re-educated" have been replaced by ethno-cultural aliens congenitally beyond redemption. From Europe to the Far East, ancient grievances are rising to the surface, societies are rediscovering (or inventing) ethno-cultural roots and nations are resurrecting old, often arcane claims on neighbouring territory.

Yet most of these disputes and antagonisms would be little more than rhetorical if the material means were not becoming readily available to act upon them.

For much of the post-war period, money was a necessary, but not a sufficient condition to open the doors of the international arms black market to a guerrilla movement. For decades the market was, if not totally controlled, at least highly influenced by the intelligence agencies of the major powers. Indeed, in the period just after the second world war the US and the USSR had the business of supplying the market for new weapons virtually to themselves; while the US arranged to have an ex-CIA agent-turned-international-weapons-merchant buy up most of the world's stock of surplus small arms.

But that comfortable control was shortlived. Duopoly in new weapons with a controlled black market in light arms gave way in the 1960s and 1970s to oligopoly in new weapons production, a controlled black market in second hand heavy material and a free-for-all in lighter weapons. First Bangkok, flush with Viet Nam war surplus material, and then Beirut, the unfortunate recipient of the attentions of the intelligence services and associated arms peddlers of at least a dozen countries, emerged as sources of supply to all who had the cash to buy.

Finally, by the end of the 1980s all vestiges of control with respect to heavy weapons had vanished. Apart from a plethora of suppliers of new material, the second hand market in major weapons systems has been abundantly nourished, first by the overflow from Afghanistan and the Middle East, and now by another, perhaps even more dangerous source of supply, the disintegrating Red Army. In the future the only restriction on the amount and type of arms an insurgent group can acquire is likely to be how much money it has to spend.

And the impact of that restriction is likely to be minimized by the results of a dramatic process of restructuring of economic life taking place all across the globe.

Paralleling the delegitimation of the extant political order, the old instruments and institutions of economic organization are also obsolete. In one country after another not only is the "underground" – the informal, unrecorded and unregulated – part of the economy growing faster than the official part, but in many countries of the developing world it is now larger in absolute terms. It is not a matter merely of unlicensed street vendors but of entire large-scale production units that are operating in an environment over which the formal state apparatus has no control.

It was not accidental that, in the past, insurgencies thrived in precisely those societies where the delegitimation of the state was paralleled by the spread of underground economic activity. And it will not be accidental that, in the future, the spread of the underground economy will be a political and financial breeding ground for the forces most anxious to challenge the status quo distribution of power and wealth. In years to come the underground riches of bank robbery and ransom kidnapping may pale in comparison the returns from international electronic funds transfer fraud and thermonuclear and chemical blackmail.

48

## Acknowledgements

Thanks to the following individuals for their comments and criticism: Rex Brynen; Fernando Cepeda; Paul Clare; Andrew Fischer; Abdo Kassir; Peter Lupsha (whose theoretical "model" is so important for the core of the argument); Sam Noumoff; James Putzel; Filipo Sabetti; and Brenda Spotton. Thanks to my research assistants, Rafy Kourouian and Paulo Bilizerkjian for their zealous digging. And thanks to the Social Sciences and Humanities Research Council of Canada for financial support during the research for this paper.

## Notes and references

While the literature on guerrilla and insurgent groups in many languages is enormous, the amount of discussion in that literature of the financial aspects of guerrilla activity is surprisingly limited. This in part reflects a Cold War myth prevalent in the West, namely that anti-state activities by armed (and often unarmed) groups in the West were in some way part of an International Communist Conspiracy, and therefore their funding came directly from their political masters behind the Iron Curtain. Witness the comment by the leading exponent of the Bolshevik Conspiracy Hypothesis, Claire Sterling:

> They made an incredible assortment. By the end of the 1970s, ethnic and religious nationalists and separatists, anti-colonial patriots and anti-racists, Sardinian bandits and Mafia thugs, anarchists, Trotskyists, Maoists, unregenerate Stalinists and otherwise unclassified Marxist-Leninists. No single label could be pinned on them; but they had all come to see themselves as elite battalions in a world wide Army of Communist Combat. (The Terror Network New York: 1981 p. 16)

While such views now seem at best infantile, at worst bordering on the paranoic, the prevalence of this view in the 1980s is not accidental, reflecting as it does the then prevailing political climate and, one supposes, an adroit campaign of disinformation by the interested intelligence agencies. Not surprisingly, this is especially evident in material dealing with the Palestinian resistance groups. As a result, critical academic (and journalistic) research on the topic is rare.

A variety of published sources have been used for the current paper – some books and a wide range of periodicals. But among the most important sources of information have been comments made to me from persons who observed the events and actions directly.

1. This paper makes no effort to unscramble the terminological confusion around the phenomenon of anti-state armed insurgency. Some prefer the term "terrorist" and some prefer "freedom fighter"; some talk of "guerrilla" armies, and some of "resistance" or "national liberation" forces. And in practice these organizations vary from a handful of urban activists waving revolvers to full-fledged armies equipped with heavy artillery. Since the point of this paper is to

examine what armed anti-state insurgent forces of all sorts have in common from the fundraising side, the most neutral term, "guerrilla group", is used throughout.

2. See esp. Joseph Hanlon, *Beggar Your Neighbour: Apartheid Power in Southern Africa* London: 1986 153ff.

3. For a general overview of Sendero activities see Gabriella Tarzona-Sevillano, *Sendero Luminoso and the Threat of Narco-Terrorism* New York: 1990.

4. While the FMLN term "zones of control" is used throughout this paper, there are equivalent terms used by other insurgent groups. The New People's Army in the Phillipines refers to the same phenomena as "consolidated zones", and the Eritrean People's Liberation Front calls them "liberated zones".

   Interestingly the Mozambique National Resistance (RENAMO), a group notorious for having no political program beyond destruction, also uses a three-fold classification system for territory in which it is active: control areas where it is sufficiently well entrenched to organize forced labour; tax areas where it extorts supplies and money from the population; and destruction areas where the objective is indiscriminate slaughter. (Globe and Mail 26/5/88; Hanlon, p. 139).

5. The most outstanding recent work on the New People's Army is by Gregg Jones, *Red Revolution: Inside the Phillipines Guerrilla Movement* Boulder Colorado: 1989.

6. The literature on this phenomenon is vast. See for example the January-February 1990 issue of *Middle East Reports*.

7. For a summary of the events leading up to the Iran-contra affair, see R.T. Naylor *Hot Money and the Politics of Debt* London: 381–417, 1987.

8. A good source on the flow of aid from the US is Jack Holland *The American Connection: US Guns, Money & Influence in Northern Ireland* Penguin: 1987.

9. *Sunday Times* 1/9/91; *L'Express* 11/9/92.

10. *The Times* 29/8/92; *Sunday Times* 30/8/92; *Guardian Weekly* 20/9/92.

11. Leakage from these aid flows can be "natural" i.e. criminal – and already anticipated in the budget. Or it can be political in motivation where a donor country wants to aid a guerrilla group but maintain deniability. In cases of exceptionally large losses there is likely an element of political connivance involved. I am indebted to Professor Sam Noumoff for this point.

12. *Far Eastern Economic Review* 27/6/76. Subsequently there have been many allegations that Libya is responsible for arming the Moros. Like all stories about Libyan activities this should be assumed to be propaganda (like the ETA connection) until proven otherwise (as an IRA connection was).

13. *Far Eastern Economic Review* 5/3/89; New York Times 18/4/88; Middle East Oct. 1991.

14. The theoretical framework to follow is adopted from Peter Lupsha's "Organized Crime: Rational Choice Not Ethnic Group Behavior" in *Law Enforcement Intelligence Digest*, Winter: 1988.

16. Alfred McCoy *The Politics Of Heroin* New York: 1991 pp 146–153.

17. One example is from the experience of the Chinese People's Army. During the fight against the Japanese occupation armies and the subsequent civil war, the People's Army had substantial success recruiting social bandits and even opium traffickers to its ranks, some of whom became high ranking officers.

18. Sterling op. cit. p. 223.

19. Jones op. cit. p. 138.

20. Christopher Dobson and Ronald Payne *The Weapons of Terror* London: 1979 p. 19.

21. On the Huk rebellion in general see Benedict Kerkvliet *The Huk Rebellion* Berkeley: 1977 and Eduardo Lachica *Huk: Phillipines Agrarian Society in Revolt* Manila: 1971.

22. A good survey of racketeering by the IRA is in James Adams *The Financing of Terror* New

50

York: 1986. On the collapse of the UDA, New York Times 14/3/88.

23.  See Barbara Conway *The Piracy Business* London: 1982 and *Maritime Fraud* London: 1990; L'évenement du Jeudi 20 Avril 1989; *Middle East* August 1988.

24.  *New York Times* 27/12/84, 12/2/88.

25.  *Israeli Foreign Affairs* Vol. VIII No. 3, March 25, 1992.

26.  *Middle East* October 1990.

27.  *New York Times* 3/7/88.

28.  Richard Clutterbuck *Terrorism and Guerrilla Warfare* London: 1987 p. 53.

29.  See the memoirs of Jimmy "the Weasel" Fratianno. Ovid Desmaris, *The Last Mafiosa* New York: 1981 p. 32.

30.  Edgar O'Ballance *The Cyanide War: Tamil Insurrection in Sri Lanka* London: 1989 p. 30.

31.  Jonathan Randall *Going All the Way* New York: 1986 p. 98–.

32.  Cited in Jillian Becker *Hitler's Children: the Story of the Baader-Meinhof Terrorist Gang* New York: 1977 p. 180.

33.  Robert Moss *Urban Guerrilla* London: 1972. Chapter 11 deals with the Tupamaros.

34.  For details see Lester Sobel ed. *Political Terrorism* New York: 1975. There is an excellent analysis by Susanne Purnell in Brian Jenkins ed. *Terrorism and Personal Protection* Storeham: 1985. The entire volume is a good, factual treatment.

35.  Richard Gillespie *Soldiers of Peron: Argentina's Montoneros* Oxford: 1982 pp. 180–3.

36.  *Canadian Business* June 1983 examines the experiences of some kidnapped oil workers.

37.  *Far Eastern Economic Review* 5/10/89; *India Today* 15/1/91.

38.  See especially Adams op. cit. Chapter 7 for a survey of IRA fundraising activities. See also *Guardian Weekly* 2/10/88 and *Financial Times* 7/1/92.

39.  Another parasitical technique the IRA is alleged to have employed to great advantage (along with the mafia) is EEC subsidy fraud. See The *Times* 8/2/89.

40.  *Cambio* 16 15/1/90.

41.  *Wall Street Journal* 25/9/84: Jacques Bernadis *Diamants Connection* Paris: 1985 p. 67.

42.  *Semana*, 3 Julio, 1992.

43.  *New York Times* 29/10/90, 9/1/91, 10/11/92.

44.  Similarly, once the IRA and its rivals had bombed and destroyed the city buses, the IRA organized networks of "black taxis" – which pay de facto licence fees to the IRA and purchase fuel and make repairs only at IRA-linked garages.

45.  *Middle East Times* 1/10/88.

46.  *New York Times* 12/8/92.

47.  See especially Andre and Louis Boucaud *Sur la Piste des Seigneurs de la Guerre* Paris: 1985.

48.  *The Economist* 6/4/91; *Far Eastern Economic Review* 22/2/90; *Le Monde Diplomatique* August 1989.

49.  *Asiaweek* 11/10/91.

50.  *Far Eastern Economic Review* 7/2/91.

51.  McCoy op. cit. 170–2, 351–2.

52.  In general see Bertil Lintner *The Rise and Fall of the Burmese Communist Party* New York: 1990.

53.  *The Economist* 6/4/91; *Far Eastern Economic Review* 28/6/90.

54.  *Far Eastern Economic Review* 3/3/88, 14/4/88.

55.  Cited in *New York Times* 18/6/86.

56.  See especially the excellent discussion in Rensaaler Lee III *White Labyrinth: Cocaine and Political Power* New Brunswick: 1989.

57.  The standard view of Sendero was challenged by research on the ground conducted by Edmundo Morales *Cocaine – White Gold Rush in the Andes* Tuscon: 1989.

58. *The Times* 26/11/88.

59. See, among many other works, Peter Dale Scott and Jonathan Marshall *Cocaine Politics: Drugs, Armies and the CIA in Central America* Berkeley: 1991.

60. See the analysis of K.R. Singh in S.C. Tiwari ed. *Terrorism in India* New Delhi: 1990.

61. *The Times* 6/10/88.

62. *Africa Analysis* 3/4/92.

63. *Far Eastern Economic Review* 28/7/88, 19/5/88.

64. A basic book on PLO finances is Cheryl Rubenberg *The PLO: Its Institutional Infrastructure* New York: 1982. There is less reliable material in Adams, *The Financing of Terror* and material that verges on the preposterous in Neil Livingston and David Halevy *Inside the PLO* New York: 1990.

65. For a time most of the support money went into the Territories in cash using returning residents, sympathetic tourists, orthodox priests and even anti-Israeli Hassidic Jews as couriers. (*Middle East Reporter* 30/7/88).

66. *Sunday Times* 24/2/85.

67. *Latin America Weekly Report* 29/3/85.

68. *Barron's* 28/9/81.

69. Peter Lupsha op. cit. comments that "This would be roughly equivalent in the United States to the Rockefellers and the Kennedys having a regular Sunday brunch with Carlo Gambino or John Gotti."

70. *Illustrated Weekly of India* 18/7/92.

71. Sterling op. cit. 175, 181.

72. Lintner op. cit. 35.

# [19]

# Addressing identity crime in crime management information systems: Definitions, classification, and empirics

*Rodger Jamieson*[a], *Lesley Pek Wee Land*[a], *Donald Winchester*[a], *Greg Stephens*[a], *Alex Steel*[b], *Alana Maurushat*[b], *Rick Sarre*[c]

[a] *The Australian School of Business, School of Information Systems, Technology and Management, University of New South Wales, Australia*
[b] *Faculty of Law, University of New South Wales, Australia*
[c] *School of Commerce, the University of South Australia, Australia*

## ABSTRACT

Identity fraud as a term and concept in its formative stages was often presumed to be identity theft and visa versa. However, identity theft is caused by the identities (or tokens) of individuals or organisations being stolen is an enabling precursor to identity fraud. The boundaries of identity fraud and identity theft are now better defined. The absence of specific identity crime legislation could be a cause of perpetrators not classified as breaching identity crimes but under other specific entrenched law such as benefit fraud, or credit card fraud. This metrics overlap can cause bias in crime management information systems. This study uses a multi-method approach where data was collected in both a quantitative and qualitative manner. These approaches are used as a lens for defining different classes of online identity crimes in a crime management (IS) security context. In doing so, we contribute to a deeper understanding of identity crime by specifically examining its hierarchical classes and definitions; to aid clearer structure in crime management IS. We seek to answer the questions: should current law around identity fraud continue to be reinforced and measures introduced to prevent identity crime; should laws be amended; or should new identity crime laws be constructed? We conclude and recommend a solution incorporating elements of all three.

*Keywords:*
Identity crime
Identity fraud
Identity theft
Identity deception
Computer crime
Internet
Information systems security (ISS)
Taxonomy
Personnel identifying information (PII)
Crime management information systems

## 1. Introduction

The illegal online use or trade in identities of individuals and organizations is recognized to have a substantial influence on other crimes such as frauds and money laundering; seriously impacting the real economy.[1] The global economic cost of these identity crimes was estimated to be "US\$2 trillion in 2005".[2] In the United States the annual estimated cost of identity crime alone in 2009 was "US\$54 billion".[3] These survey figures may not reflect the actual figures if real cases were to be analysed.[4] A major concern with the costing of identity crimes is the potential bias, error, and lack of

---

[1] Goode, S., and Lacey, D. 2010 "Detecting Complex Account Fraud in the Enterprise: The Role of Technical and Non-Technical Controls", Decision Support Systems. Ngai, E. W. T., Hu, Y., Wong, Y. H., Chen, Y., and Sun, X. 2011. "The Application of Data Mining Techniques in Financial Fraud Detection: A Classification Framework and an Academic Review of Literature", Decision Support Systems (50:4) or (50), pp. 559–569.

[2] Hurley, J., and Veytsel, A. 2003. "Identity Theft: A \$2 Trillion Criminal Industry in 2005", The Aberdeen Group 13 May, p. 1.

[3] Miceli, D., and Kim, R. 2010. "2010 Identity Fraud Survey Report: Consumer Version", Javelin Strategy & Research February, p. 5.

[4] For example, the Uniform Crime Reports have different statistics than the National Crime Victimisation Surveys in the US. See Chen, H., Schroeder, J., Hauck, R. V., Ridgeway, L., Atabakhsh, H., Gupta, H., Boarman, C., Rasmussen, K., and Clements, A. W. (2002). "COPLINK Connect: Information and Knowledge management for Law Enforcement", Decision Support Systems (34), pp. 271–285.

**382**              COMPUTER LAW & SECURITY REVIEW 28 (2012) 381–395

consistency in how they are defined and classified.[5] As crime management information systems (IS) transition from paper-based to digital systems to ease storage and aid retrieval (often remotely for law enforcement), there is an emergent need to classify the fields accurately.[6]

The US leads the way in criminalizing identity crime and data breaches.[7] (IS) security research focuses on computer abuse, computer crime, and computer-related crimes. Computer crimes include "crimes whereby the computer is the target or the mechanism for committing the crime or the computer user is the target. It also includes crimes committed over the Internet or where the Internet plays a role in the commission of the crime" (see Table 6).[8] Online identity crimes are linked to computer abuse, computer crime and computer-related crime in IS security, because they are enabled by computers and/or the Internet. A difference is that identity crime involves social engineering of people and technology.

The ubiquity of information technology; computers, the Internet, mobile devices, and their interconnectedness in a digital economy enables the increase of identity crime methods, such as phishing, not previously accounted for by computer crime and abuse in IS research.[9] Internet users reached the 2 billion mark in January 2011.[10] Smart perpetrators are devising increasingly sophisticated ways of committing identity crimes. Therefore classes of IS-enabled abuse, such as identity crime, continue to evolve often ahead of IS security innovations.[11]

The remainder of this paper is structured as follows. The next section discusses the methodology.[12] Then we identify

the various definitions of identity crime and discuss our results. The final sections discuss the contributions, implications, limitations, conclusion and future research in this area.

## 2.    Methodology

We use a multi-method research design consisting of qualitative methods and quantitative methods via secondary data to investigate how identity crime terms are defined and how the categories shape organizational actions for measuring and improving IS security to reduce identity crimes.[13] We collected qualitative data from Australia via 10 face-to-face interviews and two by teleconference in 2002. In 2002 Australia had no legislation that specifically targeted identity crime and this was a unique out-of-sample setting to study identity crimes as other jurisdictions such as the United States had enacted identity crime legislation. We also gathered data from communications with Attorney Generals and Crime Collection agencies until 2010 from many countries. All qualitative data has been continuously updated from secondary sources. From our interview transcripts, we derived themes using NVivo qualitative software.[14] The data was collected from Attorney General's departments and Government Statistics Agencies from Australia (Federal and States), Canada, European Union, Ireland, Netherland, United Nations, United Kingdom, and the US (Federal and States). The data was based on questions of identity crime definitions and their crime classification systems in use. We also obtained conditional access to the ABS Personal Fraud data collection to reclassify their identity crime data[15] for our empirical quantitative identity crime data testing, using our definitions and classification.

Interviewees were drawn from diverse industries such as banks, retailers, telecommunications, utilities, State Government licensing authorities, Federal Government agencies (welfare, immigration), and a US academic/criminologist for insights from the US. The organizations selected for interviewing represented those most targeted by identity crime perpetrators. Their credibility can be attested by the senior positions they held for instance in fraud, fraud management, compliance, and/or internal auditing. Some of the interviewees were previously employed in law enforcement or the legal profession. The interview instrument contained mainly 13 questions. Each interview lasted approximately one and a half hours. Interviewee recordings were professionally transcribed, checked for reliability and accuracy, and corroborated by members of the research team. The rich data and information gathered via email correspondence and/or telephone

[5] Romanosky, S., Telang, R., and Acquisti, A. 2008. "Do Data Breach Disclosure Laws Reduce Identity Theft?", Carnegie Mellon University pp. 1–30.

[6] Chen, above note 4. See also Orlikowski, W. J., and Iacono, C. S. 2001. "Research Commentary: Desperately Seeking the "IT" in IT Research – A Call to Theorizing in the IT Artifact", Information Systems Research (12:2), pp. 121–134, and Sproule, S., and Archer, N. 2007. "Defining Identity Theft", IEEE Computer Society, Eighth World Congress on the Management of eBusiness pp. 1–11.

[7] Romanosky, above note 5. See also Maurushat, A., "Data Breach Notification Law Across the World from California to Australia" Privacy Law and Business International, April, 2009.

[8] Douglas, J. E., Burgess, A. W., Burgess, A. G., and Ressler, R. K. (Eds. 2nd edition). 2006. Crime Classification Manual, San Francisco, CA, Jossey-Bass. Parker, D. B. 1976. Crime by Computer. New York, Charles Scribner's Sons.

[9] Bryant, R. (Ed.) 2008. Investigating Digital Crime. England, John Wiley & Sons Ltd.

[10] Statement of ITU Secretary General, Dr. Hamadoun Toure, January 26, 2011 available at http://www.who.int/topics/millennium_development_goals/accountability_commission/ITU_SG_statement_26Jan2011.pdf.

[11] Biegelman, M. T. (ed.) 2009. Identity Theft Handbook: Detection, Prevention, and Security. John Wiley & Sons, Inc. See also Berg, S. 2008. "Preventing Identity Theft Through Information Technology", in Perspectives on Identity Theft, M. M. McNally, and G. R. Newman (Eds.), Crime Prevention Studies, (23), pp. 151–167. Monsey, NY, U.S.A., Criminal Justice Press.

[12] McKelvey, B. 1982. Organizational Systematics: Taxonomy, Evolution, Classification. Berkeley, CA. University of California Press. See also Stuessy, T. F. (2nd edition) 2009. Plant Taxonomy: The Systematic Evaluation of Comparative Data. New York, Columbia University Press.

[13] Ashakkori, A., and Teddlie, C. 1998. Mixed Methodology: Combining Qualitative and Quantitative Approaches. Thousand Oaks, CA, Sage Publications. Corbin, J., and Strauss, A. 1990. "Grounded Theory Research: Procedures, Canons, and Evaluative Criteria", Qualitative Sociology (13:1), pp. 3–21. Glaser, B. G., and Strauss, A. L. 1967. The Discovery of Grounded Theory. Chicago: Aldine.

[14] QSR NVivo. 2008. Version 2.0. Melbourne, Australia, QSR International Pty. Ltd.

[15] Australian Bureau of Statistics. 2008a. 4528.0 Personal Fraud 2007. Australian Bureau of Statistics, June, pp. 1–40.

| **Table 1 – Proposed identity crime definitions.** |
|---|
| **Identity crime** is a generic term that covers identity fraud, identity theft, and identity deception acts or events. It also applies to identity crime related crimes such as terrorism, money laundering, and trafficking (people, drugs, weapons, illicit material) enabled by identity fraud, identity theft, and identity deception where the purpose of the perpetrator is to seek anonymity, avoid detection, or shift the blame. |
| **Identity fraud** is the deliberate use (in criminal law terminology the combination of a physical act element and a mental fault element of intention, knowledge or recklessness) of identity theft and/or identity deception details (documentation or personal identifying information) for a financial gain, avoidance of a loss, or to seek anonymity to commit identity-related crimes (money laundering, trafficking, or terrorism acts). |
| **Identity theft** is the unlawful obtaining of identity documentation details (including personal identifying information used in customer not present situations or when customers interface with machines to authenticate, for instance personal identification numbers (PINs), passwords, key tokens, or biometrics). |
| **Identity deception** is misrepresentation through: |
|    i.  Creation of a false identity or changes to an existing identity through alteration of existing data, or the context of the data, relating to the identification of a real individual or entity, such as via a change of name, change of initials, change of residency details, change of date of birth etc. |
|    ii.  Creation of a false identity based on fake (i.e. fictitious) identification data |
|    iii.  Creation of false identification documentation both novel and counterfeit. |
| Source: Extended from Jamieson et al. (2008). |

communications with government Attorney Generals and Statistic agencies were similarly analysed for main themes. Secondary data collected on the relevant literature by key word searches of library, Internet, legislation and other proprietary databases using terms such as, identity crime, identity fraud, identity theft, and identity deception or synonyms. Data obtained from secondary sources, enabled the discovery of more detailed and refined concepts.

## 3. Identity crimes

The major objective for this paper is to refine identity definitions and improve identity crime classes reducing class overlap or ambiguity. Identity crime involves the illegal use of any part of a biometric, attributed or biographical identity of an individual and entity.[16] These three identity components are used by governments and organizations to identify and authenticate customers in everyday business transactions. The identity crime label is an overarching class that encompasses identity fraud. Identity fraud is enabled by identity crime sub-classes identity theft and identity deception. The following Tables define and refine existing identity definitions. Fig. 1

Confusion between the labels – identity theft and identity fraud – was due to the evolving nature of the definitions within different countries (see Table 6). Second, within the sub-class 'identity deception', numerous other labels are often used, for example identity falsification, identity fabrication, fake identity, false identity, or synthetic identity. Similarly, within the 'identity theft' sub-class other names in use may include identity appropriation, and true name identity. The variety of terminology and the dynamic nature of identity crimes' sub-classes exacerbate definitional and classificatory uncertainty.

In the development of identity crime legislation and its judicial interpretation, legal authorities would be assisted by a shared vocabulary and classification of crime types. While the full range of identity-related crimes is too broad and evolving to be able to precisely or usefully define in legislation, significant clarity can be achieved in definition of sub-categories of identity crime. Reaching a consensus among stakeholders for the meaning of identity crime terms also has major implications in data and information collection, analysis, and dissemination of outputs across time and locations for comparison.[17]

As a result of ambiguous crime class definitions and the lack of crime theories used in IS research, the metrics used to record trends in newer computer-related crime facilitated abuse methods like identity crime are not consistently collated or comparable.[18] Hence specific information about these crimes is not easily retrievable.[19] This is a critical research gap when determining the theory for explaining computer and online identity crime situations.[20] Recently, there is support in an IS security context to investigate identity theft, Cybercrime, electronic fraud, credit card fraud, antiphishing and privacy methods by applying criminological theories.[21] Proper classifications will enable a better understanding of the relative level of this identity crime activity and

---

[16] Kim, R. 2008. "2008 Identity Fraud Survey Report Consumer Version: How Consumers Can Protect Themselves", Javelin Strategy & Research pp. 1–23.

[17] Model Criminal Law Officers' Committee. 2008. Final Report Identity Crime. Commonwealth of Australia, March, 1–46.
[18] Goode, above note 1.
[19] OECD. 2008. Scoping Paper on Online Identity Theft. Organisation for Economic Co-operation and Development, DSTI/CP(2007)3/FINAL, January, pp. 1–69.
[20] Liang, H., and Xue, Y. 2009. "Avoidance of Information Technology Threats: A Theoretical Perspective", MIS Quarterly (33:1), pp. 71–90. See also Berg, above note 12; and Orlikowski, above note 6.
[21] Mahmood, M. A., Siponen, M., Straub, D., and Rao, H. R. 2008. "Special Issue – Call for Papers – Information Systems Security in a Digital Economy", MIS Quarterly pp. 1–6. Smith, S., Winchester, D., Bunker, D., Jamieson, R. 2010. A Study of Mandated Compliance to an Information Systems Security de jure Standard in a Government Organization. MIS Quarterly (34), 463–486.

its impact on organizations and individuals, in making generalizations over time nationally and internationally.[22] This process is complicated when there may be more than one (legal) jurisdiction within a country, as in Australia, Canada or the US, among others.

The main purpose of crime metrics in management IS gathered by national statistics collecting bodies or at the law enforcement case level is to have a history of relationships that could help authorities to understand and develop counter-measures for crimes.[23] However, these relationships are often unclear or imprecise, due to method biases. This is in part due to perpetrator acts not given proper definitions to determine classification boundaries.[24] In fact, in some instances in the US and Australia, State statistic collecting bodies have more granular data collection categories than a Federal agency and they must periodically align their more granular crime data via conversion tables.[25] In other cases, if only aggregated data is kept, then the advantages of precision in collections are lost by merging data with another less granular crime data class potentially subverting the original data collection purpose(s) of the IS. The similarities between identity crimes, computer crime, and fraud in general, give us a clue as to where we can start to refine identity crime definitions and classifications, and to observe linkages, or find overlaps, whether by homogeneity or heterogeneity, between classes.

## 4.    Discussion of results

Identity theft and identity deception are also enablers of identity fraud as well as other related economic crimes such as money laundering, terrorist financing, drug trafficking and people smuggling.[26] In Australia, people committing identity crimes may be prosecuted under current legislation such as bank fraud, credit card fraud, or mail fraud (see Table 5), or under some other legislation where specific identity crime

laws are absent such as in certain Australian States. Herein lies a dilemma for government, law enforcement, practitioners, and academic researchers[27]; should current law continue to be reinforced, laws be amended, or new identity crime laws be constructed? Based on our findings in this study, we promote a combination of these options. We now outline our reasons.

The evolution of identity crimes such as identity theft had its beginnings well before 1964 when the term 'identity theft' was first documented. Similar crimes were well known to US law enforcement agencies in postal services and the credit card industry.[28] These criminal behaviours of committing fraud were perpetrated by stealing credit cards from the mail from the 1960s. Mail theft itself was a problem in the US from the start of the US Postal Service in 1775. United States legislation was subsequently passed in the late 18th century to criminalize mail theft.[29] Similarly, 'wire fraud' was and continues to be a problem in the US and other jurisdictions as communications technology evolves from fixed line to mobile telephony and the Internet or a hybrid system (for example Voice over Internet Protocol). Some forms of conduct have been criminalized, as policy-makers (often due to public pressure) have sought to use the legal system to establish or to reinforce acceptable social norms, culture, and attitudes.

A reasonable starting point to assess the general evolution of crime leading to identity crime sub-classes is to investigate the norms or attitudes that may have influenced the cultures in countries that currently have identity crime laws (Australia, Canada, US). Thus, crime classification systems vary by jurisdiction although there are some commonalities. Major crime categories (for example, murder, fraud, or theft) and their heuristics also determine how sub-classes of these crimes have evolved. The evolutionary changes in fraud in Australia have been documented and changes may differ when compared with other countries.[30] Fraud, while not being a new crime, is a crime that is in a state of change and evolution due to shifting IS technologies.[31] As the scope of the identity crime problem (in both economic and societal terms) increases, similar pressures have been placed on government policy makers to legislate against it.[32] The use of identity deception techniques for committing crimes is not a recent phenomenon. For example, the English Forgery Act was passed in 1870 to legislate against false share certificates. The evolution of specific identity crime taxonomy via a classification (process) correlates closely with the introduction of legislation firstly in the US and subsequently in Australia or

[22] Sproule, S., and Archer, N. 2008. "Measuring Identity Theft in Canada: 2008 Consumer Survey", McMaster eBusiness Research Centre (MeRC) DeGroote School of Business (23), pp. 1–70. Foley, L., Barney, K., and Foley, J. 2010. "Identity Theft: The Aftermath 2009", Identity Theft Resource Center, pp. 1–45. Halperin, R., and Backhouse, J. 2008. "A Roadmap for Research on Identity in the Information Society", Identity in the Information Society Journal (1:1), pp. 1–17. Parsons, J., and Wand, Y. 2008. "Using Cognitive Principles to Guide Classification in Information Systems Modeling", MIS Quarterly (32:4), pp. 839–868. US General Accounting Office. 2002. Identity Theft: Greater Awareness and Use of Existing Data are Needed. June, pp. 1–72. See also OECD, note 20.
[23] Kraus, L. I., and MacGahan, A. 1979. Computer Fraud and Countermeasures. Englewood Cliffs, New Jersey, Prentice-Hall, Inc. See also Mahmood, note 21.
[24] Warner, S. B. 1931. "Crimes Known to the Police: An Index of Crime?", Harvard Business Review (45:2), pp. 307–331.
[25] Australian Bureau of Statistics. 2008b. Australian Standard Offence Classification (ASOC) 1234.0, (2nd Ed.), Australian Bureau of Statistics, August, pp. 1–172. Castle, C., and Sampson, L. 2008. JANCO Classification System. Government of South Australia – Office of Crime Statistics and Research, May, pp. 1–41.
[26] Chen, above note 4. Wang, G., Chen, H., and Atabakhsh, H. 2004. "Automatically Detecting Deceptive Criminal Identities", Communications of the ACM (47:3), pp. 71–76.

[27] Gill, G., and Bhattacherjee, A. 2009. "Whom are we Informing? Issues and Recommendations for MIS Research from an Informing Sciences Perspective", MIS Quarterly (33:2), pp. 217–235.
[28] Straub, D. 1989. "Validating Instruments in MIS Research", MIS Quarterly (13:2), pp. 147–169.
[29] Biegelman, above note 11.
[30] Goode, above note 1.
[31] Goode, above note 1. See also US Government. 2007. Combating IDENTITY THEFT: A Strategic Plan. The President's Identity Theft Task Force, April, pp. i-110.
[32] Stephan, M., Pennington, S., Krishnamurthi, G., and Reidy, J. 2009. Identity Burglary. Texas Review of Law and Politics (13:1), pp. 401–418. Stevenson, C. L. 1944. Ethics and Language. New Haven, Connecticut, Yale University Press.

**Table 2 – Hierarchically ordered identity crimes sub-classes.[a]**

| Identity act or event name | Classification | Context | Region | Reference |
|---|---|---|---|---|
| Identity crime | Top category | Tax Crime | Australia | Australian Tax Office (2009) |
| Identity fraud | Category | | | |
| Identity creation | Category | | | |
| Identity theft/takeover | Sub-category | | | |
| Database identity (Population), | Category | Legislation, | Australia, UK | Sullivan (2009) |
| Token identity (Individual) | Sub-category | | | |
| Identity crime | Category | Legislation, maintaining the | US, International | US Secret Service (2010, |
| Credit card/access | Sub-category | integrity of the nation's (US) | | http://www.secret |
| Device fraud (Skimming), | | financial infrastructure and | | service.gov/criminal.shtml) |
| Identity theft, | Sub-category | payment systems | | |
| False identification | Sub-category | | | |
| Passport fraud, | Sub-category | | | |
| Bank/check fraud | Sub-category | | | |
| Identity (Theft) appropriation | Category | Identity crime legislation | Australia | Model Criminal Law Officers' Committee (2008) |
| Identity fraud | Category | Extent and nature survey | Canada | Sproule and Archer (2008; 2007) |
| Identity theft | Sub-category | | | |
| ID-related crime | Category | Conceptual, | UK | Koops et al. (2009) |
| Identity deletion | Sub-category | Technical, legal | | |
| ID-related crime | Umbrella term | Policy, Research | UK | Koops and Leenes (2006) |
| Identity fraud | Category | | | |
| Identity theft | Sub-category | | | |
| Identity crime | Top category | Policy, research, meaningful | Australia, | Jamieson et al. (2008) |
| Identity fraud | Category | data collection, analysis and | New Zealand, | |
| Identity theft | Sub-category | comparisons across jurisdictions | Asia-Pacific | |
| Identity deception | Sub-category | | | |
| Identity-related crime | Category | | | |
| Identity collision | Category | Policy, research | UK | Leenes (2006b, ed.) Rost, |
| Identity change | Category | | | Meints, and Hansen (2006) |
| Identity takeover | Sub-category | | | |
| Identity exchange | Sub-category | | | |
| Identity delegation | Sub-category | | | |
| Identity creation | Sub-category | | | |
| Identity deletion | Category | | | |
| Identity restoration | Category | | | |
| Identity[b] | Category | Information society | UK, EU | Anrig et al., 2005 |
| Subjects | Sub-category | (A set of concepts) | | |
| Virtual persons | Sub-category | | | |
| Identity crime | Top Category | Policy, Research | Australia | Australasian Centre for |
| Identity fraud | Category | | | Policing Research 2006 |
| Identity theft | Sub-category | | | |
| Identity theft | Category | | US | Cheney 2005 |

a  Legislation makes an act or event a crime.
b  Identity: identification, anonymity, pseudonymity, (un)observability, (un)traceability.

Canada, with other countries beginning to follow, for example the UK. The basis of taxonomy is evolutionary connectedness.

Identity crimes are a problem directly associated with identity attribution and system authentication such as a credit card PIN or username and password. Identity crime is not an industry specific crime. Identity crime permeates across all sectors and countries where personal and organizational identity information is used for economic gain or avoidance of cost or loss. The grouping and ranking in hierarchies, by similarities or differences between identity crime classes are shown in Table 2.

Reading Table 2, we see the many different identity crime nomenclature, classifications by rank, context, and jurisdictional region; these identifications by the individuals gave referral to their taxon referenced by author(s). Table 2 column 1, shows a vast array of identity crime nomenclature used across and within regions as well as their evolving classification labels.

Both identity theft and identity deception have many crime sub-class methods at the most granular level. Well-known examples of offline identity theft are caused by wallet theft, mail redirection, and dumpster diving, while an example of an online identity theft method is war-driving. Online examples for identity deception are phishing, vishing, and smishing.[33]

---

[33] Urban, M. 2006. "The Evolution of Phishing", ISSA Journal September, pp. 1–53.

**Table 3 – Participant interviewees insights on the meaning of identity crime.**

| Participant | Selected interviewee insights on the meaning of identity crimes |
|---|---|
| | **Australian private organizations** |
| 1 | "We have no document (in Australia) that was originally designed and/or issued with all the necessary checks, balances data matching and enquiries to prove someone's identity. If we can get that process right then you can start building the process, working up from that and that is where it simply falls over." |
| 2.1 | "if identity crime was easy to describe we probably wouldn't be sitting here because there would have been a measure around it. I mean that's the problem." |
| 3.2 | "In terms of what we've got to get down to is defining exactly what identity theft or identity fraud is. What it requires is the actual adoption or use of someone else's identity in order to commit that fraud. Where banks mainly see identity fraud is in the false applications for things like credit cards and so forth." |
| 3.1 | "I think there's some use in defining or distinguishing between identity theft and identity takeover (identity deception), in that we categorize frauds where a person has been in fact made up, if you like fictitious, using false identification documentation. We categorize that differently to takeover of a legitimate person's identity. It is somewhat easier to perpetrate a takeover and obviously there is social engineering involved. "I think it is worthwhile to note that historically the bank has classified identity fraud, based on product or service delivery channel. We've classified that as by the product it's been paid for." |
| 6 | "Identity fraud for me indicates that the identity that's been presented is false, like counterfeit or something like that. We get a lot of true name fraud, but it's usually new accounts. They are not usually existing customers or added onto an existing customer account. It is usually dealers." |
| | **Australian Government – federal and state agencies** |
| 4 | "From an external fraud point of view, [what] we try to address are; illegitimately issued and fraudulently obtained State photo driver licenses; Motor vehicle re-birthing associated with fraudulent identities; fake State driver licenses used as proof of identity in commercial frauds; fraudulently obtained, misused, or manufactured Proof of Age cards; gun and security licenses and associated impact on the integrity of the XXX Transport Authority's policies/procedures and records; and fraudulently obtained, misused or manufactured mobility parking system authorities." |
| 7 | "We define identity fraud as relating to the actual, the physical person, and their name." |
| 8 | "We have a definition for identity fraud where it is "the misuse of an identity to claim, to receive government payments in excess of the general entitlement. We certainly sub-define it down to different levels of fictitious identity, created identity, assumed identity. Accordingly, each one of those would be approached in a different way because they manifest themselves differently. Each type of category requires a different approach." |
| 9 | "identity fraud under two broad categories; assumed identity (identity deception) and stolen identity (identity theft)". |
| 10 | The big area where there are issues, is in account opening identification, is of course fake or stolen documents. That's actually prohibited by legislation."[a] |
| 11 | "We say identity fraud is basically someone saying who they are not. They pretend to be someone else". |
| | **US Academic** |
| 12 | "Earlier on when the identity crime literature started to develop people were referring to it as identity theft. That has now migrated to a new term, identity fraud, because identity frauds are a larger category. There is a need to create some type of typology of identity frauds because there are new forms emerging all the time and maybe more than one typology would be better. For a while there were no statutes governing or very loose statutes governing identity crimes (such as identity theft or identity fraud) those statutes have tightened up so now. What makes anything a crime is a statute." |

a The Anti-Money Laundering and Counter-Terrorism Financing Act 2006 (AML/CTF Act) received Royal Assent on 12 December 2006. In the US a similar law is; Provide Appropriate Tools Required to Intercept and Obstruct Terrorism (PATRIOT) Act of 2001.

Identity deception is a broader cause of criminality than identity theft because stealing an identity is just one of many classes of identity crime that allows someone to assume an identity of another individual or entity (real or fictitious). The identity deception class has been recommended to be further classified into sub-classes identity manipulation and identity falsification and each has been given similar labels.[34] The Australasian Centre for Policing Research (2006) and Model

Crime Law Officer's Committee (2008) identity crime definition also includes the situation for when someone creates a false identity that is not based on a real person; a fictitious identity. We label this identity deception. Identity crime generally means activity in which a perpetrator utilizes a false identity in order to facilitate the commission of a crime; with nomenclature labelled identity fraud or sub-classes ranked identity theft and identity deception categories.

Interview quotes from Participant 12 in Table 3 illustrate the need for and problems around, the requirement to initially define a new phenomenon such as identity fraud and identity theft or to classify the many other labels for identity deception. Until the terms are defined within statutes and improved upon with amendment(s) and/or case law, law enforcement case charges are usually laid against an identity crime (or any

---

[34] Australasian Centre for Policing Research. 2006. "Standardisation of Definitions of Identity Crime Terms: A Step Towards Consistency", Report Series, (145.3), March, pp. 1–17. United Kingdom Home Office Identity Fraud Steering Committee. 2004. Identity Crime Definitions. 9 December. v1.0. Also see Table 3 interviewee 3.1 quotes for example.

| US State | Correspondence feedback |
|---|---|
| **Table 4 – Selected examples of participant feedback from email correspondence with US experts within a specific jurisdiction.** | |
| California | "Although the California Penal Code does differentiate crime against property from other crimes, identity theft is not one of the crimes that are required to be tracked in California. One of the major challenges in tracking identity theft crimes in California is that an identity theft crime may be charged as a number of different crimes. For example, an identity theft case that involves stalking may resolve as stalking." |
| Delaware | "The (identity theft) law was enacted in 2000 as a class E felony but was changed to the more serious Class D felony in 2004". |
| Idaho | "Idaho state law pertaining to identity theft is codified under Title 18 of the Idaho Code, Chapter 31 ("false pretenses, cheats, and misrepresentations"), [see http://www.legislature.idaho.gov/idstat/Title18/T18CH31.htm]. Section 18–3126 relates specifically to identity theft". |
| Indiana | "I work in the Attorney General's Identity Theft Unit, and we worked with our legislature to pass an identity theft bill earlier this year. Our identity deception (and new synthetic identity deception) statutes can be found at http://www.in.gov/legislative/ic/code/title35/ar43/ch5.html. Other criminal offences are contained in Title 35 of the Indiana Code (see http://www.in.gov/legislative/ic/code/title35/)". |
| Montana | "Theft is a "top-level" classification. I'm sure you have heard the expression "index crimes". According to the index, MN statutes (and therefore offences) on identity theft are categorized under 'theft'. However, the Montana Incident-Based Reporting System (MTIBRS) (Montana's crime data collection system), identity theft is classified as a fraud. But depending on the incident, any number of offences could be included with the identity theft, such as writing a bad check, credit card theft/unlawful use of a credit card, or embezzlement. Montana does not use any sub-classification in any data collection efforts. In MT's crime incident reporting handbook, we have a number of indexes that show the relationship between Montana's MCA/MTIBRS codes and how they relate to the FBI's codes. Lastly, you would be correct by saying that our "fraud" category would be inflated by including identity theft". |
| North Carolina | "The law gets divided into criminal or civil law. So depending on the severity and nature of the act, identity theft could be a crime or a civil issue. Most of the identity crimes are handled on the local level, not the state level. We spend most of our time educating citizens on how to protect themselves". |
| North Dakota | "We do not have statistics relating to identity theft because it is not, generally, prosecuted as a criminal offense and because reports can be filed with local law enforcement OR with this office (AG's) OR with the Federal Trade Commission. There is no requirement for reporting among agencies". |
| New Mexico | "The Attorney General's Office is now required by law to collect statistics on identity theft (passed this year). As they have just started this collection process they do not have any figures currently available. Statistics on identity theft in the US are fairly non-existent. Here is an excerpt from the US Department of Justice Website: In contrast to Federal Trade Commission extensive database of consumer complaints and victimization, the criminal justice system lacks any such information related to identity theft. No criminal justice agency maintains a national database of the number of identity theft cases". |
| Nevada | "In Nevada by various statutes, crimes are classified as Category A, B, C, D, and E felonies, Gross Misdemeanors, and Misdemeanors". |
| Ohio | "Ohio is a Home Rule State and with that we do not have any one entity that governs the other when it relates to identity crimes. Law enforcement would be the entity that would investigate any of the white collar crimes such as identity theft, economic, cyber, computer, or organized crime, theft and fraud". |
| Oregon | "Identity theft is one of those offences that tend to get lost among other offences because of the grouping we have to do. In Oregon we have 2 crime reporting formats. Law enforcement agencies reporting in our older format (about 68%) report identity theft as 'Fraud-By Deception'. The remaining 32% of the law enforcement agencies in Oregon who use our newer reporting format (called O-NIBRS) report identity theft as 'Fraud-Impersonation'". |
| Tennessee | "Identity theft is generally categorized as an economic crime though it begins quite often as simple theft." |

other 'new' crime for that matter) perpetrator under a current statute, for example, mail fraud, telephone fraud, credit card fraud, or check fraud. There is a need to define identity crimes in legislation because 'identity theft' and 'identity deception' are enablers of 'identity fraud'. There is a range of crimes then which impact communities in devastating ways.[35] All these intricacies in identity crime terms we clearly define in Table 1 grounded from interviewee data collection; this is the level at which identity crime definitions need to be considered for accurate research and comparison of results across time and location.[36] We attained these definitions upon considering themes from coded data.

Participant 8 alludes to perpetrators using fictitious identities, which can manifest itself in different ways. With fictitious identity, perpetrators may eventually exist within organizational knowledge management systems. Organizations or government can find it difficult to discover false identities within their databases, or in via other interactions in the community. This is because identity fraud perpetrators can create an identity by registering on other databases, or with other organizations through exploiting weak attribute checks or authentication systems. Perpetrators might for instance register on the electoral roll, create bank accounts or to obtain a driver's license if the authenticity checks of any of these systems can be circumvented. If successful, perpetrators have then created an identity which is likely to be able to authenticate further uses in other databases, because organizations are unlikely to look behind

[35] Chua, C. E. H., Wareham, J., and Robey, D. 2007. "The Role of Online Trading Communities in Managing Internet Auction Fraud", *MIS Quarterly* (31:4), pp. 759–781.
[36] Corbin, above note 13.

**388**            COMPUTER LAW & SECURITY REVIEW 28 (2012) 381–395

**Table 5 – Identity crime legislation.**

| Country/Level | Legislation | Effective | Description (Abridged) |
|---|---|---|---|
| Australia[a]<br>Federal Level<br>(Commonwealth and the Territories): | Criminal Code Act 1995, Schedule ('The Criminal Code') Part 10.8—Financial information offences | 31 August 2004 | These provisions prohibit dishonestly obtaining, or dealing in, "personal financial information"[b] without the consent of the person to whom the information relates; or possessing, controlling or importing any "thing" with the intention that the thing be used to commit the offence of dishonestly obtaining or dealing in personal financial information. These offences are primarily directed at: "credit card skimming" and "phishing" but may have a broader reach. |
|  | Criminal Code Act 1995, Schedule ('The Criminal Code') Part 9.5—Identity crime | 3 March 2011 | Under these provisions a person (the first person) commits an offence if: (a) the first person deals in identification information; and (b) the first person intends that any person (the user) (whether or not the first person) will use the identification information to pretend to be, or to pass the user off as, another person (whether living, dead, real or fictitious) for the purpose of: (i) committing an offence; or (ii) facilitating the commission of an offence; and (c) the offence referred to in (b) is an indictable offence against a law of the Commonwealth |
| State Level:<br>South Australia | Criminal Law Consolidation Act 1935 Part 5A—Identity Theft | 5 September 2004 | These provisions make it an offence for a person to assume a false identity, or falsely pretend to have particular qualifications or a particular capacity, intending, by doing so, to commit, or facilitate the commission of, a serious criminal offence. It is also an offence to use another person's personal identification information to commit, or facilitate the commission of, a serious criminal offence. |
| Queensland | Criminal Code Act 1899s 408D—Obtaining or dealing with identification information | 7 February 2007 | Under these provisions, it is a 'misdemeanour' for a person to obtain or deal with another entity's identification information for the purpose of committing, or facilitating the commission of, an indictable offence. It is also an offence to possess equipment for the purpose of committing, or facilitating the commission of, the aforementioned misdemeanour. |
| Western Australia | Criminal Code Act Compilation Act 1913, Appendix B (Criminal Code Act 1913) Schedule (The Criminal Code) Division III Chapter LI—Identity crime | Assented 25 June 2010 (Criminal Code Amendment (Identity Crime) Bill 2009), not yet commenced | Upon commencement of these provisions, it would be an offence for a person to make, use, possess or supply identification material with the intention that material will be used, by the person or some other person, to commit, or facilitate the commission of, an indictable offence. |
| Victoria | Crimes Act 1958 Part 1 Division 2AA—Identity crime | 17 June 2009 | It is an offence for a person to make, use, possess or supply identification information (not relating to that person), if the person is aware that the information is identification information (or is aware that there is a substantial risk that the information is identification information), and intends to use or supply the information to commit, or facilitate the commission of, an indictable offence. |
| New South Wales | Crimes Act 1900 Part 4AB—Identity offences | 12 November 2009 | It is an offence for a person to possess or deal in identification information with the intention of committing, or facilitating the commission of, an indictable offence. It is also an offence for a person to possess any equipment, material or other thing to make identification documents or other things with the intention to use these documents or things to commit, or facilitate the commission of, an indictable offence. |

COMPUTER LAW & SECURITY REVIEW 28 (2012) 381–395 **389**

| Table 5 – *(continued)* | | | |
| --- | --- | --- | --- |
| Country/Level | Legislation | Effective | Description (Abridged) |
| **Canada** *National Level:* | Criminal Code (RSC, 1985, c C-46) Sections 402.2, 403 | 22 October 2009 (S-4 *An Act to Amend the Criminal Code (Identity Theft and Related Misconduct)*) | It is an offence for a person to knowingly obtain or possess another person's identity information in circumstances giving rise to a reasonable inference that the information is intended to be used to commit an indictable offence that includes fraud, deceit or falsehood as an element of the offence. It is an offence for a person to transmit, make available, distribute, sell or offer for sale another person's identity information, or have it in their possession for any of those purposes, knowing that or being reckless as to whether the information will be used to commit an indictable offence that includes fraud, deceit or falsehood as an element of the offence. It is an offence for a person to fraudulently personate another person, living or dead, with the intent: to gain advantage for themselves or another person; or to obtain property; or to cause disadvantage to the person being personated or another person; or to avoid arrest or prosecution; or to obstruct, pervert or defeat the course of justice. |
| **Norway** *National Level:* | The Penal Code | 2009 | It is an offence to, without authority, possesses of a means of identity of another, or to act with the identity of another or with an identity that easily may be confused with the identity of another person, and with the intent of a) procuring an economic benefit for oneself or for another person, or b) causing a loss of property or inconvenience to another person." |
| **United States** *Federal Level:* | False Identification Crime Control Act of 1982, Pub L No 97-398, 96 Stat. 2009; 18 USC § 1028 | 31 December 1982 | Under certain circumstances, it is an offence for a person to knowingly and without lawful authority produce an identification document, authentication feature, or a false identification document ('ID documents'); to transfer ID documents knowing that they are stolen or produced without lawful authority; to possess ID documents with the intention that they be used to defraud the United States; to produce, transfer or possess a document-making implement or authentication feature with the intention such document-making implement or authentication feature will be used in the production of a false identification document; or to knowingly traffic in false or actual authentication features for use in false identification documents, document-making implements, or means of identification. It is also an offence for a person to knowingly transfer, possess, or use, without lawful authority, a means of identification of another person with the intent to commit, or to aid or abet, or in connection with, any unlawful activity that constitutes a violation of Federal law, or that constitutes a felony under any applicable State or local law. |
| | Internet False Identification Act of 2000, Pub L No 106-578, 114 Stat 3075; 18 USC § 1028 | 28 December 2000 | These provisions cover computer-facilitated crimes of false identity and prohibit the possession, production, or transfer of false identification documents or identification documents that were not legally issued to the possessor. They also prohibit the production, transfer, or possession of any "document making implement" that is intended for use in manufacturing false identification documents. |
| | Identity Theft and Assumption Deterrence Act of 1998 Pub L No 105–318, 112 Stat 3007; 18 USC § 1028A | 30 October 1998 | Under these provisions, it is an offence for a person, during and in relation to certain listed felonies, to knowingly transfer, possess, or use, without lawful authority, a means of identification of another person or a false identification document. |

*(continued on next page)*

390        COMPUTER LAW & SECURITY REVIEW 28 (2012) 381–395

| Table 5 – *(continued)* | | | |
|---|---|---|---|
| Country/Level | Legislation | Effective | Description (Abridged) |
| | Identity Theft Penalty Enhancement Act, as amended by Pub L No 108-275, 118 Stat 831; 18 USC § 1028A | 15 July 2004 | The Identity Theft Penalty Enhancement Act amends the US Code to establish penalties for aggravated identity theft in addition to the existing punishments for related felonies. The act adds 2 years to prison sentences for "knowingly transferring, possessing, or using, without lawful authority, a means of identification of another person" and 5 years for false identification in the commission of "terrorist acts." |
| *State Level:* | All US States have some form of identity crime (labelled identity theft, identity fraud, or identity deception) legislation | Beginning with Arizona in 1996 | Crime offence reports can be filed with local law enforcement or at a state Attorney General's office (for example, under North Dakota consumer fraud division) or with the Federal Trade Commission. There is no requirement for reporting among agencies. Each State has their own rules on legislation matters. Most state agencies use the Uniform Crime Reporting Manual for reporting crime statistics which is published by the Federal Bureau of Investigation. |

a  For a detailed critical analysis of all Australian identity crime offences see Steel, A. "The True Identity Of Australian Identity Theft Offences: A Measured Response Or An Unjustified Status Offence?" 33 (2010) University of New South Wales Law Journal 503–531.
b  "Personal financial information" is, for constitutional reasons, defined as information relating to a person that may be used to access funds, credit or other financial benefits, where those funds are deposited with, or the credit is offered by, a corporation or an authorized deposit-taking institution within the meaning of Banking Act 1959. Practically speaking, this will cover almost all financial institutions.

these apparently genuine documents.[37] Alternatively, a perpetrator could also create another identity under a different name by simply transposing letters or by dropping a letter in a first or last name. Similar instances have occurred by mistakes in administration, for example a clerk might make a spelling or typing error on an identity document and this allows a perpetrator to opportunistically represent that altered name as their own. Assumed identities emerge also, where one can either take on the identity of a living person, a genuine person, or a dead person. Therefore systems need resilience to be able to absorb and recover from such perpetrator attacks.[37] A recent Australian innovation is for organizations to set up processes to trawl through 'fact of death' files to determine identities on their databases are deceased.

Private organizations see identity fraud, identity theft and identity deception (or synonyms) in a much narrower nomenclature than government agencies. While Australian Federal and State agencies in some cases adopt their own internal group labelling for the various identity crime sub-class names, they often have a broader description for identity crime. This could have been driven from government initiatives for defining identity crime labels over time.[38]

Table 4 illustrates a sample of the rich responses received from the various US Federal and State Attorney Generals and US Statistic Bureaus. In Table 4 the feedback correspondence from Montana describes clearly the issues this paper is endeavouring to rectify. They point out the divergence and evolution of all groups; that for index crimes 'theft' is the highest rank in their crime classification but that under the Montana Incident-Based Reporting Scheme identity theft is categorized as a 'fraud' thereby potentially inflating fraud levels. Table 6 illustrates the various modes of researcher and legal definitions of identity crimes across different countries over time. In Australia, government and law enforcement have agreed on the following standard terminology: "Identity theft is the theft or assumption of a pre-existing identity (or a significant part thereof), with or without consent, and whether, in the case of an individual, the person is living or deceased".[39] However, Australian legislation does not in the main use this terminology (see Table 5), due to concerns over limitations related to legal definitions of theft.[40]

The US federal government led the way in defining identity theft by way of legislation in the form of Identity Theft and Assumption Deterrence Act (1998) (see Table 6). This Act was introduced in order to mitigate the economic cost to victims, both entity and individual, by making identity theft a crime with substantial penalties in the form of fines or jail as a deterrent to future perpetrators. All US States subsequently followed this lead. We argue that the assumption part of the US Identity Theft and Assumption Deterrence Act (1998) identity theft definition is not identity theft but identity deception (see Table 5). We show that identity deception is a clearer referral, encompasses all similar labels, has

---

[37] Sommer, P., and Brown, I. 2011. "Reducing Systemic Cybersecurity Risk. OECD/IFP Project on "Future Global Shocks", January, pp. 1–121.
[38] See, The Anti-Money Laundering and Counter-Terrorism Financing Act 2006 (AML/CTF Act) received Royal Assent on 12 December 2006. In the US a similar law is; Provide Appropriate Tools Required to Intercept and Obstruct Terrorism (PATRIOT) Act of 2001.

[39] Council of Australian Governments Agreement to a National Identity Security Strategy 2007, p. 3.
[40] See e.g., Steel, A. "The True Identity Of Australian Identity Theft Offences: A Measured Response Or An Unjustified Status Offence?" 33 (2010) University of New South Wales Law Journal 503–531.

COMPUTER LAW & SECURITY REVIEW 28 (2012) 381–395

**Table 6 – Computer, cyber, and identity crime definitions (Researcher and legal).**

| Author | Region | |
|---|---|---|
| | | **Computer crime** |
| Furnell 2002 | UK | A crime in which the perpetrator uses special knowledge about computer technology (p. 21) |
| | | **Cybercrime** |
| Furnell 2002 | UK | A crime in which the perpetrator uses special knowledge about cyberspace (p. 21) |
| | | **Identity crime** |
| ACPR 2006; MCLOC 2008 | Australia | Refers to identity crime as: "offences in which a perpetrator uses a false identity in order to facilitate the commission of a crime" |
| COAG, Council of Australian Governments Agreement | Australia | Is a generic term to describe activities/offences in which a perpetrator uses a fabricated identity, a manipulated identity, or a stolen/assumed identity to facilitate the commission of crime (2007, p. 3). |
| UK Home Office Identity Fraud Steering Committee (2004) | UK | Classifies identity crime as "a generic term for identity theft, creating a false identity or committing identity fraud. False identity is: a fictitious (invented) identity; or (b) an existing (genuine) identity that has been altered to create a fictitious identity." |
| | | **Identity fraud** |
| GAO 1998 | US | Generally, identity fraud involves "stealing" another person's personal identifying information, for example, Social Security number, date of birth, and mother's maiden name. Criminals use such information to fraudulently establish credit, run up debt, or to take over existing financial accounts. |
| Cabinet Office 2002 | UK | Identity fraud arises when someone takes over a totally fictitious name or adopts the name of another person with or without their consent. |
| ACPR2006[a] | Australia | Identity fraud refers to the gaining of money, goods, services or other benefits through the use of a false identity |
| COAG 2007 | Australia | "Is the gaining of money, goods, services or other benefits or the avoidance of obligations through the use of a fabricated identity, a manipulated identity, or a stolen/assumed identity" (p. 3). |
| | | **Identity theft** |
| Oxford English Dictionary | UK | Identity theft (noun.), "the dishonest acquisition of personal information in order to perpetrate fraud, typically by obtaining credit, or loans, in someone else's name." |
| ITADA, Public Law 105-318 – October. 30, 1998 | US | An identity thief is anyone who "[k]nowingly transfers or uses, without lawful authority, a means of identification of another person with the intent to commit, or to aid or abet, any unlawful activity that constitutes a violation of Federal law, or that constitutes a felony under any applicable State or local law." |
| Fair and Accurate Credit Transactions Act, 2003 | US | Identity theft is "a fraud committed using the identifying information of another person", subject to such further definition as the FTC may prescribe, by regulation (15 U.S.C. §1681a(q)(3)) (also see Cheney 2005). |
| Home Office 2004 | UK | Identity theft occurs when your personal information is used by someone else without your knowledge. It may support criminal activity, which could involve fraud, deception, or obtaining benefits and services in your name |
| CIFAS Online 2006 | UK | Identity theft (also known as impersonation fraud) is the misappropriation of the identity (such as the name, date of birth, current address or previous addresses) of another person, without their knowledge or consent. These identity details are then used to obtain goods and services in that person's name |
| Office of the Privacy Commissioner of Canada 2007 | Canada | Identity theft – or perhaps more accurately, identity fraud – occurs when someone uses your personal information, your Social Insurance Number (SIN) or birth date, for example, to pose as you and then apply for credit cards and loans, open bank accounts to write bad checks and to get new government documents such as driver's licenses and SIN cards |
| COAG 2007 | Australia | "Is the theft or assumption of a pre-existing identity (or a significant part thereof), with or without consent, and whether, in the case of an individual, the person is living or deceased" (p. 3) |
| | | **Identity deception** |
| Wang et al., 2004 | US | "Identity deception is an intentional falsification of identity in order to deter investigations" (p. 71) |

a ACPR, The Australasian Centre for Policing Research (2006, p.9 footnote 7), makes the point that "the issue of intention (or the most appropriate fault element) may need to be considered in determining whether a criminal offense is involved in the use of a false identity".

**392** COMPUTER LAW & SECURITY REVIEW 28 (2012) 381-395

**Fig. 1 – Conceptual model of identity definitions. Source: Jamieson et al., 2008.**

precedence from a historical crime perspective,[41] academia,[42] and US State legislation (see Table 4).[43]

Identity deception (Table 1) is the rapidly growing phenomenon where fraudsters create identities and then steal goods and services from businesses (i.e. identity fraud). According to ID Analytics, Inc., identity deception accounted for about 85 percent of identity frauds compared to 15 percent for identity theft.[44] Those experiencing this phenomenon appreciate its far-reaching consequences versus those falling under the sub-class of identity theft.[45] Wang et al. describe their different criminal identity deception categories that fall under their labels of name, residency, identity and date-of-birth of deception, and each has sub-categories.[46] In Wang et al.'s identity deception taxonomy, reference to any identity crime act or event to obtain by a perpetrator proof of identity (POI) documentation or personally identifiable information, PII (personal identifying numbers, PIN or passwords), other than by identity theft methods may be more accurately classified as identity deception (see Table 1).[47] The basic premise of an identity theft act is that the perpetrator steals an individual or entity's POI or PII. Thus all other methods such as inventing, falsifying, altering or fabricating are classified as identity deception.

In mid 2008 the Australian Bureau of Statistics published the results of a personal fraud survey that asked questions to measure various types of identity crime incidents.[48] The publicly available results are at a reasonably high level across what we term the identity crimes sub-classes, in order to maintain survey respondent anonymity. A year after release of the data to the public, researchers who meet ABS research criteria could apply to access the data at more granular levels than was made public. We gained access to the data at a more

atomistic level and made various integrity checks. For brevity and to maintain respondent anonymity, we reclassified and consequently recalculated the data at the publicly available level following our Table 1 (identity crime definitions and classes). This better ensured that results could be replicated by others.[49]

The identity crime portion of Fig. 3 identity fraud under the ABS classification is 3.1% with 499,500 victims made up of 124,000 identity theft victims (0.8%) and 383,300 (2.4%) credit or bank card fraud victims. The remainder are victims of personal fraud or scams.[50] However, using our definitions and classifications, phishing (57,800 victims or 0.4%) is an identity crime method (taxon), specifically it is grouped within the identity deception class that may cause identity fraud or be part of a related identity crime. In Fig. 2 we show the reclassified identity crime components that constitute the identity fraud portion (now 557,300 victims or 3.5%) of the ABS Personal Fraud Survey and the corresponding number of victims in each class where they can be categorically shown without ambiguity at this domain level. The broken uni-directional lines in Fig. 2 from 'credit or bank card fraud' to identity deception and identity theft are because at this level we cannot say the exact amount apportioned to either class, but we know over half of the new identity fraud victims are caused by this fraud (383,300 or 2.4%). We could apportion the 383,300 victims to identity deception and identity theft based on prior findings of 85 percent and 15 percent respectively,[51] but again this would not be accurate.

## 5. International context

The *Council of Europe's Convention on Cybercrime* ('*Convention*')[52] is the only binding international treaty on cybercrime. The *Convention* was negotiated and written in the earlier days of cybercrime – the late 1990s – with a final draft introduced in 2001. The *Convention* entered into force on 7 January 2004.

The *Convention on Cybercrime*, an agreement between member nations of the European Union is the only international agreement in the area of cybercrime. It is unique in that it is open for signature by non-European member states. The United States, Canada, Australia and Japan have all signed the *Convention*, with the United States also ratifying.

The *Convention* may be divided into three key divisions: substantive law, procedural requirements and international cooperation. All signatories to the *Convention* must criminalise certain activities.

The *Convention* creates four main categories of substantive offences:

---

[41] Stephan, see note [32].
[42] Chen, see note 4.
[43] Michigan or Indiana.
[44] ID Analytics. 2007. "US Identity Fraud Rates by Geography", ID Analytics, Inc. February, pp. 1–12.
[45] Chen, see note 4.
[46] Above note 4.
[47] See note 4.
[48] Above note 15.

[49] McKelvey, B. 1978. "Organizational Systematics: Taxonomic Lessons from Biology", Management Science (24:13), pp. 1428–1440.
[50] Above note 15.
[51] See note 39.
[52] Seger, A. 'The Convention on Cybercrime – Meeting a Global Challenge' (Speech delivered at the AusCERT Asia Pacific Information Security Conference 2008; Gold Coast, 19 May 2008); *Convention on Cybercrime*, opened for signature 23 November 2001, 2296 UNTS 167 (entered into force 1 July 2004) ('*Convention*').

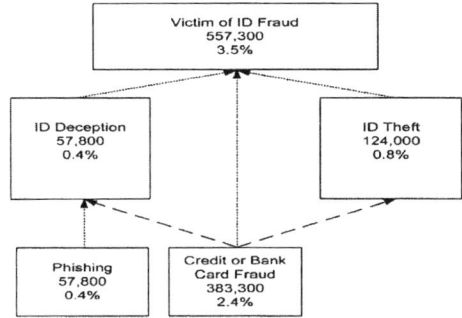

Fig. 2 – **Identity crime Reclassification of ABS Fig. 2 personal fraud survey. Source: Australian Bureau of Statistics (2008, p. 7). Note: 'Credit or Card Fraud' methods (if caused by identity crime) should be apportioned to identity (ID) deception sub-class or identity theft sub-class. 'Phishing' is an identity crime method belonging to the identity deception sub-class.**

1) offences against the confidentiality, integrity and availability of computer data and systems, comprising interference and misuse of devices;
2) computer-related offences such as forgery and computer fraud;
3) content-related offences, in particular the production, dissemination and possession of child pornography; and
4) offences related to infringement of copyright.

The *Convention* also addresses the procedural aspects of cybercrime. The main categories here are:

1) expedited preservation of stored computer data;
2) expedited preservation and partial disclosure of traffic data;
3) production orders;
4) search and seizure of stored computer data;
5) real-time collection of traffic data; and
6) interception of content data.

Finally, the *Convention* contains provisions relating to international cooperation. While some of these provisions are contentious, the *Convention* allows a certain amount of flexibility in terms of how a nation might negotiate some of the issues. These may broadly be categorised as:

1) extradition;
2) mutual assistance; and
3) designation of a 24/7 network contact.

Although the Convention criminalises computer-related offences and fraud, it does not specifically criminalise identity theft.

Alexandr Seger, Head of Economic Crime Division, the Council of Europe has spoken on the issue of identity theft stating:

*"It is nevertheless worthwhile to continue the discussion as to whether in addition it is necessary to criminalise identity-theft as a separate offence or to develop a separate national instrument on the criminalization of identity theft in general, ... , or whether the full use of the existing legal framework and a stronger emphasis on prevention would serve the purpose."*[53]

One significant disadvantage of not specifically including identity theft in the Convention is the inability to take advantage of the cooperative procedural elements such as cooperation with overseas law enforcement, real-time data collection, preservation of data, and immediate designated 24/7 points of contacts. As we have seen in this paper, identity theft is often retro-fitted into poorly-suited frameworks, or the individual is charged with a less relevant offence. A coherent and harmonized criminalization of identity theft as a separate offence (whether this is achieved through a separate international treaty or as a protocol to the existing *Convention*) would be beneficial.

## 6.    Contribution, implication and limitations

Researchers and practitioners reviewing law enforcement practices may currently find it hard to scope, conceptualize, and understand the causal factors influencing the real underlying identity crime classes, as the definitions, taxonomies, classes and names adopted are non-standardized and have differing meanings especially across jurisdictions. There are currently few instances where there is common terminology used, that researchers can use with confidence in developing models that would help to predict and explain identity crime behaviour. This study makes a contribution to IS security via identity crime definitions and also contributes to other IS related disciplines for classifying crime incidents. Benefits for practice will flow from research accuracy facilitating clearer mandates and policy from governments directing monies for mitigation based on robust metrics. A limitation of this research is the limited access to data in most instances because collection of data and statistics on identity crimes are only just beginning to be collated and released.[54] While these definitional and classificatory outcomes may contribute to better research outcomes and practice policies, caution is required as we do not wish to make casual inferences.

## 7.    New identity crime and future research

Legal definitions of crime are developed and amended by legislation. Such legislation often seeks to describe a prohibited behaviour in ways analogous to existing crimes, but legislators can struggle to find the best way to describe

---

[53] Seger, A., "Identity Theft and the Convention on Cybercrime" (2007) UN ISPAC Conference on the Evolving Challenge of Identity-Related Crime, Courmayer, Italy, available at http://www.coe.int/t/dghl/cooperation/economiccrime/cybercrime/documents/reports-presentations/567%20UN%20id%20theft%20and%20CCC_en.pdf.
[54] Goode, above note 1.

**394**      COMPUTER LAW & SECURITY REVIEW 28 (2012) 381−395

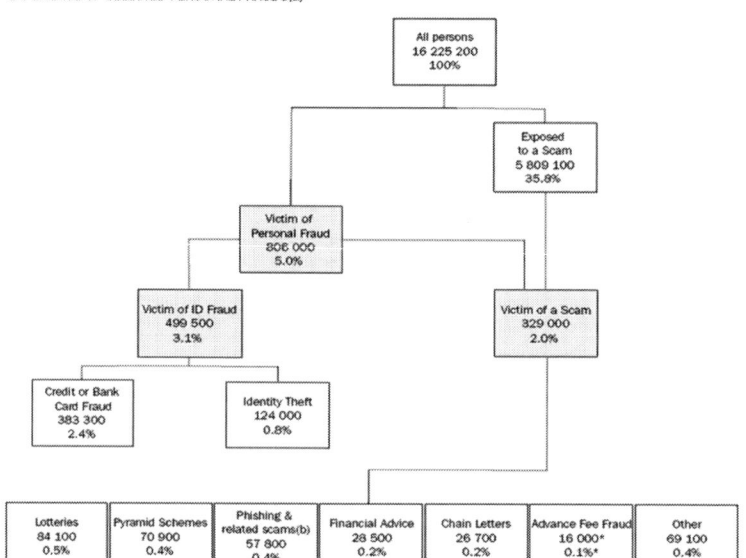

EXPERIENCE OF SELECTED PERSONAL FRAUDS(a)

Fig. 3 – Australian Bureau of Statistics (2008) personal fraud survey classification. Source: Australian Bureau of Statistics (2008, p. 7).

evolving phenomenon. Identity fraud as a term and concept in its formative stages was often presumed to be identity theft and visa versa. However, identity theft is caused by individuals or organizations identities (or tokens) being stolen and is an enabling precursor to identity fraud. The boundaries of identity fraud and identity theft are now better defined.[55] The absence of specific identity crime legislation could be a cause of perpetrators not being convicted of identity crimes but rather under other specific entrenched law such as benefit fraud, or credit card fraud (or stalking; see Table 4). In crime management (IS) this means metrics overlap causing bias. On the other hand to redefine all frauds involving some degree of false identity as identity crimes may create the opposite bias. What is clear however is that there is significant advantage to a clear set of offences separately prohibiting behaviours amounting to identity theft and identity deception as precursor offences to other specific result oriented offences such as bank and benefit fraud.

We argue that the IS artefacts resulting from the collection, collation, storage and retrieval of identity crime research data and that the accumulation, refinement, and critical analysis of results should be greatly simplified by the availability of a dependable identity crime management IS

classification scheme. Our discussion of identity crime evolution gives consideration to other areas of technology and crime that may have further impact on identity crime in the future.[56] Law enforcement, in general, takes the policy lead from government while constrained within a set of boundaries enacted by legislation, public harmony (voter empathy), and/or economic considerations. Sectors within law enforcement look forward to successful prosecutions of perpetrators of identity crime by the public prosecutors as an accomplished operation. Successful identity crime prosecutions act as a general deterrence to other identity crime perpetrators. Getting the major identity crime definitions and classes correct will ensure that prosecutions and sentencing procedures will be conducted without errors, according to the crime committed[57]; as well as correctly directing resources to well defined identity crime classes where they are most

---

[55] Sproule, above note 6.

[56] Bigelow, above note.[11] Orlikowski, above note 6.

[57] Mennens, A., De Wever, W., Dalamanga, A., and Kalamara, A., Kazlauskaité, G., Vermeulen, W., and De Bondt, W. (Eds.) 2009. Developing an EU Level Offence Classification System: EU Study to Implement the Action Plan to Measure Crime and Criminal Justice (34), Maklu, Antwerp, IRCP-Series. Vermeulen, G., and De Bondt, W. (Eds.). EULOCS. The EU Level Offence Classification System: A Bench-Mark for Enhanced Internal Coherence of the EU's Criminal Policy. IRCP-series, (39), Maklu, Antwerp, 2009.

needed.[58] Our research supports and commends efforts to devise and promote the use of a coherent identity crime classification framework via identity crime management IS for identity crimes within and across jurisdictions.[59]

A coherent identity crime classification framework could be achieved by the reinforcement around identity fraud, the laws could be fine-tuned and amended, or new identity crime laws could be introduced. Based on our findings in this study, we promote a combination of all three. Enforcement of existing identity fraud law is important, as is the education and prevention of such fraud. It is equally important that existing laws be fine-tuned in a manner which better relates to IS management systems or vice versa. Lastly, the introduction of a separate identity theft provision that was agreed to by members of the *Convention on Cybercrime* C would be beneficial.[60]

**Rodger Jamieson** *(r.jamieson@unsw.edu.au)*, **Lesley Pek Wee Land** *(l.land@unsw.edu.au)*, **Greg Stephens** *(g.stephens@unsw. edu.au)* & **Donald Winchester** *(d.winchester@unsw.edu.au) are members of The Australian School of Business, School of Information Systems, Technology and Management;* **Alex Steel** *(a.steel@unsw. edu.au)* & **Alana Maurushat** *(a.maurushat@unsw.edu.au) are members of the Faculty of Law; all of University of New South Wales, Australia; and* **Rick Sarre** *(Rick.Sarre@unisa.edu.au) is a member of the School of Commerce of the University of South Australia, Australia.*

---

[58] Brennan, T. 1987, "Classification: An Overview of Selected Methodological", Crime and Justice (9), pp. 201–248. Goode, above note 1. Kraus, above note 23.

[59] Sproule, above note 6; Stephan, above note 32.

[60] For analysis of the issues relating to such enactment in domestic contexts see above note 40.

# [20]

# Transnational organised cyber crime: distinguishing threat from reality

**Rob McCusker**

**Abstract** Cybercrime has become an integral part of the transnational threat landscape and conjures up pressing images of nefarious and increasingly complex online activity. More recently, the concept of 'organised crime' has been attributed to cybercriminality. There has been subsequent disagreement and confusion concerning whether such crime is a derivation of traditional organised crime or an evolution of such crime within the online space. This opaque state of affairs has been exacerbated by the relative lack of clear evidence attesting to and supporting either scenario. Technological advances have always been used to the advantage of the criminal fraternity. The crucial question that remains is whether those advances have merely *facilitated* the commission of physical crime or whether in fact they have led to the *creation* of a new wave of traditional, but virtual, organised crime.

## Introduction

In broad terms, the debate surrounding the actual and/or prospective involvement of traditional organised crime groups in cybercriminal activity is characterised by a tension between logic and pragmatism. Logic would dictate that traditional organised crime groups will engage with cybercriminal endeavours as fervently as they will with any low risk, high profit non-virtual criminal activity. Pragmatism on the other hand would suggest that it remains questionable whether such groups either need that engagement or indeed have the capacity to exploit the cyber environment to the extent that their capital investment would produce the desired and appropriate financial gains.

Rob McCusker is a Research Analyst in Transnational Crime, Australian Institute of Criminology.

R. McCusker (✉)
Australian Institute of Criminology, Canberra, Australia
e-mail: rob.mccusker@aic.gov.au

**Defining 'cybercrime'**

Yar argues that '[i]t has become more or less obligatory to begin any discussion of "cybercrime" by referring to the most dramatic criminological quandary it raises, namely, does it denote the emergence of a "new" form of crime and/or criminality?'[1] Grabosky sought at a relatively early juncture to address that question by suggesting that cybercrime was simply a case of 'old wine in new bottles,' that is '...less a question of something completely different than a recognizable crime committed in a completely different way.'[2] In a similar vein, Nisbett has argued that '[c]yber crime is on the increase. This does not necessarily mean that there are in fact any new crimes; rather there are new methods of committing existing crimes and better ways of detecting them.'[3] Interestingly, Wall has noted that '...when so-called cases of cybercrime come to court, they often have the familiar ring of the "traditional" rather than the "cyber" about them.'[4]

Crime, like nature, however, abhors a vacuum. It has accordingly always seemed inevitable perhaps that traditional organised crime groups would positively rush to fill the void for illicit product placement deemed to present itself in the context of cyberspace. It might be assumed, therefore, that an evaluation of the purported involvement of traditional crime groups in cyber crime would be a relatively simple affair. Certainly, the literature, broadly defined, is replete with references to 'cybercrime' and more recently to 'organised' cybercrime. Unfortunately, the mere assertion in much of that literature that such crime exists (both in a general sense and in an organised form) has been routinely transmuted, as if by osmosis, into tangible fact. Arguably, however, in many cases those 'facts' appear to rely as much upon anecdote, hearsay, extrapolation and assumption as they do upon objectively obtained and verified evidence.

At the basic level of analysis there is no discernible control mechanism in place insofar as terminology is concerned. Thus, one might speak of 'cybercrime,' 'high tech crime,' 'computer crime,' 'technology crime,' 'digital crime' and 'IT crime' and be discussing the same and/or different concepts, respectively. Achieving any vestige of comparative analysis of the impact of cybercrime therefore is fraught with difficulties. Beyond that, the increasingly common conflation of cybercrime with the prefix 'organised' infers the involvement of traditional organised crime groups but ultimately alludes to 'ordinary' criminals who happen to operate in cyberspace in an organised manner. Equally, it seems common to refer to cybercriminal 'groups' as if they were of equivalent size, complexity, 'stature' and duration as their traditional, non-virtual counterparts. This effectively allows cybercriminal groups to achieve the *semblance* of the organisational evolution *actually* achieved by those traditional organised crime groups they are deemed to emulate. In short, there remains a confused and confusing plethora of terminology, purported parameters and alleged participants of cybercrime as well as concerns over the provenance and quality of evidence elicited in support of such activity. These are certainly subtle differences but they are important differences nevertheless.

[1]Majid Y. (2005). The novelty of 'cybercrime': An assessment in light of routine activity theory. *European Journal of Criminology, 2*(4), 407–427:408.

[2]Grabosky, P. N. (2001). Virtual criminality: Old wine in new bottles? *Social and Legal Studies, 10*(2), 243–249:243

[3]Nisbett, C (2002). New directions in cyber-crime. White Paper, QineticQ, http://www.qinetiq.com/home/security/information_and_network_security/white_paper_index.Par.0012.File.pdf

[4]Wall, D. S.(2004). The internet as a conduit for criminal activity. In A. Pattavina (Ed.), *Information technology and the criminal justices system* (Chapter 4:77). Sage

In consequence the term 'cybercrime' has rapidly become a generic descriptor for any malfeasant online behaviour (whatever the relative differences in complexity and seriousness) ranging from spam emails and denial of service attacks to malware and botnet infiltration. Indeed, a recent IBM survey on cybercrime globally did not in fact define 'cybercrime' and yet sought information from business participants on every continent on the impact of such crime.[5] The net effect of such surveys is that the myth of cybercrime is perpetuated and the facts of cybercrime become sacrificed at the altar of public perception. It is the very imprecision of the term which has given rise to the hyperbole and opacity that surrounds it.

Beyond the broad non-specificity of definition lies an equally amorphous conundrum, which forms the heart of this piece, namely, whether 'organised' cyber crime is crime committed by traditional organised crime groups or 'merely' that it is crime committed online in an organised manner. Even at this juncture the question is fraught with difficulty. The term 'organised,' when applied to traditional organised crime groups, *is* defined (see, inter alia, the UN Convention against Transnational Crime [6]) and subsequently assessments of organised crime can gravitate to and from a fixed point. However, 'cybercrime' is seemingly deemed to be 'organised' once the perpetrator ceases to be the archetypal lonely hacker and gravitates instead towards a group of fellow lonely hackers. If acting in illegal concert were the *sole* arbiter of 'organised' crime then *any* form of criminal behaviour which necessitated *any* degree of planning might be deemed de facto to be organised crime.

Ultimately, however, the Council of Europe has argued that '[d]ata on connections between organised crime and cybercrime are still scarce and do not permit a reliable analysis.'[7] Thoumi suggested that technology can democratise crimes because '[t]he fact that smaller players have an easier time entering the market is one reason why the notion of the great crime "cartels" may increasingly be a myth as the contemporary criminal market places changes in origin.'[8] The definitional waters have been muddied somewhat by comparisons of cyber criminals with traditional organized crime groups. FBI agent Thomas Grasso Jr. argued that Carderplanet '...organized [itself] into the same structure as the Italian Mafia.'[9] Grasso also suggested that the International Carders' Alliance, to which Carderplanet, Mazafaka and IAACA (the International Association for the Advancement of Criminal Activity) belonged '...is really the heart of organized cybercrime.'[10] Christopher Painter, of the Computer Crimes and Intellectual Property Section at the US Department of Justice, noted in 2006 that '...[w]e are seeing organized criminal groups' but that they were in fact '...groups that are organized online targeting victims via the Internet.'[11]

---

[5]IBM (2006). *IBM B2B security survey: Australia/Global summary report* (provided to author by IBM)

[6]Article 2 (a) of the UN Convention Against Transnational Organized Crime defines an 'organised criminal group' as a '...structured group of three or more persons, existing for a period of time and acting in concert with the aim of committing one or more serious crimes or offences established in accordance with [the] Convention, in order to obtain, directly or indirectly, a financial or other material benefit.'

[7]Council of Europe (2004). *Organised crime situation report: Focus on the threat of cybercrime*, http://www.coe. int/T/E/Legal_Affairs/Legal_co-operation/Combating_economic_crime/8_Organised_crime/Documents/ Organised%20Crime%20Situation%20Report%202004.pdf

[8]Cited in Naylor, R. T. (2000). *Expert panel on emerging crimes*:4, Research and Statistics Division, Department of Justice, http://www.justice.gc.ca/en/ps/rs/rep/2002/expertpanel.pdf

[9]Cited in McMillan, R (2006). *FBI: Cybercriminals taking clues from Mafia*, http://www.pcworld.com/ article/id, 126664-c,cybercrime/article.html

[10]Ibid

[11]Cited in Wired News (2006), *Cybercrime is getting organized*, http://www.wired.com/news/technology/ internet/0,71793-0.html?tw=rss.index

These assertions are somewhat incongruous and consequently both sets of assertions do little to clarify the distinction between traditional organised crime involvement in cyber-space and criminals who simply operate in the online space.

## The law enforcement perspective

In truth, fewer terms are destined to create a greater state of apoplexy within law enforcement agencies than 'cybercrime,' a fact reflected in part by their usual depiction of such crime as 'high tech' rather than 'cyber' in nature. Indeed, even the term 'high tech' crime has drawn criticism. Hynds, for example, noted that '[h]igh tech crime is an oxymoron; a classic contradiction in terms...It's not about technology, it's about people.'[12] The dislike of the term 'cybercrime,' and particularly its increasing association with the term 'organised,' reflects a common belief in such quarters that cybercrime is nothing more than ordinary traditional crime enhanced in terms of its distribution and impact by the facilitation of technology. Nisbett maintained that '[e]very advance in technology appears to create a new crime alongside it'[13] and indeed, technological advances from the mobile telephone to the police scanner have historically been used by the criminal fraternity. That the complexity of such technology has increased, and continues to increase, exponentially does not detract from that fact.

The tension between the law enforcement perspective on the one hand, and the assertions within oft-accessed and cited literature on cybercrime on the other, may appear to be a little odd given the accepted use of technology by criminals generally. It might be argued that to admit the involvement of traditional organised crime groups in cybercriminal activity would place law enforcement agencies in the unenviable position of having to investigate yet more complex virtual crimes within a still predominantly physical law enforcement environment. Whilst at the helm of the Federal Bureau of Investigation, J. Edgar Hoover refused to acknowledge the existence of organised crime until the Kefauver[14] and McClellan[15] committees and the highly visible Apalachin[16] meeting rendered continued denial superfluous. For Hoover to have admitted the arrival of organised crime would have necessitated a concerted response designed to curb it and this was something Hoover could not at that time guarantee. Given the general advantage transnational crime groups have over law enforcement agencies in terms of the distance they are able to place between the commission of crime and its ultimate resolution at the hands of the criminal justice system, it might be suggested that a Hoover-like dread currently rests upon the heads of law enforcement agencies. However, this would be a tad disingenuous given the fact that unlike organised crime in the twentieth century, cybercrime in the twenty-first century is arguably more akin to an *adaptation* of existing crime to new technology than the *creation* of a brand new crime type and/or structure. Equally, one might assume that in order to

---

[12]Cited in Thomson, I (2003). *NHTCU issues stark cyber-crime warning*, http://www.managementconsultancy. co.uk/vnunet/news/2122171/nhtcu-issues-stark-c

[13]Nisbett, op. cit

[14]U.S. Congress (1951). Special Committee on Organized Crime in Interstate Commerce

[15]U.S. Congress (1963). Senate Permanent Subcommittee on Investigations of the Committee on Government Operations

[16]A meeting of crime Bosses at the home of Joseph Barbara in Appalachian, New York, in 1957

operate effectively within the relative complexity of the online environment one would have to be organised as a matter of course. In this sense, the debate as to whether criminality is organised or not might be deemed somewhat redundant. However, given the finite nature of law enforcement resources it remains important strategically and logistically for cybercrime efforts to be directed at the *actual* rather than *supposed* criminals. That, in turn, renders the question as to whether one is confronting traditional organised crime in an online context, or online criminals who happen to be organised, a practical and serious one.

## The generic relationship between technology and crime

In 1992 the United Nations Economic and Social Council observed that '[i]nternational experience shows that organized crime has long ago crossed national borders and is today transnational...It should be noted that aspects of the evolutionary process undergone by society may make powerful criminal organizations even more impenetrable and facilitate the expansion of their illegal activities.'[17] An integral feature of that societal evolution has of course been the development and use of technology and its associated components. More than a decade ago it was suggested that information and communication technology would play a prominent role in defining what was likely to become of greater value to a criminal in the future and might dictate that 'electronic property,' such as video-on-demand, knowledge and information such as copyrights or trademarks, or identity devices such as biometric smart cards, would be the assets of interest in the future.[18] Naylor had suggested that there had been a deal of hyperbole over the role of technology and argued that in the early to mid nineteenth century the impact of the railway, steamship and telegraph was far more revolutionary than the Internet or mass air travel.[19] Indeed, he noted, '...virtually every kind of crime now conducted through modern electronic communications technology had some equivalent in the telegraph age - which saw everything from insider trading to price fixing to financial fraud conducted by and through the telegraph, while telegraph companies faced problems of breaches of security by hackers threatening, in particular, telegraphic money transfers.'[20] Zittrain convincingly argues that '[e]very technological development...has to varying degrees been a source of criminal opportunity, be it as a target or facilitator of criminal or malicious activity. Increasingly, however, we are seeing the compounding of criminal opportunity as technologies converge.'[21] In support of this apparent convergence Sussman suggests that '[t]here is a revolution going on in criminal activity...The revolution lies in the ways that networked computers and other technologies permit crimes to be committed remotely, via the Internet and wireless communications.'[22]

---

[17]UN Commission on Crime Prevention and Criminal Justice (2001). *Conclusions of the study on effective measures to prevent and control high-technology and computer-related crime*, 10th Session, 8–17 May, http://www.unodc.org/pdf/crime/10_commission/4e.pdf

[18]Davis, R and Pease, K (2001). Crime, technology and the future, Security Journal, 59–61, Perpetuity Press Ltd.

[19]Naylor, op.cit

[20]Ibid: 4

[21]Zittrain, J. L. (2006). The generative internet, Harvard Law Review (119:7), http://www.harvardlawreview.org/issues/119/may06/may06.shtml

[22]Sussman, M. A. (1999). The critical challenges from international high-tech and computer-related crime at the millennium. *Duke Journal of Comparative and International Law, 9,* 451–489):451

Indeed, one might argue that the potential future of cybercrime sits within the broader digital environment, an environment created primarily to facilitate social and business relationships and transactions but one which is increasingly prone to degradation, infiltration and subsequent malfeasant activity. Although the precise future characteristics of cybercrime cannot be accurately determined it remains both possible and appropriate to frame potential cybercrime activities within the context of developments in technology more broadly and of the digital environment it supports and operates within.

## The target environment

As suggested at the outset, logic alone would suggest that the digital environment will be increasingly targeted by traditional organised crime groups. The recognition by the business sector of the wealth of product placement opportunities available on the Internet will not have escaped the notice of traditional organised crime entities. Conversely, the extent to which there has been a major development in traditional organised criminal behaviour and activity, as a direct or indirect result of cybercrime developments per se, is starting to be questioned.

The Internet, for example, was never designed to be a highly developed or intelligent system. The basic purpose of the Internet, a vehicle for conveying packets of data between devices (the "end to end principle"), has remained unchanged and the resultant architecture, whilst embracing the original unfettered communication precept of the Internet, has facilitated an increasing vulnerability to inadvertent technical failings as well as advertent criminal and other malfeasants. It is clear that it is becoming less and less able to cope with the exponential demands, in terms of information storage and exchange, being placed upon it. In addition, globalisation requires, and will continue to necessitate, an increased connectivity of the world's computer, banking and financial systems. Globalisation has increased the free movement of capital between the world's developed and underdeveloped economies. Globalisation operates in cyberspace, which by definition is extraterritorial. This means that the regulatory practices which purport to exist and operate in the land-locked world, and which should be the sine qua non of the globalised economy, are missing.

Furthermore, the Internet was never designed to be secure from exploitation. The strength of the Internet in terms of its rapid communication facility has become one of its undermining weaknesses. The criminal fraternity operates online under the same free market principles and the legislative and law enforcement endeavours launched against them suffer from geographical and practical restrictions. The potential for an increase in the number of victims of economic crime, as well as cybercrime more broadly, is likely to rise. The dissemination, storage and protection of information lie at the heart of the Internet, e-commerce and the online environment per se. Personal information about clients and customers is increasingly being lodged in digital documentation and that digital documentation is being routinely disseminated between computer networks. This distributed digital identity places confidential information in the ether with only the security processes of the organisation to prevent its exploitation. The acquisition and abuse of such information is likely to continue to form the basis of the future cyber crime threat. The sheer wealth of information likely to become available (if Google™ and similar search engines are any indication of future provision) to the average private user may, it is suggested, lead to the use of "knowbots" (knowledge robots) to navigate on a person's behalf through such data more effectively and even organise part of their daily routine such as scanning email for particular addresses or subject matter.[23] The dangers of such knowbots being controlled by a malicious third party might of course facilitate the navigation of bank accounts etc with equal aplomb. A recent report has suggested that the new threat landscape may be typified by malware attacks which facilitate subsequent criminal endeavours.[24] Attacks are deemed to be moving away from large affairs (such as global spam incidents) to smaller, more focused attacks upon particular clients. The motivation has become largely profit-oriented and such attacks may facilitate those activities which increase profits most readily such as identity theft, fraud and extortion. Symantec noted that in the latter half of 2005, 80% of the top 50 reported threats could be used for data theft. 'Unfortunately,' it went on to observe, 'it appears profit is the new motive for Internet threats, and the pride of one-upmanship - which used to inspire cyberattacks - is giving way to calculated criminal intent.'[25] CipherTrust has supported this assertion by noting that '[w]hen information gained through phishing is sold, profits often get routed to international criminals and activities.'[26]

Corresponding risks have of course been identified with advances in technology. Increasing dependency upon computer systems to control and operate key infrastructure may leave such control systems, and the populations who depend upon their effective operation, prone to the consequences of any subsequent breach. Importantly, the wider dissemination and availability of technology may render it a far easier task for criminals to engage fraud and fraud-related endeavours.

Technology is destined to become increasingly ubiquitous. Established technologies such as mobile phones and computers will continue to widely used but there is likely to be a proliferation of auxiliary devices aimed at improving the performance and flexibility of those established products. The key threat emanating from the ubiquity and complexity of technology in an era of increasing connectivity will be viral contamination. This threat will be exacerbated by the reliance placed by businesses and individuals upon the technology to function in their daily lives. Communication vehicles will increase exponentially and the danger of such communication conduits being breached and exploited by cybercriminals is likely to rise in tandem. As the Commission on Crime Prevention and Criminal Justice once noted '...as the degree of reliance placed on networks increases, the potential harm from criminal offences also increases.'[27]

The fact, for example, that the computer can be left permanently on and connected to the Internet, when coupled with the poor security awareness of many domestic users, renders such computers prone to criminal attack. The potential rationale for such attacks could include the obtaining of personal information for identity theft, the use of the computer as a 'zombie' or storage facility for illegal material (as has been found to be the case with commercial and university systems). These dangers are likely to be exacerbated by activities such as peer-to-peer file sharing programs or the downloading of files from unknown senders. Rapid download times have also facilitated the dissemination of content

---

[23]Miller, R, Michalski, W, & Stevens, B (1998). The promises and perils of 21st century technology: An overview of the issues in 21st century technologies. Promises and perils of a dynamic future, OECD.

[24]Symantec (2006). Symantec internet security threat report: Trends for January 06–June 06, http://www.symantec.com/specprog/threatreport/ent-whitepaper_symantec_internet_security_threat_report_x_09_2006.en-us.pdf

[25]Symantec (2006). *Cybercrime: A disturbing trend* http://www.symantec.com/home_homeoffice/library/article.jsp?aid=cybercrime_a_disturbing_trend

[26]CipherTrust (2005). Phishing: Organized crime for the 21st century, http://www.ciphertust.com

[27]UN Commission on Crime Prevention and Criminal Justice (2001), op. cit

such as pornographic images and pirated software and music particularly through Peer to peer (P2P) platforms. Most P2P software is free and it is believed may contain overt or covert advertising related software. There is a danger that the software may also contain spyware.[28]

The increasing use of mobile phones and PDAs (Personal Digital Assistants), each with ever-increasing storage capacity and ever-diminishing security protocols, constitutes another potential threat. Such devices are routinely used to store personal data and corporate information and the advent of wireless networking increases the likelihood of such information being uploaded and downloaded. In 2005, 22% of people reported losing their mobile devices and of those 81% had not encrypted the information contained therein.[29] Wireless networks themselves may bring a number of vulnerabilities. Key amongst these is the fact that the network and its data can be accessed without physical access or presence being required. This facility assists the user but more importantly constitutes a positive boon to the criminal.

### Traditional organised groups in cyberspace

Brenner has argued that '...nothing has been written about whether organized criminal activity will emerge in cyberspace and, if so, what forms it may take.'[30] This may in part be attributed to the fact that traditional organised crime groups '...evolved in the context of real-world endeavors [sic], mankind having lived exclusively in the real world until quite recently.' Nisbett has posited the notion that '[t]he current absence of organized cybercriminality makes a consideration whether organization will likely become an aspect of crime on the virtual frontier particularly topical and appropriate.'[31] Given the assertions made concerning organised cybercrime, however, the capacity for, and desire of, traditional organised crime groups to engage in cybercrime should be evaluated. Brenner ascribes the relative lack of analysis of traditional organised crime intent and/or desire to engage in cyberspace to '...the perception that cybercrime is perpetrated by hackers, who are loners, and are therefore not inclined to engage in group criminality; and the fact that, to date, most documented cybercrime reveals that a majority of incidents involve individuals, not groups.'[32] Given also the fact that it is the application and definition of the word 'organised,' which has caused much of the current disquiet, discussion ought to be had as to whether the structures of traditional organised crime groups could, or would, conform to the rather sleeker organisational models deemed essential for the smooth infiltration and exploitation of cyberspace. Nisbett suggests that '...empirical differences between the real world and the cyberworld will prevent the effective transfer of existing forms of real-world criminal organization modalities into cyberspace.'[33] For Nisbett '...the very nature of cyberspace is inconsistent with hierarchy. Cyberspace is a network, or, more properly, a network of networks. Networks are lateral, diffuse, fluid, and evolving. Hierarchies are

---

[28]Morris, S. (2004). The future of netcrime now: Part 1 - Threats and challenges, Home Office.

[29]Millman, R. (2005). *IT managers fail to protect mobile devices*, SC Magazine, 11 November, http://www.scmagazine.com/asia/news/article/527520/it-managers-fail-protect-mobile-devices/

[30]Brenner, op.cit, 24

[31]Nisbett, op.cit

[32]Brenner, op. cit, 24

[33]Nisbett, op. cit

vertical, concentrated, and tend to be rigid and fixed.'[34] This seemingly presumes, however, that traditional organised crime groups retain the degree of hierarchical structure which Cressey asserted,[35] and Valachi confirmed,[36] in the 1960s.

It is recognised that in fact, flatter, more horizontal networks, comprising cell-like 'crews,' have become the norm in much of the organised crime environment (though Chinese triads and Japanese yakuza have remained traditionally hierarchical in nature) with the United Nations having identified a number of structural variations within organised crime groups.[37] Nisbett suggests that '[l]ogically, the first issue to consider when analysing forms criminal organization may take in cyberspace is the extent to which already-evolved forms of criminal organization are likely to migrate to the virtual frontier. Since the already-evolved forms of criminal organization have proven successful in the real world, it is reasonable to expect that they will enjoy at least a measure of success in the cyberworld.'[38] The flexibility of the organisation and control of traditional crime groups has in part derived from a proactive reaction by such groups to law enforcement endeavours and operations against such groups. Whilst one might argue that such structural changes have resulted more from the necessity of protection than through freedom of choice, this demonstrated ability to make such organisational changes augurs well for similar adaptations to be made by traditional organised crime groups in reaction to, and after reflection of, changes in their operating environment, namely, cyberspace. Olson maintains that '[o]rganized crime is perfectly suited to profit from the information revolution. Its existence relies on innovating, adapting strategies and operations, and evading detection. These attributes complement the ever-changing nature and unpredictability of the information revolution. The Internet offers an array of lucrative opportunities with little or no risk.'[39]

Europol has indeed suggested that, at the meta level, '[t]he advantages the internet offers in terms of information and communication technology are extremely beneficial to [organised crime]. The underground cultures built around some of the high technology phenomena such as hacking and cracking are perfect for support, contacts, recruitment, advice and clients.'[40] By way of tacit support for such a notion, McAfee asserts that '[o]rganised crime gangs are starting to actively recruit skilled young people into cybercrime. They are adopting KGB-style tactics to recruit high flying IT students and graduates and targeting computer society members, students of specialist computer skills schools and graduates of IT technology courses.'[41] For Williams, the transition of traditional organised crime from the physical to the virtual environment is as much about a natural progression in criminal behaviour as it is about a determined course of action given the fact that as

---

[34]Ibid

[35]Cressey, D. R. (1969). *Theft of a nation: The structure and operations of organized crime in America*. New York: Harper & Row.

[36]Joseph V, A mafia member, testified before the McClellan Committee (n.17 supra). Details of his life may be found in Maas, P. (1968), *The Valachi papers*, New York: G.P. Putnam

[37]United Nations Office on Drugs and Crime (2002). *Results of a pilot study of forty selected organized crime groups in sixteen countries*, http://www.unodc.org/pdf/crime/publications/Pilot_survey.pdf

[38]Nisbett, op.cit

[39]Olson, J. L. (2004). *The threat of systematic and organized cybercrime and information warfare*: 17 http://www.american.edu/traccc/resources/publications/students/olson01.pdf

[40]Europol (2006). *Organised Crime Threat Assessment 2006*: 18 http://www.europol.europa.eu/publications/OCTA/OCTA2006.pdf

[41]McAfee (2006). *McAfee virtual criminology report: Organised crime and the internet*, http://www.softmart.com/mcafee/docs/McAfee%20NA%20Virtual%20Criminology%20Report.pdf

'[o]rganized crime has always selected particular industries as targets for infiltration and the exercise of illicit influence...[f]rom an organized crime perspective, the Internet and the growth of e-commerce present a new set of targets for infiltration and the exercise of influence...'[42]

Conversely, there has been a degree of rumination over whether the 'organised crime in cyberspace' versus 'crime in cyberspace which is organised' debate is itself being taken over rapidly by events. Clarberg has pointed out that '...high technology crime is often not a crime in isolation, and forms part of a crime which is also occurring within the physical world. It is very difficult to find a real world crime that does not have a high technology element, even if it is as common and straightforward as the use of a mobile telephone.'[43]

There have also been suggestions that in fact, as with the purported convergence of organised crime and terrorism in light of perceived mutual benefits, the two sides of the 'organised' debate may in fact find greater solace, reward and operational fluidity through a combination of their efforts.[44] Olson maintains that '[e]lements of both the cybercrime and organized crime worlds have encouraged the two to merge. Hackers were traditionally anti-social loners, operating without any monetary motivation. Their motivations have now shifted from mere curiosity to more self-serving and lucrative attacks. But hackers now frequently work together in loosely knit units or cells.'[45] Furthermore, she notes that '[m]any of the characteristics traditionally attributed to organized crime can also be attributed to cybercriminals and hackers. This overlap in skill and motivation has created a natural bond between the two underground networks.'[46]

**The possible redundancy of the term 'organised'**

More radically still is the notion that the intrinsic nature of cyberspace will in fact alter the very notion of the term 'organised' whether applied within the context of organised crime of the traditional-oriented or cyber-born complexion. Nisbett has observed a truism that '[i]n the cyberworld...one's aptitude as a cybercriminal is a function of his or her technical expertise...While there may be opportunistic reasons to affiliate with a cybercriminal group, such an affiliation is not essential for the pursuit of a criminal career, as it is for members of real-world gangs.'[47] As Brenner has it, '[t]he characteristics of cyberspace, the absence of fixed, empirical constraints and a diffuse, fluid, evolving environment, indicate that hierarchical organizational structures are at once not needed in and not appropriate for activities conducted in cyberspace. What, then, will criminal organization look like in cyberspace?...will organized criminal activity in cyberspace ever actually exist?'[48]

[42]Williams, P. (2001). Organized crime and cybercrime: Synergies, trends and responses. *Global Issues* 6(2), 25, US Department of State, http://usinfo.state.gov/journals/itgic/0801/ijge/ijge0801.pdf

[43]Clarberg, B. (2003). *Cyber crime*, Paper presented at the conference on international cooperation on transnational crime, The Hague, 9–10 October (unpublished)

[44]See, for example, McCusker, R. (2006) Organised crime and terrorism: Convergence or separation?, ECPR Standing group on organised crime newsletter (5:2) 2–5 http://www.essex.ac.uk/ecpr/standinggroups/crime/documents/SGOC_Vol5_2.pdf

[45]Olson, op.cit: 15

[46]Ibid:16

[47]Nisbett, op.cit

[48]Brenner, op.cit: 39

Some authors have posited that cybercrime itself may alter the structure of traditional organised crime groups. The Council of Europe notes, for example, that '[c]ybercrime requires less control over a geographical territory, less violence and intimidation, less personal contacts and thus less relationships based on trust and enforcement of discipline between criminals, in short less need for formal organisations.'[49] Brenner has suggested that '[o]nline criminal organization will tend to de-emphasize formal, hierarchical organizational structures. At the same time, it will emphasize a broader, lateral contextual structure. Online criminal organization has no reason to be circumscribed, in its membership or in its operations, by national, territorial boundaries or by cultural differences because cybercriminals...share a culture that transcends national borders and context. So, as opposed to the localized, rigid, and often provincial hierarchical organizations that have so far characterized criminal groups, regional, or even global, coalitions will develop.'[50]

Such coalitions are likely to comprise a mixture of '...cybercrime entrepreneurs...' and '...diffuse, loosely-structured opportunity groups...'[51] which are, in a manner currently typical of 'Russian' organised crime groups in the physical environment, likely to collude in relation to a specific offence and thereafter disband. The ties that bind and typify traditional organised crime groups in terms of membership criteria and strategic alliances are likely to become less constricting. The '...traditional indicia of commitment, and of membership, will decline in importance. Instead of multi-generational criminal enterprises, cybercriminal organization will emphasize arm's length, instrumental associative alliances.'[52]

### Traditional organised crime online or online crimes which are organised?

The catalyst behind the current debate concerning traditional organised crime online, or online crime that is organised, is the nature and quality of evidence adduced in support of either and/or both camps. As a point of origin, Clarberg has asserted that '[t]here is very little, if any quantitative data available for assessment of the size and impact of high-technology crime...'[53] That of course has not prevented the production of a wealth of information asserting its existence, its composition and its impacts. Williams once suggested that '[t]he synergy between organized crime and the Internet is not only natural but also one that is likely to flourish and develop even further in the future.'[54] He posited that safe havens used in the physical environment are likely to be replaced with similar havens in the cyberworld and that the Internet provides a range of criminal opportunities in terms particularly of the commission of old crimes in new ways as envisaged by Grabosky.[55] In essence, Williams maintained that '...[t]he Internet provides both channels

---

[49]Council of Europe (2005). *Organised crime situation report: Focus on the threat of economic crime*, http://www.coe.int/t/e/legal_affairs/legal_co-operation/combating_economic_crime/8_Organised_crime/Documents/Report2005E.pdf

[50]Brenner, op. cit: 45

[51]Ibid

[52]Ibid: 47

[53]Clarberg: op.cit

[54]Williams, op.cit: 23

[55]Grabosky, op.cit

and targets for crime and enables them to be exploited for considerable gain with a very low level of risk. For organized crime it is difficult to ask for more.'[56]

These observations and assertions reflect the logic component of the tension noted above.[57] Indeed, Williams conceded that '[m]ost organized crime will continue to operate in the real world rather than the cyberworld and most cybercrime will be perpetrated by individuals rather than criminal organizations per se.'[58] This position reflects the oft-neglected issue of motivation, that is, what might prompt organised crime groups to gravitate away from the target-rich physical environment to the relatively unknown quantity of the virtual world? Nevertheless, Williams maintained, '...the degree of overlap between the two phenomena is likely to increase considerably in the next few years' and argued that '...there is growing evidence that organized crime groups are exploiting the new opportunities offered by the Internet.'[59] The potential problem of Williams' assertion is not that it might *not* be accurate (which, given Williams' reputation, is highly unlikely) but rather that the evidence adduced *publicly* to support that assertion is not conspicuously nor overwhelmingly present. Assertions without *cited* supportive evidence are quickly trans-formed into hearsay and anecdote which are in turn recycled within other authors' assertions concerning cybercriminal activity. At the point at which citations by one author, of examples provided by another (who may not have provided tangible evidence for those examples), become the norm, the task of distinguishing the true nature of cybercriminal behaviour from its presumed characteristics will becomes an increasingly difficult task. Furthermore, the capacity for law enforcement agencies to engage with the relatively unknown quantity of 'organised' cybercrime amidst a plethora of contradictory and unsubstantiated or under substantiated reports and conjecture will be further diminished.

A number of generic cyber crime threats have been identified consisting of:

(1) Offences against the confidentiality, integrity and availability of computer data and systems (via activities such as hacking, deception, interception and espionage)
(2) Computer-related 'traditional' crimes (fraud and forgery), content-related computer offences (such as website defacement and dissemination of false information) and
(3) Offences relating to the infringement of copyright and related rights (such as the unauthorised reproduction and use of programmes and databases)[60]

Given the accepted precept that opportunity, tempered by an evaluation of relative risk, provides the key incentive to criminal endeavour, logic, if not evidence, would suggest that traditional organised crime groups and/or networks are fully engaged in the exploitation of the cyber environment. An oft-cited example of the systemic nature of transnational organised crime groups' lateral thinking and exploitative powers was witnessed in October 2000 when a Sicilian mafia group, together with twenty other strategically placed individuals, created a digital clone of the Bank of Sicily's online component.[61] Its plan, thwarted at the last moment by an informant, involved the diversion of $400 million allocated to the Bank by the European Union for regional projects within Sicily. The fact

---

[56]Williams, op.cit: 23

[57]See 'Introduction' at p.1 supra

[58]Williams, op.cit: 22

[59]Ibid

[60]Council of Europe (2004), op.cit: 169

[61]Cited in Williams (2001), op.cit: 23

that the group tried and failed is not the key issue debated. That they actually conceived the idea is. Sadly, this example has often been cited as evidence of organised cybercrime and whilst it undoubtedly indicates a propensity for such crime by organised crime groups it remains in desperate need of the company of related organised crime endeavours to strengthen and/or clarify the debate. As Morris argues '[d]espite the diverse and often interconnectedness of many of the threats and challenges that have been highlighted [in the Future of Netcrime Survey], this complexity should not obscure the fact that much of what is seen is merely old crimes committed in new ways. Human motivations, needs and frailties are relatively consistent. Criminals and offenders are largely driven by finding ways of making money...'[62]

Parizo suggests that there is a common misconception in relation to cybercrime that '... organized crime on the Internet manifests itself just like traditional mafia.'[63] According to Peretti (of the US Department of Justice Computer Crime and Intellectual Property Division) '...it is virtually impossible to find any true crime families in cyberspace.'[64] Indeed, in annual reviews and prognoses of future conduct, the level of actual or perceived involvement by organised crime groups in cybercrime remains peripheral to other traditional activities such as the trafficking of arms, drugs and people. However, such reports do note a connection between cyberspace and traditional organised crime but this is largely in the context of using cyberspace to facilitate old physical rather than new virtual criminality. It has been argued that '...only a few cases are known in which organised crime elements have been active in the area of criminal offences against the confidentiality, integrity, or availability of computer data and systems.'[65] Conversely, in relation to computer-related traditional crimes '[o]rganised crime groups are especially involved in acts of sophisticated computer fraud, credit card fraud, and telephone fraud.'[66] The Council of Europe argues that '[i]n the area of content-related offences, organised crime groups are heavily involved in the production and distribution of child pornography.'[67]

Europol also notes that '[organised crime] groups rely on fast and secure means of communication. E-mail, internet chat rooms and instant messaging all offer new opportunities, as do web-based and client server mail accounts, websites and message boards. It provides speed of communication and, combined with encryption tools, offer unprecedented security for the data they store and exchange.'[68] Furthermore, the Criminal Intelligence Service of Canada (CISC) suggests that '[t]echnology facilitates increasingly secure, anonymous and rapid communication, through tools like encryption software, wireless devices, encrypted cellular phones and anonymous re-mailers that forwards emails without revealing their origins. Criminal groups exploit tools like this to plan and undertake criminal activities, such as drug trafficking, without physical interactions, thereby reducing the risks of detection and prosecution.'[69]

---

[62]Morris, op.cit: 28

[63]Parizo, E.B. (2005). *Busted: The inside story of 'Operation Firewall'*, Security.com, http://searchsecurity. techtarget.com/originalContent/0,289142,sid14_gci1146949,00.html

[64]Cited in Parizo, op.cit

[65]Council of Europe, op.cit: 118

[66]Ibid: 119

[67]Ibid: 121

[68]Europol, op.cit: 18

[69]Criminal Intelligence Service of Canada (2005). http://www.cisc.gc.ca/annual_reports/annual_report2005/ document/annual_report_2005_e.pdf :15

In 2006, a joint US/Canadian organised crime threat assessment noted that criminal enterprises and loosely organised criminal networks perpetrate identity theft throughout Canada and the US.[70] It suggested that '...new technologies and the Internet provide identity thieves with innovative tools for acquiring large amounts of personal data with minimal effort.'[71] Asian Organized Crime Groups are deemed to have successfully combined 'traditional' activities such as extortion to technology related crimes including '... sophisticated credit card fraud, counterfeiting, and thefts of high tech components, such as computer chips.'[72]

In 2005, the CISC argued that '[o]rganized crime groups are broadening their exploitation of technological vulnerabilities by targeting individuals and businesses that rely on technology, e-commerce and the on-line storage of valuable personal, financial and intellectual property data.'[73] In 2006, the CISC reiterated this belief by suggesting that '[c]riminal groups are increasingly targeting communication devices to obtain sensitive personal and financial information in order to undertake theft and fraud.'[74]

Europol noted that '[t]echnology is increasingly becoming a main facilitator of [organised crime]. New types of fraud such as data streaming of payment card details have emerged in recent years, and traditional forms of crime such as money laundering, drug sales, the dissemination of child abuse material and prostitution have evolved as a result of technological developments. The Internet has had an especially profound effect on crime.'[75] The Serious Organised Crime Agency has noted that '[s]erious organized criminals are exploiting the Internet as a commercial medium as well as for their communications.'[76] The use of botnets has also been attributed to organised crime groups and Hynds has noted that '[t]he trade of BotNets on compromised machines is becoming an industry in itself. Organized crime is making use of this industry.'[77]

The Financial Action Task Force has indicated a new and prospective avenue for the illicit transfer of money (or more appropriately 'value') is that of new payment methods (NPTs) such as internet payment systems, mobile payments and digital precious metals. Designed primarily to facilitate cross-border funds transfer they contain a number of potential risk factors given that the distribution channel is the internet, that no face to face contact with the 'customer' occurs (a process known as disintermediation) and that the NPM process operates through an open and accessible network.[78]

---

[70]Drug Enforcement Administration, Federal Bureau of Investigation and Royal Canadian Mounted Police (2006). *2006 Canada/US organized crime threat assessment*, http://www.psepc.gc.ca/prg/le/_fl/2006_Canada-US_OC-TA_en.pdf

[71]Ibid: 13

[72]Ibid: 5

[73]Criminal Intelligence Service of Canada (2005). 2005 Annual report on organized crime in Canada: 13, http://www.cisc.gc.ca/annual_reports/annual_report2005/document/annual_report_2005_e.pdf

[74]Criminal Intelligence Service of Canada (2006), op.cit: 9

[75]Europol, op.cit: 18

[76]Serious Organised Crime Agency (2006). The United Kingdom threat assessment of serious organised crime 2006/7: 23 http://www.soca.gov.uk/assessPublications/downloads/threat_assess_unclass_250706.pdf

[77]Hynds, L (2005). *Organized crime offers rent-a-zombie deals*, http://www.spamdailynews.com/publish/Organized_crime_offers_rent-a-zombie_deals.asp

[78]Financial Action Task Force (2006). *Report on new payment methods*, http://www.fatf-gafi.org/dataoecd/30/47/37627240.pdf

In 2001, Kubic of the FBI Criminal Investigative Division argued that '[a]s worldwide dependence on technology increases, high-tech crime is becoming an increasingly attractive source of revenue for organized crime groups, as well as an attractive option for them to make commercial and financial transactions that support criminal activity.'[79] Suggestions that organised crime groups recognise the benefits and utility of the Internet may be found in recent reports which argue that criminals are targeting universities, computer clubs and online forums to find students to write computer viruses, commit identity theft and launder money (money mules).[80] McAfee maintains that '[a]lthough organised criminals may have less of the expertise needed to commit cybercrimes, they have the funds to buy the necessary people to do it for them.'[81] Stone argues that '[c]yber criminals have advanced from fairly simple virus writing to more clever attacks, sometimes using more than one attack mechanism. These range from elaborate note phishing scams...; fraudulent spam that launches viruses or spyware; and malware such as Trojans, which enable criminals to take remote control over thousands of computers for massive, distributed attacks.'[82]

Equally, there are law enforcement representatives and/or reports drawing upon law enforcement assertions which support the notion of traditional organised crime involvement in cybercrime. In 2001 the FBI announced that ongoing computer hacking by organized crime groups in Russia and the Ukraine had resulted in more than 1 million stolen credit card numbers.[83] McCafferty suggested that '[o]rganized criminals work together, with clearly defined roles. The execution is as finely crafted as the best of business plans. The capital investment is staggering.'[84] In support of this assertion McCafferty cited the example of Kansas based company, Lexitrans. Officials there were indicted in February 2004 after allegedly running a shell-company operation to market adult websites and 900 numbers that advertised for free trials but instead charged the unwary user. The illegal business generated US $750 million and Lexitrans and its shell companies were linked to the Gambino crime family.[85]

Fisher has argued, on the basis of information relayed by Larkin of the Cyber Initiative and Resource Fusion Unit (FBI), that organised crime groups range from '...so-called traditional organized crime groups, such as the Russian and Eastern European mafia, to loosely affiliated crews who pool their resources and skills in online forums.'[86] Neate (the e-crime liaison for the United Kingdom's Serious Organised Crime Agency - SOCA) noted

---

[79]Kubic, T. T. (2001). *The FBI's perspective on the cyber crime problem.* Testimony before the House Committee on the Judiciary, Subcommittee on Crime, http://www.fbi.gov/congress/congress01/kubic061201.htm

[80]Griffiths, P (2006). *Internet gangs hiring students for cybercrime*, http://www.nzherald.co.nz/section/3/story.cfm?c_id=3&objectid=10414819

[81]McAfee (2006) op.cit

[82]Stone, G (2005). *Microsoft partners with Australian law enforcement agencies to combat cyber crime*, Microsoft press release, http://www.ahtcc.gov.au/__data/assets/pdf_file/13952/MR050330_ForensicWorkshop.pdf

[83]CNN (2001). *FBI warns companies about Russian hacker attacks*, http://archives.cnn.com/2001/TECH/internet/03/08/hacker.attacks/index.html

[84]McCafferty,D.(2004).*Organized cyber crime*, http://www.thewhir.com/features/organized-cybercrime.cfm

[85]ibid

[86]Fisher, D. (2006). *Feds court infosec pros in fight against cybercrime*, http://searchsecurity.techtarget.com.au/topics/article.asp?DocID=1207228

in 2006 that '[organized crime] has changed. [There is] still...traditional organized crime, but now they have learned to compromise employees and contractors. [They are] new-age, maybe have computer degrees and are enterprising themselves. They have a wide circle of associates and new structures.'[87]

Horn argues that '[c]yber crime is rapidly evolving from the domain of misguided pranksters, to elaborate, profit-driven schemes involving organized-crime syndicates that may be based around the block, or halfway around the world.'[88] Hynds, formerly of the United Kingdom's National High Tech Crime Unit (recently absorbed into SOCA) argued in 2002 that '[w]e now have reliable intelligence showing major drugs and arms traffickers using sophisticated and disciplined methods of communication using internet relay chat and ICQ [I seek you] protocols as well as encrypted emails.'[89] He suggested that in addition '[w]e are also seeing these groups using hacking skills to access and compromise IT systems, in order to secrete their illicit material on the servers of unsuspecting businesses.'[90]

APACS has argued that '[t]he primary threat to UK e-banking services has come from eastern European crime gangs...[which] have managed to meld their criminal skills along with the technology skills of a ready pool of highly educated IT professionals to find ways of developing many criminal business streams from the internet.'[91] In an indication of increasing mastery over the transition from syntactic (targeting the computer) to semantic (targeting the computer user) attacks, the use of people to transfer drugs and/or money, a long standing practice of the criminal fraternity, is being replicated in the cybercrime environment. 'Money mules' (ostensibly innocent people unrelated to the criminal activity that creates the illicit funds) transfer relatively small amounts of money lodged in their bank accounts to overseas accounts held by criminals. Money mules are a consequence of the need for criminals to transfer, and disguise the origins of, illicit proceeds of crime. Money mules seem to be recruited largely from the US, UK and Australia and transfer illegal funds to criminals located primarily, in the former Soviet Union.[92]

## Conclusion

There are undoubtedly criminal elements (known colloquially as 'super-empowered criminals') operating in the online environment as obtainers and disseminators of identity and identity-related information. Operation Firewall, for example, in 2004 in the US and Canada culminated in the arrest of 28 people from six countries for offences including the buying and selling of 1.7 million credit card numbers.[93] Such groups may be typified as

---

[87]Cited in Ilett, D (2006). *Mafia insiders infiltrating firms, U.K. cops warn*, http://news.com.com/Mafia+insiders+infiltrating+firms%2C+U.K.+cops+warn/2100-7348_3-6064954.html?tag=mainstry

[88]Horn, P. (2006). *It's time to arrest cyber crime*

[89]Cited in Thomson, I. (2002). *Organised crime goes digital*, http://www.crime-research.org/news/2002/12/Mess1201.htm

[90]Ibid

[91]Association for Payment Clearing Services (2006). *A vulnerability and threat assessment of authentication mechanisms for internet based financial services: 2006 review*, London

[92]McCusker, R. (2007). The ultimate work at home scam. *Money Laundering Intelligence* (14)

[93]McAfee (2005). *McAfee virtual criminology report: North American study into organized crime and the internet*, http://www.mcafee.com/us/local_content/misc/mcafee_na_virtual_criminology_report.pdf

criminal individuals and/or groups online who are organised rather than traditional organised crime groups who are online. It seems certain, however, that traditional organised crime groups are nevertheless prepared to pay for such information in order to facilitate the commission of physical rather than virtual crimes. However, it remains unclear, and indeed doubtful, whether currently there are traditional organised crime groups operating within the cyber environment. Equally, it seems likely that traditional organised crime groups will not shy away from using the cyber environment to facilitate the operation, and / or to disguise the illicit proceeds, of physical world-based crimes. The use, for example, of denial of service attacks to pursue extortion, of online banking to transfer laundered funds and the use of malware and/or botnet operators to acquire pertinent personal information for use in identity related financial crime is likely to continue to develop. The wholesale or partial mutation of traditional organised crime groups into fully-fledged cybercriminals will ultimately be determined as much by the diminished profitability, or increased risk, of real world criminal activities as it will by the innate attractiveness and relatively low risk of virtual criminality.

# [21]

# Intellectual capital and economic espionage: new crimes and new protections

Herbert Snyder

*Department of Accounting and Information Systems,*
*North Dakota State University, Fargo, North Dakota, USA, and*

Anthony Crescenzi

*Baldwinsville, New York, USA*

## Abstract

**Purpose** – Intellectual capital's (IC's) rising value in the production of wealth has been mirrored by its increasing vulnerability to crime. Among these are the increasing frequency of cybercrime, the intangible nature of IC which facilitates theft and the lack of legal remedies for the theft of IC. Taken together, these factors have created a new environment in which IC is uniquely at risk from financial crime. The purpose of this paper is to attempt to examine the efficacy in current legal remedies and formulate suggestions for better protecting IC.

**Design/methodology/approach** – The analysis is conceptual, using frameworks drawn from legal scholarship and traditional views of law-enforcement practice.

**Findings** – This paper explores the risks of crime inherent in IC and a distributed cyber environment in greater detail in order to demonstrate that traditional legal remedies are largely ineffective to protect IC property rights and that, given this policy environment and the nature of IC itself, prevention is the only reasonable means for protecting IC.

**Research limitations/implications** – Conceptual papers offer an intrinsically different form of evidence than empirical studies. Significant public debate prior to enacting legislation and subsequent empirical testing of the paper's propositions, if enacted into legislation, are strongly encouraged.

**Practical implications** – The paper includes implications for the development of legal protections based on guarding sensitive information at its source, rather than traditional reactive policing and legal actions after a theft has been committed.

**Originality/value** – This paper fulfils an identified need to propose useful and concrete legal solutions that deal with the increasing importance of IC and the concomitant frequency of crimes that involve its theft.

**Keywords** Intellectual capital, Crime, Theft, Data security

**Paper type** Conceptual paper

## Introduction

Intellectual capital's (IC) rising value in the production of wealth has been mirrored by its increasing vulnerability to crime. It is estimated that a majority of the productive capacity of organizations is tied up in IC and even a significantly more conservative estimate leaves IC as a major force in organizational competitiveness (Daum, 2001; Lev, 2001; Guthrie and Petty, 2000; Stewart, 1997). The move from tangible to intangible assets as a major productive force has produced a number of challenges to management and financial reporting. This shift has also resulted in a new vulnerability to financial crime that organizations face as a result of their reliance on IC.

Among these are:

- *The increase of economic espionage and cybercrime.* Economic espionage is an increasingly prevalent threat to organizational assets. Moreover, since IC is not tangible, physical access is not necessarily a requirement for theft. The misappropriation of IC is further facilitated by computer-based crime which needs only network access (ONCIX, 2007, 2006; Effron, 2003).
- *The nature of IC as an asset.* Tangible assets are finite. In the event of theft, the subsequent return of the asset prevents the criminal or anyone else from using it. IC, in contrast, can be infinitely expandable and the return of IC to its original owner does not guarantee exclusive benefit. Nor does the return of the asset guarantee that its original owner will not suffer damages (Pagano, 2007).
- *The lack of legal remedies for the theft of IC.* Traditional remedies for property-based crime rely on the physical restrictions of property to be effective. Those laws which do purport to guard against cybercrime (e.g. the Economic Espionage Act – EEA) are largely ineffective (Brenner and Clarke, 2007; Brenner and Crescenzi, 2006; Brenner, 2001, 2004).

Taken together, these factors have created a new environment in which IC is uniquely at risk from financial crime. This paper explores these risks in greater detail in order to demonstrate that traditional legal remedies are largely ineffective to protect IC property rights and that given this policy environment and the nature of IC itself, prevention is the only reasonable means for protecting IC.

## Understanding economic espionage

Successful businesses have always gathered and used intelligence to increase their competitiveness. Economic espionage may be distinguished from this legitimate business or competitive intelligence in that its practitioners steal the information rather than infer it from legitimate sources. More specifically, this paper adapts and broadens the definition of "economic espionage" included in EEA (1996), i.e. economic espionage consists of misappropriating trade secrets belonging to citizens of one country in order to benefit another country to include the unlawful taking use of proprietary information by anyone not lawfully entitled to it.

The definition is in one sense more generic than that incorporated in the EEA. The Act differentiates between the theft of trade secrets, carried out without the intent to benefit a foreign sovereign, and economic espionage, intended to further the strategic initiatives of a sovereign state and/or damage those of a rival state. The definition of economic espionage used in this paper considers the nature of the conduct at issue and therefore encompasses those who steal to benefit either a sovereign state or private parties. The broader definition is necessary to implement the paper's focus on economic espionage as a unique type of criminal activity, one with effects beyond the parameters of current policy and legal redress (Brenner and Crescenzi, 2006).

## The nature and proliferation of economic espionage

The essence of economic espionage has remained unchanged when observed from a historical perspective. Economic espionage continues to consist of covert actions intended to eliminate market advantages. There is, for example, a long history of such actions in the

# IC and economic espionage **247**

USA, dating back to the late seventeenth and early eighteenth centuries, when intellectual piracy was the *de facto* policy of the fledgling republic (Ben-Atar, 2004).

The convergence of technology, economic, demographic, and social factors has resulted in the emergence of the "Flat world" described by author Thomas Friedman. Friedman asserts that these factors have resulted in a leveling of the economic playing field and allowed developing nations like China, India, states comprising the former Soviet Union, Eastern Europe, and South America to compete more evenly with more developed nations. The case Friedman posits is a compelling one, amply demonstrated by the recent growth in gross domestic product in China, India and to a lesser extent the other geographic areas mentioned. Factors leading to a "flat world" have also altered the methods and operations of those engaging in economic espionage (Friedman, 2007).

Prior to globalization, economic espionage practitioners were constrained by traditional factors of proximity, scale, physical constraints, and patterns. These factors required that espionage tradecraft be conducted in a high-risk environment by professional intelligence operatives (case officers) trained to recruit agents and manage agent networks. Typically, this required elaborate coordination and planning to accomplish meetings or exchanges. Proximity between agents and handlers could not be avoided. Case officers were limited in the number of agents they could manage ensuring a scale of operations contingent on resources. The physical constraints of operating in a foreign environment were a constant challenge with respect to logistical support and operational techniques. Additionally, the need to follow established tradecraft protocols resulted in patterns that could be discerned by counterintelligence personnel increasing the risk of discovery and apprehension (Dulles, 1963; Johnson, 2000).

In today's so-called "flat world", the entire operational landscape has been transformed. The need for proximity with respect to agent operations has been lessened by the ability to remotely and anonymously target data contained on information networks. The scale of operations has been greatly expanded by the ability to simultaneously target multiple objectives, increasing potential collection capabilities by an order of magnitude far exceeding what was formerly available to traditional agent networks. The absence of physical constraints in cyberspace provides an unbounded virtual operational venue characterized by speed and an immediacy of results absent in traditional espionage operations. The ability of operators to implement a variety of targeting techniques crossing multiple international jurisdictions reduces the likelihood of a successful counterintelligence operation and affords a much lower risk environment. This reduction of risk combined with a commensurate opportunity for higher rewards will result in an increase of trade secret and intellectual property theft since there is so much to be gained in comparison with the flattened cost of espionage efforts.

Practitioners of economic espionage consist primarily of two groups: state sponsors and business competitors. The overexpansion of broadband capacity during the dot.com bubble era had some unanticipated consequences relative to Friedman's flat world scenario. This overexpansion resulted in increased world-wide connectivity, collaboration and information sharing to an extent not previously attainable. The ability to aggregate and disaggregate information remotely provides numerous electronic targets of opportunity. The dark side of the flat world is that the productivity-enhancing factors are vulnerable to a variety of electronic targeting and attack methodologies by adversaries engaged in economic espionage collection pursuits.

The proliferation of state-sponsored theft of IC has proven especially problematic to those businesses which on IC for the creation of wealth and to maintain a competitive position in the market (ONCIX, 2007) First, the centrality of IC assets to competitiveness has made them an increasingly attractive target for all competitors, but particularly those with more capabilities in production and fewer in research and development (R&D). An extreme case is that of software piracy in which programs that required millions in R&D to produce can be duplicated for a few cents per CD-ROM.

A second aspect of state-sponsored economic espionage is the difficulty of bringing legal remedies to bear against the perpetrators of the crime. As subsequent sections of the paper will argue, conventional law enforcement is predicated on the identification of individuals responsible for committing the crime and for their extradition to the USA to face charges if they are outside the physical jurisdiction of the courts. The theft of IC by sovereign states makes this model problematic in practice due to the likelihood that responsible individuals will be shielded from investigation by the sponsoring state and likelihood that the sponsoring state will bar extradition even in the event that specific perpetrators are discovered. Since the primary beneficiary of the crime is the state itself rather than the individual perpetrators, prosecution of individuals is unlikely to deter future thefts. Even worse, they may operate under the protections of diplomatic immunity and escape criminal responsibility altogether (Effron, 2003; Blood, 2002).

The conduct of business, particularly electronic commerce (e-commerce), has further facilitated the ease with which IC can be targeted. The nature of e-commerce requires remote, electronic access to company resources to pace, pay for and track the progress of shipments. Moreover, the expansion of customer management services allows and even encourages outside users to access company files to update individual data. While protections against intrusion can be built into e-commerce systems, the conduct of e-commerce creates access to a firm's IC assets that would have been unprecedented even ten years ago. Moreover, the trend is likely to increase in the future as customers demand greater services and access to information.

### IC assets: increased risk of theft and subsequent damage from loss
Unlike tangible assets, there is no limit to the number of usable copies that can be made from IC. The distinction may seem obvious, but it has a number of important implications in the context of IC theft, among which are those below.

*Ease of theft*
Unlike cash or paintings, which require the criminal to enter a vault or museum and subsequently carry off the stolen objects, IC requires only that the criminal make a copy. Historically, even this may have inhibited theft and increased the likelihood of detection. For example, when IC was available primarily in the form of documents, theft required the copying and/or carrying away of bulky paper files. For example, Jose Lopez, a former Executive at General Motors, was indicted in 1993 by a Detroit Grand Jury for the theft of numerous paper documents and computer discs. Such a charge is unlikely to be made today when the same amount of information can easily fit on a portable data drive (Lopez' case is also notable as an illustration of the difficulties of bringing an economic espionage case under existing law at the time. Had Lopez not taken the documents in physical form or otherwise run afoul of the provisions of wire fraud by e-mailing them to himself, he would have remained beyond the jurisdiction of US Federal Law.) (Effron, 2003).

# IC and economic espionage                    **249**

Lopez' crime, in fact, is largely a thing of the past. Since IC usually has no tangible embodiment, it is not necessary to be in physical contact in order to steal it, nor does it occupy anything but a negligible physical space. As noted above, the "flat world" of cyberspace has created an operational space in which physical proximity is unnecessary to effect a theft of IC. The ease with which IC can be stolen is further exacerbated by the increasing connectivity required to conduct business.

*Restoring the asset does not prevent others from using it*
The classic remedy in cases of theft is to return the property to its original owner. This has the two-fold outcome of preventing the asset's use by the thief and restoring exclusive use to the rightful owner. An automobile, for example, can be driven by only one person at a time. Nor must the asset always be in a tangible form for the restoration to work. Restoring cash, even in a digitized form, prevents a competitor from using the asset.

In the case of productive business assets, denying the use of the asset by a competitor may be as important as the return of the asset itself. The concept, in fact, really has no application outside intangible assets. A competitor, for example, could not simultaneously return and continue to use stolen machinery. However, since copies of IC are often as useful as the originals, there is little benefit in simply restoring the stolen information to its original owner. Anyone with copies of the IC can still use the assets for competitive advantage.

A simple example of the use/but return problem can be seen in the theft and subsequent piracy of intellectual property such as music or movies. The pirated copies can be produced at a low cost by manufacturers with no initial investment to recoup even if the originals remain in the possession of their legal owners. Patent and copyright law offer relatively sparse protection, particularly since many nations have official or unofficial policies of using pirated IC with little or no legal protections against its unauthorized use. (Note the subsequent section concerning state-sponsored theft of IC).

A situation with even less legal recourse might result from the disclosure of unpatented research-in-progress. When a firm has patented its research, it obtains legally enforceable intellectual property rights. However, research has value long before it becomes patentable. The research itself might not be at a stage in which it was possible to claim intellectual property rights, but could still be valuable to competitors as an indication of new avenues of research. Nothing would prevent competitors from pursuing successful parallel research once they were aware of its underlying concepts.

*It can be difficult to prove exclusive ownership of some IC assets*
Even in cases where control of the IC can be made, it may be extremely difficult for the original owners to prove that they had exclusive ownership. Software, in particular, is extremely problematic in this regard. It is more difficult task to prove exclusive ownership of a series of bits than tangible property. The issue becomes even more complicated due to the ease with which IC such software is distributed, raising the question of multiple sources of ownership or creation. Further, since most software is produced using a variety of development tools such as compliers, CASE tools and dis-assemblers, a software developer may create a product in which he or she has not written a line of original code (Coombs, 2005).

Nor is the problem confined to software. Much of the value of IC comes from the value added by the collection and organization of what may be public information. Thus, the selection of property owners to create a mailing list for marketing provides the real value of the asset, but the names themselves are public property. Once the list has been copied, the burden of proving exclusive ownership based on the selection criteria is problematic.

*The damage from the theft of IC may be irreversible even if the asset cannot be used directly by a competitor*

In some cases, information theft may be less for the direct use by the thief than to cause damage to the original owner or its customers. An extreme example of this situation would be the release of previously confidential information which proved damaging to the original owner. Such information might provide evidence of criminal activity or simply activities which are embarrassing. Even if the assets were returned to the original owner, the damage which resulted from their disclosure could not be undone with the return.

Blackmail is a classic case of information that produces gain in cases where it has no intrinsic value to the thief and a tactic that has become increasingly common with data thieves. A recent case involved the threaten release of stolen medical records from the Express Scripts prescription company. Express Script refused payment and reported the attempt to the FBI (Rubenstein, 2008). However, according to security experts, a number of firms, particularly in the financial services sector have already paid substantial amounts to prevent the release of their data (Krebs, 2008).

Less extreme (but no less damaging) are situations in which the IC is stolen and distributed with the intent of encouraging third parties to use it to cause damage. In 2004, more than 13.5 million lines of code from Microsoft's Windows 2000 operating systems were leaked and exchanged by thousands of hackers through file-sharing programs. The release was without any immediate gain to the original thieves and judging from the traffic at the time, was done simply to damage the software manufacturer (CNN, 2004). Similarly, the source code for Valve Software's popular Half-life 2 computer game was stolen and released on the Internet. Other game companies such as ID (producer of *Quake*) have suffered releases, sometimes for games still in development (Morris, 2003; Ratan, 2003).

Finally, the damage to information's owner may be as the result of liability issues. As the incidence of crimes such as identity theft increase, there are increasing calls for the initial owners of the data to be held accountable for both criminal and civil damages from victims whose personal information was compromised (Wernick, 2006; Wildstrom, 2005).

## Legal remedies for the theft of IC

Prior to 1996, there was little legislation that protected owners of IC. The passage of EEA (1996) finally provided legislation which made the theft of trade secrets and proprietary information a federal crime. Although the EEA has been widely promoted as a crime-fighting tool, its effectiveness in dealing cybercrime and the theft of IC remains problematic. This is due largely to the manner in which police work has been traditionally been carried out and the nature of cybercrime rather than specific shortcomings in the EEA.

There are two aspects to prosecution and punishment in criminal matters, which together with the nature of cybercrime and IC make the EEA and (or any criminal legislation) unlikely to be effective protection for IC assets. The first is the apprehension and trial of the perpetrators and the second is the restoration of stolen property (or, at a

# IC and economic espionage 251

minimum, preventing the criminals from profiting from the theft). As noted earlier, restoration is extremely problematic in the case of IC. Not only does the return of the asset fail to prevent its use by other parties, but also the original owner may still suffer significant damage even if the exclusive use of the assets is returned (Brenner, 2001, 2005).

Apprehension and punishment of the criminals is also extremely difficult in the case of online crime. Conventional crime investigation and prosecution assumes normative conditions of crime among which are:

- *Reactive responses by police to crime.* While police regularly provide anti-crime programs and a public presence to deter crime, the classic procedure is for police agencies to investigate crimes after they occur, apprehend suspects and eventually bring them to trial (Brenner, 2001; Brenner and Clarke, 2007).
- *Physical proximity.* Conventional law enforcement assumes that the perpetrator and victim will be near one another in space. Crime investigation as a result focuses on physical jurisdictions such as cities or states.
- *Limited frequency.* In some respects, this condition is an outgrowth of the physical proximity assumption. A criminal who is in the act of murdering one individual cannot carry out the same crime against another at the same time. Limited frequency also allows reactive policing to be an effective strategy since crimes are rare enough occurrences to be dealt after the fact.
- *Cooperation among states.* Crime is generally seen as a threat to order in all states. As such, the norm among political entities such as towns, counties, states and countries has been cooperation in remanding individuals from one state to another in order to face trial. There are notable exceptions and the act of extradition itself can be cumbersome and time-consuming, but the principles of mutual help to preserve order are widely accepted and practiced (Blood, 2002).

All of these assumptions are regularly violated in the case of cybercrime and the theft of IC. Unlike traditional crime, the theft of IC does not require physical proximity of the criminal, nor indeed does it necessarily require a human agent for a specific theft. Many instances of cybercrime are carried out by simultaneous, automated attacks on multiple company information systems. Further, these thefts may be planned and orchestrated by criminal enterprises which are not only located in foreign states, but in several foreign states, acting as a distributed, virtual crime organization (ONCIX, 2006, 2007). The problems for traditional, reactive police enforcement are significant. No longer are criminals limited by time and geography, and even as police are investigating a crime, a number of others may still be taking place (Brenner and Clarke, 2007).

Even assuming the perpetrators can be identified, however, bringing them to trial is challenging if they reside outside the USA. This has always been true, of course, but extradition becomes even more difficult when the theft is state-sponsored. As noted earlier, the state-sponsored theft of IC by countries such as China, France, Israel, and Russia has become common-place (ONCIX, 2006; Fialka, 1999). Unlike traditional crime, theft of economically useful information does not threaten the order of sponsoring states, and in fact creates a benefit. The injured nation can hardly expect help in extraditing criminals if they are in the employ of the host nation (Blood, 2002).

## Protection and remedies for the theft of IC

The frequency and virulence of economic espionage attacks has increased markedly over the last ten years and will almost certainly continue to grow as the importance of IC grows and as criminals (both private and state-sponsored) increase in number and sophistication. As this paper as previously noted, the traditional, reactive model of law-enforcement has not proven effective in reducing the frequency of economic espionage or in mitigating the damages of such crimes. And while statutes such as the EEA have provided improved legal remedies in cases of IC theft, they are clearly insufficient to control the burgeoning industry of economic espionage. This really leaves only one venue to control the problem, prevention, but how best to implement it?

The conventional wisdom to date has been to allow firms that own IC to protect it voluntarily. Given the rising tide of identity theft and related security breaches, this has clearly been an unworkable strategy (Wildstrom, 2005). Mandating compliance, however, is nearly as challenging since it adds an additional layer of policing. Given that the number of potential victims is even greater than the number of potential attackers, this is hardly more effective than simply increasing the number of investigators. A more effective strategy under the circumstances is to devolve both the responsibility for protecting valuable and liability for losing it on the owners.

There are several ways in which this responsibility could be enforced. One is civil liability. However, since the company losing the information is both victim as well as the party responsible for causing its loss, finding an individual with standing to bring litigation is unwieldy. One proposed solution in this situation is to allow the federal government to bring suit against those firms which lose information as they do in similar actions such as antitrust suits. Another possibility for enforcement is criminal liability for data breaches. The option may seem draconian in that it appears to punish the victim (i.e. the firm which has suffered the theft). The firm, however, is not the only the only party suffering damages in the event of IC theft. The federal government also suffers damages, particularly as the economic importance of the lost assets grows. As noted earlier, economic intelligence is taking on the same importance to state security as traditional state secrets and as such be protected in a similar manner.

The logic in this set of recommendations is not to punish the victims, but to recognize first that traditional, reactive law enforcement tactics are insufficient either to prevent crimes, or to receive the support necessary from sovereign states to bring suspected criminals to trial. Second is the realization that protecting IC assets is best done by those who own them, but that voluntary efforts at protection are insufficient. Criminal statutes are imposed on those who control IC because they are also best able to protect them. The intent of criminal statutes on the owners of IC is not to deter criminal acts, but rather to foster a climate in which commercially and strategically valuable assets are stringently protected (Brenner and Crescenzi, 2006).

## References

Ben-Atar, D. (2004), *Trade Secrets: Intellectual Piracy and the Origins of American Industrial Power*, Yale University Press, New Haven, CT.

Blood, C. (2002), "Holding foreign nations civilly accountable for their economic espionage practices", *IDEA*, No. 42, p. 229.

Brenner, S. (2001), "Is there such a thing as 'virtual crime'?", *The California Criminal Law Review*, No. 4, p. 11.

# IC and economic espionage                                    **253**

Brenner, S. (2004), "Toward a criminal law for cyberspace: distributed security", *Boston University Journal of Science & Technology Law*, No. 10, p. 229.

Brenner, S. (2005), "Distributed security: moving away from reactive law enforcement", *International Journal of Communications Law and Polic*, No. 9, p. 18.

Brenner, S. and Clarke, L. (2007), "Distributed security: a new model of law enforcement", *John Marshall Journal of Computer & Information Law*, SSRN, available at: http://ssrn.com/abstract=845085 (accessed November 12, 2008).

Brenner, S. and Crescenzi, A. (2006), "State sponsored crime and the futility of the Economic Espionage Act", *Houston Journal of International Law*, No. 27, p. 389.

CNN (2004), "Microsoft grapples with leak of source code online", *CNN.com Technology*, available at: www.cnn.com/2004/TECH/internet/02/13/microsoft.code.ap/ (accessed November 12, 2008).

Coombs, J. (2005), "Investigating software and source-code theft", *Dr Dobb's Portal*, available at: www.ddj.com/windows/184406134 (accessed November 12, 2008).

Daum, J. (2001), *Intangible Assets and Value Creation*, Wiley, Hoboken, NJ.

Dulles, A. (1963), *The Craft of Intelligence*, Harper & Row, New York, NY.

EEA (1996), *Economic Espionage Act of 1996*, Pub. L. No. 104-294, 110 Stat. 3488.

Effron, R. (2003), "Secrets and spies: extraterritorial application of the Economic Espionage Act and the Trips Agreement", *New York University Law Review*, No. 78, p. 1475.

Fialka, J. (1999), *War by Other Means: Economic Espionage in America*, W.W. Norton, New York, NY.

Friedman, T. (2007), *The World is Flat – Brief History of the Twenty-first Century*, Picador, New York, NY.

Guthrie, J. and Petty, R. (2000), "Intellectual capital literature review measurement, reporting and management", *Journal of Intellectual Capital*, Vol. 1 No. 2, p. 155.

Johnson, L. (2000), "Spies", *Foreign Policy*, Vol. 120, p. 18.

Krebs, B. (2008), "Extortion used in prescription data breach", *Washington Post*, p. D01, November 8.

Lev, B. (2001), *Intangibles: Management, Measurement, and Reporting*, Brookings Institute Press, Washington, DC.

Morris, C. (2003), "Playable version of Half-Life 2 stolen", *CNNMoney*, available at: money.cnn.com/2003/10/07/commentary/game_over/column_gaming/ (accessed November 12, 2008).

ONCIX (2006), *Annual Report to Congress on Foreign Economic Collection and Industrial Espionage – 2005*, U.S. GPO: NCIX 2006-009, Office of the National Counterintelligence Executive, available at: www.ncix.gov/publications/reports/fecie_all/FECIE_2005.pdf (accessed February 29, 2008).

ONCIX (2007), "Counterintelligence in the 21st century: not just a government problem", remarks presented at the AFCEA Counterintelligence Conference. Sunnyvale, CA, December 4, Office of the National Counterintelligence Executive, available at: www.ncix.gov/publications/speeches/AFCEASpeech.pdf (accessed November 12, 2008).

Pagano, U. (2007), "Cultural globalisation, institutional diversity and the unequal accumulation of intellectual capital", *Cambridge Journal of Economics*, Vol. 31 No. 5, p. 649.

Ratan, S. (2003), "Game biz mystified by code theft", *Wired Online*, available at: www.wired.com/gaming/gamingreviews/news/2003/10/60701 (accessed November 12, 2008).

Rubenstein, S. (2008), "Express scripts says clients received threats", *Scripts Says Clients Received Threats*, available at: http://online.wsj.com/article/SB122645284841119467.html (accessed November 12, 2008).

Stewart, T.A. (1997), *Intellectual Capital*, Doubleday, New York, NY.

Wernick, A. (2006), "Data theft and state law", *Journal of AHIMA*, November/December, p. 40.

Wildstrom, S. (2005), "Personal data theft: it's outrageous", *BusinessWeek Online*, available at: www.businessweek.com/technology/content/apr2005/tc20050415_5345_tc120.htm (accessed November 12, 2008).

### About the authors

Herbert Snyder is an Associate Professor of Accounting and Information Systems at North Dakota State University. He received his PhD from Syracuse. He has published in the areas of scholarly communication, accounting for information assets and white-collar crime. During 2003, he was a Fulbright scholar in Ukraine. Prior to entering the academic world, he worked as a Fraud Investigator and an Intelligence Analyst for the US Army. Herbert Snyder is the corresponding author and can be contacted at: herbert.synder@ndsu.edu

Anthony Crescenzi served as an Intelligence Officer in the US Army. Upon his retirement he worked as an Investigator for the US Defense Investigative service. He now runs his own intelligence consulting firm.

# [22]

# Cross-border Crime and the Interface between Legal and Illegal Actors

*Nikos Passas[1]*

*The debate on whether the problem of transnational crime is growing or not rages on. Yet, basic research and reliable data on which to inform this debate are lacking. As a consequence, anecdotal and incomplete information leads to analyses that focus on individual problems and neglect serious structural problems underlying the demand for illegal goods and services. Both theoretical endeavors and policy construction would thus benefit from some corrective analysis. This paper paves the ground for such analysis by focusing on the interface of legal and illegal actors. It first seeks to clarify the meaning of the terms 'international crime' and 'cross-border crime', often referred to as 'transnational crime'. Secondly, it separates for analytical purposes 'enterprise crime' from 'political crime', while recognizing that the two are often combined in practice. Thirdly, it attempts to construct a typology of legal–illegal links and associations, in order to better organize the existing knowledge and data on this subject. Fourthly, it addresses the question of whether the problem is growing, and if so, why. Finally, it outlines research and policy implications.*

**Key words: Transnational crime; cross-border crime; terrorism; organized crime; white-collar crime; corporate crime; state crime; theory; policy**

### Introduction

Processes of globalization have multiplied cross-border links and intensified interconnectedness in the economic, political and cultural spheres. Inevitably, criminal enterprises have also become global. At the same time, they have shown that they can exploit the weaknesses of the existing regulatory patchwork. Nationalisms, concerns about sovereignty, and the lack of clear international rules and effective enforcement mechanisms have led to a situation in which cosmopolitan offenders easily escape the nets of 'parochial' controllers. Many governments have publicly voiced anxiety over the risks posed by global 'organized crime', which many in the USA and the European Union consider as a serious threat to national and international security.[2]

There are calls from different quarters to do something about this problem. Declaring a 'war' on transnational crime conveys the idea of the militarization of law enforcement. In addition, even before the attacks on 11th September 2001, calls were made for an active role for intelligence services in anti-crime and control efforts. These are drastic steps in a direction that may bring about risks of their own for democratic states (both established and, most importantly, those in transition). As these and other measures are being contemplated or implemented, one would have thought that the policy-making process is informed by solid data and an adequate understanding of the problem.

Unfortunately, even a cursory review of media and other reports, as well as of public statements by officials, indicates that the nature and causes of the problem have not been studied fully. There are many inaccuracies, simplifications, exaggerations and mis-conceptualizations, suggesting

**20    Security Journal**                                           *Nikos Passas*

that either we do not have adequate information or we have not properly analyzed the available evidence (or both). The debate regarding the potential risks and the need for draconian or exceptional measures is ongoing in the academic community.[3] In the context of the fight against terrorism, this debate takes on added significance and urgency.

Official discourses focus on the ethnic and foreign elements of crime. However, portrayals of the phenomenon as a 'global conspiracy' or a 'Pax Mafiosa'[4] have been challenged as unfounded and misleading.[5] There is evidence to suggest that cross-border crime is not always as well organized as commonly assumed and that alliances among criminal groups are opportunistic and ad hoc rather than long-lasting.[6] Most importantly, there are complex and diverse relationships between criminals and respected actors.[7]

The roots of the problem often escape our attention, as many observers effectively individualize the problem and neglect systemic and structural causes of the demand for goods and services which are outlawed, in short supply or embarrassing. Underestimating the significance of such factors leads to false impressions of the risks posed by such crimes, to scapegoating, to injustice, and to an illusionary comfort that control systems do function satisfactorily. So, before we get down to policy construction, a great deal of 'corrective' analysis needs to be done.

### Distinctions between international and cross-border crime

There are two general types of misconduct that transcend the interests of individual nation states: international crimes and transnational crimes. International crimes are acts prohibited by international criminal law on the basis of the 1994 draft code, multilateral treaties or customary practice.[8] Transnational or cross-border crimes, on the other hand, are sometimes defined as acts which violate the laws of more than one country.[9] It is probably preferable not to rely entirely on legal definitions of crime for social studies. In a global community made up of extremely diverse legal systems, it is particularly limiting to employ the rules of select countries, in order to delimit the scope of scientific research. It is possible to define cross-border crime in a more abstract and principled way while also taking into account legal norms: cross-border crime is conduct which jeopardizes legally protected interests in more than one national jurisdiction and which is criminalized in at least one of the states concerned.

The process of globalization has contributed to the growth of this phenomenon through the use of new technologies, the more frequent and faster movement of people, capital and goods across national borders, and the integration of markets. Not all cross-border crimes are equally serious, sophisticated or 'organized'. The recent concern about global crimes has been fuelled primarily by illegal drug-trafficking, terrorism, trading in illegal arms or technology, the smuggling of aliens, frauds, corruption and money-laundering. The list of serious transnational crime includes tax evasion, capital flight, the theft of art and cultural property, smuggling of legal goods (minerals, agricultural produce, cigarettes, etc) as well as endangered species, environmental crimes, and the use of child labor. Computer crimes are also frequently mentioned as 'the crime of the future', but they constitute for the most part a new modus operandi, rather than a different type of crime: the computer, in other words, is used as an *instrument* to commit an offense.[10]

This paper focuses on cross-border crimes, and considers international ones only when the two overlap. It will also shun the term 'organized crime', and follow the concept of 'enterprise crime'.[11] It will also use the term 'political crime' in order to underline that, while financial gain is the main goal in most cases, we also need to consider political, ideological, and religious motives for a more complete understanding of the phenomenon.

## Interface analysis I: goals of transnational offenders

It took years of hard work to effectively challenge false conventional wisdom about illegal enterprises within the US. Positivist and stereotypical conceptions drew clear lines dividing the law-abiding and conventional society from 'the underworld'. Misconceptions about la Cosa Nostra as 'the' organized crime problem, alien conspiracies leading to nation-wide hierarchical organizations, monopoly control over illegal markets, and the clear separation between organized criminals and legitimate organizations have been dispelled.[11] It appears that similar research and analytical efforts are now necessary with respect to transnational crime.

At a Hearing on International Crime before the Senate Appropriations Committee Subcommittee on Foreign Operations, the FBI's Director referred to organized crime as 'a continuing criminal conspiracy having a firm organizational structure, a conspiracy fed by fear and corruption' (12th March 1996). Such descriptions, frequently with a high degree of tautology, cloud the nature and causes of serious crime and do not advance the careful study of facts relative to the social organization of the best organized and most sophisticated misconduct that crosses national boundaries.

As corporate and other actors become transnational or engage increasingly in cross-border transactions, so do illegal enterprises, if only because of price differences. As illegal enterprises commit offenses, so do legitimate actors. The line between the legal and the criminal is often fuzzy, especially when actors from opposite ends of the continuum come into contact and transact with each other. This empirical claim is much less controversial now than it was a few years ago, thanks to recent revelations with respect to the Iran-Contra affair,[12] BCCI,[13] BNL and the arming of Iraq,[14] systemic corruption in Italy[15] and throughout Europe,[16] and links between the Yakuza and Japanese politicians.[17] After all, it is plain that the goods and services offered by illegal actors are in demand by not only other criminals but legal actors too. Moreover, many 'legal' actors act as crime entrepreneurs by systematically offering legitimate goods and services made cheap because of fraud.[18]

So, how do the underworld and conventional society interact? Which parts of the latter have dealings or links with what sort of criminal actors? What are the main characteristics of the legal–illegal interface? As one explores this interface, there are different ways of going about it, depending on the criteria and variables one prioritizes. For instance, one may wish to concentrate on the relative power and autonomy of legal and illegal actors, in order to assess possibilities of intervention and the chance of criminal justice policies succeeding. Alternatively, one could focus on temporal issues by asking whether legal and illegal actors work together or whether their interactions take place primarily before and after crimes are committed. It would assist studies asking whether illegal actors work *with* legal actors or *for* them. The legal–illegal links are not always known, suspected or direct (there may be degrees of directness). Analyses in that direction could be useful in determining the benefits, risks or crime-facilitative role of legal actors. It would be also interesting to consider the strength of legal–illegal links (eg measured by the frequency, duration and intensity of interactions). A typology catering for such concerns might be as follows, with each box highlighting different relationships:

|  | Strong links | Loose links |
|---|---|---|
| Sequential links | 1 | 2 |
| Parallel links | 3 | 4 |

**22   Security Journal**                                    *Nikos Passas*

This typology, however, may not take sufficiently into account the question of reciprocity. Illegal actors can also work *against* legal ones. In addition, one may want to center on the causes of various types of interface, differentiating among both legal and illegal actors. For this paper, it was thought most productive to organize the discussion around two main criteria: motivation, and mutuality of interests. This will hopefully assist in the study of the social organization of cross-border crime, with emphasis on the questions of why, who and how. So, by looking into the primary objective of the actors involved, we can differentiate between 'enterprise crime', 'political crime' and 'hybrid crime'. At a second level of differentiation, we can distinguish between the two broad categories of 'antithetical' or 'symbiotic' relationships.

But first, a key issue as we explore the legal–illegal interface is the ultimate objective of the actors in question. What are the underlying motivations of those prepared to break the law or to take the risk of transacting with law violators? True, most criminal actors are for-profit enterprises or use such enterprises for other goals. However, ideological, religious or political goals may be the driving force behind transnational organized misconduct. The two objectives may also be equally important. In any event, the distinction on the basis of motive is important for both theoretical and policy reasons. First, no complete account of the root causes of such crimes can be offered without an account of motives. Second, different types of policy interventions would be required for long-term and effective solutions. So, we can conceive of three types of misconduct. It can be hypothesized that each of these types fosters different kinds of associations between legal and illegal actors.

*Enterprise crime (or crime for profit)*
Enterprise crime refers to criminal acts carried out within an entrepreneurial structure, motivated primarily by financial gain. This is by far the most common type. The entrepreneurial structure may be outright criminal. Analysts almost automatically assume that what they call 'transnational organized crime' is entirely enterprise crime. A 'transnational criminal organization' has been regarded as 'an organisation with a single purpose or goal, which is the maximisation of profit'.[19] Illegal actors of this type take advantage of the demand for certain goods and services. They can act on their own or collaborate with other criminal enterprises, which is historically the rule in cases of cross-border crime trafficking of prohibited substances. We have seen this in the illegal trade in drugs or arms, for example.[20]

At the other end of the legal–illegal continuum, the criminal activities of legitimate actors may reflect the organizational skills or level of their corporations. Since these actors are legal, their offenses are quite often of a predatory nature. There are plenty of examples, ranging from the looting of savings and loan institutions (eg David Paul's CenTrust was seriously damaged by insider fraud and abuse, with the assistance of foreign individuals and organizations), to insurance and other types of fraud, systematic tax and customs levies evasion,[21] the pharmaceutical and oil industries,[22] defense contractors[23]—and the list goes on.[24]

In this light, there is little surprise when legitimate and illegal entrepreneurs act together. Indeed, this is the type of crime where most links to legitimate businesspeople and corporations can be expected. For instance, we have seen links in the disposal of toxic waste,[25] insurance fraud and arson for profit,[26] and in money laundering.[27] The black market for pesos has brought together drug traffickers, Colombian brokers, and traders who need US dollars in order to buy goods in the United States. The broker sells drug money at a 20 per cent discount to the businessman, who deposits his payment in pesos in the trafficker's account in Colombia.[28]

Official corruption cases provide possibly the best illustrations of this sort of interface, as illegal marketeers seek regulatory or political protection ('blind eyes'), preferential treatment, inside information, and relative certainty in their environment.[29]

*Nikos Passas*                            *Security Journal*    23

## Political crime

There is more to crime causation and weaknesses in control than strictly rational-economic motivation. Many criminal actors pursue chiefly political or religious goals. As clearly illustrated in the attacks in the USA, there is no material gain in suicide-bombing attacks. The main goal ranges from the overthrow of the government to political independence or land rights (eg sabotage of oil company facilities in order to protect indigenous people's rights; political violence in the Middle East). There are sufficient ethnic, regional and religious conflicts around the globe involving transnational crime to make us transcend the assumption that all such crime is rational and based on the pursuit of maximization of profit. Of course, financial considerations are still important. Such crime requires financing, training, ammunition, information, protection, fighters and 'welfare systems' for the families of the perpetrators.[30] However, profit is not the primary consideration here. Money is only the means to another end. Maximization of financial gains may not be a goal at all; rather, ideology, higher loyalties, cultural or political ties, and the desire for revenge or to make a point can be much more important issues.

As political groups resort to violent and criminal methods, they seek allies, supporters, sympathizers and protectors (just like conventional political groups). In addition, foreign policy by most countries is not carried out exactly as it is officially announced. Covert operations (legal or illegal even under domestic laws) often bring government agents into contact with criminal actors, irrespective of their actual crime-trade.[31] When it comes to political transnational crime, therefore, we should expect connections with political and government agents and agencies. Typical examples can be found in cases of states accused of supporting terrorism (eg, at different times, East Germany, Syria, Libya, Iran, Iraq, etc). US agencies have also been involved in such associations (the Contras and the intelligence services, the Afghani rebels before the end of the Cold War, etc).[32] As with enterprise crime, legal actors may be involved in political cross-border crime on their own too (eg when French agents blew up the *Rainbow Warrior*, the Greenpeace ship, in Auckland; or when Israeli agents assassinated political actors outside Israel, including an innocent Norwegian citizen, for which they later apologized; or US-sponsored terror).[33]

Where political crimes are concerned, the causes, networks, associations, as well as conceivable policy and enforcement responses to them, are obviously very different from those of economic crimes.

## Hybrid crime

Hybrid crime amounts to a combination of the above two types. It may be that financial and political motives are of almost equal importance. In such cases, the networks of crime, corruption and other misconduct are likely to include both businesses and political or administrative actors. It has been claimed that the communist government of Bulgaria set up Kintex, a state corporation, in order to sell arms in Europe and the Middle East and to accept drugs as payment. With high-ranking security service officials on its board, Kintex was allegedly also playing a political role by furnishing weapons to Palestinians and Turkish terrorist groups.[34] The evidence supporting this allegation has been seriously challenged; however, taken as a hypothetical scenario, it illustrates the hybrid type of crime.

The alleged communist conspiracy had its counterpart in the US. In the course of the Iran-Contra investigation, the testimony of Richard Secord (a retired General in the US Air Force) was instructive. He was asked before Congress why the US was selling the Contras arms bought from a communist nation, at exorbitant profit rates. His answer was that there were two objectives: helping the Contras and managing a commercial enterprise. 'Cannot I have two purposes? I did.'

The par-excellence illustration of this nexus, however, is provided by the BCCI affair, which revealed extensive networks of 'ordinary criminals', white-collar offenders, and respected professionals and organizations from a number of industries—banking, insurance, commodities trade, telecommunications, etc. Holy and unholy alliances with mixed ideological, geo-political and financial motives operated through this bank.[35]

Under this category we can also consider those crimes committed in the context of anti-American, anti-West and anti-capitalism sentiments. Faulty policies and Western government mistakes affecting mostly Third World countries have generated such sentiments, which may neutralize law-abiding values and principles held by people who feel justified in targeting symbolic victims.

Nigerian people, for example, are worse off now than before the discovery of oil in their soil. Transnational corporations have exploited the environment and resources of the country and taken advantage of its corrupt regime.[36] Nigeria subsequently became fertile ground for the recruitment of members in criminal organizations. 'We stick it to the Americans' is the kind of self-justifying argument that may make ordinary people do extraordinary things. Similarly, many Latin Americans, having suffered through West-supported dictatorships and corporate exploitation, may afford little sympathy for US kids abusing drugs. These become loyal supporters of criminals and their enterprises. By analogy to the point that chemical weapons are poor countries' nuclear arms, cross-border crime feeds off desires for independence, autonomy and self-determination. It must be emphasized that none of this implies that this is the only or most important cause of Nigerian or Latin American crime. The point here is that this is a contributing factor, which we often neglect or overlook.

A different kind of hybrid crime can be seen in the context of international finance and assistance offered by regional banks. Institutions like the IMF and World Bank offer loans and fund projects in developing countries. The terms of the loans frequently involve austerity measures that recipient governments must impose, if these governments wish to either refinance the loans or get new lines of credit. However, this process increases dependence on Western sources and creates discontent conducive to regional or civil conflicts.[37] Projects funded by such institutions have sometimes been of more assistance to Western corporations than to the countries meant to benefit most. Companies have often got contracts to deliver works that were not needed, for which there was no commitment on the part of the recipient country, and which were left incomplete.[38] As Falk has noted,[39] the Permanent Peoples Tribunal in Rome has in the past condemned certain IMF conditions as illegal. In the past, some Third World governments have sought to circumvent IMF conditions, and turned to the BCCI for assistance.[40] Resolving the controversy over the appropriate role and responsibilities of regional banks is beyond the scope of this paper. The point is that not everyone in the recipient countries has a positive opinion of the lending institutions. In this context, it is not hard to imagine self-justifying arguments on the part of some government officials to the effect that 'we are defending the national interest, we are resisting unreasonable measures forced on us, we need to prevent crises of legitimacy and bloodshed in our country'. This may lead to 'extra-legal' circumvention of the conditions imposed.

### Interface analysis II: the nature of the legal–illegal interface

The legal–illegal interface can have either antithetical or symbiotic relationships. We will examine each in turn.

*Antithetical relationships*
*Antagonistic* relationships obtain when there is competition between legal and illegal actors. Actors may be vying for market share independently, as in the case of state-run lotteries, casinos, and illegal gambling operations. Similarly independent is the antagonistic relationship between crooked

*Nikos Passas* **Security Journal** **25**

financial institutions on the Internet or offshore, offering illegal services to clients who would otherwise do business with conventional banks (eg the European Union Bank in the Caribbean).

In the political, ideological or religious spheres, the competition may be for legitimacy. Actors may seek to gain popular support and a following in the same geographic area by legal and criminal means. Illustrations of such antagonisms can be found in political conflicts such as those in Northern Ireland, the Middle East, former Soviet Republics, Angola, Peru, parts of Northern India and Sri Lanka.

*Injurious* relationships occur when actors undermine, attack or harm each other. This is typified by groups which may sabotage a foreign corporation they consider exploitative or corrupt. Another example is when offenders commit robbery in order to finance guerilla operations.

The above two analytically separate categories may overlap in practice: a combination of antagonistic and injurious relationship is when activists employ violent means against a state, its symbols or its citizens.

The relationship is *predatory* when the aim or effect is to destroy or bleed to death an organization— eg to control and then fraudulently bankrupt a business.

The relationship is *parasitical* when the aim is to preserve the viability of the target, eg illegal benefits can be extorted on a more or less regular basis. For example, triad members selling protection to Asian business owners; or surplus line insurance companies selling a mixture of sound and bogus policies to foreign institutions keen to enter the US market.[41]

Counterfeiting goods may be a mixed antithetical/symbiotic (systemic) relationship: criminal entrepreneurs take advantage of and profit from a brand name, which becomes better known and popular. So, the owner of the brand may not make all the possible sales, but expands and gains market share in additional regions.

*Symbiotic relationships*
A widespread belief is that when legal and illegal actors come into contact, it is because criminals seek to infiltrate, extort, or bankrupt legal enterprises. Nevertheless, there is accumulating evidence of symbiotic relations between them. Again, illegal markets operate because there is a demand for what they offer. Very often their clients are conventional and respected actors (users of illegal narcotics, prostitution, gambling, etc). Such relationships can be of various types, depending on several factors, such as the mutuality or one-sidedness of benefits, awareness of the links, the intent of participants and their degree of collaboration.

*Outsourcing* refers to a division of labor between legal and illegal actors, where one party offers specialized services to the other. This mainly covers cases where the 'dirty work' is done by 'criminals', while the main benefit is reaped by a legal actor. It can be a one-off or a continuous relationship between a client and a provider. The dirty work may be delegated to actors outside an organization or agency for reasons of convenience, efficiency or plausible deniability. The blame is thus externalized, if the misdeed or the offenders are ever discovered (eg Iran-Contra and other intelligence-related activities, such as the use of death squads by Turkish governments against Kurd nationalists;[42] or the use of agents or subsidiaries to bribe foreign officials in order to avoid scrutiny and sanctions under the law.)

In the above cases, legal actors are the clients. The reverse, however, is also possible. Legal actors may provide financial or other support to criminal groups. It is possible that only one of the parties is aware of the quasi-contractual relationship. The Abu Nidal organization, for example, has used a network of legitimate companies whose proceeds financed terrorist activities without the knowledge of the managers and workers in these companies.

*Collaboration.* In this case, the links become stronger and more direct as legal and illegal enterprises or actors work together for the commission of the same offense. For instance, police officers may work with drug traffickers or an art gallery owner may fence stolen cultural property. Under this category, we can also include various types of professionals—such as lawyers, politicians, accountants, bankers or casino managers—who knowingly offer their services to criminal operators.

*Cooption.* In this category, there may be some arm-twisting or voluntary interaction. So, while it involves mutual benefits, there are uneven power relations between the parties. For example, a deal may be struck for a company to operate, or to operate unimpeded, in a country, if a government agency is allowed to monitor its computers and collect information on its clients. For example, BCCI has been accused of being a bedfellow of intelligence services in several countries. Some BCCI managers have argued that this was the only way BCCI could hope to survive and do business internationally. They added (in personal interviews) that this sort of relationship is common in the banking sector. Interviews the present author has conducted with retired cosmopolitan businessmen and reporters indicate that many business deals in 'high-risk' countries or regions receive an OK from certain government officials or agencies (eg to build an oil pipeline through areas of conflict). Some of the business transactions may violate domestic or international laws. In return, businesspeople may have to share their knowledge about particular projects or simply allow themselves and their companies to become the eyes and ears of government agencies. The top executive of Matrix Churchill, the company charged in England with illegal exports to Iraq prior to the Gulf war, was an informant for British intelligence services.[43]

*Reciprocity* (or 'even exchanges'). This is the case when there are consciously mutual benefits between the legal and illegal actors (eg legal brothel manager working with smugglers of aliens). This type includes possibly the most common interface, whereby legitimate or conventional actors are the clients for goods and services offered by criminals (eg drugs, gambling, weapons, prostitutes, etc). Other examples of reciprocity include dictators or government officials who receive rich commissions and kickbacks in exchange for favors to transnational corporations. The latter are then allowed to exploit the land, people or entire country for financial benefits (eg Somoza in Nicaragua or Marcos in the Philippines;[44] logging companies and the political elite in Papua New Guinea[45]). Similar offers of safe haven and protection are made to illegal entrepreneurs, and to criminal organizations too (examples may be found in Bolivia, Aruba, Italy, or Russia).

We can speak of *systemic synergy* when legal and illegal actors benefit each other while they go about their business independently promoting their interests and objectives. The practical effects of synergy are similar to those of outsourcing. In this case, however, there is no conspiracy or client-provider relationship. The synergy is a consequence of structural factors. There may be no knowledge, intent or reasonable suspicion of such a link (in some cases, suspicions may be 'cured' by efforts to avoid any knowledge). Legitimate actors merely reap the benefits of others' criminal activities. For example, financial institutions in the West may receive from overseas substantial funds that are proceeds of crime. In such cases, the laundering has taken place elsewhere, and intermediary transactions have hidden the traces of illegality. In the chemical industry, companies benefit from the operations of networks illegally disposing of toxic waste—if there is conspiracy to do so, we have a case of 'outsourcing'; if not,[46] we have synergy. Combinations are more likely than not, as in the toxic waste dumping scandal in South Holland, and dumping toxic waste in Belgium.[47] Financial institutions are the main beneficiaries of certain arson-for-profit schemes without their being aware or liable.[48] The smuggling of cigarettes across borders in order to avoid taxes and customs dues ultimately helps tobacco companies sell cheaper products

*Nikos Passas* *Security Journal* 27

to their clients and thereby increase their market share, which in the end creates an elaborate underground economy. Japanese banks have in the past avoided consumer loan restrictions by lending to *sarakin* (akin to our loanshark), who in turn was lending to the wider public.[49]

The reverse is also possible: that is, criminal actors can benefit from the activities and practices of legal actors. For instance, secrecy jurisdictions and tax havens do not serve only the criminals. If that were the case, there would be little resistance to calls for action against such jurisdictions (or indeed, their very existence). The market for secrecy caters to a wide range of customers, including corporations, government agencies, and law-abiding individuals.[50] Attempts to reform the system or to sanction anyone operating or doing business in these jurisdictions can expect strong lobbying and pressure from the conventional society to let things be.

*Funding* relationships are also possible, with legitimate organizations providing, knowingly or not, essential financial support for the operation of criminal groups. A recent example is provided, after the 11th September 2001 attacks on the USA, by agencies around the world which are looking for charities and other legal entities (eg farming businesses) that may have fuelled the Al-Qaeda network.

*Legal interactions*. No criminal actor commits only and always crime. Diversification is required not only for money-laundering purposes but also for the reduction of risk and the maximization of benefits. Some may do this in order to leave the life of crime eventually, others seek protective shields, while still others strive for respectability. So, they all have legal aspects or faces (eg Cali drug traffickers). Inevitably, then, they interact with conventional actors. The latter's knowledge of their counterparts' 'diverse background' ranges from complete ignorance to benign neglect, perhaps anesthetizing their conscience by rationalizing that their transactions are only above board and legitimate (eg the acceptance of campaign contributions from criminals); BCCI offered many examples of lawful interaction with elites all over the world.

*Legal actors committing organized crimes*. In this instance, there is no interface between legal and illegal actors. Rather, legal actors engage in well-organized and sophisticated crimes on their own; legal actors behave in a typical illegal-actor fashion. An illustration of this type is provided by the East German state authorities, which used to run a well-organized illegal trade in stolen art;[51] in another case, Citicorp systematically evaded taxes by booking European transactions in a tax haven;[52] and yet another example is offered by the BCCI affair, which has been branded a criminal enterprise by New York City prosecutors. In such cases one can differentiate between legal actors who commit criminal acts and legal actors who are only 'legal' because of the formal corporate structures they abuse.

## Growth of cross-border crime?

If cross-border crime is growing, how can we tell? What parameters need to be examined to reach a reasonable conclusion? Do we have sufficient and solid evidence on which to build policies?

The present author has argued elsewhere that the causes of transnational crime can be traced to 'criminogenic asymmetries'.[53] These are defined as structural disjunctions, mismatches and inequalities in the spheres of politics, culture, the economy and the law. Asymmetries are criminogenic in that:

• they generate or strengthen the demand for illegal goods and services;

• they generate incentives for particular actors to participate in illegal transactions; and

• they reduce the ability of authorities to control illegal activities.

**28    *Security Journal***                                         *Nikos Passas*

For example, political and economic asymmetries between China and Western countries have fuelled the smuggling of both commodities and humans. Asymmetries in environmental regulation facilitate the illegal trade in toxic and other hazardous waste. Asymmetries between art-rich and art-collecting countries underlie the trade in stolen art and national cultural property. In the global age, such asymmetries are multiplied and their criminogenic potential is more easily activated. At the same time, certain control capacities are undermined. As the world 'shrinks' and becomes a 'global village', controllers remain constrained by their divergent domestic rules and limited by their own jurisdiction.

Just as globalization serves well the needs of legal capital, so it facilitates criminal enterprises. Both ordinary and illegal international business transactions can be concluded at the speed of light (though safety still requires much crime-business to be handled in a face-to-face fashion). Just as local destinies often cannot be explained without taking into account global factors, local crime victimization may not be fully understood without reference to global forces. As the autonomy of nation states is reduced, even domestic crimes can be neither prevented nor sanctioned without cross-national collaboration.

In the past we have seen how organizations became a weapon for crime,[54] and distanced the criminal hand from the criminal mind.[55] In the global age, this distance is stretched further as organizations are more compartmentalized and spread throughout the world. In addition, both criminal hands and criminal minds may be absent, far away from the locus of the crime. In many instances, crimes are so well camouflaged that only experts and specialists can detect them and realize the risks involved.

Globalization processes relate to all three types of criminogenic conditions. Illicit opportunities are produced by the fragmentation of enterprises and transactions over more than one country. For instance, lawyers who form and represent a shell corporation in a secrecy jurisdiction on behalf of someone overseas may not even know (nor prefer to know) who is the owner of the company for which they are working. Such corporations offer tax advantages and shelter against regulation and the detection of misconduct. They also help to hide criminals' assets that victims and prosecutors are looking for. Lawyers may see no problem with participating in such affairs. Not knowing the identity of their client, they do not have to know whether he is a drug trafficker, a corrupt dictator or a devious executive. Even if required to testify, lawyers cannot offer any significant assistance to investigating authorities. So, controls get weaker.

Secrecy and anonymity hinder investigators by covering the tracks of the global offender. Illegal financial transactions and losses that must be reported can be conducted and hidden through offshore entities of global enterprises. Secrecy jurisdictions serve as a 'black box' through which all manner of illegal activities can be shielded against prosecution and punishment.[56]

Globalization also facilitates 'jurisdiction shopping': finding jurisdictions which allow conduct outlawed in one's own state. Thus, it contributes to 'crimes without law violation'.[57] Toxic waste may be dumped in countries with lax or no regulation of such waste. The bribing of foreign government officials (in order to ensure a contract is gained or renewed) has been treated by some countries as a tax-deductible business expense. Lawyers, accountants, and former government or military officials often act as consultants or private businessmen after they leave public office, offering advice on how to engage in risky and harmful practices without breaking the laws of the countries where different operations take place. Transactions criminalized in many parts of the world may be concluded in countries that allow them. Particularly, corporate entities are expert in this kind of criminal evasion (on the pharmaceutical industry, for instance, see Braithwaite[58]).

Other examples of cross-border crimes without law violations include the use of child labor in poor countries that condone it, by companies that then export the manufactured goods to countries that criminalize the practice. Taxes may be evaded legally through the practice of transfer pricing, which allows the profits to be booked in countries with no income tax;[59] (see also illegal cases of transfer pricing by Asian logging companies in Papua New Guinea.[60]) Dirty money can be laundered in countries requiring no reporting of even substantial amounts of cash deposits, and then transferred to Western banks that may not know its criminal origin (or care to find out[61]).

At first sight, this analysis suggests that cross-border crime may be on the increase. However, the process of globalization also offers new opportunities for better controls. Thanks to new technologies in communications, more people can participate and make a difference in the fight against transnational and domestic crime. For example, a process of 'globalization from below'[62] enables relatively weak actors to influence decisions at home and overseas (eg in the case of indigenous people and Occidental Petroleum in Colombia[63]).

To the extent that criminal entrepreneurs rationally seek profit (whether as a goal or as a means to other ends important to them), the fear that they will destabilize nation states may be out of proportion. There is always such a risk, of course, especially for those countries which are the target of politically motivated groups or organizations. However, the extensive legal–criminal interface, and especially the symbiotic aspects of it, suggest that the nullification or destabilization of governments is against the interest of criminal organizations. Given that these organizations in many ways operate according to market principles, they generally also need a comparatively stable and predictable environment. The government provides that for free. Even though many criminal enterprises thrive in the midst of bad governance, some of the best/costliest organized crimes take place in strong states.

The number of reports and debates on this phenomenon also suggest that the threat might be growing. However, it must be emphasized that not all information is accurate. Careful investigations and analyses have repeatedly shown reports and statements to be alarmist and exaggerated. Congressional hearings examined the risk posed by counterfeit dollars, for instance, and subsequent GAO reports and testimony from the Secret Service suggested that the danger was much lower than previously feared. The volume of drug proceeds in the US has also been exaggerated,[64] while in general the volume of the proceeds of crime has been inflated for political purposes. The extent of credit card fraud and computer-assisted crimes is unknown, because of victims' unwillingness to report and thereby reveal vulnerabilities. Embarrassment prevents many victims of advance-fee frauds from coming foreword, collaborating with investigators or even admitting that they have been fooled. The brutality of criminals and problems of Chinese illegal aliens in the US have also been exaggerated.[65] Finally, there has been more speculation than solid evidence on nuclear material smuggling,[66] and reports on 'underground banking' were full of 'facts by repetition'.[67]

As with many other crime problems, media and official reports raise a broad awareness rather than provide valid indications of the extent of the reported phenomenon; more reports and debate about it do not demonstrate an increase of the problem.

## Research implications

There are two main research implications of the foregoing discussion. First, we need to develop *solid empirical data*. Second, we need to engage in more *analytical work* towards a better understanding of the causes of the problem at hand. These two steps should provide the basis on which to build better theories and sound policies.

**30**   *Security Journal*                                    *Nikos Passas*

## Developing a solid empirical ground

Despite all the attention the problem of cross-border crimes has attracted, the information base remains remarkably weak. Many analyses are based on theoretical expectations, anecdotal evidence, unreliable data, and sheer speculation, as well as ideological commitments and vested interests.

This lack of reliable data reflects years of neglect by the research and policy community. This is partly due to methodological hurdles one has to overcome and partly due to the lack of adequate funding for researching cross-border crime. This leaves the field open for journalistic, politically motivated or simply not very sophisticated accounts to shape conventional wisdom. This wisdom often equates cross-border crime with the stereotyped 'organized crime', when the latter becomes international. This, however, erroneously limits the scope of the field. A number of concrete steps may be taken to remedy this situation.

First of all, we need to reach as wide an agreement as possible on what constitutes cross-border crime. The definition offered in this paper is unambiguous as well as succinct, while it encompasses criminal phenomena which go *beyond* single national jurisdictions. It is not legalistic, while still law-oriented. A related problem is that the concept of cross-border crime tends to become associated with or even classified under the categories of 'organized crime', 'white-collar crime' or 'state crime'. This does not help very much, as these concepts are ambiguous, due to the preponderance of political or emotional attempts to define them over clear analytical delineation. Frequently there is a confusion between actors and acts. Though this contribution has stressed the importance of the wide range of symbiotic relationships between legal and illegal actors, empirically and conceptually the general area of cross-border crime ought to be based on acts.

The second task is to establish what we know, what we think we know and what we need to know about these acts. Despite our common admission that we do not have adequate information on the nature of the problem, there is a plethora of articles, books, official reports, media accounts, databases and web sites with material relevant to our subject matter. It is quite possible that valuable and solid evidence can be found in this labyrinth of information. However, we currently have no way of assessing the validity and reliability of existing data. How can we evaluate the strength of the evidence used by other researchers and separate it from commercial and journalistic works or unsubstantiated 'conspiracy theories'? Because it is sometimes easy to identify inaccuracies, gross mistakes, contradictions, half-truths and exaggerations in these publications, the whole notion of interconnection and interdependence among various criminal and legitimate actors gets discarded or overlooked. We need, therefore, an instrument (eg a reliability scale) to evaluate the various sources and types of secondary data.

The third task is the collection of original reliable data. The methodological hurdles we face are legion. From domestic experience, we are familiar with the unreliability of official and government records, with the distortion of information coming from journalistic sources, with the risks to researchers of serious crime, and with the high financial cost when data collection must be undertaken in several jurisdictions. The scarcity of prosecutions related to corporate and state crimes, lack of access to informants and privileged information, confidentiality of various types of records, classification of reports and other data—all this compounds the problem. Even if we wished to consider official statistics seriously, there are no such statistics kept on crimes which cross national borders, or the available statistics are non-comparable. Given the misgivings even about legal trade figures (cf Enron), quantitative studies on illegal transnational enterprises do not look particularly promising. Such studies may yield some gross estimates on the volume of certain transactions, but they will have to be read with more than a grain of salt.

*Nikos Passas*                              *Security Journal*    **31**

Qualitative studies are not without problems, but they appear more appropriate for this field. Case studies, for example, always run the risk of furnishing non-generalizable results. In such cases, however, we can gain invaluable insights for theoretical elaborations. Moreover, policy-making can benefit even from unique or atypical incidents, which occasionally reveal systemic problems and sound alarm bells before such cases become more common. Qualitative methods are also more adequate for the study of networks and of the interface between legal and illegal actors, the points at which criminals and conventional society meet. Methodological hurdles have turned the study of criminal enterprises into a business of accumulating (not always valid) information about either specific groups of people (eg la Cosa Nostra, the *yakuza*, or the Russian *mafiya*) or particular offenses (drug-trafficking, arms-trafficking, smuggling of aliens, etc). Even the best works on 'organized crime' are group-, offense-, or institution-specific.

Although valuable insights are offered by such studies, there is a huge gap in the literature relative to the *social organization* of crime. We know very little about the modi operandi and methods used, the ultimate beneficiaries and victims of these crimes, the degree of specialization, short or long-term alliances, or division of labor. We have incomplete knowledge of the role of professionals and of the relationship between illegal markets, on the one hand, and that of legitimate corporations and government agencies, on the other. The links among criminal organizations are also under-studied. In short, we need more research into the multiple and complex links and associations among both legitimate and illegitimate actors. Findings of researchers, though usually rather fragmented, do indicate the plausibility of the hypothesis of the existence of crime networks, but there is no systematic study of such interconnections. No one has attempted to put the various pieces of the global crime puzzle together. Again, a major difficulty is methodological. Advancements in technology allow us to experiment with new software programs for a better organization and more systematic analysis of both primary and secondary data, especially in the area of networks and complex transactions.

Finally, as we collect and analyze our data, it important to remember that the problem of cross-border crime is not uni-dimensional or monolithic. By its very nature it can only be studied from a *comparative* perspective.

## Understanding the causes of transnational crime

Analytical studies are also in short supply on the nature, causes, risks and growth of the problem. We need to focus more on the fundamental causes of the problem and spend more energy on the demand side rather than solely on the supply side. For instance, the above typology of the interface between legal and illegal actors can assist in understanding various sources of demand for prohibited goods and services, but requires some fine-tuning. It needs to be tested and elaborated on the basis of empirical data.

Any attempt to explain crime requires an examination of opportunities to commit the crime in question, of motives leading actors to take advantage of such opportunities, and of control options and weaknesses. While much of the literature on cross-border crime deals with the issue of opportunity, most observers neglect the question of motives. The profit motive is widely assumed to be the main or only reason behind transnational crime. Yet, political, religious or ideological motivations can be an important causative element (as 11th September showed). Also, cultural differences are often overlooked. For example, the question of software piracy is approached differently in Asia, where the sharing of social knowledge is considered more important than proprietary rights.[68]

Most analyses concentrate on the mounting problems in controlling certain types of cross-border misconduct (eg the drugs trade, political violence or corrupt practices) rather than seeking to better understand the nature of the more general problem. Explanations of even spectacular disasters, such as the BCCI scandal or the Barings collapse, focus on corrupt, inept or greedy individuals out of control. Such explanations conceal the systemic causes of problems.

The above analysis suggests that structural problems—criminogenic asymmetries—may be a key to understanding, preventing and fighting serious crime. However, not all asymmetries produce the same crime problems. A number of issues remain unclear and need further elaboration. For example, when do asymmetries become criminogenic? Is it possible that all asymmetries are potentially crime-inducing, but only some of them get 'activated'? If so, when is the criminogenic potential activated? Alternatively, one could ask whether there are asymmetries with no such potential. Are there any asymmetries with positive effects? In that case, how could one maximize such effects?

## Policy implications

The foregoing discussion points to the need for restraint before adopting drastic measures against the perceived threat of transnational crime. Given that there are still too many open questions, careful and thoughtful cost-benefit analyses are of critical importance. Some of the policies currently debated or partially implemented are themselves risky (eg militarization of law enforcement, merging law enforcement with intelligence operations, international undercover investigations, extraterritorial application of domestic laws, etc). Some measures may be costlier than the problem they are designed to remedy. A cost of the militarization of law enforcement, for example, is that the discourse of a 'war on crime' paves the ground for the acceptance of 'collateral damage'. This sort of collateral damage can take several forms, most importantly the harm to democratic processes and accountability. Excesses, abuses of power, limitations of freedom and of collective or individual rights are a corollary of the war metaphor, even in domestic cases.[69] In short: the maintenance of law is not a war, but a civil task for a civil society.

It is important to differentiate according to the nature of the criminal activity, because the distinction between political and economic crimes has practical implications beyond the theoretical significance of motive. It draws attention to different root problems, which require different strategies and tactics, especially with respect to prevention. A demand-side approach to politically motivated crimes may be to seek peaceful resolution of a conflict, democratization, decolonalization, the granting of independence or autonomy, etc. The intensity of beliefs held by political offenders will also require different assessment of risks (eg suicide and more audacious attacks). In addition, the associations or alliances political criminals will form are likely to be different from those of profit-seekers.

This brings us to the policy implications of the legal–illegal interface. Overwhelmingly, the debate and policy-making energy centers on activities that resemble the stereotypical conception of 'organized crime'. As a result, better organized crimes, more harmful malpractices, and more dangerous networks of crime and corruption do not receive the attention that is due. We need to find out more about the relative frequency, cost and significance of various types of interface, as we seek to assess risks, estimate costs, sort out priorities, allocate scarce resources, and maximize the effect of our anti-crime efforts. It is commonplace to call for more cooperation and collaboration among various control and other agencies at all levels. Yet certain crimes or associations may produce locally positive consequences. They may help with the balance of payments, by increasing wealth, by lowering unemployment rates, etc. Other crimes may have little or no effect on regional economies or other interests (on the European Union context, see Passas[70]). A blind eye, indifference or cooption will inevitably affect the degree of cooperation with outsiders. In this light, there is a need to generate incentives for local action and mutual assistance.

The foregoing analysis of criminogenic asymmetries also suggests that many systemic sources fuelling the demand for illicit goods and services can be traced back to nation states. In some cases they are complicit; in other cases they are unable or unwilling to take remedial action. It is national policies and agencies, the exercise of asymmetric state powers, an obsession with sovereignty and nationalist resistance against international regulation that account for criminogenic asymmetries. It is their economic policies which bear responsibility for relative and objective deprivation. It is their protectionism and subsidization of domestic industries that impair the efforts of less-developed countries to narrow the gaps. It is their monetary policies and control of international organizations that preserve asymmetric development and growth. It is authoritarian regimes that cause ethnic and political violence. It is their hegemonic policies and support for dictatorial regimes overseas that provoke international terrorism and fundamentalism. It is their selective control and promotion of domestic military industries that fuel armed conflicts (note that industries from the permanent members of the UN Security Council produce the overwhelming majority of weapons). It is their unwillingness to share knowledge, information and technology that breeds unease and inequalities. It is their prohibitions of commodities and services in demand that create illegal opportunities. It is their inability or unwillingness to reduce the demand for prohibited goods and services that perpetuates the illegal markets. It is their imposition of quotas for new immigrants that gives rise to the inhumane smuggling of illegal aliens. It is their resort to criminal justice methods to deal with the consequences of their policies that provides incentives for more sophisticated organization of crime and raises the price of corruption. Even if these policies are understandable from a national perspective, their hidden costs may be cross-border crime.

There is little doubt that the process of globalization has fostered more and new types of transnational crime. However, globalization also furnishes new opportunities for more effective controls, some of them rather informal in nature (eg the use of the Internet to shame powerful actors into socially responsible policies). A detailed discussion of these control opportunities is beyond the scope of this paper. Yet it is plain that we need to detect, create and maximize the use and effectiveness of such opportunities. We can make the public as well as controllers aware of them and fortify the process of 'globalization from below' and the 'democratization of control'.

Finally, we urgently need an evaluation instrument, so that we know in advance what will constitute a success and what will be a failure of contemplated and existing policies. This is important both for line agents, who should know whether they are doing a good and efficient job, and for policy makers, who must have the ability to measure the progress, success or failure of particular strategies and methods.

In conclusion, serious as the threat of transnational crime is, it is perhaps too early to panic about it. We are not helpless and powerless against it. Clearly, more systematic (and well-funded) studies are necessary to ensure that our analyses and policies are based on sound evidence rather than conjuncture and speculation. There are plenty of things, however, that we can undertake in the meantime.

## Notes

1    Nikos Passas is Professor of Criminal Justice at Temple University, Philadelphia; email: passas@temple.edu.

2    See for instance Godson, R. and Olson, W.J. (1993) *International Organized Crime: Emerging Threat to US Security.* Washington, DC: National Strategy Information Center; Paine, L.P. and Cilluffo, F.J. (eds) (1994) *Global Organized Crime: The New Empire of Evil.* Washington, DC: Center for Strategic and International Studies.

3	See for instance Andreas, P. (1997) The Rise of the American Crimefare State. *World Policy Journal.* Vol. 14, No. 3, pp 37–45; Lupsha, P.A. (1996) Transnational Organized Crime Versus the Nation-State. *Transnational Organized Crime.* Vol. 2, No. 1, pp 21–48; Naylor, R.T. (1995) From Cold War to Crime War: The Search for a New 'National Security' Threat. *Transnational Organized Crime.* Vol.1, No. 4, pp 37–56. Reprinted in Passas, N. (ed.) (1998) *Transnational Crime.* Aldershot: Dartmouth; Shelley, L. (1995) Transnational Crime: An Imminent Threat to the Nation-State? *Journal of International Affairs.* Vol. 48, No. 2, pp 463–89; van Dyune, P.C. (1996) The Phantom and Threat of Organized Crime. *Crime, Law and Social Change.* Vol. 29, No. 4, pp 341–77; Williams, P. (1994) Transnational Criminal Organisations and International Security. *Survival.* Vol. 36, No. 1, pp 96–113. Reprinted in Passas, op cit.

4	Sterling, C. (1994) *Thieves' World.* New York: Simon and Schuster.

5	Naylor, op cit.

6	See for instance Observatoire Géopolitique des Drogues (1996) *The Geopolitics of Drugs: 1996 Edition.* Boston, MA: Northeastern University Press; Williams, P. (1995) Transnational Criminal Organizations: Strategic Alliances. *Washington Quarterly.* Vol. 18, No. 1, p 57; Williams, P. and Woessner, P.N. (1996) The Real Threat of Nuclear Smuggling. *Scientific American.* Vol. 274, January, pp 40–4. Reprinted in Passas, op cit.

7	See for instance Arlacchi, P. (1992) Large Scale Crime and World Illegal Markets. In United Nations and the University of New Mexico (eds) *Organized Crime: International Strategies.* Albuquerque, NM: Latin American Institute, University of New Mexico; Block, A.A. (1991) *Masters of Paradise: Organized Crime and the Internal Revenue Service in the Bahamas.* New Brunswick, NJ: Transaction; Chambliss, W.J. (1989) State-Organized Crime. *Criminology.* Vol. 27, No. 2, pp 183–208; Naylor, R.T. (1995/96) From Underworld to Underground. *Crime, Law and Social Change.* Vol. 24, No. 2, pp 79–150; Passas, N. (1995a) The Mirror of Global Evils: A Review Essay on the BCCI Affair. *Justice Quarterly.* Vol. 12, No. 2, pp 801–29; Passas, N. and Nelken, D. (1993) The Thin Line Between Legitimate and Criminal Enterprises: Subsidy Frauds in the European Community. *Crime, Law and Social Change.* Vol. 19, No. 3, pp 223–43; Ruggiero, V. (1996) *Organized and Corporate Crime in Europe.* Aldershot: Dartmouth.

8	See for instance Bassiouni, C. (1983) The Penal Characteristics of Conventional International Criminal Law. *Case Western Reserve Journal of International Law.* Vol. 15, pp 27–37; Malekian, F. (1991) *International Criminal Law.* Uppsala.

9	Bossard, A. (1990) *Transnational Crime and Criminal Law.* Chicago, IL: Office of International Criminal Justice.

10	Grabosky, P.N. and Smith, R.G. (1998) *Crime in the Digital Age: Controlling Telecommunications and Cyberspace Illegalities.* New Brunswick, NJ: Transaction.

11	See for instance Anderson, A. (1979) *The Business of Organized Crime.* Stanford, CA: Hoover Institution Press; Block, A.A. (1983) *East Side-West Side: Organizing Crime in New York, 1930–1950.* New Brunswick, NJ: Transaction; Brady, J. (1983) Arson, Urban Economy and Organized Crime. *Social Problems.* Vol. 31, pp 1–27; Chambliss, W.J. (1988) *On the Take: From Petty Crooks to Presidents.* Bloomington, IN: Indiana University Press; Reuter, P. (1983) *Disorganized Crime: Illegal Markets and the Mafia.* Cambridge, MA: MIT Press; Reuter, P. and Rubinstein, J. (1978) Fact, Fancy and Organized Crime. *The Public Interest.* Vol. 53, Fall, pp 45–68; Scott, P.D. (1996) *Deep Politics and the Death of JFK.* Berkeley and Los Angeles, CA: University of California Press; Smith, D.C. (1990) *The Mafia Mystique.* Lanham, NY: University Press of America.

12	Walsh, L.E. (1993) *Final Report of the Independent Counsel for Iran/Contra Matters.* Washington, DC: US Court of Appeals for the District of Columbia Circuit.

13	See for instance Kerry Report (1992) *The BCCI Affair.* Washington, DC: Government Printing Office; Passas (1995a) op cit.

14	See for instance Mantius, P. (1995) *Shell Game.* New York: St. Martin's Press; Phythian, M. (1996) *Arming Iraq: How the U.S. and Britain Secretly Built Saddam's War Machine.* Boston, MA: Northeastern University.

15    See for instance Colombo, G. (1996) *Il Vizio della Memoria*. Milan: Feltrinelli; Tribunale di Milano, V Sezione Penale (1997) *La Maxitangente Enimont*. Milan: Kaos.

16    Della Porta, D. and Mény, Y. (eds) (1995) *Démocratie et Corruption en Europe*. Paris: La Découverte.

17    See for instance *The Economist* (1992) Money, Gangsters and Politics: An Everyday Story of Japan. 26th September–2nd October, pp 31–2; Kerbo, H.R. and Inoue, M. (1990) Japanese Social Structure and White Collar Crime: Recruit Cosmos and Beyond. *Deviant Behavior*. Vol. 11, pp 139–54; Yayama, T. (1990) The Recruit Scandal: Learning from the Causes of Corruption. *Journal of Japanese Studies*. Vol. 16, No. 1, pp 93–114.

18    See for instance Passas and Nelken, op cit; van Duyne, op cit.

19    Williams, op cit, p 111.

20    Observatoire Géopolitique des Drogues, op cit.

21    See for instance Magnusson, E. (1981) *Ekonomisk Brottslighet vid Export och Export*. Stockholm: Brottsforebyggande Radet; Passas, N. (1994) European Integration, Protectionism and Criminogenesis: A Study on Farm Subsidy Frauds. *Mediterranean Quarterly*. Vol. 5, No. 4, pp 66–84. Reprinted in Passas (1998) op cit; US House Committee on Energy and Commerce (1982) *SEC and Citicorp*. Washington, DC: US Government Printing Office.

22    See for instance Andvig, J.C. (1995) Corruption in the North Sea Oil Industry: Issues and Assessments. *Crime, Law and Social Change*. Vol. 23, No. 4, pp 289–313; Braithwaite, J. (1984) *Corporate Crime in the Pharmaceutical Industry*. London: Routledge and Kegan Paul; Eaton, J.P. (1997) The Nigerian Tragedy, Environmental Regulation of Transnational Corporations, and the Human Right to a Healthy Environment. *Boston University International Law Journal*. Vol. 15, pp 261–307.

23    Seagull, L.M. (1994/95) Whistleblowing and Corruption Control: The GE Case. *Crime, Law and Social Change*. Vol. 22, No. 4, pp 381–90.

24    See for instance Clinard, M.B. (1990) *Corporate Corruption: The Abuse of Power*. New York: Praeger; Michalowski, R.J. and Kramer, R.C. (1987) The Space Between Laws: The Problem of Corporate Crime in a Transnational Context. *Social Problems*. Vol. 34, No. 1, pp 34–53. Reprinted in Passas (1998) op cit.

25    See for instance Szasz, A. (1986) Corporations, Organized Crime, and the Disposal of Hazardous Waste: An Examination of the Making of a Criminogenic Regulatory Structure. *Criminology*. Vol. 24, No. 1, pp 1–27. Reprinted in Passas (1995b) op cit; van Duyne, P. (1993) Implications of Cross-Border Crime Risks in an Open Europe. *Crime, Law and Social Change*. Vol. 20, pp 99–111.

26    Brady, op cit.

27    See for instance Buffle, J.-C. (1993) L'Argent du Crime et les Banques Suisses. In Labrousse, A. and Wallon, A. (eds) *La Planète des Drogues*. Paris: Seuil; Levi, M. (1991) Pecunia non Olet: Cleansing the Money-Launderers from the Temple. *Crime, Law and Social Change*. Vol. 16, No. 3, pp 217–302; Passas, N. and Groskin, R.B. (2001) Overseeing and Overlooking: The US Federal Authorities' Response to Money Laundering and Other Misconduct at BCCI. *Crime, Law and Social Change*. Vol. 35, Nos. 1–2, pp 141–75.

28    Passas, N. (1999b) *Informal Value Transfer Systems and Criminal Organizations: A Study into So-Called Underground Banking Networks*. The Hague: Netherlands Ministry of Justice.

29    See for instance della Porta and Mény, op cit; Popescu-Birlan, L. (1994) Privatization and Corruption in Romania. *Crime, Law and Social Change*. Vol. 21, No. 4, pp 375–9; Reed, Q. (1994/95) Transition, Dysfunctionality and Change in the Czech and Slovak Republics. *Crime, Law and Social Change*. Vol. 22, No. 4, pp 323–37.

30    See for instance Adams, J. (1986) *The Financing of Terror*. London: New English Library; Naylor, R.T. (1993) The Insurgent Economy: Black Market Operations of Guerilla Organizations. *Crime, Law and Social Change*. Vol. 20, No. 1, pp 13–51.

31    McCoy, A. (1991) *The Politics of Heroin in Southeast Asia*. New York: Lawrence Hill.

32    Ibid.

33    Herman, E.S. (1987) U.S. Sponsorship of International Terrorism: An Overview. *Crime and Social Justice*. Nos. 27–28, pp 1–31.

34    Sterling, op cit, p 159.

35    Truell, P. and Gurwin, L. (1992) *False Profits*. Boston, MA and New York: Houghton Mifflin; Passas, N. (1993) Structural Sources of International Crime: Policy Lessons from the BCCI Affair. *Crime, Law and Social Change*. Vol. 20, No. 4, pp 293–305; Passas (1995a) op cit; Passas, N. (1996) The Genesis of the BCCI Scandal. *Journal of Law and Society*. Vol. 23, No. 1, pp 52–72; Passas, N. (2001) False Accounts: Why do Company Statements Often Offer a True and Fair View of Virtual Reality? *European Journal on Criminal Policy and Research*. Vol. 9, No. 2, pp 117–35.

36    Eaton, op cit.

37    See for instance Bello, W. (1998/1999) The Asian Economic Implosion: Causes, Dynamics, Prospects. *Race and Class*. Vol. 40, Nos. 2/3, pp 133–43; Mander, J. and Goldsmith, E. (eds) (1996) *The Case Against the Global Economy*. San Francisco, CA: Sierra Club Books; Passas, N. (2000) Global Anomie, Dysnomie, and Economic Crime: Hidden Consequences of Globalization and Neo-liberalism in Russia and Around the World. *Social Justice*. Vol. 27, No. 2, pp 16–44.

38    Plater, Z.J.B. (1988) Damming the Third World: Multilateral Development Banks, Environmental Diseconomies, and International Reform Pressures on the Lending Process. *Denver Journal of International Law and Policy*. Vol. 17, No. 1, pp 121–53.

39    Falk, R. (1993) Rethinking the Agenda of International Law. In Nordenstreng, K. and Schiller, H.I. (eds) *Beyond National Sovereignty: International Communication in the 1990s*. Norwood, NJ: Ablex.

40    Passas (1993) op cit.

41    Lupsha (op cit) has used the terms 'predatory' and 'parasitical' to define different stages in the evolution of criminal organizations. I am using these terms in a different way. I am not concerned with the evolution of single organizations here. Indeed, for many of the organizations I have in mind, there is no evolution from one type to another. The terms are employed here to denote different types of relationship between legal and illegal enterprises.

42    Bovenkerk, F. and Yesilgoz, Y. (1998) *De Maffia van Turkjie*. Amsterdam: Meulenhoff.

43    Phythian, op cit.

44    Clinard, op cit.

45    Barnett, T. (1990) *The Barnett Report: Commission of Inquiry into Aspects of the Forest Industry in Papua New Guinea: Final Report*. Hobart: Asia Pacific Action Group.

46    Szasz, op cit.

47    van Duney (1993) op cit.

48    Brady, op cit.

49    Naylor (1995/1996) op cit.

50    Walter, I. (1985) *Secret Money: The World of International Financial Secrecy*. London: George Allen & Unwin.

51    Conklin, J.E. (1994) *Art Crime*. Westport, CT: Praeger.

52    US House Committee on Energy and Commerce, op cit.

53    See for instance Passas (2000) op cit; Passas, N. (1999a) Globalization, Criminogenic Asymmetries and Economic Crime. *European Journal of Law Reform*. Vol. 1, No. 4, pp 399–423; Passas, N. (1998) A Structural Analysis of Corruption: The Role of Criminogenic Asymmetries. *Transnational Organized Crime*. Vol. 4, No. 1, pp 42–55.

54    Wheeler, S. and Rothman, M.L. (1982) The Organization as Weapon in White-Collar Crime. *Michigan Law Review*. Vol. 80, pp 1403–27.

55    Braithwaite, J. (1989) Criminological Theory and Organizational Crime. *Justice Quarterly*. Vol. 6, No. 3, pp 333–58.

56    Blum, J. and Block, A. (1993) Le Blanchiment de l'Argent dans les Antilles: Bahamas, Saint Maartin et Iles Caïmans. In Labrousse and Wallon, op cit.

57    Passas (1999) op cit; Passas (2000) op cit.

58    Braithwaite, op cit.

59    Picciotto, S. (1992) *International Business Taxation*. New York: Quorum Books.

60    Barnett, op cit.

61    Levi, op cit.

62    Falk, op cit.

63    *The Economist*, op cit.

64    Reuter, P. (1996) The Mismeasurement of Illegal Drug Markets. In Pozi, S. (ed.) *Exploring the Underground Economy*. Kalamazoo, MI: W.E. Upjohn Institute for Employment Research.

65    Chin, K.-L. (1999) *Smuggled Chinese: Clandestine Immigration to the United States*. Philadelphia, PA: Temple University Press.

66    William and Woessner, op cit.

67    Passas (1999b) op cit.

68    Swinyard, W.R., Rinne, H. and Kau, A.K. (1990) The Morality of Software Piracy: A Cross-Cultural Analysis. *Journal of Business Ethics*. Vol. 9, pp 655–64.

69    Skolnick, J.H. and Fyfe, J.J. (1993) *Above the Law: Police and the Excessive Use of Force*. New York: Free Press.

70    Passas (1994) op cit.

# Part III
# Control Issues

# [23]

# Criminalizing Consequences of Sanctions: Embargo Busting and Its Legacy

Peter Andreas

*Brown University*

The upsurge in the use of economic sanctions in the post-Cold War era has prompted much scholarly and policy debate over their effectiveness and humanitarian consequences. Remarkably little attention, however, has been devoted to their criminalizing consequences and legacy for the post-sanctions period. In this article, I develop an analytical framework identifying and categorizing the potential criminalizing effects of sanctions across place (within and around the targeted country) and time (during and after the sanctions period), and apply and evaluate this framework through an in-depth examination of the case of Yugoslavia. For comparative leverage and to assess the applicability of the argument beyond the Yugoslavia case, the analysis is briefly extended to other cases both within and outside the Balkans (Croatia and Iraq). The article suggests that sanctions can unintentionally contribute to the criminalization of the state, economy, and civil society of both the targeted country and its immediate neighbors, fostering a symbiosis between political leaders, organized crime, and transnational smuggling networks. This symbiosis, in turn, can persist beyond the lifting of sanctions, contributing to corruption and crime and undermining the rule of law. The article is one of the first efforts to integrate the study of sanctions and transnational crime, and suggests that the criminalized collateral damage from sanctions and its post-sanctions legacy should be made a more central part of the evaluation of sanctions.

Multilateral economic sanctions have been a popular policy instrument in the post-Cold War era. During the 1990s, the United Nations (UN) imposed sanctions six times as often as in the prior 45 years, leading some scholars to label it "the sanctions decade" (Cortright and Lopez, 2000). The heightened use of sanctions has generated enormous scholarly and policy debate over their effectiveness and humanitarian consequences. Remarkably little attention, however, has been devoted to their criminalizing consequences and legacy for the post-sanctions period. This article is one of the first efforts to integrate the study of sanctions and transnational crime, and it suggests that the criminalized collateral damage of sanctions and its post-sanctions legacy should be made a more central part of the evaluation of

*Author's note*: I especially thank Peter Romaniuk for his valuable research assistance. Helpful comments and criticisms were provided by Jasmina Burdžovic Andreas, Christopher Corpora, Neta Crawford, Josip Dasovic, Daniel Drezner, Jonathan Kirshner, Audie Klotz, Roger Haydon, Aida Hozic, Marc Lynch, Tom Naylor, Aaron Presnall, Darius Rejali, Norrin Ripsman, James Ron, Herman Schwartz, Michael Soussan, and three anonymous reviewers. An earlier version of this article was presented at the 2004 annual meeting of the International Studies Association, Columbia University, and the International Peace Academy. Research funding was provided by the Smith Richardson Foundation and the Watson Institute for International Studies (Brown University).

TABLE 1. Potential Criminalizing Consequences of Sanctions*

| Location | Sanctions Period | Post-Sanctions Period |
|---|---|---|
| State apparatus | State sponsors organize crime to generate funds and secure supplies; foster alliances with clandestine transnational economic actors; subcontract out sanctions busting tasks and provide privileged access in exchange for loyalty and support | Persistence of symbiosis between state and organized crime; high levels of corruption and entrenched resistance to reform and establishment of rule of law |
| Economy | Underground economy expands through sanctions evasion while aboveground economy contracts and goes into crisis; emergence of new elite as power and wealth of smuggling entrepreneurs grows while those in the aboveground economy are marginalized | Continued high levels of underground economic activity as sanctions-busting networks adapt and diversify while the aboveground economy struggles to recover from sanctions; new elite selectively move into other sectors of the economy |
| Civil society | Broad societal tolerance of smuggling; smuggling perceived as "normal;" "uncivil society" empowered | Continued high societal acceptance of smuggling; engagement in smuggling economy broadly viewed as a legitimate avenue of upward social mobility |
| Regional repercussions | Regional sanctions-busting networks develop with official complicity of neighbors; aboveground trade relations with targeted country collapse while underground trade relations expand (clandestine side of economic interdependence becomes dominant); cross-border crime linkages grow | Lifting sanctions generates shock wave through regional sanctions evading trade routes; sanctions-busting networks persist and are adapted for other smuggling activities |

*Modifies and extends the framework in Crawford and Klotz (1999:30).

sanctions. I develop an analytical framework (summarized in Table 1) identifying and classifying the potential political, economic, and societal criminalizing effects of sanctions across place (within and around the targeted country) and time (during and after the sanctions period).

At the political level, the most important criminalizing effect of sanctions is that the targeted regime may go into the business of organized crime to generate revenue, secure supplies, and strengthen its hold on power, fostering an alliance with clandestine transnational economic actors for mutual gain. This alliance may, in turn, persist beyond the sanctions period. At the economic level, the most profound criminalizing result of sanctions can be to push economic activity underground and dramatically inflate the profitability of illicit commerce. Aboveground trading relations can be supplanted by underground trading relationships, creating clandestine region-wide sanctions-evading networks that reshape the political economy of the region and that may endure beyond the sanctions. Sanctions can create an economic opportunity structure that privileges those best positioned in the underground economy, enhancing the value of their smuggling skills and connections.[1] This, in turn, can redistribute wealth and favor, helping to propel the emergence of a *nouveau riche* elite. Unable or unwilling to shift to legal trading after sanctions are

---

[1] There is no consensus in the literature on the use and definition of the term "underground economy," but for my purposes here I am mostly interested in those underground economic activities related to the evasion of sanctions, which largely involves some form of smuggling.

lifted, sanctions evaders may simply engage in substitution strategies, turning to other illegal trading activities. Incentives to enter or continue operating in the underground economy can be reinforced by the devastated condition of the aboveground economy after sanctions. At the societal level, the most significant criminalizing consequence of sanctions is the potential of fostering "uncivil society," reflected in a higher level of public tolerance for lawbreaking and an undermined respect for the rule of law. Smuggling may not only become perceived as "normal" rather than deviant, but it may even be celebrated as patriotic. Even in countries with extreme levels of corruption, there tends to be official disapproval of smuggling, but this may be eroded under sanctions. The result can be a general legal demoralization as society becomes accustomed to practices that do not conform to modern legal standards. Reestablishing societal acceptance of legal norms can be one of the most challenging tasks after sanctions are lifted, as old habits can be difficult to break. Table 1 summarizes these potential political, economic, and societal criminalizing consequences of sanctions.

In this article, I apply and evaluate this analytical framework through a detailed examination of sanctions evasion in the case of the Federal Republic of Yugoslavia (FRY, now Serbia and Montenegro). The FRY case represents a particularly important and high profile sanctions episode that "featured unprecedented international cooperation in sanctions monitoring and enforcement" (Cortright and Lopez, 2000:63). As a centerpiece of the post-Cold War upsurge of multilateral sanctions efforts, the 1992–1995[2] FRY sanctions experience has weighed heavily in sanctions deliberations and has contributed to the move toward more targeted sanctions (Popovski, 2002). For comparative leverage and to determine the applicability of the analytical framework beyond the FRY case, I also briefly examine two other cases within and outside the Balkans (Croatia and Iraq).

As I document in this article, the FRY case closely matches the patterns of criminalization identified in Table 1, while the Croatia and Iraq cases partially match. My focus on the criminalizing effects of the sanctions in the FRY does not suggest that there was little or no criminalization of the state, economy, and society before sanctions, or that criminalization would not have been a problem in the absence of sanctions. Sanctions were part of a larger enabling environment for criminalization. Other variables contributed to criminalization, particularly the challenges of post-Communist transition[3] and the context of prolonged war. The FRY's involvement in the war in Bosnia and Herzegovina (BiH), for example, provided incentives and opportunities for criminal activity, including war profiteering from smuggling and selling looted goods.[4]

Given these important contextual variables, it is difficult to precisely measure what part and what proportion of criminalization is attributed to sanctions. The argument here is not that sanctions are the only criminalizing force, but rather that they produce much higher levels of criminalization than would otherwise have been the case in the absence of the sanctions. The limited comparative case extensions help to support this argument. In the absence of comprehensive sanctions, I suggest, the FRY would likely have more closely resembled neighboring Croatia—also a former Yugoslav republic run by a nationalist authoritarian leadership in the midst of post-Communist transition and war, but one not facing comprehensive economic sanctions. The criminalization of the state, economy, and

---

[2] Partial sanctions were later imposed on the FRY during the Kosovo conflict but will not be examined here because of space limitations.

[3] See the special issue of *Problems of Post-Communism* (May/June 2004) focusing on transnational crime and conflict in the Balkans.

[4] These criminalizing effects of the war have been analyzed in detail elsewhere. See, for example, Andreas (2004a). For a more general discussion, see John Mueller, *The Remnants of War* (Ithaca:Cornell University Press, 2004).

TABLE 2. Case Comparisons

| | Sanctions Type | |
| Prolonged War | Comprehensive Sanctions | Arms Embargo |
|---|---|---|
| Yes | Federal Republic of Yugoslavia: transition country; criminalization: high | Croatia: transition country; criminalization: medium |
| No | Iraq: non-transition country; criminalization: high | Slovenia: transition country; criminalization: low |

society is a serious problem in both cases, but much more so in the FRY. Slovenia, the former Yugoslav republic that has had the smoothest transition and the fewest problems of criminalization, has also been the least affected by war and sanctions. Finally, the Iraq sanctions case comparison not only shows the applicability of the analytical framework beyond the Balkans but is also a sanctions case involving high criminalization in a non-transition and largely non-war context. These case variations are captured in Table 2.

In the next section, I briefly review the sanctions debate. I then trace the political economy of sanctions evasion in the Yugoslav case and its regional support structure in the 1992–1995 period. This is followed by an evaluation of the lifting and legacy of sanctions. For comparative leverage and to evaluate the applicability of the analytical framework beyond the FRY case, I provide a limited extension of the analysis to other cases within and outside the Balkans (Croatia and Iraq). The concluding section points to the broader lessons for sanctions-related research and policy debates.

## The Sanctions Debate

The scholarly and policy debates on sanctions have traditionally focused primarily on the narrow question of whether sanctions work in achieving their stated policy objective (Wallensteen, 2002). This ongoing debate has almost entirely overshadowed the criminalizing consequences of sanctions and their legacy for the post-sanctions period.[5] Although Galtung (1967) long ago pointed to smuggling as an effective sanctions evasion method, the specific dynamics of such evasion and their criminalizing side effects are rarely made the center of analysis or traced in detail. This is part of the larger tendency in much of the literature to gloss over the political economy of how targeted states strategically cope and adapt to sanctions.[6] As Rowe (2001:6) rightly points out, "the central theoretical puzzle posed by economic sanctions, how governments can often survive and even benefit from severe disruptions to the national economy, remains largely unanswered." Unlike most sanctions scholars, policy practitioners are very much focused on problems of evasion, as evident in UN Security Council debates and sanctions implementation manuals.[7] Nevertheless, the criminalizing impact of sanctions and their longer-term legacy are generally not central policy considerations when officials contemplate their imposition.

One reason why the dominant focus in the sanctions literature on the question of whether sanctions work is so unsatisfactory is that it pays inadequate attention to the mechanisms by which sanctions change behavior in the targeted country.[8]

---

[5] This is reflected, for example, in the extensive sanctions bibliography compiled by Mikael Eriksson, Department of Peace and Conflict Research, Uppsala University, 2002.

[6] Notable exceptions are Crawford and Klotz (1999), Naylor (1999), Brooks (2002), and Rowe (2001).

[7] For example, Part IV of the Stockholm Process Report (Wallensteen et al., 2003) provides an extended discussion of evasion problems.

[8] My assessment of the sanctions literature has been greatly aided by Romaniuk's (2003) insightful review.

Scholars who stress greater complexity regarding the domestic consequences of sanctions enforcement necessarily have more to say about evasion. For example, Kirshner's (1997:41) emphasis on the "microfoundations" of sanctions draws attention to the fact that sanctions can have substantial economic effects without producing the intended policy outcome, and it suggests that the analysis of sanctions should be recast to look more closely at how groups within a target state are affected differently by sanctions. Other sanctions scholars, such as Brooks (2002), Rowe (2001), and Selden (1999), also point to the often perverse and unintended distributional effects of sanctions, which create new winners and losers. These various lines of analysis all point to the utility of broadening the sanctions debate and looking more closely at the political economy of sanctions enforcement and evasion, including their criminalizing consequences. In this regard, the analytical framework developed by Crawford and Klotz (1999:30) for understanding how sanctions work in general can be usefully modified and extended to identify and categorize the range of potential criminalizing side effects of sanctions (see Table 1).

There has also been an upsurge of scholarly and policy interest in the unintended negative consequences of sanctions, but this has almost exclusively been interpreted to mean unintended *humanitarian* consequences. The heightened attention to targeted sanctions reflects these concerns, as the main goal of these sanctions (or "smart sanctions") is to limit humanitarian damage while retaining effective pressure on the targeted regime. Indeed, this has been the primary motivation for the move away from comprehensive sanctions and toward more targeted sanctions in recent years (Wallensteen, Staibano, and Eriksson, 2003).[9] But while the criminalizing damage from economic sanctions may be acknowledged or mentioned in passing, this is rarely highlighted in these evaluations (let alone made a central part of the rationale for change in sanctions instruments). Equally important, evaluations of sanctions typically tend to stop at the point of sanctions termination, with sanctions observers quickly turning their attention to other cases. Although this is understandable, it unfortunately overlooks the potentially profound aftereffects of sanctions.

In this article, I evaluate the criminalizing side effects of sanctions through a detailed examination of the political economy of sanctions evasion and their legacy in the case of the FRY. Interestingly, this case tends to be one of the few sanctions episodes that many scholars and practitioners tend to categorize as a "success." The view that the FRY sanctions were successful in achieving the aims of the UN Security Council (1996) is stated most boldly in the *Report of the Round Table on United Nations Sanctions in the Case of the Former Yugoslavia*, which claims that the sanctions were "remarkably effective." Although the document provides a list of lessons learned and recommendations for future sanctions regimes, it does not include the challenge of dealing with the criminalized residue of sanctions. Cortright and Lopez (2000:69, 75) similarly claim that the FRY sanctions were "among the most effective in history," but they also acknowledge that sanctions fueled "corruption, smuggling, and criminality. .... A vast network of black marketers emerged, much of it connected to and protected by the government." However, these observations are not explored at greater length. Part of the reason they give for the "success" of sanctions is that the sanctions did not produce a humanitarian crisis. The criminalizing side effects are thus presumably viewed as much less consequential.

If most assessments of the Yugoslav sanctions neglect or under-explore the unintended criminalizing effects of sanctions, a report prepared by the Inter-Agency Task Force on Serbian Sanctions of the United States Department of State (1996) tackles the issue directly but minimizes and downplays its importance. Criminalization is considered a regrettable but tolerable side effect of sanctions that are judged to have been reasonably successful. The Task Force asserts that sanctions

---

[9] Also see the website of the Special Program on the Implementation of Targeted Sanctions (www.smartsanctions.se).

enforcement measures in the FRY meant that smugglers were reduced to operating in smaller volumes, but whether such smuggling had other deleterious consequences was not considered. As discussed below, the sanctions-busting smuggling economy was not only far more significant in terms of organization and scale than acknowledged by this official assessment, but the negative political, economic, and social consequences of criminalization have been profound and long lasting—not only for the targeted country but also for the region as a whole.

Interestingly, even the harshest critics of the FRY sanctions tend not to make the criminalizing collateral damage of sanctions the focus of their critiques. For example, Woodward refers to "sanctions-runners" as part of the local "economic elite" that gained an interest in maintaining the sanctions (Woodward, 1995:294). Licht's (1995:158) evaluation of the sanctions notes in passing that "Life under sanctions forced a significant portion of society to live on the fringes of legality. The black market became a way of life." These authors thus make some important initial claims about the criminalizing consequences of sanctions. In this article, I follow this line of analysis in a more systematic and detailed manner, tracing the political, economic, and societal criminalizing consequences of sanctions across time (during and after the sanctions period) and place (within and outside of the targeted country).

## The Imposition of Sanctions

In response to charges of the Milošević regime's complicity in the war in BiH (Gagnon, 1994; Ron, 2000), comprehensive sanctions were imposed with the UN Security Council resolution 757 on May 30, 1992, covering trade, air travel, financial transactions, scientific and technical cooperation, and sports and cultural exchanges. Certain exemptions for humanitarian goods and transshipment were included in the sanctions resolution, although permission of the UN Sanctions Committee was required. Some six months later the transshipment of goods was barred and maritime shipping on the Danube was halted (Resolution 787 of November 1992). Later still, Yugoslav assets abroad were frozen, Yugoslav vessels were denied transit, and transshipment was further limited (resolution 820 of April 1993). In September 1994, these sanctions were extended to the Bosnian-Serb controlled areas of BiH. In return for Belgrade's cooperation in enforcing these amended measures, the UN ban on cultural and sporting events was lifted, and air and ferry service between Montenegro and Italy was resumed.

The objective of the sanctions was to pressure the Milošević government to curtail support to the rebel Serbs in Bosnia, which in turn would presumably make the Bosnian Serb leadership more willing to negotiate an end to the war. To enforce the sanctions, the Western European Union (WEU) and NATO commenced interdiction patrols in the Adriatic Sea in the summer of 1992. In an unprecedented initiative to enhance regional enforcement capacity on the ground, UN Sanctions Assistance Missions (SAMs) were set up in Bulgaria, Hungary, Romania, Albania, Croatia, Macedonia, and Ukraine, and were staffed by U.S., Canadian, and European customs agents at border posts and coordinated via a Sanctions Assistance Missions Communications Center (SAMCOMM) headquartered in Brussels.[10] For Cortright et al. (2000:219), "the SAMs were the most elaborate and highly developed monitoring program ever established," making the sanctions "the most rigorously enforced in history." One UN-sponsored report (Garfield, 2001:64) claims that the SAMs made the sanctions "the most effective of the post-Cold War sanctions regimes ..."

---

[10] A U.S.-provided and maintained satellite system linked SAMCOMM with the New York-based UN sanctions committee and enabled customs agents at border posts to check cargo documents and curb use of falsified or forged paperwork. See Cortright and Lopez (2000:69).

*The Mechanisms and Criminalizing Consequences of Sanctions Evasion*

International isolation through sanctions hit the FRY economy hard. The U.S. State Department estimated that the Serbian economy contracted by 26 percent in 1992 and 37 percent in 1993 (Cosgrove, 2002). The sanctions were only partly to blame for the sharp economic downturn: the economy was in trouble well before the sanctions were in force, trade relations were already greatly disrupted by the outbreak of conflict, and the government's own policies made a rapidly deteriorating economic situation even worse. Sanctions did, however, greatly exacerbate the economic crisis and, equally important, gave the Milošević regime a convenient external source to blame for the growing economic hardship—even as those close to the regime were becoming rich from war profiteering and sanctions evasion.

Moreover, the sanctions not only provided Slobodan Milošević with a way to distract and deflect domestic criticism but also provided him a rationale to reassert state controls and avoid market reforms (Mijatovic, 1998:175). The economy remained highly regulated, and for sanctions busting this meant that many economic tasks were subcontracted out by the state to those most loyal to the regime and with the greatest skills and connections to smuggling. While the underground economy is conventionally viewed as operating outside of state controls, in the case of sanctions evasion in the FRY, it was to a substantial extent state directed and promoted as "patriotic smuggling" (Antonic, 2002:371).[11] Sanctions were central to both the rapid growth of the underground economy and its state-directed restructuring toward organized smuggling and clandestine financial transactions.[12] Milošević was able to command loyalty and collect sanctions rents by providing preferential access to the sanctions-busting trade, which in turn helped to prop up the regime. In short, sanctions enhanced the criminalization of politics and the politicization of criminality (Vasilijevic, 1995).

The importation and distribution of oil was particularly important in this regard. The FRY's substantial military self-sufficiency meant that the UN's region-wide arms embargo had little impact; however, the country was financially vulnerable and highly dependent on imported oil. The initial effect of the imposition of comprehensive sanctions in May 1992 was to induce an oil shortage. Road traffic was reportedly halted during the summer as queues for petrol emerged across the country. However, later that year, Serbia secured new supplies, reducing the price of petrol.[13] The new suppliers were black marketeers, importing Russian oil through the Montenegrin port of Bar, over the Bulgarian border at Kalotina, and via the Danube.

At the low end of the petrol trade were small-scale local freelancers, engaged in gasoline smuggling using private cars customized to carry extra tanks. The greatest profits and risks were at the high end of the trade, which was more organized and required official connections. In some places, small traders would over time be pushed out by more organized smuggling operations (as was the case in early 1993 when Milošević's son, Marko, took over much of the cross-border smuggling in the town of Bela Crkva on the Romanian border).[14] Domestic distribution was also farmed out to those closest to the regime. Some 40 percent of Serbia's petrol stations were controlled by banks with close links to Milošević, those with links to his Socialist party, or military leaders who laundered war profits through them.[15] For

---

[11] Also see Antic (1998).

[12] The underground economy made up an estimated 23.7 percent of the Yugoslav economy in 1991, but then mushroomed in size under sanctions (Minic, 1993:6).

[13] Silber, Laura. November 16, 1992. Fuel Embargo on Serbia Flouted: Queues Vanish as Petrol Tankers Violate United Nations Sanctions. *Financial Times*.

[14] Zavrtanje Mafifaških Slavina (Tightening of the Mafiosi Spigots), April 10, 2003. Dnevnik (Belgrade). Retrieved from ⟨http://www.dnevnik.co.yu⟩.

[15] Awash in Oil. November 21, 1992. *Economist*, 60.

example, Mirko Marjanović was both Serbia's Prime Minister and the head of Progres, the country's leading gas and oil importing firm. Earnings from smuggled oil during the sanctions period reportedly financed the firm's new five-story, marble-and-chrome office building in central Belgrade, and Marjanović apparently amassed a personal fortune of some $50 million.[16] Another well-known case is that of Željko Ražnatović, or "Arkan," Serbia's most infamous paramilitary leader and underworld figure. Arkan was reportedly as skilled at sanctions busting as he was at ethnic cleansing and looting. Milošević rewarded Arkan for his oil smuggling successes by giving him ownership of several gas stations. For each tanker truckload of oil Arkan managed to bring in, it was estimated that he made $30,000 (United Nations Experts, 1994: Annex III. A). Through these kind of embargo-busting commercial deals, the ties between organized crime and the state deepened and expanded.

A state-sponsored embargo-busting system eventually became institutionalized with the help of key actors close to Milošević in the State Security and the Interior Ministry of which it was a part. To oversee and regulate sanctions busting, Milošević appointed Mihalj Kertes—who had earlier played a leadership role in coordinating the smuggling of arms to Croatian and Bosnian Serbs—as head of the customs office in 1994. As the institution that could most effectively collect currency, the Customs Service became the heart of the regime's clandestine financial structure. As the head of Serbia's Central Bank observed in 2001, the Customs Service "was Milošević's primary source of cash, and it never ran dry."[17] Kertes was crucial to the organization of the embargo-busting trade, as his office provided import and export permits to those loyal to Milošević and those who proved most adept at circumventing UN monitors. Some members of the regime came to wealth and power owing to these customs office permits. The customs post allowed Kertes to generate substantial revenue for the regime by organizing and taking a cut of the illicit commerce. In September 1994, Kertes explained, "I don't care if it's legal or not, I only care if it makes a profit."[18]

The Customs service thus became the central office for state-organized crime. Kertes restructured the Customs Service, replacing trained and experienced staff with people he trusted, from his home town of Bačka Palanka, whom he personally hired by invitation.[19] They were then assigned to border crossings, where there were the biggest opportunities to skim from the smuggling trade. Those who complained had their goods seized or would have to pay more. The Customs Service also selectively confiscated money from locals and foreigners who were carrying cash over the border. As all formal international financial transactions were frozen by the sanctions, most remittances entered the FRY as smuggled German marks (DEM). Disciplinary action against Customs officials would only be taken against those who stole from someone who was under Kertes' protection.[20] The highly selective nature of customs enforcement thus provided windfall profits for those with official connections. The result was a massive redistribution of wealth via state-sponsored clandestine commerce. "Sanctions are paradise," one sanctions buster told a foreign journalist. "Normally you import and pay duties and then taxes. But under sanctions, if you know the right people, you pay no duties and no

---

[16] Pomfret, John. November 21, 1996. Serbia's Duty-free Road to Europe's Markets. *Washington Post*. See also Antonic (2002:374).

[17] Quoted in Purvis, Andrew. April 12, 2001. The Song of the Insider. *Time* (European edition). Retrieved from ⟨http://www.balkanpeace.org/hed/archive/apr01/hed3058.shtml⟩.

[18] Vasic, Miloš, Dulovic, Jovan, and Konjikušic, Davor. December 20, 2000. Hapšenje Direktora Savezne Uprave Carina (The Arrest of the Federal Customs Director). *Vreme* (Belgrade), 27–30.

[19] Roughly 800 of the 2,300 Customs officials in the country came from Bačka Palanka. Dobbs, Michael. November 29, 2000. Crash of Yugoslavia's Money Man. *Washington Post*.

[20] Vasic, Miloš, Dulovic, Jovan, and Konjikušic, Davor. December 20, 2000. Hapšenje Direktora Savezne Uprave Carina (The Arrest of the Federal Customs Director). *Vreme* (Belgrade), 27–30.

taxes, and you have the excuse of charging more. Sanctions are what cemented Milošević's power."[21]

Successfully evading the sanctions through clandestine imports required not only porous borders but also access to foreign exchange to pay for the smuggled goods. The Milošević government therefore turned to various financial schemes. One method was to simply print large quantities of dinar notes and then deploy money changers to buy up foreign exchange on the black market. The currency black market predated the sanctions, but it became far more important under sanctions because the country's international economic isolation meant that imports had to be paid for in cash. By early 1993, 40 percent of the supply of dinars were being used to sop up hard currency on the currency black market (Minić, 1993:6). The large-scale printing of dinars, in turn, generated one of the most extreme episodes of hyperinflation in history.

Another method to absorb hard currency was state sponsorship of two pyramid banks offering extraordinarily high interest rates. As these two banks also had leased a large number of the country's gasoline stations from the government, the cash deposits could be used to import oil in violation of sanctions (Naylor, 1999:360–61). The largest of the banks, Dafiment Bank, was owned and operated by Dafina Milanović, a former cashier who had a criminal record for embezzlement and forging documents. She was given her banking license partly as a reward for her pension fund contributions and key role in sanctions busting (Naylor, 1999:361; Judah, 2000:264). Her professional rise was facilitated by close ties to criminal business associates such as Arkan. In 1993, the *Economist* reported that "Arkan's men help protect Dafina Milanović, a formidable lady who went from bank teller to bank proprietor in 2 years. Sanctions made her, and other bankers, suddenly rich by increasing the value of hard currency, pushing dollar interest rates to stratospheric levels and by providing opportunities to import sanctions-busting oil."[22] These classic pyramid schemes eventually collapsed, with few (other than government officials and paramilitary leaders) able to salvage their deposits (Naylor, 1999:363).[23]

Sanctions busting also propelled the growth of the international side of the regime's clandestine financial apparatus. As explained by the financial investigator for the International Criminal Tribunal (Torkildsen, 2002:3): "The necessity to create the international part of the financial structure and to locate its operation and organization in Cyprus grew from the international economic sanctions that were in place against the FRY." This external apparatus helped to fund imports through front companies and banks based in Nicosia, Cyprus. In the first half of 1992, roughly 500 Serbian firms were added to the island's list of 8,000 offshore companies, some of which were set up for sanctions evasion (International Crisis Group, 2000:16). Cyprus also hosted branches of various Serbian banks, which became especially important after Serbia sent a large part of its foreign exchange reserves to the island in anticipation of the international asset freeze in 1993 (Naylor, 1999:354). Through this convenient offshore sanctions-busting base, imports could be ordered and paid for and then clandestinely diverted to the FRY. Similarly, the FRY could arrange the sale of its exports via Cyprus with the origins of the goods camouflaged (Naylor, 1999:354).

While those closest to the regime enjoyed the most profitable sanctions-busting opportunities, sanctions also helped prompt broader participation in and tolerance of the underground economy. Sanctions created powerful incentives for law-abiding middle-class professionals to either turn to the underground economy or join the swelling ranks of the Serb diaspora community abroad. The only alternative was a kind of "dignified poverty" that became less viable over time (Antonić, 2002:379). One Belgrade surgeon, for example, quit his job to become a gasoline smug-

---

[21] Harden, Blaine. August 29, 1999. The Milosevic Generation. *New York Times Magazine*, 30.

[22] Serbia; Profits and Losses under Sanctions. March 20, 1993. *Economist*, 55.

[23] For a detailed account of these financial schemes and their impact, see Dinkic (1995).

gler during the sanctions, boosting his monthly income from $140 a month to many thousands of dollars a month.[24] One smuggler selling contraband goods during the sanctions commented, "If one had ever told me that I'd be a smuggler I would have spat in his face. Today, even my father, a high school principal, works for me at the market."[25]

Although sanctions busting generated high profits for some, for most people the turn to the underground economy was simply part of a survival strategy. Indeed, as Dinkić has argued, the Milošević government "deliberately encouraged black markets" to prevent social unrest. "Everyone realized that it was far more profitable to smuggle or sell goods on the street. These activities at first served as an additional source of income but for many people soon became a full-time occupation." This, however, had socially corrosive effects. According to Dinkić (1995:229–30), the black market "encouraged the complete collapse of moral standards. Honesty became a burden, while dishonesty was a virtue and a basic condition of survival. This inevitably led to an increase in corruption and crime, which assumed staggering proportions." In other words, the societal effect of sanctions was to propel the growth of "uncivil society."

Smuggling is present in all societies, but in the FRY under sanctions it became "normal"—that is, the expected and accepted method of trade. Indeed, in contrast to other countries where smuggling is at least condemned even if not fully confronted by the authorities, in the FRY it was elevated to the status of a patriotic duty in the early 1990s. The Belgrade government publicly praised those who became "entrepreneurial" under the sanctions.[26] A recent study of corruption in the Serbian Customs Administration (Begović et al., 2001:99) noted that under the sanctions, "all dealings bringing goods into the state (smuggling, corruption, and so on) were not viewed as breaking the law but rather as holy patriotic missions." In this fertile environment for criminality, high-profile criminals such as Arkan became local celebrities and role models, and were treated as patriots by the Belgrade media.

As criminals were empowered, law-abiding professionals were disempowered. As one UN-sponsored study of the FRY (Garfield, 2001:66) in the 1990s has observed, "The large middle class of engineers, teachers, and government bureaucrats lost income, status, and options throughout the 1990s. A new and much smaller class of people involved in smuggling and the black market took their place." In this context, "Those engaged in criminal activities looked increasingly attractive as models of success" (Garfield, 2001:63). Sanctions were not singularly responsible for, but significantly contributed to, this criminalized social transformation of the country. As a Belgrade sociologist has described it, "An intensive and hasty criminalization of the society contributed to the springing up of a new elite, which was recruited from criminals. No other sphere of society was impacted so strongly by the sanctions . . . Beginning with sanctions (and probably with war), a new period in social development commenced—the state apparatus and organized crime grew together" (quoted in Babić, 2000). Importantly, the regime could simply rationalize this as a necessary response to sanctions: In January 1996, Serbian Prosecutor-General Dragan Petković commented that if there had been no sanctions violators or smugglers, the country's banking and commercial infrastructure would have found it very hard, if not impossible, to survive.[27]

[24] Harden, Blaine. August 29, 1999. The Milošević Generation. *New York Times Magazine.*

[25] Anastasijevic, Duška, and Jovanovic, Tatjana. June 27, 1994. Novi Pazar, Balkanski San Antonio (Novi Pazar: The Balkan San Antonio). *Vreme* (Belgrade), 30–31.

[26] Bogosavljević, Srđan. August 31, 1992. Srbija na Dve Stolice (Serbia on Two Chairs). *Vreme* (Belgrade), 1–2.

[27] Stan Markotich. January 23, 1996. *OMRI Daily Digest.*

*The Criminalizing Consequences of Sanctions for Neighboring States*

Following the patterns outlined in Table 1, the criminalizing effects of sanctions were not restricted to the targeted state but extended throughout the Balkans. The Milošević regime's sanctions-busting apparatus relied on a regional support structure utilizing immediate neighbors as transshipment points. Thus, even while not directly targeted by international sanctions, countries such as Albania, Romania, Bulgaria, and Macedonia directly experienced their criminalizing effects. While aboveground trade relations in the region were crippled by the imposition of sanctions, underground trade relations blossomed. Thus, regional economic interdependence did not simply cease but turned into a clandestine form of interdependence.

Neighboring states were all confronted with a similar dilemma regarding their official endorsement of the sanctions and their interest in maintaining trading links with the FRY. Milošević's sanctions-busting advisor, Radoje Đukić, noted at the time that there was very little incentive for neighboring states to fully implement the sanctions, given their potential economic losses.[28] Although all neighboring states reported enormous losses in trade with Serbia (Romania said to have lost $8 billion, Bulgaria and Hungary $1.5 billion, and Macedonia "stricken"),[29] this was partly cushioned by a growing underground trade relationship. For instance, according to a recent study (Dadak, 2003), underground trade from Bulgaria to Serbia reached more than $5 billion in 1994.

Rather than deterring sanctions busting, the gradual tightening of sanctions enforcement had displacement and rerouting effects. For example, when the WEU's Danube Mission became operational in June 1993 and Romania and Bulgaria increased their cooperation with sanctions enforcement, the sanctions-busting contraband trade increased from Greece passing through Macedonia.

Neighboring countries all found a place in sanctions busting, especially in the oil trade. In the case of Greece, the European Commission presented evidence in December 1992, indicating the systematic violation of sanctions by Greek companies, which were sending several thousand tons of oil per week to Serbia via Romania and Bulgaria.[30] A confidential EU report from March 1995 indicated a pattern of continuous sanctions busting by Greece (Michas, 2002:69). In the case of Albania, the country's impoverished Shkoder Lake region became an oil transshipment hub. Tellingly, in 1994, Albania imported twice as much oil as it consumed (Naylor, 1999:435). And in 1995, the country was believed to be illegally exporting north between 100 and 150 percent in excess of domestic oil consumption.[31] EU sanctions monitor Richardt Vork estimated at that time that 40 percent of the fuel smuggled into the FRY was entering via Albania.[32] The sanctions created extreme price differentials: a 210 liter barrel of oil purchased for 160–190 DEM in Albania could be sold for 300–340 DEM in Montenegro (Hajdinjak, 2002:15). While publicly declaring its commitment to sanctions, the Albanian government was complicit in the oil smuggling business. The ruling party ran the biggest oil company in the country, and taxing oil shipments became a leading generator of state revenue. Albania became more important as a sanctions-busting conduit as sanctions enforcement increased elsewhere in the region. To try to impress international observers, the government would occasionally crack down on small-time smugglers

---

[28] Beating the Sanctions on Serbia. July 2, 1994. *Economist*, 49.

[29] Traynor, Ian. August 4, 1994. Poor Neighbors Bear the Burden. *Guardian*, 10.

[30] Silber, Laura. December 9, 1992. EC Accuses Greeks over Serb Boycott. *Financial Times*, 3.

[31] Schmidt, Fabian. May 4, 1995. UN Security Council Concerned over Albania's Sanctions Busting. *OMRI Daily Digest*, II, No. 87. 〈http://www.hri.org/news/balkans/omri/1995/95-05-04.omri.html#11〉.

[32] Schmidt, Fabian. May 16, 1995. Update on Albanian Embargo-Busting. *OMRI Daily Digest*, II, No. 94 〈http://www.hri.org/news/balkans/omri/1995/95-05-16.omri.html〉.

while more organized smuggling operations with connections to the regime would be overlooked (Naylor, 1999:358, 366).

Romania also became an important smuggling transshipment point and, in the process, fostered closer ties between the state and organized crime. Poor Romanian towns near the Serbian border experienced an economic boom owing to the clandestine cross-border trade. In the city of Timisoara, "Hundreds of trading companies, many Serbian owned, set up shop along streets lined with gasoline stations. They were watched by Romanian Customs officers who were content to supplement their meager salaries by picking up a little hush money" (Naylor, 1999:354). Gasoline could be sold in Serbia at three times the Romanian price. Each fully loaded smuggling boat from the town of Moldova Veche in Romania reportedly made a profit of about $2,500 per trip across the Danube into Serbia—an enormous amount in a country where the average monthly salary was $100.[33] While the Romanian government publicly insisted that it was strictly applying sanctions (pointing to hundreds of cases of confiscating fuel from smugglers), the oil continued to flow across the border to Serbia. In May 2000, Romania's former intelligence chief, Virgil Magureanu, claimed that "The violation by Romania of the embargo against Yugoslavia was a political decision at the highest level." A probe by Romanian investigators discovered that 695 train cars carrying 36,500 tons of fuel were smuggled into Serbia via the Romanian-Serb border crossing of Jimbolia during the sanctions period. The trains apparently crossed at night with their lights off escorted by the secret service.[34]

The awkward dilemmas of enforcing the sanctions were particularly acute for neighboring Macedonia, which was economically integrated with Serbia and had long served as a transit point for Serbia-bound commerce. It had achieved independence and broke away from Yugoslavia less than a year before it was called upon to implement the sanctions. Communications and transportation were also routed through Serbia, with whom it had 60 percent of its trade.[35] Macedonia's independence was convenient for sanctions evasion: formal independence meant that the tiny neighboring country would not be targeted by sanctions, even though it was dominated by sanctions-busting economic interests. The government estimated that in the first full year of sanctions, they would cost the country $1.3 billion,[36] and in the second year, losses were put at $1.7 billion—a massive amount considering the country's GNP was a mere $3 billion.[37] Given these high costs, sanctions busting was one of the only viable economic activities and sources of foreign currency (Judah, 2000:272). Although Macedonian Customs officials, supervised by Canadian sanctions monitors, oversaw border crossings during the day, trucks could pass through unchecked to Serbia after dark.[38] It became an "open secret" that between 7 P.M. and 7 A.M., when the border was supposed to be closed, trucks would cross the border in both directions.[39] Macedonia became a particularly important sanctions-busting hub following the November 1992 UN prohibition on transshipment through Serbia, and when Romania and Bulgaria are reported to have improved their enforcement of the sanctions. The result was a greater concentration of contraband passing through Macedonia, much of it from

---

[33] Evans, Simon. October 6, 1995. Danube Fishermen Net Cash at Night Smuggling to Serbs. *Christian Science Monitor.*

[34] Porte, Jean-Luc. May 26, 2000. Probe into Romania's Role in Breaching Yugo Sanctions. *Agence France-Presse.*

[35] Landay, Jonathan S. July 9, 1993. No Hitch for Truckers Busting Sanctions through Macedonia. *Christian Science Monitor.*

[36] Macedonia: The Price of a Name. August 1, 1992. *Economist,* 39.

[37] Landay, Jonathan S. July 9, 1993. No Hitch for Truckers Busting Sanctions through Macedonia. *Christian Science Monitor.*

[38] Chazan, Yigal. July 3, 1993. Macedonia Mocks Yugoslav Embargo. *The Guardian.*

[39] Landay, Jonathan S. July 9, 1993. No Hitch for Truckers Busting Sanctions through Macedonia. *Christian Science Monitor.*

Greece.[40] In early 1995, *Jane's Intelligence Review* reported that "Economically, it is now an open secret in Skopje that Macedonia would have completely collapsed long ago had it attempted to avoid such regional sanctions busting."[41]

Macedonia also became a leading outlet for smuggling Serbian exports out of the region—with forged paperwork indicating Macedonia as the point of origin—in violation of UN sanctions (Naylor, 1999:354). Many Serbian front companies were set up in the capital city of Skopje to facilitate the process of importing and exporting via Macedonia. For example, one shell company, BOMIL, had branches in Skopje and in Limassol, Cyprus. During the sanctions years, the company reportedly bought oil (mostly in Greece and Macedonia) and paid Macedonian officials a "commission" of about 30 percent for clandestine passage across the border to Serbia (Cohen, 1998:180). Similarly, Radoje Đukić, the owner of a Serbian knitwear firm, specialized in exports to Germany via his Skopje-based company. He became the Serbian Minister for Small Business, which involved advising local businesses on how to circumvent sanctions (Judah, 2000:273).[42]

But while sanctions busting helped Macedonia cope under precarious economic circumstances, this activity also had serious and long-lasting criminalizing consequences. Large-scale smuggling became institutionalized as a mode of wealth accumulation and smugglers acquired much greater power in Macedonian society. As the *Financial Times* reported at the time, the main side effect of the "embargoes has been the encouragement of widespread smuggling which has created mafia-style economic gangs throughout the region. A new brash and violent "business class" has emerged which poses a long-term threat to the development of legitimate, tax-paying business in the Balkans as a whole."[43] As discussed below, these problems have left a powerful and enduring imprint.

## The Lifting and the Legacy of Sanctions

In November 1995, UN Security Council resolutions 1021 and 1022 specified the terms for suspending (conditionally) the sanctions against Belgrade and the Bosnian-Serb controlled areas of BiH. Some commentaries and reporting at the time gave an indication of what lay ahead, with fears raised that "[T]he most lasting and overlooked damage of sanctions may have been the corruption they encouraged in surrounding countries" and that high-level involvement in sanctions busting would bequeath an unfortunate legacy.[44] The criminalization of society "has reached its highest levels," commented Budimir Babović in 1996, a former deputy director of Interpol and a retired Yugoslav federal police official. "Reversing the process will not be easy."[45]

### The Economic Shock of Lifting the Sanctions

Given the centrality of sanctions busting in the economies of the Western Balkans, the lifting of sanctions had immediate region-wide ripple effects. For example, the spoils of sanctions busting in Macedonia was part of the glue that held together an uneasy ethnic peace in the 1990s (Hislope, 2003:7). Lifting the sanctions contributed to the unraveling of a multiethnic economic alliance of convenience, heightening ethnic tensions. Similarly, Strazzari (2003) has argued that ethnic unrest in

---

[40] Marsh, Virginia. June 4, 1993. Sanctions Against Serbia and Montenegro Enforced on Danube. *Financial Times;* Landay, Jonathan. S. July 9, 1993. No Hitch for Truckers Busting Sanctions through Macedonia. *Christian Science Monitor.*

[41] Milivojevic, Marko. February 1, 1995. The Balkan Medellin. *Jane's Intelligence Review,* 68.

[42] See also Beating the Sanctions on Serbia. July 2, 1994. *Economist,* 49.

[43] Robinson, Anthony. July 7, 1995. Survey of the Republic of Macedonia. *Financial Times.*

[44] Bonner, Raymond. November 19, 1995. How Sanctions Bit—Serbia's Neighbors. *New York Times.*

[45] Pomfret, John. November 21, 1996. Serbia's Duty-Free Road to Europe's Markets. *Washington Post.*

Kosovo was partly contained in the early 1990s by the profits generated from sanctions busting and other underground economic activities, contributing to a Serbian-Albanian "pax Mafiosi" during the sanctions years. Worsening economic conditions following the lifting of sanctions further exacerbated ethnic tensions in the area. The ending of sanctions had the most destabilizing effects for neighboring Albania, which had grown dependent on sanctions busting. Wallensteen (2002:13, footnote 14) observes that "the ending of sanctions by 1996 resulted in a complete economic collapse [in Albania] in 1997, leading to a Western peace operation to help stabilize the country." Naylor (1999:372) argues that the drying up of sanctions-evasion profits provided a "fatal blow" to Albania's pyramid financial schemes, and their collapse in 1997 brought down the Albanian government. An estimated $1.5 billion moved through the pyramid banks between 1992 and 1996, partly sustained by revenue generated from sanctions busting and other smuggling activities (Hajdinjak, 2002:32). When the pyramids collapsed, so did the government. The resulting chaos brought with it the looting of government armories and an influx of more than a million weapons onto the black market. Most of these weapons were then reportedly smuggled into Kosovo (Judah, 2000:320), providing a leading source of arms for the KLA (which until that point had had only limited success in its arming efforts).

### The Criminalized Legacy of Sanctions

Beyond the immediate aftershocks of lifting sanctions, sanctions have left a criminalized legacy in the region with major economic, societal, and political repercussions (closely paralleling the outcomes identified in Table 1). A particularly important criminalized economic legacy of the sanctions has been the persistence of sanctions-busting networks. Rather than sanctions evaders simply being put out of business with the lifting of sanctions, there has been a displacement effect as smugglers have turned to other commodities. The White House International Crime Threat Assessment observed (National Security Council, 2000:18): "Many of the criminal business enterprises set up to circumvent earlier sanctions are still operating." In Serbia and Montenegro, many of the state-sponsored smuggling networks that expanded under sanctions have endured. As Naylor (1999:363) explains the process, "Out of the deals to link Serbian intelligence to professional smugglers emerged new networks dealing in stolen cars, cigarettes, arms, illegal aliens and heroin that were the scourge of Europe. Government functionaries who had begun smuggling to earn money to prop up the regime, continued to smuggle to prop up their own bank accounts." For example, Milošević's son, Marko, who carved out a dominant position in the cigarette-smuggling business under sanctions, reportedly continued business in collaboration with Italian-organized crime figures, clandestinely shipping cigarettes from Montenegro through Italy into Western Europe. A perverse negative feedback effect of the sanctions was that the same smuggling channels that helped Serbia get around the sanctions turned to dumping smuggled cigarettes inside the country (Naylor, 1999). In the year following the sanctions, the government estimated that it was losing almost 20 percent of its potential budget revenue to the cigarette-smuggling trade. In 2002, Serbian tax authorities estimated that about half of the country's financial transactions were being made via illegal channels.[46] In 2003, Belgrade-based Western bankers estimated that only 30–40 percent of trade in the country was legal.[47]

Part of the reason that sanctions-busting networks have persisted long after the sanctions period is that once a state goes into the business of sponsoring smuggling to evade sanctions it can be difficult to get out of the business. Nowhere is this more

---

[46] Cvijanovic, Željko. June 12, 2002. Serbia: Government Facing Mafia Dilemma. Balkan Crisis Report, No. 342.

[47] Jansson, Eric. July 30, 2003. My Friend the Black Market. *Financial Times.*

evident than in Montenegro, where the smuggling apparatus built up during sanctions has not only stayed in place but has also continued to grow. As the *Financial Times* reported in August 2001 "What began as an attempt to circumvent a UN trade embargo on Yugoslavia has mushroomed into an international business spreading from the Balkans into Italy and other European Union states."[48] According to German customs investigators, "Since 1992, Montenegro has become one gigantic marketplace for smuggled cigarettes."[49] Italian investigators claim that cigarette smuggling accounts for nearly 50 percent of Montenegrin GDP, making it the tiny republic's most important economic activity. Some estimates (Hajdinjak, 2002:26–27, 41) suggest that by the end of the 1990s, the Montenegrin government was earning as much as $700 million annually from the clandestine cigarette trade. In 1999, it was reported that earnings from smuggling cigarettes and other goods were flowing into a parallel government budget, which was then used to support the official budget.[50] In a 365-page July 2003 indictment, Milo Đukanović, prime minister of Montenegro since 1991 and president since 1998, was accused by Italian prosecutors of collaborating with Italian crime organizations in smuggling mass quantities of untaxed cigarettes into the European Union.[51] Montenegro's links to the Italian mafia grew and were cemented during the sanctions period, with some mafia leaders relocating to the Montenegrin port of Bar in the early 1990s.[52]

Another related legacy of the sanctions period has been the emergence of a *nouveau riche* elite. New elite formation in the post-Communist transition process throughout Eastern Europe has also involved corruption and crime, but in the Western Balkans, the criminalization of the transition was reinforced under conditions of sanctions busting and war profiteering.[53] A few brief individual profiles illustrate how sanctions busting provided a mechanism for upward social mobility and criminalized elite formation. In the early 1990s, the Milošević government reportedly gave Vladimir Bokan a monopoly license for clandestinely importing cigarettes into Montenegro.[54] In an October 2000 interview, Bokan confessed that he had earned as much as $10,000 a day from embargo busting and smuggling items such as oil and cigarettes in the 1990s, making him a multimillionaire (five days after this interview, Bokan was gunned down in front of his villa near Athens by two gunmen) (Michas, 2002). One of the wealthiest individuals in the Balkans is Stanko "Cane" Subotić, who apparently earned his initial fortune during the sanctions period. The Zagreb weekly *Nacional* describes Subotić as the "European king of cigarette smuggling." He allegedly got his start as a tailor in Belgrade boutiques owned by the sanctions-busting tycoon Bokan, and in the early 1990s, he became a leading figure in the underground economy when war broke out and sanctions were imposed. Subotić reportedly spent the years under sanctions setting up a vast regional cigarette-smuggling and distribution network in close collaboration with Montenegrin Prime Minister Milo Đukanović and Serbian secret police chief Jovica Stanišić.[55]

In Serbia, the most successful entrepreneurs to emerge from the 1990s were those with close ties to the regime who were given informal monopolies, including the business of sanctions evasion.[56] Those who made fortunes from sanctions bust-

[48] Forster, Nicholas, and Husic, Sead. August 9, 2001. Probe into Montenegro's Role at Illegal Cigarette Trade. *Financial Times*.

[49] Quoted in ibid.

[50] Vukovic, Dragoljub. November 13, 1999. Montenegrin Parallel Budget. AIM.

[51] Traynor, Ian. July 11, 2003. Montenegrin PM Accused of Link with Tobacco Racket. *Guardian*.

[52] Vukovic, Marko. April 10, 1998. Bar Chief of Police Arrested by Italian Police. AIM.

[53] On the creation of new elites during the Milošević era, see Antonic (2002).

[54] Forster, Nicholas, and Husic, Sead. August 9, 2001. Probe into Montenegro's Role at Illegal Cigarette Trade. *Financial Times*.

[55] Babic, Jasna. May 17, 2001. The Balkan Godfather (Part 1): Nacional Reveals the Head Mafia Boss of the Balkans. *Nacional* (Zagreb); Pukanic, Ivo. May 24, 2001. The Balkan Godfather (Part 2). *Nacional* (Zagreb).

[56] Author interview with Milko Štimac, director of the G-17 Institute and member of the Serbian Securities and Exchange Commission, June 30, 2003 (Belgrade).

ing and other illicit activities during the Milošević years have successfully used their financial power to protect their illicit gains. This has been facilitated by the fact that the competitiveness of the new political parties requires financing and that there are few alternatives to turn to for funding. A report from the Sofia-based Center for the Study of Democracy (2004:13) observes that "Former criminals and organized crime lords have become the top business class in post-Milošević Serbia. They own banks, newspapers and TV channels, import and export companies and supermarket chains, and are among the main financiers of political parties."

Tackling economic crimes from the Milošević era has been a difficult and politically sensitive task. For example, in the summer of 2001, a new "extra profit tax" was introduced in Serbia to target war profiteers, criminal organizations, and Milošević-era cronies and front companies (United States Institute of Peace, 2002:8). Two years later, only a handful of individuals had paid extra taxes under the new law, and its application appeared to be highly selective (International Crisis Group, 2003:17). Prominent members of the new elite have strongly resisted establishing the rule of law.[57] Many have gone legitimate by becoming dominant players in the legal sectors of the economy, but the manner in which many conduct business continues to blur the distinction between legality and illegality.[58] Public opinion surveys have revealed broad societal tolerance and acceptance of illegal practices such as bribery and smuggling. In one survey in Serbia (Vasovic, 2000:15–16), more than 50 percent of respondents indicated that smuggling was (always or under certain conditions) a morally acceptable activity. Seventy-four percent of respondents agreed with the statement that "Only criminals and thieves are getting on well in this society," and some 70 percent of respondents agreed that "People in Serbia respect the law only when it suits them."

The most difficult political challenge in post-Milošević Serbia has been breaking the close symbiosis between the state and organized crime, which was nurtured by sanctions and war during the 1990s. The seriousness of the problem was most dramatically exposed by the March 2003 assassination of Serbian Prime Minister Zoran Đinđić. The alleged leader of the assassination plot is Milorad Lukovic ("Legija") and his so-called Zemun clan, a well-known Belgrade criminal group specializing in the smuggling of drugs, cigarettes, and oil.[59] The power of Lukovic and his associates can be traced back to the Milošević era, when crime, business, and the state security apparatus became closely linked in the effort to evade international sanctions and support the wars in the 1990s. Lukovic, a former French foreign legionnaire and commander of the "Red Berets" special unit within the Serbian Ministry of the Interior, had retired from state service into criminal enterprise while retaining ties to the security apparatus. Lukovic and Belgrade's criminal underworld played an important role in Đinđić's rise to power and removal of Milošević. Lukovic met with Đinđić in October 2000 days before Milošević was ousted, and, according to Đinđić, Lukovic agreed to disobey any Milosevic order to shoot opposition supporters converging on Belgrade from across the country on October 5. He and other key leaders in the state security apparatus kept their promise.[60] Moreover, Lukovic's men also assisted in June 2001 with Milošević's deportation.[61] Some of Serbia's leading crime groups, having abandoned their former

---

[57] Author interview with Mlađan Dinkic, the then Governor of the National Bank of Serbia (currently Minister of Finance), June 30–July 4, 2003 (Belgrade).

[58] Author interviews, G-17 Institute, International Crisis Group, National Bank of Serbia, June 30–July 4, 2003 (Belgrade).

[59] Drenča, Boris, and Šunter, Daniel. May 23, 2003. Serbia: Further Action against Mafia Demanded. Balkan Crisis Report, No. 432.

[60] Griffiths, Hugh. March 31, 2003. Balkan Reconstruction Report: A Mafia Within the State. Transitions Online. Article available at: ⟨http://www.tol.cz/look/TOL/article.tpl?IdLanguage=1&IdPublication=9&NrIssue=1&NrSection=4&NrArticle=9149⟩.

[61] Jansson, Eric, and Wagstyle, Stefan. March 14, 2003. The Cancer of Organized Crime that Riddles Serbia. *Financial Times.*

patron and sided with Đinđić, had been given an implicit amnesty after Milošević's capture and extradition. However, facing pressure from the international community and pragmatically accepting the need for reform to secure much-needed foreign aid, Đinđić had started to crack down on organized crime figures—including individuals who had assisted his rise to power.[62] Some observers have therefore cynically described the assassination as a "small killing among friends."[63] Loosening the entrenched ties between the state security apparatus and criminal enterprise in Serbia remains a daunting task for Đinđić's successors—and many have questioned whether there exists sufficient political will.[64] A recent International Crisis Group report (2004:I–II) emphasizes that, in order to become a stable state, Serbia must undergo the transition "from the Milosevic-era criminalized state to a more normal society."

## Comparative Extensions

Although a comprehensive comparison is beyond the scope of this article, a brief extension of the analysis to cases both within and outside the Balkans provides useful comparative leverage and helps to assess the applicability of the analytical framework beyond the FRY case.

### *Extensions Within the Balkans: Croatia*

In assessing the causal importance of sanctions relative to other variables that may have criminalizing effects—particularly prolonged war conditions and the post-Communist transition process—it is helpful to use counterfactual reasoning to ask how criminalized the state, economy, and society in the FRY would have been in the absence of comprehensive sanctions. My analysis suggests that the FRY would have more closely resembled neighboring Croatia—also a former Yugoslav republic in the midst of a post-Communist transition, also involved in prolonged warfare, and also run by an authoritarian nationalist leadership, but not subjected to comprehensive economic sanctions. Likewise, it is likely that if Croatia had faced comprehensive economic sanctions, it would have had a profile more closely resembling that of the FRY. The criminalization of the state, economy, and society has been a major problem for both countries, but much more so in the FRY than in Croatia.

Rather than being subjected to comprehensive sanctions, Croatia was part of the region-wide UN arms embargo imposed in 1991. The arms embargo had criminalizing consequences, but not nearly to the same degree as comprehensive economic sanctions. As in the FRY, smuggling took place under wartime conditions, and smuggling-generated wealth accumulation provided a path of rapid upward social mobility for some well-placed entrepreneurs. But importantly, in Croatia this did not reach as widely or as deeply into the broader economy and society because smuggling was mostly restricted to arms trafficking.

The arms embargo itself, however, had a much greater criminalizing effect on Croatia than it did on the FRY. This is owing to the fact that the FRY was more self-sufficient militarily, whereas Croatia was more dependent on clandestine weapons imports. A weapons procurement system based on smuggling invited war profiteering and corruption as it involved cash transactions with no paper trail and much greater interaction between state institutions and criminal networks. As a former Croat soldier who had been involved in an illegal weapons import scheme has put it, the arms embargo had the perverse consequence of making smuggling patriotic and nurturing

---

[62] LeBor, Adam. March 13, 2003. Brussels Fears Serbian Gangsters. *Balkan Crisis Report*, No. 414.

[63] Author interview with former federal judge, July 3, 2003 (Belgrade).

[64] Author interview, International Crisis Group, June 30, 2003 (Belgrade); and author interview, Helsinki Committee on Human Rights, June 30, 2003 (Belgrade).

state tolerance for illegality.[65] Retired Croatian General Martin Špegelj, who organized the initial covert acquisition of weapons from Hungary to supply the expanding Croatian police forces in 1990, claims that embargo-evading weapons smuggling after the initial stage of the defense effort degenerated into war profiteering and corruption.[66] Moreover, Croatia was the primary conduit for smuggling weapons to the Bosnian government in violation of the UN arms embargo, and it informally collected hefty transshipment fees (typically 30 percent, with payment in kind).[67] Given the state-directed nature of much of this smuggling, this had a particularly powerful criminalizing effect on state institutions such as the customs service. As a recent study of organized crime in the region describes it (Center for the Study of Democracy, 2004:73): "One of the main tasks of the Croatian customs service after its establishment was to facilitate the illegal weapons imports before and during the 1991–1995 war.... However, the "state-building" role of the smuggling networks soon transformed into criminal cooperation between organized crime and corrupt state institutions." One Croatian economist (Bičanić, 2001:169) has similarly argued that the lack of transparency in weapons purchases during the war "forged a close link between politicians, arms dealers, smugglers, and other underworld figures," and this nexus persisted throughout the decade.

There is another crucial difference between the two cases: whereas the economic sanctions dealt a crippling blow to the formal economy in the FRY, the same was not true of the arms embargo in Croatia. Unlike in the FRY, the country's aboveground trade and financial relations with the rest of the world were not pushed underground by sanctions. Consequently, a greater proportion of the population turned to the smuggling economy in the FRY than in Croatia. Further, while the harsh economic conditions under sanctions contributed to a significant exodus of the professional middle class that had been the backbone of the formal economy in the FRY, a similar exodus did not take place in Croatia. This economically driven Serbian "brain drain" was especially evident in 1993 at the height of the sanctions (Grečić, 2002).

Unlike in the FRY, a leading source of corruption in Croatia was the misappropriation of financial donations for the war effort from émigré communities abroad (Hokenos, 2003) and an ill-conceived wartime privatization process that was manipulated to reward and enrich those closest to the Tudjman regime and the ruling nationalist political party. Even under the best of conditions, privatization in transition economies can be corruption-prone. However, it is far more problematic to do this in the midst of the distractions of war where the rule of law is low and tolerance for corruption is high.[68]

Given these legacies of the 1990s, it is perhaps not surprising that the privatization agency and the customs service are viewed as Croatia's two most corrupt state institutions (Center for the Study of Democracy, 2002:54). Nevertheless, few today would disagree that the state, economy, and society in Croatia are, overall, much less criminalized than in Serbia and Montenegro. While the indicators are admittedly highly imperfect, they include much lower levels of corruption and underground economic activity (Ott, 2002).[69] Zagreb's criminal groups, while not insignificant, are a shadow of their Belgrade counterparts.[70] World Bank surveys

---

[65] Author interview with former Croatian soldier, June 28, 2002 (Zagreb). The soldier was involved in covertly importing howitzers, which he officially listed as "giraffes" on the import paperwork.

[66] Author interview with retired Croatian Army General Martin Špegelj, July 23, 2002 (Zagreb).

[67] Author interview with retired Croatian Army General Špegelj, July 23, 2002 (Zagreb), and the retired BiH Army Generals Rasim Delic, July 8, 2002 and Stjepan Šiber, July 17, 2002 (Sarajevo).

[68] Croatia apparently implemented the privatization plan despite the war conditions because of pressure from the International Monetary Fund, which agreed to formally recognize Croatia if the government pushed forward with privatization. Author interview with economist Ivo Bičanić, June 28, 2002 (Zagreb).

[69] Ott (2002:6) notes the problematic nature of corruption measurements.

[70] For comparisons between the Zagreb and Belgrade criminal groups, see the interview with Jasna Babic, author of *Zagreb Mafia*, in *Novi List*, June 28, 2003. Available at ⟨http://www.hsp1861.hr/vijesti4/030628jb.htm⟩.

have placed Croatia in the intermediate group of transition countries in terms of corruption,[71] while Serbia and Montenegro, in contrast, has been grouped amongst the most corrupt countries in the world. In 2003, Croatia ranked 59 while Serbia and Montenegro ranked 106 out of 133 countries in Transparency International's Corruption Perception Index. Interestingly, neighboring Slovenia—also a former Yugoslav republic going through a post-Communist transition process but has been least affected by sanctions and war—ranked 29th and in 2004 was admitted to the European Union.[72] Although Slovenia was already the wealthiest of the republics before Yugoslavia broke apart, avoiding the devastating effects of sanctions and prolonged war have contributed to its impressive post-Communist transition success.[73] Slovenia did play a limited support role in covertly circumventing the arms embargo, but this did not have broadly felt criminalizing consequences (in sharp contrast, for example, to the high levels of criminalization resulting from Macedonia's support role in circumventing the comprehensive sanctions on the FRY).

### Extensions Outside the Balkans: Iraq

A brief examination of the Iraq case provides additional comparative leverage and tests the applicability of the argument beyond the Balkans. The Iraqi experience in some ways parallels the FRY experience, but there are striking differences between the two cases that reveal important variation in the political economy of sanctions evasion and its aftermath. For the purposes of the argument in this article, it should be stressed that, unlike in the FRY, the comprehensive sanctions against Iraq for more than a decade took place in a non-transition and mostly non-wartime context—but still had high criminalizing effects. Thus, in addition to extending the analysis beyond the Balkans, the Iraq case helps to show how sanctions can have serious criminalizing effects largely in the absence of these other factors.

Recent and ongoing investigations have revealed that the Iraqi regime generated substantial illicit revenue by exploiting, manipulating, and evading the UN sanctions system (Coalition for International Justice, 2002). In April 2004, the U.S. General Accountability Office, the investigative arm of the U.S. Congress, calculated that Iraq illegally earned over $10 billion from oil smuggling and the systematic extortion of kickbacks from firms trading with Iraq through the UN's Oil for Food Program between 1997 and 2002 (U.S. Government Accountability Office, 2004). In October 2004, a report by the lead U.S. arms inspector provided detailed evidence showing how the Iraq regime created clandestine trade agreements and a vast international bribery network. According to the *New York Times*, the oil deals documented in the report "seem certain to spark scandals and set off investigations in a dozen countries."[74] Created in 1996, the Oil for Food Program "quickly evolved into an open bazaar of payoffs, favoritism and kickbacks."[75] The UN's former program coordinator claims that there was no self-policing of the program and that the UN chain of command was aware of the kickback scheme years before it became a public scandal but "chose to turn a blind eye."[76] Much of the funds were apparently deposited in Iraqi embassies, bank accounts, and front companies,

---

[71] See Kregar, Josip (nd) Corruption in Croatia: Risks and Actions. Available at: ⟨http://www.transparency.hr/dokumenti/tekstovi/deloitt_kregar.pdf⟩.

[72] See ⟨http://www.transparency.org/pressreleases_archive/2003/2003.10.07.cpi.en.html⟩.

[73] On Slovenia's transition process, see Ramet (1997).

[74] Shane, Scott. October 7, 2004. Report Says Iraq Misused UN Oil Plan. *New York Times*.

[75] Sachs, Susan. February 29, 2004. Hussein's Regime Skimmed Billions from Aid Program. *New York Times*. A review of remaining oil-for-food contracts revealed that 70 percent of the suppliers had agreed to pay a 10 percent kickback.

[76] Author telephone interview with Michael Soussan, former coordinator of the oil-for-food program, August 13, 2004.

and then funneled back to Iraq as cash.[77] Seven separate official inquiries have been initiated to investigate the full extent of the corruption surrounding the Oil for Food Program.[78]

An elaborate regional clandestine trading network developed in the 1990s to evade sanctions, largely involving the smuggling of oil by truck to neighboring Turkey and Jordan, by ship to Iran, and by pipeline through Syria. So much oil was being smuggled out of Iraq that the country sometimes experienced domestic fuel shortages.[79] To assist in sanctions evasion, Hussein released convicted smugglers from jail and supplied some of them with trucks and Jordanian passports. This move, Naylor (1999:320) notes, "created a *nouveau riche* class of black-marketeers beholden to the regime." As in the case of the FRY, sanctions busting in Iraq enriched a small class of politically protected "businessmen" while the traditional middle class became impoverished and marginalized. A world food program official said of the damage done by sanctions in Iraq: "If help does not come soon, the survivors will be the sanctions breakers, the black marketeers, and the thieves" (Graham, 1999:190). Similar to the FRY, those with close ties of one kind or another to the ruler had the benefits of sanctions evasion distributed to their advantage. At least one other commentator has compared Milošević and Hussein in similar terms, noting that:

> Regimes like Milošević's and Hussein's are propped up not only by official state institutions but also by sprawling and overlapping matrixes of underworld criminal groups, shadowy commercial clans and quasi-legal paramilitary units. International sanctions and embargoes like those imposed on the FRY and Iraq tend to strengthen these elements, which are adept at the smuggling and subterfuge necessary to keep the economy puttering along.[80]

Also similar to the FRY experience, the dynamics of Iraqi sanctions evasion had powerful regional repercussions. Under sanctions, relations between the Kurds and Baghdad, and between those parties and the Turks, were substantially driven by smuggling interests (Naylor, 1999:327). This was based on an informal tripartite arrangement between Baghdad officials, the Turkish military and the Kurdistan Democratic Party (which controlled the trade routes) to smuggle oil.[81] Paralleling the experience in the Balkans, even as Iraq's aboveground trade relations with its neighbors were massively disrupted by sanctions (with devastating repercussions for the legal economies of the region), underground trade linkages greatly expanded. Iraqi Vice Foreign Minister Nizar Hamdoun acknowledged in early 2001 that trading with Iraq's neighbors is "the only way we can bust the sanctions regime."[82] Thus, some reports of UN efforts to monitor Iraq's borders are reminiscent of the situation in the Balkans. For instance, the claims that "for every truck crossing the Turkish-Iraqi border that is checked by UN oil-for-food monitors, 200 pass by unchecked" and that "the same is true at other points of entry into Iraq such as Syria, Jordan, and Iran"[83] echo observations at Serbia's border crossings. At the same time, variation in the nature of supply and demand in each case (most

[77] Bone, James. April 23, 2004. Saddam, the Politicians, the Kickbacks and the $4.4 billion UN Oil-for-Food Scandal. *The Times* (London).

[78] The Biggest Scandal Ever? May 1, 2004. *Economist*, 46.

[79] Soussan, Michael. May 31, 2004. Black Gold. *The New Republic*, 42.

[80] Whitmore, Brian. May 5, 2003. Letter from Belgrade. *Nation*, Vol. 276, Issue 17. Available at ⟨http://www.thenation.com/doc.mhtml?i=20030505&s=whitmore⟩.

[81] Whitelaw, Kevin, and Strobel, Warren P. September 11, 2000. Inside Saddam's Iraq. *U.S. News and World Report*.

[82] Barr, Cameron. W. February 23, 2001. Iraq Trades its Way into the Arab Fold. *Christian Science Monitor*.

[83] Shahin, Mariam. June 2000. Where the Rich Get Poorer and the Poor Die. Middle East, No. 302, 9–11.

notably, smuggling to export rather than import oil) and the structure of sanctions enforcement efforts generated different patterns of evasion.

Another important difference is that the structure of sanctions busting in the FRY was "flatter," in that Milošević relied more on his ability to cooperate and form alliances with quasi-private criminal actors. In Iraq, reports suggest a more tightly controlled and rigidly centralized system in operation, with brutal coercive power exercised directly by Hussein and his close-knit inner circle.[84] Therefore, while Milošević oversaw "state-directed" smuggling, providing privileged access to the clandestine sanctions-busting trade, centralized control was comparatively greater in the Iraq case, with Hussein's sons Uday and Qusay playing lead roles. This is not to suggest that the regime monopolized the market and that other sanctions busters were entirely under the regime's control. But those that grew too powerful did so at great personal risk. In 1992, for instance, Hussein ordered the hanging of 42 merchants accused of profiteering.[85]

After the U.S.-led military defeat of the Iraqi regime in early 2003, the way was cleared for the lifting of sanctions. Differences between the Iraq and Yugoslav cases are most evident here. In both cases, the jolt of lifting sanctions has contributed to a realignment of winners and losers in the political economy of the region. The basic difference is that, for the FRY, an important part of the criminalized legacy of the sanctions has been the degree of institutionalization of the Milošević-era sanctions-busting networks. For Iraq, almost the opposite problem has emerged: a vacuum created by the apparent destruction of previously dominant institutions.

Some remnants of the old Iraqi sanctions-busting system nevertheless remain in the absence of direct state sponsorship. A fact-finding mission of the UN Office on Drugs and Crime warned in August 2003 that "The evolving nature of organized crime in Iraq is based on sophisticated smuggling networks, many established under the previous regime to circumvent UN sanctions."[86] Targeted or repeated looting also points to the potential influence of highly organized smugglers (nowhere more evident than in the quick looting of the Iraq national museum during the fall of Baghdad). In the case of oil, some reports indicate that the system of organized smuggling under sanctions has largely been dismantled, with those involved at the lower level looking for alternative work.[87] But oil smuggling has continued in some places, such as in the small river port of Abu Fulus—a favorite place for sanctions busting during the Hussein regime.[88]

Although understandably difficult to measure, the tolerance of widespread corruption in Iraqi society encouraged under the sanctions conditions has very much persisted into the post-sanctions era. As described by the *Financial Times*:

> When UN sanctions were imposed on Saddam Hussein's regime after his invasion of Kuwait in 1990, the former Iraqi leader instructed ministries to fend for themselves. As they sought their own sources of financing, they created a web of corruption that spread throughout society. . ... Most Iraqis earning a few dollars a month in salary started to look for other, illegal sources of income. Theft became widespread and bribes became a part of the daily struggle for survival. Mr. Hussein's late son Uday led the way, acting as the godfather of the smuggling networks that circumvented the UN sanctions and fed the coffers of the regime. Now, as the U.S. battles to stem the deterioration of postwar Iraq and restore a semblance of security, this pervasive culture of corruption is emerging as one of the main obstacles to stability.[89]

---

[84] McGeary, Johanna et al. May 13, 2002. Inside Saddam's World. *Time* (European edition), 24.

[85] They had been tied to poles in public with signs that read, "We are bloodsuckers." Coughlin, Con. Jan/Feb 2003. The Savage Sunset of Saddam Hussein. *American Spectator*, 46.

[86] UN Warns of Organized Crime Threat in Post-War Iraq. August 27, 2003. *Deutsche Presse-Agentur*.

[87] Goodman, Peter. S. May 7, 2003. Iraqi Oil Smugglers Eluded U.S. Patrols. *Washington Post*.

[88] Andrews, Edmund. L. June 23, 2003. After the War: Economy. *New York Times*.

[89] Khalaf, Roula. May 22, 2004. Even the Anti-Corruption Investigators are on the Make. *Financial Times*, 7.

Nevertheless, if the main pillars of Hussein's sanctions evasion infrastructure have indeed been removed along with the regime, the longer-term criminalizing effects of sanctions should be less evident and less consequential than in the FRY case. In the FRY, the architecture of the Milošević regime has undergone much more modest change,[90] and most of the country's new economic elites were leading beneficiaries of sanctions busting. In Iraq, a more profound realignment of political-economic power has taken place, with those privileged by the regime and given preferential access to sanctions evasion profits now marginalized.

## Conclusions

Tracing the criminalizing consequences of sanctions contributes to the larger effort to broaden the sanctions debate and better understand the effects of sanctions across time and place. It also helps to include sanctions evasion within the broader study of transnational crime and the illicit side of the global economy, which have been substantially neglected by international relations scholars (Friman and Andreas, 1999; Andreas, 2004b). Placing the unintended criminalizing effects of sanctions and their legacy front and center in the analysis highlights dynamics that are typically missing or under-explored in the scholarly literature and policy debates on sanctions. Although it is often recognized that sanctions are undermined by circumvention, too rarely are the political, economic, and societal criminalizing consequences fully acknowledged and critically evaluated.

Bridging the study of sanctions and transnational crime, I have developed an analytical framework (summarized in Table 1) identifying and classifying the potential domestic and regional criminalizing effects of sanctions, both during and after sanctions, and evaluated these effects through a detailed examination of the FRY case with some limited secondary case comparisons. The experience of sanctions evasion in the FRY closely fits the patterns of political, economic, and societal criminalization identified and categorized in Table 1, while the secondary cases fit to varying degrees.

In Croatia, the presence of the arms embargo but the absence of comprehensive sanctions meant that criminalizing effects were substantial but more muted and narrowly confined than in the case of the FRY. During the sanctions period, the Iraq case largely confirms the patterns of criminalization identified in Table 1, but the specific mode of regime change (external military invasion and occupation) has both limited and made it more difficult to identify the criminalized legacy in the post-sanctions period. The more delayed and less dramatic mode of regime change in the FRY, in contrast, has made the criminalized residue of sanctions more durable and evident (although the more time passes, the more difficult it is to clearly attribute what aspects of criminalization reflect the legacy of sanctions). Both the FRY and Croatia experienced prolonged war conditions and the difficulties of the post-Communist transition process, but the fact that criminalization has been both deeper and more widespread in the FRY—which, unlike Croatia, faced comprehensive economic sanctions—suggests that sanctions have independent causal importance. If prolonged war were a more important variable, one may expect to see more criminalization in Croatia than in the FRY, given that Croatian territory was more affected by war (armed conflict never directly took place on Serbian territory, while about one-third of Croatia was militarily contested). As expected, levels of criminalization are lowest in Slovenia, the former Yugoslav republic that was the least affected by war and sanctions. The Iraq case provides additional comparative evidence for the independent causal significance of comprehensive sanctions, given

---

[90] According to a 2004 International Crisis Group report (2004:i–ii): "Milošević era structures and personnel are still relatively intact in the judiciary, police, army and other key institutions."

that sanctions had high criminalizing effects in a non-transition country during a largely non-war period. These case variations are outlined in Table 2.

Although a case study has inherent explanatory limitations, it nevertheless offers some important general lessons that are relevant to the broader sanctions debate. First, moving beyond asking whether sanctions work and assessing their humanitarian consequences, the evidence presented in this article suggests the utility of bringing a more criminological perspective to the study of sanctions. Sanctions reflect an effort to manipulate the vulnerabilities that come from economic interdependence, but sanctions can unintentionally foster clandestine forms of interdependence that enable adaptation and evasion. As we have seen in the FRY case, sanctions can create incentives and opportunities for the targeted regime to co-opt, empower, and ally with those local and transnational actors that have the greatest connections and skills in smuggling. Although underground economies are typically thought of as operating outside of state controls, the dynamics of sanctions evasion traced in this article reveal the extent to which underground economic activity can be state sponsored and organized.

This article also points to the importance of geographically extending the focus of analysis to include an evaluation of the criminalizing repercussions of sanctions for neighboring countries. The typical focus in the sanctions literature on "senders" and "targets" pays far too little attention to third parties and the regional context within which sanctions take place.[91] As we have seen, the criminalizing consequences of sanctions can have significant regional ripple effects. Equally important, just as the analysis of sanctions should be extended geographically for a region-wide perspective, it should also be extended temporally. It is striking that the sanctions debate has so little to say about the aftermath and legacy of sanctions, including the criminalized residue that may be left over from sanctions. For example, the European Union now considers Serbia and Montenegro as an organized crime gateway to Western Europe. The imposition of comprehensive sanctions by the international community unintentionally encouraged much closer state-criminal ties and large-scale smuggling, and now in the post-sanctions period, the international community has blamed organized crime and corruption for blocking much needed reforms. Rarely is there any Western acknowledgment of having contributed to the problem in the first place. A notable exception is the notes of a Stockholm Process Working Group (2002): "Regarding measures for dealing with those who have enriched themselves under sanctions and who continue to present obstacles to reform in Serbia, the international community should consider working with the Serbian government to create a "cordon sanitaire" around the most important offenders." The Working Group also observed that "patterns of smuggling and unofficial economic activity" originating in sanctions busting have now "made it extremely difficult for the new government to collect taxes."

Some might be tempted to conclude that the main lesson to be learned from these patterns of sanctions evasion is the need to bolster the UN's enforcement capacity. Cortright and Lopez (2000:5) echo the common view that the UN system "lacks the ability to administer sanctions." But while there is certainly much truth in this claim, they also consider the FRY sanctions case to be a rare model of high enforcement capacity and effectiveness, describing it as the most rigorous implementation effort ever attempted in the history of sanctions. Thus, unfortunately, if the experience in the FRY is any indicator, more rigorous sanctions enforcement runs the risk of unintentionally exacerbating the criminalizing consequences of sanctions without necessarily making sanctions much less porous. Further tightening the sanctions net around a targeted country may simply push out small-time freelance operators while further inflating profits and enhancing market position

---

[91] But see Doxey (2002), Khadiagla (1999), Romaniuk (2003), and Rowe (2001).

for the most sophisticated and well-organized smugglers. It may also geographically spread the sanctions evasion problem, as enforcement pressure in one area leads to more evasion elsewhere. Some of these dynamics have long been evident in law enforcement efforts to curb other market-driven transnational crimes such as drug trafficking and migrant smuggling. In this regard, sanctions enforcement and sanctions evasion should be viewed as part of the much broader set of interactions between transnational crime and crime control (Andreas, 1998).

Drawing greater attention to the negative criminalizing side effects of sanctions does not imply that sanctions should never be used, or that concerns over criminalization should trump all other considerations. However, it does suggest that this concern should be brought more centrally into the design, implementation, and evaluation of sanctions. Largely in response to the experiences of the 1990s in places such as the FRY and Iraq, there has been a push in recent years to fine-tune and more sharply focus sanctions to reduce their negative consequences. The findings in this article suggest that this reassessment and retooling of sanctions mechanisms should also include more self-conscious efforts to minimize the criminalizing effects of sanctions. In this regard, it should be stressed that comprehensive sanctions are likely to generate much more criminalized collateral damage than more narrowly and selectively targeted sanctions. As Mack and Khan (2004:117) point out, "In denying target regimes the black-market opportunities provided by comprehensive sanctions, smart sanctions reduce perverse incentives for elite members to benefit from sanctions."

Targeted sanctions such as aviation bans, travel bans for regime members and their families and close associates, freezing of personal overseas assets of regime leaders, and diplomatic isolation and denial of accreditation are far less likely to have serious criminalizing effects. Even in those cases involving black-market substitution (such as using fraudulent documents in response to a travel ban), this does not have broad criminalizing repercussions. At the same time, it should be recognized that some targeted sanctions have more criminalizing repercussions than others. And indeed, some targeted sanctions—particularly commodity sanctions such as arms embargoes [92] (as we have seen in the case of Croatia)—can still have enormous criminalizing consequences, even if less so than the comprehensive sanctions applied in cases such as the FRY and Iraq.

## References

ANDREAS, P. (1998) Smuggling Wars: Law Enforcement and Law Evasion in a Changing World. *Transnational Organized Crime* **4**:75–90.

ANDREAS, P. (2004a) The Clandestine Political Economy of War and Peace in Bosnia. *International Studies Quarterly* **48**:29–51.

ANDREAS, P. (2004b) Illicit International Political Economy: The Clandestine Side of Globalization. *Review of International Political Economy* **11**:634–645.

ANTIĆ, S. (1998) "Sankcije i Ekonomska Politika (Sanctions & Economic Politics)." In *Ekonomske Sankcije UN: Uporedna Analiza i Slucaj Jugoslavije (UN Economic Sanctions: A Comparative Analysis and the Case of Yugoslavia)*, edited by M. Prokopijevic and J. Teokarovic. Beograd: Institut za Evropske Studije.

ANTONIĆ, S. (2002) *Zarobljena Zemlja: Srbija za Vlade Slobodana Miloševica (A Captive Country: Serbia Under the Rule of Slobodan Milošević)*. Beograd: Otkrovenje.

BABIĆ, S. (2000) "The Political Economy of Adjustment to Sanctions: The Case of Serbia." *Medunarodni Odnosi* 2, np. Available at ⟨http://www.geocities.com/CapitolHill/Parliament/6682/babic.html⟩.

---

[92] This is recognized in the Stockholm report (Wallensteen et al., 2003:105): "Targeted actors frequently evade arms sanctions by turning to criminal networks or enlisting the services of organized or transnational criminal groups."

BEGOVIĆ, B., B. MIJATEYIĆ, R. SEPI, M. VASOVIĆ, AND S. VUKOVIĆ (2001) *Corruption in the Customs: Combating Corruption at the Customs Administration.* Belgrade: Center for Liberal-Democratic Studies.

BIČANIĆ, I. (2001) Croatia. *Journal of Southeast European Politics and Black Sea Studies (Special Issue: Balkan Reconstruction)* 1:158–173.

BROOKS, R. A. (2002) Sanctions and Regime Type: What Works, and When? *Security Studies* 11:1–50.

CENTER FOR THE STUDY OF DEMOCRACY (2002) *Anti-Corruption in Southeast Europe: First Steps and Policies.* Sofia: Center for the Study of Democracy.

CENTER FOR THE STUDY OF DEMOCRACY (2004) *Partners in Crime: The Risks of Symbiosis Between the Security Sector and Organized Crime in Southeast Europe.* Sofia: Center for the Study of Democracy.

COALITION FOR INTERNATIONAL JUSTICE (2002) *Sources of Revenue for Saddam & Sons: A Primer on the Financial Underpinnings of the Regime in Baghdad.* Washington, DC: Coalition for International Justice.

COHEN, R. (1998) *Hearts Grown Brutal.* New York: Random House.

COSGROVE, E. (2002) "The Efficacy of Sanctions." International Security Policy Paper No. 82. Available at: ⟨http://www.isisuk.demon.co.uk/0811/isis/uk/regpapers/no82_paper.html⟩.

CORTRIGHT, D., AND G. A. LOPEZ (2000) *The Sanctions Decade: Assessing UN Strategies in the 1990s.* Boulder: Lynne Rienner.

CRAWFORD, N. C., AND A. KLOTZ (1999) "How Sanctions Work: A Framework for Analysis." In *How Sanctions Work: Lessons from South Africa*, edited by N. C. Crawford and A. Klotz. New York: St. Martin's Press.

DADAK, C. (2003) The 1992–1996 Trade Data Puzzle: A Case of Sanctions Breaking. *Cato Journal* 22:511–532.

DINKIĆ, M. (1995) *The Economics of Destruction.* Beograd: Video Nedeljnik.

DOXEY, M. P. (2002) "United Nations Economic Sanctions: Minimizing Adverse Effects on Nontarget States." In *Smart Sanctions: Targeting Economic Statecraft*, edited by D. Cortright and G. A. Lopez. Lanham, MD: Rowman & Littlefield.

FRIMAN, H. R., AND P. ANDREAS EDS. (1999) *The Illicit Global Economy and State Power.* Lanham, MD: Rowinan and Littlefield.

GAGNON, V. P. (1994) Ethnic Nationalism and International Conflict: The Case of Serbia. *International Security* 19:130–166.

GALTUNG, J. (1967) On the Effects of International Sanctions. *World Politics* 3:378–416.

GARFIELD, R. (2001) *Economic Sanctions, Health, and Welfare in the Federal Republic of Yugoslavia, 1990–2000.* Belgrade: OCHA/UNICEF.

GRAHAM, B. S. (1999) *Sanctioning Saddam: The Politics of Intervention in Iraq.* New York: St. Martin's Press.

GREČIĆ, V. (2002) The Role of Migrant Professionals in the Process of Transition in Yugoslavia. *International Problems* 3. Available at ⟨http://www.diplomacy.bg.ac.yu/mpro2002.htm⟩.

HAJDINJAK, M. (2002) *Smuggling in Southeast Europe: The Yugoslav Wars and the Development of Regional Criminal Networks in the Balkans.* Sofia: Center for the Study of Democracy.

HISLOPE, R. (2003) "Political Corruption and Interethnic Coalitions: The Crisis in Macedonia." Paper Presented at the Watson Institute for International Studies, Brown University, May 6, 2003.

HOKENOS, P. (2003) *Homeland Calling: Exile Patriotism and the Balkan Wars.* Ithaca: Cornell University Press.

INTERNATIONAL CRISIS GROUP (May 2, 2000) *Serbia's Grain Trade: Milošević's Hidden Cash Crop.* ICG Balkans Report No. 93.

INTERNATIONAL CRISIS GROUP (July 17, 2003) *Serbian Reform Stalls Again.* ICG Balkans Report No. 145.

INTERNATIONAL CRISIS GROUP (March 26, 2004) *Serbia's U-Turn.* ICG Europe Report No. 154.

JUDAH, T. (2000) *The Serbs.* New Haven: Yale University Press.

KHADIAGLA, G. M. (1999) ""Regional Dimensions of Sanctions," in Crawford and Klotz." In *How Sanctions Work: Lessons from South Africa*, edited by N. C. Crawford and A. Klotz. New York: St. Martin's Press.

KIRSHNER, J. J. (1997) The Microfoundations of Economic Sanctions. *Security Studies* 6:32–64.

LICHT, S. (1995) "The Use of Sanctions in the Former Yugoslavia." In *Economic Sanctions: Panacea or Peace Building in a Post-Cold War World?*, edited by D. Cortright and G. A. Lopez. Boulder: Westview Press.

MACK, A., AND A. KHAN (2004) "UN Sanctions: A Glass Half Full?" In *The United Nations and Global Security*, edited by R. M. Price and M. W. Zacher. London: Palgrave/MacMillan.

MICHAS, T. (2002) *Unholy Alliance: Greece and Milošević's Serbia.* College Station, TX: Texas A&M University Press.

MIJATOVIĆ, B. (1998) "O Politickom i Ekonomskom Aspektu Sankcija (Of Political and Economic Aspect of the Sanctions)." In *Ekonomske Sankcije UN: Uporedna Analiza i Slucaj Jugoslavije (UN*

*Economic Sanctions: A Comparative Analysis and the Case of Yugoslavia*), edited by M. Prokopijević and J. Teokarović. Beograd: Institut za Evropske Studije.

MINIĆ, J. (1993) The Black Economy in Serbia: Transition from Socialism? *RFE/RL Research Report* **2**:6.

MUELLER, J. (2001) *The Remnants of War*. Ithaca: Cornell University Press.

NATIONAL SECURITY COUNCIL (2000) *International Crime Threat Assessment*. Washington, DC: White House.

NAYLOR, R. T. (1999) *Patriots and Profiteers: On Economic Warfare, Embargo Busting and State-Sponsored Crime*. Toronto: McLelland and Stewart Inc.

OTT, K. (2002) *The Underground Economy in Croatia*. Occasional Paper No. 12. Zagreb: Institute of Public Finance

POPOVSKI, V. (2002) The UN Security Council Approach to the Conflicts in the Former Yugoslavia. *Journal of Southeast European and Black Sea Studies* **2**:39–62.

RAMET, S. P. (1997) "Democratization in Slovenia—The Second Stage." In *Politics, Power, and the Struggle for Democracy in South-East Europe*, edited by K. Dawisha and B. Parrott. Cambridge: Cambridge University Press.

ROMANIUK, P. (2003) "Beyond Senders and Targets: The Enforcement of Multilateral Sanctions." Paper Prepared for the International Studies Association annual Conference, February 26–March 1, 2003, Portland, OR.

RON, J. (2000) Boundaries and Violence: Patterns of State Action along the Bosnia–Yugoslavia Divide. *Theory and Society* **29**:609–647.

ROWE, D. M. (2001) *Manipulating the Market: Understanding Economic Sanctions, Institutional Change, and the Political Unity of White Rhodesia*. Ann Arbor: University of Michigan Press.

SELDEN, Z. (1999) *Economic Sanctions as Instruments of American Foreign Policy*. Westport: Praeger.

STOCKHOLM PROCESS WORKING GROUP No. 3 (July 15, 2002, published August 12, 2002) Notes from the Meeting with Experts in Brussels. Available at: ⟨http://www.smartsanctions.se/stockholm_process/reports/Brussels_rep1.htm⟩.

STRAZZARI, F. (2003) "Between Ethnic Collision and Mafia Collusion: The Balkan Road to State Making." In *Shadow Globalization, Ethnic Conflict and New Wars*, edited by D. Jung. London: Routledge.

TORKILDSEN, M. (2002) "Amended Expert Report Prepared for the ICTY, Case No. IT-02-54-T." Available at: ⟨http://hague.bard.edu/reports/Torkildsen_financing.pdf⟩.

UNITED NATIONS SECURITY COUNCIL (1996) "Report of the Round Table on United Nations Sanctions in the Case of the Former Yugoslavia (Copenhagen)." Available at: ⟨http://www.un.org/sc/committees/sanctions/s96776.pdf⟩.

UNITED NATIONS, SECURITY COUNCIL COMMISSION OF EXPERTS (1994) *Final Report of the United Nations Commission of Experts Established Pursuant to Security Council Resolution 780 (1992) (Annex III.A. Special Forces)*. Available at: ⟨http://www.ess.uwe.ac.uk/comexpert/ANX/⟩.

UNITED STATES DEPARTMENT OF STATE, INTER-AGENCY TASK FORCE ON SERBIAN SANCTIONS (1996) *UN Sanctions Against Belgrade: Lessons Learned for Future Regimes*. Washington, DC: U.S. Government Printing Office.

UNITED STATES GOVERNMENT ACCOUNTABILITY OFFICE (April 7, 2004) Testimony of Joseph Christoff, before the Committee on Foreign Relations, U.S. Senate.

UNITED STATES INSTITUTE OF PEACE (March 15, 2002) *Special Report No. 84: Serbia Still at the Crossroads*. Washington, D.C.: United States Institute of Peace.

VASILIJEVIĆ, V. A. (1995) "Epilogue." In *Kriminal Koji Je Izmenio Srbiju (The Crime which Changed Serbia)*, 2nd ed., edited by A. Knežević and V. Tufegdžić. Beograd: Radio B-92.

VASOVIĆ, M. (2000) "Survey report, Part IV (Citizens Moral Position and Accounts of the Social Anomic Condition)." In *Korupcija i Podmićivanje: Pogled iz Ugla Javnog Mnenja Srbije (Corruption and Bribery: How Serbian Public Opinion Sees Corruption)*, edited by Center for Policy Studies, Public Opinion Survey Report (Serbian language version). Belgrade: Center for Policy Studies. Available at: ⟨http://www.cpa-cps.org.yu/cpa-cps/cpa/index_html⟩.

WALLENSTEEN, P. (2002) "A Century of Economic Sanctions: A Field Revisited." Uppsala Peace Research Papers, No. 1. Uppsala: Uppsala University, Department of Peace and Conflict Research.

WALLENSTEEN, P., C. STAIBANO, AND M. ERIKSSON, eds. (2003) *Making Targeted Sanctions Effective: Guidelines for the Implementation of UN Policy Options*. Uppsala: Uppsala University, Department of Peace and Conflict Research.

WOODWARD, S. (1995) *Balkan Tragedy: Chaos and Dissolution after the Cold War*. Washington, DC: Brookings Institution.

# [24]

FINANCIAL CONTROLS AND COUNTER-PROLIFERATION OF WEAPONS
OF MASS DESTRUCTION

*Nikos Passas**

*This paper focuses on financial controls and vigilance against the proliferation of Weapons of Mass Destruction (WMD). It refers to the new Financial Action task Force (FATF) Recommendations on this subject and outlines relevant provisions of the U.N. Security Council Resolutions (UNSCRs) and the considerable challenges facing the international community in their implementation. While it suggests that there is a good deal of work underway towards consistent and effective implementation, it points to some concrete measures and areas where counter-proliferation finance efforts could focus, particularly in the area of commerce and trade.*

## I. INTRODUCTION

Neither the use of financial sanctions as a tool to apply pressure on governments nor controversies and diverse interpretations of their effects are new. An early example from classical Greece is the Megarian Decree, under which Athens introduced a trade embargo on Megara merchants during the Pericles era.[1] Aristophanes,[2] Thucydides[3] and others[4] offered

---

\*   Nikos Passas is a Professor at Northeastern University. His law degree is from the University of Athens, his Master's from the University of Paris II, and his Ph.D. from the University of Edinburgh. He is a member of the Athens Bar. Passas is fluent in six languages and specializes in the study of corruption, terrorism, money laundering, illicit flows, informal fund transfers, white-collar crime, targeted sanctions, organized crime and international crimes. He has more than 140 publications in thirteen languages. Passas offers public and private sector training, serves as an expert witness and consults with law firms, financial institutions, international organizations and government agencies on all continents. He serves as the Editor-in-Chief of *Crime, Law and Social Change: An International Journal*, and as an associate editor in several others. He is a member of the Board of Directors of the International Society of Criminology.

[1]   Carl A. Alex, Updating Economic Operations in the Post Industrial Age (March 1998) (unpublished Master of Science in Defense Analysis thesis, Naval Postgraduate School), *available at* http://www.dtic.mil/cgi-bin/GetTRDoc?AD=ADA343821.

very different views: some suggested that it was effective, while Thucydides regarded it as a pretext for the war that followed.

The U.N. first introduced sanctions in the 1920s, but it employed them seldom in the years that followed. It was the 1990s that witnessed a significant growth in the use of such coercive measures.[5] Aimed at global security threats in ways that could be effective but less radical than the use of force,[6] their scope has widened, ranging from aggression and conflict to international terrorism and proliferation of weapons of mass destruction (WMD).[7] Multilateral sanctions have been considered and applied due to proliferation concerns in several countries,[8] but the most recent ones focus on non-state actors, the Islamic Republic of Iran, and the Democratic People's Republic of Korea (DPRK).[9] Originally, counter-proliferation measures revolved chiefly around export controls, but these are now supplemented by financial control requirements for both governmental and private sector actors.

At the same time, "follow-the-money" approaches to crime control have been applied at both the national and international levels.[10] Financial

---

[2]   ARISTOPHANES, THE ACHARNIANS (S. Douglas Olson ed., 2002).

[3]   THUCYDIDES, HISTORY OF THE PELOPONNESIAN WAR (Richard Crawley trans., 1903).

[4]   Jona Lendering, *Megarian Decree*, LIVIUS.ORG, http://www.livius.org/mea-mem /megara/decree.html (last updated Mar. 31, 2006); James McDonald, *Supplementing Thucydides' Account of the Megarian Decree*, 2 ELECTRONIC ANTIQUITY, no. 3 1994, http://scholar. lib.vt.edu/ejournals/ElAnt/V2N3/mcdonald.html.

[5]   ENRICO CARISCH & LORAINE RICKARD-MARTIN, GLOBAL THREATS AND THE ROLE OF UNITED NATIONS SANCTIONS 2 (2011); *see also* GEORGE A. LOPEZ & DAVID CORTRIGHT, THE SANCTIONS DECADE: ASSESSING UN STRATEGIES IN THE 1990s (2000).

[6]   *See* GARY CLYDE HUFBAUER, ECONOMIC SANCTIONS RECONSIDERED (3d ed. 2007); PETER WALLENSTEEN & CARINA STAIBANO, INTERNATIONAL SANCTIONS: BETWEEN WORDS AND WARS IN THE GLOBAL SYSTEM (2005).

[7]   CARISCH & RICKARD-MARTIN, *supra* note 5, at 3.

[8]   *See* BERNARD SITT ET AL., SANCTIONS AND WEAPONS OF MASS DESTRUCTION IN INTERNATIONAL RELATIONS 28 (2010) (noting that suspected WMD-producing states such as the Islamic Republic of Iran, Syria and the Democratic People's Republic of Korea are among the states targeted by WMD-related sanctions).

[9]   NIKOS PASSAS, IAN ANTHONY, GENEVIEVE DEANAZ & JANET WALKER, PREVENTION OF CBRN ILLICIT TRAFFICKING AND DECEPTIVE FINANCIAL PRACTICES: REPORT TO THE COMMISSION OF THE EUROPEAN UNION (2010).

[10]   This has been marked by differing degrees of success and heated debates among observers, such as JEFF BREINHOLT, TAXING TERRORISM FROM AL CAPONE TO AL QAIDA: FIGHTING VIOLENCE THROUGH FINANCIAL REGULATION 1 (2005) (discussing the importance of follow the money methods as counterterrorism strategy); Nikos Passas, *Terrorism Financing Mechanisms and Policy Dilemmas*, in TERRORISM FINANCING AND STATE RESPONSES: A COMPARATIVE PERSPECTIVE 21–38 (Jeanne K. Giraldo & Harold A. Trinkunas eds., 2007) (arguing for a better balance of the costs and benefits of certain "follow the money" strategies); PETER REUTER & EDWIN M. TRUMAN, CHASING DIRTY MONEY 73 (2004) (suggesting that technological developments promote follow the money methods); Michael Levi & Peter

controls have been increasingly employed to address serious crime and security problems ranging from organized criminal group activities to corruption and the support of terrorism. These can be used for investigative and intelligence-gathering objectives—they assist in identifying co-conspirators, facilitators, and supporters—as well as for deterrence, disruption, punishment and confiscation purposes. The most recent addition to the list of unlawful practices targeted with this approach is the financing of WMD proliferation. In February 2012, the Financial Action Task Force (FATF), a body setting international standards on money laundering and terrorism finance, revised its Recommendations and incorporated the issue of proliferation finance.[11] New Recommendation 7 is entitled "Targeted financial sanctions related to proliferation" and states that:

> Countries should implement targeted financial sanctions to comply with United Nations Security Council resolutions relating to the prevention, suppression and disruption of proliferation of weapons of mass destruction and its financing. These resolutions require countries to freeze without delay the funds or other assets of, and to ensure that no funds and other assets are made available, directly or indirectly, to or for the benefit of, any person or entity designated by, or under the authority of, the United Nations Security Council under Chapter VII of the Charter of the United Nations.[12]

There is no legal and universally adopted definition of "proliferation finance." However, the FATF's working definition can be used for our purposes here:

> Proliferation finance refers to the act of providing funds or financial services which are used, in whole or in part, for the manufacture, acquisition, possession, development, export, trans-shipment, brokering, transport, transfer, stockpiling or use of nuclear, chemical or biological weapons and their means of delivery and related materials (including both technologies and dual use goods used for non-legitimate purposes), in

---

Reuter, *Money Laundering*, 34 CRIME & JUST. 289, 294 (2006) ("[T]he [anti-money laundering] regime does facilitate investigation and prosecution of some criminal participants who would otherwise evade justice, but fewer than expected and hoped for by advocates of 'follow the money' methods."); R.T. NAYLOR, SATANIC PURSES: MONEY, MYTH, AND MISINFORMATION IN THE WAR ON TERROR (criticizing measures imposed by the Patriot Act to facilitate follow the money strategies) (2008), *and* J.C. SHARMAN, THE MONEY LAUNDRY: REGULATING CRIMINAL FINANCE IN THE GLOBAL ECONOMY 71 (2011) (arguing that the ability to obscure transactions defeats follow the money efforts).

[11] *See* FINANCIAL ACTION TASK FORCE [FATF], INTERNATIONAL STANDARDS ON COMBATING MONEY LAUNDERING AND THE FINANCING OF TERRORISM AND PROLIFERATION: THE FATF RECOMMENDATIONS 47 (2012) (noting the new focus on proliferation financing in these Recommendations).

[12] *Id.* at 13.

contravention of national laws or, where applicable, international obligations.[13]

This paper focuses on proliferation finance, outlines relevant provisions of the U.N. Security Council Resolutions (UNSCRs) and the challenges facing the international community in their implementation. While it suggests that there is a good deal of work towards consistent and effective implementation, it points to some concrete measures and areas where counter-proliferation finance efforts could focus.[14]

## II. U.N. SECURITY COUNCIL RESOLUTIONS AND PROLIFERATION FINANCE

Chapter VII of the U.N. Charter provides that when the Security Council establishes a threat or breach of the peace or acts of aggression, it has the power to introduce measures ranging from "provisional measures" to the use of force.[15] Article 41 lays down the legal basis on which sanctions can be applied:

> The Security Council may decide what measures not involving the use of armed force are to be employed to give effect to its decisions, and it may call upon the Members of the United Nations to apply such measures. These may include complete or partial interruption of economic relations and of rail, sea, air, postal, telegraphic, radio, and other means of communication, and the severance of diplomatic relations.[16]

The obligations stemming from Resolutions issued under Chapter VII of the U.N. Charter are generally mandatory. Yet, room for interpretation exists in the language of some provisions. For instance, when the Resolutions state that Security Council "decides" or that Member States "shall" do something, there is no debate about their mandatory nature. However, when Member States are "called upon" to take certain measures,

---

[13]  FATF, COMBATING PROLIFERATION FINANCING: A STATUS REPORT ON POLICY DEVELOPMENT AND CONSULTATION (2010).

[14]  The paper draws largely on work I conducted while I was privileged to be part of a study team that produced a report for the Commission of the European Union, titled PREVENTION OF CBRN ILLICIT TRAFFICKING AND DECEPTIVE FINANCIAL PRACTICES. PASSAS ET AL., *supra* note 9.

[15]  U.N. Charter arts. 39–42.

[16]  U.N. Charter art. 41.

> The Security Council may decide what measures not involving the use of armed force are to be employed to give effect to its decisions, and it may call upon the Members of the United Nations to apply such measures. These may include complete or partial interruption of economic relations and of rail, sea, air, postal, telegraphic, radio, and other means of communication, and the severance of diplomatic relations.

*Id.*

some argue that these provisions are not mandatory, while others believe that they are mandatory nonetheless. Such diverse interpretations obviously affect different countries' implementation and practices.

The international community has reached a broad consensus on the need to prevent WMD proliferation, but the use of financial controls to this effect is novel to both government agencies and the private sector. How exactly the new counter-proliferation tools can be integrated with or supplement more traditional controls is not entirely clear—even in countries strongly supportive of the new measures.

It is important to clarify what sort of measures are provided for by the various UNSCRs. The UNSCRs most relevant to a review of financial vigilance measures are:

- 1540, 1673, 1810, 1887, 1977 on non-state actor proliferation;
- 1695, 1718, 1874 on DPRK; and
- 1696, 1737, 1747, 1803, and 1929 on Iran.

These Resolutions establish Committees and occasionally Expert Groups in order to support and monitor their implementation. Their measures cover not only export- and border-control issues, but also:

- financial controls and vigilance;
- activity-based financial prohibitions;
- specific vigilance measures and actions on designated banks;
- freezing of assets;
- international cooperation and information sharing; and
- financial and technical assistance.

Resolution 1540 requires that States refrain from supporting by any means non-State actors from developing, acquiring, manufacturing, possessing, transporting, transferring or using nuclear, chemical or biological weapons and their delivery systems.[17] The Resolution obliges States to establish domestic controls to prevent the proliferation of nuclear, chemical and biological weapons, and their means of delivery, including by establishing appropriate controls over related materials.[18]

It also mandates that States:

[A]dopt and enforce appropriate effective laws which prohibit any non-State actor to manufacture, acquire, possess, develop, transport, transfer or use nuclear, chemical or biological weapons and their means of delivery, in particular for terrorist purposes, as well as attempts to engage

---

[17] S.C. Res. 1540, ¶ 1, U.N. Doc. S/RES/1540 (Apr. 28, 2004).

[18] *Id.* ¶ 3.

in any of the foregoing activities, participate in them as an accomplice, assist or finance them.[19]

Subsequently, the Security Council stressed the need for work under this and successor Resolutions to be coordinated with that of Committees operating under counter-terrorism Resolutions. Thus, UNSCR 1810 urged the enhanced cooperation "between the 1540 Committee, the Security Council Committee established pursuant to resolution 1267 (1999), concerning Al-Qaida and the Taliban, and the Security Council Committee established pursuant to resolution 1373 (2001) . . . ."[20]

With respect to Iran, UNSCR 1737 (2006) and subsequent Resolutions, the Security Council has adopted measures that include:

- An embargo on providing to Iran proliferation-sensitive nuclear and ballistic missile-related items listed in the main text or in annexes;[21]

- A ban on the procurement of any arms and related materiel from Iran and a ban on the supply of seven categories of conventional weapons and related materiel to Iran;[22]

- A travel ban and an assets freeze on specific persons and entities listed in annexes. This assets freeze also applies to any individuals or entities acting on behalf of, or at the direction of, the designated persons and entities, and to entities owned or controlled by them.[23]

The UNSCR financial measures regarding Iran are more specific than those relative to non-state actors. Some are broad-based and preventive in nature, but they contain specific and targeted sanctions as well. They also refer to obligations of both governments and financial institutions.

UNSCR 1737 contains several financial measures. Among other things, it requires that all States:

> [S]hall . . . take the necessary measures to prevent the provision to Iran of any technical assistance or training, financial assistance, investment, brokering or other services, and the transfer of financial resources or services, related to the supply, sale, transfer, manufacture or use of the prohibited items, materials, equipment, goods and technology specified [in paragraphs 3 and 4].[24]

It further mandates that all States:

---

[19]   *Id.* ¶ 2.

[20]   S.C. Res. 1810, ¶ 12, U.N. Doc. S/RES/1810 (Apr. 25, 2008).

[21]   S.C. Res. 1737, ¶ 3, U.N. Doc. S/RES/1737 (Dec. 23, 2006).

[22]   S.C. Res. 1747, ¶¶ 5–6, U.N. Doc. S/RES/1747 (Mar. 24, 2007).

[23]   S.C. Res. 1737, *supra* note 21, ¶¶ 10, 12.

[24]   *Id.* ¶ 6.

[S]hall freeze the funds, other financial assets and economic resources which are on their territories at the date of adoption of this resolution or at any time thereafter, that are owned or controlled by the persons or entities designated in the Annex, as well as those of additional persons or entities designated by the Security Council or by the Committee as being engaged in, directly associated with or providing support for Iran's proliferation sensitive nuclear activities or the development of nuclear weapon delivery systems, or by persons or entities acting on their behalf or at their direction, or by entities owned or controlled by them, including through illicit means . . . .[25]

UNSCR 1803 introduced provisions that applied the measures of Paragraph 12 of UNSCR 1737 to expanded lists of persons and entities and increasingly called for vigilance over all trade and finance—as well as financial institutions—to prevent any support to Iran's nuclear proliferation activities.[26] It also focused on financial institutions and two specific Iranian banks by:

*Call[ing] upon* all States to exercise vigilance over the activities of financial institutions in their territories with all banks domiciled in Iran, in particular with Bank Melli and Bank Saderat, and their branches and subsidiaries abroad, in order to avoid such activities contributing to the proliferation sensitive nuclear activities, or to the development of nuclear weapon delivery systems, as referred to in resolution 1737 (2006).[27]

UNSCR 1929 expanded the measures and extended some to explicitly cover insurance and re-insurance.[28] Additional measures applied to financial institutions as UNSCR 1929 called upon States to:

[T]ake appropriate measures that prohibit financial institutions within their territories or under their jurisdiction from opening representative offices or subsidiaries or banking accounts in Iran if they have information that provides reasonable grounds to believe that such financial services could contribute to Iran's proliferation-sensitive nuclear activities or the development of nuclear weapon delivery systems.[29]

With respect to DPRK, UNSCRs 1695 (2006) and especially 1718 (2006) and 1874 (2009) introduced a regime intended to force DPRK to comply with demands related to its nuclear and ballistic missile programs. The measures in this regime include:

---

[25]   *Id.* ¶ 12.

[26]   *See* S.C. Res. 1803, ¶¶ 9–10, U.N. Doc. S/RES/1803 (Mar. 3, 2008).

[27]   *Id.* ¶ 10.

[28]   *See* S.C. Res. 1929, ¶ 21, U.N. Doc. S/RES/1929 (June. 9, 2010).

[29]   *Id.* ¶ 24.

- An embargo on the supply of nuclear, ballistic missiles and other weapons of mass destruction program-related items listed in UNSC documents;[30]

- A complete arms embargo with the exception of small arms and light weapons and their related materiel, which can be supplied using controlled channels and after prior notification to the Security Council;[31]

- Individual targeted sanctions in the form of a travel ban and an assets freeze on designated persons and entities;[32] and

- A ban on the export of luxury goods to the North Korea.[33]

UNSCR 1718 mandated a freeze of:

[F]unds, other financial assets and economic resources which are on their territories at the date of the adoption of this resolution or at any time thereafter, that are owned or controlled, directly or indirectly, by the persons or entities designated by the Committee or by the Security Council as being engaged in or providing support for, including through other illicit means, DPRK's nuclear-related, other weapons of mass destruction-related and ballistic missile related programmes, or by persons or entities acting on their behalf or at their direction, and ensure that any funds, financial assets or economic resources are prevented from being made available by their nationals or by any persons or entities within their territories, to or for the benefit of such persons or entities.[34]

Extending further previous sanctions, UNSCR 1874 called upon Member States:

[T]o prevent the provision of financial services or the transfer to, through, or from their territory, or to or by their nationals or entities organized under their laws (including branches abroad), or persons or financial institutions in their territory, of any financial or other assets or resources that could contribute to the DPRK's nuclear-related, ballistic missile-related, or other weapons of mass destruction-related programs or activities, including by freezing any financial or other assets or resources on their territories or that hereafter come within their territories, or that are subject to their jurisdiction or that hereafter become subject to their jurisdiction, that are associated with such programs or activities and

---

[30]   S.C. Res. 1718, ¶ 8(a)(ii), U.N. Doc. S/RES/1718 (Oct. 14, 2006).

[31]   S.C. Res. 1874, ¶ 10, U.N. Doc. S/RES/1874 (June 12, 2009).

[32]   S.C. Res. 1718, *supra* note 30, ¶¶ 8 (d) & (e).

[33]   *See Security Council Imposes Sanctions on DPR Korea After its Claimed Nuclear Test*, UN NEWS CENTRE (Oct. 14, 2006), http://www.un.org/apps/news/story.asp?NewsID=20261 &Cr=DPRK&Cr1 ("Also prohibited from export to the DPRK are luxury goods.").

[34]   S.C. Res. 1718, *supra* note 30, ¶ 8(d).

applying enhanced monitoring to prevent all such transactions in accordance with their national authorities and legislation.[35]

UNSCR 1874 also called upon:

[A]ll Member States and international financial and credit institutions not to enter into new commitments for grants, financial assistance, or concessional loans to the DPRK, except for humanitarian and developmental purposes directly addressing the needs of the civilian population, or the promotion of denuclearization, and also calls upon States to exercise enhanced vigilance with a view to reducing current commitments.[36]

In practical terms, implementing such measures may require new domestic legislation; the introduction of preventive measures and monitoring; enhanced enforcement capacity; and actions to be taken by private-sector entities, especially financial institutions.

Two categories of measures can be usefully distinguished in these provisions. One category includes targeted financial sanctions centered on actors of concern, while the other is based on activities that support proliferation efforts or programs.

Targeted financial sanctions generally "entail the use of financial instruments and institutions to apply coercive pressure on transgressing parties—government officials, elites who support them, members of non-governmental entities—in an effort to change or restrict their behavior."[37] This type of measure can thus target specific persons or entities, their assets, and their transactions because of their involvement in proliferation activities. Occasionally, the names of targets are cited in the main text of Resolutions.[38] More often, however, the list of targeted actors is appended.

For example, UNSCR 1737 Paragraph 5's provisions on asset freezes cited earlier should be applied to any other persons or entities "engaged in, directly associated with or providing support for Iran's proliferation sensitive nuclear activities or the development of nuclear weapon delivery systems, or by persons or entities acting on their behalf or at their direction, or by entities owned or controlled by them, including through illicit means . . . ."[39] It also required that all States "shall ensure that any funds, financial assets or economic resources are prevented from being

---

[35]  S.C. Res. 1874, *supra* note 31, ¶ 18.

[36]  *Id.* ¶ 19.

[37]  WATSON INST. FOR INT'L STUDIES, TARGETED FINANCIAL SANCTIONS: A MANUAL FOR DESIGN AND IMPLEMENTATION, at ix (2001).

[38]  *See* S.C. Res. 1929, *supra* note 28, ¶¶ 8, 10 (discussing measures to restrict the Islamic Republic of Iran Shipping Lines (IRISL), or those acting on their behalf or at their direction).

[39]  S.C. Res. 1737, *supra* note 21, ¶ 12.

made available by their nationals or by any persons or entities within their territories, to or for the benefit of these persons and entities."[40] The provisions cited above regarding specific Iranian banks and entities of the Islamic Republic of Iran Shipping Lines also fall in this category. An example from the DPRK regime is provided by Paragraph 8(d) of UNSCR 1718 as cited above.

On the other hand, activity-based measures relate to specific actions and transactions, such as financing or insurance, linked to proliferation efforts. For example, UNSCR 1540 requires states to establish "appropriate laws and regulations to control export, transit, trans-shipment and re-export and controls on providing funds and services related to such export and trans-shipment such as financing . . . ."[41] According to UNSCR 1540, financial controls should be available for application to any exports of controlled items, regardless of destination.[42] How and when these legal instruments are applied is left to the discretion and best judgment of the national authorities in the exporting state concerned.

There are also provisions that require countries to apply activity-related controls against particular countries, such as Iran and DPRK. An illustration of this type are the measures of Paragraph 6 of UNSCR 1737 regarding technical assistance or training, financial assistance, etc., related to the prohibited items specified in that resolution.[43] More recently, UNSCR 1929 mandates that States "prevent the provision to Iran by their nationals or from or through their territories of technical training, financial resources or services, advice, other services or assistance related to the supply, sale, transfer, provision, manufacture, maintenance or use" of specified conventional arms and related materiel.[44] In such cases, the Security Council targets financial, commercial and service flows connected to activities supportive of programs of concern in these countries while allowing other transactions with these countries that are not subject to restrictions.

The exhaustive listing of requirements and obligations of U.N. Member States is beyond the scope of this paper, but it is clear that they vary not only by type of measure, but also by the particular targets, the implementing national authorities, and the responsibilities of individuals and private sector entities.

---

[40]   *Id.*

[41]   S.C. Res. 1540, *supra* note 17, ¶ 3(d).

[42]   *Id.*

[43]   S.C. Res. 1737, *supra* note 21, ¶ 6.

[44]   S.C. Res. 1929, *supra* note 28, ¶ 8.

III.  IMPLEMENTATION CHALLENGES

A review of Member State reports to the various U.N. Security Council sanctions committees on what they have done to implement the Resolutions discussed here reveals a wide variety of approaches with respect to financial vigilance. Many States refer to their money laundering, terrorism or terrorism-finance laws as measures responsive to the UNSCRs. Other States simply notify national authorities of the UNSCRs' passage. A small number of governments have considered or introduced specific new measures and laws. France, for instance, has passed a law with three separate offenses against the finance of proliferation of nuclear, chemical, and biological weapons.[45] On the other extreme, some countries have not even filed a required progress report to the relevant committees.[46]

This global asymmetry of national laws against proliferation finance is matched by the asymmetry in the existence, strength and application of national export controls. While there is no systematic and comprehensive review of these diverse laws and practices, it is crystal clear that there is plenty of room for improving the way the global community addresses proliferation threats.

The challenges are legion. We have already noted the lack of a universal definition of the term "proliferation finance" and the uncertainty about which obligations stemming from the different UNSCRs are mandatory, even when they are under Chapter VII of the U.N. Charter. This uncertainty is of course not coincidental, as it indicates the diverse interests, priorities, and objectives of the members of the Security Council. Consensus has not been reached even within the group of the five permanent members of the Security Council. The ambiguity of terms, such as "financial services," "other services," "Iranian-controlled bank," "reasonable grounds to believe," and "entity under control,"—which are neither defined nor operationalized—makes it unclear what concrete steps are required.[47]

---

[45]  *See* Loi 2011-266 du 14 mars 2011 relative à la lutte contre la prolifération des armes de destruction massive et de leurs vecteurs [Law 2011-266 of March 14, 2011 on the Fight Against the Proliferation of Weapons of Mass Destruction and their Delivery], Journal Officiel de la République Française [J.O.] [Official Gazette of France], Mar. 15, 2011, p. 4577, arts. 2, 5, 11, *available at* http://legifrance.gouv.fr/affichTexte.do?cidTexte=JORFTEXT 000023707202&categorieLien=id.

[46]  *See* Cole J. Harvey, *Two Steps Forward, One Step Back: Slow, but Steady Progress Implementing UNSCR 1540*, NUCLEAR THREAT INITIATIVE (July 20, 2011), http://www.nti. org/analysis/articles/unscr-1540/ (noting that only 59 states met the deadline to submit national implementation reports six months following the passage of Resolution 1540).

[47]  The FATF has issued three helpful sets of non-binding guidance. *See generally* FATF, GUIDANCE REGARDING THE IMPLEMENTATION OF FINANCIAL PROVISIONS OF UNITED NATIONS SECURITY COUNCIL RESOLUTIONS TO COUNTER THE PROLIFERATION OF WEAPONS OF MASS DESTRUCTION, Annex (June 29, 2007), *available at* http://www.fatf-gafi.org/dataoecd/23/16

A complicating factor for both government bodies and financial institutions is the existence of related sanction regimes and financial controls at the regional and national level, notably by the EU[48] and the U.S.[49] These controls go beyond the requirements of the Security Council, have extra-territorial implications, and have been the subject of frequent additions and amendments, reflecting geo-political developments and perceptions of proliferation risks.

Beyond legal uncertainties, other implementation difficulties range from lack of capacity and awareness, political will, commercial concerns, and lack of coordination to the neglect of guidance and outreach to the private sector.[50] One particular issue worth dwelling upon is the issue of proliferators' increased sophistication in recent years and the connection between proliferators and other crime or security concerns.

Proliferating networks appear to be involving multiple production facilities, more countries, intermediaries, and trans-shipment points, all while compartmentalizing operations and occasionally breaking procurement down to parts and small amounts, which are difficult to detect or trace. As the FATF notes, "while proliferators previously attempted to buy or sell whole manufactured systems with the effective control systems, there is a growing trend to purchase or sell more elementary components. Proliferation networks continuously seek out and exploit weaknesses in the global export control system and international financial system."[51]

Moreover, rising trade volumes coupled with technological advances have led to more complex trading patterns, rendering export controls more difficult to manage and maintain. In the area of WMD components, the same FATF report has noted the difficulty in dealing with "dual-use" goods with both commercial applications and applications for WMD.[52] By masking WMD-related procurement activities as legitimate trade, proliferators tend to exploit global commerce by operating in and

---

/39318680.pdf; FATF, PROLIFERATION FINANCING REPORT (June 18, 2008), *available at* http://www.fatf-gafi.org/dataoecd/14/21/41146580.pdf; FATF, BEST PRACTICES PAPER: SHARING AMONG DOMESTIC COMPETENT AUTHORITIES INFORMATION RELATED TO THE FINANCING OF PROLIFERATION (Feb. 2012), *available at* http://www.fatf-gafi.org/dataoecd/5/31/49848736.pdf (explaining the terms in more context).

[48] *Consolidated List of Persons, Groups, and Entities Subject to EU Financial Sanctions*, EU: EXTERNAL ACTION, http://eeas.europa.eu/cfsp/sanctions/consol-list_en.htm (last updated May 4, 2012).

[49] *See Sections Programs and County Information*, U.S. DEP'T TREASURY, http://www.treasury.gov/resource-center/sanctions/Programs/Pages/Programs.aspx (last visited Apr. 14, 2012) (listing the OFAC sanctions programs).

[50] *See* PASSAS ET AL., *supra* note 9.

[51] PROLIFERATION FINANCING REPORT, *supra* note 47, at 3.

[52] *See id.* at 6.

through countries with high volumes of cross-border trade or free-trade zones, where their illicit shipments may escape close scrutiny.

Even though we lack perfect knowledge of the social organization of proliferation networks and their interface with organized criminal groups or public officials, there is information to suggest that they resort to nominees, front companies, informal channels and methods employed in the commission of other offences (e.g., Customs, commercial and subsidy frauds, tax evasion, corruption, trade-based money laundering, etc.).

The open-source literature has not yet discussed proliferation finance in detail. Indeed, this topic may be neglected even within governments and international organizations. Typically, agencies and countries do not share such information, which has hampered some study efforts. Yet we do know that financial institutions' suspicious activity reports have triggered some such cases.[53] We also know that financial transaction information has served well intelligence gathering, investigative, and prosecutorial efforts in various countries.[54] Quite often, investigations and prosecutions were initiated under laws targeting money laundering, fraud or corruption.

As proliferators seek to circumvent sanctions and other measures, their open-account, nominee, compartmentalized and deceptive practices become harder for financial institutions and government agencies to detect. Additionally, as efforts focus on the financial sector, proliferators may make more use of informal financial and trade networks, which are misunderstood in many parts of the world and difficult to monitor.[55] Quite extensive informal financial, remittance, and trade networks operate in key areas—such as South and Southeast Asia, the Middle East, the Caribbean and South America—have been connecting jurisdictions of concern and neighboring countries.

Whether or not sanction regimes and financial controls are successful in producing the intended outcomes, they generate effects and raise the cost of proliferation efforts. Past experiences show that among the unintended consequences of sanctions is a certain criminalization of both

---

[53]   *See* PASSAS ET AL., *supra* note 9.

[54]   *See* CATHERINE COLLINS & DOUGLAS FRANTZ, FALLOUT: THE TRUE STORY OF THE CIA'S SECRET WAR ON NUCLEAR TRAFFICKING 126 (2011); GORDON CORERA SHOPPING FOR BOMBS: NUCLEAR PROLIFERATION, GLOBAL INSECURITY, AND THE RISE AND FALL OF THE A.Q. KHAN NETWORK 166 (2006); *see also* CATHERINE COLLINS & DOUGLAS FRANTZ, THE NUCLEAR JIHADIST: THE TRUE STORY OF THE MAN WHO SOLD THE WORLD'S MOST DANGEROUS SECRETS...AND HOW WE COULD HAVE STOPPED HIM (2007).

[55]   *See* Nikos Passas, Informal Value Transfer Systems, Terrorism and Money Laundering 16, 96–97, 100 (2003) (report to the National Institute of Justice (NIJ) and Financial Crimes Action Network (FINCEN)), *available at* https://www.ncjrs.gov/pdffiles1/nij/grants/208301.pdf (discussing that informal systems and trade facilitated transfer need to be monitored and should be kept in line with FATF recommendations).

public- and private-sector actors in target and neighboring countries through which illegal flows are routed.[56] Criminal infrastructures, methods, networks, and associations brought about by the demand for prohibited goods and services survive sanctions regimes and pose a longer-term governance threats.

Confronting such threats necessitates the consideration of five key points emerging from research into financial crime and specifically relevant to money laundering, terrorism finance and corruption that are common to proliferation finance. These five key points consist of the need for: (1) evidence-based policy making; (2) practices that transcend the current fragmentation of controls that focus on particular offenses; and (3) a strategic approach that (4) includes outreach and partnership with the private sector as well as the academic community and (5) ensures that data on the global flows of information, commerce and finance are collected, rendered traceable, analyzed, and matched in order to identify irregular and suspicious activities, to piece together the bigger picture of serious financial misconduct and networks, illuminating the economic activity currently taking place in the shadows.

Briefly, here are the main issues from each point:

1) Too much crime control and policy has been based on assumptions, suspicions and theories rather than carefully collected and strong evidence about the problem at hand.[57] As with terrorism finance, we must gather the facts and understand well proliferation activities and networks, their division of labor and methods of operation.

2) Unusual activities that raise suspicion and initial investigations will often not flag a particular underlying offense. The details about the motives and aims of the offenders emerge gradually as inquiries progress. The same applies to sanctions violations and proliferation efforts. Firewalls and strict division of labor that discourage or prevent sharing of information among different control agencies undermine the fight against serious crime and security threats.

3) Given the plethora of challenges facing the implementation of a counter-proliferation finance regime, success and effectiveness is a long-term goal that can be reached progressively and systematically. The project is complex, sensitive and in need of consensual knowledge and a thoughtful sequencing of immediate steps and medium term objectives, while anticipating and minimizing as much as possible adverse consequences.

---

[56]   GARY CLYDE HUFBAUER, ECONOMIC SANCTIONS RECONSIDERED 44–48 (2007).

[57]   Cynthia Lum & Leslie W. Kennedy, *Evidence-Based Counterterrorism Policy*, *in* SPRINGER SERIES ON EVIDENCE-BASED CRIME POLICY 3, 3–8 (Cynthia Lum & Leslie W. Kennedy eds., 2012) (stating that crime policy ought to be based on scientific studies and on valid empirical data analysis).

4) The best ideas and sustainable solutions can only be achieved through multi-stakeholder interactions and collaborations. Guidance from government agencies help private sector entities and compliance officers better identify irregular and problematic accounts, clients or transactions and report them to appropriate authorities, such as the Financial Intelligence Units. Better quality and targeted reporting assists investigations and intelligence analysis as it often provides information otherwise unavailable to government agencies. Risk-based approaches can only be done effectively, when the risks are properly identified, understood and prioritized. Academic and research institutions can assist in this effort by creating new technologies enhancing controls and by engaging in systematic, comprehensive and critical analysis of data and evidence contributing to improved rule-making, policy construction, planning, facilitating multi-stakeholder interactions and training.

5) Research has shown that significant numbers of abuses, irregular and suspicious commercial activities involving billions of U.S. dollars in value every year go undetected due to lack of transparency, traceability and analysis of these transactions on their own and in comparison with the financial data that relate to them. This is a major vulnerability undermining all financial controls the global community has been implementing over the years.[58] As Passas and Flynn point out:

> The fundamental challenge that remains to be faced head on is how the global flows of information/intelligence, finance, trade and services can be made traceable and analyzed at the same time, in the same place. This is the only way one can piece together the puzzle so as to reveal a comprehensive picture of how criminal global networks are able to move and benefit from billions of dollars of profits generated from illicit activities.[59]

## IV. Conclusion

Proliferation of WMD is a top priority security concern, and financial controls are a recent and necessary addition to the international community's toolkit. The policy implications of the challenges discussed in this paper can be a rather lengthy report *per se*. The urgent needs include clearer UNSCR mandates, guidance to implementers, and analysis of the relationship correspondence between them and regional or national sanction

---

[58] *See* Nikos Passas, *Setting Global CFT Standards: A Critique and Suggestions*, 9 J. MONEY LAUNDERING CONTROL 281(2006); Nikos Passas, *Terrorist Finance, Informal Markets, Trade and Regulation: Challenges of Evidence in International Efforts*, *in* SPRINGER SERIES ON EVIDENCE-BASED CRIME POLICY 255 (Cynthia Lum & Leslie W. Kennedy eds., 2011).

[59] *See* Nikos Passas & Stephen Flynn, Overcoming the Mexican Trade Facilitated Money Laundering Challenge (this paper is to be presented at the Southwest Border Anti-Money Laundering Alliance, June 13–14, 2012, in Scottsdale, Arizona) (on file with author).

*Transnational Financial Crime*

regimes. One helpful precedent to consider is the approach taken by the U.N. Office on Drugs and Crime, which published legislative guides for the implementation of recent and complex international conventions against transnational organized crime and against corruption.[60] The task there was to explain what is necessary for effective implementation without interpreting the conventions. This took painstaking effort to negotiate and reach consensus on their language and requirements, while giving examples of implementation in different legal traditions. Given the sensitivity around proliferation finance issues and controls, an equivalent initiative on UNSCRs would be welcome by Member States and the private sector. The FATF's forthcoming methodology for the assessment of compliance with its new 40 Recommendations could possibly pave the ground for more harmonized approaches too.

The study of proliferation cases and the mapping of proliferation networks, their operations, and their nexus with conventional, informal, and illegal actors is a necessary step towards the construction of an evidence-based strategy in cooperation with the private sector as well as academia.

An important issue raised above is the need to rethink crime control beyond specific offenses and defenses against them. The same methods, routes, and infrastructures can be used for a whole range of crimes: offenders most often do not specialize in one crime. Crime controls, especially for serious security threats, must be better organized and coordinated. Financial controls are sometimes resisted as an unnecessary distraction from border and expert controls. Increasingly, they are seen as very useful supplements to all kinds of serious crime. Ideally, they do not just supplement other controls but they all get integrated, which is arguably the only way in which national, regional, and international efforts will be truly effective.

Awareness-raising, training- and capacity-building, gaming exercises, technical assistance to countries and international bodies, further elaborations and operationalization of the risk-based approach to tackling financial crimes, expert panels, and committees are all important actions and recommendations. Nevertheless, the critical objective in this global effort is to appreciate that counter-proliferation and serious crime control is one and the same enterprise. If we adequately control proliferation, we will control financial and other crime. If we effectively control serious crime in general, we will also detect, capture, and disrupt proliferation attempts. In

---

[60] U.N. Office on Drugs and Crime Division for Treaty Affairs, Legislative Guides for the Implementation of the United Nations Convention against Transnational Organized Crime and the Protocols Thereto, U.N. Sales No. E.0000000 (2004); U.N. Office on Drugs and Crime Division for Treaty Affairs, Legislative Guides for the Implementation of the United Nations Convention Against Corruption, U.N. Sales No. E.06.V.16 (2006).

order to accomplish this, we must address the challenge of the three global flows: commercial, financial and informational. Research and policy energies and brainpower ought to be invested in the quite-feasible[61] task of collecting and analyzing the data; rendering them traceable; matching them; producing investigative leads; building the "big picture" of crime and security threats; and leading to pragmatic, sustainable strategies.

---

[61] An initiative in exactly this direction is currently underway at Northeastern University as a collaboration between the Kostas Institute for Research in Homeland Security, the School of Criminology and Criminal Justice and the College of Computer Sciences.

# [25]

## Balancing financial threats and legal interests in money-laundering policy

PETRUS C. VAN DUYNE*, MARC S. GROENHUIJSEN
and A.A.P. SCHUDELARO
*Tilburg University, P.O. Box 90153, 5000 LE Tilburg, The Netherlands;*
*\*author for correspondence (e-mail: petrus@uvt.nl)*

**Abstract.** The fight against money laundering has been energetically introduced and developed into a global enforcement regime. Various economic and financial justifications have been put forward, which are not self-evident. The simple and basic foundation is that ill-gotten profits should not remain in the possession of the criminal. Nevertheless, the cause of fighting money laundering is loaded with arguments about the staggering size and the undermining effects of the crime-money, for which there is no empirical evidence. The arguments concerning the integrity of the financial system, usually taken at face value, proves to be less than coherent. Nevertheless, these (globally) politically accepted arguments prove to be effective in overruling a more careful balancing of legal interests and foundations, like the all-encompassing breadth of the money-laundering approach. This approach is compared with the computer crime legislation, in which restraint was balanced with the requirement to update the legal tools to an adequate level of effectiveness in an electronic criminal environment. This clarity contrasts strongly with the rhetoric of the money-laundering policy, in which we find neither restraint nor clarity.

### The quest for basics and balance

Wisdom develops by hindsight, sometimes by insight in simple basics and picking up evidence. That is knowledge- and experience-based conduct, which is assumed a basic principle to run public affairs. However, in many areas of policy making, legislation and law enforcement this principle often does not appear to apply (Eijlander, 2004). Policies once decided upon for certain reasons may be pursued towards other aims, while its original foundations have faded and feedback from (historical) experience is ignored. There is no hindsight and little learning. For example, the fight against drugs or organised crime, fear-driven policies, covers increasingly wider criminal phenomena that previously would not be included. Meanwhile the elusive results of organised crime or drug policy stimulated rather than discouraged an undeterred persistence, instead of leading to reflection and consideration (Van Duyne and Levi, 2005). Within such a policy attitude there is little space for weighing law enforcement interests against social and legal costs (Vruggink, 2000). Regarding organised crime or drugs this lack of weighing has already been discussed elsewhere (Wisotsky, 1986; Woodiwiss, 2003). In this paper, we will examine the anti-money laundering policy from this perspective of imbalance. We will compare that policy with an adjacent area: computer crime policy to clarify that anticipating threats from new forms of crime can proceed in a controlled, well-balanced fashion: rational versus fear-driven policy making.

The policy areas of laundering and crime-money (a shorthand for all criminally acquired assets) and computer crime are both relatively new. The anti-laundering policy is originally based on concerns about dangers stemming from organised (drug) crime (and its 'transnational' variety). It is commonly assumed that criminally derived wealth represents a threat, which may be exacerbated by laundering, as it allows the crime-money to flow freely into our law abiding society. Even modern internet "cyber" facilities may be abused, allegedly aggravating the situation. During the last fifteen years, international law enforcement has been put on the alert to protect interests threatened by crime-money and all related phenomena, like terrorist financing.

As usual in law enforcement, various interests are at stake, which require a mutual balancing. On the one hand, there is the protection against criminally inflicted harm, which in its general formulation will always be approved of. However, at closer inspection, underlying such a general formulation values and ideologies remain often implicit. If these are made explicit in their mutual relations the general formulation may appear not be so clear after all. On the other hand, there is the need for equity in substantive and procedural law requiring proportionality of the severity of the legal instruments, as well as their reach and social costs of their application. How serious is the volume of crime-money and its laundering to warrant heavy penalties and the involvement of financial and non-financial institutions and private entrepreneurs to stem this threat? Is that aggravated by 'cyber laundering'? And how serious are the threats emanating from computer crime? Given these questions, this paper reviews and compares the ways the policies in the two areas of money-laundering and computer crime evolved, thereby considering on the one hand, their foundations and on the other hand, the requirements of equity. To this end we will briefly describe some aspects, aims and evidence about the development of both policy areas starting with crime-money and its laundering.

*'Ill gotten goods (should) never thrive'*

The roots of the anti-laundering policy, as developed during the past decades, are simple and basic, as worded by the proverb: 'Ill gotten goods never thrive'. As with many proverbs, this is pious wishful thinking of the 'righteous', mostly never getting within reach of opportunities of unlawful enrichment. History invariably proves them wrong. The proceeds of loot and plunder and many other forms of illegal enrichment did and still do prosper: ancient American robber barons (Abadinsky, 1991) and their modern Russian counterparts (Varese, 2001) are only conspicuous manifestations of the falsification of this folk wisdom. However, folk wisdom is not easily brushed aside, certainly not when it converges with other folk images. Robber barons, establishing charity foundations, (legitimate) industries and other socially acceptable institutions, like universities, may be forgiven: in the end, their ill-gotten funds became 'gentrified'.[1] But lawbreakers deviating from this upperworld business-like appearance do not escape from the application of the 'ill gotten gains' principle. That is where the proverb evolved into legislation.

Despite its ancient wisdom, reinforced by the related 'crime should not pay', it took some time before legal penal and civil instruments were put into place to redress this wrong. The impetus was given by the US concern about Italian-American organised crime, first brought into the open in 1950–1951 by the Kefauver Crime Committee, to be subsequently reinforced by two successor committees on organised crime.[2] At that time, the focus of attention was directed at the ethnic alien conspiracy theme, embodied in the image of *La Cosa Nostra*, allegedly operating as a criminal 'cartel' across the US. To fight this menace the Organised Crime Control Act of 1970 was enacted, which included the Racketeer Influenced Corrupt Organizations statute. This statute provided the possibility to freeze a defendant's assets before trial and a civil and criminal forfeiture procedure against any illegally acquired property. It was a major step to honouring the principle that ill-gotten gains should be taken from the wrongdoer. However, at that time, the act of money-laundering itself had not yet become a federal offence (Hinterseer, 2002).

The fact that money-laundering itself was not yet criminalized did not imply that the financial handling of crime-moneys was neglected: the Bank Secrecy Act of 1970 required banks and non-bank financial institutions to make and retain records and report cash transactions of more than $10.000. This reporting system was designed to generate information useful for proactive and reactive investigations. Were these new legal instruments successful? The answer to that question depends on the performance measures to be applied. Among law enforcement agencies, a certain satisfaction could be noticed (Abadinsky, 1991).[3] However, measured by the effects on the crime-markets, particularly the drug market, the impact was negligible. Despite the financial onslaught provided by increasingly tough legislation, the crime-markets in the US and Europe demonstrated a remarkable resilience (Van Duyne and Levi, 2004).

The main target, the (organised) drug market proved to be evasive. The 1980s witnessed a partly successful campaign against cannabis use,[4] which was soon eclipsed by the tremendous growth of the US cocaine market

(Rasmussen and Benson, 1994). This generated substantial flows of (cash) crime-money within the US and particular towards the source countries of South America. Though the biggest price profit margin is realized after importation on the level of wholesale distribution and the middle level market, capital accumulation was most conspicuous in the source countries (Reuter and Greenfield, 2001; Thoumi, 1995). A number of historical circumstances led to the development of what are sometimes denoted as 'narcocracies': countries characterized by an institutional permeation of drug money, corrupting the administration from the lowest ranks to government officials, heads of state not excluded (Nadelmann, 1997). Depending on political expedience, the US administration left them alone, supported or intervened with such corrupt regimes, frequently aggravating its own drug problem.[5] Apart from this foreign *Realpolitik*, these countries could on solid grounds be presented as formidable warning examples of how criminals were able to penetrate the 'control chambers' of society due to their astounding wealth.

These developments, together with the 'war on crime' mood during the Reagan administration of the 1980s, contributed to a shift in attention. Forfeiting the ill-gotten profits, even after extension by the Comprehensive Forfeiture Act of 1984 proved to be insufficient. To a certain extent, this was due to the defects in compliance with the Bank Secrecy Act: many banks failed to report (Hinterseer, 2002:191–192), while the currency reporting requirements were 'an example of over-trumpeted intelligence gathering methodology' (Levi, 1991). In addition, attempts to confiscate and forfeit can be frustrated by successful laundering operations, requiring therefore complementary anti-laundering legislation. However, in wording and intentions, the enacted anti-laundering policy goes well beyond this specific aim, targeting any willful or negligent handling of crime-derived profits. This broadened aim was dressed up with an extensive ideology and 'threat imagery'.

### 'Deeply concerned' in financial nebula

Given the universal 'crime does not pay' adage, the idea of taking away the advantages obtained from lawbreaking was not something that came to the European policy makers' mind as a novelty. After the Second World War, the Dutch administration enacted severe recovery measures against so-called war-profiteers (Van der Landen, 1992, Section 7.4; Borgers, 2001, Ch. 3).[6] After a relatively long period of silence, the idea of addressing the issue of the criminal profits revived during the 1980s. In 1982, Italy put into place recovery provisions within the framework of a new law against mafia conspiracy ('La Torre Law', Arlacchi, 1986). The United Kingdom followed suit with the recommendations of the *Hodgson Committee* which stimulated the Parliament to enact the Drug Trafficking Offences Act (1986). This Act gave the courts the power to confiscate proceeds from drug trafficking. In the Netherlands, a special commission on the recovery of proceeds from serious crime issued its first report in 1987, which initiated a phase of experimenting with financial investigation.[7] Three years later the Convention on Laundering, Search, Seizure and Confiscation of the Proceeds from Crime of the Council of Europe provided a European policy framework.

The emphasis on drugs money was no coincidence. We have seen that the illicit drug market continued to expand, particularly in the US, and subsequently in European (Van Duyne and Levi, 2004). The US had (again) re-invigorated its 'war on drugs' and – as before with the Single Convention of 1961 – worked zealously within the UN to elaborate the new United Nations Convention against illicit traffic in narcotic drugs and psychotropic substances. This convention obliged the 'deeply concerned' parties to adopt measures to confiscate proceeds from drug trafficking (Bewley-Taylor, 1999). Given this clearly favourable climate of universal consensus, one may wonder why the money-laundering and drugs connection had to be brought out so heavily during the G-7 meeting of 1989. There were hardly serious 'non-believers' who could disturb the consensus, certainly not on higher policy making levels.

Despite the presence of a believing audience, a social-psychologically most interesting orchestration unfolded. With a collectively accepted libretto (the evil of the (drug) crime-money) supported by powerful stage directors (the leaders of the industrialized countries), the FATF set out to compose its anti-laundering opera in sonorous Wagnerian *Götterdämmerung* colours. For that performance it did not need to be creative, as almost everything was already in place: the US anti-laundering model only needed to be translated into 'new' recommendations. One blank area still needed to be filled: something had to be said about the magnitude of the problem, since this had to be part of the justification of the desired massive collective efforts to counter the threat. Hence, the FATF set out to fill that blank with as great an authority as the 'broad brush' it used to paint the threat.

The defects in the methodology and outcomes of the FATF estimations have been extensively analyzed and discussed by Van Duyne (1994). The presented volume of the drug money of $300 billion worldwide (1990) was huge and has been moderated by Reuter and Greenfield (2001) to a more realistic range around $25–30 billion, which pleased no one.[8] Apart from the 'creative arithmetic' yielding deliberately inflated figures, which would bring the managers of ENRON in the dock, the most interesting aspect of the whole orchestration is the surrounding political and scientific gullibility.

Even a superficial analysis of the text of the FATF would reveal its basic shortcomings: not only in the arithmetic of its unpublished addendum, but in the logic of its wording of the main text. This is illustrated by the following:

The FATF used three indirect methods to assess the volume of the production of drugs, judging the validity and reliability of each method as follows:

- the UN estimations of world drug production of $300 billion are qualified in the report as '*very uncertain*';
- the consumption needs of drug abusers are considered as of '*doubtful reliability*';
- seizures of illicit drugs, about which the rapporteurs remarked that it '*raises significant methodological problems*'.[9]

Undeterred by its own qualifications of these premises as invalid (defying the Aristotelian basic rule that no conclusions can be drawn from invalid premises), the report continues, without a single line of additional argumentation, in the next section: 'Using these [questionable] methods, the group estimated that sales [of drugs] amount to approximately $122 billion per year in the US and Europe, of which 50–70% or as much as $85 billion per year could be available for laundering and investment'.[10]

Instead of raising questions, policy makers (as expected) and scholars (surprisingly) joined without demur in the supporting chorus of common assent. When we subsequently survey the literature for a critical discussion of the FATF and the crime-money scenery presented as real (in informal conjunction with the UN and the OECD), one hardly finds a dissident voice. And if any critical comment is put forward, it does not result in a debate (Pieth, 1999; Naylor, 1999; Reuter and Greenfield, 2001; Reuter and Truman, 2004).

Given this widely shared representation of the problem and the accordingly generated fears, it is hardly surprising that there was (and still is) little or no pressure for evidence-based policy making (Van Duyne, 2002; Reuter and Truman, 2004).[11] As a matter of fact, while the ever-increasing volume of the crime-money has become as much an article of faith as the monster of Loch Ness, those who believed in the latter never abated in their zeal for research. The believers in the financial monster showed hardly any interest in facts and figures: they asked too little because they believed too much (Van Duyne, 2002). Instead, the legislative development appears to have acquired its own automated momentum, spreading its radius of application to an ever increasing group of entrepreneurs and enterprises. This was not only justified by the basic 'crime should not pay' but also by other foundations.

*The integrity of the financial system*

The most frequently mentioned foundation is the integrity of the financial system. Particularly this point has been emphasized ever since 'the deeply concerned' member states expressed in the Vienna Convention their awareness of the 'wealth enabling transnational criminal organizations to penetrate, contaminate and corrupt' the healthy tissue of trade and industry, the financial business mentioned separately. This is a lofty objective, which generated a host of policy papers, theoretical discussions and legal 'exegesis'. But how and to what extent is this integrity jeopardized?

The assumed undermining of the integrity of a financial system is a puzzling conception. It has an emotive appeal with much *a priori* validity, but it does not clarify the empirical and analytical foundations. The empirical evidence is meager and contradictory. Let us for the sake of argument assume that the official claims about the volume of the crime-money is real. If we accept (by way of hypothesis) the estimates of either the FATF or the UN (Keh, 1996) of respectively $500 billion or $1 trillion dollar of crime-money *per year* entering the system, by now the problem should not be how to *prevent* the system from becoming corrupt, but how to *cure* it from an impending disaster. Bear in mind, as soon as money starts being used economically, it becomes a part of a flow-system: money is turned into property, that is sold again, mortgaged etc. Beyond what point or stage is the crime-money no longer tainted? And every year on top of the already existing accumulated billions or trillions another trillion is added. Surely, such a globally affected financial system should reveal symptoms of a very grave illness. What are the symptoms? Do we witness global shifts in property relations due to (drug) crime-money, which should be the logical consequence?[12]

Finding an answer to this question is difficult, as most national and international financial systems look quite healthy, notwithstanding the fact that by now they should be rolling in crime-money, according to the FATF/UN assumptions. Actually, financial institutions see to it to radiate what supervisors and depositors expect: financial health and *trustworthiness*. Regarding this feature wealthy criminals do not differ from any other customer. They would not even dream of destabilizing the bank in which they deposit their hard-earned dirty money.[13] They are not only looking for discretion, but also for efficiency and financial reliability (Harvey, 2005). Likewise, most tax offenders in the European Union do not deposit their 'black' savings in grubby banks in exotic tax havens, but go to trusted banks in neighbouring countries, as became apparent with the Belgian 'tax dodgers'.[14] Once deposited, the financial processing must follow basic banking principles. The exported tax and crime-moneys are not stored in bank vaults, but they must flow into the international capital market in the same way as all other funds.

Do the Belgian, German, Swiss or Liechtenstein banks reveal 'sickness problems', which can be causally related to receiving tainted (tax) moneys and which can be observed *independently* of our moral disapproval of the free availability of the hidden funds? If we find no sickness symptoms, one should not conclude that the system or its separate component financial institutions are therefore 'beyond good and evil'. There have been sufficient banking scandals in which institutions (represented by the top managers) acted unethically and to the detriment of its customers (connivance at bad loans, dubious share emissions): e.g. the UK Barings Bank, the US Loan and Savings scandal, the French Crédit Lyonnais, in connection with the Dutch Slavenburg Bank (d'Aubert, 1993) or the skimming ('tunnelling') of financial institutions by the management in the Czech Republic (Baloun and Scheinost, 2003). However, none of these cases were (exclusively) caused by the influx or a surplus of *crime*-money.[15]

It remains difficult to find an unambiguous criterion with which to identify a causal relationship between the effects of crime-money within the financial system and its way of monetary functioning. If we cannot find any criterion, should we discard the objective 'integrity of the financial system' as mere rhetoric? As far as the justification of anti-crime money legislation is concerned, the answer is 'yes'. The integrity argument remains too weak to function as an unambiguous foundation. This does not imply the rejection of ethics within the financial system and placing it 'beyond good and evil'. Any financial system transcending pure bartering depends on *trust*. Integrity of financial institutions remains of predominant importance, not because of the colour of money, but because of the trust bestowed by customers in the promise of a proper handling of their property.

If the objective of the integrity of the financial system fails because of its elusiveness, where do we find clearly identifiable interests at risk because of laundering? An abundance of crime-money need not be without effects, though these go beyond the concerns about the financial system and may under circumstances falsify some general assumptions. As a matter of fact, the financial system may even benefit from the surfacing and integration of crime-money. Part of the debt crisis of Latin America during the 1980s was softened by the return of narco-dollars. It was a touchy subject, but none of the European creditor banks ever felt its integrity affected (Naylor, 1987). Moreover, due to a combination of conservative monetary policy and the influx of narco-dollars, Colombia, the main cocaine exporter, managed to keep its foreign debt within acceptable margins (Thoumi, 1995).

The most important harm inflicted is not to the financial system itself, but to the social-economic system when the administration fails to contain the hidden economy. In such an event the budget policy will be based on wrong assumptions about the volume of available money. If a substantial amount of unrecorded money is in circulation as disposable income, the required fiscal income will be calculated on a narrower income basis than real purchase power. This leads to various policy measures, like cutting down on expenditure, raising taxation or increasing the public debt, as few elected governments are willing to incur the wrath of an impoverished electorate. This seems to be somewhat remote from the issue of crime-money and laundering, which is misleading. A higher taxation stimulates the underground economy, part of which consists of the provision of (criminal) services and goods. A continuing expansion of this hidden (partly criminal) economy erodes the economic and social integrity of the public realm. This has been observed in Colombia (Thoumi, 1995), Morocco (De Mas, 2001), the Russian Federation (Varese, 2001) and in some EU member states (Reuter and Truman, 2004, Ch. 2). Apart from that, the surplus of purchasing power above what is officially registered can lead to inflation, particularly within economic sectors which are most targeted for spending 'hot money'. Inflation in the real estate sector has been observed in Northern Morocco and Colombia. Related to this (but not necessarily) may be the dissipation of crime-money to uneconomic investments. In short, an abundance of crime-money is not an economically or morally neutral phenomenon even if the financial system itself is not (seriously) affected.

*Financial incapacitation*

Preventing crime-entrepreneurs from returning to their crime-business after having served their prison sentence by taking away their 'criminal reserves', is also a frequently mentioned reason (Levi, 2002). Though this may be theoretically correct, empirically it is empty. Underlying this aim is the idea of a criminal corporation, which operates with a kind of emergency 'war chest'. Taking away these reserves contributes to (financial) incapacitation. It is true that some smuggling operations are expensive, incurring expenses of about one or two million euros per project. However, this is mainly the case with cross-border wholesale shipping operations (Meloen et al., 2003; Van Duyne and Levi, 2005). Apart from the fact that such expenses constitute a mere fraction of the value of the cargo, most smuggling enterprises operate on a cheaper joint venture basis, the most important assets being human capital in the form of criminal networks (Desroches, 2003).

When we look at other crime-markets, we find even cheaper operating crime-enterprises in terms of investments or reserves. In the first place a variety of investment fraudsters, the so-called 'economic nomads' (Van Duyne, 1997), who require little more than advertisement costs and a smooth telephone communication system. Sometimes they rent a plush office to evoke prestige and trust, leaving the premises with a few months rent in arrears. A second type, crime-entrepreneurs defrauding the public fund with VAT and excises operate equally cheaply. Their main investment consists of the acquisition of a series of front firms, the payment of a strawman, and the printing of invoices. The front firms are intended to go bust as soon as the Inland Revenue Service discovers the tax scam. As with juggling, while the first firm comes down, the next front firm is already thrown up in the air: hence their characterization as 'front firm jugglers'. In general one can conclude that these types of organised business crime hardly need any reserves for doing business. Their main craft is to create debts and disappear at the right moment. The third type consists of 'legitimate' entrepreneurs, producing legitimate goods, but operating systematically on a fraudulent cost price reducing basis. Mixing a flow of false invoices or documents of about 10% of the turnover with an otherwise licit bookkeeping is sufficient for out-competing most competitors. These 'mixers' are rarely the focus of the war on crime-money rhetoric, though their distortion of the market may be substantial. On the contrary, the recovery procedure does not have the nature of a rough 'freezing, seizing and forfeiting', but consists of civilized negotiations between the authorities and the perpetrators. The interested banks may look on or become involved to reduce their losses: after all, they may be the biggest losers, if the recovery policy is strictly applied.

The theory of financially crippling a crime-entrepreneur is not wrong as such, but it applies to an entrepreneurial type, which is just a rare bird in the criminal markets.

*Punishment*

Another conception concerns the 'hitting the criminal where it hurts him most: in his pocket'. To most law enforcement officers this is an understandable objective, underlined by an often quoted statement: the convict will no longer smile at a prison sentence of 20 years when he knows there are no longer funds available on his release (Hinterseer, 2002). (One may wonder how many convicts did produce such a smile at a 20 years verdict.) The punishment argument has an emotive appeal to crime-fighters and it is more frequently put forward in social contexts in which it has a convincing effect, just because it is vindictive and is correct to the extent that convicted criminals do feel likewise (Vruggink, 2000).

Given its emotional value and appeal, its proponents will be little impressed by the confusion, which surrounds recovery as a punishment. Actually, application of the punishment objective opens the gate to glaring inequality of justice. Should the defendant who has squandered his loot be meted out a longer prison sentence to make his punishment equal to his thrifty fellow criminal, who is stripped of all his criminal savings? The argument soon obtains absurdist features if one compares a serious application across the categories of crime: traditional property crime and other crimes for profit committed by the 'usual suspects' versus organised business and corporate crime committed by 'captains of industry'. Business criminals, like the insider trader Boetsky, felt more hurt by being sent to prison 'like a criminal', than by being stripped of their ill-gotten profits (Groenhuijsen and Van Kalmthout, 1989:205).

If vindictiveness should be a guidance to inflict harm, the basic aim of recovering the ill-gotten profits is likely to become distorted.

Surveying the anti-laundering landscape we observe a mixture of simple principles and a complexity of at best semi-ordered considerations and objectives, amplified by nebulous and disputable, but generally accepted threat assessments. On the one hand, there is a basic principle of restoring justice: 'ill-gotten profits' must be taken away. On the other hand, we observe a diversity of disordered justifications, partly semi-empirical, partly economic and juridical, which together look like a display of glittering Christmas tree decorations in which anyone can find something of his liking. It has a similarity with a plea of an uncertain defense lawyer, who for fear of not convincing the jury, displays one reserve argument after the other. And if 'reason' does not prevail, fear and pressure may win over residual reluctance.

## The cyber laundering challenge

Criminals operating computers, and entering the cyber space, are also considered threatening phenomena. How were these threats addressed? What do the money-laundering ICT opportunities look like and what was the law enforcement response? We will first describe the approach to this ICT menace, and compare this in a subsequent chapter with the way the Dutch legislator addressed the computer crime challenge.

*Policy making and new challenges: The case of 'cyber-laundering'*[16]

The introduction of the Internet to the general public may be the single most important technological development of the last ten years. Who can nowadays imagine a world without the World Wide Web, without email, or without almost instantaneous and global communications? Using these techniques, a large number of electronic payment systems have been developed. Systems, like on-line banking applications and personal computer-based digital cash systems, were designed specifically for use on the global computer network. Some systems have been introduced as part of an ongoing trend to make payments more efficient, whereas others aimed at facilitating electronic commerce. Together these new forms of payment are called 'cyber payments'.

Since the mid 1990s, cyber payments have attracted the attention of the anti-money laundering agencies. The fear was expressed that cyber payments might make it much easier for criminals to enter their illegal funds into the legitimate economy and launder them more efficient, aggravating the already existing threat.

Many warnings have been put forward: 'Financial crime will be a severe problem with digital money';[17] 'the potential for conducting financial transactions on-line (. . .) presents one of the most significant vulnerabilities to money laundering at present' (FATF, 2000a); and '[t]he abuse of these systems by launderers is no longer a distant possibility', are just a few of such statements (FATF, 1999:87). Some have wondered whether Internet access might be 'the new type of detergent which allows for cleaner laundry' (Bortner, 1996), or have called the increasing utilization and promotion of on-line banking and electronic payment systems '[t]he greatest boon to money launderers' (Lilley, 2000:114). Others have gone as far as presenting electronic money, together with tax evasion, as one of the horsemen of the Apocalypse, forgery, currency disruptions, and surveillance being the other three.[18] Moreover, in theoretical scenarios, developed in the second half of the 1990s, a future was sketched in which thousands, or even millions, of dollars could be loaded onto and transported using smart cards or mobile phones, in which drug dealers would store similar amounts in anonymous digital cash on their personal computers (Molander et al., 1998:19), and in which the act of money laundering could be carried out while sitting on a tropical beach with a laptop computer and sipping a Margarita (Bortner, 1996). Now, 10 years later, the question is: 'What is the evidence for these concerns?'

The most striking aspect about the claims that new electronic methods of payment pose a real money laundering threat is the lack of underlying evidence. For example, since the FATF began writing about electronic money and on-line banking, it has not been able to present any clear, real-life case payment (FATF, 1996a:24–29; FATF, 1997a:14, and Annex C, 43). Instead, between 1996 and 2001, the FATF has repeatedly reported a lack of evidence by stating with respect to electronic money, on-line banking, or both that:

- 'experts have no evidence to suggest that cyber payments technologies [mostly smart card-based electronic purses] are being manipulated by criminal interests' (FATF, 1996a:29);

- 'there have been no reported instances of money laundering through these systems' that is, electronic money systems, and that 'no case of laundering has been detected in this sector' that is, the banking sector using new technologies (FATF, 1997b, Appendix 6; FATF, 1998a,b:7);
- '[a]ll delegations continue to report that there have not been as of yet any investigated money-laundering cases involving the new payment technologies', that 'there were no reported cases of this type of laundering [that is, through on-line banking] taking place at this time' (FATF, 1999:27 and 31), that 'no money laundering cases have been detected yet which involve this mechanism [on-line banking]', that 'the FATF experts have seen few if any examples of on-line banking being used in money laundering', and that 'the experts were not yet able to provide case examples of money laundering through on-line banking' (FATF, 2000a:104. Similarly, FATF, 2000b:92; FATF, 2000b:8; FATF, 2001:11).

After reporting so many non-events, in the FATF's 2002 annual report, words like 'the Internet', 'digital', 'electronic', 'smart card', or 'electronic purse' are no longer present, a situation that is not altered in any material way by FATF publications of 2003 and 2004 (FATF, 2003a; FATF, 2002; FATF, 2004). Finally, in the 2001–2002 report on money-laundering typologies, only one case was presented in which on-line banking 'might' have been used by money launderers, but the link was weak at best. In documents about electronic money prepared by the G-10 group of countries and the US Department of the Treasury, similar statements can be found.[19]

The FATF does not consider the apparent lack of evidence as indicating that no money laundering is taking place through on-line connections. Instead, 'some experts believe that adequate means of detecting this type of laundering activity have not yet been fully developed' (FATF, 2001:11. Similarly, FATF, 1998:7 and FATF, 2002b:8). Others have voiced similar opinions, as reflected in the following statement: 'The best fraud schemes are so good that they are not discovered. So, who can tell me that it is not happening', which sounds like an article of faith: 'I believe because I cannot see it', coming close to the thesis of Tertilian: 'Credo quia absurdum'.[20]

Against this background of non-events and unwavering belief, the case that possibly comes closest to being evidence is that of the by now defunct European Union Bank. Reportedly, this Antigua-based Internet bank 'explicitly proposed completely anonymous investments' (FATF, 1998a,b:11). Such offerings have been suggested to represent money laundering services being advertised through the Internet (FATF, 2000b:4). The story of the European Union Bank played between 1994 and 1997. In 1994, the East European International Bank was established on the island of Antigua and within a few months of its establishment, the name of the bank was changed into the European Union Bank. Having set up a site on the World Wide Web, the European Union Bank was called the 'first offshore bank operating via the Internet' (FATF, 1998a, 1998b:72). Services available from the European Union Bank included numbered accounts, international wire transfers online, tax protection, and '[a] number of other specialized bank services to meet individual needs'.[21] Through the European Union Bank, customers could also register an Antiguan International Business Corporation within 48 h and for $995. Such corporations were advertised as 'a perfect privacy tool', because of the allowed use of bearer shares, the absence of a public share register, no disclosure of shareholders, no disclosure of beneficial ownership, and the absence of a requirement to file any corporate reports.

Because of these advertisements, the European Union Bank was accused of being involved in money-laundering activities. By mid-1995, auditors reported that they were unable to state whether the financial statements presented by the bank fairly presented its financial position. At the end of 1996, the Bank of England advised potential depositors to exercise appropriate due diligence with respect to the European Union Bank. Early 1997, the Ministry of Finance of Antigua told the European Union Bank that it was 'not in good standing' and later it issued a fraud warning (Blum et al., 1998:58–59 and 62). In August of the same year, the two owners of the bank absconded with the bank's deposits, which were said to amount to $10 million (Bonorris and Coates, 1997:41), apparently leaving a notice on the locked door of the bank's office above a dentist's office and Nio's Bar and Restaurant, stating that 'European Union Bank Inc. has been placed in receivership effective this eighth day of August 1997' (Rohter, 1997).

Although the case of the European Union Bank has been presented as one of money laundering through the Internet, a number of arguments can be brought forward that put matters into a different perspective.

In the first place, we already observed that owners of 'hot money' are not necessarily looking for shady banks with an unknown management, which may abscond with their funds, as happened with the European Union Bank.

A second issue concerns the funds that a money launderer would want to transfer to an institution like the European Union Bank. To deposit money, the launderer would either have to transport his funds to the bank, for instance, in cash, make a giro transfer, or use electronic money. In the first case, the Internet or electronic payment systems would not be used at all. In the second case, the money launderer would already have deposited his funds successfully in some account, circumventing anti-money laundering measures, such as the reporting requirements. In the third case, the money launderer would have to buy electronic value with cash money in the first place, dodging again anti-money laundering measures, just as in the second case.

Thirdly, it should be realised that the example of the European Union Bank appears to be the only one of its kind to date. Following the case of this bank, it was reported that 'entities are using the Internet to offer money-laundering services', sometimes styling themselves as legitimate 'offshore financial services' or 'investment opportunities', but no new concrete examples have been presented (FATF, 2000b:4). Moreover, the owners of the European Union Bank escaped with a mere $10 million: they were no launderers but thieves.

Fourthly, it can be argued that, even though warnings and injunctions may not prevent people from doing business with financial institutions of questionable repute, they can help to put pressure on local regulators to take action. In the case of the European Union Bank, the Antiguan authorities in the end took some action, which may have induced the bank owners to abscond (Blum et al., 1998:62).

Fifthly, the possible 'cascading downward' of regulatory coverage, that is, strict and effective supervision being circumvented through badly supervised issuers offering services in well-regulated territories, has been "argued to be worse in cyber space, but [it is] hardly a unique problem" (Mussington et al., 1998:47): it also exists in the world of bricks and mortar.

Just as was done just now for the case of the European Union Bank, arguments that cyber payments make money laundering much easier, "for instance because of an alleged inadequacy of rules and legislation, the supposedly anonymous character of electronic payment systems, the alleged non-availability of audit trails, large transaction volumes or ease of use" can be either put into perspective or even simply dismissed (Schudelaro, 2003, ch. 7). This leads to the conclusion that at present electronic payment systems do not present the money-laundering threat as once imagined.

This conclusion is supported from various sides. The Bank for International Settlements, for instance, has concluded with respect to electronic money that, "in most cases, the security features that suppliers intend to implement (...) might make these products less attractive for use in criminal activities than many existing payment instruments" (Bank for International Settlements, 1996:25). Others have stated that "only fully anonymous digital cash stands much chance of aiding in financial crimes such as money laundering".[22] Systems of this kind enabling users to transfer large amounts of money do not exist and are unlikely to be introduced in the future. Moreover, the question remains which rational criminal would be willing to invest in expensive efforts to launder money in a new, well-secured electronic money system (Lelieveldt,

1998:82). According to the FATF, "[t]here is no single design feature of the various e-money systems currently available or envisaged which will make them especially attractive to money launderers" (FATF, 1997b:64). Although this statement was made in 1997, there is no reason to believe the present situation is any different. More generally, and also including on-line banking systems, the FATF has stated that measures like putting limits on the amounts of value that can be transferred using cyber payment systems, linking usage of on-line payment instruments to accounts that have been established in a face-to-face manner, enforcing know-your-customer principles, and developing information technology tools to detect suspicious on-line transactions, could all help deal with the potential vulnerability of cyber payments to money laundering (FATF, 2000b:13).

Finally, the apparent lack of evidence supporting the claim that cyber payments are a money-laundering threat should be considered as well. In 1997, the FATF wrote that "it is premature to consider prescriptive solutions to theoretical problems" (FATF, 1997b:67). In 2004, problems do not appear to have developed much beyond that stage, underlining our conclusion that responsible policy makers should not raise the alarm without proper fact finding and weighing the evidence.

## Computer crime legislation

In the introduction we announced that anticipating threats from new forms of crimes can be met in a 'cool', controlled and well-balanced way. To underling this statement we will now compare the political characteristics of the war against money laundering with the tactics and strategy employed in a similar environment, i.e. the danger of computer crime: policy makers can be effective without threat images.

During the late seventies and the eighties of the past century, it became evident that the ICT-revolution would not leave substantive and procedural criminal law untouched. Little imagination was required to recognise that existing provisions of substantive law and prevailing techniques of law enforcement would quickly become obsolete. Two simple examples may suffice to underscore this point. Traditional criminal law used to be well equipped to protect against intrusions of the premises (home and property) of citizens. In the computer era many new ways would be opened to trespass someone else's domain without intruding into his physical domain. Gaining illicit entrance to a person's computer files is one case in point; copying his data and appropriating them without permission is another. Neither of these actions were covered by existing substantive criminal law, even though they represent modern equivalents of common criminal behaviour (Groenhuijsen, 1991). The second example is about procedure. In old times – i.e. until recently – bookkeeping records were nicely written down on paper and stored in folders or filing cabinets. When someone was suspected of law breaking, law enforcement officials had the power to search and seize paper evidence. Not so anymore. Bookkeeping and filing has to a large extend been automated, and at present even the most conservative enterprise has most of its records on hard discs and in computer networks rather than in print on a bookshelf. Police investigative powers at best provided for seizure of the hardware involved, but they were powerless if the data were shielded from access by complicated passwords or encryption methods.

Near the end of the previous section, we quoted the FATF in writing that "it is premature to consider prescriptive solutions to theoretical problems". How did the issues connected with looming computer crime relate to this point of departure? It is interesting to briefly outline the response of the Dutch government in this area, since it demonstrates a markedly different approach compared to the money-laundering issue.

In 1987, the Dutch authorities charged a specialist committee (the 'Franken-committee') with mapping out the field. The committee had to find out whether substantive and procedural law were inadequate in a future ICT-environment. In its final report, the committee made 29 recommendations to modernise existing statutes. The government accepted the main line of analysis of the committee, amended some of its proposals, and introduced the Computer Crime Act I, which came into force in 1993. The Act provided for some relatively moderate adaptations of the Codes of Criminal Law and Criminal Procedure. It inserted new articles criminalizing, *inter alia*, 'unlawful entry of a computer system' and 'unlawful manipulation[23] of computer stored data'. From a procedural angle, the Act introduced a new power to not only monitor telephone conversations, but to intercept all kinds of communication taking place within a telecommunication infrastructure.[24] It explicitly mandated authorities to search an automated system. In addition, it allowed investigators to issue an order to an administrator to access a secured computer system.[25] Hence, new offences were created and additional investigative powers were conferred on law enforcement officers. Yet from the point of view that concerns us in the present contribution – i.e. the comparison with the response to the perceived menace of money laundering – the Computer Crime Act I features remarkable restraint. This is confirmed by the explanatory memorandum of the Act, claiming that the government seeks to maintain a 'steady level' of penal-law protection. The objective of the Act is *not* to increase the range of criminal liability, but only to adapt an existing system to the new, computer dominated environment (Wiemans, 2004:95).

An important inference is that we find it quite natural and prudent for a legislator to intervene at a point in time when damage to society is foreseeable, but has not yet materialised (Groenhuijsen, 1990:14). This experience demonstrates that new legislation can be justified when the scope of a problem is not yet clear and when the precise extent of projected damages have not yet been determined. The condition, which has to meet in cases like these, though, is that there is indisputable consensus among all experts about the likelihood of rapidly increasing numbers of incidents in the field to be covered. If that is the case, it would even be wrong to suspend action until a series of dramatic events occurs, because that would entail the serious risk of a hasty response with unbalanced measures urged by the heat of the moment (overkill).

We do not contend that the approach adopted in this area is beyond criticism. At the time the Computer Crime Act I was introduced, many academic writers felt that parts of it were either inappropriate or undesirable. Some authors implied that there was more law on computer crime than there were criminals in this area (Kaspersen, 1993). Others disputed the claim of the government that the Computer Crime Act I did not raise the level of repressive powers of law enforcement.[26] Apart from that, the fact remains that the explicit *intention* underlying this piece of legislation was not to enhance the powers of the criminal justice system, but rather to preserve an already existing state of affairs in the face of new technological developments.

Similar observations can be made about the subsequent drafting of the Computer Crime Act II.[27] In principle, we feel it is good practice to proceed in the way elaborated above. The rationale is to maintain a piecemeal approach, based on practical experience with existing provisions and keeping track of specific new developments in ICT. Hence the draft CCA II provides for additional penal protection of e-mails which are stored with Internet providers, it criminalizes sending so-called 'email-bombs', it extends the crime of forgery to cover forged chip cards, and in procedural matters it calls for more powers to gain access to computer systems by expanding possibilities to give an order to allow access and/or to decrypt stored data.

Again, our purpose is to demonstrate fundamental differences in the approach adopted in this area compared to the efforts we have analysed in response to the perceived threat of money laundering. From this perspective 'and leaving details aside' it is significant to notice a distinct and continuing attitude of restraint and prudence in the former field. Just one example to finally underscore this point. Even though it is obvious that dealing with computer crime in a responsible way will require further expansion of substantive and procedural criminal law, the Dutch legislator has thus far proceeded with caution and recognized other interests, which need to be respected. This is exemplified by the fact that despite dire predictions of horrific consequences in the fight against organised crime, the Dutch government has thus far refrained from introducing a general obligation to decrypt data filed in an encrypted mode.[28]

The next step will be the implementation of the Convention on Cyber-crime. This Council of Europe convention calls the member States to adopt national legislation on a number of specific topics of substantive and procedural criminal law (Kaspersen, 2004). Interestingly, even on this international level it appears that more moderation is visible in connection with cyber crime than is the case in the arena of money laundering.

Returning to the main line of argument in the present contribution, we can conclude this section with two general observations:

- computer crime legislation addressed the potential of tangible harmful infringements by modernising substantive penal law, while anti-laundering policy aimed to protect an abstract legal interest like the integrity of the financial system by addressing the entire flow of money and information;
- computer crime addressed procedural law to anticipate future investigative problems with modernised criminal investigative tools for evidence finding in an electronic environment, while anti-laundering regulations cast an all-encompassing legal net bestowing law enforcement agencies with powers to catch even the smallest criminal fish.

## Nebulae still prevail

Money-laundering remains legally and empirically a hazy area. This is partly due to the phenomenon itself and partly to the way it is approached by politicians and policy makers: many of its aspects are shaped by the way it is defined. That approach is mainly determined by law enforcement perspectives and not by a phenomenological analysis. When that perspective broadens or shifts, so does the phenomenon. While the essence of laundering still is making a 'black', illegal possession 'white', the wide juridical drapery around it, enshrined in an all encompassing definition, covers *any* kind of proceeds related conduct, which may, but does not necessarily need to lead to 'whitewashing'.[29] Within the law enforcement perspective, the picture seems to be clear and mainly related to cash-based traditional crime for profit, mostly committed by the 'usual' offender. Whether the loot may eventually be 'whitened' (which happens less often than is assumed) is irrelevant, as anyone knowingly or negligently handling these proceeds may be a part in the laundering process.

This stand seems quite unambiguous, but its strict application opens the gate to ever-widening fields. Apart from the fact that a perpetrator of a predicate offence cannot escape being his own launderer, unless he destroys his loot immediately, all members of his crime-enterprise or household, who knowingly benefit from his criminal income, are guilty of laundering too. Within relationships in the criminal underground economy (mainly trade in prohibited substances) this is still rather clear. However, moving away from the initial emphasis on this cash-based underground economy, to the field of economic crime, an indeterminate horizon unfolds. This concerns the circle of suspect people involved. For example, is the staff of a fraudulent firm, not involved in the fraud itself, but receiving a 'hush bonus', as much guilty of laundering as the accountant who tampers with the books to justify the illegal revenues? Are the partners of the culprits also guilty of laundering, happily mingling the 'hush money' with their household money?[30] Apart from the circle of potential suspects, taking the Convention of the Council of Europe as a general template, and marking all illegally acquired advantages (including illicitly saved production costs) as proceeds, leads to a broadening of the application. This broadening is not only due to the fact that all economic crime-profits are 'proceeds', but also to the accountancy technique of processing these illegal savings. This entails that the subsequent interweaving of these proceeds in the books, for example for corporate or income tax declarations, can be qualified as documentary (tax) fraud as well as laundering.[31] As within corporate settings one fraudulent act requires 'successor' acts as a technical cover-up to balance the books, one can easily construct a long 'hereditary' chain of laundering actions with many accessories.

These considerations have an important bearing on the potential extent of the laundering 'problem' and on the way it may be represented. The initial official concern about laundering was focused on *drug* money. We have seen that there was a great interest in 'big numbers'. As Reuter (2000) suggested, a low estimate would not invalidate the correctness of the anti-laundering policy, but would lower the readiness to invest the huge bureaucratic efforts. Hence, Reuter's low estimate of global drug proceeds was viewed unfavourably by the FATF: indeed, no bureaucracy can live with low numbers. The inclusion of the proceeds of economic crime can heavily (and happily) contribute to the desired trillions, but certainly thicken the existing nebulae. The following example illustrates the complexity, which arises:

> How to determine what and how much is laundered in the case of a successful VAT (or excise) fraud scheme of €500.000? Such a windfall can be handled in two ways. It can be shipped out of the country, which is a single act of laundering, or it can be absorbed within the firm. In the last case it leads to a corporate increase of assets, which is covered by the original false invoices. As soon as the tax declaration is accepted by the

tax inspector that money is 'white', which would yield 35% corporate tax (€175.000). Is that tax form the laundering instrument and the after tax profits (€325.000) the laundered money?

Fraud schemes are rarely that straightforward. The firm has still some illegal payments to settle: €100.000 is used to pay the unrecorded (black) wages of the staff, the straw man of the front firm and the accessory director of the foreign delivery firm. These expenses are covered by a false invoice to another front firm, which was dissolved soon afterwards. This yields a reimbursement of 20% VAT 'paid' to the front firm: €20.000. But there are more expenses to deduct: another €50.000 is paid as bribe to a customs officer and booked as 'consultancy fee', again lowering the corporate tax. Now, the firm has to pay 35% corporate tax over €370.000 (including the false reimbursement of the VAT), which is €129.500: originally the firm would have to pay €175.000 tax, yielding an illegal saving of €45.500. Having paid €279.500 on tax plus criminal business expenses, the firm has a 'white' net profit of €220.500. The director awards himself a bonus of €200.000 and the creative accountant €20.500, whose incomes are dutifully mentioned in the income tax forms and taxed with 50%, leaving a final 'white' income of €110.250. How much has been laundered?

€500.000: the basic VAT *proceeds*;
€520.000: the initial VAT proceeds plus the falsely reimbursed VAT;
€220.500: the *net profits* mentioned in the income tax forms;[32]
€110.250: the final net profits *after* income tax;
€370.500: the net profits plus the €150.000 paid to staff, strawman, delivery firm and the corrupt official (all laundering by merely accepting their share);
€860.500: the sum of all the separate cover-up invoices, (false) tax forms and beneficiaries (corporation and private persons) of the VAT money:

$$2 \times €100.000 + €20.000 + €50.000 + €370.000 + €220.500.$$

This is not just a hypothetical case: in daily practice prosecutors and defense attorneys bicker about such calculations, as the outcome determines the amount of the money to be recovered.[33] Little surprise that there is no really right answer.

If we take into account that this is just a simplified example of (organised) business crime, we obtain a fair idea that approaching the volume of laundered money in a responsible way requires a careful analysis per economic sector, based on an unambiguous definition. It also requires a choice between a legal and an economic definition. A legal definition is *conduct* based. In our example, the corporation, as well as the natural persons each launder crime-money, which together may yield a sum larger than the original defrauded sum. From an economic point of view only the laundered ('whitened') and expended moneys are relevant, as these flow into the upperworld economy. From this perspective the economist will argue a downward correction for the amount of money, which flows directly into the public fund due to a higher 'white' income and corporate tax of the successful launderers.[34]

Such an analysis is an arduous, but necessary undertaking if we want to lift the veils surrounding the conventional threat imagery. Do we observe a willingness to shed light through those veils? Judging from the observable policy of the FATF, the member states and the FIUs involved, the situation is still little better than in 1998. At that time, the informal Money-Laundering Experts Group of Europol recommended to 'identify a uniform statistical model with minimum basic statistics formulated in a compatible manner' (Crimorg, 1998:173). To no avail: a viability study and a report later, opaqueness still prevails. Whether out of ignorance, lack of interest or sullen resistance to design a quantitative analytic tool to survey, make comparable and analyze the registered cases of suspicious transactions and/or the money-laundering prosecutions, none of the recommendations have been heeded (Van Duyne and De Miranda, 2000).

Though we do not assume an intention, maintaining the nebulae in this field (tacitly) serves certain valuable functions. The most important function is the prevention of the disclosure of the 'financial disclosers', because of a looming 'emperor's cloths-effect'. In general, the results of the anti-laundering policy hardly mirror the collective efforts of financial institutions and public agencies. Without denying that the drug markets generate much money, and substantial sums of money have occasionally been confiscated, all put together, it does not come close to the official threat imagery. There are also no indications that the drug markets are caving in as a result of the anti-crime money policy. Changes like the shrinking of the ecstasy market have been related to changes in youth culture (lower popularity of techno music) and not to law enforcement actions in general or anti-laundering in particular (Gruppo Abele, 2003).

In this context designing a transparent performance measure for the agencies involved is well-nigh impossible, and probably not welcomed. The absence of such measures allows each agency the freedom to pursue its own bureaucratic goals. For example, for the Dutch Agency for the Disclosure of Unusual Transactions, a tacit performance indicator is the number of reports they receive. In reaching a high number target, the agency is astoundingly successful. Subsequently, after a test, reports, which have certain features, will be forwarded to a police support unit for a deeper analysis in order to communicate them to detective squads for a criminal investigation and subsequent prosecution. However, this part of the system is much less successful, similar to the findings of Gold and Levi (1994) 10 years ago.

Lacking a valid overview of the crime-money landscape and indicators of the law enforcement impact, any shortcoming can be attributed to any other cause but the anti-laundering policy and its implementation. The usual culprits are the 'cunning criminals', who allegedly always succeed in finding new loopholes and out-manoeuvring the investigators: 'they are always one step ahead' and 'we run after the facts' are frequently heard complaints. Hence, 'we need more powers', is the 'conditioned response'. Here a spiral effect may be set into motion. This spiral does not contribute to a balancing of the various legal interests of law enforcement and civil rights.

**Balancing legal interests**

The policy of anti-money laundering has been disseminated with a zeal befitting a messianic message of 'apocalypse now'. As with most apocalypses, financial-economic reality proves to be highly resilient, weathering various financial storms and scandals, which did inflict harm and which may have been less pernicious, if with due diligence the sneaky ways of handling the proceeds of such misdeeds would have been prevented or interrupted. Hence, no apocalypse, but occasional criminal financial disasters and scandals did occur.[35] Despite grave warnings, the virtual cyber-laundering apocalypse did not even show a first trace of inception. The conclusion 'do not fear without facts', was not drawn: the issue simply evaporated without feedback or lessons learned. This fits into a 'policy of fear' (Van Duyne, 2004). Indeed, the phenomenon of laundering has obtained a political-emotive weight and fear component, which it shares with other whipped up fears, such as concerning drugs, organised crime (with its later fear enhancing addition 'transnational') and recently terrorism. As a matter of fact, absence of facts rather stimulated more severe legislation, instead of reflecting on the effects of the policy followed thus far. Such fear loaded perspectives, which tend to set into motion a virtual autonomous policy making of ever more severe measures, square badly to other elementary legal notions like proportionality and civil rights.

The internationally strong political emphasis on the 'threat image' of laundering has contributed to placing laundering in the higher levels of the maximum punishments in some jurisdictions: 20 years imprisonment in the US and 14 years in the UK, and (at a moderate level) 6 years imprisonment in the Netherlands or 5 years in Germany. As in most jurisdictions the laundering offence is regarded as a *separate* offence, which can be committed by the perpetrator of the predicate offence himself (the *reflexivity* principle), situations can arise in which the maximum punishment for the predicate offence is lower than for the subsequent laundering offence. Because crimes for profit (particularly when the loot cannot immediately be consumed after the act), require some form of hiding, concealing, transport etc., it is difficult to see how a perpetrator can avoid the offence of laundering, short of turning himself in or at any rate betraying himself. This is particularly the case with documentary fraud. In many fraudulent schemes – particularly within corporate settings – the predicate profit generating offence has to be complemented by additional acts to make the books (falsely) balance. The defense may plea for the merging of the two acts in a 'continuous activity', though if the laundering act is actually a separate decision, it can be counted as an offence in its own right. This implies that the offender can be charged with the heavier crime of laundering in cases in which the less punishable predicate crime entails technically the laundering. Only those who are so inapt as to forget to cover the financial or documentary 'fingerprints' of their crimes can avoid this additional charge. This can be compared with imposing an extra punishment on murder or manslaughter if the perpetrator has wiped off his fingerprints and removed other traces at the scene of crime: 'guilty of interfering with the course of justice'. How far does the reflexive application of the laundering offence go towards crossing the line of self-incrimination?

A related aspect concerns the cross-border handling of crime-money and the dual criminality of predicate offences. Laundering has been made a crime in virtually all jurisdictions, as no government dares to incur the wrath of the FATF and become blacklisted. As arrest warrants can be issued on the separate offence of laundering alone, one can be arrested for extradition for 'laundering', while the predicate offence is not punishable in the country which is requested to extradite. For example: the European Union has introduced the European arrest warrant and Poland requests the extradition of the director of an illegal abortion clinic who has wired the proceeds to Germany or the Netherlands, where abortion is legal. From the Polish point of view the director is a launderer, which makes the request for extradition difficult to refuse, even if according to Dutch or German law there is no predicate offence. But that is not the issue they have to respond to: that concerns laundering, albeit for a Polish predicate offence. There are many variations to this theme, like environmental crimes, the proceeds of which may be wired to a jurisdiction in which such offences do not exist. A Hungarian industrialist violating the strict German environmental laws transfers his illegal savings by means of false invoices to his Hungarian holding. This qualifies as laundering. Should the director of the Hungarian branch be extradited to Germany for receiving that money? In short, under the all-encompassing umbrella of the laundering offence a country can be forced to extradite someone for having handled the proceeds of offences for which extradition itself would not have been allowed.[36]

Another aspect concerns the recruitment of private partners in the fight against money-laundering. From the angle of an all-encompassing law-and-order perspective this is a natural criminal problem approach: everybody should be deployed to fend off the menace of (transnational, organised) crime. In a sense, everybody who may deal with crime-money has been turned into an obligatory financial 'deputy-sheriff' (Levi, 1997): from financial institutions to sellers of expensive items. (Willful) neglect of such a duty is punishable, justified by the proclaimed global seriousness of the money-laundering threat. This has two consequences, a practical and a theoretical one. In practical terms, complying with the anti-laundering regulations can take the form of a risk avoiding over-reporting (Harvey, 2005), clogging the system with tens of thousands never-to-processed reports. Not fear of crime-money, but fear of not reporting may be driving compliance (Van Duyne and Levi, 2005, Ch. 1). Albeit compulsory, the designated citizens have become state informants. Have the consequences of this shift in the citizen-state balance been sufficiently thought through?

Contrary to the well-balanced computer crime legislation, more attention has been devoted to fear factors of crime-money than to a detached balancing of various legal and social interests. Within such a narrowed approach, the door appears to be open to other less legal considerations, for example financial performance measures: the yearly confiscation result. The US led the way in harnessing the crime-money recovery policy for income-related criminal justice enforcement. In 1990 the US Attorney General issued a warning to the local attorneys for a 'failure to achieve the $470 million projection [as this would] expose [us] to criticism and undermine confidence in our budget projections' (Blumenson and Nilson, 1997, note 102). This implies an important shift towards a preponderantly revenue-oriented law enforcement. However, according to this view, going after the crime-money is less about restoring justice than about state income completion. When law enforcement efforts are to be measured in terms of the volume of crime-money recovery, we may end with the adage: 'Low yield, poor justice'. Without a responsible balancing of legal and social interests crime-money can be dangerous indeed.

## Notes

1. The number of entrepreneurial law breakers, who gathered huge fortunes with which they established dynasties with 'gentrified' capital, is long: Astor, Carnegie (contributed to the Peace Palace in The Hague), Vanderbilt, Stanford (established the famous university) to

142 P.C. VAN DUYNE ET AL.

mention a few historical names, who would today be prime targets of the FIU's (Abadinsky, 1991, Ch. 2).

2. McClennan Committee (1960); President's Commission on Law Enforcement and Administration of Justice (1965).

3. The RICO has particularly been successfully (or excessively) applied by private citizens in cases against swindlers, security brokers and forms of corporate crime. There were so many cases (about 1000 per year) that a new journal, *RICO Law Reporter*, was successfully launched. Despite these successes, the RICO statute has very often been (ab)used against other targets than were originally intended.

4. Perkins and Gilbert (1987) describe the 'success' of the US imposed eradication programme against cannabis in Colombia, resulting in important shifts of the merchandise to Mexico and other countries in the Caribbean and finally to California. In addition, the policy contributed to the expansion of cocaine as a replacement drug.

5. See for a detailed account of US Central American drug policy: Scott (1992, 1998) and Marshall (1991).

6. Recovery of illegal advantage became part of the Law on Economic Offences in 1947.

7. From its inception the Dutch Commission on Financial Aspects of Serious Crime broadened the scope by designing a recovery policy of illicit profits from *all* forms of (serious) crime.

8. Various increases have been suggested: $500 billion up to $1 trillion (Keh, 1996).

9. FATF 1990 report, chapter 1: Extent and nature of the money laundering process.

10. Dutifully the report mentions that 'One Task Force member estimated global profits at the main dealer level, which might be most subject to international laundering, to be about $30 billion per year'. In the subsequent consensus about the bigger numbers, this lower number was forgotten.

11. A change towards an evidence-based policy making can be observed in the Council of Europe and the European Commission. It remains to be seen whether this 'knowledge spring' will become a summer as soon as the findings from research contradicts politicians' belief's.

12. In certain regional circumstances shifts in property relations have been observed. Some of these, like farmland in Colombia, can directly be attributed to the influx of drug money (Strong, 1995; Thoumi, 1995). The property relations in the former socialist states of the erstwhile Comecon countries is another example of (half) criminal distribution of property, not primarily due to the inflow of crime-money, but to corruption, mismanagement, inexperience and economic crime (Varese, 2001). See for the South Italian criminal economic situation Paoli (2003).

13. This observation may apply generally to the Western industrialized countries; in the Russian Federation criminals often targeted banks for obtaining influence (Rawlinson, 1996).

14. In 2004, the Belgian government announces a moderate tax amnesty together with more effective controls due to improved exchange of information with foreign banks in Europe. This led to a massive repatriation of money and a huge spending on consumer articles and house improvement.

15. The Banco Ambrosiana (Cornwell, 1987) and the BCCI (Kochan and Whittington, 1991) are mixed cases, but the losses these banks incurred were not due to crime-money deposits. The BCCI is a mixed case, but its crisis and scandal had little to do with mismanagement, as the shareholders had signed a blank check to bail it out, with the blessing of the Bank of England (see Passas, 1995, 1996).

16. This section is based on Schudelaro (2003, Ch. 7).
17. Bonorris and Coates (1997, p. iv).
18. Technology writer and, since September 1996, senior editor of Newsweek magazine Steven Levy as quoted in Hoogenboom (1997).
19. US Department of the Treasury 1996, section III, Law Enforcement, and G-10 (1997:12).
20. KPMG forensic accountant F. Hoek, as quoted in Van Dinther (2000:40).
21. Website of the European Union Bank as quoted in Blum et al. (1998:60).
22. Mondex chairman Tim Jones as quoted in Froomkin (1996).
23. According to the wording of the Act, this includes altering the data, deleting data, making data inaccessible or illegally adding data to the system (viruses etc.), art. 350a Criminal Code.
24. The new powers included interception of fax-messages, emails, and online communications.
25. It must be noted, though, that such an order cannot be addressed to someone who is in the position of being a 'suspect' of the crime; the legislator considered such an extended power to be a violation of the principle against forced self-incrimination.
26. Kuitenbrouwer (1987) in response to the recommendations of the Franken-committee, a criticism, which can directly be extended to the legislative end-result.
27. The proposal for the CCA II was submitted to parliament in 1999. It now looks as if the draft might be withdrawn or adapted in order to kill two birds with one stone: improve on the CCA I and at the same time secure implementation of the Convention on Cybercrime, ETS, 185 (Wiemans, 2004:197).
28. In exercising this self restraint, the government resists the advise of some practitioners in law enforcement and accepts the recommendations from the best academic research on the subject, i.e. Koops (1999).
29. From empirical perspective it may more neutrally be called 'criminal financial management', as has been done in Van Duyne (2003) and Van Duyne and Levi (2005).
30. This is not a hypothetical option: under Dutch law partners of social security fraudsters have been prosecuted for receiving. Now they can be prosecuted for laundering as well.
31. The defendants of the ENRON and WORLDCOM scandals have been charged with fraud, conspiracy, organised crime and laundering.
32. In this paper, we have not gone into the issue of proceeds versus profits: according to the FATF the proceeds concern the total gross payments, profit that is actually received after business costs. Most money-laundering figures are based on proceeds, which increases the obscurity because business costs only enter the laundering stage if they are illegal income for the service provider too.
33. The tax authorities do not operate according to these refined calculations: they simply estimate the 'fiscal damage', which is always higher than the net profit.
34. Similarly the economist will correct for immediate consumer expenses on taxed articles and services, which leads to a direct flow-back of indirect taxes.
35. It is interesting to observe that in none of the major scandals that were unveiled in the industrialised countries in the last decades, crime-money, let alone drug money was involved. For example, all bribe moneys came from licit industries: from Lockheed to Dassault and Agusta, from Watergate, the Iran-Contra scandal to Chancellor Kohl's illegal party coffers. Sometimes the term 'laundering' has loosely been applied, though no underlying crime was proven. E.g., the flight capital from South America and Russia, or the stolen capitals of dictators in Asia and Africa, which were rather 'moral crimes' than criminal offences.

144                                     P.C. VAN DUYNE ET AL.

36. The requirement of double criminality has been abolished for a list of 32 broadly described offences, money-laundering being one of these (Malewicz and Hamer, 2004).


## References

Abadinsky, H., *Organised Crime* (Chicago: Nelson Hall, 1991).

d'Aubert, F., "L'argent sale. Enquête sur un krach rententissant" (Parijs, Plon, 1993).

Arlacchi, P., "Mafia Business," *The Mafia Ethic and the Spirit of Capitalism* (London: Verso, 1985).

Baloun, V. and M. Scheinost, "Financial Crime in the Czech Republic," in P.C. van Duyne, K. von Lampe and J.L. Newell (eds.), *Criminal Finances and Organising Crime in Europe* (Nijmegen: Wolf Legal Publishers, 2003).

Bank for International Settlements, Committee on Payment and Settlement Systems and the Group of Computer Experts of the Central Banks of the Group of Ten countries, Security of Electronic Money, August 1996.

Bewly-Taylor, D.R., The United States and International Drug Control, 1909–1997 (London: Pinter, 1999).

Blum, J., M. Levi, R. Naylor and P. Williams, "Financial Havens, Bank Secrecy and Money Laundering," United Nations Office for Drug Control and Crime Prevention, 1998.

Blumenson, E. and E. Nilson, "Policing for Profit: The Drugs War Hidden Agenda," http:www.fear.org/chicago.html.

Bonorris, S. and V. Coates, "Digital Money: Industry and Public Policy Issue," (Washington DC: The Institute for Technology Assessment (ITA), October 1997).

Borgers, M., De ontnemingsmaatregel (Den Haag: Boon uitgevers, 2001).

Bortner, R.M., "Cyberlaundering: Anonymous Digital Cash and Money Laundering," Presented as final paper requirement for Law & the Internet (LAW 745), a seminar at the University of Miami School of Law, 1996.

Cornwell, R., "God's Bankers," *The Life and Death of Roberto Calvi* (London, Unwin Hyman, 1987).

Crimorg, 173, "Multidisciplinary Working Group on Organised Crime," *Draft Report on the Informed Money Laundering Expert Group* (Den Haag: Europol, 1998).

De Mas, P., "De poreuze noordkust van Marokko," *Justitiële Verkenningen*, 2001(5), 72–86.

Desroches, F.J., "Drug Trafficking and Organised Crime in Canada: A Study of High-Level Drug Networks," in M. Beare (ed.), *Critical Reflections on Transnational Organised Crime, Money Laundering, and Corruption* (Toronto: University of Toronto Press, 2003).

Dinther, M. van, "Vrijspel voor witwassers.com," FEM/DeWeek, 18 March 2000, pp. 38–41.

Duyne, P.C. van, "Money-Laundering; Estimates in Fog," *The Journal of Asset Protection and Financial Crime*, 1994 (19), 103–142.

Duyne, P.C. van, "Organised Crime, Corruption and Power," *Crime, Law and Social Change*, 1997 (26), 201–238.

Duyne, P.C. van, "Crime Entrepreneurs and Financial Management," in P.C. van Duyne, K. von Lampe and N. Passas (eds.), *Upper World and Under World in Cross-Border Crime* (Nijmegen: Wolf Legal Publishers, 2002).

Duyne, P.C. van, "Money-Laundering Policy: Fears and Facts," in P.C. van Duyne, K. von Lampe and J.L. Newell (eds.), *Criminal Finances and Organizing Crime in Europe* (Nijmegen: Wolf Legal Publishers, 2003).

Duyne, P.C. van, "The Creation of a Threat Image: Media, Policy Making and Organized Crime," in P.C. van Duyne, M. Jager, K. von Lampe, J.L. Newell (eds.), *Threats and Phantoms of Organized Crime, Corruption and Terrorism* (Nijmegen: Wolf Legal Publishers, 2004).

Duyne, P.C. van, and H.A. de Miranda, *Report on the Falcone Project Data Base Harmonization of Suspicious Transactions* (Zoetermeer, KLPD, 2001).

Duyne, P.C. van, and M. Levi, "Drug and Money," *Managing the Drug Trade and Crime Money in Europe* (London: Routledge, 2005).

Eijlander, Ph., "Idealen en de werkelijkheid," in W. Witteveen and J. Verschuuren (eds.), *De fascinatie Wat wetgeversonderzoekers bezighoudt* (Den Haag: Boom Juridische Uitgevers, 2004).

FATF-VII Report on Money Laundering Typologies, Financial Action Task Force, June 1996.

FATF, Annual Report 1996–1997, Financial Action Task Force, June 1997a.

FATF, 1996–1997 Report on Money Laundering Typologies, Financial Action Task Force, February 1997b.

FATF, Annual Report 1997–1998, Financial Action Task Force, June 1998a.

FATF, 1997–1998 Report on Money Laundering Typologies, Financial Action Task Force, February 1998b.

FATF, 1998–1999 Report on Money Laundering Typologies, Financial Action Task Force, February 1999.

FATF, Annual Report 1999–2000, Financial Action Task Force, June 2000a.

FATF, 1999–2000 Report on Money Laundering Typologies, Financial Action Task Force, February 2000b.

FATF, Report on Money Laundering Typologies 2000–2001, Financial Action Task Force, February 2001.

FATF, Annual Report 2001–2002, Financial Action Task Force, June 2002.

FATF, Annual Report 2002–2003, Financial Action Task Force, June 2003a.

FATF, Report on Money Laundering Typologies 2002–2003, Financial Action Task Force, February 2003b.

FATF, Report on Money Laundering and Terrorist Financing Typologies 2003–2004, Financial Action Task Force, 2004.

Froomkin, A., "Flood Control on the Information Ocean: Living with Anonymity, Digital Cash, and Distributed Databases," *Pittsburg Journal of Law and Commerce* 1996, 395.

G-10 Working Party on Electronic Money, "Electronic Money, Consumer Protection, Law Enforcement, Supervisory and Cross-Border Issues," G-10, April 1997.

Gold, M. and M. Levi, *Money-Laundering in the UK: An Appraisal of Suspicion-Based Reporting* (London: Police Foundation, 1994).

Groenhuijsen, M.S., "Het wetsvoorstel Computercriminaliteit bezien vanuit het gezichtspunt van een behoorlijk wetgevingsbeleid," in F.P.E. Wiemans (ed.), *Commentaren op het wetsvoorstel Computercriminaliteit* (Maastricht: ICCSP, 1991).

Groenhuijsen, M.S. and A. van Kalmthout (eds.), *Voordeelsontneming in het strafrecht* (Arnhem: Gouda Quint, 1989).

Gruppo Abele, *TNI-IECAH and UNICRI, Synthetic Drugs Trafficking in Three European Cities: Major Trends and the Involvement of Organised Crime* (Turin: MARCveyH, 2003).

Harvey, J., "Controlling the Flow of Money-Laundering or Satisfying the Regulators," in P.C. van Duyne, K. von Lampe, M. van Dijck and J.L. Newell (eds.), *The Organized Crime Economy. Managing Crime Markets in Europe* (Nijmegen: Wolf Legal Publishers, 2005).

146 P.C. VAN DUYNE ET AL.

Hinterseer, K., "Criminal Finance," *The Political Economy of Money Laundering in a Comparative Legal Context* (The Hague: Kluwer Law, 2002).

Hoogenboom, A.B., "De vier ruiters van de Apocalyps: Openbare orde en fraude in Cyber space," in *Handboek Fraudebesctrijding*, May 1997.

Kaspersen, H.W.K., "Het Cybercrime-verdrag van de Raad van Europa," in B.J. Koops (ed.), *Strafrecht en ICT* (Den Haag: SDU Uitgevers, 2004).

Kaspersen, H.W.K., "De Wet computercriminaliteit is er–nu de boeven nog," *Computerrecht*, 1993 (4), 134–145.

Keh, D.I. *Drug Money in a Changing World: Economic Reform and Criminal Finance* (Vienna: UNDCP, 1996).

Kochan, N. and B. Whittington, "Bankrupt," *The Financial Scandal of the Century* (London: Victor Gollancz, 1991).

Koops, B.J., "The Crypto Controversy," *A Key Conflict in the Information Society* (Tilburg: Eindhoven Centre for Innovation Studies, 1999).

Kuitenbrouwer, F., "Rapport Franken, gevaar van 'overkill'," in Dossier Computercriminaliteit, *Computerrecht*, 1987 (3), 165–167.

Lelieveldt, S., "Regulering van pre-paid elektronisch geld," in Reader Elektronisch Geld, De Nederlandsche Bank, September 1998, 77–85.

Levi, M., *Customer Confidentiality, Money-Laundering, and Police-Bank Relationship: English Law and Practice in a Global Environment* (London: The Police Foundation, 1991).

Levi, M., "Evaluating the 'New Policing': Attacking the Money Trail of Organised Crime," *Australian and New Zealand Journal of Criminology*, 1997 (1), 1–25.

Levi, M., "Grossbrittanien," in M. Kilchling (ed.), *Die Praxis der Gewinnab-schöpfung in Europa* (Freiburg: Max-Planck-Institut, 2002).

Lilley, P., "Dirty Dealing," *The Untold Truth About Global Money Laundering* (London, Dover (USA): Kogan Page, 2000).

Malewicz, R. and G.P. Hamer, "Het Europese Arrestatiebevel," http://www.cleerdin-hamer.nl/publ_eurarrest.htm.

Marshall, J., "CIA Assets and the Rise of the Guadalajara Connection," *Crime, Law and Social Change*, 1991 (1), 85–96.

Meloen, J., R. Landman, H. De Miranda, J. van Eekelen and S. van Soest, "Buit en besteding. Een empoirisch onderzoek naar de omvang, de kenmerken en de besteding van misdaadgeld," 's-Gravenhage, Reed Business Information, 2003.

Molander, R., D.A. Mussington and P.A. Wilson, "Cyberpayments and Money Laundering, Problems and Promise," RAND 1998.

Mussington, D., P. Wilson and R. Molander, "Exploring Money Laundering Vulnerabilities Through Emerging Cyberspace Technologies: A Caribbean-Based Exercise," RAND 1998.

Nadelmann, E.A., "Cops Across Borders," *The Internationalisation of US Criminal Law Enforcement* (Pennsylvania: The Pennsylvania State University Press, 1997).

Naylor, R.T., "Wash-Out: A Critique of the Follow-The-Money Methods in Crime Control Policy," *Crime, Law and Social Change*, 1999 (1), 1–57.

Naylor, R.T., *Hot Money and the Politics of Debt* (London: Unwin Hyman, 1987).

Paoli, L., "Mafia Brotherhoods," *Organised Crime, Italian Style* (Oxford: Oxford University Press, 2003).

Passas, N., "The Genesis of the BCCI Scandal," *Journal of Law and Society*, 1996 (23:1), 52–72.

Passas, N., "The Mirror of Global Evils: A Review Essay on the BCCI Affair," *Justice Quarterly* 1995 (12:2), 801–829.

Perkins, M.K. and H.R. Gilbert, "An Economic Analysis of the US Drug Control Policy: The Impact of the Cannabis Trade," *Corruption and Reform*, 1987(2), 41–54.

Pieth, M., "The Harmonization of Law Against Economic Crime," *The European Journal of Law Reform*, 1999 (4), 527–546.

Reuter, P., "Transnational Crime: Drug Smuggling," Paper presented at the Conference on Transnational Crime, University of Cambridge, January 2000.

Rasmussen, D.W. and B. Benson, "The Economic Anatomy of a Drug War," *Criminal Justice in the Commons* (Lanham: Rowman and Littlefield, 1994).

Rawlinson, P. "Russian Organised Crime: A Brief History," *Transnational Organised Crime*, 1996 (1–3), 28–52.

Reuter, P. and E.M. Truman, "Chasing Dirty Money," *The Fight Against Money Laundering* (Washington: Institute for International Economics, 2004).

Reuter, P. and V. Greenfield, "Measuring Global Drug Markets. How Good Are the Numbers and Why Should We Care About Them?" *World Economics*, 2001 (4), 159–173.

Rohter, L., "New Bank Fraud Wrinkle in Antigua: Russians on the Internet," *The New York Times* 20 August, 1997.

Schudelaro, A., "Electronic Payment Systems and Money Laundering," *Risks and Countermeasures in the Post-Internet Hype Era* (Nijmegen, The Netherlands: Wolf Legal Productions, 2003).

Scott, P.D., "Honduras, the Contra Support Network and Cocaine: How the US Government has Augmented America's Drug Crisis," in A.W. McCoy and A.A. Block (eds.), *War on Drugs. Studies in the Failure of US Narcotics Policy* (Boulder: Westview Press, 1992).

Scott, P.D. and J. Marshall, *The Cocain Politics* (Berkeley: University of California Press, 1998).

Strong, S., "Whitewash," *Pablo Escobar and the Cocaine Wars* (London: Macmillan, 1995).

Thoumi, F.E., *Political Economy and Illegal Drugs in Colombia* (Boulder: Lynne Rienner Publishers, 1995).

US Department of the Treasury, "An Introduction to Electronic Money Issues, Prepared for the United States Department of the Treasury Conference 'Toward Electronic Money and Banking: The Role of Government'," Washington, September 19–20, 1996.

Varese, F., "The Russian Mafia," *Private Protection in a New Market Economy* (Oxford: University Press, 2001).

Vruggink, J., "Gepakt en gezakt. Invloed van de ontnemingsmaatregel op daders," Leyden, Ph.D. Thesis, 2000.

Wiemans, F.P.E., *Onderzoek Van Gegevens in Geautomatiseerde Werken* (Nijmegen: Wolf Legal Publishers, 2004).

Wisotsky, S., *Breaking the Impasse in the War on Drugs* (New York: Greenwood Press, 1986).

Woodiwiss, M., "Transnational Organised Crime: The Strange Career of an American Concept," in M. Beare (ed.), *Critical Reflections on Transnational Organised Crime, Money Laundering, and Corruption* (Toronto: University of Toronto Press, 2003).

# [26]

# Do European procurement rules generate or prevent crime?

Nicholas Dorn and Michael Levi
*Cardiff University, Cardiff, UK, and*

Simone White
*European Commission, Brussels, Belgium*

## Abstract

**Purpose** – The purpose of this paper is to explore whether opportunities for fraud and corruption might be reduced or increased by rules governing public procurement. The focus is on specific European legislation – Procurement Directive 2004/18 on the coordination of procedures for the award of contracts for public works, public supply and public services by public bodies within all EU Member States – however similar issues would arise in other jurisdictions.

**Design/methodology/approach** – The procurement process is examined in relation to three stages of procedure: preparation of specifications, selection of tenderers, and execution of contracts, within each of which some specific risks (red flags) are identified.

**Findings** – Particular risks that may not have been sufficiently addressed, in terms of research or legislation, arise at the first of these stages; accordingly this paper focuses there. Generally, risks are summarised in terms of insider-driven specifications, low visibility of procurement processes, and ample opportunities for renegotiation of terms. Risks may be increased by innovative procurement practices that have the effect of extending the manoeuvring between tenderers and public bodies, such as competitive dialogue.

**Research limitations/implications** – Fraud and corruption risk in public procurement is an area deserving detailed and comparative study, with special attention to the pre-contracting stage. Research on this topic within EU Member States should go hand in hand with enquiry into international procurement, and into the EC's own rules as applied by its institutions and bodies.

**Practical implications** – Suggestions for risk-reduction are put forward in relation to quality standards and pre-award publicity.

**Originality/value** – After some time as the Cinderella of crime policies, large-scale frauds attract greater interest. This paper gives grounds for asking whether, in relation to procurement fraud, a combination of traditional practices and modernisation may outpace anti-fraud measures.

**Keywords** Public procurement, Fraud, Corruption, European legislation, European directives, European Union

**Paper type** Research paper

## Introduction

This paper may be read as a scoping study, making a broad scan of important European legislation on procurement of goods and services by public bodies in

The work on which this papers is based was conducted in the context of a European Commission funded study, called MARC, on "legislative crime proofing" otherwise known as part of the security dimension of impact assessment. In funding that study, the European Commission was interested in developing a method for understanding the vulnerability of legislative proposals to exploitation by criminals. The authors gratefully acknowledge financial support to Cardiff University for this and other work within the MARC project and thank project partners for their support and suggestions.

the EU Member States, seeking to identify some potential crime risks and preventive aspects of the legislation, which might repay more focussed future study than can be attempted in an overview. The directive in question spans 120 pages and governs procedures for the award of public works contracts, public supply contracts and public service contracts (European Union, 2004). This is a consolidating measure, updating and replacing Directives 92/50/, 93/36/EEC 93/37/and 97/52 (the former Directives henceforth), which between them covered the same topics. Directive 2004/18 also takes account of European Court of Justice case law, clarifying certain matters including definition of a public body and what information should be given[1]. Procurement in the field of utilities (water, energy, transport and telecommunications sectors) is outside the scope Directive 2004/18 and there remain many specific matters, including notably public private partnership and procurement, and e-procurement, which are being further addressed by the EU. The value of making a scan of issues related to Directive 2004/18 is that it offers an opportunity to take a broad view of fraud risks in public procurement.

*Auspices, boundaries and approach*
The research was carried out within the context of an EU-funded research consortium aiming to develop the security aspects of EU impact assessment – sometimes referred to as legislative crime proofing[2]. Within that consortium, an earlier and longer version of this paper served as one of several resources feeding into the development of methods (Curtol *et al.*, 2006). The concern in the present paper, however, is not with methodology but rather with substantive and specific understanding of fraud risks within the procurement process and some practical possibilities for counter-measures.

The central question for this work is whether vulnerabilities to fraud may have been increased or decreased by the Directive, which refers to procurement by public bodies in the member states. Procurement by EC institutions and bodies (as distinct from national public bodies) is governed by a parallel but distinct set of rules, the financial regulation (European Union, 2002). Although in our opinion some read-across would be desirable between research on frauds within the member states and on frauds involving the EU Institutions and bodies, the focus here remains on the former. This reflects a preference of the European Commission as conveyed by its directorate-general for research and may, to a certain extend, relate to a division of competences between other directorates-general of the commission. Such institutional boundaries are not unknown in other organisations.

From the onset, one comes up against the question of how to "read" legislation when looking for fraud or other crime risks. Should one simply look at the words within and the structure of the text? Or should one be trying to second-guess 27 national transpositions, related national regulations, sets of guidance, approaches embedding these in "procurement cultures", contractors' understandings and business practices, administrative/judicial monitoring, remedies and controls[3], and so on? The first option may be too restrictive, because the implications of the words have to be understood with reference to specific actors, their contexts, understandings, risk assessments and willingness to take action. However, the second option would be over-ambitious, within the modest means available for this study. Faced with such challenges, this study takes a middle course, making judgements on the basis of the literatures on procurement, fraud and corruption; some discussions with specialists[4]; and professional criminological judgement.

# European procurement rules                    **245**

The research process followed was as follows. First, a search was made of academic and professional literature. Discussions were held with a small number of specialists, based in Brussels, Paris (helping to offset the English language bias of most of the literature searches) and Helsinki. As a result, a simple sequential framework of tendering was adopted – preparation, selection of tenderers and finally execution of contracts – within which specific risks (red flags) could be identified on the basis both of specialist experience and the literature. Finally, those known and suspected risks were mapped onto the specific provisions of the Directive. Such linkage was more easily demonstrated and evidenced in terms of the general experience of specialists in purchasing bodies and law enforcement agencies than in terms of court cases, simply because some of the greater risks are not easy to bring to court.

The limitations of information from court cases can be illustrated by making reference to the scope for irregularities at all stages of the procurement procedure. Risks at the pre-tender stage may at least equal risks during selection of bidders or execution of contract. There can be subtle and careful favouring by public officials or technical experts of particular specifications or tenders, when the latter are "friends of friends" or linked by political networks, through which favours later (perhaps much later) may be reciprocated. Such irregularities would usually count as corruption, however tracking their occurrence over time and social space is difficult and proving them even more difficult. Thus, risks may be greatest when direct evidence thereof is least.

The need, therefore, is to look for areas of risk and their possible abatement or exacerbation by regulation. Here, the experience of procurement specialists can be drawn upon. They of course may be rather more concerned with issues of business efficiency and public value than with fraud and/or corruption *per se*. However, specialist procurement commentaries provided us with one valuable point of departure for understanding some broad risks. For example, Christopher Bovis comments that reform of EU procurement directives has been organised around three themes: "simplification", "modernisation" and "flexibility" (Bovis, 2005). There are possible implications for understanding fraud risks, for example simplification might reduce the opportunities for fraud if it reduces ambiguities in procurement processes – through removal of scope for criminality to hide behind textual ambiguities, through enhancing legal certainty and by underpinning more robust enforcement. Moving on to modernisation, Bovis observes the introduction in the Directive of a new award procedure called "competitive dialogue", which enables the public sector to award complex projects such as public private partnerships and trans-European networks more effectively. Notable issues here include:

> The discretion of contracting authorities to initiate the procedure (who is to determine the nature of a particularly complex contract and the inability of the contracting authorities to draw precise specifications and the contract's financial and legal make-up). The internal structure and conduct of the procedure (the confusion surrounding the different stages pre-tender and post tender). [. . .] The degree of competition achieved (there is great potential for post tender negotiations) [. . .] (Bovis, 2005).

Here, legal certainty appears to be rather low, with the implication that "wriggle room" may be appreciable. Until the framework is further clarified, "competitive dialogue" may imply fresh opportunities for crime. These and other considerations are taken up below.

*An outline of Directive 2004/18*

Comparing 2004/18 with the former directives, it consolidates new provisions and in some cases new procurement concepts and procedures can be found in the following areas: framework agreements, competitive dialogues, dynamic purchasing systems, disclosure of weighting of criteria, keeping records and being ready to make reports, environmental and social issues, and electronic auction. Directive 2004/18 does not apply to "secret" or "special security measures" or "protection of the essential interests" of member states, nor to international agreements and contracts in conformity with Treaties between sovereign states, the stationing of troops abroad, work concerning international organisations, or other defined services including independent research. Much other public contracting is caught if involving a price above defined limits[5]. Subdivision of contracts into lots should not be used as a way of getting past the thresholds. Threshold calculations have to include any contractual options or renewals. In the case of renewed or recurrent contracts, a 12-month period is used to calculate thresholds. Contract award criteria may either be price alone, or "most economically advantageous", in which case criteria must be set out in the notice (call), involving either a hierarchy of criteria or weightings. Where stated in the notice, and where price is not the sole criterion, tenderers may submit variants. Contracting authorities must keep internal records about each contract call, the names of successful tenderers, the reasons for each tenderer's selection or rejection, and the circumstances justifying use of negotiated procedures or competitive dialogue[6] or framework agreements[7]. Unsuccessful tenderers must be advised of the reasons why they have not been selected[8]. However, there is no requirement for wider circulation/publication of the results of calls for tender.

Key terms and procedures include "open procedures"[9], meaning those procedures whereby any interested and capable economic operator may submit a tender. "Restricted procedures" means those procedures in which only those economic operators invited by the contracting authority may submit a tender. "Negotiated procedures" means those procedures whereby the contracting authorities consult the economic operators of their choice and negotiate the terms of contract with one or more of these. Negotiated procedure can follow if tenders offered during open procedure, restricted procedure or competitive dialogue are either absent or unacceptable or, in exceptional cases, where prior pricing cannot be done, or in certain circumstances where services are hard to specify. Negotiated procedures can proceed in stages of elimination of contractors. They can also occur without publication of a contract notice (call) in urgent or unforeseen circumstances. In a "concession", what is given is a right to exploit the work or that right together with payment. "Design contests" means those procedures that enable the contracting authority to acquire a plan or design selected by a jury after being put out to competition with or without the award of prizes.

An innovation in the Directive, "competitive dialogue" is a procedure, applicable in complex cases, in which the contracting authority conducts a dialogue with those candidates admitted to that procedure, with the aim of developing one or more suitable specifications capable of meeting its requirements, on the basis of which candidates chosen are invited to tender. In this process, chosen entities submit ideas and plans, possibly in stages, until the purchaser can identify possible solutions, whereupon it asks all tenderers to submit final tenders. In restricted procedures, negotiated procedures and competitive dialogues, the purchaser may limit the numbers of

# European procurement rules **247**

candidates according to non-discriminatory criteria that must be indicated in advance in the notice. Negotiated procedure, competitive dialogue and framework agreement all imply an extended period of discussion between public officials and representatives of firms. This must open up risks, especially when these procedures are entered into repeatedly. "Framework agreement" will be discussed below.

According to Directive 2004/18, evidence of economic stability and technical/professional ability must be provided by tenderers. The directive extended this to quality standards and (where applicable) adherence to environmental standards. An oft-remarked upon safeguard is that exclusion of tenderers is required in the case of their proven participation in a criminal organisation, corruption, fraud or money laundering as defined in EU instruments, bankruptcy, and professional misconduct, failure to pay social security or taxes or related misrepresentation[10]. In order to demonstrate good standing, tenderers may supply an extract from a judicial record, or a certificate, or a witnessed oath or, in member states lacking such possibilities, may self-certificate. We comment on the implementation of this below.

*The preparatory stage of the procurement process.* The procurement procedure occurs in stages, which may be represented as follows:

(1) preparatory stage, when procurement needs, budget and questions of procedure are settled;

(2) solicitation, bidding and selection; and

(3) the execution of contract stage, in which the work is done and delivered (however under certain conditions, fine-tuning of terms and/or possible extension of contract may also occur at that stage).

Criminality may potentially arise at any of the stages.

Although there is relatively little literature on risks associated with the preparatory stage, the following paragraphs give reasons to suggest that it is here that the risks may be greatest. Criminality and/or corruption opportunities arise as decisions are made about whether and how the provisions should be applied in the light of the needs of the purchaser, the type and scale of work envisaged, the criteria to be met by successful providers, the availability of potential tenderers, the procedures to be followed, and so on. External parties may be involved in shaping the requirements, either through their prior work and/or through a specific contract for assistance to the purchasing body. The call for tender will be advertised or not, depending on the procedure being followed.

Key decisions made at this stage will decisively shape the scope and terms of the eventual contract. Such decisions include the choice of procedure, justifications for using open, negotiated, competitive dialogue or emergency procedures, the possibility of breaking work into small packages spread across different budget headings and time-frames, and the specifications and pricing for the work/service/products to be delivered. Such decisions may narrow the field to one or a very small number of tenderers (for example in negotiated procedures or in emergencies) or may even place the work outwith the scope of application of the directive ("smurfing"[11], if carefully done).

Drawing upon the experiences of those consulted, some of the crime risks at pre-contracting stage may be summarised broadly and crudely as procurement staff corruption and/or improper involvement of contractors; fixing the specification or criteria so to unduly narrow the field; setting an unrealistically low price so as to discourage tenders and then entering into negotiated procedure with just one favoured (and possibly appreciative) contractor; "surfing" the work, etc. In the following paragraphs, we draw on available sources to give a few practical examples.

Fictitious work. A "requirement" can be entirely fictitious, invented by procurement staff in order to divert money to self, family or others, without any involvement of tenderers. One UK case illustrates the risk of staff fraud occurring within a purchasing environment:

> In this [. . .] case, a junior member of staff over a period of two years was able to defraud a department of over £100,000 by exploiting weaknesses in purchasing and payments systems. The junior clerk had been employed by the department for six years in the purchasing directorate. [. . .] He was given a password which enabled him to create and edit records. On completion of this task the junior clerk moved to a purchasing team where he was involved in the processing of purchase orders and the information needed to enable payments to be made to suppliers. Security over the computer system was lax and the junior clerk realised that the password previously given to him to carry out specific tasks still allowed him access. In particular, he was able to access the supplier database and create false supplier records [. . .]. The finance section accepted his signature as authorisation for payment. [. . .] No further checking was carried out by management (Her Majesty's Treasury, 2001).

The provisions of the Directive do not bear upon this issue.

Under and over estimation of specification or price. Turning to cases in which there really is a genuine public requirement, on the basis of experiences of anti-corruption and anti-fraud experts and from the literature, a number of procurement staff-related risks can be identified, including the following.

Purchasers may under-estimate the cost of the work, thus failing to get any bids and allowing them to enter into a negotiated procedure with a tenderer, who may give a bribe (success fee) or find a way of returning favours in future (e.g. employment, consultancy or directorships after retirement from public service).

Alternatively, an underestimated tender price may be accepted, leading to requests for more financing, such additional sums then give an opportunity for payment to officials – who may well have understood that the tender price was unrealistically low in the first place and that it would need additional support.

Overestimated tenders, if accepted, also give scope for "commission" payments. Likewise, contracting for already-existing work (or work that is actually done by the purchaser in-house and then given to the tenderer to deliver) allows considerable excess profit, which can be distributed.

Unnecessarily high-technical specifications, or over-estimates of the materials, effort or time required, allow for the possibility of later "recognition" of the "error", permitting a saving for the tenderer. Such misspecification may occur:

- through genuine error or uncertainty;
- where procurement staff naively accept technical advice from an interested party (see below);
- where the purchaser is responsible for checking the work and has no intention of requiring the successful tenderer to deliver fully; or

# European procurement rules 249

- where the purchaser may have intended the high specification to be delivered but another official, responsible for checking deliverables, decides that she can accept work of a lower standard.

In any of those cases, the tenderer may have cause to be grateful.

Political party financing and procurement. Considerable publicity has been attracted over the years to a series of scandals related to the financing of some European political parties. During 2005, persons implicated attested to a well-established "system" in which public works contracts attract a success fee, sometimes 2 per cent of the total contract price, which goes to fund political parties, networks, staff and expenses of well-disposed individuals (*Le Monde*, 2005a). Reports indicate that some of the practices may have been accepted at a high level in several European countries (Samuel, 2005), posing a counterweight to the more usual focus on corruption and bribery in developing countries (Shaxson, 2005):

> L'ancien directeur de cabinet de Jacques Chirac à la mairie de Paris, Michel Roussin, a reconnu mardi au procès des marchés publics d'Ile-de-France qu'il était au courant du système de versement des 2% du prix des marchés par les entreprises aux partis politiques. Interrogé par le président du tribunal sur ce chiffre, M. Roussin (65 ans) a déclaré, mardi, "ne pas ignorer cette histoire des 2% (*Le Monde*, 2005a).

The custom is also known in other national contexts. The reasons suggested for such behaviour vary. Transparency International (2005) points to cultural and organizational aspects, whilst others commentator has pointed to situations in which there were no (or inadequate) sources for funding of political parties. That takes us way beyond the scope of the procurement directive but could be an important contextual point.

In the view of some of those consulted, amongst the most endemic risks are contractors being involved in drawing up specifications. Contractors may assist purchasers by preparing specifications; the information may then be shared with affiliates, subsidiaries or others; or the spec may be prepared in line with a particular tenderer's capabilities and profile. This may occur in cases in which officials are incompetent, uninterested or lazy – in which case they may allow contacts to assist them in an informal (even purely verbal) manner that does not show up in any record – and/or some may be open to inducement. In that case, the persons involved may be linked though professional, social and sometimes political networks, and may show mutual appreciation over the long term, rather than through any immediate and identified "payoff". This risk would be greatest in more technically demanding projects.

Open call: a benchmark?. In considering risks of procedures other than open call, the latter is often taken as a benchmark, since it maximises transparency. However, open call procedure is by no means a guarantee of clean procurement: it may be undermined from outside (contractors), from inside (procurement staff) or from both directions. In anti-fraud investigations, data mining techniques are sometimes used. These techniques can be used to bring together scattered records on procurement, searching for repeated patterns of collusion between tenderers, sometimes referred to as "concert parties". In the following example, a "win/lose" analysis identified unusual patterns in the tendering statistics:

> There were two key elements to this: • Suppliers that consistently lost their bids; and • Suppliers that won more than 95% of bids. Suppliers that consistently lose are often referred

to as "shadow bidders". The sole purpose of such bids was to "pad out" the tendering process to ensure that a sufficient number of suppliers had been invited to bid. [...] In many cases, jobs that were signed off by a Purchasing Manager as having been completed were never started, in others the technical specification was such that costs could be saved by using different materials, and finally there were instances where the cost of the materials was grossly inflated. This was a classic example of control delusion where, just because the controls stated that each contract needed to have five bidders and there was a tender board to select the winning supplier, it was believed that collusion could not happen (Kusnierz, 2003).

According to our sources, such practices are widespread. In extreme circumstances, firms that show signs of not "playing the game" may find themselves in difficulty in their commercial relations or their managers may be disappointed in their hopes for career advancement. Whilst firms and managers have to manage reputational risk and on that score seek to steer clear of any suggestion of impropriety, they also have to get on in markets and social networks.

Inexplicable decision making by purchasing bodies' staff. Although no criminal offence has been identified, a catalogue of embarrassments in procurement of the Scottish Parliament building in Edinburgh was laid out in an investigating barrister's report. This report established that those responsible had adopted "construction management" as the basis for purchasing. It is generally acknowledged "construction management" is highly risky, especially when the purchaser is inexperienced, for the following reasons:

> [...] greater client risk; the complexity of administering many different trade packages (around 60 in the case of Holyrood [Scottish Parliament]); the requirement for the client to be informed and decisive; the need for a good team and brief; the relative difficulty of managing delay and disruption; and most important of all, the absence of any overall contractual programme or contract sum (Fraser, 2004).

Through the choice of "construction management" instead of a safer mode of purchasing, a client may end up with financial and other responsibility without power of direction. The potential benefit to the contractor can be proportional to the disadvantage to the public purse. The report continues that, in the Scottish Parliament case, officials proceeded to take this more risky procurement route, also they re-instated the most expensive bidder when normally that one might have been expected to have been dropped from further consideration[12]. Officials awarded the contract without supervision by ministers – even though clearly the work was high profile, all the more so given the newness and aspirations of the Scottish Parliament. This was an instance when the harm caused may have been broader than the financial aspects.

Remedies? Legal action ensued as McAlphine's, the tenderer that had offered the lowest price, took action against the UK Government, alleging breach of EC rules. However, as of 2005, legislation of some EC Member States did not adequately provide for a dissatisfied tenderer to stop the tender award process, enabling them to take a complaint over procurement procedure to a court with the power to stay or set aside particular decisions (Denton Wilde Sapte, 2002). Strangely, Directive 2004/18 does not incorporate the relevant judgment of the European Court of Justice in the case of Alcatel[13]. However, the member states take note of the ECJ, for example the UK took the Alcatel case into account when amending its national regulations implementing the Directive (Office of Government Commerce, 2005; Field Fisher Waterhouse, 2006).

# European procurement rules 251

Nevertheless, this might have been done in a more consistent manner across the EU had it been done via the directive.

Emergency procedures. Emergency procedures are typically used in humanitarian and security related situations – but not only then. Part of the wider problem is that they may be used in routine situations, following delays caused by the administration itself. The "emergency", in other words, is one that has been constructed, either by incompetence, by indifference or by even a positive appreciation of the lower level of transparency and checks in such procedures.

It seems well accepted, from the literature and from discussion with procurement and fraud specialists, that emergency procedures, whether they be "real" or constructed, have the effect of bypassing the usual safeguards and open the door to high levels of misappropriation. An example from the UK follows:

> [...] £50,000. A contractor performed services for a department and submitted payment requests. Payments began being made on the basis that the payment requests were valid. Further substantiation was requested from the contractor to support the payment requests. Some of the supporting documentation appeared to have been altered and departmental signatures appeared to have been forged. Management controls were not properly applied because the work was carried out during an emergency (Her Majesty's Treasury, 2001, p. 45).

The picture has been clouded further by allegations about private sectors bribes paid to a variety of individuals, private sector bodies and public sector bodies variously in Iraq, elsewhere in the Middle East and in many other countries of the world, including France (*Le Monde*, 2005b), where total, formally Elf-Aquitaine, has once again come to the fore in an unfavourable light (*Le Monde*, 2005c) in part due to US pressures on European and other companies (Katzman and Blanchard, 2005) One aspect of the affair having relevance for European procurement directives and corresponding national laws is the apparent loosening of scrutiny that often accompanies international, humanitarian or urgent contracting (Independent Inquiry into the United Nations Oil-for-Food Programme, 2005). Such problems may go hand-in-hand with a culture of tolerance in purchasing bodies for helping friends and relatives, as may have been the case in the United National central procurement department (*The Times*, 2005; Wikipedia, 2005). The world's largest catering firm, Compass, found its UK subsidiary caught up in that affair (*Financial Times*, 2005). Summarising, the emergency-humanitarian-international procurement nexus seems to present particular risks, since it brings together the use of quick and easier procedures with contracts of very large value.

Exemptions regarding business abroad. Another procurement issue with national/international ramifications is the question of rules and procedures to be followed by European governments and their export agencies when supporting private sector involvement in international development projects. During 2004, this area become noteworthy in at least one EU Member State, the UK, as there was debate on whether it is right for firms to continue to be eligible for government financial support, when they may be involved in bribery and corruption overseas and may admit as much, defending it as normal business practice (UNICORN, 2004; Institute for Public Policy Research, 2004; The Corner House, 2006; ECGD, 2004). That same behaviour in the domestic (EU) setting would result in their exclusion under Directive 2004/18. Private sector lobbyists had not evinced enthusiasm over the possibility of exclusion, saying that though bribery in matters of procurement would be indefensible in any context, all the same it may be essential in many international contexts. A number of think tanks and NGOs put forward the view that such a disparity would not be right.

The point for present purposes is that Directive 2004/18 does not govern the conduct of public bodies when supporting the private sector in procurement abroad (outside the EU). Nor it is clear if it refers to convictions outside the EU. The overall consequence could be that, whilst a public body could not (or should not) do business with a private sector firm whose managers or owners had convictions in an EU Member State, the public body could do business with the same firm if it had offended outside the EU (for example, whilst a public body was politically and/or financially supporting such a firm to gain contracts). It will be interesting to see how much the new UK "National Fraud Strategic Authority" (Attorney General's Office, 2006) would concern itself with behaviour of UK-based firms and persons in relation to bribery abroad, or if it finds its remit restricted to frauds whose recipients are within the UK. The well known case(s) of British Aerospace's alleged payments in connection with armaments for Saudi Arabia come to mind, the UK Government decision to drop the case having prompted legal action for judicial review (Campaign Against Arms Trade and the Corner House, 2007).

Of course, if the objective of 2004/18 is procurement value and probity within the EU only, and if such a restricted notion could be politically "sellable", then such considerations would be somewhat blunted. Indeed it is possible that a corporation feeling impelled to bribe outside the EU for contracts (for example, if it feels that otherwise it is a certainty that another firm would win the contract by bribery), could behave with integrity within the EU. Businesses, like individuals, may behave differently in different contexts (an everyday observation and an elementary bit of social science). At the same time, not all governments would feel comfortable in reinforcing regulatory arbitrage.

*Risks at the stage of solicitation of bids.* At this stage of procurement, there is consideration of tenderers and their offers, and selection of a provider (or consortium of providers). Decisions are made about the suitability (or barring) of specific tenderers, checks should be made to see that tenderers are independent (rather than all or some being structurally linked or formally independent but actually working in concert), and the selection criteria should be applied even-handed manner in order to choose a successful tenderer.

It is understood that internal "crime proofing" work on Directive 2004/18 by the European Commission focussed mainly on this stage and, most specifically, on the question of whether particular tenderers may have past criminal involvements and, if so, how that may be established[14]. However, other sources of risk could also be considered at contracting stage: collusion between tenderers; inadequacy of information available to purchasers for checking tenderers' status, capabilities or past performance; collusion and "concert parties" between contractors who either "take turns" in putting in winning bids or, in some cases, make a reasonable living by being paid for putting in failing bids (an example is given below).

Past participation of tenderers in crime. The consequences of the directive will depend upon how its rather loose requirements on exclusion[15] are carried through into and defined in national laws and in resulting administrative practices. As the UK independent think tank The Corner House (2005) has commented:

> Without detailed guidance on the scope for exclusion, there would be further considerable loopholes that would allow economic operators to evade exclusion on a regular basis.

# European procurement rules 253

EU economic operators may for instance seek to evade exclusion by using a subsidiary to apply for a contract, getting a "clean" company to front a bid on which it may be a subcontractor or control by covert means such as shadow directors, or by changing corporate identity.

Leaving aside the question of whether safeguards would best be take at national or EU level, the more general observation made in the quotation above seems hard to brush aside. A criminal tenderer could "ride a horse and carriage" through 2004/18. One UK case illustrates the risk of lack of proper checking of tenderers, compounded in this case by the lack of information-sharing between purchasing bodies:

> Works contract fraud. [...] A new facilities management contract worth some £1.5 million was to be let for a three-year period with possible extensions for a further two years. The contract was advertised in the European Journal and let under EC procurement rules. A short list of four contractors who expressed an interest was drawn up which included one firm which had carried out maintenance work previously at the sites. The contractors were vetted to ensure that they were financially viable and capable of carrying out the work to the standards specified, except the firm which had been used before. This firm went on to win the contract (Her Majesty's Treasury, 2005).

The Corner House (2005) draws attention to the likelihood that many tenderers with shady backgrounds may not be weeded out because, for example:

* there is an area of non-criminal law "in between" past criminal conviction on the one hand and "professional misconduct" on the other, that is not explicitly referred to;
* active checking is not required by the directive; and
* systems for making checks and sharing information across the EU and with international organisations are not required.

Unanswered questions about negotiation and dialogue. Both negotiated procedures and the new competitive dialogue blur the line between the preparatory stage and the solicitation/selection stage. Competitive dialogue goes further, opening up what may be an extended period of "shadow-boxing" between competing tenderers. Overall, competitive dialogue has been welcomed by big contractors for its "flexibility" and by governments for its ability to clarify technically complex and ambitious aspects of large contracts. However, it is something of an unknown factor from a crime and corruption point of view.

*Risks in execution of contracts.* Once the contract has been agreed in principle, there may be further negotiations on details of scope and price. Depending on the type of procedure employed – a critical issue – these negotiations and their financial and other consequences may be quite considerable. Within certain limits, prolongations or extension of contracts may be agreed, without further competition.

Risks here include "slippage" of work, which either may be inherent in the tender but not anticipated by the purchaser, or alternatively may be engineered by the tenderer in the course of the work in order to obtain an extension. In some circumstances the purchaser may prefer to issue another (differently worded) contract, rather than to admit that things are going badly. In some cases, staff changes may mean that purchasers do not understand that they are being manipulated; in other cases there may be conflicts of interest and corruption. Deliverables should be monitored to assess to what extent they meet the specification: however, if in the specifications themselves or in the checking process there is slackness or corruption, then deliverables may be substandard, replicates of previously provided deliverables, or incomplete or absent (Bueb and Ehlermann-Cache, 2005).

Strengthening the process and encouraging whistle blowing. A contribution to a UK Treasury report by a representative of the firm control risks asks the question, "are there any general principles of fraud control by which organisations can judge themselves?" (Dawson, 2003). Building on this, the present authors offer a compliance matrix (Table I). Scores or 1, 2 or 3 would be allocated (3 being highest level of fraud control). Scores represent whether fraud control policies exist on paper, are whole-heartedly accepted by management, are widely communicated to staff and any subcontractors, and are monitored to ensure compliance; and whether practical controls and procedures exist on each of these points; and whether staff is vetted where necessary; and if appropriate training is given.

It could be for managers within public bodies to require such an approach of all tenderers, and for legal officers (with pubic bodies and/or advising) to ensure such an approach was being implemented. In terms of Directive 2004/18, this might fall within the context of quality standards, which can be taken into account in drawing up and applying specifications and criteria[16]. In other words, in the interests of clean procurement practice, public bodies involved in developing capability standards to be met by tenderers might wish to consider a requirement that all tenderers present information about themselves in such a framework.

This could be a way of presenting to what extent an anti-fraud/anti-crime policy may or may not be in place in tendering firms. In order to be effective, there would need to be a power for purchasing bodies to make independent checks and, to make public and accessible (e.g. by www) the self-assessments submitted by all tendering firms, this being done some time prior to award of contracts. Alternatively, and more economically, there could be a requirement for all tenderers themselves to place such information on a public web site as a normal part of the tendering process. This might assist purchasing bodies to solicit, from the public and from industry generally, any information that might bear on questions of accuracy and fairness of tenderers' self-assessments against the quality standards, though such information (e.g. from embittered ex-employees or indirectly from competitors) would have to be managed carefully. It seems to the authors that the quality approach mentioned immediately above – see Table I – could also be applied to purchasing bodies. This might then have value in reducing procurement crime risk. It would be salutatory for checks to be run by independent entities (be they governmental, private consultants, NGOs or academics), since auditing after the event may be insufficient.

**Table I.** Compliance matrix

| | Policies | Control | Vetting | Training | Overall total |
|---|---|---|---|---|---|
| Exist? Score: | 1, 2 or 3 | 1, 2 or 3 | 1, 2 or 3 | 1, 2 or 3 | $T$ = between 16 (low) and 48 (max) |
| Accepted? | 1, 2 or 3 | 1, 2 or 3 | 1, 2 or 3 | 1, 2 or 3 | |
| Communicated? | 1, 2 or 3 | 1, 2 or 3 | 1, 2 or 3 | 1, 2 or 3 | |
| Monitored? | 1, 2 or 3 | 1, 2 or 3 | 1, 2 or 3 | 1, 2 or 3 | |
| Totals of above | 4-12 | 4-12 | 4-12 | 4-12 | |

**Notes:** Convert $T$ to a percentage; above 60 per cent regarded as acceptable

# European procurement rules 255

Publicity. Finally, the lack of a requirement for general publicity about tender awards – who bid, what in outline was the bid, who was successful, against what criteria and why, decided on what grounds, by whom, who advised – is a major fault-line running through both the former Directives and Directive 2004/18? Only in the biggest contracts does such information find its way into the public sphere; in the myriad of smaller and medium-sized procurement contracts, there is a right for competing tenderers to know the outcome but no requirement for wider publicity. This must lessen the possibility that a wide range of observers at local and regional level – be they competitors, other firms in the sector, trade unions, even academics, compliance offices, audit firms, police, or just interested citizens – could give information relevant to tenders. A timely opportunity for supply of such information could add an external dimension to the process of checking tenderers' representations regarding beneficial owners, managers and staff, and capabilities and activities. Publicity is proving its work in related fields, for example in relation to protection of the financial interests of the European community, where:

> The arguments in favour of transparency are gaining ground. If public money is being used, then its use should not be private. [. . .] Publication is a useful (and cheap) protection against fraud, since farmers may be dissuaded from making false claims if they know that their neighbours can see what they are receiving (King, 2005).

As the same source reports, some authorities have been:

> [. . .] disapproving of efforts by the European Commissioners Mariann Fischer Boel (agriculture) and Siim Kallas (administration and antifraud) to get national governments to disclose who received what money from EU coffers (King, 2005).

Nevertheless, several member states now publish such lists. It should be required at an EU level.

The argument for public disclosure of information would be stronger still if the information could be made public prior to any final decision on award of the contract/grant. The European Court of Justice has ruled that unsuccessful tenderers who allege that they are unfairly dealt with have a right of challenge in court or similar forum. Since such challenge should involve the possibility of the award being set aside, it follows that, before a tender is awarded, there has to be a "cooling off" period in which the purchasing body communicates its provisional decision to all tenderers, to see if any challenge is forthcoming from them[17]. That much is now required. What we are suggesting is that public authorities might also wish to take the opportunity to facilitate challenges from outwith the sometimes narrow ranks of tendering firms.

## Conclusion

Fraud risks in public procurement may be summarised in terms of insider-driven specifications, low visibility of procurement processes, and ample opportunities for renegotiation of terms. In order to deepen our understanding the relationships between formal policies, the contexts of their implementation, the cultural and political "climates" underpinning these and outturns in terms of value for money, fairness, fraud and corruption, we need to engage in more interdisciplinary exercises, involving lawyers, purchasers, policy makers, traders and concerned NGOs and criminologists.

As a preliminary view, the authors suggest that Directive 2004/18 does not address many well-known risks – starting with outside contractors formally or informally

**256**                                                                          JFC 15,3

being involved in drawing up many specifications, continuing with lack of timely and widespread publicity on who has been successful, and progressing through ample possibilities for slippage and re-negotiation of contract parameters (see preceding pages). It's central anti-crime measures, the exclusion of rogue tenderers, may not always be easy to implement in the context of fluidity of European, indeed global, markets; and may be easy to circumvent. Against that troubling background, Directive 2004/18 introduces new procedures that carry new risks, particularly competitive dialogue and framework contracts.

Some of these risks might be mitigated by quite simple measures: suggestions have been made regarding quality standards and publicity. Having said this, it is important to be politically realistic and to bear in mind that neither Directive 2004/18 nor the former directives it consolidates were motivated primarily by the specific objective of reducing fraud risks. Rather, they are seen as an important part of the development of the European single market. Even so, economic growth and market efficiency will hardly be maximised by maintaining opportunities for fraud in procurement and associated corruption in public bodies.

For these reasons we call for fuller study of crime risks in public bodies' procurement procedures, of the extent to which such risks may be increased or decreased by EC rules, and of the broadly corresponding risks facing the European institutions and bodies. There may be a case for more robust input into the policy-making process by the European Commission's Directorate General for Justice, Liberty and Security, and by the EU's anti-fraud body OLAF; even, dare one mention it, more visible cooperation between the two. From an institutional point of view, there may be sensitivity and a perceived need to maintain a boundary between work on frauds against member states and frauds against the EU as such, that boundary corresponding to the procurement Directives and to the EC financial regulation, respectively. This however should be no bar to cooperation on research, given that the risks may be structurally similar, may involve the same *modus operandi* and sometimes the same personalities, may cause similar economic and political harms, and may be susceptible to similar preventive and enforcement measures.

**Notes**

1. Cases C-285/99 and C-286/99 (joint), C-380/98, C-19/00, ECR I-7725. Cour de justice des Communautés européennes, Luxembourg, available at: http://curia.europa.eu/en/content/juris/index.htm

2. For the homepage of the project see, Project MARC – Developing Mechanisms for Assessing the Risk of Crime due to legislation and products in order to proof them against crime at EU level, Università Cattolica del Sacro Cuore, Milan, available at: http://marc.unicatt.it/index.html, for outcomes to date, see Savona (2006).

3. The Court has encouraged the development of decision making at national level, although both it and the commission has had to ensure some basic principles are followed, see for example the Alcatel case mentioned below.

4. The authors have drawn upon conversation with Jean-Pierre Bueb of the SCPS (anti-corruption agency in Paris) and upon his unpublished work. We also benefited from discussion with Seppo Leppa at HEUNI. Bueb (n.d.) refers to "a distinction between cases prior to decision making, cases occurring when the procurement process has been launched, cases linked with particular methods of consultation; and cases occurring during contract execution". In the current paper, Bueb's "cases linked with particular methods of consultation"

# European procurement rules 257

are considered with reference to the phases in which such cases arise, i.e. primarily the procurement planning phase and the solicitation phase. Informal 2005 discussion with OLAF staff is also drawn upon here (OLAF is the EU's anti-fraud office). See also Matechak (n.d.), who says: "Although public procurement processes are fairly complex and can be implemented differently in various jurisdictions, the three main phases of the public procurement process are: 1. procurement planning and budgeting; 2. procurement solicitation; 3. contract award and performance".

5. The financial thresholds for Directive 2004/18 are €162,000 for most supply and service contracts; or, in the case of certain contracts including some awarded by defence sector purchasers or certain telecommunications services, €249,000 or, 6,242,000 for public works; or defined limits in the case of contracts which are subsidised by more than 50 per cent by the contracting authorities. Thresholds are reviewed annually.

6. Article 29 of Directive 2004/18.

7. Article 32 of Directive 2004/18.

8. Article 41 of Directive 2004/18.

9. Article 1 of Directive 2004/18 (definitions).

10. On the topic of exclusion, see White (2000, 2005).

11. "Smurfing" is a term taken from money laundering, namely the careful framing of activities to fall just below the threshold required to trigger reporting to the authorities (or, in this case, the more formal tendering procedures).

12. A Scottish TV news video, "Holyrood building contract legal action", may be viewed on http://scotlandtoday.scottishtv.co.uk/content/default.asp?page = s1_1_1&newsid = 6186.

13. Case C 81/98 Alcatel Austria and others, reference to the Court under the Article 177 of the EC treaty.

14. Source: discussion with EC officials.

15. Article 45 of Directive 2004/18.

16. See Directive 2004/18, Annex VI, definition of certain technical specifications, paragraphs 1(a) and 1(b), page 217 and elsewhere in the main text of the directive.

17. Judgment of the Court (Sixth Chamber) of 28 October 1999 – Alcatel Austria AG and Others, Siemens AG Österreich and Sag-Schrack Anlagentechnik AG v Bundesministerium für Wissenschaft und Verkehr. Reference for a preliminary ruling: Bundesvergabeamt – Austria. Public procurement – procedure for the award of public supply and works contracts. Review procedure – Case C-81/98, available at: http://europa.eu.int/eur-lex/lex/LexUriServ/LexUriServ.do?uri = CELEX:61998J0081:EN:HTML#SM. See also earlier comments above regarding Alcatel case.

## References

Attorney General's Office (2006), *Fraud Review: Final Report*, Attorney General's Office, London, p. 377, available at: www.lslo.gov.uk/pdf/FraudReview.pdf (accessed 24 July).

Bovis, C. (2005), *Reforming the Public Sector: The New Public Procurement Regime*, eGov monitor/Knowledge Asset Management Ltd, London, available at: www.egovmonitor.com/node/1152 (accessed 31 May).

Bueb, J-P. (n.d.), *Fraud and Corruption in Public Procurement*, SCPS, Paris, (non- published, informal English translation of French language text, pp. 39).

Bueb, J-P. and Ehlermann-Cache, N. (Eds) (2005), "Inventory of mechanisms to disguise corruption in the bidding process and some tools for prevention and detection", *Fighting Corruption and Promoting Integrity in Public Procurement*, Organisation for Economic

# 258

Co-Operation and Development, Paris, pp. 161-74, available at: www1.fidic.org/resources/integrity/corrup_proc_OECD-rapport-2005-aase.pdf

Campaign Against Arms Trade and the Corner House (2007), *Legal Challenge to Decision to Drop BAE Corruption Inquiry*, CAAT and The Corner House, Sturminster Newton, update on proposed judicial review, available at: www.thecornerhouse.org.uk/subject/corruption/ (accessed 25 January).

(The) Corner House (2005), Submission from the Corner House to OGC consultation on draft regulations for EU procurement Directive 2004/18 and proposed guidance. The Corner House, Sturminster Newton, available at: www.thecornerhouse.org.uk/pdf/document/EUprocur.pdf, pp. 9-10.

(The) Corner House (2006), *Still Serious Loopholes in ECGD's Anti-Corruption Procedures*, The Corner House, Sturminster Newton, available at: www.thecornerhouse.org.uk/item.shtml?x = 400043 (accessed 21 October).

Curtol, F., Pesarin, G. and Vander Beken, T. (2006), "Testing the mechanism on EU public procurement legislation", *European Journal on Criminal Policy and Research*, Vol. 12 No. 3, pp. 337-64, available at: www.springerlink.com/content/u55422x3g5x7966w (accessed 15 December).

Dawson, S. (2003), "Is fraud benchmarking feasible?", *2002-2003 Fraud Report: Anti-fraud Advice and Guidance*, Treasury, Assurance, Control and Risk Team, London, December, available at: www.hm-treasury.gov.uk./media/389/A7/fraud_anti_fraud_adv_02-03.pdf, pp. 3-7 of 27.

Denton Wilde Sapte (2002), *The Potential Ramifications on the UK PFI Industry of the Alcatel Austria Case*, Denton Wilde Sapte, London, February, p. 4, available at: www.dentonwildesapte.com/assets/P/PFI_AlcatelAustriaCase_Feb02.pdf

ECGD (2004), *Consultation on Changes to ECGD's Anti-bribery and Corruption Procedures: Interim Response*, Export Credit Guarantee Agency, London, available at: www.ecgd.gov.uk/index/pi_home/pi_pc/abc_int_resp.htm

European Union (2002), Council Regulation (EC, Euratom) No 1605/2002 of 25 June 2002 on the Financial Regulation applicable to the general budget of the European Communities, L 248/1-48. *Brussels: Official Journal of the European Communities*, available at: www.bsrinterreg.net/programm/_downloads_No_2002_1605_en_Budgetary_principles.pdf (accessed 16 September 2002).

European Union (2004), Directive 2004/18 of the European Parliament and of the Council of 31 March 2004 on the coordination of procedures for the award of public works contracts, public supply contracts and public service contracts, *Brussels: Official Journal of the European Union*, L 134/114-240, available at: http://europa.eu.int/eur-lex/pri/en/oj/dat/2004/l_134/l_13420040430en01140240.pdf (accessed 30 April 2004).

Field Fisher Waterhouse (2006), *Public Procurement, the Modernising Regulations*, Field Fisher Waterhouse, London, p. 12, available at: www.ffwpublicsector.com/documents/Procurement_and_EU/publicprocurementmodernisingdirective.pdf

*Financial Times* (2005), "Compass dismisses chief of UK division", *Financial Times*, p. 25, available at: www.linkselection.com/detframe.asp?doit = 518258 (accessed 4 November).

Fraser, L. (2004), *The Holyrood Inquiry, A Report by The Rt Hon Lord Fraser of Carmyllie QC*, SP Paper No. 205, Scottish Parliament, Edinburgh, September, pp. 80-1, available at: www.holyroodinquiry.org/FINAL_report/chapter%2006.pdf

Her Majesty's Treasury (2001), *Fraud Casenotes*, H.M. Treasury, Assurance, Control and Risk Team, London, p. 9, available at: www.hm-treasury.gov.uk./media/90A/8A/fraud_casenotes200105.pdf

# European procurement rules **259**

Her Majesty's Treasury (2005), *2004-2005 Fraud Report: An Analysis of Reported Fraud in Government Departments*, H.M. Treasury, London, November, available at: www.hm-treasury.gov.uk/media/8E8/A9/Fraud_Report_2004-05-141105.pdf

Independent Inquiry into the United Nations Oil-for-Food Programme (2005), *Report on the Manipulation of the Oil-for-Food Programme, Chapter III – Humanitarian Goods Transactions and Illicit Payments* (so-called *Volcker Report*), United Nations Iraq Oil-for-Food Programme, United Nations, New York, NY, available at: www.iic-offp.org/documents/Final%20Report%2027Oct05/IIC%20Final%20Report%20-%20Chapter%20Three.pdf (accessed 27 October), p. 184.

Institute for Public Policy Research (2004), *Response to the ECGD Consultation on Changes to ECGD's Anti-bribery and Corruption Procedures Introduced in December 2004*, Institute for Public Policy Research, London, June, p. 4, available at: www.ecgd.gov.uk/ippr.pdf

Katzman, K. and Blanchard, M. (2005), *CRS Report for Congress [on] Iraq: Oil-For-Food Program, Illicit Trade, and Investigations*, The Library of Congress, Congressional Research Service, Washington, DC, p. 32, available at: www.fas.org/sgp/crs/mideast/RL30472.pdf (accessed 14 June).

King, T. (2005), "CAP confessions better late than never", *European Voice*, 27 October, p. 12.

Kusnierz, R. (2003), "A case for data mining – using advanced analytical data mining techniques to detect fraud", *2002-2003 Fraud Report: Anti-fraud Advice and Guidance*, H.M. Treasury, Treasury, Assurance, Control and Risk [team], London, December, pp. 8-14, available at: www.hm-treasury.gov.uk/media/389/A7/fraud_anti_fraud_adv_02-03.pdf

*Le Monde* (2005a), *Marchés publics: Michel Roussin était au courant du système des 2%*, Le Monde, Paris, available at: www.lemonde.fr/cgi-bin/ACHATS/898923.html?offre = ARCHIVES& type_item = ART_ARCH_30J&objet_id = 898923 (accessed 26 Avril).

*Le Monde* (2005b), *'L'image de la France*, Le Monde, Paris, available at: www.lemonde.fr/web/article/0,1-0@2-3232,36-698517@51-696953,0.html (accessed 12 Octobre).

*Le Monde* (2005c), *La dérive corruptive du programme Pétrole contre nourriture*, Le Monde, Paris, available at: www.lemonde.fr/web/article/0,1-0@2-3226,36-657879,0.html (accessed 3 Juin).

Matechak, J.P. (n.d.), *Fighting Corruption in Public Procurement*, Center for International Private Enterprise, Washington, DC, available at: www.cipe.org/pdf/publications/fs/matechak.pdf

Office of Government Commerce (2005), *OGC Consultation on the Amendments to Procurement Regulations [of UK] Implementing Alcatel August 2005*, Consultation document [on] draft amendments to regulations implementing the ECJ judgment in the Alcatel case, Office of Government Commerce, London, August, p. 23, available at: www.ogc.gov.uk/embedded_object.asp?docid = 1004104

Samuel, H. (2005), "Chirac allies go on trial over 'bribes scandal'", *Daily Telegraph*, available at: www.telegraph.co.uk/news/main.jhtml?xml = /news/2005/03/21/wfran21.xml (accessed 21 March).

Savona, E. (2006), "Double thematic issue on: proofing EU legislation against crime", *European Journal on Criminal Policy and Research*, Vol. 12 Nos 3/4, available at: www.springerlink.com/content/p34422451323

Shaxson, N. (2005), "The Elf trial: political corruption and the oil industry", Global Corruption Report 2005, Transparency International, Berlin, part 4, Corporate Money, available at: www.globalcorruptionreport.org/download/gcr2004/06_Corporate_money.pdf

*(The) Times* (2005), "UN budget chief on corruption charge", *Times Online*, London, available at: www.timesonline.co.uk/article/0,3-1762467,00.html (accessed 3 September).

**260**                                                        JFC 15,3

Transparency International (2005), "Political finance regulations: bridging the enforcement gap", *Policy Briefing 2/2005*, Transparency International, Berlin, p. 4, available at: www.transparency.org/content/download/1920/11242/file/02policy _brief _political _ finance_regulations.pdf

UNICORN (2004), *Submission by UNICORN to the ECGD Consultation on Changes to ECGD's Anti-bribery and Corruption Procedures Introduced in December 2004*, Export Credit Guarantee Department, London, p. 4, available at: www.ecgd.gov.uk/unicorn.pdf

White, S. (Ed.) (2000), *Procurement and Organized Crime: An EU Wide Study*, Institute of Advanced Legal Studies, London.

White, S. (2005), *Fighting Corruption and Promoting Integrity in Public Procurement*, Chapter 30, OECD Publishing, Paris, pp. 251-5.

Wikipedia (2005), "Alexander Yakovlev (on UN procurement)", Wikipedia entry, available at: http://en.wikipedia.org/wiki/Alexander_Yakovlev_%28UN_procurement%29

**Corresponding author**
Nicholas Dorn can be contacted at: dorn@cardiff.ac.uk

# [27]

# Criminal Profits, Terror Dollars, and Nonsense

**by R.T. Naylor**
*Special to CJI*

Today there seems to be a broad consensus that a complex financial investigation followed by seizure of illegal assets is the most powerful tool both to control crime and, increasingly, to preempt terror. Such a strategy has led to: the creation of an unprecedented new class of offenses; the conscription of the private financial sector in a way previously unknown even in wartime; a rollback of traditional legal protections combined with a de facto reduction in the burden of proof; a sharp shift in law enforcement priorities towards the money trail; and the introduction of a new complication in international relations. Yet these remarkable initiatives are hardly the product of careful consideration of the nature of a threat and possible responses. Rather they emerged in the 1980s in an atmosphere of inflated fears and exaggerated expectations, and have resulted in a cumbersome, costly, and increasingly intrusive regulatory framework which lacks any defensible criteria by which its success (or failure) can be judged.

### THE LOGIC OF THE STRATEGY

The U.S. was the first to implement a (more or less) coherent follow-the-money strategy, and remains the sole country with the financial and political muscle to impose some uniformity of standards abroad. The American model is built on five pillars.[1]

One is a new crime called money-laundering which makes a set of acts that are in themselves harmless (like opening an offshore account or wiring some money abroad) major crimes if committed by one group of citizens but perfectly legitimate if committed by another, and elevates to the status of serious offenses what were previously seen as minor regulatory infractions (like failure to fill out a form).

Second is a new set of reporting requirements whose purpose is not to help the government protect the solvency and liquidity of the financial system or to achieve macro-economic

---

*R.T. Naylor is a professor of economics at McGill University in Montreal, Canada. His books include among others* Hot Money and the Politics of Debt, Satanic Purses: Money, Myth and Misinformation in the War on Terror, *and* Wages of Crime.

stability, the roles played by traditional financial monitoring, but to feed information about the citizenry on an ongoing basis from the financial sector to law enforcement and, increasingly, to the national security apparatus.

Third, using these new regulations, police and prosecutors prioritize efforts to find, freeze, and forfeit something known as the "proceeds of crime," a slippery concept capable of multiple interpretations, aided by a progressive loosening of the legal grounds (from criminal to civil to sometimes merely administrative) on which such "criminal assets" get forfeited to the state or its agencies.[2]

Fourth, in the U.S. "proceeds-of-crime" go to the police forces that do the grabbing, threatening to turn them into self-financing bounty-hunting organizations. In that respect, fortunately, few places have yet followed the American lead.

Fifth, because of progressive liberalization of world financial flows, to work internationally the model demands, if not full homogenization, at least substantial coordination of regulations among countries.

These five features combined have produced a veritable revolution in criminal justice methods. Of course, there is nothing new about financial investigations or even the forfeiting by court order of illegally obtained wealth. However, traditional financial investigations were reactive—a property crime was reported and the police got on the trail. Success or failure was judged on a case-by-case basis. The target was usually predatory offenses, involving fraudulent or forcible redistribution of wealth. And the purpose of an investigation was to seek evidence against perpetrators and to make restitution to victims. By contrast, with a modern follow-the-money strategy, investigations are often proactive. Justice bureaucrats articulate objectives with respect to the criminal economy as a whole. The target is mainly market-based crimes involving consensual exchanges between suppliers and customers. The immediate target is income earned in criminal transactions, not stolen property. Since there are no direct victims to whom restitution is due, seized wealth goes to

continued from page 27

the state or its agencies. And the ultimate purpose is to deter perpetrators. Taking away the money supposedly removes both the motive (profit) for crimes and the means (criminal capital) with which to commit them. To this is sometimes added that it prevents criminals from using proceeds-of-crime to infiltrate the legal economy.

## THE STRATEGY IN ACTION

The operational core of the strategy is a profound shift in the relations of "banker," client, and police. In the past the police seemed convinced that the typical manager of financial assets and his/her client operated furtively on one side of a brick wall with the police shut out on the other. However in correcting a situation which may occasionally have gone overboard in terms of financial privacy, the pendulum has swung back so far that now it is more like police and banker forming a secret cabal (albeit with the banker often a reluctant participant) leaving the client on the far side of that wall with little or no prospect of a court-ordered window drilled through it. This has occurred because of differences in how various financial-reporting procedures operate.

A Currency Transaction Report (CTR) is automatically required when a deposit or withdrawal of monetary instruments reaches a mandated threshold; the banker asks the client for predetermined information; and the client is fully informed. Thus, whatever its other faults, the process is reasonably objective; and the banker's role is passive, simply a conduit for information flowing from client to authorities.

However a Suspicious Transaction (or Activity) Report results not from an exogenously determined limit, but from something in the transaction or transactor which appears suspicious to bank personnel. Here the bank is reactive; the information is strictly subjective; and the client is uninformed. Indeed the institution and its staff can land in serious legal trouble if they alert the client.

With Know-Your-Client (KYC) rules, the financial institution becomes proactive, seeking information about the client prior to any transaction with the client again remaining in the dark. In effect the role of the institution is no longer that of a conduit, or even of a police informant, but of a private detective agency, a role which few institutions either wish or are competent to fulfill.

Financial institutions cooperate because failure to do so can bring civil penalties (fines and forfeitures), criminal charges against the institution and/or its personnel, or a major money-laundering scandal leading to a flight of clients, private lawsuits, or the collapse of share prices.

## THE "REASON" WHY

To understand how the criminal justice system got its hands on such a blunt weapon, it is necessary to recall six erroneous or exaggerated beliefs prevalent in the 1980s.

First, reputedly enormous sums were generated by crime. Country after country reported burgeoning underground economies, sometimes exceeding legal GNP. The world's drug trade was alleged to be turning over $500 billion annually. The fortune of a notorious gangster like Pablo Escobar was pinpointed by police intelligence at somewhere in the $2-14 billion range. And so forth. Such numbers, based mainly on hype and hysteria, quickly became facts-by-repetition, while much more modest ones derived from more defensible methodologies were pointedly ignored.

Second, the threat posed by such sums was presumed all the greater because they were under the control of great "cartels"—large, durable and hierarchically structured transnationals of crime. No doubt occasionally in places lacking effective policing and burdened with corrupt judiciaries and/or complicit politicians, this model might have some relevance. But in most western countries, it was (is) absurd. Even if a big, hierarchically controlled "organization" emerges from time to time, it is highly visible, and police forces target it on a priority basis. In reality economically motivated crimes are largely the work of individuals and small groups who engage in arms-length transactions of an opportunistic nature and generate modest profits.

Third came fears (continuing to this day) that such "cartels" plotted to use their huge profits to capture and corrupt the commanding heights of the legal economy. Certainly criminals from time to time seek entry into the legal economy. They may seek long-term security, available only from legitimate income flows; they may wish to make bequests to biological rather than to criminological heirs; they may want tax cover for their illegal funds by reporting them as legal; or they may want to apply criminal methods to legal businesses to enhance profits. Only in that last case, and only if it is widespread in key sectors of the legal economy, is there a true emergency. So far such an alarming scenario exists mainly in the minds of alarmist police officers and reporters with overactive imaginations. Certainly ample criminal activity exists within the legal economy; but it is mainly the work of bent insiders. Their objective is not to convert illegal money into apparently legal via the formal financial system, but to convert legal into illegal, then hide it somewhere else—precisely the opposite sequence to that used to rationalize the anti-money laundering regime.

Furthermore "infiltration" of criminal money into the legal economy may not always be such a bad thing. Advocates of the anti-proceeds strategy sometimes cite the pioneering example of Italy's 1982 Pio La Torre law. Certainly that law tried to prevent illegal money from taking control of legal businesses with a view to enhancing profit by applying criminal methods; it also sought to prevent legally-earned money from investing in the higher returns available in the criminal economy. However, to neutralize the adverse economic impact of criminal money, its main intent was to use the threat of asset seizure not so much to confiscate criminal assets as to frighten illegal money to move from the illegal sector, and from legal businesses functioning illegally, into strictly legal operations. In other words, far from blocking the movement of funds from the illegal to the legal sector, the law hoped to encourage just such a flow with the proviso that the money would subsequently behave legitimately.[3]

In addition to concerns over huge sums supposedly in the hands of great cartels of malefactors covetously eyeing the Fortune 500, three other important beliefs drove the follow-the-money fad. One was a changing concept of criminal motivation.

The old-fashioned view was that criminals were motivated by a complex if fuzzy mix of psychological, social, and economic factors. The newer view saw the criminal as stepping straight out of an elementary university micro-economics textbook. If criminal motivation reduces to a simple cost-benefit calculation, the notion that taking away the money will also remove motive might have some merit. However if criminal motivation is considerably more complex, the result may be grossly inflated expectations about what the threat of asset seizure can possibly accomplish.

A fifth factor, whispered in private conversations rather than spelled out in formal police reports, was the view that bankers by nature were the devil's apprentices, an opinion reinforced by widely repeated stories about the misdeeds of Swiss bankers in particular.[4] If banker and client were so intent on forming a secret partnership against the probes of the law enforcement apparatus, it seemed to make sense to have an independent source of data, for example, via a flow of mandatory reports on client activities. But if bankers were normal members of civil society, some upstanding, some dodgy, most simply trying to stay out of trouble, the logic faltered.

Finally at work were corporate-cum-political agendas. American banks were fully aware that if they were precluded from offering as much client confidentiality as their main (British and Swiss) competitors, they might lose business handling the assets of what they euphemistically called the "high net-worth individual." No doubt the U.S. Treasury was also worried about spooking foreign clients who had been so eager to plant their savings, legal and illegal, in American stocks and U.S. government treasury bills, helping to finance both the budget and visible-trade deficits. The solution was articulated by presidential hopeful, Senator John Kerry. "If our banks," he said, "are required to adhere to a standard, including offshore, and other banks do not and rush for deposits in those U.S. banks, we will once again have taken a step that will have disadvantaged our economic structure and institutions relative to those against whom we must compete in the marketplace." Hence the effort to impose

continued on page 30

continued from page 29

the same level of reporting requirements on foreign banks who wanted either to do business in the U.S. or to use the American-controlled international clearing system.

## DOES IT ACTUALLY WORK?

Such political machinations would perhaps be forgivable if the resulting policy actually fulfilled its objective of shrinking the relative size of the criminal economy. The standard "proof" offered is that the police are seizing ever more assets. That is a double delusion. First, what counts is not total seized assets but seized assets relative to total criminal assets—the police could grab more each year while the criminal economy continues to expand, criminal assets along with it, even faster. Second, this criterion confuses instrument and objective. The instrument is seizure of part of the stock of criminal wealth (assets). The objective is reduction of the flow of criminal income. To determine if the instrument is actually having a serious impact requires that the ratio of seized to total criminal assets be increasing. But to find out if taking away a rising percentage of criminal wealth is effective in actually shrinking the size of the criminal economy requires that the ratio of criminal to total income be falling.

Finding the numerator of the first, the asset ratio, seems simple enough. Every year the Justice apparatus reports total seized assets. But that data may include materials with innocent co-owners. The authorities might also toss in things like "instrumentalities" of crime (cars, houses, boats, planes etc.) which have nothing to do with the proceeds therefrom, could also be of innocent origin, and in practice could have little or no real functional relationship to the offense. The figures, too, may lump together assets seized under criminal criteria with those seized under civil criteria—common sense suggests they be treated differently. Most egregiously, such data tend to conflate two quite different concepts—the assets of criminals and criminal assets—ignoring the fact that people designated as criminals, too, are capable of holding down a day job and may well have been the beneficiary of the recent demise of a well-to-do maiden aunt. And of course the relevant starting point ought to be assets ultimately adjudicated by courts not those loftily proclaimed in press releases issued by police or prosecutors.

Even if seized (and forfeited) asset figures could be suitably adjusted, the bigger problem is ascertaining the total of criminal assets actually in existence. The process would logically start with an estimate of total criminal income. Then it would be necessary to guess a profit rate. After all, criminals are motivated not by total income but by net income or profit—which is also the basis for the formation of criminal assets. But that is not enough. Some part of profits may be dissipated in consumption of legal or illegal goods and services. Hence it is also necessary to estimate a savings rate out of criminal profit. Then the figures must be summed over the appropriate number of years while adjusting for rates of return on financial assets, rates of depreciation of durable goods, and capital gains on valuables like gold jewelry or vintage cars. These adjustments can be difficult but not impossible if estimates of profit and savings rates are reasonable, and if there is also a good estimate of total criminal income with which to start the process. That key variable, aggregate criminal income, is obviously also essential to the second part of the exercise, the trend in the ratio of criminal to total income in the economy.

The obvious way to calculate criminal income is from data on the underground economy. Here there is an immediate complication. Most underground economic activity is "informal" rather than criminal—it might involve evasion of commercial regulations and taxes, but most goods and services informally traded are perfectly legal. Similarly there is probably substantial barter activity that sidesteps the formal economy, again to avoid or evade taxes. The criminal sector, dealing in explicitly prohibited goods and services, is likely much smaller. But estimates of the underground economy are aggregates. Hence what is required is both its overall size and the percentage in the criminal category.[5]

Certainly the numbers reported on the total were alarming. In the U.S. they ran as high as 35% on top of official GNP (or, as is more common today, GDP). Even more alarming figures appeared elsewhere in the world.[6] What was rarely reported along with the numbers is how they were calculated. Some were based on (highly questionable) surveys to find a hidden labor force. Some were based on (unwarranted) extrapolations from (seriously limited) tax data. Some tried to turn technical indicators (like electricity use) into estimators, a huge stretch. Some were built on a (logically and statistically) problematic notion of a measurable discrepancy between national income and national expenditure. Most popular were techniques based on monetary aggregates that were so flawed as to produce a veritable growth industry just devoted to debating and disputing their results.[7]

Not only were these techniques either too limited or fatally flawed, or both, but the results were all over the map. For example, a right-wing think-tank agitating for a roll-back of taxes and regulations in Canada, using an aggregate monetary measure, claimed an underground economy equal to 50% of measured GDP. In other words one dollar in three earned in Canada was clandestine. On the other hand, the national statistical agency broke down the Canadian economy into sub sectors and asked how much money could possibly be hidden in each of them. It arrived at an underground economy equal to about 1.5% of GDP. No matter how big (or, more likely in major western countries, small) the underground economy really is, it would be foolhardy to judge the efficacy of public policy on the results of an exercise that can yield estimates ranging from 1.5-50.0% of GDP.

Furthermore to figure out how much is actually criminal is complicated because not all economically-motivated crimes are actually part of the underground economy. Predatory crimes involve the fraudulent or forcible redistribution of existing wealth

rather than the creation of new incomes. Hence they are neutral with respect to GNP or GDP. Some crimes are commercial in nature, involving business enterprises as perpetrators and/or victims of other businesses. These redistribute existing income flows rather than creating new ones. The only crimes that matter for GNP calculations are market-based crimes which involve the generation of new income flows. But even here there is a fundamental problem.[8]

Economic activity can be underground in two quite distinct ways: Its existence can be hidden, or its nature can be disguised. A prostitute, for example, might walk the streets and accept cash. There is no record; GNP is understated; and taxes go unpaid. Going upscale, that same prostitute might work under cover of a massage parlor or escort service and accept checks or credit cards. If so, the transaction enters the national accounts, misrepresented on the micro level but captured on the macro. Because of police and tax-inspector pressures, the more illegal income someone earns, the greater will be his/her propensity to create a suitable front through which to launder it. To the extent illegal incomes are laundered, they are measured as part of the legal economy. To then add an estimator of any such activity to legal GNP would involve double counting. On the other hand, most illegal activity left in the unrecorded part is likely so small in scale and value that it is not worth the effort to measure.

There is only one sensible conclusion. Although this or that component of hidden economic activity may be estimated from time to time with some degree of accuracy, no one has any idea how big the aggregate underground economy is, or, for that matter, what percentage is actually criminal. Hence there is no basis on which to calculate the ratio of criminal to total income, or the ratio of seized to total criminal assets. Therefore there is no way of knowing whether a follow-the-money strategy can ever work.

continued on page 32

continued from page 31

## THE PROBLEM OF "COLLATERAL DAMAGE"

On the other hand, there is ample proof of social costs. Far from being aberrant, and therefore correctable to make the strategy work better, offenses against natural justice and common sense are built into the inherent logic of each of the five key components of the American model, the one that has been widely, if not completely, imitated and/or imposed around the world.

First, the new crime of money-laundering has not only elevated regulatory infractions to the status of high crimes but has so distorted natural justice that today handling the money ostensibly generated by a crime can lead to much tougher sentences than the underlying offense. Furthermore the law is unnecessary. Existing legal concepts of aiding and abetting or accessory-after-the-fact or even criminal conspiracy could do at least part of the job. Or the underlying offenses could be rewritten to make handling the money part of the primary crime. A stand-alone offense called money laundering makes as much sense as would a crime called driving-the-get-away-car for bank robbery cases.

Second, this new crime has rationalized a regulatory apparatus that has turned the domestic, and increasingly the international, financial system into a global espionage apparatus. It puts financial institutions in a position of conflict of interest between their responsibilities to clients and shareholders and their duties to police and national security agencies. It produces a self-defeating deluge of information, particularly with the CTR. It puts a premium on rumor, bias, and stereotype, especially with the STR. And it tries to convert financial managers into private detectives, as with modern KYC rules. (A KYC rule was originally supposed to help to protect an institution, for example against potential fraud by clients—now its main intent is to protect "society," a dramatic and not very well-considered shift of mandates.) The resulting information passes through the financial institution's internal hierarchy before being sent to some government bureaucracy, which sifts through it then, in turn, passes tidbits on to the fiscal authorities, police forces, or national security agencies, a remarkably indirect and cumbersome method of generating usable information. To work, it must also be broad and indiscriminate. Yet if the citizenry at large are really as inclined to violate law as such a sweeping reporting regime seems to imply, the state has a much greater problem than the criminal justice system is likely to be able ever to resolve.

Third, the point of all this is to find assets that can be seized on increasingly loose criteria. Particularly notorious is the fad of civil forfeiture. If individuals have certain guaranteed rights in criminal procedures, their assets have very little in civil procedures, which leads to the interesting result that someone can have their wealth seized on the grounds that it must be the proceeds-of-crime and the person thereby indirectly labeled a criminal (or worse, a terrorist financier) without the benefit of a criminal trial to establish truth or falsehood of the accusation. Recent "reforms" in the U.S. did eliminate the old requirement that the person losing wealth post a 10% bond before beginning recovery procedures, allowed for the first time an "innocent owner" defense, and shifted the burden of providing a preponderance of evidence onto the government. But they did nothing to impede use of civil procedures in what are to all intents and purposes criminal processes.[9]

Fourth, in the U.S. (with police in other jurisdictions agitating for like treatment), seized assets go to police forces. This puts a premium on cultivation of paid informants, detaches police

budgets from real logistical needs, subverts community control, shifts attention from violent to wealthy offenders, and leads to (amply documented) instances of police corruption.

Fifth, to function, the model has to be imposed on the rest of the world even though legal traditions, institutional capacities, and social priorities may be radically different. And all this with no proof that the strategy can actually achieve its goals.

If there is no credible basis for optimism about the policy with respect to crime control, how much more foolish to depend upon it for terror control. The logic of deterrence presumed in the follow-the-money fad is three fold—removing the money takes away the motive for crimes, the means to commit them, and the financial capacity to infiltrate the legal economy. Yet with terrorism, clearly money is not a motive; nor do terrorists have ambitions to take over (as opposed to occasionally bringing down) the commanding heights of the legal economy. All that remains is the means argument—which fails in the face of reality. In case after case around the world, horrendous acts have not required humongous sums. Ultimately the key asset for terrorist acts is determination which cannot be frozen in a bank account.[10]

## MORE THAN REASONABLE DOUBT?

Some will claim that there is no viable alternative. But presumably it ought first to be genuinely proven that a dramatic policy change was actually necessary. Even if the case can be made for special measures, in recent times various countries, prior to being bullied or bribed into following the American lead, experimented with radically different policies to deal with the problem of "black money" in terms of their own priorities.

Some issued state bearer-bonds to make underground money temporarily available for budgetary finance. Some used tax and cash-deposit amnesties to increase fiscal resources or bank liquidity. Some employed capital-flight amnesties to bring home offshore nest-eggs to bolster foreign-exchange reserves. Some attempted currency demonetizations to wipe out domestically-held black-market hoards. There are many other examples. Each policy option had flaws: but none were any more egregious than those revealed repeatedly by the current freeze-and-seize approach.[11]

Nor is it necessary to be so exotic. Using ordinary fiscal procedures law to seize unreported income produces the desired result with few if any of the undesirable side-effects. There is no need in fiscal-enforcement to suggest that unreported or misreported income is criminal in origin to justify taking it away—it suffices that such money exists. Thus there is no need to tar someone with the brush of criminality without the right to a criminal trial to determine truth or falsehood. Nor by using tax law would there be any need to contrive an offense like money laundering. In terms of the logic of deterrence espoused by advocates of the follow-the-money strategy, it matters not whether the proceeds of crime (defined as profit, income or however else) are taken by the tax collector or the cops—if the proceeds vanish, so does the motive and the means.

The flaws in the follow-the-money strategy are apparent; the damage done equally so. However once dramatic new directions in law and policy are undertaken, very quickly vested interests build up to maintain them, along with entrenched attitudes based on popular fable which are extremely difficult to dislodge. Particularly disturbing is the recent renewal of a moral panic atmosphere. If much of the original pretext for the strategy was the image of the mustachioed Colombian narco-baron reclining in a gold-plated bathtub lighting Havana cigars with hundred dollar bills while plotting to turn western youth into dope-crazed anarchists, it has now shifted to the bearded Islamic financier-of-terror hiding in a cave in Waziristan while wiring money from his Swiss bank accounts to finance the downfall of Judaeo-Christian Civilization. Today the target is no longer the consequences of something that had happened—i.e., money (however exaggerated the sum) earned from peddling drugs or committing other crimes. Now the objective is to prevent something which might possibly happen in the future. If nothing happens, supporters of the strategy can claim credit for preventing it; if something does happen (and by waiting long enough or engaging in sufficient provocative acts, something probably will), they can claim not that the previous strategy was fatally flawed, but that its laws and penalties were not strong enough. 🔊

## Notes

1. For an in-depth dissection, see R. T. Naylor, Wages of Crime: Black Markets, Illegal Finance and the Underworld Economy (Ithaca NY: 2004) Chap. IV.

2. On the controversy over the spread of civil forfeiture in the U.S. see, for example, Leonard Levy, A License to Steal: the Forfeiture of Property (Chapel Hill: 1996).

3. This was explained by Pino Arlacchi, intellectual author of the law, in "Effects of the new anti-mafia law on the proceeds of crime and the Italian economy" Bulletin on Narcotics XXXVI, No. 4, 1984.

4. See, for example, R. T. Naylor, Hot Money and the Politics of Debt (New York and London, 1985, 1986, reissued Montreal 2006).

5. On these issues see R. T. Naylor, "The Rise and Fall of the Underground Economy" Brown Journal of World Affairs XI Issue 2 2005 and R. T. Naylor "The Underground Economy: A Ruse by Any Other Name" Challenge: the Magazine of Economic Affairs 48 No. 6 Nov.-Dec. 2005.

6. In Germany they were in the 15-30% range; in India 35-50%; in Taiwan 25-45%; in Pakistan 20-50%. In Brazil the estimates started at 7% in the early 1980s and shot all the way up to more than 100% by the early 1990s. Mexico in the 1980s saw its underground economy supposedly treble while the legal one registered virtually no net growth. Argentina's underground economy in the same decade was reckoned to be rising at double the rate of the measured one.

7. See for example the critique by Richard Porter and Amanda Bayer, "Monetary Perspectives on Underground Activity in the United States" in Edgar Feige (ed.) Underground Economies: Tax Evasion and Information Distortion (Cambridge: 1989).

8. Commercial crimes may have indirect effects raising or lowering GNP. But since it is impossible to say a priori whether they do or do not, and since they all take place within a normal business context, it is safer to assume they, too, have no impact on GNP, measured or covert. On this see R.T. Naylor, "Towards a General Theory of Profit-Driven Crime" British Journal of Criminology 43, 2003.

9. On the continued scope for abuse, see Brant Hadaway" Executive Privateers" University of Miami Law Review Vol. 55. No. 1, Oct. 2000.

10. This is the main theme of R. T. Naylor, Satanic Purses: Money, Myth and Misinformation in the War on Terror (Montreal: McGill-Queen's University Press, 2006).

11. For a survey of these see R.T. Naylor "From underworld to underground: Enterprise crime, 'informal sector' business and the public policy response" Crime, Law & Social Change 24, 1996.

# [28]

# Asset and money laundering in Bolivia, Colombia and Peru: a legal transplant in vulnerable environments?

Francisco E. Thoumi · Marcela Anzola

## Introduction

The deepening of the globalization process and the growing interrelations among countries have reinforced the need for homogeneous norms and common systems not only to regulate international capital flows and international trade but also to control and combat illegal capital flows and money laundering. In this context the normalization and standardization of criminal offenses and regulatory measures seeks to facilitate the prosecution and penalization of criminal activities.

Illegal capital flows and money laundering were recognized as an international policy issue in the 1988 Convention against Illicit Traffic in Narcotic Drugs and Psychotropic Substances that was followed by substantial international developments. In 1989 the G7 countries established the FATF to attack money laundering. In 1990 it issued Forty Recommendations to fight money laundering which were revised and tightened in 1996 and 2003. In October 2001 it issued 8 recommendations on Terrorism Financing that were updated in October 2004 when a ninth was added. These revisions took into account the new United Nations Conventions against Transnational Organized Crime, 2000 (the Palermo Convention) and the 1999 International Convention for the Suppression of the Financing of Terrorism. After the UN General Assembly Special Session of 1998 (UNGASS-1998) the UN established the Global Program Against Money Laundering (GPML) within the UN Office of Drug Control and Crime Prevention (UNDCCP) that in 2003 became the UN Office on Drugs and Crime (UNODC). The GPML launched a technical assistance program to help countries enact anti money laundering legislation and to develop anti money laundering agencies and systems. This set of international arrangements and guidelines constitutes an anti-money laundering -AML- system

F. E. Thoumi (✉)
Latin American Studies, University of Texas, Austin, TX, USA
e-mail: fthoumi@hotmail.com

M. Anzola
Law School, University of Texas, Austin, TX, USA

that serves as a model to the domestic legislations and initiatives to combat money laundering.

This system is focused on the financial sector and is based on the following assumptions:

- First, asset and money laundering is defined as a process by which illegally obtained assets and money is made to appear legal in order to minimize or eliminate the risk of seizure and forfeiture. This definition implicitly divides economic activities into legal and illegal. Asset and money laundering aims to lower the risks associated to illegal activities and obtain the benefits of legality.
- Second, money laundering is defined as a three stage process focused on the financial sector. Illegally obtained cash or financial assets are first *placed* in a financial institution. Then the money is sent through various transactions involving wire transfers and many accounts. This *layering* is done to hide the origin of the funds. After the illegal origin is disguised, the assets should be *integrated* into the legal economy, that is, they are invested or spent without generating suspicion. In this laundering process the financial sector plays a key role.[1]
- Third, it assumes that individuals have a preference for legal over illegal assets; that a legally obtained dollar is worth more than an illegally obtained one because it can be used in many more ways than the illegal one and because in the illegal sector there is a risk of seizures and forfeitures that does not exist in the legal one.
- Fourth, it is also assumed that the benefits of "cleansing" assets outweigh the costs of the laundering process.

In this context, as a result of an initiative of legal unification and in order to accomplish with the acquired compromises by signing international agreements to combat money laundering, Bolivia, Colombia and Peru, the three countries that are the source of illegal cocaine, have adopted national legislations that follow the above mentioned international guidelines.

Notwithstanding the existing institutional arrangements and legal developments in these countries, actual results in terms of prevention, detection, and suppression on money laundering have been very modest. The implementation process has not been successful and in the three countries the results are unsatisfactory. These three countries have concentrated the coca-cocaine industry and the AML policies are an important part of their anti drug policies. Their AML experiences however, are not exceptional and similar failures are found across the developing world.

---

[1] The FATF 40+9 recommendations are designed to attack money laundering in each of its three steps and increase the costs and risks of laundering. The references to the real economic sector in the FATF 40+9 are marginal. Only recommendation 12 refers to "non-financial businesses and professions in the following situations: casinos, real estate agents, dealers in precious metals and in precious stones, trust and company service providers and "lawyers, notaries, other independent legal professionals and accountants when they prepare for or carry out transactions for their client concerning the following activities: buying and selling of real estate; managing of client money, securities or other assets; management of bank, savings or securities accounts; organization of contributions for the creation, operation or management of companies; creation, operation or management of legal persons or arrangements, and buying and selling of business entities." These activities are almost always related to the financial sector.

The root of the problem in this context is that the domestic legislation is more the result of an international initiative of legal unification in response to a global problem than the product of a domestic initiative. This constitutes a typical case of what in comparative law has been called "a legal transplant" [14]. National legislation based upon international guidelines and foreign principles acts as an organ that it is transplanted in a strange body and, as occurs in the case of a biological organism, the transplant of such a regime into the domestic legislation requires an adequate environment to be successful. However, as seen below, the environment of these countries has been less than welcoming to this transplant.

Money laundering in the Andean countries, as in other developing countries, transcends the financial sector; it is complex and involves the real sector to a greater extent than what is implied in the literature and in the legal transplants. All these countries have very large informal economies, a large share of which does not comply with many laws and regulations. Many economic activities that take place outside the law are considered normal and acceptable by a large share of the population. In these economies operating in either the formal and informal sectors has benefits and costs. The incentives to be simultaneously in both are high and it is common for firms to operate in both sectors in an attempt to capture the benefits of each one and to minimize their costs. This is why many formal firms simultaneously sale legally imported and contraband goods[2], have several accounting systems and balance sheets, sublease some activities to firms in the informal sector, etc.

Since AML legislation focuses almost exclusively on financial transactions, the weakness of the formal economy and property rights in the three countries are great obstacles to the successful implementation of AML policies. This poses a very difficult problem: how to make compatible the need for a harmonized transnational legislation with the institutional particularities and weaknesses of the Andean countries?

This study focuses on the AML system in the Andean countries, evaluates its advances and explains its limitations. Section II shows how the development of the AML system as the result of an international initiative of legal unification and not the product of a domestic initiative. Section III discusses some institutional problems of the AML legislation implementation. Section IV surveys the AML international and the domestic legislations in the three countries and looks at the scant evidence about the enforcement of that legislation. Finally, some conclusions are presented. It is important to mention that the data and other available information are very different in the three countries. Colombia has greater experience and a more advance AML which allows for a more detailed analysis.

## AML system in the Andean countries: a typical case of "legal transplant"

In Bolivia, Colombia and Peru, multilateral agencies and international agreements have played an important role in AML activities and as a result their national

---

[2] A significant part of incoming money laundering flows is though contraband imports sold in the domestic market. Contraband markets have been institutionalized in the Andean countries for a long time. In each of the main cities there are large commercial areas where contraband is sold openly mixed with legally imported goods.

legislations reflect international principles and guidelines. Indeed, the three countries have advanced substantially in the adoption of the FATF 40+9 recommendations (see Table 1). All of them are signatory of most conventions and international arrangements that seek to combat drug trafficking, terrorism and money and assets laundering. Bolivia is a party of the U.N. Convention against Illicit Traffic in Narcotics and Psychotropic Substances of 1988 (the 1988 Vienna Convention). In January 2002, Bolivia ratified the UN International Convention for the Suppression of the Financing of Terrorism. Colombia is a party to the 1988 Vienna Convention, the UN International Convention for the Suppression of the Financing of Terrorism and the UN Convention against Transnational Organized Crime. In October 2006 Colombia ratified the UN Convention against Corruption and in June 2008 Inter-American Convention against Terrorism. Peru is a party to the UN International Convention for the Suppression of the Financing of Terrorism and the Inter-American Convention on Terrorism, the 1988 Vienna Convention, the UN Convention against Transnational Organized Crime, and the UN Convention against Corruption.

These efforts have been complemented by regional initiatives—GAFISUD, FELABAN, and the Andean Community—that have incorporated the international principles and guidelines and have contributed to the implementation of national laws and policies.

GAFISUD[3] is a regional inter-governmental organization established in December 2000 in Cartagena, Colombia, by Argentina, Bolivia, Brazil, Chile, Colombia, Ecuador, México, Paraguay, Peru and Uruguay.[4] It follows the FATF model and adopted its Forty Recommendations and encourages the signatory countries to implement them.

The Latin American Banking Federation[5] (FELABAN) which groups bank associations from Latin American countries is also a player in AML. It approved a *Declaration of Principles* for the prevention of undue use of the financial system in laundering assets originating from drug dealings and other illegal activities.[6] It defines cooperation principles for each country's authorities regarding general information exchange, prevention methods and technical aspects between associations and entities members of FELABAN, and proposes that its members adopt prevention policies—codes of conduct—for their affiliates.

The Andean Community approved the "Andean Cooperation Plan for the Control of Illegal Drugs and Related Offenses" on June 22, 2001—Decision 505—. The Plan addresses drug production, trafficking, and consumption and related offenses. Concerning asset laundering the plan contains a set of actions and guidelines to be implemented by the Andean Countries.

---

[3] http://www.gafisud.org/home.htm

[4] The following participate as observers: World Bank, Inter-American Development Bank, Egmont Group, Germany, Spain, United States of America, IMF, France, INTERPOL, INTOSAI, Portugal and United Nations. The following fellow organizations also attend the sessions: FATF, Financial Action Task Force of the Caribbean (CFATF) and the Organization of American States, through the Inter-American Commission against Drug Abuse (CICAD).

[5] http://www.felaban.com/index.php

[6] http://www.felaban.com/lavado/boletin_comite_latinoamericano.php

Table 1 Compliance with FATF-GAFI recommendations

| FATF recommendations | | Bolivia | Colombia | Peru |
|---|---|---|---|---|
| Legal System | Scope of the criminal offence of money laundering (Recommendations: 1, 2) | Law 1768/1997 | Law 30 of 1986, Law 599/00, Article 345, Law 1121 of 2006 | Law 27765 of 2002 |
| | Provisional measures and confiscation (Recommendation 3) | Law 1786/97, article 71 bis | Law 333 of 1996, Law 785 of 2002, Law 793 of 2002 | Legislative Decree No. 992/07 |
| Measures to be taken by Financial Institutions and Non-Financial Businesses and Professions to prevent Money Laundering and Terrorist Financing | Customer due diligence and record-keeping (Recommendations: 4, 5, 6, 7, 8, 9, 10, 11, 12) | Administrative Resolution FIU 016/99 | Decree 1872 of 1992 | Supreme Decree 018-2006-JUS |
| | Reporting of suspicious transactions and compliance (Recommendations: 13, 14, 15, 16) | | Decree 663 of 1993 -Organic Statute of the Financial System, Article 102, no. 2 | |
| | Other measures to deter money laundering and terrorist financing (Recommendations: 17, 18, 19, 20) | | | |
| | Measures to be taken with respect to countries that do not or insufficiently comply with the FATF Recommendations (Recommendations: 21, 22) | | | |
| | Regulation and supervision (Recommendations: 23, 24, 25) | | | |
| Institutional and other measures necessary in systems for combating Money Laundering and Terrorist Financing | Competent authorities, their powers and resources (Recommendations: 26, 27, 28, 29, 30, 31, 32) | Supreme Decree 24771 de 1997, *Artículo 2* | Law 526 of 1999 | Supreme Decree 018-2006-JUS |
| | Transparency of legal persons and arrangements (Recommendations: 33, 34) | | | |
| | International Co-operation (Recommendation 35) | | | |
| | Mutual legal assistance and extradition (Recommendations: 36, 37, 38, 39) | | | |
| | Other forms of co-operation (Recommendation 40) | | | |

## Inadequate environment: informal economy, bancarization and property rights problems

The three countries have a very large informal economy, the access to credit and financial services (bancarization) is very low and property rights in many areas are ill defined and questionable.

### Informality

There is no consensus on the definition of the informal economy as "shown by the wide variety of terms: non-observed, unofficial, second, hidden, shadow, parallel, subterranean, informal, cash economy, black market, unmeasured, unrecorded, untaxed, non-structured, petty production and unorganized" [10]. Despite the definitional and measurement problems, there have been several efforts to measure the size of the informal economy in the three countries. The concepts used vary but the estimates are illustrative and their trends provide reasonable indications of how informal activities change through time. Schneider and Klinglmair [11:10] using a combination of statistical procedures estimate that the informal economy in 1999/2000 accounted for 67.1% of GNP in Bolivia, 39.1% in Colombia and 59.5% in Peru. This study covers 110 countries and obtains estimates of 41% for developing countries, 38% for transition countries and 18% for OECD members. A World Bank study [8] measuring informality using employment classifications found that between 1992 and 2005 Colombian independent workers increased their share in total employment by 17.3%, the Bolivian share increased 6.9% between 1990 and 2000 but Peru's declined 6.9% between 1991 and 2005. They also estimate that the share of informal independent workers plus informal wage earners in Bolivia (2005) at 81.5%, in Peru (2002) at 81.9% and in Colombia (2006) at 66.8%. These are workers that do not comply with many legal requirements, contribute little if any to social security and do not have many social security benefits.

### Bancarization

The financial sector is undeveloped in the three countries. As in most developing countries, the low level of bancarization presents a problem for AML policies designed for situation in which it is expected that most people use banks, savings institutions, obtain mortgages, etc. Data on bancarization are very general and are not available in many countries. A survey of Latin American experiences [9] obtained data for only six countries: Brazil, Chile, Colombia, El Salvador, Mexico and Peru. It shows that financial system deposits and credit relative to GNP are very low, particularly in Colombia and Peru although their trend is positive. Data for 1990–1999 and 2000–2005 show that in Colombia deposits were 14% of GNP in the first period and increased to 22% in the second. In Peru they increased from 16% to 24%. Credit in Colombia rose from 15% to 19% and in Peru from 14% to 22%. These figures are about one third of those for the developed countries included in the survey and about one half of those for Chile. Similarly, the number of bank offices and ATM machines per 100,000 inhabitants are very low; in Colombia about one half and in Peru about one third of those in Brazil, Chile and Mexico. These figures are about 10% and less of what is found in the developed world.

A more detailed study [6] shows that 26.5% of the Colombian population resides in municipalities that do not have banking services. These cover large areas of the country with strong guerrilla and paramilitary presence. Data from the large urban areas show that only 26.4% of the adult population has either deposits in or credit from the financial system. These people are mostly upper income. Colombia experienced a financial crisis in 1999 caused by a significant change in the way mortgages' balances were estimated. In response to persistent high inflation rates, in the early 1970s a "constant value unit" system was established. In essence, if set a fix interest rate on mortgages but the principal was adjusted by the inflation rate. In the 1990s the adjustment was changed to reflect high interest rates and the value of the principal ballooned. Many borrowers found themselves with mortgages that exceeded substantially the value of their properties and the real estate market collapsed. In 1999 Colombia for the first and only time during the postwar had negative GDP growth of −4.2%. After the financial and real estate crisis the financial institutions had to clean their portfolios and their total credits declined. Tafur-Saiden [13: 23] using annual data shows that during the 1990s the ratio of credit to PIB increased reaching 37.9% in 1998. Then it dropped sharply to the 24 to 25% range in 2002–2005.[7]

A tax on financial transactions of 0.002% that was raised on two occasions to 0.003% and to 0.004% was earmarked to support the troubled financial sector. The government however, found it a very expedient source of funds and maintained after the crisis was over. Today it collects about 1% of GDP [6: 58]. Increases in service costs including many difficult to see fees was another response of the financial sector to the crisis. Banks charges include account management fees, fees to use ATM machines and even to consult balances on ATM machines and the internet among many others. Besides, their intermediation interest gap is probably the largest one in Latin America.[8] Bancarization in Colombia has other obstacles like the fear of assaults after withdrawing deposits or cashing checks. This type of crime is so common that the police offers protection on demand.

Peru had a very good growth record in the 2000's and the financial sector assets grew 20% between 2001 and 2005 reaching $45.6 billion in 2005 [7: 133]. The financial sector is highly concentrated and 12 banks accounted for 54.8% of all assets in 2005 while micro-financial establishments had 3.6%. Banks supplied about 88.7% of all credits in 2001 and 87.2% in 2005. Bank lending is highly concentrated: 2% of the possible borrowers receive 62% of the loans. The government's drive to increase microcredit led to an increase in micro-financial credit from 2.9% to 5.8% of the total. In the same period the banks' share of deposits fell from 97% to 94% while micro-finance organizations increased their share from 2% to 5%. Despite these encouraging signs, the above mentioned comparison between 1990–1999 and 2000–2005 hides a declining trend in intermediation in the latter period as the ratio of credit to GNP declined from 22.4% in 2001 to 19.8% in 2005 while the ratio of deposits to GNP fell from 24.7% to 22.9% [7: 134]. Among the countries surveyed by Rojas-Suárez [9], Peru had the lowest number of bank offices for 100,000 inhabitants (4.8).

---

[7] These data are consistent with a graph in Marulanda [6: 50] that unfortunately does not provide figures. In this graph the ratio of deposits to PIB follows a similar path.

[8] One of the authors of this essay, for example, in 2008 closed a savings account that keep a balance of about $7,000 because the interest received was less than the monthly account costs.

Aggregate data on Bolivia suggest a higher degree of bancarization than in Colombia and Peru. In 2008 the ratios of loans to GNP and deposits to GNP were 0.36 and 0.49 [1]. It has a relatively low number of ATM machines per 100,000 inhabitants (9), but it has 10.3 finance offices per 100,000 inhabitants, the third highest number in Latin America. There are no studies that explain these figures but one may suggest that the strong community organizations among the countries' Indians and poor and the government led by a Bolivian Indian may be a reason for it.

The structure of the finance sector also reflects the influence of community organizations. The country has 12 banks, 8 *mutuales*, 6 private financial funds, 23 open savings and loans cooperatives, 94 closed savings and loans cooperatives and 14 financing NGO organizations.

Property rights

Property Rights in the three countries are weak and ill defined in many areas. Land property is particularly problematic. The root of this problem lays in history. The Spanish conquistadores arrived with a goal to live off the rest of the population. Indeed, they considered manual labor dishonorable not fit for any respected hidalgo. On arrival they faced a big problem: fertile land was abundant relative to the stock of labor that was decimated by the illnesses brought by the Spaniards, and the natives were used to communal property. They distributed the land among themselves but faced the problem of attaching the labor to the land and devised several systems to achieve this goal such as the *encomienda*. Indeed, if there had been a neoliberal market solution, they would have had to work by themselves to be able to survive. Since the Conquest the problem of land tenancy has been a constant in the Andean countries political economy.

For several centuries the Andean economy was characterized by a seigniorial structure, having abundant natural resources, very little capital, primitive technology and unskilled labor. This system was based on the hacienda and in some areas of Bolivia and Peru also on mining. Land tenancy was very concentrated across the region. Bolivia and Peru had important land reforms that distributed land in 1953 and 1969 respectively. In Colombia, where native communities were less organized and *mestizaje* more widespread, there was a failed attempt at land reform in the 1960s.

In the three countries rural-urban migration and the population explosion of the 1950s through the 1970s produced a sharp increase in urbanization that led to large informal and illegal urban settlements where property rights were questionable.[9]

In the last few decades in the three countries there has been a process of expansion of the rural frontier as new areas have been settled. In many cases this has been carried on without government control or support and has been related to the expansion of illegal coca crops.

Traditional economic policies in the three countries were not conducive to socially validating property rights. Government interventionism prevalent throughout history

---

[9] De Soto's acclaimed works [2, 3] stress the need to clarify and define urban and rural property rights and argue that the deficiencies in property rights are a main obstacle to development. Smolka and Mullahy [12] survey urban development in Latin America and present various typologies that show the weakness and importance of property rights.

placed the State in a position to distribute benefits. Despite the opening of the Andean economies in the last 20 years the link between privilege and wealth has persisted in the imaginary of many. For a large sector of the population individual wealth is not created but captured. The link between the social welfare and individual capital accumulation is weak at best, particularly in Colombia. In this country, extortive kidnappings may be perceived by a segment of the population as a rent transfer mechanism: if one does not have access to privilege to accumulate wealth, a seconded best strategy is to kidnap someone who has and transfer rents. One of the paradoxes of this society is that people fight to accumulate wealth but once this goal is achieved, the main problem is how to protect it. This has led to a privatization of police security services (Bogotá, for instance, has at least three times more private guards than policemen), the incorporation of heavy security systems in new construction, and the strange situation in which single family homes are substantially cheaper than apartments in similar locations simply because the latter are safer.

Consequences

Informality implies the existence of a large grey area in the economy in which some laws are respected and others don't and money laundering takes place. But money dirtying also occurs, that is, legally generated income and assets are hidden and invested in ways that violate laws. When there is little or no real risk of seizures and expropriations, these activities are frequent and accepted as normal and socially legitimate ways of "doing business". In these countries economic activities can be typified in four broad categories: legal and legitimate, legal and illegitimate, illegal but legitimate and illegal and illegitimate. A normal transaction in the modern economy is both legal and socially legitimate but illegal transactions such as buying contraband appliances are also socially legitimate; a legal abortion may be illegitimate for certain groups in the society but not for others; hiring an assassin (sicario) may be illegal and illegitimate for most people and illegal but legitimate for others. In these economies there are financial flows across these four categories.

AML policies in the Andean countries have to be implemented in an environment that is not conducive to success. To begin, the part of the economy that uses the financial system is small and the informal economy is very large. Economic activities that break laws are very common and socially accepted. To compound the problem, property rights in large sections of the economy are ill defined, difficult to enforce and lack social legitimacy. These factors have contributed to the development of a market system in which rent seeking is a very profitable activity.

Furthermore, the implementation of AML policies is done by people who have grown, have been educated and socialized in this environment and may not be committed to their success. Not surprisingly, as seen below, policy implementation is very ineffective.

**AML legislation: international standards but meager results**

As mentioned in section II, the three countries have developed institutional arrangements to comply with the 40+9 AML recommendations and meet international standards. They also have created, at least formally, financial intelligence units (FIU), which in most of the cases can request information and submit it to the competent authorities in order to initiate, when relevant, the respective criminal investigation and prosecution. The regulatory framework has focused on three dimensions: the administrative control of financial transactions; penalization of money laundering and illicit enrichment as autonomous offenses; and the development of comprehensive asset forfeiture legislation. However, the results are meager. In some cases the existing norms and organisms (political, budgetary and administrative) impede the adequate enforcement of the laws; in other cases, perhaps most dramatic, the lack of adequate regulations is an obstacle to prosecute illegal activities that are not closely related with the financial sector.

## Bolivia

Bolivia's money laundering supervision strategy has been based on the system of mandatory external audits of financial institutions. The FIU is not responsible for supervising compliance with anti-money laundering standards, but for requesting *"that external audits be carried out by the respective superintendencies to verify the compliance with the requirements imposed on the regulated entities."* (Supreme Decree 24771/1997 article 8.) The FIU was created in 1997 by Law 1768 (Article 2 no. 40) but the history of its regulation has been quite complex and it has been an obstacle to its adequate functioning.[10] Additionally, although the law grants the FIU the powers of a typical *"decentralized agency with functional, administrative, and operational autonomy"*, it does not have an independent structure. According to the law it is an organic part of the Superintendency of Banks and Financial Entities. Currently the FIU can request cooperation, obtain confidential information, and have access to any database or file of any government agency without the need to share the information obtained, but it must, however, submit to the competent authorities such duly substantiated information as may be needed for the relevant criminal investigation and prosecution.

Money laundering was criminalized by Law 1768/1997 with a penalty of 1– 6 years' imprisonment (article 185 of the Penal Code). It will apply even if the offenses giving rise to the illicit gains have been committed wholly or partly in another country, provided that the offenses are considered as such in both countries. This law establishes also the principle of seizure (Article 71 bis of the Penal Code). The instruments confiscated can be sold at public auction, if they are legally tradable, to cover civil liability in cases of insolvency; otherwise, they are destroyed or rendered useless. The *Dirección de Registro, Control y Administración de Bienes Incautados* (Directorate of Registration, Control, and Administration of Confiscated Goods)—**DIRCABI**- administers the seized goods (Article 253 of the Penal Code).

---

[10] Supreme Decree 28695 of 2006 repealed Supreme Decree 24771 and created the *Organizational Structure in the Fight against Corruption and Illicit Enrichment* and provided for the creation of a Financial and Property Intelligence Unit, to replace the FIU. Because the FIU was eliminated before its replacement was operational, the government then passed Supreme Decree 28713 on May 13, 2006, reinstating the FIU's functions and duties until January 2007 and placing the FIU under the Ministry of Finance. On November 29, 2006, the government passed Decree 28956, eliminating the portion of Decree 28695 that had repealed Decree 24771 and allowing the FIU to continue to operate.

However, the administration of these goods is commonly criticized by the media. Scandals of corruption and bad administration have been reported periodically in newspapers without legal consequences. On July 31, 2007, the Egmont Group announced the expulsion of Bolivia because of continued lack of adequate terrorist financing legislation (United States Department of State 2009).

## Colombia[11]

In Colombia, Decree 1872 of 1992 set forth the principles and procedures to combat money laundering in the financial sector. It made financial entities responsible for adopting adequate and sufficient control measures to avoid being used as instruments for concealing, handling, investing and in any way using funds or other assets originating from criminal activities, or to give an appearance of legitimacy to criminal activities or transactions and funds related to such activities.

Law 526 of 1999 created the Financial Information and Analysis Unit (UIAF), a special Administrative Unit ascribed to the Ministry of Treasury and Public Credit, charged with preventing and detecting Money Laundering in the different sectors of the economy. There is a consensus among experts that this is one of the most sophisticated intelligence units in the developing world.[12] On one hand, Colombia has made a good effort to comply with the FATF 40+9 and, on the other hand, the close oligopolistic structure of the Colombian financial sector and, paradoxically, the low level of bancarization have helped a lot. Banks have also taken strong measures. The Banco de Bogotá, for example, has a team of 50 professionals each of which visits 50 clients a month to look at how their businesses' operate. They realize that contraband is a main laundering venue and want to make sure that they know their clients well enough to prevent money laundering. The UIAF has recently turned its attention to the real sector. It is working with the Colombian Retailers Association (FENALCO) and with the Chamber of Commerce of Bogotá. It helps and encourages investigative journalism and in its efforts to expand the control illicit flows and money laundering, it now monitors the financial sector, insurance companies, the solidarity sector, the stock exchange, gambling systems, lotteries and casinos, foreign trade and customs agents, money exchange houses, businesses that transport valuables, vehicle sales and purchases, gold imports and exports, soccer teams, and arts and antique dealers.

The Colombian UIAF collects data from several sources, analyzes and cross checks it. After it finds basis for prosecution it gives the information to the Fiscalía. The UIAF believes that their actions have led to a decline in incoming flows of dirty money. They have detected a significant increase in the number of businesses that are open to provide specialized laundering services. The Fiscalía finds a similar evolution. "Ten years ago trafficking organizations were 'pyramidal'. Today they are fragmented and more collegiate." Money laundering has advanced technologically and money laundering firms have become increasingly specialized and offer their

---

[11] This section benefitted from in dept interviews with staff of UNODD, DNE, the UIAF and the office of the General Prosecutor (Fiscalía).

[12] Interviews with staff of UNODC, the National Drugs Directorate (DNE), the UIAF and the office of the General Prosecutor (Fiscalía).

services to many that need their services. In the past they were part of the main drug trafficking structures, today they are independent. Many of these firms have licit facades and provide diverse services. In one case, for example, the Fiscalía found that a firm had 1,500 "cédulas", the Colombian national identity cards. They were used to make financial transactions (smurfing) for various clients.

Colombia has also broadly criminalized money laundering. In 1997, it criminalized the laundering of the proceeds of extortion, illicit enrichment, rebellion, narcotics trafficking, arms trafficking, crimes against the financial system or public administration, and criminal conspiracy (Law 365/1997, article 9; Title VII, Volume II, Chapter III of the Penal Code).

However, the illegal drugs industry is continuously evolving and adapting to the government policies and today it is difficult to identify new drug traffickers. The Fiscalía thinks that they are chasing old traffickers and having little effect on today's drug industry. They think that new traffickers have a low profile, many are educated, some bilingual and have experience abroad. They invest in legal business and are camouflaged within the business community. The Fiscalía has a large backlog of cases. They have few prosecutors (fiscales) and the Judicial Police has only 40 officers assigned to fight money laundering. The prosecution processes are very time and labor consuming. Because of the prevalence of *testaferrato*, in order to prosecute they have to investigate the traffickers and all their family members.

A few years ago Colombia with the encouragement and support of the U. S. changed its traditional justice system to an accusatory one. The switch to the new system has not been easy and many lawyers, judges and prosecutors do not really understand the new one. Many young judges are not well qualified and do not understand money laundering issues and should be trained. A further problem is presented by high personnel turn over that requires continuous training. These have been main reasons for the large backlog of cases.

The Fiscalía also finds that there are many obstacles to its activities in small towns. Many of these are controlled by either armed groups or just local traditional landlords. The cadastre in the country is incomplete and real estate assessments grossly underestimated in many places. Municipal registries that should provide information on ownership are also woefully inadequate and frequently simply refuse to cooperate as they are controlled by those whose property rights may be challenged.

UNODC officials believe that there is a pressing need to improve the quality of the justice system personnel in all Andean countries. They think that personnel problems are behind a decline in AML sentences. UNODC personnel also think that the quality of the data available on the judicial processes is poor. The government agencies involved in money laundering supply data on processes that enter and exit the system but there is no information about the quality of what goes on during the processes themselves.

By 2008 new complex money laundering system had been developed. During the last several years pyramidal Ponzi systems attracted many Colombians. The largest and more complex was DMG, founded by David Murcia-Guzmán, a young man from La Hormiga, Putumayo, a small town near Ecuador's border that had been a main producer of coca and cocaine. DMG became wildly successful and developed a complex combination of financial pyramid, commercial enterprise and money laundering scheme. The government attempted to close DMG but it hired some of the top lawyers of the country and changed its structure to evade financial sector controls and usury laws. Depositors were not defined as savers but as associates who received a voucher that they could use in DMG's stores to buy many goods and services at about 20% to 30% above regular store prices. After some time they were paid back what they gave DMG or a higher amount. This was not interest considered as or principal but as a payment for doing word of mouth publicity. This payment could also be converted in a voucher and a new round started.

No definitive study of DMG has been possible yet. However, it grew from a very small town and it took time for it to cover large areas of the country. This allowed it to be sustained for about three years. Goods sold in the DMG warehouses were a mix of legally imported and produced and contraband used to launder money. As it expanded, it opened offices in Panama and Ecuador where it had large accounts in the financial sector of those countries whose currency is the U.S. dollar. This apparently allowed drug traffickers to make deposits in DMG accounts and receive equivalent amounts in Colombia. The government finally closed DMG when it was close to have collapsed. The amounts recovered were about $100 per depositor. The closing of DMG generated widespread civil reactions. People demanded their right to continue DMG as many did not accept that this was a Ponzi scheme. Other argued that returns of 100% and 200% were normal in today's capitalist system; that formal banks obtained those returns and the Colombian oligarchy simply did not want others to become rich. Many people became blinded by DMG and deposited their life savings. Others mortgaged their houses. Interestingly, some attribute the sharp decline in the coca acreage in Putumayo during these years to the growth of DMG as many people became dependent on it and just stopped working. In many of the pro DMG marches a common poster was "let us work", meaning let us deposit our money in DMG so that we do not have to work. Mr. Murcia-Guzmán was extradited from Panama and while awaiting trial one of the parties of Mr. Uribe's coalition attempted to nominate him as a candidate for Congress. There is no question that if he could have run in the 2010 election he would have become a very popular congressman. Such is life in the tropics.

In May 2009 Mr. Murcia-Guzmán was requested on extradition by the United States government on drug money laundering charges. He confidently expressed its trust in the American justice system and asserted that he was not afraid of extradition. In January 2010 he was extradited.

The growth in contraband trade to launder illicit drug proceeds requires greater interagency cooperation within the government, including coordination between the UIAF and DIAN. Congestion in the court system, procedural impediments and corruption are other challenges. Limited resources for prosecutors, investigators, and the judiciary hamper their ability to close cases and dispose of seized assets. Streamlined procedures for the liquidation and sale of seized assets under state management could help provide funds available for Colombia's anti-money laundering and counterterrorist financing regime. Notwithstanding the progress in combating money laundering this illegal activity still creates difficulties for legitimate businesses. The sale within Colombia of cheap, illegally imported goods continues to represent unfair competition on a major scale for local producers, importers and retailers, as well as helping the drug trade. The operation of "front" companies and other illegal businesses in construction and other sectors also undercuts legal competitors.

Concerning forfeiture, Colombian law provides also for both conviction-based and non conviction based in rem forfeiture. A general criminal forfeiture provision for intentional crimes has existed in Colombian Penal Law since the 1930s. Since then, Colombia has adopted more specific criminal forfeiture provisions in other statutes, including Law 30 of 1986 (National Drug Statute) and Law 333 of 1996. In 2002, the Colombian government enacted Law 785 and Law 793.[13]

*Dirección Nacional de Estupefacientes* (DNE) is charged with administering, managing and disposing seized goods. Its record has been quite questionable despite the efforts of most of its staff. As with the case of the Fiscalía, it continuously faces problems with many deeds of the seized properties. The cadastre and local registries are not well managed and there is a lot of corruption at the local level. Powerful local interests make sure that these offices are not modernized. Most keep all files manually. It is not convenient to the local powers to have these offices well organized because that prevents frauds and corruption. Disorganization is a good obstacle to prosecution. In many cases of seized properties, the records disappear. DNE opted to take assets to manage only after formalizing precautionary measures.

DNE currently manages assets in 7 specialized divisions: Chemical substances, urban real estate; rural real estate; land vehicles; airplanes; boats; cash, art and other goods; and businesses. The latter located mostly in the areas around Bogotá, Cali and Medellín.

DNE decides how to dispose of the forfeited assets. Both, DNE and the Fiscalía have had great difficulty separating *testaferros* from good faith asset holders. They know that a large share of seized assets is in the hands of *testaferros* but their condition is difficult to prove. A further problem is caused by the fact that many assets are not productive but should be maintained and generate substantial costs. Others require special skills to be managed properly.

When the asset seized is a business DNE confronts particular problems. The financial sector blacklists the business, cuts its credit lines and leaves it in dire straits. This is done even if the business is in the hands of the State. DNE does not have funds or the capacity to borrow from the financial system to provide working capital for those business and many just fail.

Table 2 summarizes the results the AML efforts in seized and forfeited drug traffickers' assets. Official data are aggregate and do not provide some important information. For example, there are no estimates about the value of the assets seized and forfeited. Besides, as shown below, the definition of an "asset" is not clear. Despite the deficient data, it is clear that the results are not encouraging.

---

[13] Law 785/02 strengthened the Colombian government ability to administer seized and forfeited assets. This statute provides clear authority for the DNE to conduct interlocutory sales of seized assets and contract with entities for the management of assets. Notably, Law 785 also permits provisional use of seized assets prior to a final forfeiture order, including assets seized prior to the enactment of the new law (Article 2). Law 793/02 repealed Law 333/96 and imposed strict time limits on proceedings, placed obligations on claimants to demonstrate their legitimate interest in property, required expedited consideration of forfeiture actions by judicial authorities, and established a fund for the administration of seized and forfeited assets. The amount of time for challenges was shortened and the focus was moved from the accused to the seized item (cash, jewelry, boats, etc.), placing more burdens on the accused to prove the item was acquired with legitimately obtained resources.

Asset and money laundering in Bolivia, Colombia and Peru 451

**Table 2** AML results: number of seized and forfeited assets

| Asset type | Returned by judicial decision | In judicial process | Forfeited | Total |
|---|---|---|---|---|
| Urban Real Estate | 2,571 | 11,790 | 2,965 | 17,326 |
| Rural Real Estate | 1,282 | 3,659 | 695 | 5,636 |
| Businesses | 62 | 2,541 | 287 | 2,890 |
| Cash | 410 | 5,420 | 327 | 6,157 |
| Controlled substances | 525 | 9,439 | 653 | 10,617 |
| Land vehicles | 3,823 | 9,198 | 585 | 13,606 |
| Airplanes and helicopters | 361 | 660 | 44 | 1,065 |
| Boats | 179 | 571 | 99 | 849 |
| Other | 3,184 | 17,451 | 2,079 | 22,714 |
| Total | 12,397 | 60,729 | 7,734 | 80,860 |

UIAF. Data through November 30, 2008

At the end of November 2008 DNE had received 80,860 assets to manage while the forfeiture processes were advancing. Of those, 12,397 (15.3%) had been returned to their owners who had obtained favorable judicial sentences. Only 7,734 (9.6%) had been forfeited and the rest 60,729 (75.1%) were in judicial process. The forfeiture process is very slow. Indeed, in early May 2008 DNE auctioned property seized from Pablo Escobar, killed on December 2, 1993. The fact that a larger number of assets have been returned to their owners than those forfeited also indicates significant problems in the process. DNE officials suggest that the data are misleading because the definition of an "asset" used does not refer to a single piece of property but to a set of properties believed to belong a person that are seized at one time. They claim that some of the forfeited assets include several properties. They however, do not have data to corroborate this.

DNE has substantial management problems. It has very few people relative to the size of its task. High management has frequently been appointed for political reasons and has not had the necessary skills. The Uribe administration has appointed four General Managers. The first one is currently requested for extradition by Panama where he has to face money laundering charges. The second is a very well known general who led the army's attack that destroyed the Justice Palace that had been taken over by M-19 guerrillas in 1985. He is currently facing several human rights charges on account of the disappearance of a number of magistrates and other personnel that were seen leaving the Palace alive but disappeared or later on appeared dead in the Palace's ruble. The third manager tried to modernize the operation but the results have been mixed at best. He however, had to resign over a conflict of interest scandal about his father's bids to rent DNE seized properties. Hopefully the fourth one would do better.

Some examples explain the problems faced. First, it has been very difficult to rent properties seized or to find management companies willing to run some of the businesses. DNE personnel suspect that some of those that have been hired to manage or who have rented seized properties are probably part of the criminal groups that owned those properties. The problem is that most managers and managing firms shy away from running businesses previously owned by drug traffickers. Second, the inventory of seized assets is incomplete and inaccurate. For instance, some airplanes seized have disappeared. Obviously, they have flown away. Third, they do not have control over the use of the rented property. The case of a boat seized in San Andrés Island with a cocaine cargo is perhaps extreme but points out some of the problems. The boat was rented out after the seizure and it was seized again with another cocaine load. The Fiscalía has today two separate forfeiture processes on the same asset.

DNE is making managerial advances and is in the process to hire the asset management functions to a Central de Inversiones (CISA) a mixed capital company attached to the Finance Ministry subject to the Private Law Regime. It was established mainly to manage and dispose of the homes foreclosed during the 1998–2000 real estate crises. There are questions among both government officials and analysts about CISA's ability to handle the varied assets currently in the hands of DNE. In particular, a possible problem may arise because CISA has an extensive urban management experience but a large share of the properties under DNE's supervision is made up rural properties.

Several public officials suggest other possible changes that could allow the government to sell seized properties and return the proceeds to the owners in case they win their suits. This would eliminate the problem of managing seized property. This however raises the issue of how to set sale prices in highly imperfect market environments.

Peru

Peru's AML legislation lagged several years from Bolivia's and Colombia's. During the 1990 the Fujimori government projected a strong law and order image but its main adviser, Vladimiro Montesinos, the power behind the throne, "collected bribes, dealt in drugs, weapons and other illicit markets. Montesinos directed the political life in the country using public funds to bribe judges, opposition politicians and the media and keep their loyalty" [5: 231]. Not surprisingly, the FIU was created only through law 27693 of 2002 after the Fujimori regime was forced out.[14] The FIU is the government entity responsible for receiving, analyzing and disseminating suspicious transaction reports (STRs) filed by obligated entities. This law serves as a framework for the implementation of the all AML policies.

Concerning criminalization measures, since June 2002, Peru has adopted substantial changes to its existing anti-money laundering regime, significantly broadening the definition of money laundering beyond a crime associated with narcotics trafficking. Prior to these changes, money laundering was only a crime when directly linked to narcotics trafficking and "narcoterrorism."

Legislative Decree No. 992/07, established the procedure for loss of dominion, which refers to the extinction of the rights and/or titles of assets derived from illicit sources, in favor of the government, without any compensation of any nature. This Decree has also created the Loss of Dominion Fund (FONPED) in the Justice Ministry to manage and dispose of all assets seized for forfeiture.

---

[14] It was amended partially by law 28009 of 2003.

In Peru the Government has made advances in strengthening its AML regime in recent years. However, despite these significant efforts there are still a number of weaknesses in Peru's AML system: bank secrecy must be lifted in order for the FIU to have access to certain cash transaction reports, smaller financial institutions are not regulated, and the FIU is not able to work directly with law enforcement agencies; rather, the Public Ministry must coordinate any collaboration between the FIU and other agencies.

Peru however has had an interesting experience recuperating corruption moneys deposited abroad. The Fujimori-Montesinos regime centralized corruption in the hands of Montesinos who controlled the government's security apparatus. Montesinos had a curious practice to video tape all his corruption transactions. The collapse of the Fujimori administration started when a video of Montesinos bribing a congressman became public. The about 700 "vladivideos" that appeared implicated members of the judicial system, the country's media, the legislative branch, the military and industry leaders. They also made clear the links between Montesinos, the State and the illicit drug industry.[15]

Under Fujimori, Montesinos and some very high ranking military received very large "commissions" on large military purchases particularly in Russia and Belarus.[16] This was not however the only source of illicit funds deposited in the corrupted officials' accounts abroad. Large sums were involved in a scheme to invest moneys from the armed forces retirement fund in overvalued assets. Those who managed the fund captured a large proportion of the overvaluation.

After Fujimori fell the government's efforts focused on the former government leaders' loot rather than on AML policies. The new government had to start strengthening the institutions that had been captured, co-opted and weakened by Fujimori-Montesinos. Some of the changes made were the creation of an anti corruption unit; a shift from an inquisitorial to an adversarial judicial system facilitated the use of plea bargaining that resulted in several lower level accused to provide valuable information leading to the discovery of very large bank accounts held by prominent military and Montesinos in Switzerland, the United States, Panama, the Cayman Islands, Mexico and Luxembourg; and the approval of restrictive precautionary measures that allowed the state to seize assets during the preliminary steps of an investigation [5: 233–234].

By 2008 Peru had recovered $175 million from accounts in Switzerland, the United States and the Cayman Islands and was negotiating with the other jurisdictions. The political prominence of the Fujimori-Montesinos case probably facilitated this positive result but the changes in the Peruvian legislation, the 2003 Anti Corruption Convention and the blacklisting of some jurisdictions by the FATF were also factors [5].

This case has provided positive lessons about how countries may be willing to cooperate with each other even when their own laws and regulations may not make cooperation automatic. In the United State, for instance, the General Attorney has

---

[15] Pablo Escobar's brother, for example, attests that Montesinos visited Pablo Escobar at the famous Hacienda Nápoles where they made an agreement to safely use some landing strips in Peru to move coca paste to Colombia [4: 7–11].

[16] Jorge [5] provides an excellent description and analysis of these events and the process in which Peru recovered large sums deposited in several off-shore centers.

discretionary power to decide whether to return the money to the country where corruption took place or to keep it for the U.S. government. In this case an agreement was achieved by which the returned moneys had to be used to fight drugs in Peru [5].

## Conclusions

AML legislation is the result of an international initiative of legal unification and harmonization in response to a global problem and not the product of a domestic initiative. The AML international system is based on the implicit assumption that money and assets flow from the illegal to the legal economy and that the illegal economy is not very large.

In Bolivia, Colombia and Peru most money laundering is related to the illegal cocaine industry. The main problem for money launderers is to find safe ways to bring the profits obtained in international markets to the domestic economy. Concerning terrorism, the main issue in the Andean countries is the financing of domestic terrorist organizations.

However, although these countries have made substantial efforts to adopt the international AML legislation guidelines, the implementation process has not produced a successful regime and the results are unsatisfactory. Cases like the recovery of moneys hidden abroad by Fujimori-Montesinos might have been influenced by political prominence and it is not clear if it could be easily replicated.

Lack of congruence between the international AML system and the domestic environment explains in great part the meager results of the AML legislation in the Andean countries. The fact that international AML system is focused on the financial sector has played an important role. AML international principles do not take into account that in these countries money laundering transcends the financial sector. It is complex and involves the real sector to a greater extent and a significant part of incoming money laundering flows is contraband imports sold in the domestic market. In the three countries the part of the economy that uses the financial system is small and the informal economy is very large. The informal sector does not comply with many laws and regulations. Many economic activities that take place outside the law are considered normal and acceptable by a large share of the population.

In all Andean countries a very large share has a pre-modern relationship with the State. They are not citizens with rights and duties. They are more like serfs that depend on the on the benevolence of the Lord. Not surprisingly, despite some 20 years of a sequence of elected governments in the region (and a much longer one in Colombia) today through the Andes there is a strong trend toward governments run by strong caudillos. In these environments the caudillo is able to interpret and change the rules of the game and many norms become increasingly fuzzy. In a modern system one would expect rules to be certain and results uncertain. The Andes is drifting toward the opposite, systems in which rules are uncertain but results are certain.

It is important to highlight that the success of AML policies depends critically on the type of relationship that individuals have with the State. A key issue is whether they are modern or pre-modern citizens. Legal harmonization initiatives in general must take it into account. It is true that the globalization process has reinforced the need for homogeneous norms and common systems in order to facilitate the relations among countries and as a result, guidelines and principles are directly transplanted into domestic legislations. However, it is also important to point out that in many cases a legal transplant into a hostile environment tends to be rejected. These have been the cases of AML initiatives in Bolivia, Colombia and Peru.

A key lesson learned from the experience of these three countries that may be applied to other countries and issues is that there is a big challenge making compatible the need for a harmonized legislation with the institutional particularities and weaknesses of the countries. Since legal transplants require an adequate environment, harmonization initiatives must focus more on institutional issues than on mere legislative changes. Policy and law makers, on the other hand, should not fall in the temptation of legal transplants without taking into account that in many cases international principles and guidelines are responses to the need for global harmonization that may conflict with the particular country´s environments and circumstances. In these cases, the blind adoption of international standards result in ineffective policies in which countries appear to go to the motions of complying with the international norms but are incapable to achieve significant results.

## References

1. Asobancaria Bolivia. (2008). *Bancarización en Bolivia*. Available Online: http://www.asoban.bo/publicaciones/documentosPub/2008-11-BancarizacionEnBolivia.pdf.
2. De Soto, Hernando. (1986). *El Otro Sendero*. Lima: Editorial El Barranco.
3. De Soto, H. (2000). *The mystery of capital*. Basic Books.
4. Escobar, R. (2000). *Mi Hermano Pablo*. Quintero Editores.
5. Jorge, G. (2008). La experiencia de Perú: el caso "Fujimori-Montesinos". In G. Jorge (Ed.), *Recuperación de Activos de la Corrupción*. Buenos Aires: Editores del Puerto.
6. Marulanda, B. (2006). Una nueva política para un mayor acceso a los servicios financieros en Colombia. In Secretaría General Iberoamericana, *La Extensión del Crédito y Servicios Financieros. Obstáculos, propuestas y buenas prácticas*, Madrid, September.
7. Morón, E. (2006). Los retos del sistema bancario del Perú. In Secretaría General Iberoamericana, *La Extensión del Crédito y Servicios Financieros. Obstáculos, propuestas y buenas prácticas*, Madrid, September.
8. Perry, G., Arias, O. S., Fajnzylber, P., Maloney, W. F., Mason, A. D., & Saavedra-Chanduvi, J. (2007). *Informality: Exit and exclusion*. The World Bank.
9. Rojas-Suárez, L. (2006). El panorama regional. In Secretaría General Iberoamericana, *La Extensión del Crédito y Servicios Financieros. Obstáculos, propuestas y buenas prácticas*, Madrid, September.
10. Sindzingre, A. (2006). The relevance of the concepts of formality and informality: a theoretical appraisal. In: B. Guha-Khasnobis, R. Kanbur, E. Ostrom (Eds.), *Linking the formal and informal economy: Concepts and policies*. Oxford University Press.
11. Schneider, F., & Klinglmair, R. (2004). *Shadow economies around the world: What do we know?* Department of Economics, Johannes Kepler University of Linz, Working paper 0403.
12. Smolka, M., & Mullahy, L. (eds.) (2007). *Perspectivas Críticas Urbanas. Temas críticos en políticas de suelo en América Latina*. Cambridge: Lincoln Institute of Land Policy.
13. Tafur-Saiden, C. (2009). Bancarización: una Aproximación al caso Colombiano a la Luz de América Latina. *Estudios Gerenciales*, *25*, 110. January–March, Cali: Universidad ICESI.
14. Watson, A. (1993). *Legal transplants: An approach to comparative law* (2nd ed.). Georgia: University of Georgia Press.

# [29]

# Testing the Global Financial Transparency Regime[1]

J. C. Sharman

*Griffith University*

How can we tell whether rules that apply in theory actually do so in practice? Realists argue that the gap between what formal rules proscribe and their effectiveness may be particularly wide at the international level. Furthermore, dominant states may impose costly standards on others that they themselves choose not to implement. To test these propositions, the article assesses the effectiveness of international soft law standards prohibiting anonymous participation in the global financial system by seeking to break these standards. The findings indicate that the prohibition on anonymous corporations is relatively ineffective and is flouted much more in G7 countries than in tax havens. The article contributes to and extends the work of realist scholars in international political economy, both in their skepticism of formal rules and focus on the effects of power. Evidence is drawn from the author's solicitations and purchases of anonymous shell companies from 45 corporate service providers in 22 countries.

Rules are at the heart of the study of politics. But how can we tell whether the rules that apply in theory do so in practice? It is a commonplace that laws, regulations, and policies can be a dead letter, completely ineffectual and irrelevant for actors' behavior. Yet, political scientists have rarely taken the most direct approach to testing the effectiveness of rules: attempting to break them and seeing what happens. This paper practices just such a participant approach. It is based on seeking to violate recent global soft law standards prohibiting anonymous participation in the international financial system so as to assess the effectiveness of these standards. Such a test is especially apposite in looking at the effect of international rules, long argued by realists and others to be troubled by particular enforcement difficulties due to the lack of a world government.

The argument presented aims to build on the work of realist scholars in international political economy in two ways: first, by emphasizing a healthy suspicion of the practical effectiveness of international rules and second, by focusing on the power of dominant states to impose rules on others that they do not follow themselves. Relating to the first concern, the unusually direct approach to testing the impact of global rules helps to counteract worrisome biases in much of the existing literature on global governance and international regimes, which tends to overstate the success of international rules. These biases have often meant that the study of global governance and international regimes has run counter to the

[1] The author would like to thank Lee Morgenbesser, Jo-Anne Gilbert, and Vanessa Newby for their research assistance and acknowledge the financial support of Australian Research Council Discovery Grants DP0771521 and DP0986608.

general scientific presumption of favoring tough tests over easy ones (Popper 1968; King, Keohane, and Verba 1994:100). By providing a more direct and demanding test, a participation approach helps to re-balance empirical work in this area, as well as providing support for a realist scholar's skepticism about taking formal international agreements at face value. And whether as scholars or as citizens, when we ask "do the rules make a difference?" we are asking whether rules proscribing an activity (speeding, selling cocaine, torture, genocide, nuclear proliferation, polluting, etc.) have made it significantly less likely that this activity will occur. In this context, an investigation premised on rule testing by rule breaking enjoys an advantage over less direct methods.

Turning to the second point, scholars working in the liberal tradition have focused on overcoming the obstacles to mutually advantageous co-operation in the production of international public or quasi-public goods. They have neglected the possibility that strong states might be able to hold others to international rules, while themselves opportunistically defecting and enjoying the benefits of free riding. Realists have correctly argued that power plays a central and often under-rated role in setting international rules. They have usefully demonstrated that just because all states follow the same rules, this does not mean they benefit equally, or perhaps in some cases receive any benefit at all. But once again, they have generally overlooked the idea that dominant states may in practice be able to violate formal universal standards while forcing others to apply them. The existence of such a "do as I say, not as I do" logic of standard setting has been obscured by the prevailing conceptual lens, but perhaps even more so by the lack of a direct method for testing who is actually enforcing formal rules, as opposed to just ritualistically endorsing them.

The standards in question arise from a recent international campaign to proof the international financial system against financial crime, especially money laundering, large-scale corruption, and tax evasion. The proximate goal of this campaign is to ensure that the world's financial and banking systems are transparent: every actor and transaction within the system must be able to be traced to a discrete, identifiable individual. States and international organizations have diffused rules outlawing anonymous participation in global financial networks, a provision now legislated in more than 180 countries (FATF 2010). Anonymity is forbidden precisely because it is so useful for those looking to perpetrate financial crimes.

This article tests the global transparency rules by seeking to break these same rules. The project is based on attempting to found anonymous companies that conceal the author's identity. Such a participant approach fills an important gap in our knowledge by providing direct, primary empirical evidence about the effectiveness of global governance in this realm. To the extent that the new emphasis on transparency renders these attempts difficult or impossible, this would comprise compelling testimony of the power to regulate the global financial system. But if breaking the rules by participating anonymously in the global financial system is easy, this provides a strong indication that, in this case, the rules reflect nothing more substantial than pious hopes.

The logic behind this research design is that a company is little more than an alternative legal identity. Because these legal persons can have their own bank accounts, to the extent the true owner of the company is hidden, all transactions processed through the corporate account become untraceable. Such a corporate veil is thus very useful for those looking to hide criminal profits, give or receive bribes, finance terrorists, or escape tax obligations. The research design involved electronically soliciting offers of anonymous companies from 45 different corporate service providers in 22 different countries and collating the various responses. The next step was to purchase a subset of these companies to determine whether the prohibitions on anonymous corporate entities (and thus anonymous participation in the international banking system) that apply in theory actually obtain in practice. Beyond assessing the ease or difficulty of establishing anonymous bank accounts overall, this research design also tests relative effectiveness of rules in different types of countries. Specifically, it tests the claim that these global rules are much less effective in offshore financial centers than major OECD economies. Policymakers in the major institutions of global economic governance have consistently acted on the basis that those small jurisdictions stigmatized as offshore centers or tax havens pose the greatest threat to the integrity of the financial system and tend to facilitate the conduct of financial crime by providing strict financial secrecy (FSF 2000, 2007; G20 2008, especially the sections on Promoting Integrity in Financial Markets; UNODC-World Bank 2007; European Commission 2008; Senate 2008). Yet, this presumption has remained largely untested.

To foreshadow the results, it is relatively easy to break the supposedly hard-and-fast rule prohibiting anonymous participation in the global financial system. Seventeen of the 45 attempts to solicit anonymous companies met with success. Of these, 13 of 17 approaches to service providers in OECD countries were successful, compared with only four of 28 in so-called tax havens. Establishing a corporate bank account while preserving this anonymity proved more difficult. Nevertheless, five of the solicitations were successful in obtaining offers for an anonymous company with an associated bank account without having to provide any certified identity documentation as to the true owner of the company and account. This success rate, indicating that the prohibition was effective almost 90% of the time, may seem like an endorsement of the existing rules; after all, no system is perfect. Furthermore, given the small sample size, a degree of modesty is in order. But the author's effort to procure anonymous corporate and banking services was a relatively amateurish, low-budget affair carried out in the absence of any formal legal training or advice, involving a budget of $10,000. Even such a shoe-string affair managed to break a central principle of global financial regulation relatively quickly, cheaply, and without sanction (so far).

Furthermore, policymakers have constantly portrayed global standards as being "only as strong as their weakest link," because of the ease of regulatory arbitrage. Thus, US Treasury Secretary Larry Summers remarked in 2000: "As interdependence increases, each country is as vulnerable to financial crime as the weakest link in the chain" (http://usinfo.org/wf-archive/2000/000203/epf405. htm). Gordon Brown similarly emphasized in 2006 that "[A]s terrorist finance operates on a global scale, we know that we are only as strong as our weakest links," before asserting that Britain and the United States would lead the world to tougher financial standards (http://thesop.org/index.php?article=2773). Examples of such statements can be multiplied *ad nauseam*. Thus, according to the logic of these senior British and American officials, even if only one or two countries are delinquent in enforcing global standards, they will crucially undermine the efforts of all the rest. The exceptions dominate the rule.

How does rule-effectiveness vary between the small states labeled as tax havens and OECD countries? Here, the result is exactly the opposite of what most observers have maintained: with regard to financial transparency, small island offshore centers have standards that are much higher than major OECD economies like the United States and the United Kingdom. The centers with the highest standards are those like Bermuda, the British Virgin Islands, the Bahamas, the Cayman Islands, and Panama, which uniformly require extensive identity documentation before establishing a corporate entity, let alone a bank account. A second group of centers was less observant, allowing the establishment of anonymous shell companies, but generally requiring identification before opening a bank account. These included Belize, Hong Kong, Canada, and Britain. The third group, represented by Somalia and, most surprisingly of all, the

United States, is prepared to provide corporate bank accounts without proper identity documentation. Before 2008 in the United States and pre-2007 in the United Kingdom, the situation was even worse, with providers offering companies with corporate accounts without the need for any documentation at all. This pattern of results completely contradicts the rather sanguine picture of rule-effectiveness painted by powerful G7 states and the international organizations they dominate, which are responsible for monitoring these standards. As is argued below, this provides a strong indication that powerful states are choosing to profit by not following the standards they have imposed on others. A stream of independent confirming evidence from various other sources tends to corroborate this impression.

In developing these points, the structure of the paper is as follows.

The first section reviews the literature on international rules to isolate problems of selection bias, endogeneity, and formalism, which in combination lead scholars to overstate the impact of international rules. While realists have correctly emphasized the importance of power in rule setting, they have generally neglected the possibility that powerful states may induce others to follow rules the former are not themselves adhering to. Company ownership may seem like a minor legal quibble, but the next section shows how a succession of major policy reports has identified the prohibition of anonymous shell corporations as the lynchpin of efforts to combat financial crimes ranging from tax evasion, to money laundering, to corruption. The third section argues for the merits of direct participation and field experiment methods. Despite relative neglect, such approaches are suited not only for inspiring new hypotheses, but also in testing hypotheses, even at the level of global governance. The article then describes the procedure for gathering evidence (soliciting and buying anonymous financial arrangements) and presents the findings. Chief among these are that international rules proscribing anonymous corporate entities are largely ineffective, though accessing anonymous banking is much harder. Prevailing double-standards, imposed and maintained by power, mean that the failure to apply international standards is more pervasive in G7 centers, especially the United States, than in small island countries. The conclusions of the direct test are buttressed by evidence from a variety of other sources, while a brief account of the Bahamian experience with international corporate transparency rules illustrates the coercive "do as I say, not as I do" logic at work.

## A Realist Perspective on International Rules

Realists have strongly argued that international covenants and rules are often empty formalities with no independent effect on actors' behavior. Yet, substantiating this judgement generally requires some way of assessing whether the international rules that should apply in theory do so in practice. In general, Simmons notes that "In the face of daunting conceptual and methodological issues, very little evidence has been accumulated to assess basic propositions about why governments commit to and comply with international legal obligations, and whether this makes any difference to outcomes in which we are interested" (Simmons 2000:832). But the evidence that has been collected often presents an artificially positive picture of the impact of international rules. Reviews of the compliance literature (Simmons 1998; Raustiala and Slaughter 2002) note that many studies of compliance tend to overstate success (see also Haas, Keohane, and Levy 1993:17–18). First, there is a bias because of selection effects: only "easy" issues tend come up for international negotiation in the first place. The second bias is endogeneity: governments may only sign up to commitments that they think it will be in their interest to keep. (As demonstrated below, the global financial transparency regime is an exception.) When behavior is compliant with the rules, it is very difficult to show that compliance is occurring because of those rules, as opposed to merely reflecting what the actor would have done anyway.

In the current study, what is it exactly that is being tested? To answer this question, it is important to have a clear understanding of the related yet distinct concepts of compliance and effectiveness. The most common definition of compliance in International Relations is that of Oran Young: "Compliance can be said to occur when the actual behavior of a given subject conforms to prescribed behavior, and non-compliance or violation when actual observed behavior departs significantly from prescribed behavior" (Young 1979:3). In this view, compliance is different from effectiveness (the effect on the underlying policy problem, for example torture, polluting, or money laundering). Compliance, whether states' behavior corresponds with rules, may be necessary for effectiveness, but it is definitely not sufficient (Simmons 1998:78). However, things do not stay this clear for long. Raustiala and Slaughter (2002:539) observe that because compliance is above all concerned with how legal rules affect actual behavior, notions of compliance and effectiveness tend to blur. The level of compliance may in fact say nothing about the impact of rules on behavior, that is, the outcome that is of most interest to scholars, policymakers, and citizens alike (Nye 1993:ix). Studying compliance in isolation thus poses a danger of formalism, falsely depicting a rule-governed world. Drezner (2007:12) agrees that "governments often make pledges to co-ordinate without actually doing so." Indeed, this basic objection centering on the ineffectiveness of international rules is central to realist work (Carr 1939; Mearsheimer 1994–1995). Such biases mean that empirical tests of global rules often provide only relatively easy, and thus less valuable, tests that tend to confirm the hypothesis that international rules do make a difference.

The test performed in this article relates to perhaps the single most constant preoccupation of those working in International Relations since the 1980s: explaining whether, when, and why states adhere to common rules for mutual benefit (Keohane 1984; Baldwin 1993; for the most recent "contractualist" take, see Lake 2007). Realists have made important contributions to foregrounding the exercise of power with reference to international standards but have also tended to overlook an aspect of the problem at the heart of this article. Specifically, the oversight is the ability of dominant countries to establish "hypocrite standards": costly common rules imposed on lesser states but not implemented by the dominant states themselves. Here, it is important to situate the contribution of this article within broader realist literature. Leading realist commentators on political economy questions like Krasner, Gruber, and Drezner all premise their work on what they see as the insufficient attention devoted to power in explaining international rules (for example, Krasner 1977:670, 1991:342; Gruber 2000:10; Drezner 2007:xiii). The main issue for each is how powerful states can induce others to comply with the rules that disproportionately advantage the strong. Thus, in writing on global communication standards, Krasner (1991) persuasively argues that the presence, absence, and nature of regimes are determined by states' relative power. Dominant states are able to impose their preferred standard and pick their favored point on the Pareto frontier, claiming for themselves a larger share of the benefits that eventuate, though no party is worse off from co-ordinating standards. The rules in question are biased toward the strong, but they are followed by strong and weak alike.

Lloyd Gruber (2000) takes this realist logic a step further. His innovation is that states may accede to international standards even when these standards leave them worse off than the status quo. Powerful states may exercise "go-it-alone" power by clubbing together and establishing institutions or rules that act to remove the status quo as an option for outsiders. Under the changed circumstances, states outside the club are presented with a bad option or a worse one: the first is to join up even though this will leave them worse off and the second is to pay an even heavier penalty for remaining isolated. All relevant states thus adhere to the new rule, either because they are genuinely better off or because it is the least-bad alternative open to them. Again, all follow the same rules. Drezner (2007) holds that regulatory regimes are a product of the level of agreement within and between great power and lesser state groupings, creating a four-part typology. Where all are in agreement, there are harmonized standards. Where none are in agreement, there will be either no regime or notional "sham standards," rules that remain only on paper. Where the great powers are split but each can secure allies among other lesser states, competing "rival standards" will result. Finally, where the great powers are in accord on their preferred rules, but those on the periphery are opposed, these "club standards" will be coercively imposed as far as possible. But, like Krasner and Gruber, Drezner does not consider another vital prerogative of power: the ability of the strong to impose rules on others that they have no intention of following themselves. Perhaps a fifth type to Drezner's classification might be "hypocrite standards": ostensibly universal standards that the great powers impose on others but in practice do not observe themselves. By this means, great powers can shift the expense of adjustment elsewhere while opportunistically exploiting widespread rule observance by others.

Rather than this point being only of interest to realists, it goes to the heart of other work on co-operation also. In the Prisoner's Dilemma rendering, neo-liberal work has fixated on gaining the benefits of co-operation while avoiding sucker's pay-off. But of course for any individual player, the most preferred outcome is not co-operation; it is unilateral defection when all other players are co-operating. Under the highly stylized parameters of the game, where coercion is forbidden, this is generally impossible (or at least not an equilibrium outcome). In the real world, however, and particularly in the context of the global financial transparency regime, this is not the case. For example, from the point of view of the United States, the ideal world is not one where there are no havens for foreigners to hide money away from tax collectors; the ideal world is one where the United States is the only such haven. Every other country bears the costs of being financially transparent so as to assist the United States collect its taxes, while the United States is opaque, benefiting from the illicit capital invested in its economy. Lest this example seem too farfetched, it is worth considering the verdict of one of the most authoritative commentators on international tax issues over the last 50 years:

> It does not surprise anyone when I tell them that the most important tax haven in the world is an island. They are surprised, however, when I tell them the name of the island is *Manhattan*. Moreover, the second most important tax haven in the world is located on an island. It is a city called *London* in the UK. (Langer 2008:9).

Although the detailed empirical material is left until the following sections, it is worth noting that the United States levies no taxes on the dividends, interest, or capital gains of foreign investors and has studiously ignored requests to exchange such financial information with the Mexican and other governments whose citizens use the United States to hide illicit wealth (see Goulder 2009). Among others, the American Bankers' Association has consistently and successfully argued that if such information were provided to foreign governments, the United States would suffer a massive loss of much needed foreign deposits, valued at $2.6 trillion in 2007 (http://www.aba.com/NR/rdonlyres/AF4BE30B-E70C.../HWaLetter0227095.doc).

In the instance of financial transparency, and perhaps more broadly, the existence of this "do as I say, not as I do" logic of international regulation has been obscured by an excessive preoccupation with universal formal rules, rather than the actual pattern of effectiveness. Publicly proclaiming such hypocritical double-standards runs against prevailing standards of legitimacy. As long as the field has lacked a direct means of testing effectiveness, the possibility that strong states can in practice flout the same rules they publicly support and impose on others has been overlooked. And of course because the organizations that monitor compliance with these international standards are disproportionately funded and influenced by powerful states, they have a strong incentive not to blow the whistle. The Nuclear Non-Proliferation Treaty might be another (unusually obvious) example. In principle, Article VI states: "Each of the Parties to the Treaty undertakes to pursue negotiations in good faith on effective measures relating to cessation of the nuclear arms race at an early date and to nuclear disarmament, and on a treaty on general and complete disarmament." But, in practice, it allows nuclear weapons for the powerful few while barring them to the rest.

More broadly, in looking to advance such a realist argument, the article seeks to help remedy the situation whereby realism has become, as one sympathetic observer noted, a "diminished voice" in International Political Economy scholarship (Kirshner 2009:46). It could be objected that partisans of a particular orientation love to portray themselves as an embattled and under-appreciated minority (Mearsheimer 2001:22–25). But, in their detailed and systematic review of International Political Economy articles in twelve leading journals from 1980 to 2006, Maliniak and Tierney note that realist contributions usually comprise <5% of the published output in these venues. Realist contributions are disproportionately used as "counter-arguments, framing devices and straw-men" (Maliniak and Tierney 2009:16). The purpose of reintroducing a realist perspective is not diversity for its own sake, nor the protection of some intellectual endangered species, but better explanations. No lesser figure than Robert Keohane has recently noted his "gnawing dissatisfaction" with reigning liberal IPE perspective of free agents consensually contracting for mutual advantage (Keohane 2009:37), in part because of the blind spot regarding the role of power. Keohane notes how IPE overall has suffered from a dearth of realists pushing others to be cognizant of coercion and domination (Keohane 2009:39). The results below seek to show how marrying a realist outlook with an unconventional method can produce valuable new insights.

### The Significance of Anonymous Shell Companies

Discovering who is really behind corporate vehicles and their bank accounts may sound like a trivial, esoteric accounting matter. In fact, it is the linchpin of some of the most important global governance initiatives (see G20 2009). These include the fight against tax evasion, efforts to stem corruption and corporate malfeasance, and the campaign to counter money laundering and the financing of terrorism. This section establishes that individual countries and international organizations have recognized the matter of anonymous corporate vehicles as a significant policy issue. One of the first reports to put the issue of anonymous corporations at center stage was commissioned by the United Nations in 1998. *Financial Havens, Banking Secrecy and Money Laundering* explains that "Despite a myriad of complications, there is a simple structure that underlies almost all international money-laundering activities ... The launderer often calls on one of the many jurisdictions that offer an instant corporation manufacturing business ... Once the corporation is set up in the offshore jurisdiction, a bank deposit is made in the haven country in the name of that offshore company" (United

Nations Office for Drug Control and Crime Prevention 1998:2). The authors emphasize that secrecy regarding the ownership of a corporation is a much more serious obstacle to countering money laundering than banking secrecy as such (United Nations Office for Drug Control and Crime Prevention 1998:31). Subsequent analysis by the Financial Action Task Force on money laundering (FATF) has reiterated this conclusion that shell companies and other vehicles, set up by Corporate Service Providers like those contacted in this study, are fundamental to financial crimes (FATF 2006). Thus, in December 2009, a report dedicated to this issue stated:

> The FATF has for many years noted the importance of corporate vehicles as one of the key mechanisms used in money laundering schemes ... Indeed, the beneficial ownership of legal persons is important not only for anti-money laundering purposes, but is also fundamental for other important areas such as anti-corruption, corporate governance and work to combat tax evasion, to name a few. (FATF 2009:2)

In 2001, the OECD released the report *Behind the Corporate Veil: Using Corporate Entities for Illicit Purposes*, responding to a request from the Financial Stability Forum to investigate the problem of anonymous corporations. The report was subsequently endorsed by the G7 finance ministers (OECD 2001:3). Corporate entities where the beneficial ownership is obscured are said to be central to all economic crimes: tax evasion, money laundering, fraud, corruption, insider trading, and others. It is said that they may in the aggregate even imperil the stability of the global financial system (OECD 2001:7; see also G20 2008). Offshore centers are said to be particularly at fault through their provision of shell corporations (2001:24). More recently, a 2009 World Bank study authored by Richard Gordon sought to discover how corrupt heads of state and other senior politicians launder the bribes they receive. The key features identified in the report are anonymous shell companies and accounts linked with such entities (World Bank 2009a:15, 22), confirming the empirical focus of the participation exercise at the heart of this paper. Echoing others, Gordon notes that the most common alibi for these funds is "consultancy fees" (World Bank 2009a:18). (Gordon also notes that it is just as likely for onshore vehicles and banks to facilitate the laundering of the proceeds of grand corruption as those in small island offshore centers [World Bank 2009a:16]). In resolving this problem, however, it is not so much a case of introducing new international principles and standards as making those already on the books effective. A slew of global standards mandate the imperative for financial institutions to "Know Your Customer," meaning that beneficial ownership of corporate vehicles must be established (see Table 1 for a sample). FATF Recommendation 33 clearly states: "Countries should ensure that there is adequate, accurate and timely information on the beneficial ownership and control of legal persons that can be obtained or accessed in a timely fashion by competent authorities." There is no question that the formal rules are in place; the great unknown is their effectiveness.

TABLE 1. Prohibitions on Anonymous Companies and Accounts

| Body | Instrument | Clause |
|---|---|---|
| United Nations | Convention against corruption | Article 52 |
| OECD | Principles of corporate governance | Chapter V A 3 |
| FATF | 40+9 recommendations | Recommendations 5, 33 |
| Basel Committee | Basel core principles | Basel core principle 18 |
| IOSCO | Multilateral memorandum of understanding | Paragraph 7 b (ii) |

### Why a Participant Approach?

There are international laws and conventions against torture, corruption, gender and racial discrimination, and drugs, yet the existence of these instruments tells us nothing about their practical effectiveness. Common sense suggests that the gap between laws and standards may be very wide. A participation approach, in this case assessing the effectiveness of a rule by trying to break it, gives a particularly acute sense of the magnitude and incidence of this gap. This kind of approach is rare in political science but is closely related to field experiments (though importantly without randomization, due to the lack of a treatment). A common objection to field experiments has been that individual scholars can only test small questions, as opposed to the overarching issues of most interest to the field, especially issues in International Relations (Green and Gerber 2002). A first reply would be that even localized, direct interventions or participation can provide inspiration and insight on very important macro-matters, up to and including global governance. Even on an informal basis, participant observation has provided the stimulus for some of the most influential recent work on international organizations and global governance. Barnett and Finnemore trace their dissatisfaction with conventional wisdom on international organizations to their time working with the United Nations and the World Bank, respectively (Barnett and Finnemore 2004:vii). From a very different theoretical orientation, Daniel Drezner (2007:xii) relates that the formative incident for his realist account of global regulatory regimes took place during a year spent with the US Treasury. (Significantly, this incident concerned standards prohibiting of corporate and banking anonymity.)

But if the uses of participant observation and field experiments have been under-appreciated in generating propositions about international organizations and global governance, the same goes doubly for testing such propositions (Green and Gerber 2002:808). An example from economics of the utility of a direct approach in testing propositions is represented by "Are Emily and Greg More Employable than Lakisha and Jamal? A Field Experiment in Labor Market Discrimination." Here, the authors sent fictitious résumés in response to job advertisements in Chicago and Boston, randomly assigning black- and-white-sounding names to measure the effect of perceived race on employability. Even allowing for perceived class differences, the authors found that perceived race did make a pronounced difference. With identical résumés, white names received 50% more requests for interviews (Bertrand and Mullainathan 2004). The conclusion drawn was that racial discrimination is still a major factor in the US job market, with crucial implications for the life chances of black Americans.

An even more closely analogous method to that employed in this article is that used by Hernando de Soto ([1989], 2002, 2000) and his team of researchers looking at the causes of worldwide development failures. De Soto makes the obvious and yet under-appreciated point central to this article that "Reading the laws as they are written gives no clue to how they will work in practice" (de Soto [1989], 2002:xxii). In seeking to test their notions about the difficulty of entering the formal economy in the Third World, his team performs a number of what are referred to as "experiments" or "simulations." The team applies for a sole trader license to produce textiles in Lima, Peru, following all the requirements of the law and bureaucratic procedure. The researchers carefully recorded all the time spent filling out forms, waiting for official permission and dealing with bribe requests, mimicking as closely as possible the approach of a genuine applicant (de Soto [1989], 2002:133–134). They found that even this seemingly simple task required 11 separate procedures, taking 289 work days and cost the equivalent of 32 times the minimum monthly wage in lost profits, not counting the bribes that had to be paid. De Soto's team later repeated equivalent experiments in Egypt, Haiti, and the Philippines, with similar results (De Soto 2000:20–21). The findings give significant support to the proposition that it is extremely hard for those stuck in the underground economy in developing counties to enjoy formal property and other legal rights, which in turn greatly raises the barriers to overall national economic development.

The scale, ambition, and significance of these studies disprove the notion that participatory and field experiment designs must be limited to small questions and minor concerns. Neither do the geographical restrictions that characterized pioneering work in this vein in political science still obtain (Gosnell 1927). Of course these can be surmounted in a large-budget exercise involving a team of international researchers, as per De Soto (2000). But even when such means are lacking, modern communications can provide an answer. Working alone, the author tested the regulatory regimes of over 20 different countries without the necessity of international travel. The solicitation stage of the exercise required no funds, while the budget for purchasing shell companies and associated bank accounts was relatively modest (*c.* $10,000).

### Soliciting and Purchasing Anonymous Shell Companies

The first step in the participation exercise was to compose a short approach email to corporate service providers. This was designed to mimic the profile of a representative would-be miscreant, based on recurring elements identified in the reports of the international organizations referred to above. The first is the anonymous company itself. The approach letter asked for the provision of such a company and emphasized the need for confidentiality and tax minimization. The second is the nature of the business activity: international consultancy. Consulting fees are often a useful cover story for illicit cross-border flows (World Bank 2009a:18). Because there is a very large volume of legitimate money being moved around for this purpose, such transactions do not stand out as being unusual. Consulting fees may be very large, providing an alibi for large sums of criminal proceeds. Because consultancy does not involve the exchange of physical goods, and unlike many other services does not require buyer and seller to be in the same location, it is very hard to prove that a consultancy arrangement was *not* in place. The letter involved a permutation of the author's real name. This was done so as to avoid the legal consequences of signing financial documents in a fake name but also to complicate the efforts of corporate service providers to link the person in the approach letter to the author's related publications.

After designing the approach letter, the next step was to identify relevant corporate service providers, those firms whose business it is to establish and provide basic administration for shell companies, trusts, foundations, and so on. The aim here was to include service providers from a range of G7 countries that are portrayed (or at least portray themselves) as leaders in Know Your Customer standards like the United States and Britain, as well as jurisdictions that have commonly been stigmatized as tax havens. Specific providers were identified through advertisements in the *Economist* and in offshore finance magazines like *Offshore Investment.* The sample included a range of both on- and offshore centers in terms of the location of the service providers, and the specific corporate entities they offered. (There is no necessary reason for providers to offer companies only from their home jurisdiction.) This sample was achieved by targeted Web searches for service providers and entities in rough proportion to their national share of the total market. Also taken into consideration was the range of perceived stringency and laxity of regulatory standards according to international assessments from bodies like the OECD and FATF. Such sampling allows for testing the proposition that powerful states will choose to enforce financial transparency standards less stringently than small states. The selection process was necessarily somewhat ad hoc, as with conflicting or non-existent national definitions of corporate service providers, there is very limited knowledge of the total population or distribution of such agents (FATF 2006). The selection process for service providers was deliberately *not* just an effort to comb the murkiest recesses of international finance to find the most secretive or scofflaw providers.

This test was premised on an *a fortiori* logic: if even a relatively limited search turned up anonymous products, then how much easier would it be for the criminals that the global transparency regime is designed to stop? Similarly, choosing easy-to-find providers with a relatively high profile also acts as a tough test of the argument concerning the ineffectiveness of the rules. This kind of providers should be most visible to those responsible for enforcing the regulations and thus most likely to be applying the rules. Fifty-four service providers were contacted, of which 45 returned valid replies. In the valid replies, service providers recommended one or more corporate structures that could achieve the goals set out in the approach letter, together with a pricing schedule. These replies were tabulated in terms of whether the service provider would supply anonymous vehicles and then whether this anonymity could be maintained in establishing an associated bank account (see Table 2).

Where the response made provision of the company and/or bank account conditional on notarized copies of a passport together with birth certificate, utility bills, and the like to establish identity and residence, this was coded as not anonymous. It would have been impossible to shield true identity short of falsifying these documents (that is, committing fraud). Where the corporate service provider required only name, address, credit card details, etc. to be entered into an online form without any supporting documentation, this was coded as anonymous (remembering that credit cards can be issued for corporate vehicles or supplied by a third party). By definition, where the third party has no information as to the real owner, they cannot hand over any information to investigating authorities, representing a guarantee of anonymity. In relation to five bank accounts, providers asked only for an electronic scan of an identity document like a driver's license, but there was no requirement to have it notarized or certified as a true copy. These are individually noted in Table 2. While indicating some concern with establishing beneficial ownership, this does not meet the international standards in Table 1. Rather than stopping with offers of anonymous entities and bank accounts, it was necessary to go through and make the purchase from a sample of the service providers.

## Findings

Table 2 presents the aggregate results of approaches to different service providers. Of the 54 Corporate Service Providers approached, 45 indicated a willingness to provide a shell corporation, the first step. Of these, 28 required identification before establishing companies (a notarized copy of a passport, usually complemented by utility bills as proof of residential address, as well as sometimes bank or professional references), while 17 were content to form the company without any independent confirmation of identity, requiring only a credit card and a shipping address for documents. Although the cost varied, in all cases establishing an anonymous shell corporation is a cheap proposition, ranging from $800 to $3000 as an up-front cost followed by a slightly smaller amount on an annual basis. The cost variation is generally explained by the optional extras, in particular the extra layers of secrecy, but also various corporate accessories and accoutrements (mail- and phone-forwarding, brass plate, rubber stamp, letter head, embossed seal, etc.). Relative to the corporations

TABLE 2. Results

| Service provider | Shell company | ID required? | Bank | ID required? |
|---|---|---|---|---|
| Bahamas | Anguilla | Yes | | |
| Bahamas | Bahamas | Yes | | |
| Bahamas | Bahamas | Yes | | |
| Belize | Belize | Yes | | |
| Bermuda | Bermuda | Yes | | |
| British Virgin Islands (BVI) | BVI | Yes | | |
| Cayman Islands | Cayman Islands | Yes | | |
| Cayman Islands | Cayman Islands | Yes | | |
| Cyprus | BVI, Panama, St Vincent | Yes | | |
| Czech Republic | BVI, Seychelles | Yes | | |
| Dominica | Dominica | Yes | | |
| Gibraltar | Turks & Caicos | Yes | | |
| Gibraltar | BVI, Delaware, Gibraltar, Panama, Wyoming, etc. | Yes | | |
| Hong Kong | BVI | Yes | | |
| Hong Kong | BVI, Hong Kong, Seychelles, etc. | Yes | | |
| Hong Kong | BVI | Yes | | |
| Labuan (Malaysia) | Labuan | Yes | | |
| Liechtenstein | Liechtenstein | Yes | | |
| Nauru | Nauru | Yes | | |
| Panama | Panama | Yes | | |
| Panama | Panama | Yes | | |
| Panama | Belize, Nevis, Panama, Seychelles, Vanuatu, etc. | Yes | | |
| Sao Tome | Sao Tome | Yes | | |
| Seychelles | BVI, Seychelles | Yes | | |
| Singapore | Bahamas, BVI, Delaware | Yes | | |
| Singapore | Singapore | Yes | | |
| Switzerland | BVI, Delaware, Panama | Yes | | |
| Belize | Belize | No | Belize | Yes |
| Canada | BVI, Ontario, Panama, Wyoming, etc. | No | Latvia, Panama | Yes |
| Hong Kong | Delaware | No | Hong Kong | Yes |
| Singapore | BVI, Hong Kong, Seychelles (Gruppo 20) | No | Cyprus | Yes |
| Spain | Belize | No | Belize | Yes |
| UK | Belize, BVI England, Nevada, Panama, etc. | No | Isle of Man | Yes |
| UK | Belize | No | Hong Kong | Yes |
| UK | Cyprus | No | Cyprus | Yes |
| UK | Belize, BVI, Delaware, England, etc. | No | Hong Kong | Yes |
| UK | England (A. Pascal) | No | Latvia | No (pre-2007), Yes |
| Uruguay | Seychelles | No | Hong Kong, Panama | Yes |
| United States | Wyoming | No | United States | Yes |
| United States | Nevis | No | Belize | Yes |
| Liechtenstein | Somalia | Yes | Somalia | Yes (unnotarized) |

Table 2. (Continued)

| Service provider | Shell company | ID required? | Bank | ID required? |
|---|---|---|---|---|
| UK | Belize, BVI, Delaware, Nevada, Panama, etc. | No | St Vincent | Yes (unnotarized) |
| UK | Seychelles | No | Montenegro | Yes (unnotarized) |
| United States | Nevada (BCP consolidated) | No | United States | Yes (unnotarized) |
| United States | Wyoming | No | United States | No (pre-2008), Yes (unnotarized) |

requiring identification checks, the anonymous vehicles were slightly cheaper, depending on the accessories purchased.

Where the service provider has proof of the individual's identity, the veil of secrecy is vulnerable to being pierced. Particularly in countries with strong domestic investigative powers, local law enforcement may seize beneficial ownership documentation if such material is held by the corporate service provider within their jurisdiction. The United States has premised its strategy for controlling the existence and proliferation of anonymous shell companies on such strong investigative powers. The fatal flaw in this plan, as the OECD points out, is that it depends on local service providers having collected the ownership information in the first place (OECD 2001:10; see also FATF 2009:6), which is precisely the problem in the United States.

Even leaving aside cases where the service provider is in the same jurisdiction as the investigative authority, however, the range of risks spreads much further—first, because the hosting jurisdictions are vulnerable to pressure from foreign governments to hand over client identity documentation. For example, after repeated public assurances that the Cayman Islands would not join the EU's tax information exchange program, Britain successfully obtained a reversal by threatening to suspend the Caymans' self-government (Sharman 2008). Second, service providers themselves are vulnerable to the same sort of outside pressure. A case in point is the Swiss bank UBS, which, only a few years after sending its US clients a soothing email guaranteeing them that it would never pass their details to the IRS, passed over the details of clients to the IRS (Sheppard 2009). Finally, rogue employees of the service provider like Heinrich Kieber of Liechtenstein's LGT bank may leak sensitive material (in Kieber's case relating to 4,500 accounts in return for €4.2 million from the German intelligence service; see Fisher 2008). Clearly, however, if the service provider has no information to disclose, these threats to the integrity of the corporate veil are all obviated.

The results in Table 2 show that forming an anonymous shell company is a cheap and easy proposition. Following from this, the rules directly prohibiting such arrangements (see Table 1) are ineffective. An analysis that assumed that the mere presence of formal international rules prohibiting anonymous shell vehicles indicated that such vehicles were impossible, or even difficult, to obtain, would be wrong. Despite the near-universal coverage in terms of the countries that have committed to these rules, a significant number have merely adopted sham standards. Perhaps even more striking than the ease with which this rule can be violated is the pattern of jurisdictions that routinely violate this rule. Here, the results are closely in line with the proposition of "hypocrite standards": service providers in powerful OECD states are much more likely to offer anonymous shell companies (that is, are much less likely to enforce international rules) than those in small islands. Thus, attempts to incorporate anonymously with providers in the Bahamas, Bermuda, the British Virgin Islands, the Cayman

Islands, Dominica, Nauru, Panama, and the Seychelles all met with failure, in that these agents refused to proceed without proof of identity. In nearly all cases, these agents explicitly noted that anti-money-laundering regulations necessitated their keeping this information on file. Even the Liechtenstein-based agent of the Somali International Financial Center required notarized passport copies (though they were much less stringent about bank accounts; see below). One provider in Belize offered to incorporate a Belize shell company without identity documents, as did another in Uruguay for Seychelles companies, and one each from Hong Kong and Singapore regarding Delaware and other offshore companies.

Yet, of the seventeen providers in OECD countries approached, no <13 agreed to form shell companies without requiring identification documents. These comprised seven in the UK, four in the United States, one in Spain, and one in Canada. (The sole Swiss and Czech providers responding were more scrupulous.) Of these 13 providers, only one limited its stock to offshore shell companies (from Belize), three of the US providers offered only American companies, while the remaining US, Canadian, and all British providers sold a mix of onshore and offshore vehicles, in some cases from more than 30 jurisdictions. In every case, whether or not identity documentation was required was a function of the location of the provider, not the domicile of the legal entity created (that is, a British Virgin Islands company created from Britain would be anonymous, whereas one established from the Bahamas would not be). Although the sample size is small, these findings suggest that the problem of financial opacity is one for which the G7 countries, particularly the United States and Britain, are responsible, not palm-fringed tropical islands. While not an unprecedented finding, this does diametrically contradict the initial premises of important global regulatory campaigns. Although nearly all offshore centers regulate corporate service providers, Britain and the United States have chosen to leave them unregulated. The consequences are clear.

An example of one shell company set up for this paper, André Pascal Enterprises, may prove illustrative. The company is an England and Wales Private Company Limited by shares (with bearer shares) set up by a UK provider. Upon payment and submission of the order, the provider electronically lodged the application with UK Companies House. The provider became the initial shareholder of the company and subscriber to the Memorandum and Articles of Association for the purposes of the government records. Upon receipt of signed documents (once again, without the need supporting identification), the provider issued bearer share warrants, erasing the provider's name from the share registry without substituting any other. André Pascal Enterprises had a nominee director and nominee secretary (once more courtesy of the provider), again providing separation from the beneficial owner (the author). The incorporation process took less than a day, filling out the online forms took 45 minutes, and the total cost was GBP 515.95. The new legal person is the kind of classic anonymous shell corporation so important for perpetrating a wide range of financial crimes, which is almost impossible to obtain from offshore providers. The bonus is that as a corporate citizen of the UK, André Pascal avoids the taint associated with offshore companies while securing much tighter secrecy, an advantageous combination remarked upon by a number of other providers (see also BCP Consolidated Enterprises [Nevada], below). Significantly, until 2006, the same UK provider offered corporate accounts at a Latvian bank without the need for any supporting identity documentation.

Given that an anonymous shell corporation is generally a prerequisite for entering the international banking system while keeping one's identity secret, the 17 providers offering anonymous corporations became the target subset. In seeking to purchase a bank account associated with an anonymous company, the author soon ran into requirements for notarized identity documentation from all but five providers. Thus, the general effectiveness of the prohibition on anonymous accounts is substantially higher relative to that regarding anonymous shell companies. But the pattern of ineffective rules for providers in G7 states compared with those in so-called tax havens largely remains. At first glance, this high level of overall effectiveness (40 from 45) may seem to rehabilitate global standards on financial transparency; if a shell company is redundant without access to a banking system, and if anonymous companies are barred from the banking system, then the failure to prohibit corporate secrecy is much less serious, particularly for delinquent countries like the United States and UK. The difficulty of obtaining anonymous corporate accounts does mark an important change from the situation a decade ago (United Nations Office for Drug Control and Crime Prevention 1998). But even without direct access to the banking system, anonymous vehicles can be useful in financial crime. One of the most common forms of international tax evasion is holding share portfolios in the name of a foreign shell company so as to avoid capital gains tax that would be due at home. More importantly, in a chain of corporate entities even one anonymous vehicle (for example, a company acting as a director of another company or as a trustee) can disrupt the effort to establish the true owner at the end of the chain, rendering the whole structure opaque. Companies can be re-domiciled or transferred to re-establish anonymity broken in the process of setting up an account. Finally, however, the fact that it is difficult to retain corporate anonymity while opening a bank account is not to say it is impossible.

Only a small number of providers that responded to author were deficient in requesting proper identification documentation. The first, and most flagrantly in breach of international standards, was a US provider offering a Wyoming Limited Liability Corporation with a US bank account. The provider offered to use their employees' own Social Security Numbers in applying for an Employer Identification Number (EIN), the tax identification number for the corporate vehicle. As the provider breezily informed the author in an email, "You can open a bank account in any state in the nation. It does not have to be in Wyoming. You will need an EIN number for the LLC, which we may be able to get for you, if you elect the nominee tax ID service. There are no supporting documents required at this time, outside of your contact information." Disappointingly for would-be criminals, in the months between this receiving this email and going ahead with an attempt to buy this structure, the laws in Wyoming changed to prevent this particular service being offered. Yet, of all the countries appearing in Table 2, the United States remains in dead last place in terms of corporate and banking due diligence, behind even Somalia. A revealing comparison chart from a service provider specifies the documentation necessary to open a bank account in various countries, along with an overall difficulty rating (http://www.offshoreinc. net/new_bankcomparison.shtml). This ranges from "very high" (Seychelles, Jersey), to "high" (Hong Kong, Singapore), to "medium" (Cyprus, Dominica); the United States is the only country ranked as "low," allowing accounts to be opened with an unnotarized copy of a driver's license.

To test this ranking directly, the author established two companies with accounts in 2009, a classic offshore structure and an onshore equivalent. The first example involved approaching a large service provider in Singapore and buying the most secret vehicle and bank account available. This was a Seychelles company (Gruppo 20 Enterprises) formed with a nominee director and bearer shares, the latter meaning that whoever holds the physical share certificate owns the company. The accompanying bank account was in Cyprus, picked on the advice of the service provider because of this bank's unfastidious willingness to accept bearer share companies. Despite being the most *laissez faire* offshore bank available, the Cypriot bank still required a notarized physical passport copy, original bank reference, and original utility bill before opening the corporate account. These are also required for any person subsequently given signatory power over the account. Establishing the company and opening the account cost €1754. The second, onshore vehicle, BCP Consolidated Enterprises, is a Nevada corporation set up by a Nevada service provider with a nominee director and nominee shareholders. As such, the author's name appears nowhere on the incorporation documents, but in any case Nevada refuses to share tax information with foreign authorities. BCP Consolidated then opened an online bank account with one of the top five US banks. The cost of establishing the company and the bank account was $3695. Neither the original service provider nor the bank required more than an unnotarized scan of the author's driver's license (showing an outdated address). Thus, even the laxest offshore bank has due diligence standards far higher than those applied by major US institutions.

The final case, the Liechtenstein–Somali joint venture, is unusual in having stricter requirements for establishing a company compared with opening an account. While setting up a Somali shell company explicitly requires a notarized passport copy, both the provider's Web site and email communications repeatedly note that, although they require a scanned copy of some piece of photograph identification, there is definitely no need to get this notarized or certified as a true copy in opening a bank corporate account. The repeated emphasis on this last point suggests that the providers are broadly hinting at the possibility of a de facto anonymous account. The author tested this by successfully establishing first a personal account (€300) and then a second US-dollar corporate account for BCP Consolidated Enterprises (Nevada) in Somalia via a major Italian bank, for another €300. This required only a scan of the author's unnotarized driver's license (again, showing an old address) and the company's Articles of Association (which, to repeat, includes only the nominees' names rather than author's). Thus, rather than one of the "usual suspect" island tax havens, only a failed African state provided corporate banking facilities with as little due diligence as the United States.

### Independent Confirming Evidence

The goal of this penultimate section is twofold: first, to provide independent confirming evidence of the results of the direct test above and second, to illustrate the pressures that explain why small states have been so diligent in applying the standards flouted by the United States and others. Regarding the first point, as discussed earlier, powerful states are unlikely to stir up needless controversy by admitting their lax enforcement of the rules they impose on others. The international clubs they fund and dominate have a strong incentive to overlook their patrons' failings (for example, the G20, the OECD, and the FATF). This problem notwithstanding, however, there is good evidence from a variety of sources to support the conclusion that the United States in particular, as well as other OECD countries, is less stringent in applying the rules on corporate transparency than offshore centers. Evidence is taken from six independent sources: the NGO Tax Justice Network, the World Bank, the United States Senate, a study for the European Commission, the world's major Anti-Money Laundering software firm, and a more restricted direct test like that performed above.

In November 2009, the NGO Tax Justice Network released a Financial Secrecy Index, "a ranking which identifies the jurisdictions that are most aggressive in providing secrecy in international finance, and which most actively shun co-operation with other jurisdictions" (http://www.financialsecrecyindex.com/). Sixty jurisdictions were each assessed against 200 variables. The index aims to measure a broader range of factors than just the transparency of shell companies, but the results are broadly in agreement with those presented in the previous section. Thus, the worst offender by a large margin is Delaware (the only US state assessed), followed by Luxembourg, Switzerland, the Cayman Islands, and the United Kingdom. The Tax Justice Network concludes:

> The major global players in the supply of financial secrecy are mostly not tiny, isolated islands, but rich nations operating their own specialized jurisdictions of secrecy, often with links to smaller "satellite" jurisdictions which act as conduits for illicit financial flows into the mainstream capital markets. (Tax Justice Network 2009)

Commenting on this unflattering conclusion, one local pointed out "Delaware is no more secret than any other US state," given that the others also fail to collect beneficial ownership information (http://www.reuters.com/article/domestic-News/idUSTRE59U1VB20091101).

In the same week, Senator Carl Levin issued a damning statement regarding American delinquence in meeting international standards:

> Our 50 states are forming nearly 2 million companies each year and, in virtually all cases, doing so without obtaining the names of the people who will control or benefit from those companies ... Most of our States allow hidden owners to buy companies online within 24 hours of a request. In two States, for an extra $1,000, hidden owners can form a US company within a single hour.[2]

Levin goes on to expressly note that the United States is in violation of international standards of financial transparency, that it derives economic advantage from under-cutting the standards in this manner, and that this verdict confirms the results of the Tax Justice Network study referred to above. On each of these counts, it also confirms the conclusions of this article. An earlier Government Accountability Office survey of American practice conveys the same message with its title alone: *Company Formations: Minimal Ownership Information Is Collected and Available* (2006). Yet, the problem remains unaddressed. Giving an indication of the consequences, in 2009 the World Bank compiled a database of the corporate vehicles used to launder the proceeds of major corruption. By November 2009, the database included 104 cases of grand corruption in which more than $1 million was transferred internationally involving 295 identifiable corporate vehicles. The single most common jurisdiction of incorporation for the shell companies involved was the United States (43 instances) (see World Bank 2009b).

Although the United States is the worst offender, it is not the only one. A study for the European Commission, *Protecting the EU Financial System from the Exploitation of Financial Centers and Offshore Facilities by Organized Crime* (which did not survey the United States), also constructs an index of corporate secrecy. Despite the European Commission's premise that the problem was offshore, the report finds that "the European Union member states have not 'cleaned up their acts' before asking others to do so" (Euroshore 2000:15). Because the company law relating to beneficial ownership is "the most essential factor in the transparency of a financial system," the report concludes that EU members must first address their own serious failings in this area. Likewise, World-Check, the world's leading private firm for the provision of "Know Your Customer" (KYC) software, notes the divergence between conventional stereotypes and reality regarding the degree of due diligence exercised on- and offshore:

---

[2] Statement of Sen. Carl Levin, D-Mich., on Business Formation and Financial Crime: Finding a Legislative Solution, November 5, 2009. Available at http://levin.senate.gov/newsroom/speeches/speech/statement-of-sen-carl-levin-d-mich-on-business-formation-and-financial-crime-finding-a-legislative-solution/?section=alltypes.

> There is a false sense of security when carrying out due diligence on or dealing with an onshore company, trust, foundation or charity, in comparison to the equivalent offshore vehicles. The registration of a company in most onshore jurisdictions carries little or no KYC requirements on the beneficiaries, owners or company directors. The knowledge that a company is registered in the United Kingdom, the United States or in the EU, as opposed to some small tax haven island nation, for some reason would appear to make us think it must be above board. (World-Check 2008:9)

Coming full circle to the notion of a direct test is the exercise performed by two former US IRS officials in 2006, who used a Nevada corporate service provider to set up shell companies in New York, Florida, and Panama, each with bank accounts, before wiring money from each company to the other. One of the officials observed, "Surprisingly, it was more difficult to form an account there [in Panama] than it was in the U.S." Panama required notarized copies of the passport page and driver's license, while the American institutions required neither. He concluded, "The U.S. beats up on these small island countries, from Antigua to Nauru to everyplace else, for not having adequate (corporate) controls, yet we have control problems in our states" (Project Shows 2007).

The evidence presented above from a wide range of sources broadly confirms the main conclusion of the direct tests employed: that in practice the rules prohibiting corporate anonymity have major effectiveness problems and that powerful countries, especially the United States, are more at fault than small state offshore financial centers. The final task, then, is to briefly demonstrate why small states have been so stringent in enforcing rules that others routinely ignore. In keeping with the realist orientation of the article, the answer is that they are forced to. The example of the Bahamas is instructive in demonstrating hypocrite standards in action. This small, weak country was forced to implement expensive, purportedly international standards on corporate transparency by a coalition of powerful countries led by the United States, despite the fact that this latter group did not (and currently do not) meet the standards in question.

In June 2000, the Bahamas was blacklisted for failing to meet international standards on financial transparency, with removal from the list conditional upon adopting far-reaching regulatory reforms (Sharman 2009). A central demand was that all Bahamian shell companies be able to be traced to their real owners (FATF 2000:3). All G7 members warned their financial institutions to exercise particular caution when transacting with the Bahamas. At their July 2000 summit, the G7 heads of state announced, "We are prepared to act together ... to implement co-ordinated countermeasures against those [blacklisted jurisdictions] that do not take steps to reform their system appropriately, including the possibility to condition and restrict financial transactions with these jurisdictions" (http://www.mofa.go.jp/policy/economy/summit/2000/pdfs/action.pdf). The Bahamian negotiating team was incensed to learn in discussions with its counterpart (led by a US official), that to be removed from the list all Bahamian corporate service providers had to be licensed, even though there was (and is) no such requirement in the United States or most other OECD states (FATF 2006). The concessions extracted were far-reaching: "In a move that has their financial sector reeling, the Bahamas' Premier told bankers, in August [2000], that the Bahamas will fully co-operate in international investigations, scrap secrecy laws and share tax information with the USA" (Johnson 2001:213). The president of the Bahamas Bar Association was moved to denounce the decision as "capitulation to OECD terrorism" (http://www.freedomandprosperity.org/Papers/maynard/maynard.shtml). The Bahamas experienced considerable economic loss as a result of the concessions (Vlcek 2008:122–125). In confidential interviews with officials from the Bahamian team, the FATF, and the US Treasury, all three sources confirm that the Bahamas had simply given in to a coercive process in adopting the regulations (Drezner 2007:142–145). To add insult to injury, all sides knew that the Bahamas was being held to standards that the United States, Britain, and other powerful states did not meet. Extensive interviews in other small states confirm the Bahamas' experience as typical.[3]

## Conclusion

The article closes by re-emphasizing points on the significance of the substantive findings and the method employed to generate them. The results of the direct test show a pattern of partial effectiveness (low for the formation of anonymous companies, much higher for anonymous banking), but even so the more variation in national compliance (low by G7 countries, much higher among those small states cast as tax havens). In relation to anonymous shell companies, the United States, United Kingdom, and other OECD states, unlike the Cayman Islands and Panama, have simply chosen not to comply with international standards they had a large hand in creating. Nor is uneven progress in making these rules effective a result of a race to the bottom driven by regulatory arbitrage, or a prisoner's dilemma, whereby all states share the same preference, but rational anticipation of others' defection causes actors to refrain from co-operation. The "do as I say, not as I do" position of the G7 states toward smaller states is a good fit with a realist position concerning the power- rather than rule-governed nature of the international system. But unlike recent realist accounts of international standard setting and effectiveness, it is not a case of core states or a hegemon adopting rules and then inducing others to follow their example (Krasner 1991; Gruber 2000; Drezner 2007). Instead, the hegemon and core states induce other states to follow rules that the former are *not* following themselves, perhaps analogous to the nuclear non-proliferation regime. Realist authors may thus have actually understated the influence of power in the selective application and impact of international rules.

Concerning the field more generally, the conventional story of progress in political science emphasizes the move away from studying formal rules toward behavior, as well as the employment of increasingly scientific methods. Given this orientation and scale of values, direct approaches like field experiments and participation are curiously scarce. Such methods can potentially shed light on a class of questions of great interest to scholars, policymakers, and citizens: do rules work, that is, are they effective? Their lack of employment in political science to complement existing techniques seems to indicate much more a failure of imagination in the field than any inherent shortcomings. No doubt there are many areas of interest where participant and field experiment approaches are impractical, unethical, and/or illegal. Yet, speaking only of International Relations, the extent to which issues like legalization, global governance, and international regimes have become major controversies in the field argues for the potential of similar approaches. Soft law standards are amenable to testing by breaking. Civil society groups, epistemic communities, private firms, and international organizations and states are relatively porous to scholars looking to learn by participating

---

[3] Interviews with regulators and private sector representatives in George Town, Cayman Islands, January 19–20, 2004; regulators, government officials, and private sector representatives in Avarua, Cook Islands, July 28–29, 2008, and December 2–4, 2009; regulators and government officials in Yaren, Nauru, August 18–19, 2008; regulators and private sector representatives in Vaduz, Liechtenstein, January 29, 2009; regulators, government officials, and private sector representatives in Panama City, Panama, April 2–4, 2008; government officials in Basseterre, St Kitts and Nevis, January 22–23, 2004; regulators and private sector representatives in Victoria, Seychelles, May 30, 2005; and regulators, government officials, and private sector representatives in Porta Vila, Vanuatu, March 10, 2006, and August 4–6, 2008.

in their activities. The opportunities to advance scholarly and policy knowledge through direct approaches are there; more political scientists should seize them.

## References

BALDWIN, DAVID A., Ed. (1993) *Neorealism and Neoliberalism: The Contemporary Debate*. New York: Columbia University Press.

BARNETT, MICHAEL, AND MARTHA FINNEMORE. (2004) *Rules for the World: International Organizations in Global Politics*. Ithaca: Cornell University Press.

BERTRAND, MARIANNE, AND SENDHIL MULLAINATHAN. (2004) Are Emily and Greg More Employable than Lakisha and Jamal? A Field Experiment on Labor Market Discrimination. *American Economic Review* 94 (4): 991–1013.

CARR, E. H. (1939) *The Twenty Years' Crisis, 1919–1939*. London: Macmillan.

DE SOTO, HERNANDO. ([1989] 2002) *The Other Path: The Economic Answer to Terrorism*. New York: Basic Books.

DE SOTO, HERNANDO. (2000) *The Mystery of Capital: Why Capitalism Triumphs in the West and Fails Everywhere Else*. New York: Basic Books.

DREZNER, DANIEL. (2007) *All Politics Is Global: Explaining International Regulatory Regimes*. Princeton: Princeton University Press.

EUROPEAN COMMISSION. (2008) *Report from the Commission to the Council in Accordance with Article 18 of Directive 2003/48/EC on the Taxation of Savings Income in the Form of Interest Payments*. Brussels: Commission to the European Communities.

EUROSHORE. (2000) *Protecting the EU Financial System from the Exploitation of Financial Centers and Offshore Facilities by Organized Crime*. Prepared for the European Commission. Trento, Italy.

FATF (FINANCIAL ACTION TASK FORCE). (2000) *First Review to Identify Non-Co-operative Countries and Territories*. Paris: FATF.

FATF (FINANCIAL ACTION TASK FORCE). (2006) *The Misuse of Corporate Vehicles, Including Trust and Corporate Service Providers*. Paris: FATF.

FATF (FINANCIAL ACTION TASK FORCE). (2009) Securing Timely Access to Beneficial Ownership Information (Legal Persons). Working Group on Evaluation and Implementation. Washington, DC.

FATF (FINANCIAL ACTION TASK FORCE). (2010) *Policy Brief*. Paris: FATF.

FISHER, HOWARD. (2008) The Death of Offshore Secrecy—And It's Not Resting in Peace. *Offshore Investment* 187: 11–19.

FSF (FINANCIAL STABILITY FORUM). (2000) *Report of the Working Group on Offshore Financial Centers*. Basel: FSF.

FSF (FINANCIAL STABILITY FORUM). (2007) Financial Stability Forum Review of Its Offshore Financial Centers Initiative. Press release, September 26.

G20. (2008) Declaration of the Summit on Financial Markets and the World Economy. November 15. Available at http://www.whitehouse.gov/news/releases/2008/11/20081115-1.html. (Accessed December 8, 2008.)

G20. (2009) Communiqué: Meeting of Finance Ministers and Central Bank Governors. November 7. Available at http://www.g20.org/Documents/2009_communique_standrews.pdf. (Accessed November 15, 2009.)

GOSNELL, HAROLD. (1927) *Getting Out the Vote: An Experiment in the Stimulation of Voting*. Chicago: University of Chicago Press.

GOULDER, ROBERT. (2009) How the U.S. Is a Tax Haven for Mexico's Wealthy. Available at http://www.taxanalysts.com/www/features.nsf/Articles/522A39903AFD6CFB8525761D004F113B?OpenDocument. (Accessed November 26, 2009.)

GREEN, DONALD P., AND ALAN S. GERBER. (2002) Reclaiming the Experimental Tradition in Political Science. In *Political Science: State of the Discipline*, edited by Ira Katznelson and Helen V. Milner. New York: W.W. Norton.

GRUBER, LLOYD. (2000) *Ruling the World: Power Politics and the Rise of Supranational Institutions*. Princeton: Princeton University Press.

HAAS, PETER M., ROBERT O. KEOHANE, AND MARC A. LEVY., Eds. (1993) *Institutions for the Earth: Sources of Effective International Environmental Protection*. Cambridge, MA: MIT Press.

JOHNSON, JACKIE. (2001) Blacklisting: Initial Reactions, Responses and Repercussions. *Journal of Money Laundering Control* 4 (3): 211–225.

KEOHANE, ROBERT O. (1984) *After Hegemony: Co-operation and Discord in the World Political Economy*. Princeton: Princeton University Press.

KEOHANE, ROBERT O. (2009) The Old IPE and the New. *Review of International Political Economy* 16 (1): 34–46.

KING, GARY, ROBERT O. KEOHANE, AND SIDNEY VERBA. (1994) *Designing Social Inquiry: Scientific Inference in Qualitative Research.* Princeton: Princeton University Press.

KIRSHNER, JONATHAN. (2009) Realist Political Economy: Traditional Themes and Contemporary Challenges. In *Routledge Handbook of International Political Economy: IPE as a Global Conversation*, edited by Mark Blyth. London: Routledge.

KRASNER, STEPHEN D. (1977) US Commercial and Monetary Policy: Unravelling the Paradox of External Strength and Internal Weakness. *International Organization* 31 (4): 635–671.

KRASNER, STEPHEN D. (1991) Global Communications and National Power: Life on the Pareto Frontier. *World Politics* 43 (3): 336–366.

LAKE, DAVID A. (2007) Escape from the State of Nature: Authority and Hierarchy in World Politics. *International Security* 32 (1): 47–79.

LANGER, MARSHALL J. (2008) Offshore for More than 50 Years. *Offshore Investment* 182: 9–10.

MALINIAK, DAN, AND MICHAEL J. TIERNEY. (2009) The American School of IPE. *Review of International Political Economy* 16 (1): 6–33.

MEARSHEIMER, JOHN J. (1994–1995) The False Promise of International Institutions. *International Security* 19 (3): 5–49.

MEARSHEIMER, JOHN J. (2001) *The Tragedy of Great Power Politics.* New York: W.W. Norton.

NYE, JOSEPH S. (1993) Foreward. In *Institutions for the Earth: Sources of Effective International Environmental Protection*, edited by Peter M. Haas, Robert O. Keohane and Marc A. Levy. Cambridge, MA: MIT Press.

OECD (ORGANIZATION FOR ECONOMIC CO-OPERATION, DEVELOPMENT). (2001) *Behind the Corporate Veil: Using Corporate Entities for Illicit Purposes.* Paris: OECD.

POPPER, KARL. (1968) *The Logic of Scientific Discovery.* New York: Harper and Row.

PROJECT SHOWS EASE OF MONEY LAUNDERING IN THE UNITED STATES. (2007) *USA Today*, March 19.

RAUSTIALA, KAL, AND ANNE-MARIE SLAUGHTER. (2002) International Law, International Relations, and Compliance. In *Handbook of International Relations*, edited by Walter Carlsnaes, Thomas Risse and Beth A. Simmons. Thousand Oaks, CA: Sage.

SENATE PERMANENT SUBCOMMITTEE ON INVESTIGATIONS. (2008) *Tax Haven Banks and US Tax Compliance.* Washington, DC: United States Senate.

SHARMAN, J. C. (2008) Regional Deals and the Global Imperative: The External Dimension of the European Union Savings Tax Directive. *Journal of Common Market Studies* 46 (4): 1049–1069.

SHARMAN, J. C. (2009) The Bark *Is* the Bite: International Organizations and Blacklisting. *Review of International Political Economy* 16 (5): 573–596.

SHEPPARD, LEE A. (2009) Dear Former Tax Evasion Services Customer. *Tax Notes International* 56 (2): 91–95.

SIMMONS, BETH A. (1998) Compliance with International Agreements. *Annual Review of Political Science* 1: 75–93.

SIMMONS, BETH A. (2000) International Law and State Behavior: Commitment and Compliance in International Monetary Affairs. *American Political Science Review* 94 (4): 819–835.

TAX JUSTICE NETWORK. (2009) Financial Secrecy Index. Available at http://www.financialsecrecyindex.com/. (Accessed December 30, 2009.)

UNITED NATIONS OFFICE FOR DRUG CONTROL AND CRIME PREVENTION. (1998) *Financial Havens, Banking Secrecy and Money Laundering.* Prepared by Jack A. Blum, Michael Levi, R. Thomas Naylor, and Phil Williams. Washington, DC: UNODC.

UNODC-WORLD BANK. (2007) *Stolen Assets Recovery (StAR) Initiative: Challenges, Opportunities and Action Plan.* Washington, DC: UNODC.

VLCEK, WILLIAM. (2008) *Offshore Finance and Small States: Sovereignty, Size and Money.* New York: Palgrave.

WORLD BANK. (2009a) *Laundering the Proceeds of Public Sector Corruption.* Prepared by Richard Gordon. Washington, DC: World Bank.

WORLD BANK. (2009b) Misuse of Corporate Vehicles in Grand Corruption Cases. Progress Report 5, November 13.

WORLD-CHECK. (2008) *Refining the PEP Definition*, 2nd edn. World-Check: Global Objectives Limited. Available at http://www.world-check.com/media/d/content_whitepaper_reference/Refining_the_PEP_Definition_-_EditionII.pdf. (Accessed October 7, 2009.)

YOUNG, ORAN. (1979) *Compliance with Public Authority.* Baltimore: Johns Hopkins University Press.

# Name Index